The Great Writings in Marketing

SELECTED READINGS TOGETHER WITH THE AUTHORS' OWN RETROSPECTIVE COMMENTARIES

Howard A. Thompson
EASTERN KENTUCKY UNIVERSITY

The Commerce Press Plymouth, Michigan

To Ike and Mary Hatch

Cover design by Tom Chilton

Manufactured in the United States of America.

Library of Congress Catalog Number 75-22965
ISBN: 0-916162-00-1

Contents

Foreword

Publication of *Great Writings in Marketing* will be hailed as a milestone in the maturation of marketing thought. Professor Thompson has assembled in one volume the writings that have stood the test of time and are truly deserving of the title *Great Writings*.

But this book is so much more than a simple compilation of *Great Writings*. In this book the reader can call the writer of each classic article to the present and ask him to explain his contributions in light of the events of the 1970s. In some cases, the authors modify their articles significantly; in others the modifications are slight. These *Retrospective Comments* by each living author represent a major contribution of the book. The updating of each article to match the environment of the 1970s ensures the timelessness of the contributions.

Important learning aids accompany each selection. These include an *article preview* in outline form and a *learning review* at the end of each selection. These devices serve to reinforce the reader's understanding of the major points in each article.

The materials in *Great Writings in Marketing* represent the cornerstones of the marketing discipline. They are writings to which every serious student of marketing should be exposed. This volume should serve the marketing student and practitioner in the same way that law books serve the attorney, that medical books serve the physician. It belongs on the shelf of every professional marketer.

Louis E. Boone
The University of Tulsa

Preface

Never say "Never!"

The editor of *Great Writings in Marketing* had been known to comment that he would "never be an assembler of articles written by others into a collection known as a 'reader.'" Nevertheless, when a colleague suggested the notion of developing a *Great Writings* reader, he said he would think about it.

Naiveté said "Yes."

The thinking stage took about twenty-four hours during which time he thumbed through various readings collections already available. It was soon evident that, although each one represented considerable effort to assemble the articles, obtain permissions, write prefaces and sectional introductions, etc., his first reaction to reader editing was basically correct. That is, the editorship involved no real creative flair of original contribution to the field; albeit it was a definite service to students and teachers of the discipline.

Does anyone really need this?

But what if the basic product could be built upon by adding new and needed features to meet an unsatisfied demand from knowledge-hungry business marketers, college students, and marketing professors? An informal survey of students and marketing colleagues identified several needs not being met which *a new type of readings collection* could satisfy. The framework for *Great Writings in Marketing* began to take shape in various brainstorming sessions and a *new product*—rather than just another reader—was created.

How great is great?

First, there was the problem of which articles to select as being representative of the entire field of marketing. This was resolved by choosing broad articles often footnoted in the marketing texts and literature. Although it is not possible to cover all of the marketing concepts in one volume, the 38 articles represent a great many of the foundation principles on which the discipline has been built. Many of the articles also represent one of the first definitive statements of the marketing principle or concept involved. The authors are often footnoted and may be found in the name index of nearly every marketing textbook. Other individual authors, contributors to the marketing literature of today, are not represented; it would be impracticable to include them all. But those included would certainly find their way into anyone's *Who's Who* of marketing's contributors to its great writings. Peer influence in selecting the readings included is reflected by the fact that a number of them have received the American Marketing Association's annual Alpha Kappa Psi award for the outstanding *Journal of Marketing* article that year.

"What I really meant was . . ."

Secondly, there was the problem of how to bring the time-honored and widely quoted articles up to date. Many of them had been written during the 1950s and early 1960s. An exciting solution was suggested: *Ask the authors to update their own articles*. This was done and they responded enthusiastically, many times noting to the editor their pleasure to have the opportunity to correct a dated comment, revise an errant prediction, or reply to a challenge or misunderstanding which appeared in subsequent marketing literature. A few of the authors are no longer living and their updates have been written by others chosen for their interest and acknowledged expertise in that specific area of marketing. Updates have been written by substitute authors in a couple of instances because the editor was unable to locate or contact the author of the original article.

An insider's point of view

Thirdly, the updating with the authors' own retrospective commentaries of these classic articles from the marketing literature also removed the editor's concern that *Great Writings in Marketing* might fail to measure as a real contribution to the marketing literature. A useful contribution has been made. Indeed, nowhere else can the student learn from one collection of readings how well in the eyes of the author himself these marketing principles and concepts have weathered the test of time and actual use by marketers. Many new insights are offered through the updates indicating what meanings and applications the author really had in mind. Future researchers of these marketing concepts will have an insider's point of view not elsewhere available in most instances.

Learning without the busywork

Finally, students have often complained that readings collections represent many pages from which they gain few insights not available from the textbook or lecture. These new insights, even when present, are often *well hidden* within the readings to anyone unwilling to carefully outline each selection for future review. In short, it was felt that the speed reader seldom benefited from his efforts. This shortcoming has been remedied by prefacing each selection with an outline of the major points and concluding each with programmed learning-type questions and answers printed upside down at the bottom of the page. Thus the reader is exposed to significant points in three ways and feedback is provided to determine whether these points are really understood. Speed reading is encouraged by the article outlines which permit the fast reader to scan for development of the ideas already noted. Additional questions to reward the reader may be selected from the special materials available to the instructor.

"Where did I read that explanation of . . ."

Reference books such as this one are made much more valuable if the user is able to turn to specific pages without having to search the text looking for the point he needs to review. For that purpose, extensive name and subject indices have been added.

Use as a supplement, base for reading list, etc.

The primary purpose of *Great Writings in Marketing* is to serve as a learning supplement to any of the basic textbooks in principles of marketing and marketing management. Once the students have added the collection to their personal library, it is hoped that, along with their other textbooks, it will become an annotated reference tool which will serve them throughout their careers. Additionally, the upper division marketing course which uses no textbook but rather a casebook or a readings list could use this collection as a base and add to it additional readings to develop these broad concepts in more detail. Finally, it is hoped that the marketing executive will find in these readings and retrospective comments a refresher-primer for stimulating new ideas to meet the challenges of an increasingly complex and competitive marketplace.

Thank you, thank you, thank you

The editor would like to thank the authors and publishers for allowing their work to be reprinted in this collection. Especially appreciated is the time and effort represented in the additional material, the retrospective commentaries, furnished by the authors and surrogate authors involved, for this became the truly unique feature and justification for the book.

Others contributed in many different ways: Dr. Louis E. Boone of The University of Tulsa, who suggested the project; Mr. Robert L. Taylor, who developed the instructor's materials; Ms. Margaret Carpenter, Kay Dautenhahn, Doris Irvine, and Carolyn Alford, who shared the typing and follow-up routines in contacting the authors and publishers; Mr. Mike Morgan, who developed the outlines, article questions, and introductory paragraphs; Mrs. Mary Sherwood, who was responsible for the indices; and The University of Tulsa and Eastern Kentucky University, which provided the environment in which these efforts could be successfully concluded.

Howard A. Thompson

Richmond, Kentucky
January 1976

PART 1

Marketing's Role in Management

Marketing: still growing up

Marketing vice presidents, university courses in marketing, marketing textbooks, and marketing degrees are all rather recent innovations in the management world. Marketing terminology in the literature today, most of it, has been conceived during this century. The first principles of marketing textbooks appeared in the 1920s and it was the decade of the 1930s before very many large companies got around to broadening the scope of the sales manager into that of the marketing manager.

Soap, senators, and scouting

Today most organizations admit the importance of the marketing function; the successful ones effectively implement it. And the present-day adopters of the marketing concept include not only those consumer product manufacturers such as the soap and cereal companies. Causes, candidates, nonprofit institutions, and governments, to name a few categories, have come to recognize the role of their various publics in the design of their respective marketing strategies.

Causing revolutions; curing myopia

Clearly essential to successful implementation of the marketing concept is the understanding of such concepts as the marketing revolution, marketing management, marketing myopia, and others which appear in this section. The writings which follow were selected in order that the reader might view in some perspective the maturing of marketing in management.

1

The Marketing Revolution

Robert J. Keith

PREVIEW

I. Consumer orientation has had far-reaching business implications
  A. Ideas which revolutionized conventional thought have parallels in science and philosophy
  B. Pillsbury epitomizes the revolution to the marketing concept

II. Pillsbury's transition can be viewed in stages:
  A. The *production era* goal was *to produce* quality flour
  B. The *sales era* goal was *to profitably dispose* of products
  C. The *marketing era* goal was *to satisfy customers*
  D. The *marketing control era* goal was *to install consumer-oriented marketing* as the basic motivating force throughout the company. . . .
    1. influencing long-range policy;
    2. bringing marketing influence to already accepted areas of research, promotion, procurement, and production;
    3. and to the not fully accepted areas of capital and financial planning.

The consumer, not the company, is in the middle.

In today's economy the consumer, the man or woman who buys the product, is at the absolute dead center of the business universe. Companies revolve around the customer, not the other way around.

Growing acceptance of this consumer concept has had, and will have, far-reaching implications for business, achieving a virtual revolution in economic thinking. As the concept gains ever greater acceptance, marketing is emerging as the most important single function in business.

Robert J. Keith, "The Marketing Revolution," is reprinted by permission from the *Journal of Marketing*, published by the American Marketing Association (January 1960), pp. 35–38.

A Revolution in Science

A very apt analogy can be drawn with another revolution, one that goes back to the sixteenth century. At that time astronomers had great difficulty predicting the movements of the heavenly bodies. Their charts and computations and celestual calendars enabled them to estimate the approximate positions of the planets on any given date. But their calculations were never exact—there was always a variance.

Then a Polish scientist named Nicolaus Copernicus proposed a very simple answer to the problem. If, he proposed, we assume that the sun, and not the earth, is at the center of our system, and that the earth moves around the sun instead of the sun moving around the earth, all our calculations will prove correct.

The Pole's idea raised a storm of controversy. The earth, everyone knew, was at the center of the universe. But another scientist named Galileo put the theory to test—and it worked. The result was a complete upheaval in scientific and philosophic thought. The effects of Copernicus' revolutionary idea are still being felt today.

A Revolution in Marketing

In much the same way American business in general—and Pillsbury in particular—is undergoing a revolution of its own today: a marketing revolution.

This revolution stems from the same idea stated in the opening sentence of this article. No longer is the company at the center of the business universe. Today the customer is at the center.

Our attention has shifted from problems of production to problems of marketing, from the product we *can* make to the product the consumer *wants* us to make, from the company itself to the market place.

The marketing revolution has only begun. It is reasonable to expect that its implications will grow in the years to come, and that lingering effects will be felt a century, or more than one century, from today.

So far the theory has only been advanced, tested, and generally proved correct. As more and more businessmen grasp the concept, and put it to work, our economy will become more truly marketing oriented.

Pillsbury's Pattern: Four Eras

Here is the way the marketing revolution came about at Pillsbury. The experience of this company has followed a typical pattern. There has been nothing unique, and each step in the evolution of the marketing concept has been taken in a way that is more meaningful because the steps are, in fact, typical.

Today in our company the marketing concept finds expression in the simple statement, "Nothing happens at Pillsbury until a sale is made." This statement represents basic reorientation on the part of our management. For, not too many years ago, the ordering of functions in our business placed finance first, production second, and sales last.

How did we arrive at our present point of view? Pillsbury's progress in the marketing revolution divides neatly into four separate eras—eras which parallel rather closely the classic pattern of development in the marketing revolution.

1st Era—Production Oriented

First came the era of manufacturing. It began with the formation of the company in 1869 and continued into the 1930s. It is significant that the *idea* for the formation of our company came from the *availability* of high-quality wheat and the *proximity* of water power—and not from the availability and proximity of growing major market areas, or the demand for better, less expensive, more convenient flour products.

Of course, these elements were potentially present. But the two major elements which fused in the mind of Charles A. Pillsbury and prompted him to invest his modest capital in a flour mill were, on the one hand, wheat, and, on the other hand, water power. His principal concern was with production, not marketing.

His thought and judgment were typical of the business thinking of his day. And such thinking was adequate and proper for the times.

Our company philosophy in this era might have been stated this way: "We are professional flour millers. Blessed with a supply of the finest North American wheat, plenty of water power, and excellent milling machinery, we produce flour of the highest quality. Our basic function is to mill high-quality flour, and of course (and almost incidentally) we must hire salesmen to sell it, just as we hire accountants to keep our books."

The young company's first new product reveals an interesting example of the thinking of this era. The product was middlings, the bran left over after milling. Millfeed, as the product came to be known, proved a valuable product because it was an excellent nutrient for cattle. But the impetus to launch the new product came not from a consideration of the nutritional needs of cattle or a marketing analysis. It came primarily from the desire to dispose of a by-product! The new product decision was production oriented, not marketing oriented.

2nd Era—Sales Oriented

In the 1930s Pillsbury moved into its second era of development as a marketing company. This was the era of sales. For the first time we began to be highly conscious of the consumer, her wants, and her prejudices, as a key factor in the business equation. We established a commercial research department to provide us with facts about the market.

We also became more aware of the importance of our dealers, the wholesale and retail grocers who provided a vital link in our chain of distribution from the mill to the home. Knowing that consumers and dealers as well were vital to the company's success, we could no longer simply mark them down as unknowns in our figuring. With this realization, we took the first step along the road to become a marketing company.

Pillsbury's thinking in this second era could be summed up like this: "We are a flour-milling company, manufacturing a number of products for the consumer market. We must have a first-rate sales organization which can dispose of all the products we can make at a favorable price. We must back up this sales force with consumer advertising and market intelligence. We want our salesmen and our dealers to have all the tools they need for moving the output of our plants to the consumer."

Still not a marketing philosophy, but we were getting closer.

3rd Era—Marketing Oriented

It was at the start of the present decade that Pillsbury entered the marketing era. The amazing growth of our consumer business as the result of introducing baking mixes provided the immediate impetus. But the groundwork had been laid by key men who developed our sales concepts in the middle forties.

With the new cake mixes, products of our research program, ringing up sales on the cash register, and with the realization that research and production could produce literally hundreds of new and different products, we faced for the first time the necessity for selecting the best new products. We needed a set of criteria for selecting the kind of products we would manufacture. We needed an organization to establish and maintain these criteria, and for attaining maximum sale of the products we did select.

We needed, in fact, to build into our company a new management function which would direct and control all the other corporate functions from procurement to production to advertising to sales. This function was marketing. Our solution was to establish the present marketing department.

This department developed the criteria which we would use in determining which products to market. *And these criteria were, and are, nothing more nor less than those of the consumer herself.* We moved the mountain out to find out what Mahomet, and Mrs. Mahomet, wanted. The company's purpose was no longer to mill flour, nor to manufacture a wide variety of products, but to satisfy the needs and desires, both actual and potential, of our customers.

If we were to restate our philosophy during the past decade as simply as possible, it would read: "We make and sell products for consumers."

The business universe, we realized, did not have room at the center for Pillsbury or any other company or groups of companies. It was already occupied by the customers.

This is the concept at the core of the marketing revolution. How did we put it to work for Pillsbury?

The Brand-Manager Concept

The first move was to transform our small advertising department into a marketing department. The move involved far more than changing the name on organizational charts. It required the introduction of a new, and vitally important, organization concept—the brand-manager concept.

The brand-manager idea is the very backbone of marketing at Pillsbury. The man who bears the title, brand manager, has total accountability for results. He directs the marketing of his product as if it were his own business. Production does its job, and finance keeps the profit figures. Otherwise, the brand manager has total responsibility for marketing his product. This responsibility encompasses pricing, commercial research, competitive activity, home service and publicity coordination, legal details, budgets, advertising plans, sales promotion, and execution of plans. The brand manager must think first, last, and always of his sales target, the consumer.

Marketing permeates the entire organization. Marketing plans and executes the sale—all the way from the inception of the product idea, through its development and distribution, to the customer purchase. Marketing begins and ends with the consumer. New product ideas are conceived after careful study of her wants and needs, her likes and dislikes. Then marketing takes the idea and marshals all the forces of the corporation to translate the idea into product and the product into sales.

In the early days of the company, consumer orientation did not seem so important. The company made flour, and flour was a staple—no one would question the availability of a market. Today we must determine whether the American housewife will buy lemon pudding cake in preference to orange angel food. The variables in the equation have multiplied, just as the number of products on the grocers' shelves have multiplied from a hundred or so into many thousands.

When we first began operating under this new marketing concept, we encountered the problems which always accompany any major reorientation. Our people were young and frankly immature in some areas of business; but they were men possessed of an idea and they fought for it. The idea was almost too powerful. The marketing concept proved its worth in sales, but it upset many of the internal balances of the corporation. Marketing-oriented decisions resulted in peaks and valleys in production, schedules, labor, and inventories. But the system worked. It worked better and better as maverick marketing men became motivated toward tonnage and profit.

4th Era—Marketing Control

Today marketing is coming into its own. Pillsbury stands on the brink of its fourth major era in the marketing revolution.

Basically, the philosophy of this fourth era can be summarized this way: "We are moving from a company which has the marketing concept to a marketing company."

Marketing today sets company operating policy short-term. It will come to influence long-range policy more and more. Where today consumer research, technical research, procurement, production, advertising, and sales swing into action under the broad canopy established by marketing, tomorrow capital and financial planning, ten-year volume and profit goals will also come under the aegis of marketing. More than any other function, marketing must be tied to top management.

Today our marketing people know more about inventories than anyone in top management. Tomorrow's marketing man must know capital financing and the implications of marketing planning on long-range profit forecasting.

Today technical research receives almost all of its guidance and direction from marketing. Tomorrow marketing will assume a more creative function in the advertising area, both in terms of ideas and media selection.

Changes in the Future

The marketing revolution has only begun. There are still those who resist its basic idea, just as there are always those who will resist change in business, government, or any other form of human institution.

As the marketing revolution gains momentum, there will be more changes. The concept of the customer at the center will remain valid; but business must adjust to the shifting tastes and likes and desires and needs which have always characterized the American consumer.

For many years the geographical center of the United States lay in a small Kansas town. Then a new state, Alaska, came along, and the center shifted to the north and west. Hawaii was admitted to the Union and the geographical mid-point took another jump to the west. In very much the same way, modern business must anticipate the restless shifting of buying attitudes, as customer preferences move north, south, east, or west from a liquid center. There is nothing static about the marketing revolution, and that is part of its fascination. The old order has changed, yielding place to the new—but the new order will have its quota of changes, too.

At Pillsbury, as our fourth era progresses, marketing will become the basic motivating force for the entire corporation. Soon it will be true that every activity of the corporation—from finance to sales to production—is aimed at satisfying the needs and desires of the consumer. When that stage of development is reached, the marketing revolution will be complete.

LEARNING REVIEW

Questions:

1. The key point in Mr. Keith's article is that the center of all business activity orientation should be ____________________.

2. If other companies experience the marketing revolution as did Pillsbury, they will move through perhaps four eras: a) ____________, b) ____________, c) ____________, and d) ____________.

3. In the last era of the revolution, ____________ will become the basic motivating force for the entire corporation until every activity is aimed at satisfying the needs and desires of the ____________________.

Answers:

1. the consumer or customer; 2. production, sales, marketing, and marketing control; 3. marketing, consumer.

Retrospective Comment by Earl A. Clasen*

I truly believe that the actions taken within the Pillsbury Company, as well as the leadership shown on the National Business Council for Consumer Affairs, are consistent with the philosophies and thought expressed by Mr. Keith as early as 1960.

In effect, he believed that (1) if a policy could be clearly stated, (2) a procedure could be put into effect that would be understood and endorsed by operating units within a company, and (3) a monitoring system could be established that left no doubt but that the Chief Executive Officer was involved, we could develop the finest form of self-regulation. This system would not only be in tune with the increasing level of consumer expectations, but would assure a highly competitive approach under our free enterprise system, in which he deeply believed.

Upon Mr. Keith's retirement, the new Executive Officer immediately reaffirmed this policy and procedure and obviously a legacy was left that has been perpetuated for the good of the consumer.

* Vice President, The Pillsbury Company

2

What Is the Marketing Management Concept?

J. B. McKitterick

PREVIEW

I. In the past 30 years businessmen have come increasingly to keep the customer's interest in mind, with a resulting de-emphasis on profit and production.
   A. In the period from 1920 to 1940, productivity increased dramatically but consumers had inadequate income to buy, and prices fell.
   B. In the period beginning with 1940 the focus in business was to make the old product better or to make a new product.

II. Business management faces very difficult planning decisions involving developments relating to its customers, its competitors, and its own resources.
   A. Customers have become more capricious as their income and leisure time have increased.
   B. Risks involved in large resource commitment have pushed businesses to add new products and new markets.
   C. As the organization structure of a business expands, it is difficult for a business to view itself, its own resources in relation to the total market.
   D. The owner-manager has generally been replaced by hired management.

III. The marketing concept was born to help establish a management philosophy in the midst of very difficult planning decisions.
   A. A company committed to the marketing concept focuses its major innovative effort on enlarging the size of the market in which it participates by:

J. B. McKitterick, "What is the Marketing Management Concept?" is reprinted by permission from Frank M. Bass (editor), *The Frontiers of Marketing Thought and Science* (Chicago: American Marketing Association, 1957), pp. 71–81.

1. introducing new products and services
2. promoting new uses for existing products
3. seeking out new classes of customers

B. Marketing affects decision policy by having all ventures revolve on the betterment of the customer.

IV. There are several implications of the marketing concept for society at large.
A. It will prepare us for economic competition for foreign markets, by emphasizing the need of the customer and better ways of selling.
B. The declining number of companies in each market has led to more markets for each company and hence to enough diversification to undertake the risks of real innovation.

Anyone who gets a new idea bearing on business philosophy and who then takes the trouble to scan corresponding utterances of preceding generations will return to this thought with increased awareness of its apparent lack of originality. In an attempt to locate the historic significance of this marketing concept that we are going to discuss today, I started reading the 1930 and 1940 issues of the *Journal of Marketing* and the *Harvard Business Review*. To my surprise, I found that many of the viewpoints expressed and the stances advocated on business philosophy bear striking resemblance to current writings. Indeed, what really seems to have changed are the phenomena—the goings on—that the authors cite to validate the importance and rationale of their message. So we have here a not unfamiliar problem in the social sciences; namely that words change their meaning much more slowly than the things to which they refer. This is particularly true of concepts such as profit, overhead, productivity and marketing orientation—which deal not so much with things that happen as with ways of thinking about them.

In order to map changing meanings, it frequently is helpful to superimpose on a history of thought some crude scheme of classification which takes its definitions from the present. If we do this in the case of the marketing concept, we will notice that over the last thirty years the preoccupation of businessmen with the customer increasingly has been formulated in terms of an end rather than in terms of a means. Correspondingly, the conception of profit as the end objective in business seems to have declined, with a tendency to view it more as a basic condition that must be satisfied. To be sure, thirty years ago businessmen admonished each other to keep the customer's interests in mind, but they usually connected this focus merely with their own need to adjust prices and volume of production to what the market would accept. Indeed, if we read between the lines, we find that the customer used to be the chap that you sent the bill to—frequently a distributor, agent, or dealer, but very rarely the actual end user. And sales tactics were conceived in terms of exploiting some scheme that would permit dealing with these trade institutions on a semi-exclusive basis. There was almost no mention of the idea that the manufacturer should focus his attention on the end user, and base his competitive footing on some superiority of value that matched with the needs of a particular group of these users. And it was obvious that few manufacturers felt that they had ability to look at the trade structure as a group of institutions for hire, to be selected and employed to perform specific functions that this end user needed. On the contrary, the trade structure was regarded as an impenetrable barrier—it *was* the market, and this fellow we have been calling the end user was the exclusive problem of the dealer, and no concern of the manufacturer.

Occasionally someone like Oswald Knauth, who has always been a bit ahead of his time, would remind the manufacturer that packaging and product styling had better be customer oriented. But by comparison to these occasional warnings to the man at the helm to keep his eye on what the customer was doing, there were urgent exhortations to the man in the engine room to get more output with less input. Indeed, the problem of winning out over competition seemed to be conceived essentially in terms of subtracting from the costs of production, and delivering an equivalent product at a lower price. So it was quite fitting that in the 1930s manufacturers studied the economies of scale, economists explored marginal concepts for setting the volume of production, and the government tried to prevent the large and efficient firm from sinking its smaller adversaries with the torpedo of lower price. In a short body of remarks it is out of scale to put a generalization such as this to adequate test, yet I cannot entirely resist some elaboration, because the social implications of what we call the marketing concept in the end are going to be of much greater importance than its bearing on management theory.

If we examine the 1920–1940 period, we find that it witnessed great gains in productivity, but not all of these gains were distributed to the labor force. The installed horsepower per production worker almost doubled, and the output per worker more than doubled. However, the average hourly wage in these twenty years increased only from 50 cents to 66 cents—not quite a third, and the number of production workers stayed almost constant at around 8½ million members in a population that actually grew by over 20 per cent. So, with rising productivity only to a limited degree passed on to the static body of production workers in the form of wage increases, consumer prices fell steadily until in 1940 they were only

70 per cent of the 1920 level, and unemployment in a growing population was a serious and long continuing problem. During this same period, the design and manner of use of most products changed only slowly, and the gross national product increased a scant 14 per cent.

To sum it up, the business ideology of producing the same product for less cost scarcely turned out to be an adequate driving force for economic growth. While a great deal of criticism was directed at the imperfections of markets organized around administered prices, subsequent events suggest that the real trouble was that most consumers had inadequate income and inadequate reason to buy. In short, productivity gains unevenly accompanied by innovation of new products and broad distribution of purchasing power resulted in a condition of chronic underconsumption.

Starting around 1940, the threat of war and the sponsorship of government combined to introduce a basic transformation in the business process which has had far reaching consequences. In a nutshell, business discovered research. On the eve of this revolution the total research outlay of businessmen stood at perhaps 100 million dollars. Today, these outlays are somewhere around four billions, and for the first time over 50 per cent of all the research done in this country is being paid for by industry out of its own pocket. If we throw in the defense effort which the government pays for, the total research outlay rises to about 7.5 billions. However, our interest here is not so much in the growth of this new industry or the sheer size of its burden, which seems likely to surpass the total cost of all advertising; rather we are concerned to learn what research did to the growth of the economy and to the problems of designing and managing an enterprise.

Where the pre-1940 period was preoccupied with trying to make the same product cheaper, the postwar period saw a new dimension added to competition, in which the focus was to try and make the old product better, or even more bold, to try and launch a new product. And as the research-equipped manufacturer looked around for applications for his new-found creative power, he frequently discovered them in markets that he heretofore had not entered. The petroleum refinery began to turn out chemicals; the rubber plant, plastics; new alloys challenged older metals; electronics cast its shadows over hydraulics; and soon, everyone's research and competitive endeavor was attacking someone else's *status quo*. Established concepts of industry alignment began to obliterate, schemes narrowly conceived to defend market position in terms of price advantage proved inadequate; and managements began to contend with problems of uncertainty that had multiple dimensions. A labor plentiful economy overnight became a labor short economy, and even though the number of employees and production workers has grown 50 per cent since 1940, and their productivity probably another 50 per cent, still the demand for their services has grown even faster, and wages have gone up some 70 per cent in constant dollars. So here we had a reversal of the conditions of the preceding twenty years; worker income rose more rapidly than productivity, competition was focused on using research to obsolete old ways of doing things, a flood of new products poured forth to meet the rising discretionary spending power, and we became so impressed with the results of focusing on what would be better for the customer rather than merely cheaper that we invented a now familiar phrase—"the marketing concept"—to describe this triumph of innovation over productive capacity.

If we look back on these basic changes in the economy, we find clues to many of the problems which have concerned management science over the last ten years. I refer especially to the constant search for means of planning and control that can contend with these rapidly changing marketing conditions. For example, many businessmen have complained that the problem of predicting the customer's behavior has been greatly complicated both by his rapidly rising discretionary income and by his growing control over the use of leisure time. Mink coats and motor cars, buying things and buying experiences all have begun to interact, and the passing fad and the more slowly changing style of life of which it is a part have become very difficult to diagnose and distinguish. And as we already have noted, the industrial customer with his multiple raw material and process alternatives, and his possibilities of sub-contracting entire operations, swimming all the while in his own competitive sea of changing functions and market alignments, presents an equally fickle target for prediction.

At the same time both the need for and difficulty of business planning have been heightened by technological trends in the production and distribution process. The long term commitments required by automated plants, guaranteed wages, basic research, and multi-million dollar national promotions imply not only irreversible decisions, but also greater lead time, because the assumptions in planning have to hold good over a longer and longer period as the separation between decision and implementation grows apace. The annual budget in many companies has been supplemented with the five-year and even the twenty-year plan. The very considerable risks entailed in these large resource commitments, combined with the increasing hazards posed by the caprice of the customer and the research efforts of a undefined arena of prospective competitors, have resulted in a powerful urge for diversification. Few businesses today seem to be able to undertake the risk of staying in a single market with a single product. Indeed, observing the pell-mell flight to add new products and markets, one might say that the most characteristic response of modern corporations to uncertainty is to refuse to choose. As new product applications emerge, as new catagories of customers come into the market, as new technologies compete to answer the old need, the corporation is inclined to embrace each in turn, forfeiting no opportunity, straddling all risks.

In due course, the organization structure begins to grow like a Christmas tree as the work of decision making is subdivided to take advantage of the specialized information and skills required. The sales executive is joined by the service manager, the product development manager, the advertising manager, the distribution planning manager, the market research director, and the whole team is duplicated anew as further lines are added. Many decisions become difficult to deal with in such a structure because they straddle the responsibilities of individuals. And when it comes to prepare purposive plans, the business is troubled by its inability to bring its own identity into view—to see entirely its unique resources, skills and commitments, and the whole market environment of which they are a part.

Finally, in analyzing this planning problem and its bearing on the marketing concept, something probably should be said about the decline of the owner-manager. The great size of modern enterprise, the progressive tax structures, and the new-found affluence of even the most lowly worker all have combined to lessen the inclination and ability of individuals to undertake an entrepreneurial role in many markets. Fortunately, the very economic growth which rules out individual enterprise in one area opens up an opportunity for it somewhere else—as in the service industries. But it is my impression that the passing of the entrepreneur, where it has occurred, has removed an important element in the planning process, because he supplied the reason for planning in the sense that he specified the objectives to be attained. Indeed, this entrepreneur made planning easy—if at the same time fickle—by telling people what he wanted to accomplish, and the whole matter was scarcely less personal or more complicated than his choice of a necktie for the day. In the modern corporation we have replaced the owner-manager with a hired management accountable in concept to a diffuse and rapidly changing body of shareholders, but actually in performance quite sensitive to the appraisal of multiple audiences among customers, suppliers, labor, financial institutions, government and the public at large. By degrees, therefore, the decline of perfect competition and the decline of the entrepreneur with his simple conception of objectives are not unrelated events. Today's complex markets with many dimensions of competition have been accompanied by a corresponding multiplication of the values to be reconciled in the policies of modern enterprises.

So to summarize, business management has very difficult planning decisions to make, requiring that it foresee and analyze many alternate developments relating to its customers, competitors, and its own resources, and management must get these decisions made by people who are organized in an enormously complex structure, in which they are aware of the interrelationships of their part and the business, but unable to adequately see the whole business and its environment, and the ends to be served by all these forecasts and decisions are becoming increasingly diffuse and uncertain. It is in this sort of setting that the marketing concept was born, and it is my belief, after reflecting both on the background of the movement and the many statements of the case which businessmen have set forth, that what this really represents is a search for a management philosophy—a primacy of decision values—that can restore order and manageability out of what threatens to seem like chaos. Indeed, at the risk of introducing controversy, I would speculate that looking back on this development twenty years hence, the marketing concept belatedly will be recognized as an appropriate voicing of the basic purpose of corporate institutions grown too large to be adequately guided by the profit interests of a single compact group of owners. Certainly anyone who carefully subtracts out of the total expenses of a modern business all of the sums expended on preparation for the future—ranging from research and advertising to new plant and training of personnel—is bound to discover that profit is a feeble measure of the current day's battle with competition, and is certainly meaningless if not considered with reference to accompanying changes in market position. With many companies today operating in conditions of oligopoly, it is small wonder that enlargement of the market and competitive share held in that market have become matters of management concern at least equal if not prerequisite to profit.

Now I want to turn from the general economic conditions and management problems which accompanied the emergency of the marketing concept to a discussion of its implications for business practices. Necessarily, this will be a highly personal statement because it is next to impossible to synthesize into a single theme what others have already set forth on this subject. It does seem to me, however, that the real distinction of the marketing concept which leads to the conclusion "this company has it" or "this one doesn't," is not so much a matter of organization structure or day-to-day tactics as it is a matter of what the management is trying to accomplish.

A moment ago I referred to the shifting focus of objectives that has characterized the evolution of modern business enterprise—first, from a focus on profit for the owner to a striving for market position and success against competition, and most recently to a focus on growth in which there is a continuing planned effort to enlarge the size of the market. It seems to me that the crux of the marketing concept is expressed in the latter not by depriving its historic competitors of the market position which they already have captured, but by the application of research and insight to the task of creating new markets—indeed, new businesses—then we know that we are dealing with a management that has fully embraced the marketing concept. To be sure, as already has been brought out rather fully, any such endeavor is not without its economic repercussions in other markets and industries, but the very extent of these effects, reaching as they do to far and foreign places, confirms that something more than a minor improvement in the lot of the customer must have occurred. So to say it precisely, a company committed to the marketing concept focuses its major innovative effort on enlarging the size of the market in which it participates by introducing new generic products and services, by promoting new applications for existing products, and by seeking out new classes of customers who heretofore have not used the existing products.

In all cases the word "new" means more than just new to the company in question. It means "new," period. This is a somewhat more rigorous definition than to merely say that the business must constantly think of the customers' best interests or put supremacy in marketing functions foremost. And I might add that the rigor is deliberate, because only thinking of the customer and mere technical proficiency in marketing both turn out to be inferior hands when played against the company that couples its thoughts with action and actually comes to market with a successful innovation. To be sure, the business that seeks to apply its research and mass production and national promotion prowess to such ambitious notions as doing really new things is going to have to be knowledgeably benign with respect to the customer, and it certainly will reduce its risk to the degree that it is experienced and skillful in its marketing organization. But if the product and the service and the way they are sold are fundamentally in the customer's best interests, a great deal of amateurism in marketing tactics can be tolerated without serious consequences. Turning the issue around, if business enterprises are to compete successfully in the quicksilver of modern markets, something more than sophistication in means of doing marketing work is going to be required. Indeed, to plan at all, and think adequately of what competition might do and its possible effects before committing multi-million dollar resources, requires knowledge of the customer which penetrates to the level of theory. *So the principal task of the marketing function in a management concept is not so much to be skillful in making the customer do what suits the interests of the business as to be skillful in conceiving and then making the business do what suits the interests of the customer.* As Frank Knight observed some years ago, in conditions of real uncertainty, the outcome of a venture will be controlled much more by the entrepreneurial decision on what major course of action to undertake than by expert practice in implementation.[1] Thus, the central meaning of the marketing concept to the decision structure of a business is that the major purpose of the venture is taken from the need to solve some problem in the outer environment—some betterment for the customer—and all subsidiary decisions dealing with the acquisition and allocation of resources within the business are bent to that objective. In this light, certain tests can be applied to our daily business practices which sharpen the distinction between the marketing concept and the mere awareness in management that superiority in the marketing function is beginning to be of greater strategic importance than superiority in the production function.

For example, we might ask, is the service of customers or defense against competition the main focus of the creative search for better courses of action? Is the business in the habit of undertaking tactics which pay their way in added sales volume, but which in prompt imitation by competition fail to add to profit? If so, is the overall marketing effort really adding consumable value for the customer, or only adding cost—as for instance, advertising expenditures which seek to make like products seem unlike, and product redesign which attempts to produce obsolescence without adding to the functions performed by the product? Is the business constantly exhausting itself, trying to hold back changes introduced by its competitors—as when it refuses to recognize a new product technology, a new service, or a new sales channel which the customer seems to prefer? Is foolish pride—as the songwriter puts it—causing the management to reject the verdict of the marketplace? Is the business trying to be all things to all customers when their requirements and interests in the product are so fragmenting that some forfeiture of clientele and specialization of customer alignment obviously are needed? Is what the business considers a good salesman essentially a customer oriented man or is he a loyal "company" man, intent on making the customer understand his employer's policies? And finally, is the business using its resources and ability to innovate on tasks that smaller competitors with less overhead can handle better, or is it taxing its capacities to the fullest in undertakings that really challenge it?

These are fairly direct questions, but the answers turn on rather subtle differences in the marketing posture of a company. By and large, it is my observation that concerns which are in an active growth phase will pass this sort of test; those that have slowed down and see themselves as digging in for a defense against younger, more vigorous competitors in time will fail the test. Certainly, anyone who examines the turnover in rankings of the hundred largest corporations, or the turnover in the leadership position in even the smallest markets, cannot fail to see that the graveyards of business are full of those who conceived their obligations to the customer too narrowly.

Now, one might ask, how can the active growth phase of a company be infinitely prolonged? In the end, will not the constant adding of new products, new applications and new users lead to a loss of identity and a nomadlike wandering over the entire market terrain? And how does a company so oriented—or disoriented—respond to the attack of competition? Must every action pass the test of what is truly in the customer's interests? To be sure, these are important questions. But much of the difficulty is removed if we remember that it often is in the interests of both the customer and the company that it abandon a market, that it forego an existing product line and forfeit some present clientele to competition.

Where two groups of product users have different requirements in either the product or the services that go with it, the constant temptation is to suppress these differences, to force homogenization of the requirements, and we all are familiar with examples of the skillful use of price policy, engineering standards, advertising, and product design to such ends. Yet when such an unnatural marriage is challenged by a competitor who selects only one of the two user groups as his intended clientele, a competitor who aligns all his decisions in the interests of that single group and who brings to it a specially designed product, then the profit position of the company that is straddling the issue is likely to become quite untenable. In the same way, a company may choose to deal with two unrelated markets in a manner that is dictated by the desire to apply some common technology or shared resource of production or distribution. The endeavor in each market being limited by the requirements of the opposite market, this company, too, is vulnerable to a competitor that specializes in only one of these undertakings. So I submit, it is no prescription of dogma but the hard facts of competition that argue for coupling a program of innovation and growth with a sharp pruning knife to cut out the commitments that threaten to compromise the marketing concept. If we all freely admitted our mistakes and were prompt in forfeiting a losing battle to competition, a great deal of pointless advertising could be turned into profit, and a substantial improvement could be worked in sales to other markets where efforts have been less than customer oriented due to the conflicts that have been baked in. Indeed, it is precisely because of this constant need for pruning that companies which were guided by pre-war notions of production efficiency, and which grew along lines of by-product diversification and vertical integration are in the gravest sort of difficulty today. Hence the most cogent argument for designing an industrial enterprise from the customer backward into the factory, rather than from the production process forward, so to speak, is that the success of the venture is becoming much less dependent on its production efficiency and much more dependent on its flexibility in adjusting to the risks posed by the changing requirements of its customers.

In closing now I want to briefly refer to the implications of this marketing concept to the society at large. Recently several provocative viewpoints have been set forth on the threat of underconsumption in our economy. David Riesman had raised the question as to whether business enthusiasm for the defense effort is entirely explained by patriotic and profit considerations. Melman in his recent book has theorized that a substantial part of the productive output of our economy is burned up in the form of administrative overhead—useless labor that we enjoy doing—but which does not lead to further gains in productivity.[2] Several recent books have looked askance at trends in advertising which attempt to subversively guide buying behavior. All in all, there is considerable evidence of a somewhat latent but chronic concern among businessmen with the possibility that we are able to produce more than people will consume. Hence, perhaps we do welcome the creation of markets by the government as a source of stability, and perhaps we are elaborating a style of management and distribution functions that is sort of subconsciously wasteful and antithetical to the interests of the consumer. These are two reasons why even in the presence of scant evidence such trends deserve sober consideration.

In the first place, if, as we all pray, this armed preparedness leads to peace rather than to war, then we will be thrown into an economic contest with Russia in which their political system, through lower labor costs and near equal technology, will battle for our foreign markets. If it turns out that we have built a style of competition and type of business venture in this country that burdens our native genius of manufacturing efficiency with a staggering load of nonproductive overhead and distribution costs, we then may find ourselves a country-island of democracy in a sea of communism. More hopefully, if we conceive of marketing as the work of finding out what the customer would consider a better prooduct and a better way to sell it, and use motivation and all these other new research and communication techniques to help the customer to advise the business on such questions, and if we then apply all of our war-born technology to problems of human betterment, guiding the effort with a marketing concept that insists upon constant innovation—then the heat of competition in our economy will be made to yield up consumable value and real economic growth, and our concern with under-consumption and fear for the outcome of a contest with a state directed economic system will be pointless in the extreme.

In the second place, there has been a long continuing harangue in Washington over the state of competition in American markets. Administered prices and conditions of oligopoly are deplored as a counterfeit type of competition which resists true economic progress. Ironically, the very same postwar period that heightened these concerns has witnessed the development of an intensive form of competition that has ranged far and wide across the traditional market and industry boundaries. As I see it, the greatest asset of our present industrial structure is that the declining number of companies in each market has been accompanied by an increasing number of markets for each company, so that today, more than ever before, hundreds of American businesses are sufficiently diversified to undertake the great risks of real innovation. In the final analysis, it is the basic purpose of the marketing concept to exploit this risk-taking and product developing capacity, reckoning with all the uncertainties and making a positive virtue out of an economic system that offers the customer a choice, and at that, a choice that is not confined to price alone, but one that explores the full dimensions of the consumption experience.

NOTES

1. Frank H. Knight, *Risk, Uncertainty, and Profit*, Houghton Mifflin Company, Boston, 1921.

2. Seymour Melman, *Dynamic Factors in Industrial Productivity*, John Wiley & Sons, Inc., New York, 1956.

LEARNING REVIEW

Questions:

1. The principal task of marketing is to be skillful in conceiving and then matching marketing programs to what suits the interests of the ________________.

2. In the modern corporation the owner-manager has been replaced by ________________.

3. ________________ is a feeble measure of the current day's battle with competition.

4. The marketing concept focuses on enlarging the size of the market it serves by
   a) ________________,
   b) ________________, and
   c) ________________.

Answers:

1. customer; 2. hired management; 3. Profit; 4. a) introducing new products and services; b) promoting new applications for existing products; c) seeking out new classes of customers.

Retrospective Comment

The point which I need to make at this time is that the marketing concept of matching resources and organizations to specified consumer needs and objectives has given rise to long range planning in all institutions—corporations, labor unions, and now the government itself. So the long trend from laissez-faire markets populated by so many competitors that none could influence the overall result has slowly given way to world industries in which there may be no more than one or two competing decision groups. Under these circumstances government planning and regulation finally will have to become meshed with the corporate counterpart. Examples of this trend can be seen in the case of aircraft engines, oil, electric power and agricultural commodities.

3

Marketing and Economic Development

Peter F. Drucker

PREVIEW

I. As the process through which an economy is integrated into a society serving human needs, marketing is critical to the economic development of underdeveloped *growth* countries.
   A. All of humanity shares the same vision of industrialization as the key to improving its economic lot.
   B. There is great danger of international and interracial conflict due to unequal distribution of income.

II. Marketing may be used to organize economic efforts of underdeveloped countries.
   A. Marketing is the least developed part of the economy in underdeveloped countries.
   B. Marketing is the easiest method of increasing the number of managers and entrepreneurs who create small business.
   C. Marketing is the developer of standards.
      1. Sears stores in Latin America, by applying the same standards as in the U. S., force improvements in other retail business in the area.
      2. Sears causes a multiplication of new businesses which produce the goods it sells in these countries.
   D. Marketing is a highly developed business discipline and is, therefore, both teachable and learnable.

III. Marketing, because it is highly developed, offers much to developing economies to aid humanity socially.

Peter F. Drucker, "Marketing and Economic Development," is reprinted by permission from the *Journal of Marketing*, published by the American Marketing Association (January 1958), pp. 252–259.

Marketing as a Business Discipline

The distinguished pioneer of marketing, whose memory we honor today, was largely instrumental in developing marketing as a systematic business discipline:

—In teaching us how to go about, in an orderly, purposeful and planned way to find and create customers;
—To identify and define markets; to create new ones and promote them;
—To integrate customers' needs, wants, and preferences, and the intellectual and creative capacity and skills of an industrial society, toward the design of new and better products and of new distributive concepts and processes.

On this contribution and similar ones of other Founding Fathers of marketing during the last half century rests the rapid emergence of marketing as perhaps the most advanced, certainly the most "scientific" of all functional business disciplines.

But Charles Coolidge Parlin also contributed as a Founding Father toward the development of marketing as a *social discipline*. He helped give us the awareness, the concepts, and the tools that make us understand marketing as a dynamic process of society through which business enterprise is integrated productively with society's purposes and human values. It is in marketing, as we now understand it, that we satisfy individual and social values, needs, and wants—be it through producing goods, supplying services, fostering innovation, or creating satisfaction. Marketing, as we have come to understand it, has its focus on the customer, that is, on the individual making decisions within a social structure and within a personal and social value system. Marketing is thus the process through which economy is integrated into society to serve human needs.

I am not competent to speak about marketing in the first sense, marketing as a functional discipline of business. I am indeed greatly concerned with marketing in this meaning. One could not be concerned, as I am, with the basic institutions of industrial society in general and with management of business enterprise in particular, without a deep and direct concern with marketing. But in this field I am a consumer of marketing alone—albeit a heavy one. I am not capable of making a contribution. I would indeed be able to talk about the wants and needs I have which I, as a consumer of marketing, hope that you, the men of marketing, will soon supply;—a theory of pricing, for instance, that can serve, as true theories should, as the foundation for actual pricing decisions and for an understanding of price behavior; or a consumer-focused concept and theory of competition. But I could not produce any of these "new products" of marketing which we want. I cannot contribute myself. To use marketing language, I am not even "effective demand," in these fields as yet.

The Role of Marketing

I shall today in my remarks confine myself to the second meaning in which marketing has become a discipline: The role of marketing in economy and society. And I shall single out as my focus the role of marketing in the economic development, especially of under-developed "growth" countries.

My thesis is very briefly as follows. Marketing occupies a critical role in respect to the development of such "growth" areas. Indeed marketing is the most important "multiplier" of such development. It is in itself in every one of these areas the least developed, the most backward part of the economic system. Its development, above all others, makes possible economic integration and the fullest utilization of whatever assets and productive capacity an economy already possesses. It mobilizes latent economic energy. It contributes to the greatest needs: that for the rapid development of entrepreneurs and managers, and at the same time it may be the easiest area of managerial work to get going. The reason is that, thanks to men like Charles Coolidge Parlin, it is the most systematized and, therefore, the most learnable and the most teachable of all areas of business management and entrepreneurship.

International and Interracial Inequality

Looking at this world of ours, we see some essentially new facts.

For the first time in man's history the whole world is united and unified. This may seem a strange statement in view of the conflicts and threats of suicidal wars that scream at us from every headline. But conflict has always been with us. What is new is that today all of mankind shares the same vision, the same objective, the same goal, the same hope, and believes in the same tools. This vision might, in gross over-simplification, be called "industrialization."

It is the belief that it is possible for man to improve his economic lot through systematic, purposeful, and directed effort—individually as well as for an entire society. It is the belief that we have the tools at our disposal—the technological, the conceptual, and the social tools—to enable man to raise himself, through his own efforts, at least to a level that we in this country would consider poverty, but which for most of our world would be almost unbelievable luxury.

And this is an irreversible new fact. It has been made so by these true agents of revolution in our times: the new tools of communication—the dirt road, the truck, and the radio, which have penetrated even the furthest, most isolated and most primitive community.

This is new, and cannot be emphasized too much and too often. It is both a tremendous vision and a tremendous danger in that catastrophe must result if it cannot be satisfied, at least to a modest degree.

But at the same time we have a new, unprecedented danger, that of international and interracial inequality. We on the North American continent are a mere tenth of the world population, including our Canadian friends and neighbors. But we have at least 75 per cent of the world income. And the 75 per cent of the world population whose income is below $100 per capita a year receive together perhaps no more than 10 per cent of the world's income. This is inequality of income, as great as anything the world has ever seen. It is accompanied by very high equality of income in the developed countries, especially in ours where we are in the process of proving that an industrial society does not have to live in extreme tension between the few very rich and the many very poor as lived all earlier societies of man. But what used to be national inequality and economic tension is now rapidly becoming international (and unfortunately also interracial) inequality and tension.

This is also brand new. In the past there were tremendous differences between societies and cultures: in their beliefs, their concepts, their ways of life, and their knowledge. The Frankish knight who went on Crusade was an ignorant and illiterate boor, according to the standards of the polished courtiers of Constantinople or of his Moslem enemies. But economically his society and theirs were exactly alike. They had the same sources of income, the same productivity of labor, the same forms and channels of investment, the same economic institutions, and the same distribution of income and wealth. Economically the Frankish knight, however much a barbarian he appeared, was at home in the societies of the East; and so was his serf. Both fitted in immediately and without any difficulty.

And this has been the case of all societies that went above the level of purely primitive tribe.

The inequality in our world today, however, between nations and races, is therefore a new—and a tremendously dangerous—phenomenon.

What we are engaged in today is essentially a race between the promise of economic development and the threat of international world-wide class war. The economic development is the opportunity of this age. The class war is the danger. Both are new. Both are indeed so new that most of us do not even see them as yet. But they are the essential economic realities of this industrial age of ours. And whether we shall realize the opportunity or succumb to danger will largely decide not only the economic future of this world—it may largely decide its spiritual, its intellectual, its political, and its social future.

Significance of Marketing

Marketing is central in this new situation. For marketing is one of our most potent levers to convert the danger into the opportunity.

To understand this we must ask: What do we mean by "under-developed"?

The first answer is, of course, that we mean areas of very low income. But income is, after all, a result. It is a result first of extreme agricultural over-population in which the great bulk of the people have to find a living on the land which, as a result, cannot even produce enough food to feed them, let alone produce a surplus. It is certainly a result of low productivity. And both, in a vicious circle, mean that there is not enough capital for investment, and very low productivity of what is being invested—owing largely to misdirection of investment into unessential and unproductive channels.

All this we know today and understand. Indeed we have learned during the last few years a very great deal both about the structure of an under-developed economy and about the theory and dynamics of economic development.

What we tend to forget, however, is that the essential aspect of an "under-developed" economy and the factor the absence of which keeps it "under-developed," is the inability to organize economic efforts and energies, to bring together resources, wants, and capacities, and so to convert a self-limiting static system into creative, self-generating organic growth.

And this is where marketing comes in.

Lack of Development in "Under-developed" Countries

(1) First, in every "under-developed" country I know of, marketing is the most under-developed—or the least developed—part of the economy, if only because of the strong, pervasive prejudice against the "middleman."

As a result, these countries are stunted by inability to make effective use of the little they have. Marketing might by itself go far toward changing the entire economic tone of the existing system—without any change in methods of production, distribution of population, or of income.

It would make the producers capable of producing marketable products by providing them with standards, with quality demands, and with specifications for their product. It would make the product capable of being brought to markets instead of perishing on the way. And it would make the consumer capable of discrimination, that is, of obtaining the greatest value for his very limited purchasing power.

In every one of these countries, marketing profits are characteristically low. Indeed the people engaged in marketing barely eke out a subsistence living. And "mark-ups" are minute by our standards. But marketing costs are outrageously high. The waste in distribution and marketing, if only from spoilage or from the accumulation of unsalable inventories that clog the shelves for years, has to be seen to be believed. And marketing service is by and large all but non-existent.

What is needed in any "growth" country to make economic development realistic, and at the same time produce a vivid demonstration of what economic development can produce, is a marketing system:

—A system of physical distribution;
—A financial system to make possible the distribution of goods; and
—Finally actual marketing, that is, an actual system of integrating wants, needs, and purchasing power of the consumer with capacity and resources of production.

This need is largely masked today because marketing is so often confused with the traditional "trader and merchant" of which every one of these countries has more than enough. It would be one of our most important contributions to the development of "under-developed" countries to get across the fact that marketing is something quite different.

It would be basic to get across the triple function of marketing:

—The function of crystallizing and directing demand for maximum productive effectiveness and efficiency;
—The function of guiding production purposefully toward maximum consumer satisfaction and consumer value;
—The function of creating discrimination that then gives rewards to those who really contribute excellence, and that then also penalize the monopolist, the slothful, or those who only want to take but do not want to contribute or to risk.

Utilization by the Entrepreneur

(2) Marketing is also the most easily accessible "multiplier" of managers and entrepreneurs in an "under-developed" growth area. And managers and entrepreneurs are the foremost need of these countries. In the first place, "economic development" is not a force of nature. It is the

result of the action, the purposeful, responsible, risk-taking action, of men as entrepreneurs and managers.

Certainly it is the entrepreneur and manager who alone can convey to the people of these countries an understanding of what economic development means and how it can be achieved.

Marketing can convert latent demand into effective demand. It cannot, by itself, create purchasing power. But it can uncover and channel all purchasing power that exists. It can, therefore, create rapidly the conditions for a much higher level of economic activity than existed before, can create the opportunities for the entrepreneur.

It then can create the stimulus for the development of modern, responsible, professional management by creating opportunity for the producer who knows how to plan, how to organize, how to lead people, how to innovate.

In most of these countries markets are of necessity very small. They are too small to make it possible to organize distribution for a single-product line in any effective manner. As a result, without a marketing organization, many products for which there is an adequate demand at a reasonable price cannot be distributed; or worse, they can be produced and distributed only under monopoly conditions. A marketing system is needed which serves as the joint and common channel for many producers if any of them is to be able to come into existence and to stay in existence.

This means in effect that a marketing system in the "under-developed" countries is the *creator of small business*, is the only way in which a man of vision and daring can become a businessman and an entrepreneur himself. This is thereby also the only way in which a true middle class can develop in the countries in which the habit of investment in productive enterprise has still to be created.

Developer of Standards

(3) Marketing in an "under-developed" country is the developer of standards—of standards for product and service as well as of standards of conduct, of integrity, of reliability, of foresight, and of concern for the basic long-range impact of decisions on the customer, the supplier, the economy, and the society.

Rather than go on making theoretical statements let me point to one illustration: The impact Sears Roebuck has had on several countries of Latin America. To be sure, the countries of Latin America in which Sears operates—Mexico, Brazil, Cuba, Venezuela, Colombia, and Peru—are not "under-developed" in the same sense in which Indonesia or the Congo are "under-developed." Their average income, although very low by our standards, is at least two times, perhaps as much as four or five times, that of the truly "under-developed" countries in which the bulk of mankind still live. Still in every respect except income level these Latin American countries are at best "developing." And they have all the problems of economic development—perhaps even in more acute form than the countries of Asia and Africa, precisely because their development has been so fast during the last ten years.

It is also true that Sears in these countries is not a "low-price" merchandiser. It caters to the middle class in the richer of these countries, and to the upper middle class in the poorest of these countries. Incidentally, the income level of these groups is still lower than that of the worker in the industrial sector of our economy.

Still Sears is a mass-marketer even in Colombia or Peru. What is perhaps even more important, it is applying in these "under-developed" countries exactly the same policies and principles it applies in this country, carries substantially the same merchandise (although most of it produced in the countries themselves), and applies the same concepts of marketing it uses in Indianapolis or Philadelphia. Its impact and experience are, therefore, a fair test of what marketing principles, marketing knowledge, and marketing techniques can achieve.

The impact of this one American business which does not have more than a mere handful of stores in these countries and handles no more than a small fraction of the total retail business of these countries is truly amazing. In the first place, Sears' latent purchasing power has fast become actual purchasing power. Or, to put it less theoretically, people have begun to organize their buying and to go out for value in what they do buy.

Secondly, by the very fact that it builds one store in one city, Sears forces a revolution in retailing throughout the whole surrounding area. It forces store modernization. It forces consumer credit. It forces a different attitude toward the customer, toward the store clerk, toward the supplier, and toward the merchandise itself. It forces other retailers to adopt modern methods of pricing, of inventory control, of training, of window display, and what have you.

The greatest impact Sears has had, however, is in the multiplication of new industrial business for which Sears creates a marketing channel. Because it has had to sell goods manufactured in these countries rather than import them (if only because of foreign exchange restrictions), Sears has been instrumental in getting established literally hundreds of new manufacturers making goods which, a few years ago, could not be made in the country, let alone be sold in adequate quantity. Simply to satisfy its own marketing needs, Sears has had to insist on standards of workmanship, quality, and delivery—that is, on standards of production management, of technical management, and above all of the management of people—which, in a few short years, have advanced the art and science of management in these countries by at least a generation.

I hardly need to add that Sears is not in Latin America for reasons of philanthropy, but because it is good and profitable business with extraordinary growth potential. In other words, Sears is in Latin America because marketing is the major opportunity in a "growth economy"—precisely because its absence is a major economic gap and the greatest need.

The Discipline of Marketing

(4) Finally, marketing is critical in economic development because marketing has become so largely systematized, so largely both learnable and teachable. It is the discipline among all our business disciplines that has advanced the furthest.

I do not forget for a moment how much we still have to learn in marketing. But we should also not forget that most of what we have learned so far we have learned in a form in which we can express it in general concepts, in valid principles and, to a substantial degree, in quantifiable measurements. This, above all others, was the achievement of that generation to whom Charles Coolidge Parlin was leader and inspiration.

A critical factor in this world of ours is the learnability and teachability of what it means to be an entrepreneur and manager. For it is the entrepreneur and the manager who alone can cause economic development to happen. The world needs them, therefore, in very large numbers; and it needs thems fast.

Obviously this need cannot be supplied by our supplying entrepreneurs and managers, quite apart from the fact that we hardly have the surplus. Money we can supply. Technical assistance we can supply, and should supply more. But the supply of men we can offer to the people in the "under-developed" countries is of necessity a very small one.

The demand is also much too urgent for it to be supplied by slow evolution through experience, or through dependence on the emergence of "naturals." The danger that lies in the inequality today between the few countries that have and the great many countries that have not is much too great to permit a wait of centuries. Yet it takes centuries if we depend on experience and slow evolution for the supply of entrepreneurs and managers adequate to the needs of a modern society.

There is only one way in which man has ever been able to short-cut experience, to telescope development, in other words, to *learn something*. That way is to have available the distillate of experience and skill in the form of knowledge, of concepts, of generalization, of measurement—in the form of *discipline*, in other words.

The Discipline of Entrepreneurship

Many of us today are working on the fashioning of such a discipline of entrepreneurship and management. Maybe we are further along than most of us realize.

Certainly in what has come to be called "Operation Research and Synthesis" we have the first beginnings of a systematic approach to the entrepreneurial task of purposeful risk-taking and innovation—so far only an approach, but a most promising one, unless indeed we become so enamored with the gadgets and techniques as to forget purpose and aim.

We are at the beginning perhaps also of an understanding of the basic problems of organizing people of diversified and highly advanced skill and judgment together in one effective organization, although again no one so far would, I am convinced, claim more for us than that we have begun at last to ask intelligent questions.

But marketing, although it only covers one functional area in the field, has something that can be called a discipline. It has developed general concepts, that is, theories that explain a multitude of phenomena in simple statements. It even has measurements that record "facts" rather than opinions. In marketing, therefore, we already possess a learnable and teachable approach to this basic and central problem not only of the "under-developed" countries but of all countries. All of us have today the same survival stake in economic development. The risk and danger of international and interracial inequality are simply too great.

Marketing is obviously not a cure-all, not a paradox. It is only one thing we need. But it answers a critical need. At the same time marketing is most highly developed.

Indeed without marketing as the hinge on which to turn, economic development will almost have to take the totalitarian form. A totalitarian system can be defined economically as one in which economic development is being attempted without marketing, indeed as one in which marketing is suppressed. Precisely because it first looks at the values and wants of the individual, and because it then develops people to act purposefully and responsibly—that is, because of its effectiveness in developing a free economy—marketing is suppressed in a totalitarian system. If we want economic development in freedom and responsibility, we have to build it on the development of marketing.

In the new and unprecedented world we live in, a world which knows both a new unity of vision and growth and a new and most dangerous cleavage, marketing has a special and central role to play. This role goes:

—Beyond "getting the stuff out the back door";
—Beyond "getting the most sales with the least cost";
—Beyond "the optimal integration of our values and wants as customers, citizens, and persons, with our productive resources and intellectual achievements"—the role marketing plays in a developed society.

In a developing economy, marketing is, of course, all of this. But in addition, in an economy that is striving to break the age-old bondage of man to misery, want, and destitution, marketing is also the catalyst for the transmutation of latent resources into actual resources, of desires into accomplishments, and the development of responsible economic leaders and informed economic citizens.

LEARNING REVIEW

Questions:

1. The ____________ future of the world may decide its political and social future as well.

2. A marketing system in the under-developed countries is the creator of ______________________ and ______________________.

3. A major point of this article is that international and interracial inequality may be overcome by the discipline of ______________________.

Answers:

1. economic; 2. quality standards, new business; 3. marketing

---

Retrospective Comment

That this essay is still topical in the mid-seventies, twenty years after it was written, strikes me as the most remarkable thing about it. For if the high hopes in respect to the economic development of the less-developed countries we then entertained had been realized, the article would by now be "old hat." That these hopes have not been realized and that instead the gap between the industrially developed countries and the underdeveloped world has been widening, is primarily the result of an extra-economic development which no one back in the fifties foresaw: the *population explosion*. As a result, the very rapid development that actually took place, in many cases much faster than even the optimists would have dared predict back in 1957 or 1958, failed to lead to a significant increase in personal income and standard of living.

But wherever there has been the development which we then hoped for, the thesis of this essay has been borne out. In Brazil, Mexico, and Columbia, the three countries of Latin America where there has been very substantial development in the last two decades, this thrust has largely been supplied by marketing. Both the achievements and the problems of these countries have been largely the result of their success in creating customers—poor customers, to be sure, with limited purchasing power, but customers nonetheless. The tremendous growth of the three nonCommunist Chinese countries of Taiwan, Hong Kong, and Singapore has also largely been caused by marketing; that is, through the mobilization by marketers of the resources, and especially the human resources, of these areas, to supply the mass markets of the developed world and especially of the United States. The same dynamics underlie the rapid economic growth of South Korea.

The major economic event of the years since this essay was written, however, has not been the development or lack of development of the less-developed countries. It has been the emergence of the multinational corporation. This is a *marketing event*. The multinational corporation was made both possible and necessary by the emergence of a genuine world market in which, for the first time in human history, demands, wants, and even consumer values are common across political, linguistic and racial barriers. The multinational is also primarily a *marketing* organization.

But the events of the last two decades have also shown how far marketing still has to go in the developed countries. Or rather, they have shown that far too few businessmen avail themselves of the knowledge and, above all, of the vision of marketing. *Consumerism* is, as I have said before, *the shame of marketing*. It is a response to the failure of business leaders to base their business and their management on the values, expectations and wants of the consumer. It is a failure to practice marketing.

4

Marketing Myopia

Theodore Levitt

PREVIEW

I. Management is responsible for the failure when growth in an industry is slowed or stopped.

II. In every floundering growth industry there is a self-deceiving cycle of great expansion and undetected decay accompanied by these four conditions:
   A. A belief that growth is assured by an expanding and more affluent population.
      1. The oil industry may face trouble because emphasis is on getting and making the product and not on improving the product or its marketing.
      2. New ideas for improving the product and its marketing have come from outside the oil industry.
   B. A belief that there is no competitive substitute for the industry's major product.
      1. The history of oil shows a number of unexpected reprieves from oblivion.
      2. The petroleum industry is convinced there is no substitute for its product.
   C. Too much faith in mass production and in the advantages of rapidly declining unit costs as output rises.
      1. The automobile industry focuses on *selling* (satisfying its own needs) rather than on *marketing* (satisfying the needs of the customer.)
      2. The oil industry has ignored new developments in fuel cells which may meet a powerful customer need.
   D. Preoccupation with a product that lends itself to carefully controlled scientific experimentation, improvement, and manufacturing cost reduction.

1. The electronics industry is so preoccupied with creating a superior product that they ignore marketing it.
2. The oil industry uses research to do what they are doing more efficiently without probing the needs of the consumer.

Every major industry was once a growth industry. But some that are now riding a wave of growth enthusiasm are very much in the shadow of decline. Others which are thought of as seasoned growth industries have actually stopped growing. In every case the reason growth is threatened, slowed, or stopped is *not* because the market is saturated. It is because there has been a failure of management.

Fateful Purposes

The failure is at the top. The executives responsible for it, in the last analysis, are those who deal with broad aims and policies. Thus:

The railroads did not stop growing because the need for passenger and freight transportation declined. That grew. The railroads are in trouble today not because the need was filled by others (cars, trucks, airplanes, even telephones), but because it was *not* filled by the railroads themselves. They let others take customers away from them because they assumed themselves to be in the railroad business rather than in the transportation business. The reason they defined their industry wrong was because they were railroad-oriented instead of transportation-oriented; they were product-oriented instead of customer-oriented.

Hollywood barely escaped being totally ravished by television. Actually, all the established film companies went through drastic reorganizations. Some simply disappeared. All of them got into trouble not because of TV's inroads but because of their own myopia. As with the railroads, Hollywood defined its business incorrectly. It thought it was in the movie business when it was actually in the entertainment business. "Movies" implied a specific, limited product. This produced a fatuous contentment which from the beginning led producers to view TV as a threat. Hollywood scorned and rejected TV when it should have welcomed it as an opportunity—an opportunity to expand the entertainment business.

Today TV is a bigger business than the old narrowly defined movie business ever was. Had Hollywood been customer-oriented (providing entertainment), rather than product-oriented (making movies), would it have gone through the fiscal purgatory that it did? I doubt it. What ultimately saved Hollywood and accounted for its recent resurgence was the wave of new young writers, producers, and directors whose previous successes in television had decimated the old movie companies and toppled the big movie moguls.

There are other less obvious examples of industries that have been and are now endangering their futures by improperly defining their purposes. I shall discuss some in detail later and analyze the kind of policies that lead to trouble. Right now it may help to show what a thoroughly customer-oriented management *can* do to keep a growth industry growing, even after the obvious opportunities have been exhausted; and here there are two examples that have been around for a long time. They are nylon and glass—specifically, E. I. duPont de Nemours & Company and Corning Glass Works:

> Both companies have great technical competence. Their product orientation is unquestioned. But this alone does not explain their success. After all, who was more pridefully product-oriented and product-conscious than the erstwhile New England textile companies that have been so thoroughly massacred? The DuPonts and the Cornings have succeeded not primarily because of their product or research orientation but because they have been thoroughly customer-oriented also. It is constant watchfulness for opportunities to apply their technical know-how to the creation of customer-satisfying uses which accounts for their prodigious output of successful new products. Without a very sophisticated eye on the customer, most of their new products might have been wrong, their sales methods useless.

Aluminum has also continued to be a growth industry, thanks to the efforts of two wartime-created companies which deliberately set about creating new customer-satisfying uses. Without Kaiser Aluminum & Chemical Corporation and Reynolds Metals Company, the total demand for aluminum today would be vastly less than it is.

Error of Analysis

Some may argue that it is foolish to set the railroads off against aluminum or the movies off against glass. Are not aluminum and glass naturally so versatile that the industries are bound to have more growth opportunities than the railroads and movies? This view commits precisely the error I have been talking about. It defines an industry, or a product, or a cluster of knowhow so narrowly as to guarantee its premature senescence. When we mention "railroads," we should make sure we mean "transportation." As transporters, the railroads still have a good chance for very considerable growth. They are not limited to the railroad business as such (though in my opinion rail transportation is potentially a much stronger transportation medium than is generally believed).

What the railroads lack is not opportunity, but some of the same managerial imaginativeness and audacity that made them great. Even an amateur like Jacques Barzun can see what is lacking when he says:

"I grieve to see the most advanced physical and social organization of the last century go down in shabby disgrace for lack of the same comprehensive imagination that built it up. [What is lacking is] the will of the companies to survive and to satisfy the public by inventiveness and skill."[1]

Shadow of Obsolescence

It is impossible to mention a single major industry that did not at one time qualify for the magic appellation of "growth industry." In each case its assumed strength lay in the apparently unchallenged superiority of its product. There appeared to be no effective substitute for it. It was itself a runaway substitute for the product it so triumphantly replaced. Yet one after another of these celebrated industries has come under a shadow. Let us look briefly at a few more of them, this time taking examples that have so far received a little less attention:

Dry cleaning—This was once a growth industry with lavish prospects. In an age of wool garments, imagine being finally able to get them safely and easily clean. The boom was on.

Yet here we are 30 years after the boom started and the industry is in trouble. Where has the competition come from? From a better way of cleaning? No. It has come from synthetic fibers and chemical additives that have cut the need for dry cleaning. But this is only the beginning. Lurking in the wings and ready to make chemical dry cleaning totally obsolescent is that powerful magician, ultrasonics.

Electric utilities—This is another one of those supposedly "no-substitute" products that has been enthroned on a pedestal of invincible growth. When the incandescent lamp came along, kerosene lights were finished. Later the water wheel and the steam engine were cut to ribbons by the flexibility, reliability, simplicity, and just plain easy availability of electric motors. The prosperity of electric utilities continues to wax extravagant as the home is converted into a museum of electric gadgetry.
How can anybody miss by investing in utilities, with no competition, nothing but growth ahead?

But a second look is not quite so comforting. A score of nonutility companies are well advanced toward developing a powerful chemical fuel cell which could sit in some hidden closet of every home silently ticking off electric power. The electric lines that vulgarize so many neighborhoods will be eliminated. So will the endless demolition of streets and service interruptions during storms. Also on the horizon is solar energy, again pioneered by nonutility companies.

Who says that the utilities have no competition? They may be natural monopolies now, but tomorrow they may be natural deaths. To avoid this prospect, they too will have to develop fuel cells, solar energy, and other power sources. To survive, they themselves will have to plot the obsolescence of what now produces their livelihood.

Grocery stores—Many people find it hard to realize that there ever was a thriving establishment known as the "corner grocery store." The supermarket has taken over with a powerful effectiveness. Yet the big food chains of the 1930s narrowly escaped being completely wiped out by the aggressive expansion of independent supermarkets. The first genuine supermarket was opened in 1930, in Jamaica, Long Island. By 1933 supermarkets were thriving in California, Ohio, Pennsylvania, and elsewhere. Yet the established chains pompously ignored them. When they chose to notice them, it was with such derisive descriptions as "cheapy," "horse-and-buggy," "cracker-barrel storekeeping," and "unethical opportunists."

The executive of one big chain announced at the time that he found it "hard to believe that people will drive for miles to shop for foods and sacrifice the personal service chains have perfected and to which Mrs. Consumer is accustomed."[2] As late as 1936, the National Wholesale Grocers convention and the New Jersey Retail Grocers Association said there was nothing to fear. They said that the supers' narrow appeal to the price buyer limited the size of their market. They had to draw from miles around. When imitators came, there would be wholesale liquidations as volume fell. The current high sales of the supers was said to be partly due to their novelty. Basically people wanted convenient neighborhood grocers. If the neighborhood stores "cooperate with their suppliers, pay attention to their costs, and improve their service," they would be able to weather the competition until it blew over.[3]

It never blew over. The chains discovered that survival required going into the supermarket business. This meant the wholesale destruction of their huge investments in corner store sites and in established distribution and merchandising methods. The companies with "the courage of their convictions" resolutely stuck to the corner store philosophy. They kept their pride but lost their shirts.

Self-Deceiving Cycle

But memories are short. For example, it is hard for people who today confidently hail the twin messiahs of electronics and chemicals to see how things could possibly go wrong with these galloping industries. They probably also cannot see how a reasonably sensible businessman could have been as myopic as the famous Boston millionaire who 50 years ago unintentionally sentenced his heirs to poverty by stipulating that his entire estate be forever invested exclusively in electric streetcar securities. His posthumous declaration, "There will always be a big demand for efficient urban transportation," is no consolation to his heirs who sustain life by pumping gasoline at automobile filling stations.

Yet, in a casual survey I recently took among a group of intelligent business executives, nearly half agreed that it would be hard to hurt their heirs by tying their estates forever to the electronics industry. When I then confronted them with the Boston streetcar example, they chorused unanimously, "That's different!" But is it? Is not the basic situation identical?

In truth, *there is no such thing* as a growth industry, I believe. There are only companies organized and operated to create and capitalize on growth opportunities. Industries that assume themselves to be riding some automatic growth escalator invariably descend into stagnation. The history of every dead and dying "growth" industry shows a self-deceiving cycle of bountiful expansion and undetected decay. There are four conditions which usually guarantee this cycle:

1. The belief that growth is assured by an expanding and more affluent population.
2. The belief that there is no competitive substitute for the industry's major product.
3. Too much faith in mass production and in the advantages of rapidly declining unit costs as output rises.
4. Preoccupation with a product that lends itself to carefully controlled scientific experimentation, improvement, and manufacturing cost reduction.

I should like now to begin examining each of these conditions in some detail. To build my case as boldly as possible, I shall illustrate the points with reference to three industries—petroleum, automobiles, and electronics—particularly petroleum, because it spans more years and more vicissitudes. Not only do these three have excellent reputations with the general public and also enjoy the confidence of sophisticated investors, but their managements have become known for progressive thinking in areas like financial control, product research, and management training. If obsolescence can cripple even these industries, it can happen anywhere.

Population Myth

The belief that profits are assured by an expanding and more affluent population is dear to the heart of every industry. It takes the edge off the apprehensions everybody understandably feels about the future. If consumers are multiplying and also buying more of your product or service, you can face the future with considerably more comfort than if the market is shrinking. An expanding market keeps the manufacturer from having to think very hard or imaginatively. If thinking is an intellectual response to a problem, then the absence of a problem leads to the absence of thinking. If your product has an automatically expanding market, then you will not give much thought to how to expand it.

One of the most interesting examples of this is provided by the petroleum industry. Probably our oldest growth industry, it has an enviable record. While there are some current apprehensions about its growth rate, the industry itself tends to be optimistic. But I believe it can be demonstrated that it is undergoing a fundamental yet typical change. It is not only ceasing to be a growth industry, but may actually be a declining one, relative to other business. Although there is widespread unawareness of it, I believe that within 25 years the oil industry may find itself in much the same position of retrospective glory that the railroads are now in. Despite its pioneering work in developing and applying the present-value method of investment evaluation, in employee relations, and in working with backward countries, the petroleum business is a distressing example of how complacency and wrongheadedness can stubbornly convert opportunity into near disaster.

One of the characteristics of this and other industries that have believed very strongly in the beneficial consequences of an expanding population, while at the same time being industries with a generic product for which there has appeared to be no competitive substitute, is that the individual companies have sought to outdo their competitors by improving on what they are already doing. This makes sense, of course, if one assumes that sales are tied to the country's population strings, because the customer can compare products only on a feature-by-feature basis. I believe it is significant, for example, that not since John D. Rockefeller sent free kerosene lamps to China has the oil industry done anything really outstanding to create a demand for its product. Not even in product improvement has it showered itself with eminence. The greatest single improvement, namely, the development of tetraethyl lead, came from outside the industry, specifically from General Motors and DuPont. The big contributions made by the industry itself are confined to the technology of oil exploration, production, and refining.

Asking for Trouble

In other words, the industry's efforts have focused on improving the *efficiency* of getting and making its product, not really on improving the generic product or its marketing. Moreover, its chief product has continuously been defined in the narrowest possible terms, namely, gasoline, not energy, fuel, or transportation. This attitude has helped assure that:

> Major improvements in gasoline quality tend not to originate in the oil industry. Also, the development of superior alternative fuels comes from outside the oil industry, as will be shown later.
>
> Major innovations in automobile fuel marketing are originated by small new oil companies that are not primarily preoccupied with production or refining. These are the companies that have been responsible for the rapidly expanding

multipump gasoline stations, with their successful emphasis on large and clean layouts, rapid and efficient driveway service, and quality gasoline at low prices.

Thus, the oil industry is asking for trouble from outsiders. Sooner or later, in this land of hungry inventors and entrepreneurs, a threat is sure to come. The possibilities of this will become more apparent when we turn to the next dangerous belief of many managements. For the sake of continuity, because this second belief is tied closely to the first, I shall continue with the same example.

Idea of Indispensability

The petroleum industry is pretty much persuaded that there is no competitive substitute for its major product, gasoline—or if there is, that it will continue to be a derivative of crude oil, such as diesel fuel or kerosene jet fuel.

There is a lot of automatic wishful thinking in this assumption. The trouble is that most refining companies own huge amounts of crude oil reserves. These have value only if there is a market for products into which oil can be converted—hence the tenacious belief in the continuing competitive superiority of automobile fuels made from crude oil.

This idea persists despite all historic evidence against it. The evidence not only shows that oil has never been a superior product for any purpose for very long, but it also shows that the oil industry has never really been a growth industry. It has been a succession of different businesses that have gone through the usual historic cycles of growth, maturity, and decay. Its over-all survival is owed to a series of miraculous escapes from total obsolescence, of last-minute and unexpected reprieves from total disaster reminiscent of the Perils of Pauline.

Perils of Petroleum

I shall sketch in only the main episodes:

First, crude oil was largely a patent medicine. But even before that fad ran out, demand was greatly expanded by the use of oil in kerosene lamps. The prospect of lighting the world's lamps gave rise to an extravagant promise of growth. The prospects were similar to those the industry now holds for gasoline in other parts of the world. It can hardly wait for the underdeveloped nations to get a car in every garage.

In the days of the kerosene lamp, the oil companies competed with each other and against gaslight by trying to improve the illuminating characteristics of kerosene. Then suddenly the impossible happened. Edison invented a light which was totally nondependent on crude oil. Had it not been for the growing use of kerosene in space heaters, the incandescent lamp would have completely finished oil as a growth industry at that time. Oil would have been good for little else than axle grease.

Then disaster and reprieve struck again. Two great innovations occurred, neither originating in the oil industry. The successful development of coal-burning domestic central-heating systems made the space heater obsolescent. While the industry reeled, along came its most magnificent boost yet—the internal combustion engine, also invented by outsiders. Then when the prodigious expansion for gasoline finally began to level off in the 1920s, along came the miraculous escape of a central oil heater. Once again, the escape was provided by an outsider's invention and development. And when that market weakened, wartime demand for aviation fuel came to the rescue. After the war the expansion of civilian aviation, the dieselization of railroads, and the explosive demand for cars and trucks kept the industry's growth in high gear.

Meanwhile centralized oil heating—whose boom potential had only recently been proclaimed—ran into severe competition from natural gas. While the oil companies themselves owned the gas that now competed with their oil, the industry did not originate the natural gas revolution, nor has it to this day greatly profited from its gas ownership. The gas revolution was made by newly formed transmission companies that marketed the product with an aggressive ardor. They started a magnificent new industry, first against the advice and then against the resistance of the oil companies.

By all the logic of the situation, the oil companies themselves should have made the gas revolution. They not only owned the gas; they also were the only people experienced in handling, scrubbing, and using it, the only people experienced in pipeline technology and transmission, and they understood heating problems. But, partly because they knew that natural gas would compete with their own sale of heating oil, the oil companies pooh-poohed the potentials of gas.

The revolution was finally started by oil pipeline executives who, unable to persuade their own companies to go into gas, quit and organized the spectacularly successful gas transmission companies. Even after their success became painfully evident to the oil companies, the latter did not go into gas transmission. The multibillion dollar business which should have been theirs went to others. As in the past, the industry was blinded by its narrow preoccupation with a specific product and the value of its reserves. It paid little or no attention to its customers' basic needs and preferences.

The postwar years have not witnessed any change. Immediately after World War II the oil industry was greatly encouraged about its future by the rapid expansion of demand for its traditional line of products. In 1950 most companies projected annual rates of domestic expansion of around

6% through at least 1975. Though the ratio of crude oil reserves to demand in the Free World was about 20 to 1, with 10 to 1 being usually considered a reasonable working ratio in the United States, booming demand sent oil men searching for more without sufficient regard to what the future really promised. In 1952 they "hit" in the Middle East; the ratio skyrocketed to 42 to 1. If gross additions to reserves continue at the average rate of the past five years (37 billion barrels annually), then by 1970 the reserve ratio will be up to 45 to 1. This abundance of oil has weakened crude and product prices all over the world.

Uncertain Future

Management cannot find much consolation today in the rapidly expanding petrochemical industry, another oil-using idea that did not originate in the leading firms. The total United States production of petrochemicals is equivalent to about 2% (by volume) of the demand for all petroleum products. Although the petrochemical industry is now expected to grow by about 10% per year, this will not offset other drains on the growth of crude oil consumption. Furthermore, while petrochemical products are many and growing, it is well to remember that there are nonpetroleum sources of the basic raw material, such as coal. Besides, a lot of plastics can be produced with relatively little oil. A 50,000-barrel-per-day oil refinery is now considered the absolute minimum size for efficiency. But a 5,000-barrel-per-day chemical plant is a giant operation.

Oil has never been a continuously strong growth industry. It has grown by fits and starts, always miraculously saved by innovations and developments not of its own making. The reason it has not grown in a smooth progression is that each time it thought it had a superior product safe from the possibility of competitive substitutes, the product turned out to be inferior and notoriously subject to obsolescence. Until now, gasoline (for motor fuel, anyhow) has escaped this fate. But, as we shall see later, it too may be on its last legs.

The point of all this is that there is no guarantee against product obsolescence. If a company's own research does not make it obsolete, another's will. Unless an industry is especially lucky, as oil has been until now, it can easily go down in a sea of red figures—just as the railroads have, as the buggy whip manufacturers have, as the corner grocery chains have, as most of the big movie companies have, and indeed as many other industries have.

The best way for a firm to be lucky is to make its own luck. That requires knowing what makes a business successful. One of the greatest enemies of this knowledge is mass production.

Production Pressures

Mass-production industries are impelled by a great drive to produce all they can. The prospect of steeply declining unit costs as output rises is more than most companies can usually resist. The profit possibilities look spectacular. All effort focuses on production. The result is that marketing gets neglected.

John Kenneth Galbraith contends that just the opposite occurs.[4] Output is so prodigious that all effort concentrates on trying to get rid of it. He says this accounts for singing commercials, desecration of the countryside with advertising signs, and other wasteful and vulgar practices. Galbraith has a finger on something real, but he misses the strategic point. Mass production does indeed generate great pressure to "move" the product. But what usually gets emphasized is selling, not marketing. Marketing, being a more sophisticated and complex process, gets ignored.

The difference between marketing and selling is more than semantic. Selling focuses on the needs of the seller, marketing on the needs of the buyer. Selling is preoccupied with the seller's need to convert his product into cash; marketing with the idea of satisfying the needs of the customer by means of the product and the whole cluster of things associated with creating, delivering, and finally consuming it.

In some industries the enticements of full mass production have been so powerful that for many years top management in effect has told the sales departments, "You get rid of it; we'll worry about profits." By contrast, a truly marketing-minded firm tries to create value-satisfying goods and services that consumers will want to buy. What it offers for sale includes not only the generic product or service, but also how it is made available to the customer, in what form, when, under what conditions, and at what terms of trade. Most important, what it offers for sale is determined not by the seller but by the buyer. The seller takes his cues from the buyer in such a way that the product becomes a consequence of the marketing effort, not vice versa.

Lag in Detroit

This may sound like an elementary rule of business, but that does not keep it from being violated wholesale. It is certainly more violated than honored. Take the automobile industry:

> Here mass production is most famous, most honored, and has the greatest impact on the entire society. The industry has hitched its fortune to the relentless requirements of the annual model change, a policy that makes customer orientation an especially urgent necessity. Consequently the auto companies annually spend millions of dollars on consumer research. But the

fact that the new compact cars are selling so well in their first year indicates that Detroit's vast researches have for a long time failed to reveal what the customer really wanted. Detroit was not persuaded that he wanted anything different from what he had been getting until it lost millions of customers to other small car manufacturers.

How could this unbelievable lag behind consumer wants have been perpetuated so long? Why did not research reveal consumer preferences before consumers' buying decisions themselves revealed the facts? Is that not what consumer research is for—to find out before the fact what is going to happen? The answer is that Detroit never really researched the customer's wants. It only researched his preferences between the kinds of things which it had already decided to offer him. For Detroit is mainly product-oriented, not customer-oriented. To the extent that the customer is recognized as having needs that the manufacturer should try to satisfy, Detroit usually acts as if the job can be done entirely by product changes. Occasionally attention gets paid to financing, too, but that is done more in order to sell than to enable the customer to buy.

As for taking care of other customer needs, there is not enough being done to write about. The areas of the greatest unsatisfied needs are ignored, or at best get stepchild attention. These are at the point of sale and on the matter of automotive repair and maintenance. Detroit views these problem areas as being of secondary importance. That is underscored by the fact that the retailing and servicing ends of this industry are neither owned and operated nor controlled by the manufacturers. Once the car is produced, things are pretty much in the dealer's inadequate hands. Illustrative of Detroit's arm's-length attitude is the fact that, while servicing holds enormous sales-stimulating, profit-building opportunities, only 57 of Chevrolet's 7,000 dealers provide night maintenance service.

Motorists repeatedly express their dissatisfaction with servicing and their apprehensions about buying cars under the present selling setup. The anxieties and problems they encounter during the auto buying and maintenance processes are probably more intense and widespread today than 30 years ago. But the automobile companies do not *seem* to listen to or take their cues from the anguished consumer. If they do listen, it must be through the filter of their own preoccupation with production. The marketing effort is still viewed as a necessary consequence of the product, not vice versa, as it should be. That is the legacy of mass production, with its parochial view that profit resides essentially in low-cost full production.

What Ford Put First

The profit lure of mass production obviously has a place in the plans and strategy of business management, but it must always *follow* hard thinking about the customer. This is one of the most important lessons that we can learn from the contradictory behavior of Henry Ford. In a sense Ford was both the most brilliant and the most senseless marketer in American history. He was senseless because he refused to give the customer anything but a black car. He was brilliant because he fashioned a production system designed to fit market needs. We habitually celebrate him for the wrong reason, his production genius. His real genius was marketing. We think he was able to cut his selling price and therefore sell millions of $500 cars because his invention of the assembly line had reduced the costs. Actually he invented the assembly line because he had concluded that at $500 he could sell millions of cars. Mass production was the *result* not the cause of his low prices.

Ford repeatedly emphasized this point, but a nation of production-oriented business managers refuses to hear the great lesson he taught. Here is his operating philosophy as he expressed it succinctly:

> "Our policy is to reduce the price, extend the operations, and improve the article. You will notice that the reduction of price comes first. We have never considered any costs as fixed. Therefore we first reduce the price to the point where we believe more sales will result. Then we go ahead and try to make the prices. We do not bother about the costs. The new price forces the costs down. The more usual way is to take the costs and then determine the price, and although that method may be scientific in the narrow sense; it is not scientific in the broad sense, because what earthly use is it to know the cost if it tells you that you cannot manufacture at a price at which the article can be sold? But more to the point is the fact that, although one may calculate what a cost is, and of course all of our costs are carefully calculated, no one knows what a cost ought to be. One of the ways of discovering . . . is to name a price so low as to force everybody in the place to the highest point of efficiency. The low price makes everybody dig for profits. We make more discoveries concerning manufacturing and selling under this forced method than by any method of leisurely investigation."[5]

Product Provincialism

The tantalizing profit possibilities of low unit production costs may be the most seriously selfdeceiving attitude that can afflict a company, particularly a "growth" company where an apparently assured expansion of demand already tends to undermine a proper concern for the importance of marketing and the customer.

The usual result of this narrow preoccupation with so-called concrete matters is that instead of growing, the industry declines. It usually means that the product fails to adapt to the constantly changing patterns of consumer needs and tastes, to new and modified marketing institutions and practices, or to product developments in competing or complementary industries. The industry has its eyes so firmly on its own specific product that it does not see how it is being made obsolete.

The classical example of this is the buggy whip industry. No amount of product improvement could stave off its death sentence. But had the industry defined itself as being in the transportation business rather than the buggy whip business, it might have survived. It would have done what survival always entails, that is, changing. Even if it had only defined its business as providing a stimulant or catalyst to an energy source, it might have survived by becoming a manufacturer of, say, fanbelts or air cleaners.

What may some day be a still more classical example is, again, the oil industry. Having let others steal marvelous opportunities from it (e.g., natural gas, as already mentioned, missile fuels, and jet engine lubricants), one would expect it to have taken steps never to let that happen again. But this is not the case. We are now getting extraordinary new developments in fuel systems specifically designed to power automobiles. Not only are these developments concentrated in firms outside the petroleum industry, but petroleum is almost systematically ignoring them, securely content in its wedded bliss to oil. It is the story of the kerosene lamp versus the incandescent lamp all over again. Oil is trying to improve hydrocarbon fuels rather than to develop *any* fuels best suited to the needs of their users, whether or not made in different ways and with different raw materials from oil.

Here are some of the things which nonpetroleum companies are working on:

> Over a dozen such firms now have advanced working models of energy systems which, when perfected, will replace the internal combustion engine and eliminate the demand for gasoline. The superior merit of each of these systems is their elimination of frequent, time-consuming, and irritating refueling stops. Most of these systems are fuel cells designed to create electrical energy directly from chemicals without combustion. Most of them use chemicals that are not derived from oil, generally hydrogen and oxygen.
>
> Several other companies have advanced models of electric storage batteries designed to power automobiles. One of these is an aircraft producer that is working jointly with several electric utility companies. The latter hope to use off-peak generating capacity to supply overnight plug-in battery regeneration. Another company, also using the battery approach, is a medium-size electronics firm with extensive small-battery experience that it developed in connection with its work on hearing aids. It is collaborating with an automobile manufacturer. Recent improvements arising from the need for high-powered miniature power storage plants in rockets have put us within reach of a relatively small battery capable of withstanding great overloads or surges of power. Germanium diode applications and batteries using sintered-plate and nickel-cadmium techniques promise to make a revolution in our energy sources.

> Solar energy conversion systems are also getting increasing attention. One usually cautious Detroit auto executive recently ventured that solar-powered cars might be common by 1980.

As for the oil companies, they are more or less "watching developments," as one research director put it to me. A few are doing a bit of research on fuel cells, but almost always confined to developing cells powered by hydrocarbon chemicals. None of them are enthusiastically researching fuel cells, batteries, or solar power plants. None of them are spending a fraction as much on research in these profoundly important areas as they are on the usual run-of-the-mill things like reducing combustion chamber deposit in gasoline engines. One major integrated petroleum company recently took a tentative look at the fuel cell and concluded that although "the companies actively working on it indicate a belief in ultimate success . . . the timing and magnitude of its impact are too remote to warrant recognition in our forecasts."

One might, of course, ask: Why should the oil companies do anything different? Would not chemical fuel cells, batteries, or solar energy kill the present product lines? The answer is that they would indeed, and that is precisely the reason for the oil firms having to develop these power units before their competitors, so they will not be companies without an industry.

Management might be more likely to do what is needed for its own preservation if it thought of itself as being in the energy business. But even that would not be enough if it persists in imprisoning itself in the narrow grip of its tight product orientation. It has to think of itself as taking care of customer needs, not finding, refining, or even selling oil. Once it genuinely thinks of its business as taking care of people's transportation needs, nothing can stop it from creating its own extravagantly profitable growth.

"Creative Destruction"

Since words are cheap and deeds are dear, it may be appropriate to indicate what this kind of thinking involves and leads to. Let us start at the beginning—the customer. It can be shown that motorists strongly dislike the bother, delay, and experience of buying gasoline. People actually do not buy gasoline. They cannot see it, taste it, feel it, appreciate it, or really test it. What they buy is the right to continue driving their cars. The gas station is like a tax collector to whom people are compelled to pay a periodic toll as the price of using their cars. This makes the gas station a basically unpopular institution. It can never be made popular or pleasant, only less unpopular, less unpleasant.

To reduce its unpopularity completely means eliminating it. Nobody likes a tax collector, not even a pleasantly cheerful one. Nobody likes to interrupt a trip to buy a phantom product, not even from a handsome Adonis or a seductive Venus. Hence, companies that are working on exotic fuel substitutes which will eliminate the need for frequent refueling are heading directly into the outstretched arms of the irritated motorist. They are riding a wave of inevitability, not because they are creating something which is technologically superior or more sophisticated, but because they are satisfying a powerful customer need. They are also eliminating noxious odors and air pollution.

Once the petroleum companies recognize the customer-satisfying logic of what another power system can do, they will see that they have no more choice about working on an efficient, long-lasting fuel (or some way of delivering present fuels without bothering the motorist) than the big food chains had a choice about getting into the supermarket business, or the vacuum tube companies had a choice about making semiconductors. For their own good the oil firms will have to destroy their own highly profitable assets. No amount of wishful thinking can save them from the necessity of engaging in this form of "creative destruction."

I phrase the need as strongly as this because I think management must make quite an effort to break itself loose from conventional ways. It is all too easy in this day and age for a company or industry to let its sense of purpose become dominated by the economics of full production and to develop a dangerously lopsided product orientation. In short, if management lets itself drift, it invariably drifts in the direction of thinking of itself as producing goods and services, not customer satisfactions. While it probably will not descend to the depths of telling its salesmen, "You get rid of it; we'll worry about profits," it can, without knowing it, be practicing precisely that formula for withering decay. The historic fate of one growth industry after another has been its suicidal product provincialism.

Dangers of R & D

Another big danger to a firm's continued growth arises when top management is wholly transfixed by the profit possibilities of technical research and development. To illustrate I shall turn first to a new industry—electronics—and then return once more to the oil companies. By comparing a fresh example with a familiar one, I hope to emphasize the prevalence and insidiousness of a hazardous way of thinking.

Marketing Shortchanged

In the case of electronics, the greatest danger which faces the glamorous new companies in this field is not that they do not pay enough attention to research and development, but that they pay *too much* attention to it. And the fact that the fastest growing electronics firms owe their eminence to their heavy emphasis on technical research is completely beside the point. They have vaulted to affluence on a sudden crest of unusually strong general receptiveness to new technical ideas. Also, their success has been shaped in the virtually guaranteed market of military subsidies and by military orders that in many cases actually preceded the existence of facilities to make the products. Their expansion has, in other words, been almost totally devoid of marketing effort.

Thus, they are growing up under conditions that come dangerously close to creating the illusion that a superior product will sell itself. Having created a successful company by making a superior product, it is not surprising that management continues to be oriented toward the product rather than the people who consume it. It develops the philosophy that continued growth is a matter of continued product innovation and improvement.

A number of other factors tend to strengthen and sustain this belief:

(1) Because electronic products are highly complex and sophisticated, managements become topheavy with engineers and scientists. This creates a selective bias in favor of research and production at the expense of marketing. The organization tends to view itself as making things rather than satisfying customer needs. Marketing gets treated as a residual activity, "something else" that must be done once the vital job of product creation and production is completed.

(2) To this bias in favor of product research, development, and production is added the bias in favor of dealing with controllable variables. Engineers and scientists are at home in the world of concrete things like machines, test tubes, production lines, and even balance sheets. The abstractions to which they feel kindly are those which are testable or manipulatable in the laboratory, or, if not testable, then functional, such as Euclid's axioms. In short, the managements of the new glamour-growth companies tend to favor those business activities which lend themselves to careful study, experimentation, and control—the hard, practical, realities of the lab, the shop, the books.

What gets shortchanged are the realities of the *market*. Consumers are unpredictable, varied, fickle, stupid, shortsighted, stubborn, and generally bothersome. This is not what the engineer-managers say, but deep down in their consciousness it is what they believe. And this accounts for their concentrating on what they know and what they can control, namely product research, engineering, and production. The emphasis on production becomes particularly attractive when the product can be made at declining unit costs. There is no more inviting way of making money than by running the plant full blast.

Today the top-heavy science-engineering-production orientation of so many electronics companies works reasonably well because they are pushing into new frontiers in which the armed services have pioneered virtually assured markets. The companies are in the felicitous position of having to fill, not find markets; of not having to discover what the customer needs and wants, but of having the customer voluntarily come forward with specific new product demands. If a team of consultants had been assigned specifically to design a business situation calculated to prevent the emergence and development of a customer-oriented marketing viewpoint, it could not have produced anything better than the conditions just described.

Stepchild Treatment

The oil industry is a stunning example of how science, technology, and mass production can divert an entire group of companies from their main task. To the extent the consumer is studied at all (which is not much), the focus is forever on getting information which is designed to help the oil companies improve what they are now doing. They try to discover more convincing advertising themes, more effective sales promotional drives, what the market shares of the various companies are, what people like or dislike about service station dealers and oil companies, and so forth. Nobody seems as interested in probing deeply into the basic human needs that the industry might be trying to satisfy as in probing into the basic properties of the raw material that the companies work with in trying to deliver customer satisfactions.

Basic questions about customers and markets seldom get asked. The latter occupy a stepchild status. They are recognized as existing, as having to be taken care of, but not worth very much real thought or dedicated attention. Nobody gets as excited about the customers in his own backyard as about the oil in the Sahara Desert. Nothing illustrates better the neglect of marketing than its treatment in the industry press:

> The centennial issue of the *American Petroleum Institute Quarterly*, published in 1959 to celebrate the discovery of oil in Titusville, Pennsylvania, contained 21 feature articles proclaiming the industry's greatness. Only one of these talked about its achievements in marketing, and that was only a pictorial record of how service station architecture has changed. The issue also contained a special section on "New Horizons," which was devoted to showing the magnificent role oil would play in America's future. Every reference was ebulliently optimistic, never implying once that oil might have some hard competition. Even the reference to atomic energy was a cheerful catalogue of how oil would help make atomic energy a success. There was not a single apprehension that the oil industry's affluence might be threatened

or a suggestion that one "new horizon" might include new and better ways of serving oil's present customers.

But the most revealing example of the stepchild treatment that marketing gets was still another special series of short articles on "The Revolutionary Potential of Electronics." Under that heading this list of articles appeared in the table of contents:

"In the Search for Oil"

"In Production Operations"

"In Refinery Processes"

"In Pipeline Operations"

Significantly, every one of the industry's major functional areas is listed, *except* marketing. Why? Either it is believed that electronics holds no revolutionary potential for petroleum marketing (which is palpably wrong), or the editors forgot to discuss marketing (which is more likely, and illustrates its stepchild status).

The order in which the four functional areas are listed also betrays the alienation of the oil industry from the consumer. The industry is implicitly defined as beginning with the search for oil and ending with its distribution from the refinery. But the truth is, it seems to me, that the industry begins with the needs of the customer for its products. From that primal position its definition moves steadily backstream to areas of progressively lesser importance, until it finally comes to rest at the "search for oil."

Beginning & End

The view that an industry is a customer-satisfying process, not a goods-producing process, is vital for all businessmen to understand. An industry begins with the customer and his needs, not with a patent, a raw material, or a selling skill. Given the customer's needs, the industry develops backwards, first concerning itself with the physical *delivery* of customer satisfactions. Then it moves back further to *creating* the things by which these satisfactions are in part achieved. How these materials are created is a matter of indifference to the customer, hence the particular form of manufacturing, processing, or what-have-you cannot be considered as a vital aspect of the industry. Finally, the industry moves back still further to *finding* the raw materials necessary for making its products.

The irony of some industries oriented toward technical research and development is that the scientists who occupy the high executive positions are totally unscientific when it comes to defining their companies' over-all needs and purposes. They violate the first two rules of the scientific method—being aware of and defining their companies' problems, and then developing testable hypotheses about solving them. They are scientific only about the convenient things, such as laboratory and product experiments. The reason that the customer (and the satisfaction of his deepest needs) is not considered as being "the problem" is not because there is any certain belief that no such problem exists, but because an organizational lifetime has conditioned management to look in the opposite direction. Marketing is a stepchild.

I do not mean that selling is ignored. Far from it. But selling, again, is not marketing. As already pointed out, selling concerns itself with the tricks and techniques of getting people to exchange their cash for your product. It is not concerned with the values that the exchange is all about. And it does not, as marketing invariably does, view the entire business process as consisting of a tightly integrated effort to discover, create, arouse, and satisfy customer needs. The customer is somebody "out there" who, with proper cunning, can be separated from his loose change.

Actually, not even selling gets much attention in some technologically minded firms. Because there is a virtually guaranteed market for the abundant flow of their new products, they do not actually know what a real market is. It is as if they lived in a planned economy, moving their products routinely from factory to retail outlet. Their successful concentration on products tends to convince them of the soundness of what they have been doing, and they fail to see the gathering clouds over the market.

Conclusion

Less than 75 years ago American railroads enjoyed a fierce loyalty among astute Wall Streeters. European monarchs invested in them heavily. Eternal wealth was thought to be the benediction for anybody who could scrape a few thousand dollars together to put in rail stocks. No other form of transportation could compete with the railroads in speed, flexibility, durability, economy, and growth potentials. As Jacques Barzun put it, "By the turn of the century it was an institution, an image of man, a tradition, a code of honor, a source of poetry, a nursery of boyhood desires, a sublimest of toys, and the most solemn machine—next to the funeral hearse—that marks the epochs in man's life."[6]

Even after the advent of automobiles, trucks, and airplanes, the railroad tycoons remained imperturbably self-confident. If you had told them 60 years ago that in 30 years they would be flat on their backs, broke, and pleading for government subsidies, they would have thought you totally demented. Such a future was simply not considered possible. It was not even a discussable subject, or an askable question, or a matter which any sane person would consider worth speculating about. The very thought was insane. Yet a lot of insane notions now have matter-of-fact acceptance—for example, the idea of 100-ton tubes of metal moving smoothly through the air 20,000 feet above the earth, loaded with 100 sane and solid citizens casually drinking martinis—and they have dealt cruel blows to the railroads.

What specifically must other companies do to avoid this fate? What does customer orientation involve? These questions have in part been answered by the preceding examples and analysis. It would take another article to show in detail what is required for specific industries. In any case, it should be obvious that building an effective customer-oriented company involves far more than good intentions or promotional tricks; it involves profound matters of human organization and leadership. For the present, let me merely suggest what appear to be some general requirements.

Visceral Feel of Greatness

Obviously the company has to do what survival demands. It has to adapt to the requirements of the market, and it has to do it sooner rather than later. But mere survival is a so-so aspiration. Anybody can survive in some way or other, even the skid-row bum. The trick is to survive gallantly, to feel the surging impulse of commercial mastery; not just to experience the sweet smell of success, but to have the visceral feel of entrepreneurial greatness.

No organization can achieve greatness without a vigorous leader who is driven onward by his own pulsating *will to succeed.* He has to have a vision of grandeur, a vision that can produce eager followers in vast numbers. In business, the followers are the customers. To produce these customers, the entire corporation must be viewed as a customer-creating and customer-satisfying organism. Management must think of itself not as producing products but as providing customer-creating value satisfactions. It must push the idea (and everything it means and requires) into every nook and cranny of the organization. It has to do this continuously and with the kind of flair that excites and stimulates the people in it. Otherwise, the company will be merely a series of pigeonholed parts, with no consolidating sense of purpose or direction.

In short, the organization must learn to think of itself not as producing goods or services but as *buying customers*, as doing the things that will make people *want* to do business with it. And the chief executive himself has the inescapable responsibility for creating this environment, this viewpoint, this attitude, this aspiration. He himself must set the company's style, its direction, and its goals. This means he has to know precisely where he himself wants to go, and to make sure the whole organization is enthusiastically aware of where that is. This is a first requisite of leadership, for *unless he knows where he is going, any road will take him there.*

If any road is okay, the chief executive might as well pack his attaché case and go fishing. If an organization does not know or care where it is going, it does not need to advertise that fact with a ceremonial figurehead. Everybody will notice it soon enough.

NOTES

1. Jacques Barzun, "Trains and the Mind of Man," *Holiday*, February 1960, p. 21.
2. For more details see M. M. Zimmerman, *The Super Market: A Revolution in Distribution* (New York, McGraw-Hill Book Company, Inc., 1955), p. 48.
3 *Ibid.*, pp. 45–47.
4. *The Affluent Society* (Boston, Houghton Mifflin Company, 1958), pp. 152–160.
5. Henry Ford, *My Life and Work* (New York, Doubleday, Page Company, 1923), pp. 146–147.
6. *Op. cit.*, p. 20.

LEARNING REVIEW

Questions:

1. The author says there is no such thing as a ____________________.

2. The four conditions that may accompany the failure of a growth industry are
   a) ____________________
   b) ____________________
   c) ____________________
   d) ____________________

Answers:

1. growth industry; 2. a) belief growth is assured by expanding population; b) belief there is no competitive substitute for the product; c) too much faith in mass production and lowered per-item cost; d) preoccupation with scientific experimentation.

Retrospective Comment

Marketing Myopia said nothing new. Others preceded me, saying what was original and instructive about *the marketing concept* much more carefully than I, as a latecomer, did. The major purpose of the article was to communicate to a wider audience in a much more provocative way what my predecessors had pioneered. It sought to emphasize thereby the powerful relationship between marketing and the corporate purpose. It sought also to harness a knowledge and appreciation of technology to marketing thinking.

Today, I would not write the article differently, given its original purposes. If the purpose were to write something on developing balanced corporate goals and strategies, I'd write a different and more balanced article. One thing is interesting: why the enormous popularity of the article? What is the hidden message? Is it that concrete illustrations and anecdotal facts communicate better than abstract statements standing in theoretic isolation? Is it that extreme statements, vigorously asserted, are more persuasive and more memorable than balanced statements—even when they address themselves to people accustomed to balance and thoughtful calculation? Is the message that the character of the message is at least as important as its content?

5

Broadening the Concept of Marketing

Philip Kotler and Sidney J. Levy

PREVIEW

I. Many non-business organizations perform the classic business functions, including marketing.
   A. Every organization produces a product: physical products, services, personal marketing, or ideas.
   B. Organizations must deal with groups that are interested in their product and whose demand can make a difference.
      1. Suppliers provide inputs which make it necessary to perform work and produce a product for specific channels.
      2. Consumers demand specific end uses of the product.
   C. Organizations use a number of tools with counterparts in business:
      1. *Product improvement* is encouraged by competition from other organizations.
      2. *Pricing* products and services is a complex issue which organizations must face.
      3. *Distribution* to make goods conveniently accessible to buyers is a central concern.
      4. *Customer communication* is an essential activity that many non-business organizations fail to realize.

II. There are a number of main principles of effective marketing to guide business organizations which also apply to non-business organizations.
   A. Product definition emphasizes the basic customer needs being served.
   B. The target group for the product should be certain, clearly defined groups.

Philip Kotler and Sidney J. Levy, "Broadening the Concept of Marketing," is reprinted by permission from the *Journal of Marketing*, published by the American Marketing Association (January 1969), pp. 10–15.

C. If more than one target group is served, the business organization should differentiate its product offerings and communications.
D. Customer needs and behavior should be checked through formal research and analysis.
E. Differential advantages over other products should be exploited.
F. A number of different tools, or approaches, can be used to reach the consumer.
G. Integrated marketing activities will prevent the various tools from working at cross purposes.
H. Continuous feedback should be gathered from marketing activities.
I. Periodic audits of objectives, resources, and opportunities should be provided.

III. The concept of marketing as sensitively serving and satisfying human needs is useful for all organizations.

The term "marketing" connotes to most people a function peculiar to business firms. Marketing is seen as the task of finding and stimulating buyers for the firm's output. It involves product development, pricing, distribution, and communication; and in the more progressive firms, continuous attention to the changing needs of customers and the development of new products, with product modifications and services to meet these needs. But whether marketing is viewed in the old sense of "pushing" products or in the new sense of "customer satisfaction engineering," it is almost always viewed and discussed as a business activity.

It is the authors' contention that marketing is a pervasive societal activity that goes considerably beyond the selling of toothpaste, soap, and steel. Political contests remind us that candidates are marketed as well as soap; student recruitment by colleges reminds us that higher education is marketed; and fund raising reminds us that "causes" are marketed. Yet these areas of marketing are typically ignored by the student of marketing. Or they are treated cursorily as public relations or publicity activities. No attempt is made to incorporate these phenomena in the body proper of marketing thought and theory. No attempt is made to redefine the meaning of product development, pricing, distribution, and communication in these newer contexts to see if they have a useful meaning. No attempt is made to examine whether the principles of "good" marketing in traditional product areas are transferable to the marketing of services, persons, and ideas.

The authors see a great opportunity for marketing people to expand their thinking and to apply their skills to an increasingly interesting range of social activity. The challenge depends on the attention given to it; marketing will either take on a broader social meaning or remain a narrowly defined business activity.

The Rise of Organizational Marketing

One of the most striking trends in the United States is the increasing amount of society's work being performed by organizations other than business firms. As a society moves beyond the stage where shortages of food, clothing, and shelter are the major problems, it begins to organize to meet other social needs that formerly had been put aside. Business enterprises remain a dominant type of organization, but other types of organizations gain in conspicuousness and in influence. Many of these organizations become enormous and require the same rarefied management skills as traditional business organizations. Managing the United Auto Workers, Defense Department, Ford Foundation, World Bank, Catholic Church, and University of California has become every bit as challenging as managing Procter and Gamble, General Motors, and General Electric. These nonbusiness organizations have an increasing range of influence, affect as many livelihoods, and occupy as much media prominence as major business firms.

All of these organizations perform the classic business functions. Every organization must perform a financial function insofar as money must be raised, managed, and budgeted according to sound business principles. Every organization must perform a production function in that it must conceive of the best way of arranging inputs to produce the outputs of the organization. Every organization must perform a personnel function in that people must be hired, trained, assigned, and promoted in the course of the organization's work. Every organization must perform a purchasing function in that it must acquire materials in an efficient way through comparing and selecting sources of supply.

When we come to the marketing function, it is also clear that every organization performs marketing-like activities whether or not they are recognized as such. Several examples can be given.

The police department of a major U. S. city, concerned with the poor image it has among an important segment of its population, developed a campaign to "win friends and influence people." One highlight of this campaign is a "visit your police station" day in which tours are conducted to show citizens the daily operations of the police department, including the crime laboratories, police lineups, and cells. The police department also sends officers to speak at public schools and carries out a number of other activities to improve its community relations.

Most museum directors interpret their primary responsibility as "the proper preservation of an artistic heritage for posterity."[1] As a result, for many people museums are cold marble mausoleums that house miles of relics that soon give way to yawns and tired feet. Although museum attendance in the United States advances each year, a large number of citizens are uninterested in museums. Is this indifference due to failure in the manner of presenting what museums have to offer? This nagging question led the new director of the Metropolitan Museum of Art to broaden the museum's appeal through sponsoring contemporary art shows and "happenings." His marketing philosophy of museum management led to substantial increases in the Met's attendance.

The public school system in Oklahoma City sorely needed more public support and funds to prevent a deterioration of facilities and exodus of teachers. It recently resorted to television programming to dramatize the work the public schools were doing to fight the high school dropout problem, to develop new teaching techniques, and to enrich the children. Although an expensive medium, television quickly reached large numbers of parents whose response and interest were tremendous.

Nations also resort to international marketing campaigns to get across important points about themselves to the citizens of other countries. The junta of Greek colonels who seized power in Greece in 1967 found the international publicity surrounding their cause to be extremely unfavorable and potentially disruptive of international recognition. They hired a major New York public relations firm and soon full-page newspaper ads appeared carrying the headline "Greece Was Saved From Communism," detailing in small print why the takeover was necessary for the stability of Greece and the world.[2]

An anti-cigarette group in Canada is trying to press the Canadian legislature to ban cigarettes on the grounds that they are harmful to health. There is widespread support for this cause but the organization's funds are limited, particularly measured against the huge advertising resources of the cigarette industry. The group's problem is to find effective ways to make a little money go a long way in persuading influential legislators of the need for discouraging cigarette consumption. This group has come up with several ideas for marketing anti-smoking to Canadians, including television spots, a paperback book featuring pictures of cancer and heart disease patients, and legal research on company liability for the smoker's loss of health.

What concepts are common to these and many other possible illustrations of organizational marketing? All of these organizations are concerned about their "product" in the eyes of certain "consumers" and are seeking to find "tools" for furthering their acceptance. Let us consider each of these concepts in general organizational terms.

Products

Every organization produces a "product" of at least one of the following types:

Physical products. "Product" first brings to mind everyday items like soap, clothes, and food, and extends to cover millions of *tangible* items that have a market value and are available for purchase.

Services. Services are *intangible* goods that are subject to market transaction such as tours, insurance, consultation, hairdos, and banking.

Persons. Personal marketing is an endemic *human* activity, from the employee trying to impress his boss to the statesman trying to win the support of the public. With the advent of mass communications, the marketing of persons has been turned over to professionals. Hollywood stars have their press agents, political candicates their advertising agencies, and so on.

Organizations. Many organizations spend a great deal of time marketing themselves. The Republican Party has invested considerable thought and resources in trying to develop a modern look. The American Medical Association decided recently that it needed to launch a campaign to improve the image of the American doctor.[3] Many charitable organizations and universities see selling their *organization* as their primary responsibility.

Ideas. Many organizations are mainly in the business of selling *ideas* to the larger society. Population organizations are trying to sell the idea of birth control, and the Women's Christian Temperance Union is still trying to sell the idea of prohibition.

Thus the "product" can take many forms, and this is the first crucial point in the case for broadening the concept of marketing.

Consumers

The second crucial point is that organizations must deal with many groups that are interested in their products and can make a difference in its success. It is vitally important to the organization's success that it be sensitive to, serve, and satisfy these groups. One set of groups can be called the *suppliers*. *Suppliers* are those who provide the management group with the inputs necessary to perform its work and develop its product effectively. Suppliers include employees, vendors of the materials, banks, advertising agencies, and consultants.

The other set of groups are the *consumers* of the organization's product, of which four sub-groups can be distinguished. The *clients* are those who are the immediate consumers of the organization's product. The clients of a business firm are its buyers and potential buyers; of a service organization those receiving the services, such as the needy (from the Salvation Army) or the sick (from County Hospital); and of a protective or a primary organization, the members themselves. The second group is the *trustees* or *directors*, those who are vested with the legal authority and responsibility for the organization, oversee the management, and enjoy a variety of benefits from the "product." The third group is the active *publics* that take a specific interest in the organization. For a business firm, the active publics include consumer rating groups, governmental agencies, and pressure groups of various kinds. For a university, the active publics include alumni and friends of the university, foundations, and city fathers. Finally, the fourth consumer group is the *general public*. These are all the people who might develop attitudes toward the organization that might affect its conduct in some way. Organizational marketing concerns the programs designed by management to create satisfactions and favorable attitudes in the organization's four consuming groups: clients, trustees, active publics, and general public.

Marketing Tools

Students of business firms spend much time studying the various tools under the firm's control that affect product acceptance: product improvement, pricing, distribution, and communication. All of these tools have counterpart applications to nonbusiness organizational activity.

Nonbusiness organizations to various degrees engage in product improvement, especially when they recognize the competition they face from other organizations. Thus, over the years churches have added a host of nonreligious activities to their basic religious activities to satisfy members seeking other bases of human fellowship. Universities keep updating their curricula and adding new student services in an attempt to make the educational experience relevant to the students. Where they have failed to do this, students have sometimes organized their own courses and publications, or have expressed their dissatisfaction in organized protest. Government agencies such as license bureaus, police forces, and taxing bodies are often not responsive to the public because of monopoly status; but even here citizens have shown an increasing readiness to protest mediocre services, and more alert bureaucracies have shown a growing interest in reading the user's needs and developing the required product services.

All organizations face the problem of pricing their products and services so that they cover costs. Churches charge dues, universities charge tuition, governmental agencies charge fees, fund-raising organizations send out bills. Very often specific product charges are not sufficient to meet the organization's budget, and it must rely on gifts and surcharges to make up the difference. Opinions vary as to how much the users should be charged for the individual services and how much should be made up through general collection. If the university increases its tuition, it will have to face losing some students and putting more students on scholarship. If the hospital raises its charges to cover rising costs and additional services, it may provoke a reaction from the community. All organizations face complex pricing issues although not all of them understand good pricing practice.

Distribution is a central concern to the manufacturer seeking to make his goods conveniently accessible to buyers. Distribution also can be an important marketing decision area for nonbusiness organizations. A city's public library has to consider the best means of making its books available to the public. Should it establish one large library with an extensive collection of books, or several neighborhood branch libraries with duplication of books? Should it use bookmobiles that bring the books to the customers instead of relying exclusively on the customers coming to the books? Should it distribute through school libraries? Similarly the police department of a city must think through the problem of distributing its protective services efficiently through the community. It has to determine how much protective service to allocate to different neighborhoods; the respective merits of squad cars, motorcycles, and foot patrolmen; and the positioning of emergency phones.

Customer communication is an essential activity of all organizations although many nonmarketing organizations often fail to accord it the importance it deserves. Managements of many organizations think they have fully met their communication responsibilities by setting up advertising and/or public relations departments. They fail to realize that *everything about an organization talks.* Customers form impressions of an organization from its physical facilities, employees, officers, stationery, and a hundred other company surrogates. Only when this is appreciated do the members of the organization recognize that they all are in marketing, whatever else they do. With this understanding they can assess realistically the impact of their activities on the consumers.

Concepts for Effective Marketing Management in Nonbusiness Organizations

Although all organizations have products, markets and marketing tools, the art and science of effective marketing management have reached their highest state of development in the business type of organization. Business organizations depend on customer goodwill for survival and have generally learned how to sense and cater to their needs effectively. As other types of organizations recognize their marketing roles, they will turn increasingly to the body of marketing principles worked out by business organizations and adapt them to their own situations.

What are the main principles of effective marketing management as they appear in most forward-looking business organizations? Nine concepts stand out as crucial in guiding the marketing effort of a business organization.

Generic Product Definition

Business organizations have increasingly recognized the value of placing a broad definition on their products, one that emphasizes the basic customer need(s) being served. A modern soap company recognizes that its basic product is cleaning, not soap; a cosmetics company sees its basic product as beauty or hope, not lipsticks and makeup; a publishing company sees its basic product as information, not books.

The same need for a broader definition of its business is incumbent upon nonbusiness organizations if they are to survive and grow. Churches at one time tended to define their product narrowly as that of producing religious services for members. Recently, most churchmen have decided that their basic product is human fellowship. There was a time when educators said that their product was the three R's. Now most of them define their product as education for the whole man. They try to serve the social, emotional, and political needs of young people in addition to intellectual needs.

Target Groups Definition

A generic product definition usually results in defining a very wide market, and it is then necessary for the organization, because of limited resources, to limit its product offering to certain clearly defined groups within the market. Although the generic product of an automobile company is transportation, the company typically sticks to cars, trucks, and buses, and stays away from bicycles, airplanes, and steamships. Furthermore, the manufacturer does not produce every size and shape of car but concentrates on producing a few major types to satisfy certain substantial and specific parts of the market.

In the same way, nonbusiness organizations have to define their target groups carefully. For example, in Chicago the YMCA defines its target groups as men, women and children who want recreational opportunities and are willing to pay $20 or more a year for them. The Chicago Boys Club, on the other hand, defines its target group as poorer boys within the city boundaries who are in want of recreational facilities and can pay $1 a year.

Differentiated Marketing

When a business organization sets out to serve more than one target group, it will be maximally effective by differentiating its product offerings and communications. This is also true for nonbusiness organizations. Fund-raising organizations have recognized the advantage of treating clients, trustees, and various publics in different ways. These groups require differentiated appeals and frequency of solicitation. Labor unions find that they must address different messages to different parties rather than one message to all parties. To the company they may seem unyielding, to the conciliator they may appear willing to compromise, and to the public they seek to appear economically exploited.

Customer Behavior Analysis

Business organizations are increasingly recognizing that customer needs and behavior are not obvious without formal research and analysis; they cannot rely on impressionistic evidence. Soap companies spend hundreds of thousands of dollars each year researching how Mrs. Housewife feels about her laundry, how, when, and where she does her laundry, and what she desires of a detergent.

Fund raising illustrates how an industry has benefited by replacing stereotypes of donors with studies of why people contribute to causes. Fund raisers have learned that people give because they are getting something. Many give to community chests to relieve a sense of guilt because of their elevated state compared to the needy. Many give to medical charities to relieve a sense of fear that they may be struck by a disease whose cure has not yet been found. Some give to feel pride. Fund raisers have stressed the importance of identifying the motives operating in the marketplace of givers as a basis for planning drives.

Differential Advantages

In considering different ways of reaching target groups, an organization is advised to think in terms of seeking a differential advantage. It should consider what elements in its reputation or resources can be exploited to create a special value in the minds of its potential customers. In the same way Zenith has built a reputation for quality and International Harvester a reputation for service, a nonbusiness organization should base its case on some dramatic value that competitive organizations lack. The small island of Nassau can compete against Miami for the tourist trade by advertising the greater dependability of its weather; the Heart Association can compete for funds against the Cancer Society by advertising the amazing strides made in heart research.

Multiple Marketing Tools

The modern business firm relies on a multitude of tools to sell its product, including product improvement, consumer and dealer advertising, salesman incentive programs, sales promotions, contests, multiple-size offerings, and so forth. Likewise nonbusiness organizations also can reach their audiences in a variety of ways. A church can sustain the interest of its members through discussion groups, newsletters, news releases, campaign drives, annual reports, and retreats. Its "salesmen" include the religious head, the board members, and the present members in terms of attracting potential members. Its advertising includes announcements of weddings, births and deaths, religious pronouncements, and newsworthy developments.

Integrated Marketing Planning

The multiplicity of available marketing tools suggests the desirability of overall coordination so that these tools do not work at cross purposes. Over time, business firms have placed under a marketing vice-president activities that were previously managed in a semi-autonomous fashion, such as sales, advertising, and marketing research. Nonbusiness organizations typically have not integrated their marketing activities. Thus, no single officer in the typical university is given total responsibility for studying the needs and attitudes of clients, trustees, and publics, and undertaking the necessary product development and communication programs to serve these groups. The university administration instead includes a variety of "marketing" positions such as dean of students, director of alumni affairs, director of public relations, and director of development; coordination is often poor.

Continuous Marketing Feedback

Business organizations gather continuous information about changes in the environment and about their own performance. They use their salesmen, research department, specialized research services, and other means to check on the movement of goods, actions of competitors, and feelings of customers to make sure they are progressing along satisfactory lines. Nonbusiness organizations typically are more casual about collecting vital information on how they are doing and what is happening in the marketplace. Universities have been caught off guard by underestimating the magnitude of student grievance and unrest, and so have major cities underestimated the degree to which they were failing to meet the needs of important minority constituencies.

Marketing Audit

Change is a fact of life, although it may proceed almost invisibly on a day-to-day basis. Over a longer stretch of time it might be so fundamental as to threaten organizations that have not provided for periodic reexaminations of their purposes. Organizations can grow set in their ways and unresponsive to new opportunities or problems. Some great American companies are no longer with us because they did not change definitions of their businesses, and their products lost relevance in a changing world. Political parties become unresponsive after they enjoy power for a while and every so often experience a major upset. Many union leaders grow insensitive to new needs and problems until one day they find themselves out of office. For an organization to remain viable, its management must provide for periodic audits of its objectives, resources, and opportunities. It must reexamine its basic business, target groups, differential advantage, communication channels, and messages in the light of current trends and needs. It might recognize when change is needed and make it before it is too late.

Is Organizational Marketing a Socially Useful Activity?

Modern marketing has two different meanings in the minds of people who use the term. One meaning of marketing conjures up the terms selling, influencing, persuading. Marketing is seen as a huge and increasingly dangerous technology, making it possible to sell persons on buying things, propositions, and causes they either do not want or which are bad for them. This was the indictment in Vance Packard's *Hidden Persuaders* and numerous other social criticisms, with the net effect that a large number of persons think of marketing as immoral or entirely self-seeking in its fundamental premises. They can be counted on to resist the idea of organizational marketing as so much "Madison Avenue."

The other meaning of marketing unfortunately is weaker in the public mind; it is the concept of sensitively *serving and satisfying human needs*. This was the great contribution of the marketing concept that was promulgated in the 1950s, and that concept now counts many business firms as its practitioners. The marketing concept holds that the problem of all business firms in an age of abundance is to develop customer loyalties and satisfaction, and the key to this problem is to focus on the customer's needs.[4] Perhaps the short-run problem of business firms is to sell people on buying the existing products, but the long-run problem is clearly to create the products that people need. By this recognition that effective marketing requires a consumer orientation instead of a product orientation, marketing has taken a new lease on life and tied its economic activity to a higher social purpose.

It is this second side of marketing that provides a useful concept for all organizations. All organizations are formed to serve the interest of particular groups: hospitals serve the sick, schools serve the students, governments serve the citizens, and labor unions serve the members. In the course of evolving, many organizations lose sight of their original mandate, grow hard, and become self-serving. The bureaucratic mentality begins to dominate the original service mentality. Hospitals may become perfunctory in their handling of patients, schools treat their students as nuisances, city bureaucrats behave like petty tyrants toward the citizens, and labor unions try to run instead of serve their members. All of these actions tend to build frustration in the consuming groups. As a result some withdraw meekly from these organizations, accept frustration as part of their condition, and find their satisfactions elsewhere. This used to be the common reaction of ghetto Negroes and college students in the face of indifferent city and university bureaucracies. But new possibilities have arisen, and now the same consumers refuse to withdraw so readily. Organized dissent and protest are seen to be an answer, and many organizations thinking of themselves as responsible have been stunned into recognizing that they have lost touch with their constituencies. They had grown unresponsive.

Where does marketing fit into this picture? Marketing is that function of the organization that can keep in constant touch with the organization's consumers, read their needs, develop "products" that meet these needs, and build a program of communications to express the organization's purposes. Certainly selling and influencing will be large parts of organizational marketing; but, properly seen, selling follows rather than precedes the organization's drive to create products to satisfy its consumers.

Conclusion

It has been argued here that the modern marketing concept serves very naturally to describe an important facet of all organizational activity. All organizations must develop appropriate products to serve their sundry consuming groups and must use modern tools of communication to reach their consuming publics. The business heritage of marketing provides a useful set of concepts for guiding all organizations.

The choice facing those who manage nonbusiness organizations is not whether to market or not to market, for no organization can avoid marketing. The choice is whether to do it well or poorly, and on this necessity the case for organizational marketing is basically founded.

NOTES

1. This is the view of Sherman Lee, Director of the Cleveland Museum, quoted in *Newsweek*, Vol. 71 (April 1, 1968), p. 55.
2. "PR for the Colonels," *Newsweek*, Vol. 71 (March 18, 1968), p. 70.
3. "Doctors Try an Image Transplant," *Business Week*, No. 2025 (June 22, 1968), pp. 64.
4. Theodore Levitt, "Marketing Myopia," *Harvard Business Review*, Vol. 38 (July–August, 1960), pp. 45–56.

LEARNING REVIEW

Questions:

1. An increasing amount of society's work is being done by ____________ ____.

2. How does the author view use of marketing by nonbusiness organizations? ____ ____.

3. Business organizations depend on ____________________ for survival.

Answers:

1. organizations other than business firms; 2. as useful if it is conceived of as serving and satisfying human needs; 3. customer goodwill

Retrospective Comment

This article created a marketing storm when it first appeared. It advanced the thesis that marketing was a universal function of all organizations and not just business organizations. It sharply divided marketing academics and practitioners into two camps: the conservatives, who felt that marketing addressed itself strictly to the problem of private for-profit business organizations, and the universalists, who felt that marketing's broadening would contribute to the social sector and also lead to a deeper definition of its own concepts.

Professor David J. Luck spearheaded the conservative attack in a thoughtful article in the July 1969 issue of the *Journal of Marketing*; and on several subsequent occasions he called meetings of interested scholars to probe the implications of this broadening for the future of the field.

Professor Levy and I continued our investigations and writings to document the relevant ways in which hospitals, public agencies, school systems and social cause organizations could improve their effectiveness in dealing with clients and other publics through the use of marketing analysis, planning, and control. I have written a major text, *Marketing for Nonprofit Organizations* (Prentice-Hall, 1975), to make marketing more available to administrators and students of nonprofit organizations. An increasing number of articles have appeared by other marketing scholars and practitioners recognizing and endorsing the broadening concept, and many leading graduate schools of business have been introducing marketing courses addressed specifically to the nonprofit sector of the economy.

PART 2

Marketing Planning and Control

"Success? I just began!"

A definition of a successful firm might be one that knows its objectives and is taking logical progressive steps to reach them. Note that this definition does *not* insist that success be measured by the usual yardsticks of sales volume, market share, profit, or asset value. Certainly such measures are indications of success and they may even be synonymous with the firm's objectives. But the point is that there are *successful* small companies which as yet have no impressive statistics to quote. *They are successful because they are progressing toward their goals.*

Ships without rudders . . .

The tragedy is that so few companies have carefully planned marketing objectives. And without objectives, marketing planning and control are meaningless. In most companies, if you were to ask the senior executives to define their company's goals, you are likely to receive surprisingly different answers. It is little wonder that so few companies and products endure for very long if indeed such vagueness regarding objectives exists.

Plans, systems, concepts, strategies, audits

Leon Winer's challenge, "Are You Really Planning Your Marketing," provides the framework for considering the four selections that follow. The data base necessary to successful planning is outlined by David Montgomery in "Developing A Balanced Marketing Information System." The necessity for understanding and reconciling the resources of the company with the needs of the market in order to arrive at a meaningful plan is discussed by Neil Borden in "The Concept of the Marketing Mix," and by Wendell Smith in "Product Differentiation and Market Segmentation As Alternative Marketing Strategies." Lastly, to emphasize the control aspect of marketing management, Abe Shuchman explains the nature, purposes, and problems of "The Marketing Audit."

6

Are You Really Planning Your Marketing?

Leon Winer

PREVIEW

I. The marketing *plan* of many companies does not represent any real planning.
   A. An increase in market share is assumed to be profitable or possible.
   B. The cause-effect relationship between marketing effort and sales volume is reversed.
   C. The manager is expected to select the *right* market mix from a large number of possibilities.

II. A procedure consisting of the following steps was developed from a study of marketing planning procedures of leading companies in the area.
   A. Assign responsibility for marketing planning.
      1. Planning may be done by functional executives
      2. Planning may be done by a planning staff group
      3. Planning may be done by everyone who has a part to play in marketing the brand
      4. Planning may be done by brand, or product managers.
   B. Marketing Objectives
      1. Organizations may have multiple objectives which should be considered.
      2. Objectives should be set for varying lengths of time.
      3. The firm should have levels of objectives.
   C. Analyze the situation
      1. Investigate a wide range of relevant data.
      2. Classify the data.

Leon Winer, "Are You Really Planning Your Marketing?" is reprinted by permission from the *Journal of Marketing*, published by the American Marketing Association (January 1965), pp. 1–8.

   3. Draw generalizations from data.
   4. Seek causes for relationships among data.
D. Forecast the future environment
E. Develop one-year marketing programs
   1. Formulate alternative courses of action.
   2. Examine those alternatives.
   3. Compare alternatives and select the ones to be recommended
F. Management reviews plan
   1. Criteria cure: financial and subjective.
   2. Estimate percentage of "fat."
G. Formulate derivative plans
H. Develop a system of control
   1. Establish standards
   2. Measure activities and results
   3. Compare these measurements to standards
   4. Report variances between measurements and standards.

The biggest problem in marketing planning is the *planning*. Many companies have a marketing "plan," yet few of these plans represent any real planning. To demonstrate this point, five steps will describe practices encountered frequently. These practices were observed through intensive interviews with manufacturing firms and their advertising agencies, and have been reported by executives at meetings and seminars attended by the author.

Step 1: Set the market share objective of your brand by adding to its present market share, depending on how ambitious you are.

Step 2: Project total sales volume, for *all* brands of the product, in dollars, for the following year.

Step 3: Multiply the result of Step 1 by the result of Step 2. (Market share objective X projected total dollar market.) This gives the dollar sales objective for the brand.

Step 4: Subtract from the dollar sales objective: (a) total factory cost, (b) an allocated portion of the company's fixed marketing costs, and (c) desired profit. What is left, if anything, is "planned" marketing expenditure.

Step 5: Compose a "marketing mix" of advertising, marketing research, personal selling, price concessions, public relations, package design, point of sales materials, dealer aids, and so on, that will (a) just use up all the marketing funds and (b) yield exactly the forecasted sales volume.

These five steps represent the procedures of many companies, yet they are thoroughly unsound, for three reasons:

First, this procedure assumes that an increase in market share is profitable or, for that matter, possible. By definition, not *all* brands of a product can increase their market shares.

Second, this method of marketing planning reverses the cause-and-effect relationship between marketing effort and sales volume. Clearly, the sales volume forecast should depend on the amount of effort expended on marketing, not the other way around.

Third, this method requires the manager to select the "right" marketing mix from among the hundreds, or thousands, of possible marketing mixes. In other words, the manager is given a sales volume objective and a fixed amount of money for marketing, and he is expected to devise the combination of advertising, price reductions, personal selling, marketing research, public relations, point of sale materials, and so on, that will just use up the available money and will attain the sales objective. No human being has the knowledge or the calculating ability to do this, even if it were *theoretically* possible.

If the argument presented above is correct, and widely-followed practice is inadequate, what alternatives are available?

To answer this question, a study was made of the marketing planning practices of companies recognized as leaders in this area, and of planning books and articles. The conclusion was that while a certain amount of adaptation is required in each case, a general procedure exists that is applicable to marketing planning. This procedure is presented as a flow model in Figure 1.The discussion of the steps in the model will follow the sequence shown, except that "assigning responsibility for planning" will be discussed last instead of first.

Setting Marketing Objectives

In setting marketing objectives, planners should keep in mind three properties of objectives: (1) multiplicity, the fact that organizations have many objectives: (2) time, objectives need to be set for varying lengths of time; and (3) level, the firm should have many levels of objectives, or a hierarchy of objectives.

Multiplicity

Generally speaking, marketers tend to focus on maximizing next year's profits as being the only proper objective for their efforts. Actually a company may be equally interested in stabilizing profits, or in seeking opportunities for investments for the longer term. Therefore, before doing any marketing planning, it is necessary to explore thoroughly with the company's management what *it* views the company's objectives to be and to derive marketing objectives from those of the company.

Objectives and Time

Given the company's objectives, it does not necessarily follow that these can be realized directly. A firm may not be able to capture a larger share of the market, economically, unless it has an improved product. Therefore, in order to attain a more distant objective of increasing its

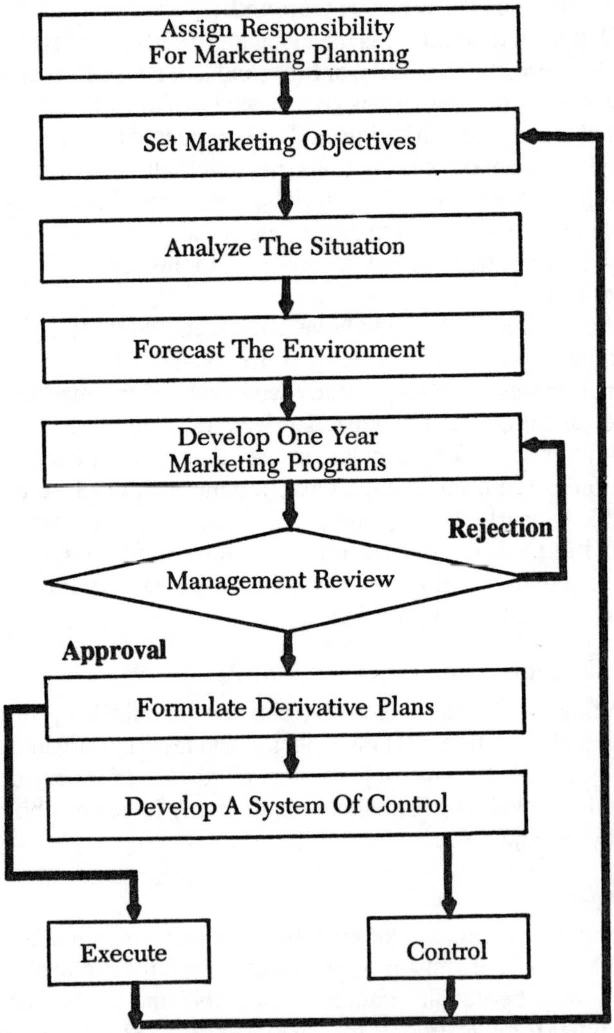

FIGURE 1. Flow model of a marketing planning procedure.

market share, it will set an intermediate objective of developing an improved product.

Since the firm possesses only limited management and financial resources, in setting the objectives described above, it will very probably have to forsake such alternative objectives as entering a foreign market or acquiring a potentially profitable competitor.

Therefore, in setting long-range objectives, and the intermediate objectives that will lead to their attainment, the firm must consider the alternatives it is forsaking, and select those most suitable to its circumstances.

Hierarchy of Objectives

Even though a firm sets long-term objectives and determines the appropriate intermediate objectives, that may not be enough. It does not do much good to tell the advertising department that the objective of the company is to increase its rate of return on investment unless this objective is translated into specific strategies. Therefore, it is necessary to develop a hierarchy of objectives.

Development of such a hierarchy of objectives is not a simple task. Careful study is required to make sure that sufficient alternatives are considered at each level and that suitable criteria are discovered for deciding which alternatives are to be selected, or emphasized.

An example, showing how a hierarchy of objectives may be derived through flow-modeling, is shown in Figure 2. This is the case of the business market (offices, factories, stores, hospitals, and so on) of the Interstate Telephone Company (a fictitious name for a real company). At the top of the chart is one of the Company's permanent objectives, that of increasing return on invested capital. A rate of return of 7½% is believed to be attainable. Two possible objectives were derived from this one: (1) increase return, or net profit, and (2) reduce the investment base on which return is computed. The second possibility was not believed to be attainable because of (1) population growth, (2) rapidly growing communications needs, and (3) trend toward mechanization and automation. Therefore, attention was focused on the first.

To increase profits, two objectives may be set, following the reasoning of the Interstate Company: (1) increase billings, or (2) reduce costs. Again, the second objective is unlikely to be attained because one of the important sources of the return on investment problem is the rising cost of labor and materials. (One exception should be noted, however. Costs may be reduced by reducing the rate of disconnections due to customer dissatisfaction, since the cost of installing complex equipment often exceeds installation charges.) This leaves the alternative of increased billings.

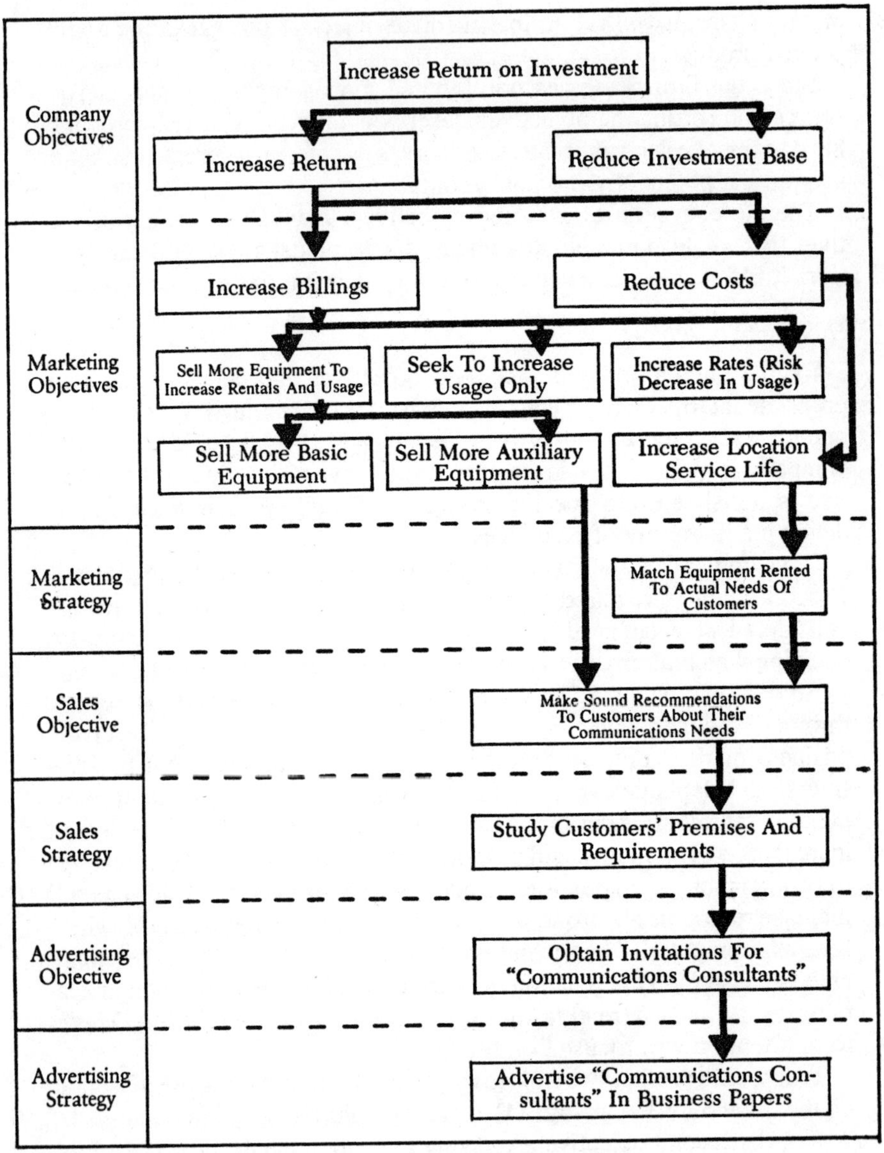

Company Objectives
Marketing Objectives
Marketing Strategy
Sales Objective
Sales Strategy
Advertising Objective
Advertising Strategy
Increase Return on Investment
Increase Return
Reduce Investment Base
Increase Billings
Reduce Costs
Sell More Equipment To Increase Rentals And Usage
Seek To Increase Usage Only
Increase Rates (Risk Decrease In Usage)
Sell More Basic Equipment
Sell More Auxiliary Equipment
Increase Location Service Life
Match Equipment Rented To Actual Needs Of Customers
Make Sound Recommendations To Customers About Their Communications Needs
Study Customers' Premises And Requirements
Obtain Invitations For "Communications Consultants"
Advertise "Communications Consultants" In Business Papers

FIGURE 2. Hierarchy of objectives for the Interstate Telephone Company.

To increase billings, the Interstate Company may (1) try to raise rates and risk reduction in usage, (2) persuade customers to increase usage of existing equipment, or (3) sell additional equipment and services in order to increase equipment rentals and, to some extent, usage. However, a public service commission will not grant a rate increase unless return on investment is below a certain minimum, say 5½%. Then a commission is not likely to grant a raise that will increase return by as much as two percentage points. The next alternative objective, persuading customers to increase usage, has been used as an objective for promotional efforts of the Company. The third objective, that of selling additional equipment and services, has been selected for particular emphasis. In particular, because of the saturation of the business market with respect to basic equipment, the marketing effort has focused on the sale of auxiliary services and equipment, such as "Call Directors," teletype units, modern switchboards, and interior dialing.

To achieve the objective of selling more auxiliary services and equipment, and reducing disconnections due to customer dissatisfaction, the Company needs to match equipment and services to the *needs* of the customers, by making recommendations based on careful study of these needs. To do this, it seeks to persuade customers, through advertising, to invite "Communications Consultants" to survey their communications problems. In this way, by deriving a hierarchy of objectives, Interstate identifies the specific marketing strategies that will lead to attainment of the Company's highest objectives.

Analyzing the Situation

Once the planner has a well-developed set of objectives, the next step is to begin discovering ways of attaining them. To do this, he has to form some ideas about what *actions* of the firm, under what *environmental conditions*, have brought about the *present* situation. He will then be able to identify courses of action that may be used in the future.

Logan[1] has suggested a four-step procedure for conducting the situation analysis:

Investigation—A wide range of data that may be relevant should be sought, with care being taken to distinguish between facts and opinions.

Classification—The planner sorts the data collected during the investigation.

Generalization—Classes of data are studied to discover relationships. Statistical techniques such as correlation analysis are used to determine whether dependable associations exist between types of events. For example, a distributor may find that least outlets are more profitable than owned outlets to a degree that prevents attributing the differences to chance.

Estimate of the Situation—Causes are sought for the associations discovered in the previous step. The planner now has some ideas about what actions under past conditions have resulted in the present situation. In this way he has learned several courses of action that he may follow to achieve his objectives. In the example cited previously, the distributor may find, on searching further, that the higher profitability of leased outlets is caused by the superior location of the leased outlets. In other words, the fact that the outlet was leased was *not* the cause of the higher profitability. Rather *both* the leasing *and* the higher profitability were caused by a third factor—superior location. (Owners of well-located outlets were not willing to sell them and therefore the distributor had been forced to lease.) Consequently, the appropriate strategy for the future would not be to prefer leasing to owning, but to seek good locations and leasing, if necessary. Inadequate search for causes might have led to very poor results.

Ideally, the situation analysis should cover other firms in the industry, so that the company may benefit from their experiences, both successes and failures.

Forecasting the Future Environment

The forecasting problem, from the viewpoint of the planner, is to determine *what* conditions he should forecast and *how* to do it. In this article we will limit ourselves to the first part of the problem because the literature of forecasting techniques is too vast to be reviewed adequately here.

Frey[2] has listed five factors that may affect purchases of a product:

1. Population changes.
2. Improvements in, and new-use discoveries for competing types of products.
3. Improvements in, and new-use discoveries for the company's own type of product.
4. Changed consumer attitudes and habits.
5. Changes in general business conditions.

Howard[3] suggests four criteria for identifying *key* factors:

1. Variability. If a factor is stable over time, there is no need to make a forecast of it.
2. Co-variation. There must be a relationship between changes in the factor and changes in demand.
3. Measurability.

4. Independence. The factor must not be closely related to another factor already considered.

Essentially, this means that the planner has to find out *which* uncontrollable factors, such as personal income, occupation of consumers, educational level, attitudes, affect sales of his brand, and then he has to forecast the future of these factors. Here, as in situation analysis, statistical methods must be used with care, to avoid erroneous conclusions.

Developing One-year Marketing Programs

Development of marketing programs requires three steps: (a) formulating alternative courses of action, (b) examining these alternatives, (c) comparing alternatives and selecting the ones to be recommended.

Formulating Alternatives

The first step in conceiving alternative courses of action was described in an earlier section on situation analysis. We reviewed a four-step process for discovering factors that had brought about the present situation, and presumably could be manipulated to achieve future objectives.

However, in addition to the cause-and-effect relationships discovered in situation analysis, there is usually room for innovation, or the development of new courses of action.

The importance of the creative process cannot be under-estimated, because a plan can only be as good as the best of the alternatives considered. Therefore, it is highly rewarding to spend time evolving alternatives. Unfortunately, there is a strong human tendency to stop the search for alternatives as soon as an apparently acceptable course of action is discovered. This is a tendency that planners must guard against.

Examining Alternatives

This step consists of projecting all the outcomes of each alternative course of action evolved above. The outcomes considered should include (1) desirable and undesirable; (2) immediate and long range; (3) tangible and intangible; and (4) certain and only possible.[4]

Clearly, one of the outcomes that must be projected in every case is sales volume and/or profit. In making this projection, errors in both directions are possible. Eldridge[5] discusses the probable consequences of these errors and suggests a solution to the problem.

"If (the marketing manager) overestimates his sales volume and gross profit, and bases his marketing expenditures on that overestimate . . . he is likely to find . . . that profits are running well below the forecast. . . .

"If he underestimates his volume and gross profit, he runs the risk of spending less than the product needs—and thereby . . . makes certain that the results are less than hoped for.

"Nevertheless, it is probably preferable for the marketing manager, when weaving his way perilously between the devil and the deep sea, to err on the side of conservatism in budgeting sales, his marketing expenditures, and his profits. . . .

"For himself, his associates, the advertising agency, and the field sales department, it is wholly desirable that objectives should be set on the high side, in order that the attainment of those objectives shall require 'reaching . . .'"

In other words, Eldridge suggests "keeping two sets of books." The implications of this suggestion will be discussed subsequently.

Comparing and Selecting Alternatives

In this step the planner compares the projected outcomes of the various alternative courses of action. The purpose is to rank the alternatives on the basis of the extent to which they achieve objectives and avoid undesirable results. Then the most desirable alternatives are recommended to management.

This point, after programs are prepared, and before they are reviewed by top management, is suitable for writing down the plans.

On the basis of the argument presented here, the written plan should discuss the following topics, if it is to enable management to evaluate it:

1. Specific objective(s) of the plan.
2. Relationship between the specific objective(s) and the objectives of the firm, or an explanation of the extent to which this plan will advance the higher-level and longer-term objectives of the firm. Quantitative measures should be included, if possible.
3. Other specific objectives considered, and the planner's opinion of the relative values of these specific objectives. This evaluation should also include quantitative measures, if possible.
4. Costs of executing the plan.
5. Forecasts of the firm's environment.
6. Course of action recommended: first, briefly, then in detail.
7. Alternative courses of action and reasons why they were considered inferior to the action recommended.
8. Projected results of the plan, if it is executed.
9. Listing of control standards and procedures to be used for controlling execution of the plan.

Before leaving this discussion of preparation of programs, an important point should be emphasized:

Marketing planning should not be done function by function, as has been the tradition for a long time and still is the practice in many firms. (By "functions" we mean the activities normally performed by a marketing department, such as advertising, personal selling, pricing, marketing research, and product and package development. *Within* these functions are many sub-functions. For example, within personal selling is recruitment, selection, and training of salesmen; assignment of territories; design of compensation system; sales analysis, and so on. At least 50 functions and sub-functions could easily be listed.)

Marketing planning should be oriented to achieving objectives. Of course, if objectives may be fulfilled entirely within one function, the objective-directed plan will also be "functional." But the approach, even then, will still be from objectives to means rather than from means to objectives.

Management Review

Criteria of reviewing executives may be grouped conveniently as follows: (1) economic, or financial; and (2) subjective.

Economic or financial criteria, such as return on investment, present discounted value of future income, alternative uses of funds, and cut-off rates, are sufficiently well known that they do not require comment here.

Subjective criteria, on the other hand, may require some discussion. Smith[6] has commented on the role of management as follows: "Management may simply accept the goals indicated. . . . More frequently . . . management's reaction will be one expressed by such comment as: 'Surely we can do better than that. . . .'"

In the case of the National Paper Company (a fictitious name for a real firm), during one year, management reduced the recommended marketing expenditures by 23%, *without* reducing the sales volume objective. Other, similar, reviewing actions could be cited. Therefore, it appears that management, in reviewing marketing plans, asks itself: "How much 'fat' does this plan contain?" and answers the question somehow, probably subjectively.

Are such reviewing actions justified? In other words, is it fair to the planner to suspect him of "padding" his plan? We have noted earlier the view that " . . . when it comes to budgeting (setting sales, profit and marketing expenditure goals), the situation is different (from setting objectives for the advertising agency, the sales force, and the like). The forecasts for financial budgeting should be sufficiently conservative that . . . they are certain to be made. . . ."[7] This commentator appears to be suggesting that the planner should overstate consistently the expenditure needed to achieve the goals of the plan. This appears to recognize that a conflict may exist between the objectives of the planner and those of the firm.

The management literature has emphasized repeatedly that differences exist between the objectives of the employee and those of the employing organization. Therefore, it seems fair to conclude that the planner, in trying to achieve his personal goals of continued employment and approval of his superiors, may undermine organizational objectives such as maximum return on marketing expenditures. Following this, the problem of the reviewing manager would then appear to be not to decide *whether* there is "fat" in the plan, but rather to estimate the percentage.

Formulating Derivative Plans

Ultimately, at the lowest level in the hierarchy, the result of planning has to be a list of actions, or a program, to be carried out.

For drawing up this program, Newman and Summer[8] suggest six steps:

1. Divide into steps the activities necessary to achieve the objective.
2. Note relations between each of the steps, especially necessary sequences.
3. Decide who is to be responsible for each step.
4. Determine the resources needed for each step.
5. Estimate the time required for each step.
6. Assign definite dates for each part.

In formulating its derivative plans, the Finchley (a fictitious name for a real company) Drug Company, uses the individual plans prepared for each of 50 products. The pertinent information is pulled out of each product plan and reassembled in three derivative plans: (a) detailing (personal selling) schedule, (b) advertising program, and (c) financial summary. These derivative plans are described below:

Detailing Schedule—The Detailing Schedule is structured very much like a calendar. For each month, three products are listed in the order in which they are to be presented to physicians. The schedule serves as a working document for the sales force. As the year passes, 500 copies of each page are made and distributed to Finchley's detail men to be carried out.

Advertising Program—The Advertising Program describes several thousand items of direct mail and journal advertising to be prepared during the course of the year. The items are arranged by month and by day of the month when they are to appear, or to be mailed. As the year progresses, this information is used by technicians and artists in the Advertising

Department and the Company's agency to prepare advertisements, buy space and materials, and so on.

Financial Summary—The Financial Summary, unlike the other two documents, is not used by any functional department as a basis for action. Instead, it is essentially a communication and control device. Probably the best way to describe the contents of this document is to list the information presented for *each* actively promoted product:

1. Total market ($).
2. Company's share (%).
3. Company's sales ($).
4. Advertising expenditure ($).
5. Allocated detailing cost ($).
6. Total marketing cost ($).
7. Marketing cost as a % of sales.
8. Gross profit ($).
9. Gross profit as a % of sales.

This information is presented both for the current year and the following year.

As plans are executed, the Financial Summary is used for comparing actual results with plans, or controlling the execution of the plan. The point is that advertising, sales, and financial plans are derived from objective-directed product marketing plans and *not* prepared independently by the separate functions: Advertising, Sales, and Finance.

Developing a System of Control

A system of control should (1) establish standards, (2) measure activities and results (3) compare these measurements to standards, and (4) report variances between measurements and standards.

Control is relevant to planning because control standards have a greater effect in determining actual results than the objectives of the plan. Therefore, it is necessary that the standards which *are* set, reflect very closely the objectives of the plan.

In addition, a system of control informs the planner of the results obtained from execution of his plans. This is helpful because it becomes possible to change plans if they are found to be ineffective either because (1) the cause and effect premise on which they were based turns out to be faulty, or (2) the actual environment is sufficiently different from the forecast environment.

In the first instance, the objectives are still valid, but the method of attaining them needs to be changed. In the second instance, the objective may no longer be appropriate. Therefore, new objectives and strategies may be required, and with them, new courses of action.

Assigning Responsibility for Marketing Planning

In practice, the management decision of assigning responsibility for marketing planning is the first step performed. In this paper, we have postponed discussion of this topic until the end, because organization of the planning function may depend on the kind of planning to be done. Therefore, it was necessary to describe first the steps in marketing planning.

Writers on the subject of marketing planning organization have described several alternatives:

1. Delegation of planning to functional executives, such as managers of the advertising, sales, pricing, sales promotion, marketing research divisions of the marketing department.
2. Planning done by a planning staff group.
3. Planning done by everyone who has a part to play in marketing the brand, including outside organizations.
4. Planning done by brand, or product managers.

However, criteria are lacking in the literature for selecting the appropriate planning organization.

Leading firms often rely on product, or brand managers for planning, although the practice is not universal, and where such managers are used, their responsibilities are not always the same.

To illustrate this point:

1. At the drug company discussed earlier, product managers plan advertising of two kinds, and personal selling.
2. At the household paper products company, brand managers plan consumer advertising and temporary reductions in price charged to retailers and consumers.
3. The telephone company, on the other hand, does not employ product managers. Instead, planning is assigned to sales and advertising executives, for their individual functions.

Possibly these differences in planning organization can be attributed to differences in the means used for communicating with the market. The telephone company needs to communicate with business market customers (that is, business firms, government agencies, and so on) on an individual basis. The reason is that no two customers (other than the very smallest) are likely to need exactly the same combination of products and services. Therefore, a centrally-conceived, uniform approach, used alone, would not be suitable. The household paper products company and the drug company deal with mass markets where the potential profit made from individual customers is small. This rules out the possibility of tailoring a specialized approach to each customer. In addition, the needs and desires of large numbers of potential and actual customers are relatively similar. Therefore, grouping large numbers of customers into a market for a brand is an economical way of approaching the planning problem.

It follows that the "brand" manager is really a *market* manager, the market being the totality of actual and potential consumers of the brand. We may conclude, therefore, that a brand or product manager has a role to play whenever there is an opportunity to use standardized appeals in communicating with numerous customers.

Nevertheless, not all firms require brand managers, even though they may use mass communication media. For example, the Interstate Telephone Company permits all the advertising planning to be done in its advertising department, and delegates the major part of its sales planning to sales executives. The question arises then: what are the key differences that cause such marked differences in planning organization?

The answer that suggests itself is that there are important differences in the marketing objectives of these firms. Two illustrations can be given.

1. At the paper company, two of the important objectives are increase in market share, and product distribution in certain areas. Programming for these objectives requires crossing of functional lines. Therefore there appears to be a need for a special planning executive.

2. At the telephone company the important marketing objectives are: (1) to increase auxiliary equipment and service billings; and (2) to increase location service life of auxiliary equipment. These objectives are interpreted to require that "communications consultants" survey the operations and premises of business market customers. To achieve this, the company tries to persuade customers to avail themselves of the free services of these consultants. Thus, we have three levels of objectives: (a) persuade the customer to invite the communications consultant, in order to (b) have the communications consultant advise the customer, in order to (c) increase billings and service life.

Achieving objectives (a) and (b), the objectives that can be achieved by direct action—(c) obviously cannot—does not require any coordination among functions. Objective (b) is achieved by the Sales Department, and objective (a), by the Advertising Department.

The conclusion is that the planning organization should mirror the hierarchy of objectives: a planning manager is needed wherever there is an objective whose achievement requires coordination of, or selection from among, several functions. In practice, the existing organization may satisfy this requirement, in which case, no new responsibilities need be assigned. However, if existing planning responsibilities dod not allow for this type of selection, or coordination, new ones need to be created.

Implications for Marketing Managers

When a new idea or concept is presented to the business world, its *form* often receives more attention than its *substance*. While attempts are made to adopt the new concept, old habits of thought, and procedures, are continued even though they may not be consistent with the new idea.

The central idea of marketing planning is to develop marketing objectives that will lead to attainment to the objectives of the firm, and then to devise programs and controls that will help to achieve these marketing objectives. In deciding to plan its marketing activities, a business firm has to stand ready to scrap its traditional budgeting and functional planning procedures and to re-think and reorganize its marketing. Only those methods and procedures should be retained that fit logically with the pattern of starting with the highest objectives of the firm and refining successive steps of instrumental objectives until courses of action are specified. Any other approach, or procedure, will give inferior results.

Admittedly, it is much easier to go through the five steps outlined in the first few paragraphs, and say that marketing is being planned, than to follow the procedure described in the body of this paper. However, in this instance, as in most, there are no easy short-cuts to the development of good, effective, and profitable plans. Also, there really is no escape from the need to plan conscientiously. Leading companies *are* planning in this way, with obvious financial success. Those who wish to attain similar success will have to apply themselves equally. Successful procedures will not be developed overnight, or even in one year. Most likely, it will take from three to five cycles of planning to establish an effective, smoothly-working procedure. However, nothing will be accomplished if a sincere beginning is not made.

NOTES

1. James P. Logan, "Economic Forecasts, Decision Processes, and Types of Plans" (unpublished doctoral dissertation, Columbia University, 1960), pp. 14–19, 76.
2. Albert W. Frey, *The Effective Marketing Mix: Programming for Optimum Results* (Hanover, New Hampshire: The Amos Tuck School of Business Administration, 1956), p. 11.
3. John Howard, *Marketing Management* (Homewood, Illinois: R. D. Irwin, Inc., 1957), Chapter VI.

4. William H. Newman and Charles E. Summer, Jr., *The Process of Management* (Englewood Cliffs, New Jersey: Prentice Hall, Inc., 1961), p. 302.
5. Clarence E. Eldridge, "Marketing Plans," in E. R. French (editor), *The Copywriter's Guide* (New York: Harper & Bros., 1958), pp. 3–28, on pp. 24–25.
6. Wendell R. Smith, "A Rational Approach to Marketing Management," in Eugene J. Kelley and William Lazer (editors), *Managerial Marketing* (Homewood, Illinois: R. D. Irwin Co., 1958), p. 154.
7. Eldridge, same reference as footnote 5, p. 25.
8. Newman and Summer, same reference as footnote 4, pp. 415–416.

LEARNING REVIEW

Questions:

1. What is the central idea of marketing planning?

____

____

____

2. The author says the problem of the reviewing manager is not to decide whether there is "fat" in the plan, but to _______________________.

3. Assigning responsibility for marketing planning is the ___________ step.

Answers:

1. to develop marketing objectives that will lead to attainment of the objectives of the firm and then to devise programs and controls that will help to achieve these objectives. 2. estimate the percentage of "fat"; 3. first

Retrospective Comment

In general, the need for marketing planning has been recognized, as indicated by the widespread preparation of marketing plans and the existence of high-priced marketing planning departments in many companies.

Yet, in spite of this, substantial disenchantment with marketing planning exists. For example, this comment by a top executive is typical: " . . . our marketing group has not done the job it should . . . I'm not sure whether it (marketing planning) is something important that we ought to do better or whether it's a fad we ought to get rid of." Other top managers have expressed similar feelings from time to time.

Of course, the only valid justification for spending time and money on marketing planning is that over the long term, *as a result of planning*:

1. Sales volume will be higher,
2. Marketing expense will be lower,

or

3. Both,

than they would have been without planning.

Unfortunately, too often creation of marketing planning departments and production of thick volumes of "plans" do not add materially to growth in sales volume or to marketing efficiency.

Most companies that have taken a serious interest in marketing planning have succeeded in following the procedural aspects. Unfortunately, the mere following of a procedure, without deep understanding of the concepts involved, will never guarantee that the hoped for results will in fact be attained. The attainment of results is heavily dependent on how the procedure is followed.

The good results obtainable from marketing planning are desired by the great majority of modern marketing executives. To obtain these results, in addition to sound procedures, we need a good understanding of the underlying concepts involved. These concepts have been developed by successful practitioners of marketing planning and the consultants who advise them. Of these concepts, the one that is absolutely essential to good planning is a careful and thoughtful structuring of the company's marketing objectives. The system of objectives forms the basis of all marketing planning and of the organizational design of the marketing planning function. The system of objectives also provides guidance for staffing of the planning department and for the kind of analytical support needed. In conclusion, we noted that the new techniques of management science can make a vital contribution if their use is planned properly.

7

Developing a Balanced Marketing Information System

David B. Montgomery

PREVIEW

I. Many business managers have made the mistake of regarding their marketing information systems too narrowly as useful merely for the generation, storage, and retrieval of data.

II. The balanced marketing decision-information system (MDIS) needed by marketing-oriented management has four major components:
   A. The *data bank* provides the capacity to store, retrieve, manipulate, and transform data.
   B. The *model bank* includes a variety of marketing models for use in planning and controlling the organization's marketing activities.
   C. The *measurement-statistics bank* provides the capacity for statistical data analysis.
   D. The *man/system communications capability*, operating through the display unit, provides a two-way link between the user and the system.

III. There are several major issues to consider in successful development and implementation of MDIS:
   A. There must be strong, unequivocal top management support.
   B. Line marketing managers should be involved in development.
   C. The system development team should be composed of representatives from each of three areas: operations research, market research, and computer systems.
   D. The system must be convenient to use.

David B. Montgomery, "Developing A Balanced Marketing Information System," (Cambridge, Mass.: Marketing Science Institute, 1970). Reprinted by permission of the author and publisher.

More and more business managers are beginning to focus in on the fact that they have perhaps been looking at their marketing information systems through the wrong end of the telescope, so to speak. In the past, they have frequently viewed their systems as useful merely for the generation, storage, and retrieval of data.

Even worse, in the basic design of their systems, they have often completely overlooked the use of data-based models and statistical methods which provide the capacity to digest, analyze, and interpret the generated data. This short-sighted perspective has carried with it the grave danger that the marketing managers will suffer data overloads and thus receive little or no help in their decision making.

In short, marketing-oriented management needs to have a balanced, decision relevant information system. This brings us to the purpose of this article—namely, to present some concepts on how to develop a balanced marketing decision-information system (MDIS). Accordingly, therefore, I shall first discuss the major components of a balanced system, and then examine the organizational aspects of the system's development, which have significance for today's technologically oriented marketing manager.

Major Elements of Balanced MDIS

The four components which comprise the major subsystems in a balanced marketing information system include: (1) a *data* bank, (2) a *model* bank, (3) a *measurement-statistics* bank, and (4) a *display* capability. The system interacts with two external elements, the user and the environment. The latter encompasses everything—both external and internal—that affects the organization's marketing activities. A diagram of the major components and their interactions is shown in *Figure 1*.

The *data* bank provides the MDIS with the capacity to store, retrieve, manipulate, and transform data. While the manager will occasionally have use for retrieval of raw information from the system, for decision purposes he will generally want the data processed in some manner. For example, he may require sales summaries to market-share information which involve further processing of the data stored in the system.

The *model* bank includes a variety of marketing models for use in planning and controlling the organization's marketing activities, such as sales effort allocation, advertising budgeting, and simulation models. Model-based analysis provides inputs to the management planning and control process, but the manager generally intervenes between the model analysis and company actions. However, in certain special cases, the models may be delegated authority to render routine decisions, as in inventory reordering.

The *measurement-statistics* bank provides the MDIS with the capacity for statistical data analysis, such as multiple regression, cluster and factor analyses, and multidimensional sealing. In addition to data analysis, this bank should contain procedures for obtaining and analyzing subjective marketing judgments, as in applications of statistical decision theory and forecasts of competitors' promotional activities.

The *man/system communications* capability, which operates through the display unit, provides a two-way link between the user and the system.

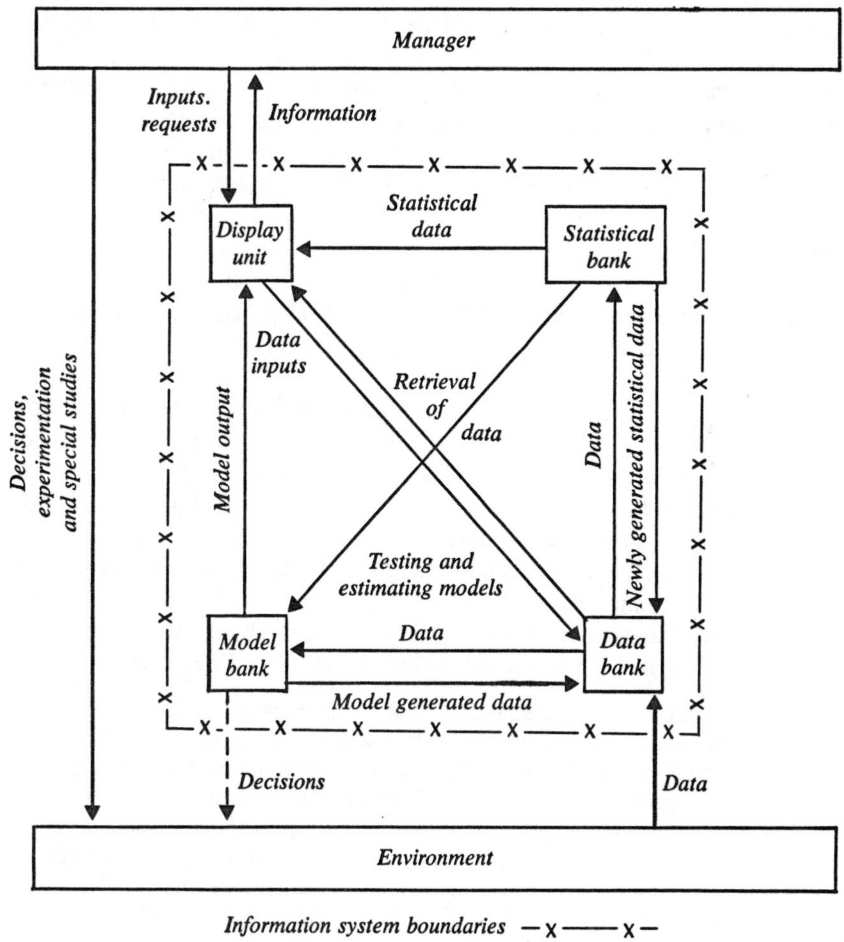

FIGURE 1. Decision-information system structure

If the MDIS is to be utilized to full advantage, this high degree of interaction between the manager and the system requires the well-coordinated development of the four subsystems.

At any point in time, the development and utilization of an organization's marketing information system are constrained by the data available. For example, important pieces of data relating to market dynamics may be missing, due to their never having been collected or to the fact that the organization has discarded them.

Consequently, decisions made today concerning what data to obtain and to retain in the data bank have long-run implications for the development and use of a balanced MDIS. Obviously, then, if a company expects to become involved in data-based marketing models at any time in the next five years, it is imperative to begin immediately to assess something of the directions its efforts will take and the requirements for data to support these efforts. This assessment should then have an impact on decisions as to what data to obtain and retain in the data bank.

The Data Bank

This major subsystem involves two primary aspects: the information categories, and the computer-based and manual processing systems for data storage, retrieval, manipulation, and transformation.

Information Categories. While an extensive discussion of all the appropriate data for the bank is outside the scope of this article, it should be noted that careful consideration must be given to the specification of what information will be maintained within the system, particularly as it affects future activities in marketing models.

Some of the categories which might be maintained in the data bank for a consumer goods manufacturer are given in *Table 1*. While this tabulation is far from exhaustive, it does illustrate some of the basic types of market data which might be maintained within the system. For example:

> The collection and maintenance of "competitive marketing activity data," as shown under "external primary data," will be increasingly important as better models are developed to assess the impact of competitive activities.
>
> Many of the data categories will subsequently be related to each other in order to gain understanding of market response. Thus the "copy and format data on company advertisements," shown under "internal corporate records report data," may be related to "advertising performance measures," tabulated under "external primary data," in order to learn systematically how the market is responding to these characteristics of ads.
>
> "External freight rate data" will support the development of distribution applications within the MDIS. Western Electric has found that such a data

base, made accessible on a computer system, enables the company to perform in a matter of hours rate analyses and studies which formerly took months.

A key design issue relates to the level of detail in which to maintain the data. In general, data should be stored in *disaggregated* form—that is, in its most elementary form. For example, salesmen's call reports might be maintained in a disaggregated form which would provide such details as person visited, place of visit, time of visit, sales aids used, and so forth. An aggregated form for this data might be the quarterly or annual call frequency of a salesman on a particular account. The goal of maintaining disaggregated data is, of course, to provide future flexibility. If data are maintained only in aggregate form, the possibility of organizing them in a different way for future, but at present unknown, purposes is sacrificed.

Processing Systems. In the data bank, these systems should be able to perform seven basic operations. Consider:

DATA PRE-PROCESSING. (The ability to clean and edit data.)

FILE CREATION, REORGANIZATION, AND DELETION.

FILE MAINTENANCE AND UPDATING.

INFORMATION RETRIEVAL.

LOGICAL OPERATIONS ON DATA. (Useful when a file is being prepared for statistical analysis.)

DATA TRANSFORMATION. (The ability to perform arithmetic operations on data is crucial to simple analysis, such as computation of market shares, as well as to more complex statistical analysis.)

REPORT GENERATION. (The ability to generate reports readily in nearly any desired format.)

Table 1. Data categories: consumer goods company

I. *Internal Corporate Records*
   A. Financial and Cost Data by Product and Time Period
   B. Internal Report Data
      1. Salesman's call reports.
      2. Marketing mix data by product, time period, and market.
      3. Sales performance information on previously implemented new products.
      4. Life cycle information on products in the line.
      5. Copy and format data on company advertisements.
   C. Judgmental Inputs
      1. Forecasts by product, time, and forecaster.

2. Estimates of market sensitivity to company and competitive marketing activities.

II. *External Data*
   A. Secondary Sources
      1. Government (e.g., population demographic data by ZIP coded area).
      2. Commercial (e.g., M.R.C.A. panel data, Nielsen store audits, B.R.I. data).
      3. Freight rate.
   B. Primary Sources
      1. Test market information.
      2. Market experiments.
      3. Market structure analysis.
      4. Competitive marketing activity.
      5. Advertising performance measures (e.g., Schwerin, Gallup-Robinson, Starch).

Two key design issues in the development of data bank processing systems are "modularity" and "flexibility." Since the data bank, and indeed the entire MDIS, will be an evolving system, it is vital that it be readily adaptable to changes in the data and in the operations performed on such data. Modularity or compartmentalization of the processing operations will help to minimize problems involved in adapting the pro cessing systems to future requirements.

Flexibility may be achieved by developing a variety of general commands for use in retrieving and manipulating data. These commands may then be called on to operate on the data. The development of these general commands, which are not specific to a particular data file, greatly reduces the kinds of problems which often result when a file is altered by additions, deletions, or reorganizations.

The data bank should maintain information regarding who used what data and for what purposes on which to base decisions regarding the data that should be kept in high-speed computer storage. Thus the data bank should include information appropriate to adapting itself to better meet the needs of its users and to developing specifications for the storage of disaggregated data.

Similarly, the system should include information on the frequency and duration of use of the data bank processing functions, as well as the procedures incorporated in the measurement-statistics and model banks. This will provide the raw material for decisions regarding the allocation of system improvement efforts.

Security Provisions. The data bank must have safeguards to ensure that both the system and the data are protected. At the *system* level, it is necessary to take steps to prevent a user from inadvertently altering or destroying one of the programs. Such user-generated accidents are both costly and frustrating.

At the *data* level, there is also a clear need for security, both vertically and horizontally. The problem is one of who may have access to what. For example, a branch manager might have access to data relative to his branch, a regional manager to data for his region, and the marketing vice president to national data. In effect, the system should allow users access to data on their individual "need-to-know" basis. This can be accomplished by assigning each user an identification code or password that specifies the data to which he may have access.

In addition, there is an obvious need for bottom-up security—e.g., individuals at a given organizational level should not have access to certain types of information relative to a higher organizational level. Similarly, there may also be a need for top-down security—e.g., particular data which should not be conveniently accessible to managers at higher organizational levels.

Likewise, too, there may be a need for horizontal security systems—e.g., the organization may not want the branch manager, say, in Boston to have access to data relative to the manager of the San Francisco branch. As with vertical security systems, horizontal systems may be implemented by means of user identification codes.

The Model Bank

This component should contain models for use in understanding market behavior, diagnosing factors underlying market results, controlling marketing operations, and planning marketing strategy. In this section, I shall first consider some of the design aspects for the model bank and then look at the emerging trends in market modeling.

Design Aspects. The bank should feature a multiplicity of models which vary according to their level of detail (or aggregation) and number and type of control variables. At the highest level of aggregation, for example, a model might reflect the market response to dollar expenditures on elements in the marketing mix, such as price, personal sales effort, advertising, and special promotions.

Having a variety of models available provides flexibility in response to any given problem situation. Thus the manager may select the level of detail and number of control variables he deems appropriate.

It may prove advantageous to have a number of alternative models at a given level of detail, since different managers may have different requirements due to variations in their areas of responsibility and decision styles.

The model bank may ultimately have multiple models available at each combination of level of detail and number of control variables in order to service the decision needs of the various marketing managers in the organization. This reinforces the important point that the development of the model bank, as is true for all aspects of the MDIS, must be an evolutionary, adaptive process which adjusts to the varied and changing needs of the managers.

The models in the bank should be designed for compatible usage—that is, they should insofar as possible be consistent with one another. The compatible use of models seeks to take advantage of the strengths of both the simple and the more complex models. The simple models may be used to explore a wide range of alternatives and to choose one or several which seem promising. More detailed models may then be called on to assess this smaller set of alternatives.

The result of the detailed simulation may in turn indicate a need for a reevaluation of one of the earlier analyses. Furthermore, it will not only provide control guidelines for evaluation of results once the policy is implemented but also an effective method for taking advantage of the strengths of the various types of models.

Emerging Trends. A number of new developments lends support to the model bank concept. *First*, there is the emergence of a problem-centered rather than technique-centered approach to marketing models. Much early work in marketing models could be characterized as techniques looking for problems. Thus marketing relevance was often sacrificed in order to achieve formulations that would satisfy the requirements of given solution techniques.

However, marketing problems are now beginning to dominate techniques in the formulation of models. Maturing experience in the structuring of marketing models, realization that successful implementation and use depend on this approach, and steady progress in management science and operations research in developing methods for approaching more realistic and complex problems have all spurred this trend. Efforts are now being expended to achieve good solutions to relevant marketing problems, rather than optimal solutions to the wrong problems.

Second, the growing availability of data for estimating and testing models is fostering the emergence of more realistic, detailed, and valid model structures. The trend toward realistic market response representation is further enhanced by a tendency toward inclusion of more behavioral phenomena, more variables, nonlinear response functions, and stochastic elements in marketing models.

Third, as a result of the development of time-shared computers, is the trend toward interactive models. Such a model, operating on a time-shared computer system, provides a decision maker with the capacity to quickly and efficiently explore the implications of his judgments relative to a given problem.

Fourth, there is the trend toward building models that consider competitive effects. This offers an opportunity for significant interaction with the data bank. Such a development needs to be supported by data bank capabilities which provide for the systematic monitoring and storing of competitive market data for use in developing, validating, and using these competitive models. Given this trend, it would seem important for organizations to consider initiating a program of competitive data generation that will match their future model intentions.

The Measurement-Statistics Bank

This essential subsystem provides the basis for measurement and estimation, as well as methods for testing response functions and models. Both data-based and judgment-based methods should be incorporated in the measurement-statistics bank. For example, the measurement-statistics bank should provide procedures for estimating the demand elasticities of marketing variables based upon data in the data bank. It should also provide for making judgmental assessments, such as the likelihood that a competitor will lower price and the reference life cycle of a new product. For testing response functions and models the measurement-statistics bank should encompass techniques for assessing the adequacy of a postulated model or function in the light of empirical evidence.

Measurement Methods. These fall into two categories: data-based and judgment-based. Some representative examples, which serve to illustrate the nature of the measurement-statistics bank, are given in *Table 2*.

In the *data-based* method, analysis of variance and other classical parametric procedures are helpful in evaluating the results of market experiments and exploring marketing data for useful relationships. Market experiments are finding increasing use in assessing the nature of market response to marketing policies. In particular, the emergence of adaptive marketing models, based on continuing market experiments, will make these statistical procedures increasingly relevant to marketing managers.

Table 2. Methods incorporated in a measurement-statistics bank

I. *Data-Based Methods*
   A. Analysis of variance and other parametric procedures
   B. Multivariate Procedures
      1. Regression analysis.

2. Discriminant analysis.
3. Factor analysis.
4. Cluster analysis.

C. Nonparametric Statistics
1. Cross-classification.
2. Goodness of fit measures.
3. Rank order measures.
4. Nonparametric analysis of variance and multivariate procedures.

D. Time-Series Analysis
E. Numeric Estimation Techniques
F. Nonmetric Scaling

II. *Judgment-Based Methods*
A. Decision Theory Program
B. Methods for Obtaining Judgmental Assessments
C. Bayesian Multivariate Analysis

Multivariate methods, which are useful in measuring and testing the multiple factor relationships that exist in marketing, ought to be included in the measurement-statistics bank. Historical information from the data bank will generally serve as input to these procedures. Perhaps the most widely used of these techniques is regression analysis, which finds many uses in estimating and testing market response functions. Since realistic representation of market response generally requires nonlinear response functions, the measurement-statistics bank should include techniques for nonlinear regression.

Data often do not satisfy the measurement assumptions of the parametric techniques. In such cases, the nonparametric statistics subsystem will be particularly useful. Tests to determine "goodness of fit" should be included in order to assess the descriptive adequacy of models or distributions in the face of data.

Procedures for time-series analysis are necessary for applications involving market dynamics.

Numeric estimation procedures should be included to provide the MDIS with the capacity to estimate and test models which involve complex estimation equations. The capacity for numeric estimation is extremely important in that it will enable the MDIS to handle realistic marketing models which are intractable in terms of analytical methods of estimation. The methods will be closely related to the techniques required to implement nonlinear regression.

Nonmetric scaling techniques have found use in the assessment of customer perceptions concerning a set of competing brands.

Statistical decision theory is perhaps the best known example of a *judgment-based* method of analysis for marketing. Applications have been proposed for a wide variety of problems, but one of the major barriers to widespread management use of this technique has been the burdensome amount of calculation required in problems of meaningful size. This barrier may be greatly reduced by development of computer programs, most likely on time sharing, to perform the necessary calculations. These programs will ask the manager the questions which must be answered in order for analysis to proceed, and they will also report the results of the analysis in a convenient format for management use. When decision theory techniques are readily available to marketing managers, it is safe to predict increasingly widespread use.

The measurement-statistics bank should provide procedures for systematic monitoring, evaluation, and improvement of the judgmental inputs provided by individuals in the organization. Monitoring and evaluation will help to identify particular valuable sources of judgmental inputs to the market planning process. For example:

Monitoring and evaluating judgmental inputs to site location problems for a chain store revealed that the best source of judgment seemed to be the operations vice president, rather than personnel on the real estate staff. Clearly, the organization would want to give his judgments greater weight in similar future decisions. In addition, the store would also know more about what it would be losing should he subsequently resign.

The monitoring and evaluation process also provides the raw material for improving performance. In the first place, feedback may be provided to the individuals concerned, which should give them the opportunity to improve over time. Secondly, the system itself may learn to adjust the judgmental inputs of given individuals for systematic market analysis. Consider:

A manufacturing company needed to develop better methods for short-run sales forecasting, because production to inventory operations were extremely expensive and sales depended heavily on delivery. Since the company's salesmen had the most direct customer contact, it was felt that they should be able to provide useful information for forecast purposes.

Accordingly, the salesmen were asked to report on a product-by-product and customer-by-customer basis their subjective probability assessment of how likely they were to achieve a given sale within 30, 60, and 90 days. Each salesman's forecasting performance was monitored in order to adjust his current predictions based on his past performance.

When the adjusted inputs were aggregated by product and customer across all salesmen, the company then had a short-run sales forecast for use in production planning.

The two examples we have just seen demonstrate that judgmental inputs are being used successfully in systematic market analysis. However, much work remains to be done on procedures for obtaining good subjective estimates.

Finally, the measurement-statistics bank should ultimately contain Bayesian multivariate procedures for use in the important task of combining data-based analysis with management judgment.

Design Considerations. Computerized statistical analysis and the widespread availability of program packages for performing such analysis carry with them a danger of abuse and misuse. Unfortunately, abuse and misuse of technique are not rare instances. Consequently, the measurement-statistics bank itself should warn the user of potential pitfalls and recommend appropriate tests and courses of action. While this will not eliminate abuse, it at least should help to minimize naive use of statistical methods.

As another design note, the techniques incorporated in the measurement-statistics bank should provide an option to have the computations performed in double precision.

An excellent source of information and programs relevant to a measurement-statistics bank is the "Computer Applications" section of the *Journal of Marketing Research*. In addition to discussions of techniques for analysis, this section also provides abstracts of computer programs which are available for performing a wide variety of statistical analyses.

The Display Capability

This major element in developing a balanced MDIS is the point of direct contact between the user and the system. If the system is to be utilized effectively, then care must be taken to provide for convenient, efficient user/system interaction.

While batch processing operations will continue to play an important role, the advent of the time-shared computer has made possible closely coupled man/system interaction in problem solving. Since the use of such on-line systems has been well covered in the growing literature on computer usage, further discussion of the user/system interface is deemed unnecessary within the scope of this article. Suffice it to say, I suggest that the reader interested in knowing more about this see, for example, the book coauthored by me and Glen L. Urban, *Management Science in*

Marketing,[1] which first proposed this structure, and also see my article "Marketing Decision-Information Systems: An Emerging View,"[2] which elaborated on it.

Organizing for MDIS

Successful development and implementation of a MDIS requires considerable attention to organizational aspects of system development. Some of the major issues to consider are:

Top management support.
Involvement of line marketing managers in system development.
Composition of the system development team.
Provision for convenient system use by marketing managers.

In this section of the article, I shall examine certain aspects of these issues a little more closely.

Top Management Support

The design, development, and implementation of a marketing decision-information system is a long-term, and often rather costly, undertaking. A substantial amount of energy and resources is required to bring such a system to successful fruition. In view of the level and time span of the resource commitment implied by system development, if the system is to command the required resources and cooperation, there must be strong and unequivocal top management support.

System development will require the cooperation of rather diverse groups within the organization, particularly the active cooperation of marketing managers. However, marketing managers are often rather wary of computers, mathematical models, and the like. The development team must demonstrate to these managers that the system is designed to assist, not replace, them. Strong top management support for the system development will also help the team gain the attention and cooperation of marketing managers.

A case in point occurred at an in-house executive seminar on management science in marketing I once conducted for a large consumer goods manufacturer. The seminar was attended by many of the company's top marketing executives. At the end of the final day's session, the senior vice president summed up the seminar with a statement to the effect that those attending would be badly mistaken if they thought they could return to their offices and simply forget about applying the content of the seminar to their own problems. In no uncertain terms, he indicated that the management science approach was indeed the way the company was headed and if those attending wanted to grow with the company they "had better get on board this effort." Since then, this company has been most progressive in applying new information technology to marketing.

The successful system requires evolution, not revolution. The system should be viewed as a dynamic development effort which can grow with, and adapt to, changing management needs. Large-scale, once and for all, system efforts are practically always doomed to failure. They inevitably exhaust their available resources and management's patience long before the systems actually work. Even if the development team does make them function properly, the chances are that the system will have a tendency to overwhelm management in terms of its complexity and comprehensiveness.

A far better development strategy is to let the system and the users develop together in a mutual interaction. This will also tend to yield useful intermediate systems and results which will provide the evidence that the development effort will indeed pay off.

Line Marketing Involvement

Applications of marketing models and other aspects of MDIS in recent years have made it abundantly clear that line marketing managers must become involved in system development. In many instances, which I have personally seen, this notion of line involvement has come as somewhat of a surprise to the managers concerned. Somehow, they often have the idea that system development can be successfully achieved by hiring a staff of technical wizards and sending them off into a corner with instructions to report back when the system is ready. It is the rare case where such an approach works. Fortunately, when the need for their direct involvement in system development is pointed out, most line managers seem willing and able to provide useful inputs to the development effort.

Why is it that the wizards-in-a-corner approach fails to work? In the first place, development of a MDIS should begin with a reassessment of the decision and information requirements of the marketing organization. Ignoring this step and plunging ahead with system development will tend to cast past mistakes in concrete. If the resultant design is to meet their decision needs, the process of reassessment clearly requires the participation of line marketing managers.

In addition, when line managers become participants in the system's evolution, it becomes "their" system and not one being imposed on them by some staff group. The fact that the evolution of the system has been in response to their decision needs will markedly enhance their utilization of it.

System Development Team

The interdependencies between the major system components in a MDIS have significant implications for staffing the system development team. The functions which are performed by the different system components have generally been in the purview of a variety of organizational units within the organization. Consider:

The operations research staff has generally been in charge of model development (model bank).

The market research staff has usually been charged (a) with the responsibility for data collection (data bank), and (b) with the methods for data analysis (measurement-statistics bank).

The computer systems group has generally had responsibility (a) for maintaining computer-based data files and computer programs for their manipulation (data bank), and (b) for generating management reports (one aspect of the man/system interface).

The system development team should be composed of representatives from each of these three areas—operations research, market research, and computer systems—in order to avoid an unbalanced system growth. For example, if the MDIS is viewed as merely a data storage and retrieval system—with perhaps some associated report generation and statistical capability—the system development team is likely to be only made up of representatives from computer systems and marketing research. Such a team is unlikely to be cognizant of the requirements of future model development efforts and is likely to make data and design decisions which will not serve the organization's future model development needs.

Convenient System Use

If the system is to achieve widespread utilization by marketing management, then provision must be made for its convenient use. On the hardware side, this will probably imply access to both time sharing and remote batch hardware. The former will provide instant access to the system, as well as a capacity for interactive operation. The latter, because it will provide convenient access to a central computer from distant locations, will enable many locations to have convenient, economical access to batch operations. Without a remote batch capability, many organizational units which will utilize the MDIS could experience significant time delays.

On the software side, convenient management use implies that the system be programmed in management's language and not vice versa. The software must be well documented and must provide the user with instructional details sufficient to make appropriate use of the system. This is an area that will witness considerable development during the 1970s.

One way to achieve convenient management access to the MDIS without requiring the manager to become a technical specialist is to provide information specialists who are trained in the operation of terminal and display devices.

These specialists could be located centrally and act in much the same way as librarians do. Thus, when a call was received for information, the information specialist would discuss the request to determine the specifics, obtain the answer in the most efficient manner, and suggest additional data which might be pertinent. The caller would then receive his answer via a terminal in his office, or by more conventional methods, such as the mail, depending on how soon he needed the information.

Finally, I wish to suggest that the system development team should have its own computer programming capability and convenient access to hardware and software, both internal and external to the organization. Without provision for these, there will be many stumbling blocks to system development and utilization.

Even with pre-MDIS systems, computer usage in marketing has often been accompanied by complaints about the service rendered by the corporate computer staff. Actually, this should not be too surprising, especially in view of the fact that most corporate computer staffs grew out of accounting-type applications. As a consequence, large-scale, routine data-processing applications, such as billings, payrolls, and orders have generally taken precedence over other applications, much to the frustration of marketing personnel.

In order to assure reasonable service in the development of the MDIS, the system development team should be free to go to outside suppliers for computer usage, should these outside sources prove to be the best choice. Hopefully, this would also tend to teach the marketing concept to corporate computer groups.

Conclusion

The major problem to date with marketing information systems has been the tendency of the marketing managers or users to overemphasize the data generation, storage, and retrieval. This tendency, of course, runs the risk that the individual manager will be inundated with data to the detriment of receiving help in his decision making.

Now marketing managers are gradually beginning to realize that in order to have a balanced data system, as well as to harness the new information technology, the system itself must be properly designed for effective and efficient utilization.

In the first section of this article, we have seen how the development of a balanced marketing decision-information system (MDIS) is based on an interacting set of four major components consisting of a data bank, a model bank, a measurement-statistics bank, and a display capability.

Then in the second section, we have examined the important organizational aspects, covering such major issues as the top management support, involvement of line marketing management, composition of the system development team, and so forth, which are significant for today's technologically oriented marketing managers.

As a final point, I offer this thought from Johann Wolfgang von Goethe (1749–1832):

> The modern age has a false sense of superiority because of the great mass of data at its disposal. But the valid criterion of distinction is rather the extent to which man knows how to form and master the material at his command.

NOTES

1. Englewood Cliffs, New Jersey, Prentice-Hall, Inc., 1969.
2. *Journal of Marketing Research*, May 1970.

LEARNING REVIEW

Questions:

1. Two key design issues in the development of data bank processing systems are ____________ and ____________.

2. The four components which comprise the subsystems in a balanced marketing information system are a) ____________, b) ____________, c) ____________, and d) ____________.

3. The major danger in regarding a marketing information system as merely for the generation, storage, and retrieval of data is that ____________ ____________.

Answers:

1. modularity, flexibility; 2. a) data bank, b) model bank, c) measurement-statistics bank, d) display capability; 3. overabundance of data may be of no aid in decision-making

Retrospective Comment

There are many successful marketing information systems in operation today. And although each of these systems can be divided into the *data bank, model bank, measurement-statistics bank,* and *man/system communication capability* components suggested in my earlier article, there is no data gathering, modeling, hardware/software, or communication interface approach common to all systems. Successful systems need to be custom fitted to organizations and management problems.

Yet there is one thing common to each successful MDIS. Those marketing managers who have developed a balanced system have done so by focusing carefully, during the developmental stages, on the *projected use* of that system. My advice today to those charged with building an MDIS would be to highlight three aspects of the use of marketing models.

First, the MDIS will be an *aid* to the decision maker, not a replacement. Second, marketing management must be committed to *use* the system, not regard it as an academic curiosity. And third, the system must be viewed as a *tool covering a wide range of activities*, not the private property of the marketing research director.

Marketing students of today have an advantage not acquired so easily by their counterparts prior to the mid-sixties. This is the ability to have by hindsight a perspective of the ways in which a marketing-decision information system can contribute to more efficient marketing management. As a result, the communication barriers of the past should be fewer and the probability of building and using a successful balanced MDIS should increase.

8

The Concept of the Marketing Mix

Neil H. Borden

PREVIEW

I. The term *marketing mix* was derived to describe the fact that a marketing manager must be able to choose and mix the many procedures and policies available.
   A. There are a number of elements of the marketing mix of manufacturers analogous to recipe ingredients.
   B. Forces arising from the behavior of individuals or groups also bear on management.

II. The marketing mix should be a product of day-to-day marketing evolution as well as longer range plans and procedures.

III. In the search for a marketing science, the concept of a mix may be viewed as a contribution to specifying areas in which facts should be assembled.

I have always found it interesting to observe how an apt or colorful term may catch on, gain wide usage, and help to further understanding of a concept that has already been expressed in less appealing and communicative terms. Such has been true of the phrase "marketing mix," which I began to use in my teaching and writing some 15 years ago. In a relatively short time it has come to have wide usage. This note tells of the evolution of the marketing mix concept.

The phrase was suggested to me by a paragraph in a research bulletin on

---

Neil H. Borden, "The Concept of the Marketing Mix," is reprinted from the *Journal of Advertising Research* (June 1964), pp. 2–7. © Copyright (1964), by the Advertising Research Foundation.

the management of marketing costs, written by my associate, Professor James Culliton (1948). In this study of manufacturers' marketing costs he described the business executive as a

> "decider," an "artist"—a "mixer of ingredients," who sometimes follows a recipe prepared by others, sometimes prepares his own recipe as he goes along, sometimes adapts a recipe to the ingredients immediately available, and sometimes experiments with or invents ingredients no one else has tried.

I liked his idea of calling a marketing executive a "mixer of ingredients," one who is constantly engaged in fashioning creatively a mix of marketing procedures and policies in his efforts to produce a profitable enterprise.

For many years previous to Culliton's cost study the wide variations in the procedures and policies employed by managements of manufacturing firms in their marketing programs and the correspondingly wide variation in the costs of these marketing functions, which Culliton aptly ascribed to the varied "mixing of ingredients," had become increasingly evident as we had gathered marketing cases at the Harvard Business School. The marked differences in the patterns or formulae of the marketing programs not only were evident through facts disclosed in case histories, but also were reflected clearly in the figures of a cost study of food manufacturers made by the Harvard Bureau of Business Research in 1929. The primary objective of this study was to determine common figures of expenses for various marketing functions among food manufacturing companies, similar to the common cost figures which had been determined in previous years for various kinds of retail and wholesale businesses. In this manufacturer's study we were unable, however, with the data gathered to determine common expense figures that had much significance as standards by which to guide management, such as had been possible in the studies of retail and wholesale trades, where the methods of operation tended toward uniformity. Instead, among food manufacturers the ratios of sales devoted to the various functions of marketing such as advertising, personal selling, packaging, and so on, were found to be widely divergent, no matter how we grouped our respondents. Each respondent gave data that tended to uniqueness.

Culliton's study of marketing costs in 1947–48 was a second effort to find out, among other objectives, whether a bigger sample and a more careful classification of companies would produce evidence of operating uniformities that would give helpful common expense figures. But the result was the same as in our early study: there was wide diversity in cost ratios among any classifications of firms which were set up, and no common figures were found that had much value. This was true whether companies were grouped according to similarity in product lines, amount of sales, territorial extent of operations, or other bases of classification.

Relatively early in my study of advertising, it had become evident that understanding of advertising usage by manufacturers in any case had to come from an analysis of advertising's place as one element in the total marketing program of the firm. I came to realize that it is essential always to ask: what overall marketing strategy has been or might be employed to bring about a profitable operation in light of the circumstances faced by the management? What combination of marketing procedures and policies has been or might be adopted to bring about desired behavior of trade and consumers at costs that will permit a profit? Specifically, how can advertising, personal selling, pricing, packaging, channels, warehousing, and the other elements of a marketing program be manipulated and fitted together in a way that will give a profitable operation? In short, I saw that every advertising management case called for a consideration of the strategy to be adopted for the total marketing program, with advertising recognized as only one element whose form and extent depended on its careful adjustment to the other parts of the program.

The soundness of this viewpoint was supported by case histories throughout my volume, *The Economic Effects of Advertising* (Borden, 1942). In the chapters devoted to the utilization of advertising by business, I had pointed out the innumerable combinations of marketing methods and policies that might be adopted by a manager in arriving at a marketing plan. For instance, in the area of branding, he might elect to adopt an individualized brand or a family brand. Or he might decide to sell his product unbranded or under private label. Any decision in the area of brand policy in turn has immediate implications that bear on his selection of channels of distribution, sales force methods, packaging, promotional procedure, and advertising. Throughout the volume the case materials cited show that the way in which any marketing function is designed and the burden placed upon the function are determined largely by the overall marketing strategy adopted by managements to meet the market conditions under which they operate. The forces met by different firms vary widely. Accordingly, the programs fashioned differ widely.

Regarding advertising, which was the function under focus in the economic effects volume, I said at one point:

> In all the above illustrative situations it should be recognized that advertising is not an operating method to be considered as something apart, as something whose profit value is to be judged alone. An able management

does not ask, "Shall we use or not use advertising," without consideration of the product and of other management procedures to be employed. Rather the question is always one of finding a management formula giving advertising its due place in the combination of manufacturing methods, product form, pricing, promotion and selling methods, and distribution methods. As previously pointed out different formulae, i.e., different combinations of methods, may be profitably employed by competing manufacturers.

From the above it can be seen why Culliton's description of a marketing manager as a "mixer of ingredients" immediately appealed to me as an apt and easily understandable phrase, far better than my previous references to the marketing man as an empiricist seeking in any situation to devise a profitable "pattern" or "formula" of marketing operations from among the many procedures and policies that were open to him. If he was a "mixer of ingredients," what he designed was a "marketing mix."

It was logical to proceed from a realization of the existence of a variety of "marketing mixes" to the development of a concept that would comprehend not only this variety, but also the market forces that cause managements to produce a variety of mixes. It is the problems raised by these forces that lead marketing managers to exercise their wits in devising mixes or programs which they hope will give a profitable business operation.

To portray this broadened concept in a visual presentation requires merely:

(1) a list of the important elements or ingredients that make up marketing programs;

(2) a list of the forces that bear on the marketing operation of a firm and to which the marketing manager must adjust in his search for a mix or program that can be successful.

The list of elements of the marketing mix in such a visual presentation can be long or short, depending on how far one wishes to go in his classification and subclassification of the marketing procedures and policies with which marketing managements deal when devising marketing programs. The list of elements which I have employed in my teaching and consulting work covers the principal areas of marketing activities which call for management decisions as revealed by case histories. I realize others might build a different list. Mine is as follows:

Elements of the Marketing Mix of Manufacturers

1. *Product Planning*—policies and procedures relating to:
   a. Product lines to be offered—qualities, design, etc.

   b. Markets to sell: whom, where, when, and in what quantity.
   c. New product policy—research and development program.
2. *Pricing*—policies and procedures relating to:
   a. Price level to adopt.
   b. Specific prices to adopt (odd-even, etc.)
   c. Price policy, e.g., one-price or varying price, price maintenance, use of list prices, etc.
   d. Margins to adopt—for company; for the trade.
3. *Branding*—policies and procedures relating to:
   a. Selection of trade marks.
   b. Brand policy—individualized or family brand.
   c. Sale under private label or unbranded.
4. *Channels of Distribution*—policies and procedures relating to:
   a. Channels to use between plant and consumer.
   b. Degree of selectivity among wholesalers and retailers.
   c. Efforts to gain cooperation of the trade.
5. *Personal Selling*—policies and procedures relating to:
   a. Burden to be placed on personal selling and the methods to be employed in:
      (1) Manufacturer's organization.
      (2) Wholesale segment of the trade.
      (3) Retail segment of the trade.
6. *Advertising*—policies and procedures relating to:
   a. Amount to spend—i.e., the burden to be placed on advertising.
   b. Copy platform to adopt:
      (1) Product image desired.
      (2) Corporate image desired.
   c. Mix of advertising: to the trade; through the trade; to consumers.
7. *Promotions*—policies and procedures relating to:
   a. Burden to place on special selling plans or devices directed at or through the trade.
   b. Form of these devices for consumer promotions, for trade promotions.
8. *Packaging*—policies and procedures relating to:
   a. Formulation of package and label.
9. *Display*—policies and procedures relating to:
   a. Burden to be put on display to help effect sale.
   b. Methods to adopt to secure display.
10. *Servicing*—policies and procedures relating to:
   a. Providing service needed.
11. *Physical Handling*—policies and procedures relating to:
   a. Warehousing.
   b. Transportation.
   c. Inventories.
12. *Fact Finding and Analysis*—policies and procedures relating to:
   a. Securing, analysis, and use of facts in marketing operations.

Also if one were to make a list of all the forces which managements weigh at one time or another when formulating their marketing mixes, it would be very long indeed, for the behavior of individuals and groups in all spheres of life have a bearing, first, on what goods and services are produced and consumed, and, second, on the procedures that may be employed in bringing about exchange of these goods and services. However, the important forces which bear on marketers, all arising from the behavior of individuals or groups, may readily be listed under four heads, namely the behavior of consumers, the trade, competitors, and government.

The outline below contains these four behavioral forces with notations of some of the important behavioral determinants within each force. These must be studied and understood by the marketer, if his marketing mix is to be successful. The great quest of marketing management is to understand the behavior of humans in response to the stimuli to which they are subjected. The skillful marketer is one who is a perceptive and practical psychologist and sociologist, who has keen insight into individual and group behavior, who can foresee changes in behavior that develop in a dynamic world, who has creative ability for building well-knit programs because he has the capacity to visualize the probable response of consumers, trade, and competitors to his moves. His skill in forecasting response to his marketing moves should well be supplemented by a further skill in devising and using tests and measurements to check consumer or trade response to his program or parts thereof, for no marketer has so much prescience that he can proceed without empirical check.

Below, then, is the suggested outline of forces which govern the mixing of marketing elements. This list and that of the elements taken together provide a visual presentation of the concept of the marketing mix.

Market Forces Bearing on the Marketing Mix

1. *Consumers' Buying Behavior*, as determined by their:
   a. Motivation in purchasing.
   b. Buying habits.
   c. Living habits.
   d. Environment (present and future, as revealed by trends, for environment influences consumers' attitudes toward products and their use of them).
   e. Buying power.
   f. Number (i.e., how many).
2. *The Trade's Behavior*—wholesalers' and retailers' behavior, as influenced by:

   a. Their motivations.
   b. Their structure, practices, and attitudes.
   c. Trends in structure and procedures that portend change.
3. *Competitors' Position and Behavior*, as influenced by:
   a. Industry structure and the firm's relation thereto.
      (1) Size and strength of competitors.
      (2) Number of competitors and degree of industry concentration.
      (3) Indirect competition—i.e., from other products.
   b. Relation of supply to demand—oversupply or undersupply.
   c. Product choices offered consumers by the industry—i.e., quality, price, service.
   d. Degree to which competitors compete on price vs. nonprice bases.
   e. Competitors' motivations and attitudes—their likely response to the actions of other firms.
   f. Trends technological and social, portending change in supply and demand.
4. *Governmental Behavior—Controls over Marketing:*
   a. Regulations over products.
   b. Regulations over pricing.
   c. Regulations over competitive practices.
   d. Regulations over advertising and promotion.

When building a marketing program to fit the needs of his firm, the marketing manager has to weigh the behavioral forces and then juggle marketing elements in his mix with a keen eye on the resources with which he has to work. His firm is but one small organism in a large universe of complex forces. His firm is only a part of an industry that is competing with many other industries. What does the firm have in terms of money, product line, organization, and reputation with which to work? The manager must devise a mix of procedures that fit the resources. If his firm is small, he must judge the response of consumers, trade, and competition in light of his position and resources and the influence that he can exert in the market. He must look for special opportunities in product or method of operation. The small firm cannot employ the procedures of the big firm. Though he may sell the same kind of product as the big firm, his marketing strategy is likely to be widely different in many respects. Innumerable instances of this fact might be cited. For example, in the industrial goods field, small firms often seek to build sales on a limited and highly specialized line, whereas industry leaders seek patronage for full lines. Small firms often elect to go in for regional sales rather than attempt the national distribution practiced by larger companies. Again, the company of limited resources often elects to limit its production and sales to products whose potential is too small to attract the big fellows. Still again, companies with small resources in the cosmetic field not infrequently have set up introductory marketing programs employing aggressive personal selling and a "push" strategy with distribution limited to leading department stores. Their initially small advertising funds have been directed through these selected retail outlets, with the offering of the products and their story told over the signatures of the stores. The strategy has been to borrow kudos for their products from the leading stores' reputations and to gain a gradual radiation of distribution to smaller stores in all types of channels, such as often comes from the trade's follow-the-leader behavior. Only after resources have grown from mounting sales has a dense retail distribution been aggressively sought and a shift made to place the selling burden more and more on company-signed advertising.

The above strategy was employed for Toni products and Stoppette deodorant in their early marketing stages when the resources of their producers were limited (cf. case of Jules Montenier, Inc. in Borden and Marshall, 1959, pp. 498–518). In contrast, cosmetic manufacturers with large resources have generally followed a "pull" strategy for the introduction of new products, relying on heavy campaigns of advertising in a rapid succession of area introductions to induce a hoped-for, complete retail coverage from the start (cf. case of Bristol-Myers Company in Borden and Marshall, 1959, pp. 519–533). These introductory campaigns have been undertaken only after careful programs of product development and test marketing have given assurance that product and selling plans had high promise of success.

Many additional instances of the varying strategy employed by small versus large enterprises might be cited. But those given serve to illustrate the point that managements must fashion their mixes to fit their resources. Their objectives must be realistic.

Long vs. Short Term Aspects of Marketing Mix

The marketing mix of a firm in large part is the product of the evolution that comes from day-to-day marketing. At any time the mix represents the program that a management has evolved to meet the problems with which it is constantly faced in an ever changing, ever challenging market. There are continuous tactical maneuvers: a new product, aggressive promotion, or price change initiated by a competitor must be considered and met; the failure of the trade to provide adequate market coverage or display must be remedied; a faltering sales force must be reorganized and stimulated; a decline in sales share must be diagnosed and remedied; an advertising approach that has lost effectiveness must be replaced; a general business decline must be countered. All such problems call for a management's maintaining effective channels of information relative to its own operations and to the day-to-day behavior of consumers, competitors, and the trade. Thus, we may observe that short range forces play a large part in the fashioning of the mix to be used at any time and in determining the allocation of expenditures among the various functional accounts of the operating statement.

But the overall strategy employed in a marketing mix is the product of longer range plans and procedures dictated in part by past empiricism and in part, if the management is a good one, by management foresight as to what needs to be done to keep the firm successful in a changing world. As the world has become more and more dynamic, blessed is that corporation which has managers who have foresight, who can study trends of all kinds—natural, economic, social, and technological—and, guided by these, devise long-range plans that give promise of keeping their corporations afloat and successful in the turbulent sea of market change. Accordingly, when we think of the marketing mix, we need to give particular heed today to devising a mix based on long-range planning that promises to fit the world of five or ten or more years hence. Provision for effective long-range planning in corporate organization and procedure has become more and more recognized as the earmark of good management in a world that has become increasingly subject to rapid change.

To cite an instance among American marketing organizations which has shown foresight in adjusting the marketing mix to meet social and economic change, I look upon Sears Roebuck and Company as an outstanding example. After building an unusually successful mail order business to meet the needs of a rural America, Sears management foresaw the need to depart from its marketing pattern as a mail order company catering primarily to farmers. The trend from a rural to an urban United States was going on apace. The automobile and good roads promised to make town and city stores increasingly available to those who continued to be farmers. Relatively early, Sears launched a chain of stores across the land, each easily accessible by highway to both farmer and city resident, and with adequate parking space for customers. In time there followed the remarkable telephone and mail order plan directed at urban residents to make buying easy for Americans when congested city streets and highways made shopping increasingly distasteful. Similarly, in the areas of planning products which would meet the desires of consumers in a fast changing world, of shaping its servicing to meet the needs of a wide variety of mechanical products, of pricing procedures to meet the challenging competition that came with the advent of discount retailers, the Sears organization has shown a foresight, adaptability, and creative ability worthy of emulation. The amazing growth and profitability of the company attest to the foresight and skill of its management. Its history shows the wisdom of careful attention to market forces and their impending change in devising marketing mixes that may assure growth.

Use of the Marketing Mix Concept

Like many concepts, the marketing mix concept seems relatively simple, once it has been expressed. I know that before they were ever tagged with the nomenclature of "concept," the ideas involved were widely understood among marketers as a result of the growing knowledge about marketing and marketing procedures that came during the preceding half century. But I have found for myself that once the ideas were reduced to a formal statement with an accompanying visual presentation, the concept of the mix has proved a helpful devise in teaching, in business problem solving, and, generally, as an aid to thinking about marketing. First of all, it is helpful in giving an answer to the question often raised as to "what is marketing?" A chart which shows the elements of the mix and the forces that bear on the mix helps to bring understanding of what marketing is. It helps to explain why in our dynamic world the thinking of management in all its functional areas must be oriented to the market.

In recent years I have kept an abbreviated chart showing the elements and the forces of the marketing mix in front of my classes at all times. In case discussion it has proved a handy device by which to raise queries as to whether the student has recognized the implications of any recommendation he might have made in the areas of the several elements of the mix. Or, referring to the forces, we can question whether all the pertinent market forces have been given due consideration. Continual reference to the mix chart leads me to feel that the students' understanding of "what marketing is" is strengthened. The constant presence and use of the chart leaves a deeper understanding that marketing is the devising of programs that successfully meet the forces of the market.

In problem solving the marketing mix chart is a constant reminder of:

(1) The fact that a problem seemingly lying in one segment of the mix must be deliberated with constant thought regarding the effect of any change in that sector on the other areas of marketing operations. The necessity of integration in marketing thinking is ever present.

(2) The need of careful study of the market forces as they might bear on problems in hand.

In short, the mix chart provides an ever ready checklist as to areas into which to guide thinking when considering marketing questions or dealing with marketing problems.

Marketing: Science or Art?

The quest for a "science of marketing" is hard upon us. If science is in part a systematic formulation and arrangement of facts in a way to help understanding, then the concept of the marketing mix may possibly be considered a small contribution in the search for a science of marketing. If we think of a marketing science as involving the observation and classification of facts and the establishment of verfiable laws that can be used by the marketer as a guide to action with assurance that predicted results will ensue, then we cannot be said to have gotten far toward establishing a science. The concept of the mix lays out the areas in which facts should be assembled, these to serve as a guide to management judgment in building marketing mixes. In the last few decades American marketers have made substantial progress in adopting the scientific method in assembling facts. They have sharpened the tools of fact finding—both those arising within the business and those external to it. Aided by these facts and by the skills developed through careful observation and experience, marketers are better fitted to practice the art of designing marketing mixes than would be the case had not the techniques of gathering facts been advanced as they have been in recent decades. Moreover, marketers have made progress in the use of the scientific method in designing tests whereby the results from mixes or parts of mixes can be measured. Thereby marketers have been learning how to subject the hypotheses of their mix artists to empirical check.

With continued improvement in the search for and the recording of facts pertinent to marketing, with further application of the controlled experiment, and with an extension and careful recording of case histories, we may hope for a gradual formulation of clearly defined and helpful marketing laws. Until then, and even then, marketing and the building of marketing mixes will largely lie in the realm of art.

References

BORDEN, NEIL H. *The Economic Effects of Advertising*. Homewood, Ill.: Richard D. Irwin, 1942.

BORDEN, NEIL H., AND M. V. MARSHALL. *Advertising Management: Text and Cases*. Homewood, Ill.: Richard D. Irwin, 1959.

CULLITON, JAMES W. *The Management of Marketing Costs*. Boston: Division of Research, Graduate School of Business Administration, Harvard University, 1948.

LEARNING REVIEW

Questions:

1. The groups and individuals whose behavior influence marketers are ____________, ____________, ____________, and ____________.

2. In addition to being a product of the evolution of day-to-day marketing, the marketing mix will also be a product of ____________________ ____________________.

Answers:

1. consumers, trade, competitors, government; 2. longer range plans and procedures

Retrospective Comment

Few analogies have endured so well as the concept of the marketer mixing his strategies to the conditions of the marketplace. Several observers of the marketing scene have added to the framework over the years. Professor E. J. McCarthy, for instance, developed a simplified model which offered the mnemonic four "P's" (Price, Product, Place, and Promotion), and which dichotomized the mix and environmental pressures into controllable and uncontrollable variables respectively.

Still, little new has been suggested which would increase the effectiveness of the original structure for teaching marketing art or analyzing marketing problems. The concept of the marketing mix remains as accurate a description of the state of marketing's progress toward becoming a science as when it was first written. That the description is still valid is not an indictment implying stagnation of marketing theory. Rather, the conclusion should be that the recipe is constantly being employed; marketers, with usage, are learning to adopt and apply more precisely the baisc ingredients.

9

Product Differentiation and Market Segmentation as Alternative Marketing Strategies

Wendell R. Smith

PREVIEW

I. There are both planned and uncontrollable differences in the products of an industry which result in different appeals by sellers in support of their marketing efforts.
   A. One type of appeal may be designed to bring convergence of individual market demands to a single product line *(product differentiation).*
   B. Another type of appeal accepts divergent demands and adjusts product lines to meet these different demands (*market segmentation*).
   C. Strategy determinations should involve an integrated approach to minimizing total costs.

II. There are a number of differences between strategies of differentiation and segmentation.
   A. Product differentiation is concerned with bending demand to the will of supply while segmentation adjusts product and marketing effort to consumer or user requirements.
   B. Successful product differentiation gives the seller a horizontal share of a broad and generalized market, while successful market segmentation give the seller depth of market position in segments that are effectively defined and penetrated.
   C. Differentiation is essentially a promotional strategy, while segmentation is a merchandising strategy.

Wendell R. Smith, "Product Differentiation and Market Segmentation as Alternative Marketing Strategies," is reprinted by permission from the *Journal of Marketing*, published by the American Marketing Association (July 1956), pp. 3–8.

III. Segmentation as a strategy is receiving increasing attention for several reasons.
   A. Improvements in technical aspects of mass production make it more feasible economically to produce different products.
   B. Minimized marketing costs of self-service impose a demand for better adjustment of products to consumer demand.
   C. General prosperity has produced sharper shopping comparison.
   D. An expanded line of goods and services is competing for the consumer's dollar.
   E. As companies grow, fringe markets become more important.
   F. Maximization of consumer satisfaction is a more secure position and helps stabilize costs.

During the decade of the 1930s, the work of Robinson and Chamberlin resulted in a revitalization of economic theory. While classical and neoclassical theory provided a useful framework for economic analysis, the theories of perfect competition and pure monopoly had become inadequate as explanations of the contemporary business scene. The theory of perfect competition assumes homogeneity among the components of both the demand and supply sides of the market, but diversity of heterogeneity had come to be the rule rather than the exception. This analysis reviews major marketing strategy alternatives that are available to planners and merchandisers of products in an environment characterized by imperfect competition.

Diversity in Supply

That there is a lack of homogeneity or close similarity among the items offered to the market by individual manufacturers of various products is obvious in any variety store, department store, or shopping center. In many cases the impact of this diversity is amplified by advertising and promotional activities. Today's advertising and promotion tends to emphasize appeals to *selective* rather than *primary* buying motives and to point out the distinctive or differentiating features of the advertiser's product or service offer.

The presence of differences in the sales offers made by competing suppliers produces a diversity in supply that is inconsistent with the assumptions of earlier theory. The reasons for the presence of diversity in specific markets are many and include the following:

1. Variations in the production equipment and methods or processes used by different manufacturers of products designed for the same or similar uses.

2. Specialized or superior resources enjoyed by favorably situated manufacturers.
3. Unequal progress among competitors in design, development, and improvement of products.
4. The inability of manufacturers in some industries to eliminate product variations even through the application of quality control techniques.
5. Variations in producers' estimates of the nature of market demand with reference to such matters as price sensitivity, color, material, or package size.

Because of these and other factors, both planned and uncontrollable differences exist in the products of an industry. As a result, sellers make different appeals in support of their marketing efforts.

Diversity or Variations in Consumer Demand

Under present-day conditions of imperfect competition, marketing managers are generally responsible for selecting the over-all marketing strategy or combination of strategies best suited to a firm's requirements at any particular point in time. The strategy selected may consist of a program designed to bring about the *convergence* of individual market demands for a variety of products upon a single or limited offering to the market. This is often accomplished by the achievement of product differentiation through advertising and promotion. In this way, variations in the demands of individual consumers are minimized or brought into line by means of effective use of appealing product claims designed to make a satisfactory volume of demand *converge* upon the product or product line being promoted. This strategy was once believed to be essential as the marketing counterpart to standardization and mass production in manufacturing because of the rigidities imposed by production cost considerations.

In some cases, however, the marketer may determine that it is better to accept *divergent* demand as a market characteristic and to adjust product lines and marketing strategy accordingly. This implies ability to merchandise to a heterogeneous market by emphasizing the precision with which a firm's products can satisfy the requirements of one or more distinguishable market segments. The strategy of product differentiation here gives way to marketing programs based upon measurement and definition of market differences.

Lack of homogeneity on the demand side may be based upon different customs, desire for variety, or desire for exclusiveness or may arise from basic differences in user needs. Some divergence in demand is the result of shopping errors in the market. Not all consumers have the desire or the ability to shop in a sufficiently efficient or rational manner as to bring about selection of the most needed or most wanted goods or services.

Diversity on the demand side of the market is nothing new to sales management. It has always been accepted as a fact to be dealt with in industrial markets where production to order rather than for the market is common. Here, however, the loss of precision in the satisfying of customer requirements that would be necessitated by attempts to bring about convergence of demand is often impractical and, in some cases, impossible. However, even in industrial marketing, the strategy of product differentiation should be considered in cases where products are applicable to several industries and may have horizontal markets of substantial size.

Long-Term Implications

While contemporary economic theory deals with the nature of product differentiation and its effects upon the operation of the toal economy, the alternative strategies of product differentiation and market segmentation have received less attention. Empirical analysis of contemporary marketing activity supports the hypothesis that, while product differentiation and market segmentation are closely related (perhaps even inseparable) concepts, attempts to distinguish between these approaches may be productive of clarity in theory as well as greater precision in the planning of marketing operations. Not only do strategies of differentiation and segmentation call for differing systems of action at any point in time, but the dynamics of markets and marketing underscore the importance of varying degrees of diversity *through time* and suggest that the rational selection of marketing strategies is a requirement for the achievement of maximum functional effectiveness in the economy as a whole.

If a rational selection of strategies is to be made, an integrated approach to the minimizing of total costs must take precedence over separate approaches to minimization of production costs on the one hand and marketing costs on the other. Strategy determination must be regarded as an over-all management decision which will influence and require facilitating policies affecting both production and marketing activities.

Differences Between Strategies of Differentiation and Segmentation

Product differentiation and market segmentation are both consistent with the framework of imperfect competition.[1] In its simplest terms, *product differentiation* is concerned with the bending of demand to the will of supply. It is an attempt to shift or to change the slope of the demand curve for the market offering of an individual supplier. This strategy may also be employed by a group of suppliers such as a farm cooperative, the members of which have agreed to act together. It results from the desire to establish a kind of equilibrium in the market by bringing about adjustment of market demand to supply conditions favorable to the seller.

Segmentation is based upon developments on the demand side of the market and represents a rational and more precise adjustment of product and marketing effort to consumer or user requirements. In the language of the economist, segmentation is *disaggregative* in its effects and tends to bring about recognition of several demand schedules where only one was recognized before.

Attention has been drawn to this area of analysis by the increasing number of cases in which business problems have become soluble by doing something about marketing programs and product policies that overgeneralize both markets and marketing effort. These are situations where intensive promotion designed to differentiate the company's products was not accomplishing its objective—cases where failure to recognize the reality of market segments was resulting in loss of market position.

While successful product differentiation will result in giving the marketer a horizontal share of a broad and generalized market, equally successful application of the strategy of market segmentation tends to produce depth of market position in the segments that are effectively defined and penetrated. The differentiator seeks to secure a layer of the market cake, whereas one who employs market segmentation strives to secure one or more wedge-shaped pieces.

Many examples of market segmentation can be cited; the cigarette and automobile industries are well-known illustrations. Similar developments exist in greater or lesser degree in almost all product areas. Recent introduction of a refrigerator with no storage compartment for frozen foods was in response to the distinguishable preferences of the segment of the refrigerator market made up of home freezer owners whose frozen food storage needs had already been met.

Strategies of segmentation and differentiation may be employed simultaneously, but more commonly they are applied in sequence in response to changing market conditions. In one sense, segmentation is a momentary or short-term phenomenon in that effective use of this strategy may lead to more formal recognition of the reality of market segments through redefinition of the segments as individual markets. Redefinition may result in a swing back to differentiation.

The literature of both economics and marketing abounds in formal definitions of product differentiation. *From a strategy viewpoint*, product differentiation is securing a measure of control over the demand for a product by advertising or promoting differences between a product and the products of competing sellers. It is basically the result of sellers' desires to establish firm market positions and/or to insulate their businesses against price competition. Differentiation tends to be characterized by heavy use of advertising and promotion and to result in prices that are somewhat above the equilibrium levels associated with perfectly competitive market conditions. It may be classified as a *promotional* strategy or approach to marketing.

Market segmentation, on the other hand, consists of viewing a heterogeneous market (one characterized by divergent demand) as a number of smaller homogeneous markets in response to differing product preferences among important market segments. It is attributable to the desires of consumers or users for more precise satisfaction of their varying wants. Like differentiation, segmentation often involves substantial use of advertising and promotion. This is to inform market segments of the availability of goods or services produced for or presented as meeting their needs with precision. Under these circumstances, prices tend to be somewhat closer to perfectly competitive equilibrium. Market segmentation is essentially a *merchandising* strategy, merchandising being used here in its technical sense as representing the adjustment of market offerings to consumer or user requirements.

The Emergence of the Segmentation Strategy

To a certain extent, market segmentation may be regarded as a force in the market that will not be denied. It may result from trial and error in the sense that generalized programs of product differentiation may turn out to be effective in some segments of the market and ineffective in others. Recognition of, and intelligent response to, such a situation necessarily involves a shift in emphasis. On the other hand, it may develop that products involved in marketing programs designed for particular market segments may achieve a broader acceptance than originally planned, thus revealing a basis for convergence of demand and a more generalized marketing approach. The challenge to planning arises from the importance of determining, preferably in advance, the level or degree of segmentation that can be exploited with profit.

There appear to be many reasons why formal recognition of market segmentation as a strategy is beginning to emerge. One of the most important of these is decrease in the size of the minimum efficient producing or manufacturing unit required in some product areas. American industry has also established the technical base for product diversity by gaining release from some of the rigidities imposed by earlier approaches to mass production. Hence, there is less need today for generalization of markets in response to the necessity for long production runs of identical items.

Present emphasis upon the minimizing of marketing costs through self-service and similar developments tends to impose a requirement for better adjustment of products to consumer demand. The retailing structure, in its efforts to achieve improved efficiency, is providing less and less sales push at point of sale. This increases the premium placed by retailers upon products that are presold by their producers and are readily recognized by consumers as meeting their requirements as measured by satisfactory rates of stock turnover.

It has been suggested that the present level of discretionary buying power is productive of sharper shopping comparisons, particularly for items that are above the need level. General prosperity also creates increased willingness "to pay a little more" to get "just what I wanted."

Attention to market segmentation has also been enchanced by the recent ascendancy of product competition to a position of great economic importance. An expanded array of goods and services is competing for the consumer's dollar. More specifically, advancing technology is creating competition between new and traditional materials with reference to metals, construction materials, textile products, and in many other areas. While such competition is confusing and difficult to analyze in its early stages, it tends to achieve a kind of balance as various competing materials find their markets of maximum potential as a result of recognition of differences in the requirements of market segments.

Many companies are reaching the stage in their development where attention to market segmentation may be regarded as a condition or cost of growth. Their *core* markets have already been developed on a generalized basis to the point where additional advertising and selling expenditures are yielding diminishing returns. Attention to smaller or *fringe* market segments, which may have small potentials individually but are of crucial importance in the aggregate, may be indicated.

Finally, some business firms are beginning to regard an increasing share of their total costs of operation as being fixed in character. The higher costs of maintaining market position in the channels of distribution illustrate this change. Total reliance upon a strategy of product differentiation under such circumstances is undesirable, since market share available as a result of such a promotion-oriented approach tends to be variable over time. Much may hinge, for example, upon week-to-week audience ratings of the television shows of competitors who seek to outdifferentiate each other. Exploitation of market segments, which provides for great maximization of consumer or user satisfactions, tends to build a more secure market position and to lead to greater over-all stability. While traditionally, high fixed costs (regarded primarily from the production viewpoint) have created pressures for expanded sale of standardized items through differentiation, the possible shifting of certain marketing costs into the fixed area of the total cost structure tends to minimize this pressure.

Conclusion

Success in planning marketing activities requires precise utilization of both product differentiation and market segmentation as components of marketing strategy. It is fortunate that available techniques of marketing research make unplanned market exploration largely unnecessary. It is the obligation of those responsible for sales and marketing administration to keep the strategy mix in adjustment with market structure at any point in time and to produce in marketing strategy at least as much dynamism as is present in the market. The ability of business to plan in this way is dependent upon the maintenance of a flow of market information that can be provided by marketing research as well as the full utilization of available techniques of cost accounting and cost analysis.

Cost information is critical because the upper limit to which market segmentation can be carried is largely defined by production cost considerations. There is a limit to which diversity in market offerings can be carried without driving production costs beyond practical limits. Similarly, the employment of product differentiation as a strategy tends to be restricted by the achievement of levels of marketing cost that are untenable. These cost factors tend to define the limits of the zone within which the employment of marketing strategies or a strategy mix dictated by the nature of the market is permissive.

It should be emphasized that while we have here been concerned with the differences between product differentiation and market segmentation as marketing strategies, they are closely related concepts in the setting of an imperfectly competitive market. The differences have been highlighted in the interest of enhancing clarity in theory and precision in practice. The emergence of market segmentation as a strategy once again provides evidence of the customer's preemience in the contemporary American economy and the richness of the rewards that can result from the application of science to marketing problems.

NOTES

1. Imperfect competition assumes lack of uniformity in the size and influence of the firms or individuals that comprise the demand or supply sides of a market.

LEARNING REVIEW

Questions:

1. From a strategy viewpoint, product differentiation is securing a measure of control over demand by advertising or promoting ____.

2. Differentiation is essentially a ____________ strategy, while segmentation is essentially a ____________ strategy.

Answers:

1. Differences between your product and the products of competitors.
2. promotional, merchandising.

Retrospective Comment

Since the publication of this article in the *Journal of Marketing*, the concept of market segmentation has become established as a significant basis for analysis and strategy determination. The concept is essentially *behavioral* in that the fundamental criteria for defining and distinguishing market segments are to be formed in differences in buying behavior. Analysis of markets based upon demographic and related criteria does not result in the identification of true market segments unless behavioral and preference homogeneity is found to be present. It is important that this essential linkage between buyer behavior and market segmentation as a marketing strategy be maintained.

While it is often true that behavior-based market segments are also homogeneous with respect to demographic characteristics, their significance for strategy determinations is fundamentally behavioral in nature.

10

The Marketing Audit: Its Nature, Purposes, and Problems

Abe Shuchman

PREVIEW

I. The marketing audit is primarily a re-examination and evaluation of marketing objectives and policies.

II. There are several purposes for a marketing audit:
   A. Prognosis is a function, as well as diagnosis.
   B. It is a search for opportunities and means of using them.
   C. It is a search for weaknesses and a way of eliminating them.
   D. The audit can help keep the operations of a marketing manager abreast of the times and in a strong position competitively.
   E. A marketing audit while a business is successful can be important in a preventative way.

III. Several problems of the marketing audit merit attention:
   A. To be successful the audit must be done by the right kind of people.
   B. A timetable for the audit should be set up and should be adhered to, or the audit will get bogged down and give inaccurate data.
   C. Marketing personnel must be educated to the fact that the audit is to help and not to harm them.

The notion of an audit—a periodic review and appraisal of a business activity—is familiar to all executives. In most companies, financial audits to establish the adequacy and accuracy of accounting and financial opera-

---

Abe Shuchman, "The Marketing Audit: Its Nature, Purposes and Problems," is reprinted by permission of the publisher from AMA Management Report No. 32, *Analyzing and Improving Marketing Performance* © 1959 by the American Management Association, Inc.

tions are accepted practice. Periodic inventories for the evaluation of physical assets are also commonplace. In addition, many firms today make periodic reviews of the records and achievements of all employees, and there is evidence that such "personnel audits" are fast becoming standard practice.

In recent years there has been increasing awareness that the future growth—indeed, the very survival—of most companies depends primarily upon the success of their marketing operations. There has been widespread recognition of the central and critical role of marketing activities in the shaping of a firm's destiny. It has not, however, been generally recognized that, because marketing operations are of such crucial importance, it is necessary to apply to these operations a type of stock-taking analogous to that currently applied to financial and personnel activities. Very few firms have yet come to realize that a *marketing audit* is as essential as an audit of the company's books, physical assets, or employees.

Most marketing executives would probably deny indignantly that they do not recognize the need for auditing the operations which are their responsibility. They would insist, in fact, that they are *constantly* evaluating these operations—and they would probably be right. Within every modern marketing organization, evaluations of many different kinds *are* constantly being made. It is important to recognize, however, that not every marketing evaluation is a marketing audit. Neither, except very rarely, does the sum of all the evaluations currently being made equal a marketing audit.

Some Distinguishing Characteristics

There are a number of reasons for asserting that current appraisals do not, either singly or as a group, constitute a marketing audit. The principal reason, however, is that they are far too limited in scope. Executives review and appraise the effectiveness of the field sales force, the advertising program, the company's product mix, and the like, but they evaluate each of these elements at different times, and in no planned or coherent pattern. They do not, within a specified interval, examine each and every facet of the *total* operation. There is no integrated, coordinated, comprehensive appraisal encompassing all marketing activities and executed systematically in accord with a planned program and schedule. Yet the principal characteristic of the marketing audit is that it *is* such a systematic and comprehensive survey and evaluation of the total marketing operation—a programed appraisal of *all* of the activities included within the marketing function.

Current appraisals are much more limited than the marketing audit in another respect. They are, in general, confined to the review and evaluation of performance, methods and procedures, and personnel, concentrating on the manpower and tactics used and the results achieved within a given framework of objectives and policies. Rarely is the framework itself subjected to systematic and critical analysis and appraisal.

Now a marketing audit is, to be sure, an appraisal of performance and tactics—of methods, procedures, personnel, and organization. Beyond this, however, it is a great deal more. In fact, its principal focus is on those elements of the marketing function which are almost never subjected to careful, regular, and orderly scrutiny but which are of fundamental importance because they comprise the base from which methods, procedures, and organization are derived. In short, the marketing audit is primarily a re-examination and evaluation of marketing objectives and policies—an appraisal not only of a company's marketing program but also of the framework which has given the program its direction, structure, and shape.

The preoccupation of the marketing audit with objectives and policies is one of its most salient and distinguishing characteristics, for it implies that, unlike other appraisals, the audit is a searching inquiry into the character and validity of the fundamental premises underlying a company's marketing operations. It is a review and evaluation of the assumptions, conceptions, and expectations that guide executives in their planning and operating decisions. It is a planned effort to test and assess executive beliefs and opinions about the character of the market, the company's position in the market, the company's objectives and capabilities, and the effectiveness of the various policies, methods, personnel, and organizational structures which are or might be employed.

As Wroe Alderson has observed:

> The marketing executive may be visualized as operating on the basis of a sort of map. There are boundaries or limits marking off the class of customers he is trying to reach or the trade channels through which he is willing to sell. There are routes over which he can move in attaining his objectives which experience or investigation has indicated are better than other routes. This map may have to be brought up to date by a validation or a revision of operating assumptions. . . .[1]

In this context, the marketing audit becomes essentially an effort to step back and take a penetrating look at the basic ideas which are the ultimate source of a company's marketing programs. It is an attempt explicitly to define and verify these ideas about the company, the market, and methods of reaching the market by testing them against current and accurate information.

The Basic Purposes

The marketing audit may thus be defined as a *systematic, critical, and impartial review and appraisal of the total marketing operation: of the basic objectives and policies of the operation and the assumptions which underlie them as well as of the methods, procedures, personnel, and organization employed to implement the policies and achieve the objectives*. This definition, however, is not complete. It conveys no sense of the purpose of the audit, as it should, for it is important to understand that the audit is a prognostic as well as a diagnostic tool—a search for opportunity as well as for malfunction.

Too many executives take a static view of appraisals. In examining the marketing operation or one of its component activities, they are concerned almost exclusively with the here and now. They are intent on identifying *existing* problems or weaknesses and discovering their causes, so that appropriate remedies can be applied. A marketing audit, too, aims at locating existing weaknesses, at pinpointing current problems and their sources. Like other types of evaluations, therefore, the audit too is a diagnostic tool. But diagnosis is not the only, or even the most important, purpose of the marketing audit. It is concerned as much with the future as with the present. It is a search not only for weaknesses that clearly exist but also for those that may arise. It is aimed at identifying current problems and determining their causes, but at the same time it probes for incipient problems—those just beginning or likely to emerge. This is what we mean when we say that the marketing audit is a prognostic as well as a diagnostic tool.

Executives tend also to conceive of audits almost exclusively as means for locating and defining problems. The identification of problems and possible remedies is, however, only one of the purposes of the marketing audit. The audit is, in addition, concerned with identifying the particular strengths of the marketing operation. It is a search for opportunities, existing and potential, to apply the factors which create strength in one marketing activity to others. And it is a search for opportunities in the market which had previously been overlooked or which have only recently emerged.

Thus, the marketing audit has several purposes. It is intended to reveal potential as well as existing strengths and weaknesses in a company's marketing operation, and it is intended also to bring into sharp focus possibilities for capitalizing on the strengths and eliminating the weaknesses. In consequence, the marketing audit is a tool that can be of tremendous value not only to the less successful, crisis-ridden company but also to the highly successful and profitable industry leader. No marketing operation is ever so good that it cannot be improved. Even the best can be made better. In fact, even the best *must* be made better, for few if any marketing operations can remain successful over the years by maintaining the status quo. Continued success requires continual adaptation to a constantly changing environment. It requires, therefore, continual scrutiny of the environment and of the firm's relationship to the environment, with the aim of spotting the cues which indicate both a need for modifying the firm's marketing program and the direction such modification should take. It requires an unremitting search for emerging opportunities that can and must be exploited if the marketing operation is to remain highly successful. The marketing audit, therefore, is not only a prescription for the sick firm but also preventive medicine for the currently healthy and successful firm.

A Total View

To summarize, then, the most prominent characteristics and most important purposes of the marketing audit are these:

It is a carefully programed appraisal of the total marketing operation.

It is centered on an evaluation of objectives and policies and of the assumptions which underlie them.

Its aim is prognosis as well as diagnosis.

It is a search for opportunities and means for exploiting them as well as for weaknesses and means for their elimination.

It is the practice of preventive as well as curative marketing medicine.

Why Audit—and When?

Every marketing executive recognizes that he operates in a highly fluid environment. He is fully aware that unceasing change is the most salient characteristic of his company's marketing situation. He knows that there is constant and continuous—sometimes even abrupt and dramatic—change in the size, composition, and geographic distribution of the population; in the size and distribution of incomes; in tastes, preferences, and habits; and in technology. He has, in short, abosrbed the truth that has so often escaped other executives: The modern market is highly dynamic.

Keeping Abreast of the Times

Unfortunately, recognition of the dynamic quality of the market has not led marketing executives to recognition of all its implications. Many executives have not yet fully realized that continual flux in the market signifies continual alteration of the relationship of a company to its market and of the competitive relationships between companies, and that such constant and widespread change in the environment makes some facet of almost every existing marketing operation obsolete. As Arthur Felton has described the situation in the *Harvard Business Review*:

> There is probably no marketing plan in industry today that is not out of date. . . . The reason is that there are so many constantly changing factors in any company's marketing situation that it is practically impossible to keep revising a plan so rapidly and so accurately that there is no lag in it. The factors that keep a plan dated are not only those of the "changing American market" which *Fortune* and other publications have discussed—suburbia, the new middle class, the Negro market, and so forth. The dating factors have also to do with changing selling problems growing out of the major upheavals—shifts in consumer psychology that necessitate different kinds of advertising and packaging, trends in distribution that affect the company's relations with wholesalers and jobbers, changes in the "customer mix" that affect the efficiency of the sales organization, and so on.[2]

The significance of market dynamism, then, is that a firm's marketing operation tends continually to fall out of phase with current conditions and incipient trends. Elements of every marketing program are always losing their effectiveness. Methods, procedures, and organizational structures rapidly become outmoded, and objectives and policies become inappropriate as the validity of the assumptions on which they are based is destroyed. The continual change in a company's marketing situation means, in fact, that no marketing program is ever completely and precisely adapted to the environment in which it is executed; indeed, it means that every program becomes ever more poorly adapted with the passage of time. This is evidenced by the fact that, almost from the moment a marketing program takes effect, a drift away from the program commences which accelerates as time goes by. This drift arises from the efforts of managers and their subordinates to cope with the many specific problems engendered by the lack of adjustment between the marketing program and the changing marketing environment. It is symptomatic of the inability to be always in perfect tune with the times. It is also dangerous if not arrested, for the drift implies that the planned marketing operation is degenerating into a patchwork of opportunistic and expedient actions. It implies that confusion and even chaos increasingly supplant the originally integrated and coherent plan for the application of marketing effort. In time, therefore, unless the marketing operation is revamped—unless objectives, policies, methods, procedures, personnel, and organization are once again combined in a carefully articulated plan which is better adapted to the company's current marketing situation—the drift and its accompanying confusion will almost certainly precipitate a company crisis.

Thus, the dynamic quality of the market implies a need for constant vigilance on the part of marketing executives. It compels recognition of the need for awareness of the nature of the changes taking place within and without the firm, and of the directions in which the marketing organization and program can be and must be modified in order to adapt to these changes. It emphasizes the need for improvement-consciousness, and thus for a continual search for new cost-reduction possibilities and new sales opportunities. In other words, the rapid pace of change in our modes of living and the continually accelerating technological revolution in industry make it imperative that the marketing executive appraise and reappraise every element of his operations and organization. Moreover, if the executive wants the best results from these appraisals he must *plan* them, for only a systematic, careful, and orderly program of appraisal can assure that no activity or element of the marketing operation is neglected or subjected to only the most cursory examination. It follows, therefore, that the marketing audit is a necessary and important tool which can provide a marketing manager with the knowledge required to keep his operations abreast of the times and thus in a strong competitive position.

Auditing under Crisis Conditions

Many executives who recognize the effectiveness of a marketing audit seem to believe that it is needed primarily by companies which are problem-ridden and which face a deteriorating market and profit position. They regard the audit as an effective remedy for a marketing operation which is in critical condition. Such a conception of the audit is entirely erroneous, however, for, as we have already noted, the audit is preventive as well as curative marketing medicine. Nevertheless, this conception of the audit is so widespread that it may be worthwhile to give some reasons for believing that it is wrong.

Executives who conceive of the marketing audit as being unnecessary for a smoothly functioning, highly successful marketing operation have really failed to udnerstand fully its nature and purposes. They fail to see, therefore, that appraisals made in an atmosphere of crisis are unlikely to have the character of a marketing audit. This is true for two reasons:

1. In a crisis situation there exists a compulsion to do something quickly which will resuscitate the marketing operation before it reaches a point of no return. Under crisis conditions, therefore, the aim of an appraisal must be to find an appropriate stimulant rather than a basic therapy. As a result, such an appraisal inevitably assumes the nature of a rapid scanning rather than a penetrating look at the marketing operation; and even this scanning is limited to those facets of the operation which experience and intuition indicate are most likely both to require attention and to respond quickly to treatment.
2. Since a crisis in a company's marketing operation often means that the company is experiencing financial difficulty, any appraisal undertaken at such a time will almost surely be allotted far less money than is required to do the job properly.

Thus, both for financial reasons and because of the need for haste, an appraisal under crisis conditions is likely to be far more superficial, far more limited in both scope and depth, than a true marketing audit.

Auditing the Successful Operation

The smoothly running and successful marketing operation can, therefore, be more effectively audited than a sick operation. More important, however, is the fact that it *needs* to be audited. Success tends to foster complacency, laxity, and carelessness. It permits tradition and habit to become the dominant shapers of marketing programs. It allows dry rot and excessive costs to develop and spread. It leads some marketing executives to become so deeply involved with existing policies and methods that they never bother to examine the possibility of performing the marketing task in other ways—ways which, although once inappropriate, may now be more closely attuned to the company's needs. Yet none of these well-known concomitants of success may be immediately apparent. A successful operation can move along well, for a time at least, propelled by the momentum which has been generated in the past. The growing waste of marketing effort and the increasing frequency of failures to pioneer innovations are not reflected at once in shrinking profits and market share. Their effect is delayed, for marketing wastes and failures erode rather than shatter the company's market position. Sooner or later, however, the erosion of market position must find expression in reduced volume and profits—and, when it does, the "healthy" marketing operation appears suddenly to have contracted a very severe illness.

The dangers of success clearly suggest that in marketing as in home maintenance the time to fix the roof is when the sun is shining. They point clearly to the need for continual, systematic, critical, and objective appraisal of even the most successful marketing operation *while it is successful*. The negligence and waste, the complacency and blind obedience to tradition and habit which breed so easily in the culture of success, can become extremely noxious viruses if permitted to develop unchecked. They can appear anywhere in a marketing organization, and they can in time sap the strength of the most vigorous marketing operation. The maintenance of health and vigor in the operation requires, therefore, that such factors be identified and eliminated just as soon as they appear. The marketing audit serves this end. It is, consequently, of considerable importance to the successful marketing organization, for it constitutes a kind of insurance against subversion by success.

Some Problems of Auditing

The dynamism of the market and the awareness that continued success may have undesirable by-products point to a general need for marketing audits. They strongly suggest that every marketing operation can be improved through a systematic and comprehensive program of evaluation. Such a program of evaluation is not likely, however, to be executed without difficulty. It may be helpful, therefore, to indicate the nature of some of the more important difficulties that are likely to be encountered.

Some of the problems that will arise as an executive seeks to inaugurate and execute a marketing audit are of such moment that they have been treated more fully than is possible here by other contributors to this volume. The problem of defining appropriate standards or criteria for each marketing activity and each element of each activity which are valid and operational measures of effectiveness is an example. Other problems, such as that of obtaining the funds needed to pay for a full-scale audit, are so obvious that they require little more than mention. In addition to these problems, however, there are three others which merit attention. These involve: (1) the selection of auditors; (2) the scheduling of the audit; and (3) the impact of the audit on marketing personnel.

Selecting the Auditors

No audit can be better than the people who make it. Consequently, no audit will yield the benefits that it is possible to obtain unless it is made by the right kind of people. As is implied by the definition of the audit, such people must be not only critical and impartial but also knowledgeable and creative. They must not be so involved with or "married" to existing policies and procedures that they cannot really be critical and objective in their assessments. In addition, they must possess the experience, know-how, and creative imagination needed to recognize problems and opportunities that are just beginning to appear on the horizon of the company's marketing situation and to define feasible courses of action for solving the problems and exploiting the opportunities. Finding enough such people to staff the audit can be a tall order. Few companies have an abundance of men with these characteristics. The quality of the audit is, nevertheless, determined largely by the extent to which the auditors possess these characteristics, and successful solution of the staffing problem is, therefore, of singular importance.

Scheduling the Audit

Since the marketing audit is an evaluation of the total marketing operation, it cannot be properly executed in a matter of days or weeks; it must be a relatively long-term project. And, as in any long-term project, there is always the danger that distractions may intervene to delay execution or that interest in the audit may be dissipated, with the result that the audit drags on and on. If the audit is permitted to drag on, however, conditions within and without the firm may change to such a degree that the findings when reported describe the marketing situation as it *was* rather than as it *is*. Any modification of the marketing operation on the basis of such findings could, of course, impair rather than improve the operation. Clearly then, the audit, if it is to yield accurate information about the company's current marketing situation, must be executed in accord with an established timetable. Preventing the many deviations from the timetable which can easily be rationalized is a central problem of any marketing audit.

Impact upon Marketing Personnel

The success of a marketing audit requires the full cooperation of all marketing personnel, from the chief executive and department heads to the salesmen in the field. The evaluation of an activity for which one is responsible, however, is often regarded by those carrying on the activity as a personal evaluation. These people often perceive in the audit a threat to their status and aspirations, and they therefore tend to resist it. They do not necessarily refuse to cooperate, but they may attempt to sabotage the audit wherever they feel it is possible to do so with impunity. Their resistance may make it extremely difficult—if not, in fact, impossible—to obtain accurate information. Moreover, the feeling that they are being threatened may impair their morale and reduce their effectiveness on the job.

It is extremely important to be aware of these possible side-effects of the audit so that pains are taken to obviate them through precautionary measures. Every effort must be made to create a genuine appreciation of the fact that the audit is not a fault-finding expedition but a search for ideas and tools that will enable everyone to do a better job. Marketing personnel must be educated to the fact that the audit is a management tool used to "help us help you" and not a device for "getting" anybody. They must be convinced that the audit is a full-scale effort to provide everyone in the marketing organization with important information that could not possibly be obtained through normal channels and routines. Before inaugurating a marketing audit, therefore, the possibilities of resistance and lowered morale must be dealt with through an educational campaign within the marketing organization.

NOTES

1. Wroe Alderson, *Marketing Behavior and Executive Action* (Homewood, Ill.: Richard D. Irwin, Inc., 1957), p. 419.
2. Arthur P. Felton, "Conditions of Marketing Leadership," *Harvard Business Review*, March-April, 1956, p. 119.

LEARNING REVIEW

Questions:

1. The audit is a ____________ as well as a diagnostic tool.

2. The marketing audit actually centers on an evaluation of the firm's marketing ____________ and ____________ and of the assumptions which underlie them.

3. The problem with scheduling an audit is that it is relatively ____________ project.

Answers:

1. prognostic 2. potential and problems (or strengths and weaknesses)
3. long-term

Retrospective Comment by Howard A. Thompson*

In the nearly two decades since this article was written the term *marketing audit* has become prominent in the marketing literature but remains a seldom-used planning and control approach in guiding the entire marketing effort. Nor has application of the concept been emphasized extensively in most marketing management courses. If the vice president of marketing suggested to the newly-hired marketing major that the first assignment would be to perform a company-wide marketing audit, the reaction might be panic rather than pleasure.

Why have the consumer-oriented companies not established *marketing auditors* to implement an idea borrowed from the somewhat more quantitative finance and accounting area and which has such obvious practical justification? There are at least three reasons that come to mind.

One reason is that in a behavioral area such as marketing, success and failure are more difficult to assess than in the more quantitative fields. It is easier to determine that dollars were embezzled, that they did not earn interest at the highest available rate, or that prompt payment discounts were not earned, than it is to determine that a salesperson spent the right amount of time calling on the small, less profitable customers (they may grow!) versus the larger ones, or that the increase in direct mail advertising had a greater influence on the increase in consumer awareness than a redesigned package (involving the same amount of money as the direct mail campaign would have). Accountability for efficiency in the marketing area is evaluated less accurately and, usually, with considerable delay. Recognizing these difficulties, it could be that many rationalize "what's the use?" and resist installing any marketing audit system, much less a marketing auditor.

Another reason is that marketing audits are already being performed but at different levels and may not be recognized as a part of a system which needs to be installed company-wide. Frequent and considerable planning and "post mortem" evaluations often audit the marketing effort which executes this year's advertising campaign for an existing product. The audit approach is seldom used, however, to ask whether or not that same product should have been modified significantly in its features or packaging before the advertising campaign planners and evaluators began.

The audit approach may be used in a new product launch which does consider the product features and packaging requirements along with the advertising campaign. It may accept as a "given," nevertheless, that the new product will be offered through the same dealer sales force channels as used in previous years. Since the audits are already being performed at different levels, more often than not the need to extend the audit to the highest level which will increase *corporate* opportunities and efficiency, as suggested by Abe Shuchman's article, is not recognized. As William Lazer has written,[1] although a marketing audit should in theory evaluate every aspect of marketing activity, this may be impossible in practice. Lazer discusses four levels of auditing: 1) an audit of the total marketing system, 2) an audit of the marketing mix, 3) an audit of the submixes, and 4) an audit of the individual marketing elements such as the selection, training, and compensation of salesmen.

A third reason that the usual company does not have an office door lettered with the title MARKETING AUDITOR is perhaps that marketing academicians have tended to avoid providing extensive "cookbook" checklists for the necessary levels of the marketing audit. This is one of the first resources a good marketing consultant develops, but consultants are seldom invited to perform a preventative audit or a company-wide audit at the highest level. If they are, the secondary and tertiary level audits are usually carried out by company personnel and the subsequent self-examinations become temporary extra research assignments which briefly illuminate the problem as would a flashbulb in a dark room. Rather, the audit should continue as would a lamp (even if low wattage!). Using carefully defined company objectives, a series of marketing performance budgets (standards) could be established which would offer continuing control using the management by exception method.

With improvement in information system management, the marketing audit and the position of Marketing Auditor are certain someday to become the norm rather than the exception. Newly-employed business graduates planning to succeed in the marketing area should hold on to their marketing texts; they are excellent sources of those necessary checklists when the Marketing V.P. says, "Your first assignment is to conduct a company-wide marketing audit." It is still not a very likely quote but the probabilities are increasing every year.

* Dr. Thompson, editor of *The Great Writings of Marketing*, is currently Dean, College of Business, Eastern Kentucky University, Richmond, Kentucky.

1. William Lazar, *Marketing Management* (New York: John Wiley & Sons, Inc., 1971), pp. 136–39.

PART 3

Understanding Consumer Behavior

"It's like . . . well, like elephant touching!"

The final selection in this section, "A Theory of Buyer Behavior," uses the analogy of blind men describing an elephant. One can imagine that each man's description would be completely different depending upon his point of contact with so large a beast. Perhaps the attempts of marketing scholars to understand consumer behavior parallel the blind men's problem. The human mind is a relatively unexplored area; inputs to it and outputs from it are observable, but neither the variables which influence the equations inside the mind nor the weights given to each variable will be *seen* in the sense of the *givens* of a math problem. All of us are blind when probing so large a beast as consumer behavior. Fortunately, however, some are more perceptive than others.

You need those pegs

Some of these perceptive frameworks now follow. With such matrices the student of consumer behavior is supplied with a peg on which to hang the many—sometimes conflicting, often confusing, always complex—observations and postulates in this field of *elephant touching.*

. . . and some frameworks

Philip Kotler's "Behavioral Models for Analyzing Buyers" shows that the different approaches used among behavioralists are all useful in understanding consumers. Abraham Maslow added a need hierarchy theory which was later criticized for failing to encompass the concept that the need levels exist together and that people may be elevated to higher levels. Yet he added a new dimension to the elephant even if accompanied by a later-to-be-corrected mismeasurement. George Katona explains why psychological theory permits a clearer understanding of such rational economic concepts as maximization of utility. Pierre Martineau offered a social class framework within which consumption patterns could be better understood. And John Howard and Jagdish Sheth draw upon stimulus-response learning theory to flow chart the phenomenon of repeat buying.

11

Behavioral Models for Analyzing Buyers

Philip Kotler

PREVIEW

I. The *Marshallian* model of buyer behavior emphasizes economic motivations.
   A. This model has been refined into modern utility theory: economic man is bent on maximizing his utility, and does this by carefully calculating the *felicific* consequences of any purchase.
   B. This model, holding that the buyer acts in the light of his best interest, offers several behavioral hypotheses to marketing:
      1. The lower the price of the product, the higher the sales.
      2. The lower the price of substitute products, the lower the sales of this product; and the lower the price of complementary products, the higher the sales of this product.
      3. The higher the real income, the higher the sales of this product, provided that it is not an *inferior* good.
      4. The higher the promotional expenditures, the higher the sales.

II. The *Pavlovian* model proposes that learning is an associative process and that a large component of behavior is conditioned in this way.
   A. This model is based essentially on four central concepts:
      1. *Drive* refers to strong stimuli internal to the individual which impel action.
      2. *Cues* are weaker stimuli in the environment and/or in the individual which determine when, where, and how the subject responds.
      3. The *response* is the organism's reaction to the configuration of cues.

Philip Kotler, "Behavioral Models for Analyzing Buyers," is reprinted by permission from the *Journal of Marketing*, published by the American Marketing Association (October 1965), pp. 37–45.

4. *Reinforcement* is anything that strengthens a response and creates a tendency for it to be repeated when the same configuration of cues re-appears.

B. Pavlovian theory offers several propositions to marketing.
   1. Strong cues may be necessary in markets characterized by strong brand loyalties.
   2. Enough similarity to other brands should be provided.
   3. Quality must be such as to provide reinforcement.
   4. Repetition in advertising fights forgetting and provides reinforcement.
   5. The strongest product related drives must be identified.

III. The *Freudian* model offers psychoanalytic motivations in explanation of behavior.

A. The Freudian model says motivations may arise or be affected in any of three parts of the psyche:
   1. The id is the reservoir of strong drives and urges.
   2. The ego is the conscious planning center for finding outlets for drives.
   3. The super-ego channels instinctive drives into socially approved outlets to avoid the pain of guilt or shame.

B. The most important marketing implication is that buyers are motivated by *symbolic* as well as economic-functional product concerns.

IV. The *Veblenian* model emphasizes the social-psychological factors.

A. Veblen's hypothesis is that much of economic consumption is motivated not by intrinsic needs or satisfaction so much as by prestige-seeking.

B. The marketing applications of the Veblenian model revolve around the fact that man's attitudes and behavior are influenced by several levels of society.
   1. Humanity tends to assimilate the mores and folkways of its *culture*.
   2. *Subcultures* are often regional entities which affect a person's attitude formation.
   3. *Social class* is a useful independent variable for segmenting markets and predicting reaction.
   4. *Reference groups* are those in which the individual does not have membership, but to which he aspires.
   5. Groups that have the most immediate influence on a person's tastes and opinions are *face-to-face groups*.
   6. Attitudes of the *person* do not automatically guarantee certain types of behavior.

V. The *Hobbesian* model emphasizes organizational factors.

A. Hobbes held that people are instinctively oriented toward preserving and enhancing their own well-being, but fear leads them to unite with others in a corporate body.

B. The major implication of the Hobbesian model for marketing is that organizational buyers can be appealed to on both personal and organizational grounds.

In times past, management could arrive at a fair understanding of its buyers through the daily experience of selling to them. But the growth in the size of firms and markets has removed many decision-makers from direct contact with buyers. Increasingly, decision-makers have had to turn to summary statistics and to behavioral theory, and are spending more money today than ever before to try to understand their buyers.

Who buys? How do they buy? And why? The first two questions relate to relatively overt aspects of buyer behavior, and can be learned about through direct observation and interviewing.

But uncovering *why* people buy is an extremely difficult task. The answer will tend to vary with the investigator's behavioral frame of reference.

The buyer is subject to many influences which trace a complex course through his psyche and lead eventually to overt purchasing responses. This conception of the buying process is illustrated in Figure 1. Various influences and their modes of transmission are shown at the left. At the right are the buyer's responses in choice of product, brand, dealer, quantities, and frequency. In the center stands the buyer and his mysterious psychological processes. The buyer's psyche is a "black box" whose workings can be only partially deduced. The marketing strategist's challenge to the behavioral scientist is to construct a more specific model of the mechanism in the black box.

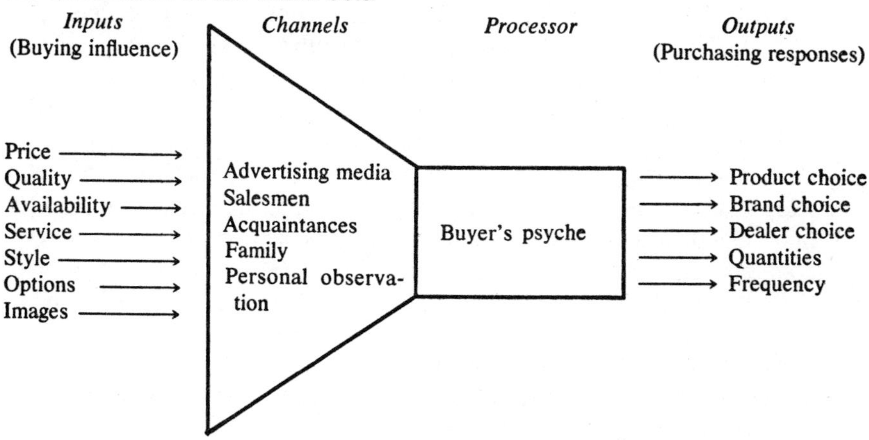

FIGURE 1. The buying process conceived as a system of inputs and outputs.

Unfortunately no generally accepted model of the mechanism exists The human mind, the only entity in nature with deep powers of understanding, still remains the least understood. Scientists can explain planetary motion, genetic determination, and molecular behavior. Yet they have only partial, and often partisan, models of *human* behavior.

Nevertheless, the marketing strategist should recognize the potential interpretative contributions of different partial models for explaining buyer behavior. Depending upon the product, different variables and behavioral mechanisms may assume particular importance. A psychoanalytic behavioral model might throw much light on the factors operating in cigarette demand, while an economic behavioral model might be useful in explaining machine-tool purchasing. Sometimes alternative models may shed light on different demand aspects of the same product.

What are the most useful behavioral models for interpreting the transformation of buying influences into purchasing responses? Five different models of the buyer's "black box" are presented in the present article, along with their respective marketing applications: (1) the Marshallian model, stressing economic motivations; (2) the Pavlovian model, learning; (3) the Freudian model, psychoanalytic motivations; (4) the Veblenian model, social-psychological factors; and (5) the Hobbesian model, organizational factors. These models represent radically different conceptions of the mainsprings of human behavior.

The Marshallian Economic Model

Economists were the first professional group to construct a specific theory of buyer behavior. The theory holds that purchasing decisions are the result of largely "rational" and conscious economic calculations. The individual buyer seeks to spend his income on those goods that will deliver the most utility (satisfaction) according to his tastes and relative prices.

The antecedents for this view trace back to the writings of Adam Smith and Jeremy Bentham. Smith set the tone by developing a doctrine of economic growth based on the principle that man is motivated by self-interest in all his actions.[1] Bentham refined this view and saw man as finely calculating and weighing the expected pleasures and pains of every contemplated action.[2]

Bentham's "felicific calculus" was not applied to consumer behavior (as opposed to entrepreneurial behavior) until the late 19th century. Then, the "marginal-utility" theory of value was formulated independently and almost simultaneously by Jevons[3] and Marshall[4] in England, Menger[5] in Austria, and Walras[6] in Switzerland.

Alfred Marshall was the great consolidator of the classical and neoclassical tradition in economics; and his synthesis in the form of demand-supply analysis constitutes the main source of modern micro-economic thought in the English-speaking worlds. His theoretical work aimed at realism, but his method was to start with simplifying assumptions and to examine the effect of a change in a single variable (say, price) when all other variables were held constant.

He would "reason out" the consequences of the provisional assumptions and in subsequent steps modify his assumptions in the direction of more realism. He employed the "measuring rod of money" as an indicator of the intensity of human psychological desires. Over the years his methods and assumptions have been refined into what is now known as *modern utility theory*: economic man is bent on maximizing his utility, and does this by carefully calculating the "felicific" consequences of any purchase.

As an example, suppose on a particular evening that John is considering whether to prepare his own dinner or dine out. He estimates that a restaurant meal would cost $2.00 and a home-cooked meal 50 cents. According to the Marshallian model, if John expects less than four times as much satisfaction from the restaurant meal as the home-cooked meal, he will eat at home. The economist typically is not concerned with how these relative preferences are formed by John, or how they may be psychologically modified by new stimuli.

Yet John will not always cook at home. The principle of diminishing marginal utility operates. Within a given time interval—say, a week—the utility of each additional home-cooked meal diminishes. John gets tired of home meals and other products become relatively more attractive.

John's *efficiency* in maximizing his utility depends on the adequacy of his information and his freedom of choice. If he is not perfectly aware of costs, if he misestimates the relative delectability of the two meals, or if he is barred from entering the restaurant, he will not maximize his potential utility. His choice processes are rational, but the results are inefficient.

Marketing Applications of Marshallian Model

Marketers usually have dismissed the Marshallian model as an absurd figment of ivory-tower imagination. Certainly the behavioral essence of the situation is omitted, in viewing man as calculating the marginal utility of a restaurant meal over a home-cooked meal.

Eva Mueller has reported a study where only one-fourth of the consumers in her sample bought with any substantial degree of deliberation.[7] Yet there are a number of ways to view the model.

From one point of view the Marshallian model is tautological and therefore neither true nor false. The model holds that the buyer acts in the light of his best "interest." But this is not very informative.

A second view is that this is a *normative* rather than a *descriptive* model of behavior. The model provides logical norms for buyers who want to be "rational." Although the consumer is not likely to employ economic analysis to decide between a box of Kleenex and Scotties, he may apply economic analysis in deciding whether to buy a new car. Industrial buyers even more clearly would want an economic calculus for making good decisions.

A third view is that economic factors operate to a greater or lesser extent in all markets, and, therefore, must be included in any comprehensive description of buyer behavior.

Furthermore, the model suggests useful behavioral hypotheses such as: (a) The lower the price of the product, the higher the sales. (b) The lower the price of substitute products, the lower the sales of this product; and the lower the price of complementary products, the higher the sales of this product. (c) The higher the real income, the higher the sales of this product, provided that it is not an "inferior" good. (d) The higher the promotional expenditures, the higher the sales.

The validity of these hypotheses does not rest on whether *all* individuals act as economic calculating machines in making their purchasing decisions. For example, some individuals may buy *less* of a product when its price is reduced. They may think that the quality has gone down, or that ownership has less status value. If a majority of buyers view price reductions negatively, then sales may fall, contrary to the first hypothesis.

But for most goods a price reduction increases the relative value of the goods in many buyers' minds and leads to increased sales. This and the other hypotheses are intended to describe average effects.

The impact of economic factors in actual buying situations is studied through experimental design or statistical analyses of past data. Demand equations have been fitted to a wide variety of products—including beer, refrigerators, and chemical fertilizers.[8] More recently, the impact of economic variables on the fortunes of different brands has been pursued with significant results, particularly in the case of coffee, frozen orange juice, and margarine.[9]

But economic factors alone cannot explain all the variations in sales. The Marshallian model ignores the fundamental question of how product and brand preferences are formed. It represents a useful frame of reference for analyzing only one small corner of the "black box."

The Pavlovian Learning Model.

The designation of a Pavlovian learning model has its origin in the experiments of the Russian psychologist Pavlov, who rang a bell each time before feeding a dog. Soon he was able to induce the dog to salivate by ringing the bell whether or not food was supplied. Pavlov concluded that learning was largely an associative process and that a large component of behavior was conditioned in this way.

Experimental psychologists have continued the mode of research with rats and other animals, including people. Laboratory experiments have been designed to explore such phenomena as learning, forgetting, and the ability to discriminate. The results have been integrated into a stimulus-response model of human behavior, or as someone has "wisecracked," the substitution of a rat psychology for a rational psychology.

The model has been refined over the years, and today is based on four central concepts—those of *drive, cue, response,* and *reinforcement.*[10]

Drive. Also called needs or motives, drive refers to strong stimuli internal to the individual which impels action. Psychologists draw a distinction between primary physiological drives—such as hunger, thirst, cold, pain, and sex—and learned drives which are derived socially—such as cooperation, fear, and acquisitiveness.

Cue. A drive is very general and impels a particular response only in relation to a particular configuration of cues. Cues are weaker stimuli in the environment and/or in the individual which determine when, where, and how the subject responds. Thus, a coffee advertisement can serve as a cue which stimulates the thirst drive in a housewife. Her response will depend upon this cue and other cues, such as the time of day, the availability of other thirst-quenchers, and the cue's intensity. Often a relative change in a cue's intensity can be more impelling than its absolute level. The housewife may be more motivated by a 2-cents-off sale on a brand of coffee than the fact that this brand's price was low in the first place.

Response. The response is the organism's reaction to the configuration of cues. Yet the same configuration of cues will not necessarily produce the same response in the individual. This depends on the degree to which the experience was rewarding, that is, drive-reducing.

Reinforcement. If the experience is rewarding, a particular response is reinforced; that is, it is strengthened and there is a tendency for it to be repeated when the same configuration of cues appears again. The housewife, for example, will tend to purchase the same brand of coffee each time she goes to her supermarket so long as it is rewarding and the cue configuration does not change. But if a learned response or habit is not reinforced, the strength of the habit diminishes and may be extinguished eventually. Thus, a housewife's preference for a certain coffee may become extinct if she finds the brand out of stock for a number of weeks.

Forgetting, in contrast to extinction, is the tendency for learned associations to weaken, not because of the lack of reinforcement but because of nonuse.

Cue configurations are constantly changing. The housewife sees a new brand of coffee next to her habitual brand, or notes a special price deal on a rival brand. Experimental psychologists have found that the same learned response will be elicted by similar patterns of cues; that is, learned responses are *generalized.* The housewife shifts to a similar brand when her favorite brand is out of stock. This tendency toward generalization over less similar cue configurations is increased in proportion to the strength of the drive. A housewife may buy an inferior coffee if it is the only brand left and if her drive is sufficiently strong.

A counter-tendency to generalization is *discrimination.* When a housewife tries two similar brands and finds one more rewarding, her ability to discriminate between similar cue configurations improves. Discrimination increases the specificity of the cue-response connection, while generalization decreases the specificity.

Marketing Applications of Pavlovian Model

The modern version of the Pavlovian model makes no claim to provide a complete theory of behavior—indeed, such important phenomena as perception, the subconscious, and interpersonal influence are inadequately treated. Yet the model does offer a substantial number of insights about some aspects of behavior of considerable interest to marketers.[11]

An example would be in the problem of introducing a new brand into a highly competitive market. The company's goal is to extinguish existing brand habits and form new habits among consumers for its brand. But the company must first get customers to try its brand; and it has to decide between using weak and strong cues.

Light introductory advertising is a weak cue compared with distributing free samples. Strong cues, although costing more, may be necessary in markets characterized by strong brand loyalties. For example, Folger went into the coffee market by distributing over a million pounds of free coffee.

To build a brand habit, it helps to provide for an extended period of introductory dealing. Furthermore, sufficient quality must be built into the brand so that the experience is reinforcing. Since buyers are more likely to transfer allegiance to similar brands than dissimilar brands (generalization), the company should also investigate what cues in the leading brands have been most effective. Although outright imitation would not necessarily effect the most transference, the question of providing enough similarity should be considered.

The Pavlovian model also provides guide lines in the area of advertising strategy. The American behaviorist, John B. Watson, was a great exponent of repetitive stimuli; in his writings man is viewed as a creature who can be conditioned through repetition and reinforcement to respond in particular ways.[12] The Pavlovian model emphasizes the desirability of repetition in advertising. A single exposure is likely to be a very weak cue, hardly able to penetrate the individual's consciousness sufficiently to excite his drives above the threshold level.

Repetition in advertising has two desirable effects. It "fights" forgetting, the tendency for learned responses to weaken in the absence of practice. It provides reinforcement, because after the purchase the consumer becomes selectively exposed to advertisements of the product.

The model also provides guide lines for copy strategy. To be effective as a cue, an advertisement must arouse strong drives in the person. The strongest product-related drives must be identified. For candy bars, it may be hunger; for safety belts, fear; for hair tonics, sex; for automobiles, status. The advertising practitioner must dip into his cue box—words, colors, pictures—and select that configuration of cues that provides the strongest stimulus to these drives.

The Freudian Psychoanalytic Model

The Freudian model of man is well known, so profound has been its impact on 20th century thought. It is the latest of a series of philosophical "blows" to which man has been exposed in the last 500 years. Copernicus destroyed the idea that man stood at the center of the universe; Darwin tried to refute the idea that man was a special creation; and Freud attacked the idea that man even reigned over his own psyche.

According to Freud, the child enters the world driven by instinctual needs which he cannot gratify by himself. Very quickly and painfully he realizes his separateness from the rest of the world and yet his dependence on it.

He tries to get others to gratify his needs through a variety of blatant means, including intimidation and supplication. Continual frustration leads him to perfect more subtle mechanisms for gratifying his instincts.

As he grows, his psyche—the id—remains the reservoir of his strong drives and urges. Another part—the ego—becomes his conscious planning center for finding outlets for his drives. And a third part—his super-ego—channels his instinctive drives into socially approved outlets to avoid the pain of guilt or shame.

The guilt or shame which man feels toward some of his urges—especially his sexual urges—causes him to repress them from his consciousness. Through such defense mechanisms as rationalization and sublimation, these urges were denied or become transmuted into socially approved expressions. Yet these urges are never eliminated or under perfect control; and they emerge, sometimes with a vengeance, in dreams, in slips-of-the-tongue, in neurotic and obsessional behavior, or ultimately in mental breakdown where the ego can no longer maintain the delicate balance between the impulsive power of the id and the oppressive power of the super-ego.

The individual's behavior, therefore, is never simple. His motivational wellsprings are not obvious to a casual observer nor deeply understood by the individual himself. If he is asked why he purchased an expensive foreign sports-car, he may reply that he likes its maneuverability and its looks. At a deeper level he may have purchased the car to impress others, or to feel young again. At a still deeper level, he may be purchasing the sports-car to achieve substitute gratification for unsatisfied sexual strivings.

Many refinements and changes in emphasis have occurred in this model since the time of Freud. The instinct concept has been replaced by a more careful delineation of basic drives; the three parts of the psyche are regarded now as theoretical concepts rather than actual entities; and the behavioral perspective has been extended to include cultural as well as biological mechanisms.

Instead of the role of the sexual urge in psychic development—Freud's discussion of oral, anal, and genital stages and possible fixations and traumas—Adler[13] emphasized the urge for power and how its thwarting manifests itself in superiority and inferiority complexes; Horney[14] emphasized cultural mechanisms; and Fromm[15] and Erickson[16] emphasized the role of existential crises in personality development. These philosophical divergencies, rather than debilitating the model, have enriched and extended its interpretative value to a wider range of behavioral phenomena.

Marketing Applications of Freudian Model

Perhaps the most important marketing implication of this model is that buyers are motivated by *symbolic* as well as *economic-functional* product concerns. The change of a bar of soap from a square to a round shape may be more important in its sexual than its functional connotations. A cake mix that is advertised as involving practically no labor may alienate housewives because the easy life may evoke a sense of guilt.

Motivational research has produced some interesting and occasionally some bizarre hypotheses about what may be in the buyer's mind regarding certain purchases. Thus, it has been suggested at one time or another that

> Many a businessman doesn't fly because of a fear of posthumous guilt—if he crashed, his wife would think of him as stupid for not taking a train.
>
> Men want their cigars to be odoriferous, in order to prove that they (the men) are masculine.
>
> A woman is very serious when she bakes a cake because unconsciously she is going through the symbolic act of giving brith.
>
> A man buys a convertible as a substitute "mistress."
>
> Consumers prefer vegetable shortening because animal fats stimulate a sense of sin.
>
> Men who wear suspenders are reacting to an unresolved castration complex.

There are admitted difficulties of proving these assertions. Two prominent motivational researchers, Ernest Dichter and James Vicary, were employed independently by two separate groups in the prune industry to determine why so many people dislike prunes. Dichter found among other things, that the prune aroused feelings of old age and insecurity in people, whereas Vicary's main finding was that Americans had an emotional block about prunes' laxative qualities.[17] Which is the more valid interpretation? Or if they are both operative, which motive is found with greater statistical frequency in the population?

Unfortunately the usual survey techniques—direct observation and interviewing—can be used to establish the representativeness of more superficial characteristics—age and family size, for example—but are not feasible for establishing the frequency of mental states which are presumed to be deeply "buried" within each individual.

Motivational researchers have to employ time-consuming projective techniques in the hope of throwing individual "egos" off guard. When carefully administered and interpreted, techniques such as word association, sentence completion, picture interpretation, and role-playing can provide some insights into the minds of the small group of examined individuals; but a "leap of faith" is sometimes necessary to generalize these findings to the population.

Nevertheless, motivation research can lead to useful insights and provide inspiration to creative men in the advertising and packaging world.

Appeals aimed at the buyer's private world of hopes, dreams, and fears can often be as effective in stimulating purchase as more rationally-directed appeals.

The Veblenian Social-psychological Model

While most economists have been content to interpret buyer behavior in Marshallian terms, Thorstein Veblem struck out in different directions.

Veblen was trained as an orthodox economist, but evolved into a social thinker greatly influenced by the new science of social anthropology. He saw man as primarily a *social animal*—conforming to the general forms and norms of his larger culture and to the more specific standards of the subcultures and face-to-face groupings to which his life is bound. His wants and behavior are largely molded by his present group-memberships and his aspired group-memberships.

Veblen's best-known example of this is in his description of the leisure class.[18] His hypothesis is that much of economic consumption is motivated not by intrinsic needs or satisfaction so much as by prestige-seeking. He emphasized the strong emulative factors operating in the choice of conspicuous goods like clothes, cars, and houses.

Some of his points, however, seem overstated by today's perspective. The leisure class does not serve as everyone's reference group; many persons aspire to the social patterns of the class immediately above it. And important segments of the affluent class practice conspicuous underconsumption rather than overconsumption. There are many people in all classes who are more anxious to "fit in" than to "stand out." As an example, William H. Whyte found that many families avoided buying air conditioners and other appliances before their neighbors did.[19]

Veblen was not the first nor the only investigator to comment on social influences in behavior; but the incisive quality of his observations did much to stimulate further investigations. Another stimulus came from Karl Marx, who held that each man's world-view was determined largely by his relationship to the "means of production."[20] The early field-work in primitive societies by social anthropologists like Boas[21] and Malinowski[22] and the later field-work in urban societies by men like Park[23] and Thomas[24] contributed much to understanding the influence of society and culture. The research of early Gestalt psychologists—men like Wertheimer,[25] Köhler,[26] and Koffka[27]—into the mechanisms of perception led eventually to investigations of small-group influence on perception.

Marketing Applications of Veblenian Model

The various streams of thought crystallized into the modern social sciences of sociology, cultural anthropology, and social psychology. Basic to them is the view that man's attitudes and behavior are influenced by several levels of society—culture, subcultures, social classes, reference groups, and face-to-face groups. The challenge to the marketer is to determine which of these social levels are the most important in influencing the demand for his product.

Culture

The most enduring influences are from culture. Man tends to assimilate his culture's mores and folkways, and to believe in their absolute rightness until deviants appear within his culture or until he confronts members of another culture.

Subcultures

A culture tends to lose its homogeneity as its population increases. When people no longer are able to maintain face-to-face relationships with more than a small proportion of other members of a culture, smaller units or subcultures develop, which help to satisfy the individual's needs for more specific identity.

The subcultures are often regional entities, because the people of a region, as a result of more frequent interactions, tend to think and act alike. But subcultures also take the form of religions, nationalities, fraternal orders, and other institutional complexes which provide a broad identification for people who may otherwise be strangers. The subcultures of a person play a large role in his attitude formation and become another important predictor of certain values he is likely to hold.

Social Class

People become differentiated not only horizontally but also vertically through a division of labor. The society becomes stratified socially on the basis of wealth, skill, and power. Sometimes castes develop in which the members are reared for certain roles, or social classes develop in which the members feel empathy with others sharing similar values and economic circumstances.

Because social class involves different attitudinal configurations, it becomes a useful independent variable for segmenting markets and predicting reactions. Significant differences have been found among different social classes with respect to magazine readership, leisure activities, food imagery, fashion interests, and acceptance of innovations. A sampling of attitudinal differences in class is the following:

> Members of the *upper-middle* class place an emphasis on professional competence; indulge in expensive status symbols; and more often than not

show a taste, real or otherwise, for theater and the arts. They want their children to show high achievement and precocity and develop into physicists, vice-presidents, and judges. This class likes to deal in ideas and symbols.

Members of the *lower-middle* class cherish respectability, savings, a college education, and good housekeeping. They want their children to show self control and prepare for careers as accountants, lawyers, and engineers.

Members of the *upper-lower* class try to keep up with the times, if not with the Joneses. They stay in older neighborhoods but buy new kitchen appliances. They spend proportionately less than the middle class on major clothing articles, buying a new suit mainly for an important ceremonial occasion. They also spend proportionately less on services, preferring to do their own plumbing and other work around the house. They tend to raise large families and their children generally enter manual occupations. This class also supplies many local businessmen, politicians, sports stars, and labor-union leaders.

Reference Groups

There are groups in which the individual has no membership but with which he identifies and may aspire to—reference groups. Many young boys identify with big-league baseball players or astronauts, and many young girls identify with Hollywood stars. The activities of these popular heroes are carefully watched and frequently imitated. These references figures become important transmitters of influence, although more along lines of taste and hobby than basic attitudes.

Face-to-face Groups

Groups that have the most immediate influence on a person's tastes and opinions are face-to-face groups. This includes all the small "societies" with which he comes into frequent contact: his family, close friends, neighbors, fellow workers, fraternal associates, and so forth. His informal group memberships are influenced largely by his occupation, residence, and stage in the life cycle.

The powerful influence of small groups on individual attitudes has been demonstrated in a number of social psychological experiments.[28] There is also evidence that this influence may be growing. David Riesman and his coauthors have pointed to signs which indicate a growing amount of *other-direction*, that is, a tendency for individuals to be increasingly influenced by their peers in the definition of their values rather than by their parents and elders.[29]

For the marketer, this means that brand choice may increasingly be influenced by one's peers. For such products as cigarettes and automobiles, the influence of peers is unmistakable.

The role of face-to-face groups has been recognized in recent industry campaigns attempting to change basic product attitudes. For years the milk industry has been trying to overcome the image of milk as a "sissified" drink by portraying its use in social and active situations. The men's-wear industry is trying to increase male interest in clothes by advertisements indicating that business associates judge a man by how well he dresses.

Of all face-to-face groups, the person's family undoubtedly plays the largest and most enduring role in basic attitude formation. From them he acquires a mental set not only toward religion and politics, but also toward thrift, chastity, food, human relations, and so forth. Although he often rebels against parental values in his teens, he often accepts these values eventually. Their formative influence on his eventual attitudes is undeniably great.

Family members differ in the types of product messages they carry to other family members. Most of what parents know about cereals, candy, and toys comes from their children. The wife stimulates family consideration of household appliances, furniture, and vacations. The husband tends to stimulate the fewest purchase ideas, with the exception of the automobile and perhaps the home.

The marketer must be alert to what attitudinal configurations dominate in different types of families, and also to how these change over time. For example, the parent's conception of the child's rights and privileges has undergone a radical shift in the last 30 years. The child has become the center of attention and orientation in a great number of households, leading some writers to label the modern family a "filiarchy." This has important implications not only for how to market to today's family, but also on how to market to tomorrow's family when the indulged child of today becomes the parent.

The Person

Social influences determine much but not all of the behavioral variations in people. Two individuals subject to the same influences are not likely to have identical attitudes, although these attitudes will probably converge at more points than those of two strangers selected at random. Attitudes are really the product of social forces interacting with the individual's unique temperament and abilities.

Furthermore, attitudes do not automatically guarantee certain types of behavior. Attitudes are predispositions felt by buyers before they enter the buying process. The buying process itself is a learning experience and can lead to a change in attitudes.

Alfred Politz noted at one time that women stated a clear preference for G.E. refrigerators over Frigidaire, but that Frigidaire continued to outsell G.E.[30] The answer to this paradox was that preference was only one factor entering into behavior. When the consumer preferring G.E. actually undertook to purchase a new refrigerator, her curiosity led her to examine the other brands. Her perception was sensitized to refrigerator advertisements, sales arguments, and different product features. This led to learning and a change in attitudes.

The Hobbesian Organizational-factors Model

The foregoing models throw light mainly on the behavior of family buyers.

But what of the large number of people who are organizational buyers? They are engaged in the purchase of goods not for the sake of consumption, but for further production or distribution. Their common denominator is the fact that they (1) are paid to make purchases for others and (2) operate within an organizational environment.

How do organizational buyers make their decisions? There seem to be two competing views. Many marketing writers have emphasized the predominance of rational motives in organizational buying.[31] Organizational buyers are represented as being most impressed by cost, quality, dependability, and service factors. They are protrayed as dedicated servants of the organization, seeking to secure the best terms. This view has led to an emphasis on performance and use characteristics in much industrial advertising.

Other writers have emphasized personal motives in organizational buyer behavior. The purchasing agent's interest to do the best for his company is tempered by his interest to do the best for himself. He may be tempted to choose among salesmen according to the extent they entertain or offer gifts. He may choose a particular vendor because this will ingratiate him with certain company officers. He may shortcut his study of alternative suppliers to make his work day easier.

In truth, the buyer is guided by both personal and group goals; and this is the essential point. The political model of Thomas Hobbes comes closest of any model to suggesting the relationship between the two goals.[32] Hobbes held that man is "instinctively" oriented toward preserving and enhancing his own well-being. But this would produce a "war of every man against every man." This fear leads men to unite with others in a corporate body. The corporate man tries to steer a careful course between satisfying his own needs and those of the organization.

Marketing Applications of Hobbesian Model

The import of the Hobbesian model is that organizational buyers can be appealed to on both personal and organizational grounds. The buyer has his private aims, and yet he tries to do a satisfactory job for his corporation. He will respond to persuasive salesmen and he will respond to rational product arguments. However, the best "mix" of the two is not a fixed quantity; it varies with the nature of the product, the type of organization, and the relative strength of the two drives in the particular buyer.

Where there is substantial similarity in what suppliers offer in the way of products, price, and service, the purchasing agent has less basis for rational choice. Since he can satisfy his organizational obligations with any one of a number of suppliers, he can be swayed by personal motives. On the other hand, where there are pronounced differences among the competing vendors' products, the purchasing agent is held more accountable for his choice and probably pays more attention to rational factors. Short-run personal gain becomes less motivating than the long-run gain which comes from serving the organization with distinction.

The marketing strategist must appreciate these goal conflicts of the organizational buyer. Behind all the ferment of purchasing agents to develop standards and employ value analysis lies their desire to avoid being thought of as order-clerks, and to develop better skills in reconciling personal and organizational objectives.[33]

Summary

Think back over the five different behavioral models of how the buyer translates buying influences into purchasing responses.

> Marshallian man is concerned chiefly with economic cues—prices and income—and makes a fresh utility calculation before each purchase.
>
> Pavlovian man behaves in a largely habitual rather than thoughtful way; certain configurations of cues will set off the same behavior because of rewarded learning in the past.
>
> Freudian man's choices are influenced strongly by motives and fantasies which take place deep within his private world.
>
> Veblenian man acts in a way which is shaped largely by past and present social groups.
>
> And finally, Hobbesian man seeks to reconcile individual gain with organizational gain.

Thus, it turns out that the "black box" of the buyer is not so black after all. Light is thrown in various corners by these models. Yet no one has succeeded in putting all these pieces of truth together into one coherent instrument for behavioral analysis. This, of course, is the goal of behavioral science.

NOTES

1. Adam Smith, *An Inquiry into the Nature and Causes of the Wealth of Nations*, 1776 (New York: The Modern Library, 1937).
2. Jeremy Bentham, *An Introduction to the Principles of Morals and Legislation*, 1780 (Oxford, England: Clarendon Press, 1907).
3. William S. Jevons, *The Theory of Political Economy* (New York: The Macmillan Company, 1871).
4. Alfred Marshall, *Principles of Economics*, 1890 (London: The Macmillan Company, 1927).
5. Karl Menger, *Principles of Economics*, 1871 (Glencoe, Illinois: Free Press, 1950).
6. Leon Walras, *Elements of Pure Economics*, 1874 (Homewood, Illinois: Richard D. Irwin, Inc., 1954).
7. Eva Mueller, "A Study of Purchase Decisions," Part 2, *Consumer Behavior, The Dynamics of Consumer Reaction*, edited by Lincoln H. Clark (New York: New York University Press, 1954), pp. 36–87.
8. See Erwin E. Nemmers, *Managerial Economics* (New York: John Wiley & Sons, Inc., 1962), Part II.
9. See Lester G. Telser, "The Demand for Branded Goods as Estimated from Consumer Panel Data," *Review of Economics and Statistics*, Vol. 44 (August, 1962), pp. 300–324; and William F. Massy and Ronald E. Frank, "Short Term Price and Dealing Effects in Selected Market Segments," *Journal of Marketing Research*, Vol. 2 (May, 1955), pp. 171–185.
10. See John Dollard and Neal E. Miller, *Personality and Psychotherapy* (New York: McGraw-Hill Book Company, Inc., 1950), Chapter III.
11. The most consistent application of learning-theory concepts to marketing situations is found in John A. Howard, *Marketing Management: Analysis and Planning* (Homewood, Illinois: Richard D. Irwin, Inc., revised edition, 1963).
12. John B. Watson, *Behaviorism* (New York: The People's Institute Publishing Company, 1925).
13. Alfred Adler, *The Science of Living* (New York: Greenberg, 1929).
14. Karen Horney, *The Neurotic Personality of Our Time* (New York: W. W. Norton & Co., 1937).
15. Erich Fromm, *Man For Himself* (New York: Holt, Rinehart & Winston, Inc., 1947).
16. Erik Erikson, *Childhood and Society* (New York: W. W. Norton & Co., 1949).
17. L. Edward Scriven, "Rationality and Irrationality in Motivation Research," in Robert Ferber and Hugh G. Wales, editors, *Motivation and Marketing Behavior* (Homewood, Illinois: Richard D. Irwin, Inc., 1958), pp. 69–70.
18. Thorstein Veblen, *The Theory of the Leisure Class* (New York: The Macmillan Company, 1899).
19. William H. Whyte, Jr., "The Web of Word of Mouth," *Fortune*, Vol. 50 (November, 1954), pp. 140 ff.
20. Karl Marx, *The Communist Manifesto*, 1848 (London: Martin Lawrence, Ltd., 1934).
21. Franz Boas, *The Mind of Primitive Man* (New York: The Macmillan Company, 1922).
22. Bronislaw Malinowski, *Sex and Repression in Savage Society* (New York: Meridian Books, 1955).
23. Robert E. Park, *Human Communities* (Glencoe, Illinois: Free Press, 1952).
24. William I. Thomas, *The Unadjusted Girl* (Boston: Little, Brown and Company, 1928).
25. Max Wertheimer, *Productive Thinking* (New York: Harper & Brothers, 1945).
26. Wolfgang Köhler, *Gestalt Psychology* (New York: Liveright Publishing Co., 1947).
27. Kurt Koffka, *Principles of Gestalt Psychology* (New York: Harcourt, Brace and Co., 1935).

28. See, for example, Solomon E. Asch, "Effects of Group Pressure Upon the Modification & Distortion of Judgments," in Dorwin Cartwright and Alvin Zander, *Group Dynamics* (Evanston, Illinois: Row, Peterson & Co., 1953), pp. 151–162; and Kurt Lewin, "Group Decision and Social Change," in Theodore M. Newcomb and Eugene L. Hartley, editors, *Readings in Social Psychology* (New York: Henry Holt Co., 1952).
29. David Riesman, Reuel Denney, and Nathan Glazer, *The Lonely Crowd* (New Haven, Connecticut: Yale University Press, 1950).
30. Alfred Politz, "Motivation Research—Opportunity or Dilemma?", in Ferber and Wales, same reference as footnote 17, at pp. 57–58.
31. See Melvin T. Copeland, *Principles of Merchandising* (New York: McGraw-Hill Book Co., Inc., 1924).
32. Thomas Hobbes, *Leviathan*, 1651 (London: G. Routledge and Sons, 1887).
33. For an insightful account, see George Strauss, "Tactics of Lateral Relationship: The Purchasing Agent," *Administrative Science Quarterly*, Vol. 7 (September, 1962), pp. 161–186.

LEARNING REVIEW

Questions:

1. Behavioral models are designed to probe the question of " ____________ people's buy."

2. Match the model on the left with the appropriate response in the column on the right:

___ A. Marshallian	1. Symbolic buyer behavior
___ B. Pavlovian	2. Organizational buyer behavior
___ C. Freudian	3. Social buyer behavior
___ D. Veblenian	4. Rational buyer behavior
___ E. Hobbesian	5. Learned response behavior

3. Hobbesian theory says that the buyer is guided by both ____________ and ____________ goals.

4. The stimulus-response model of behavior is a result of the ____________________ model.

5. The Freudian model implies that buyers are motivated by ____________ as well as economic-functional product concerns.

Answers:

1. Why; 2. A.–4, B.–5, C.–1, D.–3, E.–2; 3. personal, group; 4. Pavlovian learning; 5. symbolic

Retrospective Comment

Most of the writings on buyer behavior analysis before this article was written were addressed to single relationships that might exist between some aspect of buyer behavior and some demographic or psychological variable that might influence or explain it. A few writings were more systematic and comprehensive, leaning heavily on one school of thought about buyer behavior, such as learning theory or Freudian theory.

My purpose in this article was to suggest several competing *grand theories* for attempting to explain large ranges of observable buyer behavior. I identified five schools of thought and called them the Marshallian model, the Pavlovian model, the Freudian model, the Veblenian model, and the Hobbesian model. Each involved an interrelated and self-contained set of concepts that could throw theoretical and practical light on concrete buying situations. Subsequently, the field of consumer behavior began to experience a major boom in grand theory with efforts of such scholars as John A. Howard, Jagdish N. Sheth, Francesco M. Nicosia, Alan R. Andreasen, James F. Engel, David T. Kollat, and Roger D. Blackwell. Many of these models took their lead from stimulus-response learning theory or *gestalt* tradition and still neglect some of the factors suggested in my article. For example, the current buyer behavior models almost completely disregard Freudian psychological mechanisms and Hobbesian motivations.

The still unanswered questions is whether the field will ever be able to forge one model that answers all purposes of buyer behavior analysis or should attempt to create a repertoire of several self-contained models that are eminently suitable for analyzing particular problems in buyer behavior.

12

A Theory of Human Motivation

A. H. Maslow

PREVIEW

I. Physiological needs are first in the hierarchy of human needs.
   A. When these needs are not met, they become the major motivating force.
   B. In the United States most people have their physiological needs met.
   C. When these needs are continuously met they cease to exist as active determiners of behavior.

II. Safety needs come into play as physiological needs are met.

III. Love needs follow the physiological and safety needs.
   A. The thwarting of love and belongingness needs is the most commonly found core of maladjustment.
   B. The love need is not synonymous with sex.

IV. Esteem or self-respect is a need which has two subsidiary sets.
   A. The first is a need for achievement and adequacy.
   B. The second is a need for reputation or prestige.

V. The need for self-actualization follows the need for self-esteem.
   A. This is the need to become everything one is capable of becoming.
   B. Not much is known about these needs since their emergence depends on satisfaction of the higher-order needs.

VI. There are certain conditions which are immediate prerequisites for the basic need satisfactions.
   A. Because these conditions are close to the basic needs, they must be defended.

A. H. Maslow, "A Theory Of Human Motivation" is abridged from *Psychological Review* (July, 1943), pp. 370–396. This version is based on the abridgement that appeared in *Readings In Managerial Psychology*, ed. Harold J. Leavitt and Louis R. Pondy. (The University of Chicago Press, 1964), pp. 6–24.

B. These conditions include freedoms of action and freedom to defend one's self.

VII. There may also be a basic need to know and to understand.

The "Physiological" Needs

The needs that are usually taken as the starting point for motivation theory are the so-called physiological drives. Two recent lines of research make it necessary to revise our customary notions about these needs: first, the development of the concept of homeostasis, and, second, the finding that appetites (preferential choices among foods) are a fairly efficient indication of actual needs or lacks in the body.

Homeostasis refers to the body's automatic efforts to maintain a constant, normal state of the blood stream. Cannon[1] has described this process for (1) the water content of the blood, (2) salt content, (3) sugar content, (4) protein content, (5) fat content, (6) calcium content, (7) oxygen content, (8) constant hydrogen-iron level (acid-base balance) and (9) constant temperature of the blood. Obviously this list can be extended to include other minerals, the hormones, vitamins, etc.

Young[2] has summarized the work on appetite in its relation to body needs. If the body lacks some chemical, the individual will tend to develop a specific appetite or partial hunger for that food element.

Thus it seems impossible as well as useless to make any list of fundamental physiological needs for they can come to almost any number one might wish, depending on the degree of specificity of description. We cannot identify all physiological needs as homeostatic. That sexual desire, sleepiness, sheer activity, and maternal behavior in animals are homeostatic, has not yet been demonstrated. Furthermore, this list would not include the various sensory pleasures (tastes, smells, tickling, stroking) which are probably physiological and which may become the goals of motivated behavior.

In a previous paper[3] it has been pointed out that these physiological drives or needs are to be considered unusual rather than typical because they are isolable and because they are localizable somatically. That is to say, they are relatively independent of each other, of other motivations and of the organism as a whole, and, in many cases, it is possible to demonstrate a localized, underlying somatic base for the drive. This is true less generally than has been thought (exceptions are fatigue, sleepiness, maternal responses), but it is still true in the classic instances of hunger, sex, and thirst.

It should be pointed out again that any of the physiological needs and the consummatory behavior involved with them serve as channels for all sorts of other needs as well. The person who thinks he is hungry may actually be seeking more for comfort or dependence than for vitamins or proteins. Conversely, it is possible to satisfy the hunger need in part by other activities such as drinking water or smoking cigarettes. In other words, these physiological needs are only relatively isolable.

Undoubtedly these physiological needs are the most prepotent of all needs. What this means specifically is that, in the human being who is missing everything in life in an extreme fashion, it is most likely that the major motivation would be the physiological needs rather than any others. A person who is lacking food, safety, love, and esteem would most probably hunger for food more strongly than for anything else.

If all the needs are unsatisfied, and the organism is then dominated by the physiological needs, all other needs may become simply non-existent or be pushed into the background. It is then fair to characterize the whole organism by saying simply that it is hungry, for consciousness is almost completely pre-empted by hunger. All capacities are put into the service of hunger-satisfaction, and the organization of these capacities is almost entirely determined by the one purpose of satisfying hunger. The receptors and effectors, the intelligence, memory, habits, all may now be defined simply as hunger-gratifying tools. Capacities that are not useful for this purpose lie dormant or are pushed into the background. The urge to write poetry, the desire to acquire an automobile, the interest in American history, the desire for a new pair of shoes are, in the extreme case, forgotten or become of secondary importance. For the man who is extremely and dangerously hungry, no other interests exist but food. He dreams food, he remembers food, he thinks about food, he emotes only about food, he perceives only food, and he wants only food. The more subtle determinants that ordinarily fuse with the physiological drives in organizing even feeding, drinking, or sexual behavior, may now be so completely overwhelmed as to allow us to speak at this time (but *only* at this time) of pure hunger drive and behavior, with the one unqualified aim of relief.

Another peculiar characteristic of the human organism when it is dominated by a certain need is that the whole philosophy of the future tends also to change. For our chronically and extremely hungry man, utopia can be defined very simply as a place where there is plenty of food. He tends to think that, if only he is guaranteed food for the rest of his life, he will be perfectly happy and will never want anything more. Life itself tends to be defined in terms of eating. Anything else will be defined as unimportant. Freedom, love, community feeling, respect, philosophy, may all be waved aside as fripperies which are useless, since they fail to fill the stomach. Such a man may fairly be said to live by bread alone.

It cannot possibly be denied that such things are true, but their *generality* can be denied. Emergency conditions are, almost by definition, rare in the normally functioning peaceful society. That this truism can be forgotten is due mainly to two reasons. First, rats have few motivations other than physiological ones, and since so much of the research upon motivation has been made with these animals, it is easy to carry the rat-picture over to the human being. Second, it is too often not realized that culture itself is an adaptive tool, one of whose main functions is to make the physiological emergencies come less and less often. In most of the known societies, chronic extreme hunger of the emergency type is rare rather than common. In any case, this is still true in the United States. The average American citizen is experiencing appetite rather than hunger when he says, "I am hungry." He is apt to experience sheer life-and-death hunger only by accident and then only a few times through his entire life.

Obviously a good way to obscure the "higher" motivations, and to get a lopsided view of human capacities and human nature, is to make the organism extremely and chronically hungry or thirsty. Anyone who attempts to make an emergency picture into a typical one and who will measure all of man's goals and desires by his behavior during extreme physiological deprivation is certainly being blind to many things. It is quite true that man lives by bread alone—when there is no bread. But what happens to man's desires when there is plenty of bread and when his belly is chronically filled?

At once other (and "higher") needs emerge and these, rather than physiological hungers, dominate the organism. And when these in turn are satisfied, again new (and still "higher") needs emerge and so on. This is what we mean by saying that the basic human needs are organized into a hierarchy of relative prepotency.

One main implication of this phrasing is that gratification becomes as important a concept as deprivation in motivation theory, for it releases the organism from the domination of a relatively more physiological need, permitting thereby the emergence of other more social goals. The physiological needs, along with their partial goals, when chronically gratified cease to exist as active determinants or organizers of behavior. They now exist only in a potential fashion in the sense that they may emerge again to dominate the organism if they are thwarted. But a want that is satisfied is no longer a want. The organism is dominated and its behavior organized only by unsatisfied needs. If hunger is satisfied, it becomes unimportant in the current dynamics of the individual.

This statement is somewhat qualified by a hypothesis to be discussed more fully later, namely, that it is precisely those individuals in whom a certain need has always been satisfied who are best equipped to tolerate deprivation of that need in the future; furthermore, those who have been deprived in the past will react to current satisfactions differently from the one who has never been deprived.

The Safety Needs

If the physiological needs are relatively well gratified, there then emerges a new set of needs, which we may categorize roughly as the safety needs. All that has been said of the physiological needs are equally true, although in lesser degree, of these desires. The organism may equally well be wholly dominated by them. They may serve as the almost exclusive organizers of behavior, recruiting all the capacities of the organism in their service, and we may then fairly describe the whole organism as a safety-seeking mechanism. Again we may say of the receptors, the effectors, of the intellect and the other capacities that they are primarily safety-seeking tools. Again, as in the hungry man, we find that the dominating goal is a strong determinant not only of his current world-outlook and philosophy but also of his philosophy of the future. Practically everything looks less important than safety (even sometimes the physiological needs which being satisfied, are now underestimated). A man, in this state, if it is extreme enough and chronic enough, may be characterized as living almost for safety alone.

Although in this paper we are interested primarily in the needs of the adult, we can approach an understanding of his safety needs perhaps more efficiently by observation of infants and children, in whom these needs are much more simple and obvious. One reason for the clearer appearance of the threat or danger reaction in infants is that they do not inhibit this reaction at all, whereas adults in our society have been taught to inhibit it at all costs. Thus even when adults do feel their safety to be threatened, we may not be able to see this on the surface. Infants will react in a total fashion and as if they were endangered, if they are disturbed or dropped suddenly, startled by loud noises, flashing light, or other unusual sensory stimulation, by rough handling, by general loss of support in the mother's arms, or by inadequate support.[4]

In infants we can also see a much more direct reaction to bodily illnesses of various kinds. Sometimes these illnesses seem to be immediately and per se threatening and seem to make the child feel unsafe. For instance, vomiting, colic, or other sharp pains seem to make the child look at the whole world in a different way. At such a moment of pain, it may be postulated that, for the child, the appearance of the whole world suddenly changes from sunniness to darkness, so to speak, and becomes a place in which anything at all might happen, in which previously stable things have suddenly become unstable. Thus a child who because of some bad food is taken ill may, for a day or two, develop fear, nightmares, and a need for protection and reassurance never seen in him before his illness.

Another indication of the child's need for safety is his preference for some kind of undisrupted routine or rhythm. He seems to want a predictable, orderly world. For instance, injustice, unfairness, or inconsistency in the parents seems to make a child feel anxious and unsafe. This attitude may be not so much because of the injustice per se or any particular pains involved, but rather because this treatment threatens to make the world look unreliable or unsafe or unpredictable. Young children seem to thrive better under a system which has at least a skeletal outline of rigidity, in which there is a schedule of a kind, some sort of routine, something that can be counted upon, not only for the present, but also far into the future. Perhaps one could express this more accurately by saying that the child needs an organized world rather than an unorganized or unstructured one.

The central role of the parents and the normal family setup are indisputable. Quarreling, physical assault, separation, divorce, or death within the family may be particularly terrifying. Also parental outbursts of rage or threats of punishment directed to the child, calling him names, speaking to him harshly, shaking him, handling him roughly, or actual physical punishment sometimes elicit such total panic and terror in the child that we must assume more is involved than the physical pain alone. While it is true that in some children this terror may represent also a fear of loss of parental love, it can also occur in completely rejected children, who seem to cling to the hating parents more for sheer safety and protection than because of hope of love.

Confronting the average child with new, unfamiliar, strange, unmanageable stimuli or situations will too frequently elicit the danger or terror reaction, as, for example, getting lost or even being separated from the parents for a short time, being confronted with new faces, new situations, or new tasks, the sight of strange, unfamiliar or uncontrollable objects, illness, or death. Particularly at such times, the child's frantic clinging to his parents is eloquent testimony to their role as protectors (quite apart from their roles as food-givers and love-givers).

From these and similar observations, we may generalize and say that the average child in our society usually prefers a safe, orderly, predictable, organized world which he can count on and in which unexpected, unmanageable, or other dangerous things do not happen and in which, in any case, he has all-powerful parents who protect and shield him from harm.

That these reactions may so easily be observed in children is in a way a proof of the fact that children in our society feel too unsafe (or, in a word, are badly brought up). Children who are reared in an unthreatening, loving family do *not* ordinarily react as we have described above.[5] In such children the danger reactions are apt to come mostly to objects or situations that adults too would consider dangerous.[6]

The healthy, normal, fortunate adult in our culture is largely satisfied in his safety needs. The peaceful, smoothly running, "good" society ordinarily makes its members feel safe enough from wild animals, extremes of temperature, criminals, assault and murder, tyranny, etc. Therefore, in a very real sense, they no longer have any safety needs as active motivators. Just as a sated man no longer feels hungry, a safe man no longer feels endangered. If we wish to see these needs directly and clearly we must turn to neurotic or near-neurotic individuals, and to the economic and social underdogs. In between these extremes, we can perceive the expressions of safety needs only in such phenomena as, for instance, the common preference for a job with tenure and protection, the desire for a savings account, and for insurance of various kinds (medical, dental, unemployment, disability, old age).

Other broader aspects of the attempt to seek safety and stability in the world are seen in the very common preference for familiar rather than unfamiliar things, or for the known rather than the unknown. The tendency to have some religion or world-philosophy that organizes the universe and the men in it into some sort of satisfactorily coherent, meaningful whole is also in part motivated by safety-seeking. Here too we may list science and philosophy in general as partially motivated by the safety needs (we shall see later that there are also other motivations to scientific, philosophical, or religious endeavor).

Otherwise the need for safety is seen as an active and dominant mobilizer of the organism's resources only in emergencies, e.g., war, disease, natural catastrophes, crime waves, societal disorganization, neurosis, brain injury, chronically bad situation. . . .

The Love Needs

If both the physiological and safety needs are fairly well gratified, then there will emerge the love and affection and belongingness needs, and the whole cycle already described will repeat itself with this new center. Now the person will feel keenly, as never before, the absence of friends or a sweetheart or a wife or children. He will hunger for affectionate relations with people in general, namely, for a place in his group, and he will strive with great intensity to achieve this goal. He will want to attain such a place more than anything else in the world and may even forget that once, when he was hungry, he sneered at love.

In our society the thwarting of these needs is the most commonly found core in cases of maladjustments and more severe psychopathology. Love and affection, as well as their possible expression in sexuality, are generally looked upon with ambivalence and are customarily hedged about with many restrictions and inhibitions. Practically all theorists of psychopathology have stressed thwarting of the love needs as basic in the picture of maladjustment. Many clinical studies have therefore been made of this need and we know more about it perhaps than any of the other needs except the physiological ones.[7]

One thing that must be stressed at this point is that love is not synonymous with sex. Sex may be studied as a purely physiological need. Ordinarily sexual behavior is multi-determined, that is to say, determined not only by sexual but also by other needs, chief among which are the love and affection needs. Also not to be overlooked is the fact that the love needs involve both giving *and* receiving love.[8]

The Esteem Needs

All people in our society (with a few pathological exceptions) have a need or desire for a stable, firmly based, (usually) high evaluation of themselves, for self-respect, or self-esteem, and for the esteem of others. By firmly based self-esteem, we mean that which is soundly based upon real capacity, achievement, and respect from others. These needs may be classified into two subsidiary sets. These are, first, the desire for strength, for achievement, for adequacy, for confidence in the face of the world, and for independence and freedom.[9] Second, we have what we may call the desire for reputation or prestige (defining it as respect or esteem from other people), recognition, attention, importance, or appreciation.[10] These needs have been relatively stressed by Alfred Adler and his followers, and have been relatively neglected by Freud and the psychoanalysts. More and more today, however, there is appearing widespread appreciation of their central importance.

Satisfaction of the self-esteem need leads to feelings of self-confidence, worth, strength, capability, and adequacy, of being useful and necessary in the world. But thwarting of these needs produces feelings of inferiority, of weakness, and of helplessness. These feelings in turn give rise to either basic discouragement or else compensatory or neurotic trends. An appreciation of the necessity of basic self-confidence and an understanding of how helpless people are without it, can be easily gained from a study of severe traumatic neurosis.[11]

The Need for Self-Actualization

Even if all these needs are satisfied, we may still often (if not always) expect that a new discontent and restlessness will soon develop, unless the individual is doing what he is fitted for. A musician must make music, an artist must paint, a poet must write, if he is to be ultimately happy. What a man *can* be, he *must* be. This need we may call self-actualization.

This term, first coined by Kurt Goldstein, is being used in this paper in a much more specific and limited fashion. It refers to the desire for self-fulfillment, namely, to the tendency for one to be actualized in what one is potentially. This tendency might be phrased as the desire to become more and more what one is, to become everything that one is capable of becoming.

The specific form that these needs take will of course vary greatly from person to person. In one individual it may be expressed maternally, as the desire to be an ideal mother, in another athletically, in still another aesthetically, in the painting of pictures, and in another inventively in the creation of new contrivances. It is not necessarily a creative urge although in people who have any capabilities for creation it will take this form

The clear emergence of these needs rests upon prior satisfaction of the physiological, safety, love and esteem needs. We shall call people who are satisfied in these needs, basically satisfied people, and it is from these that we may expect the fullest (and healthiest) creativeness.[12] Since, in our society, basically satisfied people are the exception, we do not know much about self-actualization, either experimentally or clinically. It remains a challenging problem for research.

The Preconditions for the Basic Need Satisfactions

There are certain conditions which are immediate prerequisites for the basic need satisfactions. Danger to these is reacted to almost as if it were a direct danger to the basic needs themselves. Such conditions as freedom to speak, freedom to do what one wishes so long as no harm is done to others, freedom to express one's self, freedom to investigate and seek for information, freedom to defend one's self, justice, fairness, honesty, orderliness in the group are examples of such preconditions for basic need satisfactions. Thwarting in these freedoms will be reacted to with a threat or emergency response. These conditions are not ends in themselves but they are *almost* so, since they are closely related to the basic needs, which are apparently the only ends in themselves. These conditions are defended because without them the basic satisfactions are quite impossible, or at least, very severely endangered.

If we remember that the cognitive capacities (perceptual, intellectual, learning) are a set of adjustive tools, which have, among other functions, that of satisfaction of our basic needs, then it is clear that any danger to them, any deprivation or blocking of their free use, must also be indirectly threatening to the basic needs themselves. Such a statement is a partial solution of the general problems of curiosity, the search for knowledge, truth, and wisdom, and the ever persistent urge to solve the cosmic mysteries.

We must therefore introduce another hypothesis and speak of degrees of closeness to the basic needs, for we have already pointed out that *any* conscious desires (partial goals) are more or less important as they are more or less close to the basic needs. The same statement may be made for various behavior acts. An act is psychologically important if it contributes directly to satisfaction of basic needs. The less directly it so contributes, or the weaker this contribution is, the less important this act must be conceived to be from the point of view of dynamic psychology. A similar statement may be made for the various defense or coping mechanisms. Some are very directly related to the protection or attainment of the basic needs, others are only weakly and distantly related. Indeed, if we wished, we could speak of more basic and less basic defense mechanisms and then affirm that danger to the more basic defenses is more threatening than danger to less basic defenses (always remembering that this is so only because of their relationship to the basic needs).

The Desires to Know and to Understand

So far, we have mentioned the cognitive needs only in passing. Acquiring knowledge and systematizing the universe have been considered as, in part, techniques for the achievement of basic safety in the world, or, for the intelligent man, expressions of self-actualization. Also freedom of inquiry and expression have been discussed as preconditions of satisfactions of the basic needs. True though these formulations may be, they do not constitute definitive answers to the question as to the motivation role of curiosity, learning, philosophizing, experimenting, etc. They are, at best, no more than partial answers.

This question is especially difficult because we know so little about the facts. Curiosity, exploration, desire for the facts, desire to know may certainly be observed easily enough. The fact that they often are pursued even at great cost to the individual's safety is an earnest of the partial character of our previous discussion. In addition, the writer must admit that, though he has sufficient clinical evidence to postulate the desire to know as a very strong drive in intelligent people, no data are available for unintelligent people. It may then be largely a function of relatively high intelligence. Rather tentatively, then, and largely in the hope of stimulating discussion and research, we shall postulate a basic desire to know, to be aware of reality, to get the facts, to satisfy curiosity, or as Wertheimer phrases it, to see rather than to be blind.

This postulation, however, is not enough. Even after we know, we are impelled to know more and more minutely and microscopically, on the one hand, and, on the other, more and more extensively in the direction of a world philosophy, religion, etc. The facts that we acquire, if they are isolated or atomistic, inevitably get theorized about, and either analyzed or organized or both. This process has been phrased by some as the search for "meaning." We shall then postulate a desire to understand, to systematize, to organize, to analyze, to look for relations and meanings.

Once these desires are accepted for discussion, we see that they too form themselves into a small hierarchy in which the desire to know is prepotent over the desire to understand. All the characteristics of a hierarchy of prepotency that we have described above, seem to hold for this one as well.

We must guard ourselves against the too easy tendency to separate these desires from the basic needs we have discussed above, i.e., to make a sharp dichotomy between "cognitive" and "conative" needs. The desire to know and to understand are themselves conative, i.e., have a striving character, and are as much personality needs as the "basic needs" we have already discussed.[13]

Summary

1. There are at least five sets of goals which we may call basic needs. These are briefly physiological, safety, love, esteem, and self-actualization. In addition, we are motivated by the desire to achieve or maintain the various conditions upon which these basic satisfactions rest and by certain more intellectual desires.

2. These basic goals are related to one another, being arranged in a hierarchy of prepotency. This means that the most prepotent goal will monopolize consciousness and will tend of itself to organize the recruitment of the various capacities of the organism. The less prepotent needs are minimized, even forgotten or denied. But when a need is fairly well satisfied, the next prepotent ("higher") need emerges, in turn to dominate the conscious life and to serve as the center of organization of behavior, since gratified needs are not active motivators.

Thus man is a perpetually wanting animal. Ordinarily the satisfaction of these wants is not altogether mutually exclusive but only tends to be. The average member of our society is most often partially satisfied and partially unsatisfied in all of his wants. The hierarchy principle is usually empirically observed in terms of increasing percentages of non-satisfaction as we go up the hierarchy. Reversals of the average order of the hierarchy are sometimes observed. Also it has been observed that an individual may permanently lose the higher wants in the hierarchy under special conditions. There are not only ordinarily multiple motivations for usual behavior but, in addition, many determinants other than motives.

3. Any thwarting or possibility of thwarting of these basic human goals, or danger to the defenses which protect them or to the conditions upon which they rest, is considered to be a psychological threat. With a few exceptions, all psychopathology may be partially traced to such threats. A basically thwarted man may actually be defined as a "sick" man.

4. It is such basic threats which bring about the general emergency reactions. . . .

NOTES

1. W. B. Cannon, *Wisdom of the Body* (New York: Norton, 1932).

2. P. T. Young, "The Experimental Analysis of Appetite," *Psychological Bulletin*, XXXVIII (1941), 129–64.

3. A. H. Maslow, "A Preface to Motivation Theory," *Psychosomatic Medicine*, (1943), 85–92.

4. As the child grows up, sheer knowledge and familiarity as well as better motor development make these "dangers" less and less dangerous and more and more manageable. Throughout life it may be said that one of the main conative functions of education is this neutralizing of apparent dangers through knowledge, e.g., I am not afraid of thunder because I know something about it.

5. M. Shirley, "Children's Adjustments to a Strange Situation," *Journal of Abnormal and Social Psychology*, XXXVII (1942), 201–17.

6. A "test battery" for safety might be confronting the child with a small exploding firecracker or with a bewhiskered face, having the mother leave the room, putting him upon a high ladder, giving him a hypodermic injection, having a mouse crawl up to him, etc. Of course I cannot seriously recommend the deliberate use of such "tests," for they might very well harm the child being tested. But these and similar situations come up by the score in the child's ordinary day-to-day living and may be observed. There is no reason why these stimuli should not be used with, for example, young chimpanzees.

7. Maslow and Mittelmann, *op. cit.*

8. For further details see A. H. Maslow, "The Dynamics of Psychological Security-Insecurity," *Character and Personality*, X (1942), 331–44, and J. Plant, *Personality and the Cultural Pattern* (New York: Commonwealth Fund, 1937), chap. v.

9. Whether or not this particular desire is universal we do not know. The crucial question, especially important today, is, "Will men who are enslaved and dominated inevitably feel dissatisfied and rebellious?" We may assume on the basis of commonly known clinical data that a man who has known true freedom (not paid for by giving up safety and

security but rather built on the basis of adequate safety and security) will not willingly or easily allow his freedom to be taken away from him. But we do not know that this is true for the person born into slavery. The events of the next decade should give us our answer. See discussion of this problem in E. Fromm, *Escape from Freedom* (New York: Farrar Rinehart, 1941), chap. v.

10. Perhaps the desire for prestige and respect from others is subsidiary to the desire for self-esteem or confidence in one's self. Observation of children seems to indicate that this is so, but clinical data give no clear support of such a conclusion.

11. A. Kardiner, *The Traumatic Neuroses of War* (New York: Hoeber, 1941). For more extensive discussion of normal self-esteem, as well as for reports of various researches, see A. H. Maslow, "Dominance, Personality, and Social Behavior in Women." *Journal of Social Psychology*, X (1939), 3–39.

12. Clearly creative behavior, like painting, is like any other behavior in having multiple determinants. It may be seen in "innately creative" people whether they are satisfied or not, happy or unhappy, hungry or sated. Also, it is clear that creative activity may be compensatory, ameliorative, or purely economic. It is my impression (as yet unconfirmed) that it is possible to distinguish the artistic and intellectual products of basically satisfied people from those of basically unsatisfied people by inspection alone. In any case, here too we must distinguish, in a dynamic fashion, the overt behavior itself from its various motivations or purposes.

13. M. Wentheimer, unpublished lectures at the New School for Social Research.

LEARNING REVIEW

Questions:

1. The basic human needs are organized into a ____________.

2. The five most basic needs according to the author are ____________, ____________, ____________, ____________, ____________.

3. The desire to know and understand is as much a ____________ need as the basic needs.

Answers:

1. hierarchy 2. physiological, safety, love, esteem, self-actualization
3. personality

Retrospective Comment by Frederick Herzberg*

You can name very few psychologists who have captured the imagination of both professionals and the general public. Freud, Skinner, Binet, Rogers, are a few; Abraham Maslow was among them. As it is with scientists and scholars achieving both professional and public acclaim, they suffered from intense criticism, being caught in a crossfire between two parties that have a great dislike for each other, the academician and the general public. As for Maslow, he was criticized in industry for talking "gobbledygook" (humanism) and praised by the same industrial audience for talking about their lives rather than their job specifications. The academic psychologist, on the other hand, saw the humanism only as "gobbledygook" especially since Maslow did not do "basic" research. But the professional psychologist saw Abraham Maslow as giving him hope of being able to investigate outside of "Mickey Mouse" laboratories and gave him something to do besides evaluating the responses of undergraduate students in psychology. Maslow was a brilliant mind with a Lincolnesque style that attracted many thinkers as he elevated the study of man from the haunts of Freudian psychology.

His writings were better than his theory; the theory was wrong. His theory gained great popularity, however, and all of the things that the man was saying was lost; therein lies the tragedy of Abraham Maslow. His basic theory can be summarized in two parts. The first is a complete tautology in the style of Gertrude Stein—a need that is not a need is not a need. The second and most important part of his theory which has tremendous face validity, failed to hold up to critical analysis either through empirical investigations or conventional wisdom. He rank ordered man's needs in a hierarchy such that the satisfaction of higher order needs awaited the satisfaction of lower order needs. By conventional wisdom we can see clearly the difficulty with this conception of man; we would have no art if man needed to have a full belly in order to be creative. What Maslow forgot were the rising expectations. Lower order needs are never satisfied; they are only replaced by psychologically equivalent needs which are qualitatively or quantitatively more demanding. Simply put, status needs are never satisfied. The graduate student looks for an office in which to do his work, the assistant professor needs a window and the associate professor needs a private secretary.

Maslow was accepted, particularly by industry and students because he was a humanist, and he provided a theory which was, in the first part, a self-evident truth which automatically provides great popularity as do all self-evident truths. Secondly, and contrary to the basic theme in his works, his hierarchy exonerated the failure of man to grow rather than elevating man. The hierarchy became an excuse for non-self actualization. Since lower order needs are never satisfied (they need to be replenished), the results of his efforts were a most "scientific" and "humanistic" theory that became, in reality, an excuse for the failure of humanism in man.

* Dr. Herzberg is currently University Distinguished Professor, The University of Utah, Salt Lake City, Utah.

13

Rational Behavior and Economic Behavior

George Katona

PREVIEW

I. The methods of psychological theory have much to offer to formulation of economic theory and in trying to understand rationality.
   A. There are two groups of economic theorists.
      1. One group develops an *a priori* system from which they deduce propositions about how people should act.
      2. A second group regards the purpose of a theory as providing hypotheses to be tested, but they begin with simplified propositions and models which are unreal and untestable.
   B. Psychologists can draw on the theory of learning and thinking, the theory of group belonging, and the theory of motivation.

II Psychological theory and traditional rational theory offer differing views on habitual behavior as opposed to problem-solving behavior.
   A. Psychological theory offers several empirical generalizations and hypotheses:
      1. Problem-solving behavior is rare.
      2. Main alternative to problem-solving behavior is not whimsical or impulsive behavior, but habitual behavior.
      3. Problem-solving behavior is recognized most commonly as a deviation from habitual behavior.
      4. Strong motivational forces must be present to call forth problem-solving behavior.
      5. Group belonging and group reinforcement play a substantial role in change of behavior due to problem-solving.

George Katona, "Rational Behavior and Economic Behavior," is reprinted by permission from *Psychological Review* (September 1953), pp. 307–318.

6. Changes in behavior due to genuine decision-making will tend to be substantial and abrupt rather than small and gradual.

B. The traditional theory of rationality offers several propositions that seem untenable.
 1. The individual lists all conceivable consequences of his action.
 2. An individual makes the same choice each time he is confronted with the same set of alternatives.
 3. The three concepts—action, decision, and choice—are used without differentiation.

III. Psychological theory is helpful in explaining the maximization of utility concept of economic theory.
 A. The end of rational behavior according to economic theory is maximization of utility.
 B. Economic theory is a single motive theory, but psychological theory offers a multiplicity of motives.
 C. Psychological hypotheses, based on a theory of motives which change with circumstances and influence behavior, stimulate empirical studies.

IV. The levels of aspiration theory of psychology is strongly related to the concepts of diminishing utility and saturation of economic theory.
 A. Economic theory makes the mistake of postulating a one-dimensional ordering of all alternatives.
 B. Neither the saturation theory nor the levels-of-aspiration theory sufficed to explain empirical findings about the influence of assets on saving.

V. Psychology may profit from a study of economic behavior, and economic theory may profit from methodological approaches and hypotheses of psychology.

While attempts to penetrate the boundary lines between psychology and sociology have been rather frequent during the last few decades, psychologists have paid little attention to the problems with which another sister discipline, economics, is concerned. One purpose of this paper is to arouse interest among psychologists in studies of economic behavior. For that purpose it will be shown that psychological principles may be of great value in clarifying basic questions of economics and that the psychology of habit formation, of motivation, and of group belonging may profit from studies of economic behavior.

A variety of significant problems, such as those of the business cycle or inflation, of consumer saving or business investment, could be chosen for the purpose of such demonstration. This paper, however, will be concerned with the most fundamental assumption of economics, the principle of rationality. In order to clarify the problems involved in this principle, which have been neglected by contemporary psychologists, it will be necessary to contrast the most common forms of methodology used in economics with those employed in psychology and to discuss the role of empirical research in the social sciences.

Theory and Hypotheses

Economic theory represents one of the oldest and most elaborate theoretical structures in the social sciences. However, dissatisfaction with the achievements and uses of economic theory has grown considerably during the past few decades on the part of economists who are interested in what actually goes on in economic life. And yet leading sociologists and psychologists have recently declared "Economics is today, in a theoretical sense, probably the most highly elaborated, sophisticated, and refined of the disciplines dealing with action."[1]

To understand the scientific approach of economic theorists, we may divide them into two groups. Some develop an a priori system from which they deduce propositions about how people *should* act under certain assumptions. Assuming that the sole aim of businessmen is profit maximization, these theorists deduce propositions about marginal revenues and marginal costs, for example, that are not meant to be suited for testing. In developing formal logics of economic action, one of the main considerations is elegance of the deductive system, based on the law of parsimony. A wide gap separates these theorists from economic research of an empirical-statistical type which registers what they call aberrations or deviations, due to human fraility, from the norm set by theory.

A second group of economic theorists adheres to the proposition that it is the main purpose of theory to provide hypotheses that can be tested. This group acknowledges that prediction of future events represents the most stringent test of theory. They argue, however, that reality is so complex that it is necessary to begin with simplified propositions and models which are known to be unreal and not testable.[2] Basic among these propositions are the following three which traditionally have served to characterize the economic man or the rational man:

1. The principle of complete information and foresight. Economic conditions—demand, supply, prices, etc.—are not only given but also known to the rational man. This applies as well to future conditions about which there exists no uncertainty, so that rational choice can always be made. (In place of the assumption of certainty of future developments, we find nowadays more frequently the assumption that risks prevail but the

probability of occurrence of different alternatives is known; this does not constitute a basic difference.)

2. The principle of complete mobility. There are no institutional or psychological factors which make it impossible, or expensive, or slow, to translate the rational choice into action.

3. The principle of pure competition. Individual action has no great influence on prices because each man's choice is independent from any other person's choice and because there are no "large" sellers or buyers. Action is the result of individual choice and is not group-determined.

Economic theory is developed first under these assumptions. The theorists then introduce changes in the assumptions so that the theory may approach reality. One such step consists, for instance, of introducing large-scale producers, monopolists, and oligopolists, another of introducing time lags, and still another of introducing uncertainty about the probability distribution of future events. The question raised in each case is this: Which of the original propositions needs to be changed, and in what way, in view of the new assumptions?

The fact that up to now the procedure of gradual approximation to reality has not been completely successful does not invalidate the method. It must also be acknowledged that propositions were frequently derived from unrealistic economic models which were susceptible to testing and stimulated empirical research. In this paper we shall point to a great drawback of this method of starting out with a simplified a priori system and making it gradually more complex and more real—by proceeding in this way one tends to lose sight of important problems and to disregard them.

The methods most commonly used in psychology may appear at first sight to be quite similar to the methods of economics which have just been described. Psychologists often start with casual observations, derive from them hypotheses, test those through more systematic observations, reformulate and revise their hypotheses accordingly, and test them again. The process of hypotheses-observations-hypotheses-observations often goes on with no end in sight. Differences from the approach of economic theory may be found in the absence in psychological research of detailed systematic elaboration prior to any observation. Also, in psychological research, findings and generalizations in one field of behavior are often considered as hypotheses in another field of behavior. Accordingly, in analyzing economic behavior[3] and trying to understand rationality, psychologists can draw on *(a)* the theory of learning and thinking, *(b)* the theory of group belonging, and *(c)* the theory of motivation. This will be done in this paper.

Habitual Behavior and Genuine Decision Making

In trying to give noneconomic examples of "rational calculus," economic theorists have often referred to gambling. From some textbooks one might conclude that the most rational place in the world is the Casino in Monte Carlo where odds and probabilities can be calculated exactly. In contrast, some mathematicians and psychologists have considered scientific discovery and the thought processes of scientists as the best examples of rational or intelligent behavior.[4] An inquiry about the possible contributions of psychology to the analysis of rationality may then begin with a forumulation of the differences between *(a)* associative learning and habit formation and *(b)* problem solving and thinking.

The basic principle of the first form of behavior is repetition. Here the argument of Guthrie holds: "The most certain and dependable information concerning what a man will do in any situation is information concerning what he did in that situation on its last occurrence."[5] This form of behavior depends upon the frequency of repetition as well as on its recency and on the success of past performances. The origins of habit formation have been demonstrated by experiments about learning nonsense syllables, lists of words, mazes, and conditioned responses. Habits thus formed are to some extent automatic and inflexible.

In contrast, problem-solving behavior has been characterized by the arousal of a problem or question, by deliberation that involves reorganization and "direction," by understanding of the requirements of the situation, by weighing of alternatives and taking their consequences into consideration and, finally, by choosing among alternative courses of action.[6] Scientific discovery is not the only example of such procedures; they have been demonstrated in the psychological laboratory as well as in a variety of real-life situations. Problem solving results in action which is new rather than repetitive; the actor may have never behaved in the same way before and may not have learned of any others having behaved in the same way.

Some of the above terms, defined and analyzed by psychologists, are also being used by economists in their discussion of rational behavior. In discussing, for example, a manufacturer's choice between erecting or not erecting a new factory, or raising or not raising his prices or output, reference is usually made to deliberation and to taking the consequences of alternative choices into consideration. Nevertheless, it is not justified to identify problem-solving behavior with rational behavior. From the point of view of an outside observer, habitual behavior may prove to be fully rational or the most appropriate way of action under certain circumstances. All that is claimed here is that the analysis of two forms of behavior—habitual versus genuine decision making—may serve to clarify problems of rationality. We shall proceed therefore by deriving six propositions from the psychological principles. To some extent, or in certain fields of behavior, these are findings or empirical generalizations; to some extent, or in other fields of behavior, they are hypotheses.

1. Problem-solving behavior is a relatively rare occurrence. It would be incorrect to assume that everyday behavior consistently manifests such features as arousal of a problem, deliberation, or taking consequences of the action into consideration. Behavior which does not manifest these characteristics predominates in everyday life and in economic activities as well.

2. The main alternative to problem-solving behavior is not whimsical or impulsive behavior (which was considered the major example of "irrational" behavior by nineteenth-century philosophers). When genuine decision making does not take place, habitual behavior is the most usual occurrence: people act as they have acted before under similar circumstances, without deliberating and choosing.

3. Problem-solving behavior is recognized most commonly as a deviation from habitual behavior. Observance of the established routine is abandoned when in driving home from my office, for example, I learn that there is a parade in town and choose a different route, instead of automatically taking the usual one. Or, to mention an example of economic behavior: Many businessmen have rules of thumb concerning the timing for reorders of merchandise; yet sometimes they decide to place new orders even though their inventories have not reached the usual level of depletion (for instance, because they anticipate price increases), or not to order merchandise even though that level has been reached (because they expect a slump in sales).

4. Strong motivational forces—stronger than those which elicit habitual behavior—must be present to call forth problem-solving behavior. Being in a "crossroad situation," facing "choice points," or perceiving that something new has occurred are typical instances in which we are motivated to deliberate and choose. Pearl Harbor and the Korean aggression are extreme examples of "new" events; economic behavior of the problem-solving type was found to have prevailed widely after these events.

5. Group belonging and group reinforcement play a substantial role in changes of behavior due to problem solving. Many people become aware of the same events at the same time; our mass media provide the same information and often the same interpretation of events to groups of people (to businessmen, trade union members, sometimes to all Americans). Changes in behavior resulting from new events may therefore occur among very many people at the same time. Some economists[7] argued that consumer optimism and pessimism are unimportant because usually they will cancel out; in the light of sociopsychological principles, however, it is probable, and has been confirmed by recent surveys, that a change from optimistic to pessimistic attitudes, or vice versa, sometimes occurs among millions of people at the same time.

6. Changes in behavior due to genuine decision making will tend to be

> substantial and abrupt, rather than small and gradual. Typical examples of action that results from genuine decisions are cessation of purchases or buying waves, the shutting down of plants or the building of new plants, rather than an increase or decrease of production by 5 or 10 per cent.[8]

Because of the preponderance of individual psychological assumptions in classical economics and the emphasis placed on group behavior in this discussion, the change in underlying conditions which has occurred during the last century may be illustrated by a further example. It is related—the author does not know whether the story is true or fictitious—that the banking house of the Rothschilds, still in its infancy at that time, was one of the suppliers of the armies of Lord Wellington in 1815. Nathan Mayer Rothschild accompanied the armies and was present at the Battle of Waterloo. When he became convinced that Napoleon was decisively defeated, he released carrier pigeons so as to transmit the news to his associates in London and reverse the commodity position of his bank. The carrier pigeons arrived in London before the news of the victory became public knowledge. The profits thus reaped laid, according to the story, the foundation to the outstanding position of the House of Rothschild in the following decades.

The decision to embark on a new course of action because of new events was then made by one individual for his own profit. At present, news of a battle, or of change of government, or of rearmament programs, is transmitted in short order by press and radio to the public at large. Businessmen—the manufacturers or retailers of steel or clothing, for instance—usually receive the same news about changes in the price of raw materials or in demand, and often consult with each other. Belonging to the same group means being subject to similar stimuli and reinforcing one another in making decisions. Acting in the same way as other members of one's group or of a reference group have acted under similar circumstances may also occur without deliberation and choice. New action by a few manufacturers will, then, frequently or even usually not be compensated by reverse action on the part of others. Rather the direction in which the economy of an entire country moves—and often the world economy as well—will tend to be subject to the same influences.

After having indicated some of the contributions which the application of certain psychological principles to economic behavior may make, we turn to contrasting that approach with the traditional theory of rationality. Instead of referring to the formulations of nineteenth-century economists, we shall quote from a modern version of the classical trend of thought. The title of a section in a recent article by Kenneth J. Arrow is "The Principle of Rationality." He describes one of the criteria of rationality as follows: "We can imagine the individual as listing, once and for all, all conceivable consequences of his actions in order of his preference for them."[9] We are first concerned with the expression "all conceivable consequences." This expression seems to contradict the principle of selectivity of human behavior. Yet habitual behavior is highly selective since it is based on (repeated) past experience, and problem-solving behavior likewise is highly selective since reorganization is subject to a certain direction instead of consisting of trial (and error) regarding all possible avenues of action.

Secondly, Arrow appears to identify rationality with consistency in the sense of repetition of the same choice. It is part and parcel of rational behavior, according to Arrow, that an individual "makes the same choice each time he is confronted with the same set of alternatives."[10] Proceeding in the same way on successive occasions appears, however, a characteristic of habitual behavior. Problem-solving behavior, on the other hand, is flexible. Rationality may be said to reflect adaptability and ability to act in a new way when circumstances demand it, rather than to consist of rigid or repetitive behavior.

Thirdly, it is important to realize the differences between the concepts, action, decision, and choice. It is an essential feature of the approach derived from considering problem-solving behavior that there is action without deliberate decision and choice. It then becomes one of the most important problems of research to determine under what conditions genuine decision and choice occur prior to an action. The three concepts are, however, used without differentiation in the classical theory of rationality and also, most recently, by Parsons and Shils. According to the theory of these authors, there are "five discrete choices (explicit or implicit) which every actor makes before he can act;" before there is action "a decision must always be made (explicitly or implicity, consciously or unconsciously)."[11]

There exists, no doubt, a difference in terminology, which may be clarified by mentioning a simple case: Suppose my telephone rings: I lift the receiver with my left hand and say, "Hello." Should we then argue that I made several choices, for instance, that I decided not to lift the receiver with my right hand and not to say "Mr. Katona speaking"? According to our use of the terms decision and choice, my action was habitual and did not involve "taking consequences into consideration."[12] Parsons and Shils use the terms decision and choice in a different sense, and Arrow may use the terms "all conveivable consequences" and "same set of alternatives" in a different sense from the one employed in this paper. But the difference between the two approaches appears to be more far-reaching. By using the terminology of the authors quoted, and by constructing a theory of rational action on the basis of this terminology, fundamental problems are disregarded. If every action by definition presupposes decision making, and if the malleability of human behavior is not taken into consideration, a one-sided theory of rationality is developed and empirical research is confined to testing a theory which covers only some of the aspects of rationality.

This was the case recently in experiments devised by Mosteller and Nogee. These authors attempt to test basic assumptions of economic theory, such as the rational choice among alternatives, by placing their subjects in a gambling situation (a variation of poker dice) and compelling them to make a decision, namely, to play or not to play against the experimenter. Through their experiments the authors prove that "it is feasible to measure utility experimentally,"[13] but they do not shed light on the conditions under which rational behavior occurs or on the inherent features of rational behavior. Experiments in which making a choice among known alternatives is prescribed do not test the realism of economic theory.

Maximization

Up to now we have discussed only one central aspect of rationality—means rather than ends. The end of rational behavior, according to economic theory, is maximization of profits in the case of business firms and maximization of utility in the case of people in general.

A few words, first, on maximizing profits. This is usually considered the simpler case because it is widely held (*a*) that business firms are in business to make profits and (*b*) that profits, more so than utility, are a quantitative, measurable concept.

When empirical research, most commonly in the form of case studies, showed that businessmen frequently strove for many things in addition to profits or in place of profits, most theorists were content with small changes in their systems. They redefined profits so as to include long-range profits and what has been called nonpecuniary or psychic profits. Striving for security or for power was identified with striving for profits in the more distant future; purchasing goods from a high bidder who was a member of the same fraternity as the purchaser, rather than from the lowest bidder—to cite an example often used in textbooks—was thought to be maximizing of nonpecuniary profits. Dissatisfaction with this type of theory construction is rather widespread. For example, a leading theorist wrote recently:

> If *whatever* a business man does is explained by the principle of profit

maximization—because he does what he likes to do, and he likes to do what maximizes the sum of his pecuniary and non-pecuniary profits—the analysis acquires the character of a system of definitions and tautologies, and loses much of its value as an explanation of reality.[14]

The same problem is encountered regarding maximization of utility. Arrow defines rational behavior as follows: " . . . among all the combinations of commodities an individual can afford, he chooses that combination which maximizes his utility or satisfaction"[15] and speaks of the "traditional identification of rationality with maximization of some sort."[16] An economic theorist has recently characterized this type of definition as follows:

> The statement that a person seeks to maximize utility is (in many versions) a tautology: it is impossible to conceive of an observational phenomenon that contradicts it. . . . What if the theorem is contradicted by observation: Samuelson says it would not matter much in the case of utility theory; I would say that it would not make the slightest difference. For there is a free variable in his system: the tastes of consumers. . . . Any contradiction of a theorem derived from utility theory can always be attributed to a change of tastes, rather than to an error in the postulates or logic of the theory.[17]

What is the way out of this difficulty? Can psychology, and specifically the psychology of motivation, help? We may begin by characterizing the prevailing economic theory as a single-motive theory and contrast it with a theory of multiple motives. Even in case of a single decision of one individual, multiplicity of motives (or of vectors or forces in the field), some reinforcing one another and some conflicting with one another, is the rule rather than the exception. The motivational patterns prevailing among different individuals making the same decision need not be the same; the motives of the same individual who is in the same external situation at different times may likewise differ. This approach opens the way *(a)* for a study of the relation of different motives to different forms of behavior and *(b)* for an investigation of changes in motives. Both problems are disregarded by postulating a single-motive theory and by restricting empirical studies to attempts to confirm or contradict that theory.

The fruitfulness of the psychological approach may be illustrated first by a brief reference to business motivation. We may rank the diverse motivational patterns of businessmen by placing the striving for high immediate profits (maximization of short-run profits, to use economic terminology; charging whatever the market can bear, to use a popular expression) at the extreme of the scale. At the other extreme we place the striving for prestige or power. In between we discern striving for security, for large business volume, or for profits in the more distant future. Under what kinds of business conditions will motivational patterns tend to conform with the one or the other end of the scale? Preliminary studies would seem to indicate that the worse the business situation is, the more frequent is striving for high immediate profits, and the better the business situation is, the more frequent is striving for nonpecuniary goals.[18]

Next we shall refer to one of the most important problems of consumer economics as well as of business-cycle studies, the deliberate choice between saving and spending. Suppose a college professor receives a raise in his salary or makes a few hundred extra dollars through a publication. Suppose, furthermore, that he suggest thereupon to his wife that they should buy a television set while the wife argues that the money should be put in the bank as a reserve against a "rainy day." Whatever the final decision may be, traditional economic theory would hold that the action which gives the greater satisfaction was chosen. This way of theorizing is of little value. Under what conditions will one type of behavior (spending) and under what conditions will another type of behavior (saving) be more frequent? Psychological hypotheses according to which the strength of vectors is related to the immediacy of needs have been put to a test through nationwide surveys over the past six years.[19] On the basis of survey findings the following tentative generalization was established: Pessimism, insecurity, expectation of income declines or bad times in the near future promote saving (putting the extra money in the bank), while optimism, feeling of security, expectation of income increases, or good times promote spending (buying the television set, for instance).

Psychological hypotheses, based on a theory of motivational patterns which change with circumstances and influence behavior, thus stimulated empirical studies. These studies, in turn, yielded a better understanding of past developments and also, we may add, better predictions of forthcoming trends than did studies based on the classical theory. On the other hand, when conclusions about utility or rationality were made on an a priori basis, researchers lost sight of important problems.[20]

Diminishing Utility, Saturation, and Aspiration

Among the problems to which the identification of maximizing utility with rationality gave rise, the measurability of utility has been prominent. At present the position of most economists appears to be that while interpersonal comparison of several consumers' utilities is not possible, and while cardinal measures cannot be attached to the utilities of one particular consumer, ordinal ranking of the utilities of each individual can be made. It is asserted that I can always say either that I prefer A to B, or that I am indifferent to having A or B, or that I prefer B to A. The theory of indifference curves is based on this assumption.

In elaborating the theory further, it is asserted that rational behavior consists not only of preferring more of the same goods to less ($2 real wages to $1, or two packages of cigarettes to one package, for the same service performed) but also of deriving diminishing increments of satisfaction from successive units of a commodity.[21] In terms of an old textbook example, one drink of water has tremendous value to a thirsty traveler in a desert; a second, third, or fourth drink may still have some value but less and less so; an *n*th drink (which he is unable to carry along) has no value at all. A generalization derived from this principle is that the more of a commodity or the more money a person has, the smaller are his needs for that commodity or for money, and the smaller his incentives to add to what he has.

In addition to using this principle of saturation to describe the behavior of the rational man, modern economists applied it to one of the most pressing problems of contemporary American economy. Prior to World War II the American people (not counting business firms) owned about 45 billion dollars in liquid assets (currency, bank deposits, government bonds) and these funds were highly concentrated among relatively few families; most individual families held no liquid assets at all (except for small amounts of currency). By the end of the year 1945, however, the personal liquid-asset holdings had risen to about 140 billion dollars and four out of every five families owned some bank deposits or war bonds. What is the effect of this great change on spending and saving? This question has been answered by several leading economists in terms of the saturation principle presented above. "The rate of saving is . . . a diminishing function of the wealth the individual holds"[22] because "the availability of liquid assets raises consumption generally by reducing the impulse to save."[23] More specifically: a person who owns nothing or very little will exert himself greatly to acquire some reserve funds, while a person who owns much will have much smaller incentives to save. Similarly, incentives to increase one's income are said to weaken with the amount of income. In other words, the strength of motivation is inversely correlated with the level of achievement.

In view of the lack of contact between economists and psychologists, it is hardly surprising that economists failed to see the relevance for their postulates of the extensive experimental work performed by psychologists on the problem of levels of aspiration. It is not necessary in this paper to describe these studies in detail. It may suffice to formulate three generalizations as established in numerous studies of goal-striving behavior.[24]

1. Aspirations are not static, they are not established once for all time.

2. Aspirations tend to grow with achievement and decline with failure.
3. Aspirations are influenced by the performance of other members of the group to which one belongs and by that of reference groups.

From these generalizations hypotheses were derived about the influence of assets on saving which differed from the postulates of the saturation theory. This is not the place to describe the extensive empirical work undertaken to test the hypotheses. But it may be reported that the saturation theory was not confirmed; the level-of-aspiration theory likewise did not suffice to explain the findings. In addition to the variable "size of liquid-asset holdings," the studies had to consider such variables as income level, income change, and savings habits. (Holders of large liquid assets are primarily people who have saved a high proportion of their income in the past!)[25]

The necessity of studying the interaction of a great number of variables and the change of choices over time leads to doubts regarding the universal validity of a one-dimensional ordering of all alternatives. The theory of measurement of utilities remains an empty frame unless people's established preferences of *A* over *B* and of *B* over *C* provide indications about their probable future behavior. Under what conditions do people's preferences give us such clues, and under what conditions do they not? If at different times *A* and *B* are seen in different contexts—because of changed external conditions or the acquisition of new experiences—we may have to distinguish among several dimensions.

The problem may be illustrated by an analogy. Classic economic theory postulates a one-dimensional ordering of all alternatives; Gallup asserts that answers to questions of choice can always be ordered on a yes—uncertain (don't know)—no continuum; are both arguments subject to the same reservations? Specifically, if two persons give the same answer to a poll question (e.g., both say "Yes, I am for sending American troops to Europe" or "Yes, I am for the Taft-Hartley Act") may they mean different things so that their identical answers do not permit any conclusions about the similarity of their other attitudes and their behavior? Methodologically it follows from the last argument that yes-no questions need to be supplemented by open-end questions to discern differences in people's level of information and motivation. It also follows that attitudes and preferences should be ascertained through a multi-question approach (or scaling) which serves to determine whether one or several dimensions prevail.

On Theory Construction

In attempting to summarize our conclusions about the respective merits of different scientific approaches, we might quote the conclusions of Arrow which he formulated for social science in general rather than for economics:

> To the extent that formal theoretical structures in the social sciences have not been based on the hypothesis of rational behavior, their postulates have been developed in a manner which we may term *ad hoc*. Such propositions . . . depend, of course, on the investigator's intuition and common sense.[26]

The last sentence seems strange indeed. One may argue the other way around and point out that such propositions as "the purpose of business is to make profits" or "the best businessman is the one who maximizes profits" are based on intuition or supposed common sense, rather than on controlled observation. The main problem raised by the quotation concerns the function of empirical research. There exists an alternative to developing an axiomatic system into a full-fledged theoretical model in advance of testing the theory through observations. Controlled observations should be based on hypotheses, and the formulation of an integrated theory need not be delayed until all observations are completed. Yet theory construction is part of the process of hypothesis-observation-revised hypothesis and prediction-observation, and systematization should rely on some empirical research. The proximate aim of scientific research is a body of empirically validated generalizations and not a theory that is valid under any and all circumstances.

The dictum that "theoretical structures in the social sciences must be based on the hypothesis of rational behavior" presupposes that it is established what rational behavior is. Yet, instead of establishing the characteristics of rational behavior a priori, we must first determine the conditions a_1, b_1, c_1 under which behavior of the type x_1, y_1, z_1, and the conditions a_2, b_2, c_2 under which behavior of the type x_2, y_2, z_2, is likely to occur. Then, if we wish, we may designate one of the forms of behavior as rational. The contributions of psychology to this process are not solely methodological; findings and principles about noneconomic behavior provide hypotheses for the study of economic behavior. Likewise, psychology can profit from the study of economic behavior because many aspects of behavior, and among them the problems of rationality, may be studied most fruitfully in the economic field.

This paper was meant to indicate some promising leads for a study of rationality, not to carry such study to its completion. Among the problems that were not considered adequately were the philosophical ones (rationality viewed as a value concept), the psychoanalytic ones (the relationships between rational and conscious, and between irrational and unconscious), and those relating to personality theory and the roots of rationality. The emphasis was placed here on the possibility and fruitfulness of studying forms of rational behavior, rather than the characteristics of *the* rational man. Motives and goals that change with and are adapted to circumstances, and the relatively rare but highly significant cases of our becoming aware of problems and attempting to solve them, were found to be related to behavior that may be called truly rational.

NOTES

1. T. Parsons and E. A. Shils (Editors), *Toward a General Theory of Action* (Cambridge, Mass.: Harvard University Press, 1951).

2. A variety of methods used in economic research differ, of course, from those employed by the two groups of economic theorists. Some research is motivated by dissatisfaction with the traditional economic theory; some is grounded in a systematization greatly different from traditional theory (the most important example of such systematization is national income accounting); some research is not clearly based on any theory; finally, some research has great affinity with psychological and sociological studies.

3. The expression "economic behavior" is used in this paper to mean behavior concerning economic matters (spending, saving, investing, pricing, etc.) Some economic theorists use the expression to mean the behavior of the "economic man," that is, the behavior postulated in their theory of rationality.

4. Reference should be made first of all to Max Wertheimer who in his book *Productive Thinking* uses the terms "sensible" and "intelligent" rather than "rational." Since we are mainly interested here in deriving conclusions from the psychology of thinking, the discussion of psychological principles will be kept extremely brief. See M. Wertheimer, *Productive Thinking* (New York: Harper, 1945); G. Katona, *Organizing and Memorizing* (New York: Columbia University Press, 1940); and G. Katona, *Psychological Analysis of Economic Behavior* (New York: McGraw-Hill, 1951), especially Chapters 3 and 4.

5. E. R. Guthrie, *Psychology of Learning* (New York: Harper, 1935), p. 228.

6. Cf. the following statement by a leading psychoanalyst: "Rational behavior is behavior that is effectively guided by an understanding of the situation to which one is reacting." French adds two steps that follow the choice between alternative goals, namely, commitment to a goal and commitment to a plan to reach a goal. See T. M. French, *The Integration of Behavior* (Chicago: University of Chicago Press, 1952).

7. J. M. Keynes, *The General Theory of Employment, Interest and Money* (New York: Harcourt, Brace, 1936), p. 95.

8. Some empirical evidence supporting these six propositions in the area of economic behavior has been assembled by the Survey Research Center of the University of Michigan. See G. Katona, "Psychological Analysis of Business Decisions and Expectations," *American Economic Review* (1946), pp. 44–63.

9. K. J. Arrow, "Mathematical Models in the Social Sciences," in D. Lerner and H. D. Lasswell, (Editors), *The Policy Sciences* (Stanford: Stanford University Press, 1951), p. 135.

10. In his recent book Arrow adds after stating that the economic man "will make the same decision each time he is faced with the same range of alternatives": "The ability to make consistent decisions is one of the symptoms of an integrated personality." See K. J. Arrow, *Social Choice and Individual Values* (New York: Wiley, 1951), p. 2.

11. T. Parsons and E. A. Shils, *op. cit.*

12. If I have reason not to make known that I am at home, I may react to the ringing of the telephone by fright, indecision, and deliberation (should I lift the receiver or let the telephone ring?) instead of reacting in the habitual way. This is an example of problem-solving behavior

characterized as deviating from habitual behavior. The only example of action mentioned by Parsons and Shils, "a man driving his automobile to a lake to go fishing," may be habitual or may be an instance of genuine decision making.

13. F. Mosteller and P. Nogee, "An Experimental Measurement of Utility," *Journal of Political Economy* (1951), pp. 371–405.

14. F. Machlup, "Marginal Analysis and Empirical Research," *American Economic Review* (1946), p. 526.

15. K. J. Arrow, *op cit.*

16. K. J. Arrow, *Social Choice and Individual Values* (New York: Wiley, 1951). The quotation refers specifically to Samuelson's definition but also applies to that of Arrow.

17. G. J. Stigler, "Review of P. A. Samuelson's Foundations of Economic Analysis," *Journal of American Statistical Association* (1948), p. 603.

18. G. Katona, *Psychological Analysis of Economic Behavior* (New York: McGraw-Hill, 1951), pp. 193–213.

19. In the Surveys of Consumer Finances, conducted annually since 1946 by the Survey Research Center of the University of Michigan for the Federal Reserve Board and reported in the *Federal Reserve Bulletin*. See a forthcoming publication of the Survey Research Center on consumer buying and inflation during 1950-52.

20. It should not be implied that the concepts of utility and maximization are of no value for empirical research. Comparison between maximum utility as determined from the vantage point of an observer with the pattern of goals actually chosen (the "subjective maximum"), which is based on insufficient information, may be useful. Similar considerations apply to such newer concepts as "minimizing regrets" and the "minimax."

21. This principle of diminishing utility was called a "fundamental tendency of human nature" by the great nineteenth century economist, Alfred Marshall.

22. G. Haberler, *Prosperity and Depression*, 3rd ed. (Geneva: League of Nations, 1941), p. 199.

23. The last quotation is from the publication of the U.S. Department of Commerce, *Survey of Current Business*, May 1950, p. 10.

24. K. Lewin, et al., "Level of Aspiration," in J. Hunt (Editor), *Personality and the Behavior Disorders* (New York: Ronald, 1944).

25. The empirical work was part of the economic behavior program of the Survey Research Center under the direction of the author.

26. K. J. Arrow, "Mathematical Models in the Social Sciences," in D. Lerner and H. D. Lasswell, (Editors), *The Policy Sciences* (Stanford: Stanford University Press, 1951), p. 137.

LEARNING REVIEW

Questions:

1. Katona's main concern is to emphasize the relation between what two sciences in studying rational behavior? a) ____________ b) ____________.

2. To analyze rational behavior, one must keep in mind the differences between what two types of consumer behavior? a) ______________________
b) ______________________

3. ____________ and ____________that change with and are adapted to circumstance were found to be related to behavior that may be called truly rational.

4. The end of rational behavior, according to economic theory, is ______________________ in the case of business firms.

Answers:

1. a) Economics b) Psychology 2. a) Habitual behavior b) Methodological or problem solving behavior 3. Motives, goals 4. maximization of profits.

Retrospective Comment

More than 20 years have passed since I wrote this essay. In the meantime I have conducted numerous studies on economic behavior and have written three books on psychological economics. There are reasons for both satisfaction and dissatisfaction with developments in these 20 years.

To speak of the dissatisfactions first, many economic theorists and even econometricians still start out by presenting a model of rational behavior and of maximization of utilities; the model is then stepwise modified so as to approximate "real" conditions. This procedure usually does not do justice to the powerful influence of subjective factors in economic decisions.

On the other hand, we know much more today than 20 years ago of the circumstances under which rational and calculating behavior or other forms of sensible and intelligent behavior occur. To illustrate newly won insights by an example of both theoretical and practical importance, I refer to consumer response to inflation. It has been postulated by theorists that rational people, when they expect prices to go up, will stock up and hoard in order to beat inflation. But in the U.S. during the last 25 years, this form of behavior was found to occur rarely and only under the influence of specific threatening developments. Most usually, anxiety about price increases makes for uncertainity, malaise, and misgivings which paralyze action. People then respond to inflationary expectations by spending less and saving more, rather than by spending more and saving less. This is not rational, as economists define the term, but it is sensible and explainable by psychological considerations.

14

Social Classes and Spending Behavior

Pierre Martineau

PREVIEW

I. Studies of social class by Lloyd Warner and others provided for the present study a series of hypotheses grounded in assumptions about saving of money and accumulation of objects:
   A. There will be a relationship between the values a person holds and the extent to which a product exemplifies those values.
   B. There is a differential hierarchy of things for which it is worth spending money.
   C. Conspicuous spending runs all the way through the social system.
   D. At different class levels, symbols of mobility will differ.
   E. The place in the home where these symbols will be displayed will shift at different class levels.
   F. Non-mobile people tend to rationalize purchases in terms of cost or economy.

II. Placement of subjects into five different classes was made using an Index of Status Characteristics (ISC).
   A. The five classes were: upper class, upper-middle class, lower-middle class, upper-lower class, and lower-lower class.
   B. The characteristics used in the ISC were occupation, sources of income, and housing type.

III. Analysis of subject responses to questions revealed a number of class differences.
   A. Subjects tended to choose stores whose tone and physical character of advertising appealed to their class level.

Pierre Martineau, "Social Classes and Spending Behavior," is reprinted by permission from the *Journal of Marketing*, published by the American Marketing Association (October 1958), pp. 121–130.

B. Subjects showed a difference in communication skill by class level.
C. The higher a subject's class level, the more likely he was to have saving aspirations, while the lower his class level, the more likely he was to mention spending only.

IV. There are a number of psychological differences between middle-class buyers and lower-class buyers:
A. Middle class is more pointed to the future and long expanses of time while the lower class is oriented to the present and past and short periods of time.
B. Middle class is urban-oriented; lower class is rural oriented.
C. Middle class stresses rationality; lower class is non-rational.
D. Middle class has wide horizons and greater sense of choice-making; lower class has sharply defined horizons and limited sense of choice making.
E. Middle class is self-confident and willing to take risks; lower class is much concerned with security and insecurity.
F. Middle class is immaterial and abstract in thinking with well-structured sense of the universe; lower class is concrete and perceptive in thinking with vague and unclear structuring of the world.
G. Middle class sees the self tied to national happenings; lower class sees world revolving around family and self.

All societies place emphasis on some one structure which gives form to the total society and integrates all the other structures such as the family, the clique, voluntary association, caste, age and sex groupings into a social unity.

Social stratification means any system of ranked statuses by which all the members of a society are placed in some kind of superordinate and subordinate hierarchy. While money and occupation are important in the ranking process, there are many more factors, and these two alone do not establish social position. The concept of social class was designed to include this process of ranking people in superior and inferior social position by any and all factors.

Class System

It has been argued that there cannot be a class system existent in America when most individuals do not have the slightest idea of its formal structure. Yet in actuality every individual senses that he is more at home with and more acceptable to certain groups than to others. In a study of department stores and shopping behavior, it was found that the Lower-

Status woman is completely aware that, if she goes into High-Status department stores, the clerks and the other customers in the store will punish her in various subtle ways.

"The clerks treat you like a crumb," one woman expressed it. After trying vainly to be waited on, another woman bitterly complained that she was loftily told, "We thought you were a clerk."

The woman who is socially mobile gives considerable thought to the external symbols of status, and she frequently tests her status by shopping in department stores which she thinks are commensurate with her changing position. She knows that, if she does not dress correctly, if she does not behave in a certain manner to the clerks, if she is awkward about the proper cues, then the other customers and the clerks will make it very clear that she does not belong.

In another study, very different attitudes in the purchase of furniture and appliances involving this matter of status were found. Middle-class people had no hesitancy in buying refrigerators and other appliances in discount houses and bargain stores because they felt that they could not "go wrong" with the nationally advertised names. But taste in furniture is much more elusive and subtle because the brand names are not known; and, therefore, one's taste is on trial. Rather than commit a glaring error in taste which would exhibit an ignorance of the correct status symbols, the same individual who buys appliances in a discount house generally retreats to a status store for buying furniture. She needs the support of the store's taste.

In a very real sense, everyone of us in his consumption patterns and style of life shows an awareness that there is some kind of a superiority-inferiority system operating, and that we must observe the symbolic patterns of our own class.

Lloyd Warner and Paul Lunt have described a six-class system: the Upper-Upper, or old families; Lower-Upper, or the newly arrived; Upper-Middle, mostly the professionals and successful businessmen; Lower-Middle, or the white collar salaried class; Upper-Lower, or the wage earner, skilled worker group; and Lower-Lower, or the unskilled labor group.[1] For practical purposes, in order to determine the individual's class position, Warner and his associates worked out a rating index, not based on amount of income but rather on type of income, type of occupation, house type, and place of residence.

Although the Warner thesis has been widely used in sociology, it has has not generally been employed in marketing. As a matter of fact, some critics in the social sciences have held that, since Warner's thesis rested essentially on studies of smaller cities in the 10,000–25,000 class, this same system might not exist in the more complex metropolitan centers, or might not be unravelled by the same techniques. Furthermore, many marketers did not see the application of this dimension to the individual's economic behavior, since the studies of Warner and his associates had mostly been concerned with the differences in the broad patterns of living, the moral codes, etc.

Social Class in Chicago

Under Warner's guidance, the *Chicago Tribune* has undertaken several extensive studies exploring social class in a metropolitan city, and its manifestations specifically in family buying patterns. The problem was to determine if such a social-class system did exist in metropolitan Chicago, if the dimensions and the relationships were at all similar to the smaller cities which were studied before the far-reaching social changes of the past fifteen years. The studies were undertaken to see if there were any class significances in the individual family's spending-saving patterns, retail store loyalties, and his expressions of taste in typical areas such as automobiles, apparel, furniture, and house types.

It seems that many an economist overlooks the possibility of any psychological differences between individuals resulting from different class membership. It is assumed that a rich man is simply a poor man with more money and that, given the same income, the poor man would behave exactly like the rich man. The *Chicago Tribune* studies crystallize a wealth of evidence from other sources that this is just not so, and that the Lower-Status person is profoundly different in his mode of thinking and his way of handling the world from the Middle-Class individual. Where he buys and what he buys will differ not only by economics but in symbolic value.

It should be understood, of course, that there are no hard and fast lines between the classes. Implicit in the notion of social class in America is the possibility of movement from one class to another. The "office boy-to-president" saga is a cherished part of the American dream. Bobo Rockefeller illustrates the female counterpart: from coal miner's daughter to socialite. As a corollary of the explorations in class, the study also tried to be definitive about the phenomenon of social mobility—the movement from one class to another.

There are numerous studies of vertical mobility from the level of sociological analysis, mostly by comparing the individual's occupational status to that of his father. There are also studies at the level of psychological analysis. This study attempted to combine the two levels, to observe the individual's progress and also to understand something of the dynamics of the mobile person as compared to the stable individual. The attempt was to look both backward and forward: tracing such factors as occupation, place of residence, and religion back to parents and grandparents, and then where the family expected to be in the next five or ten years, what were the educational plans for each son, each daughter, a discussion of future goals.

Because this article is confined primarily to social class, this section may be concluded by saying that the studies show a very clear relationship between spend-saving aspirations and the factors of mobility-stability.

Framework of Study

Following are Warner's hypotheses and assumptions for the study:

I. Assumptions about symbols and values and about saving of money and accumulation of objects.

Our society is acquisitive and pecuniary. On the one hand, the values and beliefs of Americans are pulled toward the pole of the accumulation of money by increasing the amount of money income and reducing its outgo. On the other hand, American values emphasize the accumulation of objects and products of technology for display and consumption. The self-regard and self-esteem of a person and his family, as well as the public esteem and respect of a valued social world around the accumulator, are increased or not by such symbols of accumulation and consumption.

The two sets of values, the accumulation of product symbols and the accumulation (saving) of money, may be, and usually are, in opposition.

General working hypotheses stemming from these assumptions were: (1) People are distributed along a range according to the two-value components, running from proportionately high savings, through mixed categories, to proportionately high accumulation of objects. (2) These value variations conform to social and personality factors present in all Americans.

II. Assumptions about product symbols, savers, and accumulations.

American society is also characterized by social change, particularly technological change that moves in the direction of greater and greater production of more kinds and more numerous objects for consumption and accumulation.

Hypothesis: New varieties of objects will be most readily accepted by the accumulators, and most often opposed by the savers.

III. Assumptions about the social values of accumulators and savers.

American society is characterized by basic cultural differences, one of them being social status. Social class levels are occupied by people, some of whom are upward mobile by intent and fact. Others are non-mobile, by intent and fact. The values which dictate judgments about actions, such as the kinds of objects which are consumed and accumulated, will vary by class level and the presence or absence of vertical mobility.

IV. Assumptions about the personal values of accumulators and savers.

The personality components are distributed through the class levels and through the mobility types. By relating the social and personality components, it is possible to state a series of hypotheses about accumulators and savers as they are related to the object world around them, particularly to objects which are new and old to the culture, those which are imposing or not and those which are predominantly for display or for consumption.

At the direct, practical level, all of these theoretical questions can be summarized by one basic question: *What kinds of things are people likely to buy and not buy if they are in given class positions and if they are or are not socially mobile?* In other words, what is the effect on purchasing behavior of being in a particular social class, and being mobile or non-mobile?

If this is the crucial question, theoretically grounded, then a whole series of hypotheses can be laid out concerning values about money and values about buying various kinds of objects for consumption and for display. Some of these are:

1. *There will be a relationship between values held by a particular subject and the extent to which particular products exemplify those values.*

2. *There is a differential hierarchy of things for which it is worth spending money.*

3. *Veblen's theory that conspicuous expenditure is largely applied to the Upper Class is erroneous. It runs all the way through our social system.*

From these statements certain other hypotheses follow:

4. *At different class levels, symbols of mobility will differ.*

There is a differential hierarchy of things on which it is worth spending money. Class and mobility will be two of the dimensions that will differentiate—also personality and cultural background.

5. *The place in the home where these symbols will be displayed will shift at different class levels.*

The underlying assumption here is that there is hierarchy of importance in the rooms of the house. This hierarchy varies with social class, mobility, age, ethnicity. The studies also revealed clear-cut patterns of taste for lamps, furnishings, house types, etc.

6. *The non-mobile people tend to rationalize purchases in terms of cost or economy.*

In other words, non-mobile people tend to be oriented more toward the pole of the accumulation of money. Purchases, then, are rationalized in terms of the savings involved.

The basic theses of all the hypotheses on mobility is this: Whereas the stable individual would emphasize saving and security, the behavior of the mobile individual is characterized by spending for various symbols of upward movement. All of the evidence turned up indicates that this difference in values does exist, and futhermore that notable differences in personality dynamics are involved. For instance, the analysis of how families would make investments shows that stable people overwhelmingly prefer insurance, the symbol of security. By contrast, the mobile people at all levels prefer stocks, which are risk-taking. In Warner's words, the mobile individual acts as if he were free, white, and twenty-one, completely able to handle the world, and perfectly willing to gamble on himself as a sure bet to succeed.

Class Placement

Returning to the factor of social class, in this study class placement was based on a multi-state probability area sample of metropolitan Chicago, involving 3,880 households. It was found that the matter of placement could not be done by the relatively simple scoring sufficient for the smaller cities. To secure house typings, it was necessary to provide the field investigators with photographs covering a wide range of dwelling types, all the way from exclusive apartments to rooms over stores. Because of the very complexity of metropolitan life, occupations provided the biggest problem. To solve this operational problem, it was necessary to construct an exhaustive list of occupational types involving degree of responsibility and training required by each. The data finally used to calculate the Index of Status Characteristics (ISC) were:

(weighted by 5)
Occupation (from 1 to 7 broad categories)
(weighted by 4)
Sources of Income (from 1 to 7 types)
(weighted by 3)
Housing Type (from 1 to 7 types)

The sum of the individual's weighted scores was used to predict his social class level as follows:[2]

ISC Scores	*Predicted social class placement*
12–21	Upper Class
22–37	Upper-Middle Class
38–51	Lower-Middle Class
52–66	Upper-Lower Class
67–84	Lower-Lower Class

The study very clearly shows that there is a social-class system operative in a metropolitan area which can be delineated. Furthermore, class membership is an important determinant of the individual's economic behavior, even more so than in the smaller city. The one department store in the smaller city may satisfy almost everyone, whereas in the metropolitan city the stores become sharply differentiated.

This is the social-class structure of Metropolitan Chicago, typifying the transformation of the formerly agrarian Midwestern cities from Pittsburgh to Kansas City into a series of big milltowns:

Upper and Upper-Middle	8.1%
Lower-Middle	28.4%
Upper-Lower	44.0%
Lower-Lower	19.5%

While the Old Families and the Newly Arrived are still recognizable as types, they constitute less than 1 per cent of the population. A similar study in Kansas City turned up so few that they could not be counted at all. On the other hand, we see the emergence of a seventh class, the Upper-Lower "Stars" or Light-Blue Collar Workers. They are the spokesmen of the Upper-Lower Class groups—high income individuals, who have the income for more ostentatious living than the average factory worker but who lack the personal skills or desire for high status by social mobility.

There is certainly a rough correlation between income and social class. But social class is a much richer dimension of meaning. There are so many facets of behavior which are explicable only on a basis of social class dynamics. For instance, this analysis of the purchase of household appliances in Chicago over a four-year period shows a very different picture by income and by class:

Nine Appliance Types—Four-Year Period

By Income

Over $7,000	36.2%
4,000–6,999	46.0%
Under 4,000	17.8%

By Social Class

Upper and Upper-Middle	16.6%
Lower-Middle	29.2%
Upper-Lower	45.7%
Lower-Lower	8.5%

Income analysis shows that the lowest income group represents an understandably smaller market, but nevertheless a market. Social-class analysis highlights a fundamental difference in attitudes toward the home between the two lower classes. The Upper-Lower Class man sees his home as his castle, his anchor to the world, and he loads it down with hardware—solid heavy appliances—as his symbols of security. The Lower-Lower Class individual is far less interested in his castle, and is more likely to spend his income for flashy clothes or an automobile. He is less property-minded, and he has less feeling about buying and maintaining a home.

Several *Tribune* studies have explored the way of life and the buying behavior in many new suburbs and communities. All of them quickly become stratified along social-class and mobility dimensions, and, therefore, differ tremendously among themselves. *Fortune* has reported on Park Forest, Illinois, a middle-class suburb of 30,000 and only ten years old. It is characterized by high degrees of both upward and geographical mobility. The people are overwhelmingly those who had moved from other parts of the United States, who had few local roots, and who consequently wanted to integrate themselves in friendship groups. But this was not typical of the new Lower-Status suburbs where the women did relatively little fraternizing. It was not typical of the new Upper-Middle Class mobile suburbs where the people were preoccupied with status symbols, not in submerging themselves in the group.

One new community had crystallized as being for Higher-Status Negroes. This was a resettlement project with relatively high rents for Negroes. Eighty-five per cent of them had come from the South where social class was compressed. But, as soon as they came to Chicago, the class system opened up and they were anxious to establish a social distance between themselves and other Negroes. Almost all of them said they enjoyed the "peace and quiet" of their neighborhood, which was their way of insisting that they were not like the "noisy" lower-class Negroes. They deliberately avoided the stores patronized by other Negroes.

Choice of Store

All of these studies reveal the close relation between choice of store, patterns of spending, and class membership. In the probability sample delineating social class, such questions were asked in the total metropolitan area as:

> "If you were shopping for a good dress, at which store would you be most likely to find what you wanted?"
> "For an everyday dress?"
> "For living room furniture?"
> "At which store do you buy most of your groceries?"

To assume that all persons would wish to shop at the glamorous High-Status stores is utterly wrong. People are very realistic in the way they match their values and expectations with the status of the store. The woman shopper has a considerable range of ideas about department stores; but these generally become organized on a scale ranking from very High-Social Status to the Lowest-Status and prestige. The social status of the department store becomes the primary basis for its definition by the shopper. This is also true of men's and women's apparel stores, and furniture stores, on the basis of customer profiles. The shopper is not going to take a chance feeling out of place by going to a store where she might not fit.

No matter what economics are involved, she asks herself who are the other customers in the store, what sort of treatment can she expect at the hands of the clerks, will the merchandise be the best of everything, or lower priced and hence lower quality? Stores are described as being for the rich, for the average ordinary people, or for those who have to stretch their pennies.

The most important function of retail advertising today, when prices and quality have become so standard, is to permit the shopper to make social-class identification. This she can do from the tone and physical character of the advertising. Of course, there is also the factor of psychological identification. Two people in the same class may want different stores. One may prefer a conservative store, one may want the most advanced styling. But neither will go to stores where they do not "fit," in a social-class sense.

In contrast to the independent food retailer, who obviously adapts to the status of the neighborhood, the chain grocers generally invade many income areas with their stores. Nevertheless, customer profiles show that each chain acquires a status definition. The two largest grocery chains in the Chicago area are A. & P. and Jewel; yet they draw very different customer bodies. A. & P. is strong with the mass market, whereas Jewel has its strength among the Middle Class.

While the national brand can and often does cut across classes, one can think of many product types and services which do have social class labels. The Upper-Middle Class person rarely travels by motor coach because none of his associates do so, even though there is certainly nothing wrong with this mode of transportation. On the other hand, even with low air-coach fares, one does not see many factory workers or day laborers on vacation around airports. Such sales successes as vodka and tonic water, and men's deodorants and foreign sports cars, were accomplished without benefit of much buying from this part of the market.

Communication Skills

There is also a relation between class and communication abilities which has significance for marketing. The kind of super-sophisticated and clever advertising which appears in the *New Yorker* and *Esquire* is almost meaningless to Lower-Status people. They cannot comprehend the subtle humor; they are baffled by the bizarre art. They have a different symbol system, a very different approach to humor. In no sense does this imply that they lack intelligence or wit. Rather their communication skills have just been pressed into a different mold.

Here again, style of advertising helps the individual to make class identification. Most of the really big local television success stories in Chicago have been achieved by personalities who radiate to the mass that this is where they belong. These self-made businessmen who do the announcing for their own shows communicate wonderfully well with the mass audience. While many listeners switch off their lengthy and personal commercials, these same mannerisms tell the Lower-Status individual that here is someone just like himself, who understands him.

Social Research, Inc. has frequently discussed the class problem in marketing by dividing the population into Upper-Middle or quality market; the middle majority which combines both the Lower-Middle and Upper-Lower; and then the Lower-Lower. The distinction should be drawn between the Middle Classes and the Lower-Status groups. In several dozen of these store profiles, there is scarcely an instance where a store has appeal to the Lower-Middle and Upper-Lower classes with anything like the same strength.

It would be better to make the break between the Middle Class, representing one-third of the population and the Lower-Status or Working-Class or Wage-Earner group, representing two-thirds of metropolitan Chicago. This permits some psychological distinctions to be drawn between the Middle-Class individual and the individual who is not a part of the Middle-Class system of values. Even though this is the dominant American value system, even though Middle-Class Americans have been taught by their parents that it is the only value system, this Lower-Status individual does not necessarily subscribe to it.

Who Saves, Who Spends?

Another important set of behavioral distinctions related to social class position was revealed in the "save-spend aspiration" study. The question was asked: "Suppose your income was doubled for the next ten years, what would you do with the increased income?" This is a fantasy question taken out of the realm of any pressing economic situation to reflect aspirations about money. The coding broke down the answers to this question into five general categores: (1) the mode of saving, (2) the purpose of saving, (3) spending which would consolidate past gains, meet present defensive needs, prepare for future self-advancement, (4) spending which is "self-indulgent-centered," (5) spending which is "house-centered."

Here are some of our findings:[3] The higher the individual's class position, the more likely is he to express some saving aspirations. Conversely, the lower his class position, the more likely is he to mention spending only. Moreover the higher the status, the more likely is the individual to specify *how* he will save his money, which is indicative of the more elaborate financial learning required of higher status.

Proceeding from the more general categories (such as saving versus spending only) to more specific categories (such as non-investment versus investment saving and the even more specific stock versus real estate investment, etc.) an increasingly sharper class differentiation is found. It is primarily *non-investment* saving which appeals to the Lower-Status person. Investment saving, on the other hand, appeals above all to the Upper-Status person.

Investors almost always specify how they will invest. And here in mode of investment are examples of the most sharply class-differentiated preferences. Intangible forms of investment like stock and insurance are very clearly distinguished as Upper-Status investments. Nearly four times as many Upper-Middles select insurance as would be expected by chance, whereas only one-fifth of the Lower-Lowers select it as would be expected by chance. By contrast, Lower-Status people have far greater preference for tangible investments, specifically ownership of real estate, a farm, or a business.

To sum up, Middle-Class people usually have a place in their aspirations for some form of saving. This saving is most often in the form of investment, where there is a risk, long-term involvement, and the possibility of higher return. Saving, investment saving, and intangible investment saving—successively each of these become for them increasingly symbols of their higher status.

The aspirations of the Lower-Status person are just as often for spending as they are for saving. This saving is usually a non-investment saving where there is almost no risk, funds can be quickly converted to spendable cash, and returns are small. When the Lower-Status person does invest his savings, he will be specific about the mode of investment, and is very likely to prefer something tangible and concrete—something he can point at and readily display.

Turning from mode of saving to purpose of saving, very significant class relationships are likewise evident. Consider the verbalization of saving purpose. Lower-Status people typically explain why one should save—why the very act of saving is important. On the other hand, Middle-Class people do not, as if saving is an end-in-itself, the merits of which are obvious and need not be justified.

Spending is the other side of the coin. Analysis of what people say they will spend for shows similar class-related desires. All classes mention concrete, material artifacts such as a new car, some new appliance. But the Lower-Status people stop here. Their accumulations are artifact-centered, whereas Middle-Class spending-mentions are experience-centered. This is spending where one is left typically with only a memory. It would include hobbies, recreation, self-education and travel. The wish to travel, and particularly foreign travel, is almost totally a Middle-Class aspiration.

Even in their fantasies, people are governed by class membership. In his daydreaming and wishful thinking, the Lower-Status individual will aspire in different patterns from the Middle-Class individual.

Psychological Differences

This spending-saving analysis has very obvious psychological implications to differentiate between the classes. Saving itself generally suggests foresightedness, the ability to perceive long-term needs and goals. Non-investment saving has the characteristics of little risk-taking and of ready conversion, at no loss, into immeidate expenditures—the money can be drawn out of the account whenever the bank is open. Investment spending, on the other hand, has the characteristics of risk-taking (a gamble for greater returns) and of delayed conversion, with possible loss, to expenditures on immediate needs.

Here are some psychological contrasts between two different social groups:

Middle-Class

1. Pointed to the future
2. His viewpoint embraces a long expanse of time
3. More urban identification

4. Stresses rationality
5. Has a well-structured sense of the universe
6. Horizons vastly extended or not limited
7. Greater sense of choice-making
8. Self-confident, willing to take risks
9. Immaterial and abstract in his thinking
10. Sees himself tied to national happenings

Lower-Status

1. Pointed to the present and past
2. Lives and thinks in a short expanse of time
3. More rural in identification
4. Non-rational essentially
5. Vague and unclear structuring of the world
6. Horizons sharply defined and limited
7. Limited sense of choice-making
8. Very much concerned with security and insecurity
9. Concrete and perceptive in his thinking
10. World revolves around his family and body

Conclusions

The essential purpose of this article was to develop three basic premises which are highly significant for marketing:

I. *There is a social-class system operative in metropolitan markets, which can be isolated and described.*

II. *It is important to realize that there are far-reaching psychological differences between the various classes.* They do not handle the world in the same fashion. They tend not to think in the same way. As one tries to communicate with the Lower-Status group, it is imperative to sense that their goals and mental processes differ from the Middle-Class group.

III. *Consumption patterns operate as prestige symbols to define class membership, which is a more significant determinant of economic behavior than mere income.* Each major department store, furniture store, and chain-grocery store has a different "pulling power" on different status groups. The usual customers of a store gradually direct the store's merchandising policies into a pattern which works. The interaction between store policy and consumer acceptance results in the elimination of certain customer groups and the attraction of others, with a resulting equilibration around a reasonably stable core of specific customer groups who think of the store as appropriate for them.

Income has always been the marketer's handiest index to family consumption standards. But it is a far from accurate index. For instance, the bulk of the population in a metropolitan market today will fall in the middle-income ranges. This will comprise not only the traditional white collar worker, but the unionized craftsman and the semi-skilled worker with their tremendous income gains of the past decade. Income-wise, they may be in the same category. But their buying behavior, their tastes, their spending-saving aspirations can be poles apart. Social-class position and mobility-stability dimensions will reflect in much greater depth each individual's style of life.

NOTES

1. W. Lloyd Warner and Paul Lunt, *The Social Life of a Modern Community* (New Haven: Yale University Press, 1950). Also, W. Lloyd Warner, Marchia Meeker, and Kenneth Eells, *Social Class in America* (Chicago: Science Research Associates, 1949).
2. Dr. Bevode McCall helped to solve the ISC scoring problem for Metropolitan Chicago.
3. The saving-spending aspiration analysis was carried out by Roger Coup, graduate student at the University of Chicago.

LEARNING REVIEW

Questions:

1. The main point expressed in Martineau's article is that metropolitan markets can be isolated as to__________________________________.

2. The two sets of values in the human society, which are usually in opposition are: (a) __________________________________
(b) __________________________________.

3. The Warner study revealed four important class relationships that are relevant to marketing. These four are:
(a) __________________________________
(b) __________________________________
(c) __________________________________
(d) __________________________________

4. The ____________ the individual's class position, the more likely he is to express some saving aspirations.

5. The most important function of retail advertising today, when prices and quality have become so standard, is to permit the shopper to make ______ ______________________________.

6. Whereas the stable individual would emphasize ______________ ________________, the behavior of the mobile individual is characterized by spending for ________________________.

Answers:

1. Social class 2. a) accumulation of product symbols, b) accumulation (saving) of money 3. a) choice of stores, b) communications skills, c) save-spend aspiration, d) psychological 4. higher 5. social class identification 6. saving and security, (symbols of upward movement.)

Retrospective Comment by Richard Coleman*

Pierre Martineau's article deserves the label *Great Writing in Marketing*, because upon its appearance in the *Journal of Marketing* in 1958 it effectively established a new concept in the field: social class as a key to understanding consumption patterns. Its importance was recognized almost instantly, winning Alpha Kappa Psi's award as "best article of the year."

Martineau's article, like any pioneering work, persuasively argued the central truths of the matter—that social class is a potent, not-to-be-ignored influence on spending behavior. It did so, however, partly by overlooking some of the complexities. This "defect," which we see now in retrospect, is an inevitable by-product of the path-breaker's task, that his major ideas must be clearly, unequivocally established.

One of "the complexities"—or "elaborations," if you will—in this matter of social class impact on consumption, which this first Martineau article did not detail, is that within each social class one finds different life styles, as well as vast differences in income level. My own article, "The Significance of Social Stratification in Selling," which appeared two years later in the *Proceedings of the Winter Conference of the American Marketing Association*, 1960, and has been reprinted subsequently in many marketing books, dealt with some of these differences. As a prime example, I pointed out that each social class could be divided into three income segments—the *Underprivileged*, *Over-*

privileged, and *Average*. This segmentation is determined individually for each class group according to what is indeed "average" within the class (i.e., the expected income level for full marketplace functioning as a class member) and what is in turn considerably above average and considerably below. The most beautiful illustration for the significance of such a breakdown to the marketing fraternity was that compact cars, far from being bought by the "poorest" of new car buyers in the early 1960s, were being purchased by the Underprivileged members of each social class (at the upper-middle and upper class level no less than at the lower-middle and working class). At the same time, the "gas-guzzling monsters"—Cadillacs, Continentals, and Chryslers—were being bought, not necessarily by the "wealthiest" people in the market, but rather by each class's Overprivileged members, of which the Upper-Lower *Stars* mentioned by Martineau were perhaps the most colorful category. Much the same kind of purchasing behavior was found in other consumer markets, with each class's Underprivileged members sometimes spending very differently from its Overprivileged and at other times—on things crucial to class identity—spending indentically. Introduction of this "complexity" into application of the social class concept confirmed the concept's importance, as Martineau was the first to acknowledge in subsequent speeches and writings.

There are probably more life styles found at each social class level today than there were in the late 1950s and early 1960s, when Martineau and I were most involved in market research. Some of these life styles are based on age, others on income level, still others on region—and many of the most significant are based on "brow" level differences, as wed to liberal-conservative political attitudes, that are found at each class level. Finally, there is possibly a greater variety of life styles today precisely because there seem to be so many more options.

Even so, there are considerable differences in the way that those of the upper-middle class, whose recreational lives center on outdoor sports and back-to-nature adventures, pursue this enthusiasm from the paths followed by working class or lower-middle outdoor fans. The prosperous working class family, for example, is a leading purchaser of all manner of expensive recreational equipment—campers and boats most notable—and shows its purchases off at home in driveway and front yard, a behavior which is close to taboo in middle class neighborhoods. Among American families today in the $12,000–$20,000 income bracket, of which there are many representatives in each major class, one would find very distinctively working class styles, lower-middle class styles, and professional upper-middle styles. Their houses, even when dating from the same era, and the same in size and basic cost as well, would be found very differently equipped inside and differently maintained on the outside—and, of course, they tend to be in different neighborhoods. Each American city has its differentiated slightly-wrong-side-of-town Blue Collar suburbs, better-side-of-town White Collar districts, and enclaves of moderate-income, usually younger, professionals trying to be upper-middle class without the $25,000 a year salaries required for easy claim to that estate.

To demonstrate the importance of social class, Martineau opened his article by using the example of a "study of department stores and shopping behavior (where) it was found that the lower-status woman is completely aware that, if she goes into high-status department stores, the clerks and the other customers in the store will punish her in various subtle ways." I think that this same kind of illustration could not be used so significantly today. I believe that in the suburban shopping malls of the 1970s, where discount stores are merged under one roof with relatively fashionable specialty shops and old-line major department stores, the status differential in which any given man or woman feels comfortable shopping has all but vanished. Indeed, it would seem that the merchants themselves have encouraged such a change, the high-status stores attempting to lure an increasing number of working class customers into their patronage and the low-status stores eager to cut in on the upper-middle class family's dollar.

There are other illustrations in Martineau's article which today are anachronisms. Certainly it could not be said any more that "even with low air-coach fares, one does not see many factory workers . . . on vacation around airports." I am sure, to the contrary, that now one *does* see a great many factory workers and their wives and children at airports—but then, how does one know? Today, the white-collar worker and the professional, when traveling and vacationing, dress so far down the scale from the levels of decency and propriety in public appearance they maintained in the 1950s that I personally find it difficult to tell at casual glance the difference between vacationing factory workers and relaxing professionals when I am waiting for a plane. This in itself—this blurring in the difference of public presentation by social class—represents a change in the comportment of our population that has not been sufficiently researched, either for its significance to the class system itself or for its consequences to marketers.

None of this is to say that social class is not now important, or no longer as important in explaining spending behavior as it was fifteen or twenty years ago. Social class is a difficult concept, however, and not as often employed in full depth as I think it should be. If it is not as "popular," or as much of an "in" idea, now as in the early 1960s, such is the case more because it is so expensive and time-consuming a research variable to consider than because it is any less applicable. I believe that one cannot easily question Martineau's essential conclusions: that (1) "there is a social class system," (2) that "there are far-reaching psychological differences between the various classes," and (3) that "class membership is a more significant determinant of economic behavior than mere income," of which the latter is admittedly the "marketer's handiest index to family consumption standards." Income level only explains certain of the most obvious spending choices—and even then as often baffles as explains. Social class, to the contrary, explains more often than it baffles—and explains the less obvious even more than the obvious.

In concluding this retrospective, then, let me urge continuing research into status phenomena and into the relationship between social class and marketplace behavior, for, as I concluded in 1960, "As of the moment the marketing analyst allows his stratification concept to become dated, his use of it will cease to be sophisticated."

* Dr. Coleman is currently Senior Research Associate at the Joint Center for Urban Studies of the Massachusetts Institute of Technology and Harvard University in Cambridge, Massachusetts.

15

A Theory of Buyer Behavior

John A. Howard and Jagdish N. Sheth

PREVIEW

I. It is reasonable to attempt a comprehensive theory of buyer behavior based on research in the behavioral sciences and in consumer behavior.

II. The theory of buyer behavior has four major components:
   A. Stimulus variables may be social or commercial.
      1. Significant commercial stimuli are communicated through the physical brands.
      2. Symbolic commercial stimuli are communicated in linguistic or pictorial stimuli.
      3. Social stimuli are provided from information in the buyer's social environment.
   B. Hypothetical constructs fall into two classes:
      1. Those dealing with perception:
         a. sensitivity to information
         b. perceptual bias
         c. search for information
      2. Those dealing with learning:
         a. motive—specific and nonspecific
         b. brand potential of evoked set
         c. decision mediators
         d. predisposition toward the brands
         e. inhibitors
         f. satisfaction with the purchase of a brand
   C. Response variables include all of the buyer's responses which are relevant for market strategy.
      1. attention

John A. Howard and Jagdish N. Sheth, "A Theory of Buyer Behavior," is reprinted by permission from Reed Moyer (editor), *Changing Marketing Systems* (Chicago: American Marketing Association, 1967), pp. 253–262.

2. comprehension
3. attitude toward a brand
4. intention to buy
5. purchase behavior

D. Exogenous variables are those factors which the theorist does not try to explain in terms of formation and change.
1. importance of purchase
2. time pressure
3. financial status
4. personality traits
5. social and organizational setting
6. social class
7. culture

In the last fifteen years, considerable research on consumer behavior both at the conceptual and empirical levels has accumulated. This can be gauged by reviews of the research.[1] As a consequence we believe that sufficient research exists in both the behavioral sciences and consumer behavior to attempt a comprehensive theory of buyer behavior. Furthermore, broadly speaking, there are two major reasons at the basic research level which seem to have created the need to take advantage of this opportunity. The first reason is that a great variety exists in today's effort to understand the consumer, and unfortunately there is no integration of this variety. The situation resembles the seven blind men touching different parts of the elephant and making inferences about the animal which differ, and occasionally contradict one another. A comprehensive theory of buyer behavior would hopefully not only provide a framework for integrating the existing variety but also would prepare the researcher to adopt appropriate research designs which would control sources of influences other than those he is immediately interested in. The difficulty of replicating a study and the possibility of getting contradictory findings will be minimized accordingly.

The second major basic research reason for a comprehensive theory is the potential application of research in buying behavior to human behavior in general. In asserting the need to validate psychological propositions in a real world context Sherif has repeatedly and eloquently argued for applied research.[2] Also, McGuire argues that social psychology is moving toward theory-oriented research in *natural settings* because a number of forces are encouraging the movement away from laboratory research, and he cites the current work in buyer behavior as one of these forces.[3]

Again, one way that we can contribute to "pure" areas of behavioral science is by attempting a comprehensive theory which would help to identify and to iron out our own inconsistencies and contradictions. Such an attempt looks ambitious on the surface, but after several years of work and drawing upon earlier work,[4] we are confident that it can be achieved.

A Brief Summary of the Theory

Before we describe each component of the theory in detail, it will be helpful to discuss briefly the essentials of our view of the consumer choice process.

Much of buying behavior is more or less repetitive brand choice decisions. During his life cycle, the buyer establishes purchase cycles for various products which determine how often he will buy a given product. For some products, this cycle is very lengthy, as for example in buying durable appliances, and, therefore, he buys the product quite infrequently. For many other products, however, the purchase cycle is short and he buys the product frequently as is the case for many grocery and personal care items. Since there is usually the element of repeat buying, we must present a theory which incorporates the dynamics of purchase behavior over a period of time if we wish to capture the central elements of the empirical process.

In the face of repetitive brand choice decisions, the consumer simplifies his decision process by storing relevant information and routinizing his decision process. What is crucial, therefore, is to identify the elements of decision making, to observe the structural or substantive changes that occur in them over time due to the repetitive nature, and show how a combination of the decision elements affect search processes and the incorporation of information from the buyer's commercial and social environment.

The buyer, having been motivated to buy a product class, is faced with a brand choice decision. The elements of his decision are: (1) a set of motives, (2) several courses of action, and (3) decision mediators by which the motives are matched with the alternatives. Motives are specific to a product class, and they reflect the underlying needs of the buyer. The alternative courses of actions are the purchase of one of the various brands with their potential to satisfy the buyer's motives. There are two important notions involved in the definition of alternatives as brands. First, the brands which are alternatives of the buyer's choice decision at any given time are generally a small number, collectively called his "evoked set." The size of the evoked set is only two or three, a fraction of the brands he is aware of and a still smaller fraction of the total number of brands actually available in the market. Second, any two consumers may have quite different alternatives in their evoked sets.

The decision mediators are a set of rules that the buyer employs to match his motives and his means of satisfying those motives. They serve the function of ordering and structuring the buyer's motives and then ordering and structuring the various brands based on their potential to satisfy these ordered motives. The decision mediators develop by the process of learning about the buying situation. They are, therefore, influenced by information from the buyer's environment and even more importantly by the actual experience of purchasing and consuming the brand.

When the buyer is just beginning to purchase a product class such as when a purchase is precipitated by a change in his life cycle, he lacks experience. In order, therefore, to develop the decision mediators, he *actively seeks information* from his commercial and social environments. The information that he either actively seeks or accidentally receives is subject to perceptual processes which not only limits the intake of information (magnitude of information is affected) but modifies it to suit his own frame of reference (quality of information is affected). These modifications are significant since they distort the neat "marketing stimulus-consumer response" relation.

Along with active search for information, the buyer may, to some extent, generalize from past similar experiences. Such generalization can be due to physical similarity of the new product class to the old product class. For example, in the initial purchases of Scotch whisky, the buyer may generalize his experiences in buying of gin. Generalization can also occur even when the two product classes are physically dissimilar but have a common meaning such as deriving from a company-wide brand name. For example, the buyer could generalize his experiences in buying a refrigerator or range to his first purchase of a dishwasher of the same brand.

Whatever the source, the buyer develops sufficient decision mediators to enable him to choose a brand which seems to have the best potential for satisfying his motives. If the brand proves satisfactory, the potential of that brand to satisfy his motives is increased. The result is that the probability of buying that brand is likewise increased. With repeated satisfactory purchases of one or more brands, the buyer is likely to manifest a routinized decision process whereby the sequential steps in buying are well structured so that some event which triggers the process may actually complete the choice decision. Routinized purchasing implies that his decision mediators are well established and that the buyer has strong brand preferences.

The phase of repetitive decision making, in which the buyer reduces the complexity of a buying situation with the help of information and experience, is called the *psychology of simplification*. Decision making can be divided into three stages and used to illustrate the psychology of simplification: Extensive Problem Solving, Limited Problem Solving and Routinized Response Behavior. The further he is along in simplifying his environment, the less is the tendency toward active search behavior. The evvironmental stimuli related to the purchase situation become more meaningful and less ambiguous. Furthermore, the buyer establishes more cognitive consistency among the brands as he moves toward routinization and the incoming information is then screened both with regard to its magnitude and quality. He becomes less attentive to stimuli which do not fit his cognitive structure and he distorts those stimuli which are forced upon him.

A surprising phenomenon, we believe, occurs in many instances of frequently purchased products such as in grocery and personal care items. The buyer, after attaining routinization of his decision process, may find himself in too simple a situation. He is likely to feel the monotony or boredom associated with such repetitive decision making. It is also very likely that he is dissatisfied with even the most preferred brand. In both cases, he may feel that all existing alternatives including the preferred brand are unacceptable. He therefore, feels a need to *complicate* his buying situation by considering new brands, and this process can be called the *psychology of complication*. The new situation causes him to identify a new brand, and so he begins again to simplify in the manner described earlier. Thus with a frequently-purchased item buying is a continuing process with its ups and downs in terms of information seeking analogous to the familiar cyclical fluctuations in economic activity.

Elements of Theory

Any theory of human behavior needs some means for explaining individual differences. The marketing manager also is interested in differentiated masses of buyers. He wants to understand and separate individual differences so that he can classify or segment the total market based upon individual differences. By understanding the psychology of the individual buyer we may achieve this classification. Depending on the internal state of the buyer, a given stimulus may result in a given response. For example, one buyer who urgently needs a product may respond to the ad of a brand in that product class by buying it whereas another buyer who does not need the product may simply notice the ad and store the information or ignore the ad. A construct such as "level of motivation" will then explain the divergent reactions to the same stimulus. Alternately, two buyers may. both urgently need a product, but they buy two different brands. This can be explained by another construct: predisposition toward a brand.

Figure 1 represents the theory of buyer behavior. The central rectangular box isolates the various internal state variables and processes which combined together show the state of the buyer. The inputs to the rectangular box are the stimuli from the marketing and social environments. The outputs are a variety of responses that the buyer is likely to manifest based on the interaction between the stimuli and his internal state. Besides the inputs and outputs, there are a set of seven influences which affect the variables in the rectangular box.[5] These variables appear at the top of the diagram and are labelled "exogenous variables." Their function is to provide a means of adjusting for the interpersonal differences discussed above. The variables within the rectangular box serve the role of endogenous variables in the sense that changes in them are explained but they are something less than endogenous variables. They are not well defined and hence are not measurable. They are hypothetical constructs. Their values are inferred from relations among the output intervening variables. Several of the exogenous variables such as personality, social class and culture have traditionally been treated as part of the endogenous variables. We believe that they affect more specific variables, and by conceptualizing their effect as via the hypothetical constructs, we can better understand their role.

Thus it will be seen that the theory of buyer behavior has four major components: the stimulus variables, the response variables, the hypothetical constructs and the exogenous variables. We will elaborate on each of the components below both in terms of their substance and their interrelationships.

Stimulus Variables

At any point in time, the hypothetical constructs which reflect the buyer's internal state are affected by numerous stimuli from the environment. The environment is classified as Commerical or Social. The commercial environment is the marketing activities of various firms by which they attempt to communicate to the buyer. From the buyer's point of view, these communications basically come either via the physical brands themselves or some linguistic or pictorial representations of the attributes of the brands. If the elements of the brands such as price, quality, service, distinctiveness or availability are communicated through the physical brands (significates) then the stimuli are defined and classified as significative stimuli. If, on the other hand, the attributes are communicated in

FIGURE 1. A Theory of buyer behavior

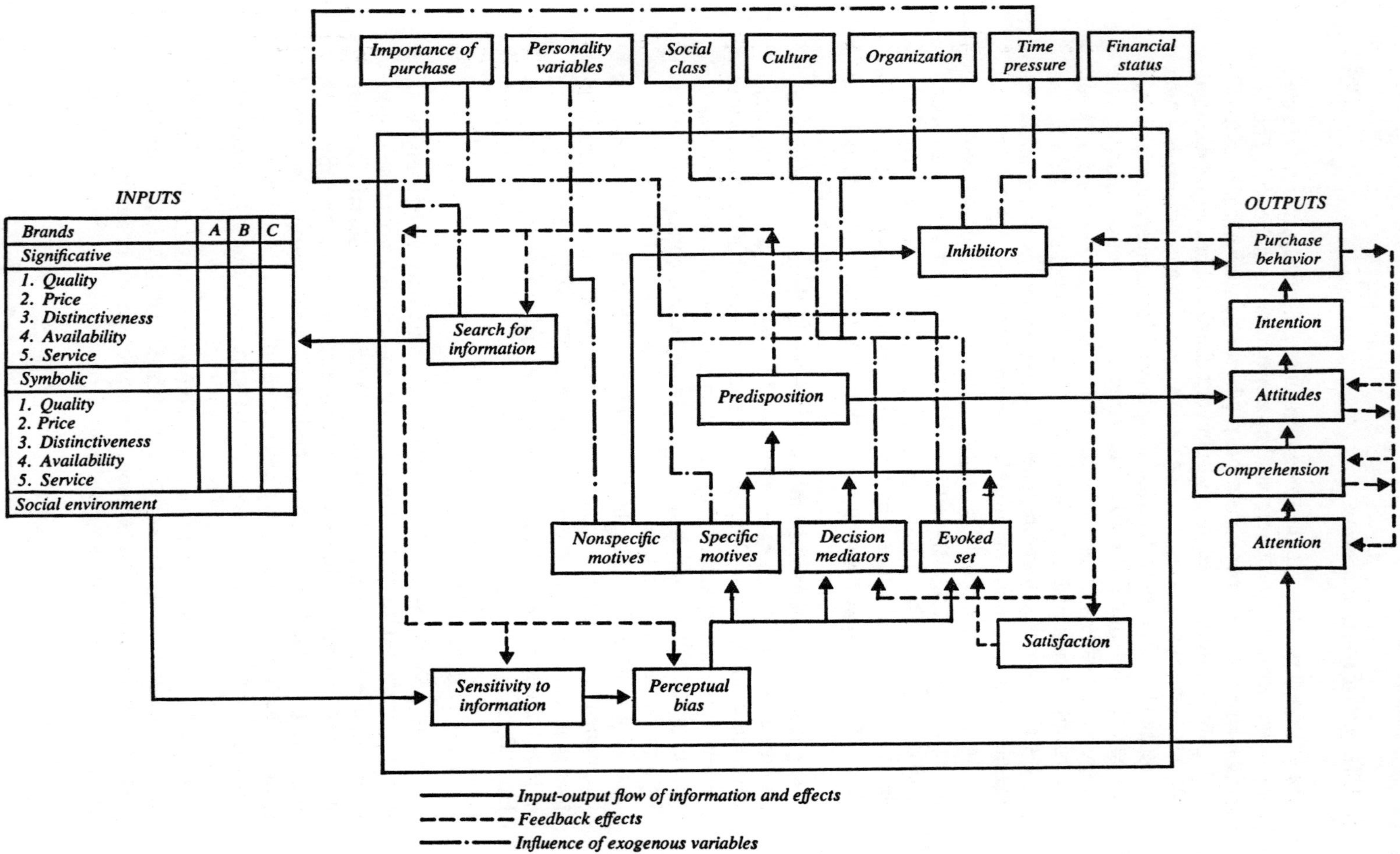

linguistic or pictorial symbols such as in mass media, billboards, catalogs, salesmen, etc. then the stimuli from commercial sources are classified as symbolic stimuli. We view the marketing mix as the optimum allocation of funds between the two major channels of communication—significative or symbolic—to the buyer.

Each commercial input variable is hypothesized to be multivariate. Probably the five major dimensions of a brand—price, quality, distinctiveness, availability and service—summarize the various attributes. The same dimensions are present in both significative or symbolic communication which become the input stimuli for the buyer. However, certain dimensions may be more appropriately conveyed by significative rather than symbolic communication and vice versa. For example, price is easily communicated by both channels; shape may best be communicated by two-dimensional pictures rather than verbal communication. Finally, size may not be easily communicated by any symbolic representation: the physical product (significate) may be necessary.

The third stimulus input variable is social stimuli. It refers to the information that the buyer's social environment provides regarding a purchase decision. The most obvious is word of mouth communication.

The inputs to the buyer's mental state from the three major sources are then processed and stored by their interaction with a series of hypothetical constructs, and the buyer may react immediately or later.

Hypothetical Constructs

The hypothetical constructs and their interrelationships are the result of an integration of Hull's learning theory,[6] Osgood's cognitive theory,[7] and Berlyne's theory of exploratory behavior[8] along with other ideas.

We may classify the constructs into two classes: (i) those that have to do with perception, and (ii) those having to do with learning. Perceptual constructs serve the function of information processing while the learning constructs serve the function of concept formation. It is interesting that, after years of experience in advertising, Reeves has a very similar classification:[9] his "penetration" is analogous to perceptual variables and his "unique selling propositions" is analogous to learning variables. We will at first describe the learning constructs since they are the major components of decision making; the perceptual constructs which serve the important role of obtaining and processing information are more complex and will be described later.

Learning Constructs. The learning constructs are labeled as (1) Motives—Specific and Nonspecific, (2) Brand Potential of Evoked Set, (3) Decision Mediators, (4) Predisposition toward the brands, (5) Inhibitors, and (6) Satisfaction with the purchase of the brand.

Motive is the impetus to action. Motives or goals may be thought of as constituting a means-end chain and hence, as being general or specific depending upon their position in the chain. Motives can refer to the buyer's specific goals in purchasing a product class. The buyer is motivated by the expectation or anticipation due to past learning of outcome from the purchase of each of the brands in his evoked set.

The specific motives—lower level motives in the means-end chain—are very closely anchored to the attributes of a product class and in this way they become purchase criteria. Examples of specific motives for buying a dietary product such as Metrecal or Sego are low calories, nutrition, taste, and value.

Very often, several specific motives are nothing more than indicators of some underlying more general motive, that is, some motive that is higher in the means-end chain. In the above example, the specific motives of nutrition and low calories might be merely indicators of the common motive of good health.

Motives also serve the important function of raising the buyer's general motivational state or arousal and thereby tuning up the buyer, causing him to pay attention to environmental stimuli. Examples of nonspecific motives are probably anxiety, fear, many of the personality variables such as authoritarianism, exhibitionism, aggressiveness, etc., and social motives of power, status, prestige, etc. Although they are nonspecific, they are not innate, but rather learned, mostly due to acculturation. The nonspecific motives also possess a hierarchy within themselves. For example, anxiety is considered to be the source of another motive, that of the need for money.[10]

Brand Potential of Evoked Set is the second learning construct. A buyer who is familiar with a product class has an evoked set of alternatives to satisfy his motives. The elements of his evoked set are some of the brands that make up the product class. The concept is important because for this buyer the brands in his evoked set constitute competition for the seller.

A brand is, of course, a class concept like many other objects or things. The buyer attaches a *word* to this concept—a label—which is the brand name such as "Campbell's Tomato Soup." Whenever he sees a can of Campbell's Tomato Soup or hears the phrase, the image conveys to him certain satisfactions, procedures for preparation, etc. In short, it conveys certain meaning including its potential to satisfy his motives.

Various brands in the buyer's evoked set will generally satisfy the goal structure differently. One brand may possess potential to the extent that it is an ideal brand for the buyer. Another brand, on the other hand, may satisfy motives just enough to be part of his evoked set. By the process of learning the buyer obtains and stores knowledge regarding each brand's potential and then rank orders them in terms of their want-satisfying potential. The evoked set, in short, is a set of alternatives with each alternative's payoff. Predisposition mentioned below enables the buyer to choose one among them.

Decision Mediator is the third learning construct and it brings together motives and alternatives. The brand potential of each of the brands in his evoked set are the decision alternatives with their payoffs. Decision mediators are the buyer's mental rules for matching the alternatives with his motives, for rank-ordering them in terms of their want-satisfying capacity. As mental rules, they exhibit reasons wherein the cognitive elements related to the alternatives and the motives are structured. The words that he uses to describe these attributes are also the words that he thinks with and that he finds are easy to remember. The criterial attributes are important to the manufacturer because if he knows them he can deliberately build into his brand and promotion those characteristics which will differentiate his brand from competing brands.

The decision mediators thus represent enduring cognitive rules established by the process of learning, and their function is to obtain meaningful and congruent relations among brands so that the buyer can manifest goal-directed behavior. The aim of the theory of buyer behavior is not just the identification of motives and the respective brands but to show their structure as well. It is the decision mediators which provide this structure.

In view of the fact that decision mediators are learned, principles of learning become crucial in their development and change over time. There are two broad sources of learning: (1) actual experience, and (2) information. Actual experience can be either with the *same* buying situation in the past or with a *similar* buying situation. The latter is generally labelled as generalization as discussed earlier. Similarly, information as a source of learning can be from: (1) the buyer's commercial environment, or (2) his social environment. Later, we will elaborate on each of the sources of learning.

Predisposition, the fourth construct, is the summary effect of the previous three constructs. It refers to the buyer's preference toward brands in his evoked set. It is, in fact, an aggregate index which is reflected in attitude which, in turn, is measured by attitude scales. It might be visualized as the "place" where brands in Evoked Set are compared with Mediator's choice criteria to yield a judgment on the relative contribution of the brands to the buyer's motives. This judgment includes not only an estimate of the value of the brand to him but also an estimate of the confidence with which he holds that position. This uncertainty aspect of

Predisposition can be called "brand ambiguity," in that, the more confident he holds it, the less ambiguous is the connotative meaning of the brand to the buyer and the more likely he is to buy it.[11]

Inhibitors, the fifth learning construct, are forces in the environment which create important disruptive influences in the actual purchase of a brand even when the buyer has reasoned out that that brand will best satisfy his motives. In other words, when the buyer is both predisposed to buy a brand and has the motivation to buy some brand in the product class, he may not buy it because several environmental forces inhibit its purchase and prevent him from satisfying his preferences.

We postulate at least four types of inhibitors. They are: (1) high price of the brand, (2) lack of availability of the brand, (3) time pressure on the buyer, and (4) the buyer's financial status. The first two are part of the environmental stimuli, and therefore, they are part of the input system. The last two come from the two exogenous variables of the same name. It should be pointed out that social constraints emanating from other exogenous variables may also create temporary barriers to the purchase of a brand.

An essential feature of all inhibitors is that they are *not internalized* by the buyer because their occurrence is random and strictly situational. However, some of the inhibitors may persist systematically over time as they concern a given buyer. If they persist long enough, the buyer is likely to incorporate them as part of his decision mediators and thus to internalize them. The consequence is that they may affect even the structure of alternatives and motives.

Satisfaction, the last of the learning constructs, refers to the degree of congruence between the actual consequences from purchase and consumption of a brand and what was expected from it by the buyer at the time of purchase. If the actual outcome is adjudged by the buyer as *at least* equal to the expected, the buyer will feel satisfied. If, on the other hand, the actual outcome is adjudged as less than what he expected, the buyer will feel dissatisfied and his attitude will be less favorable. Satisfaction or dissatisfaction with a brand can exist with respect to any one of the different attributes. If the brand proves more satisfactory than he expected, the buyer has a tendency to enhance the attractiveness of the brand. Satisfaction will, therefore, affect the reordering of the brands in the evoked set for the next buying decision.

Relations Among Learning Constructs. Underlying Predisposition toward the brands and related variables, several important notions are present. The simplest way to describe them is to state that we may classify a decision process as either Extensive Problem Solving, Limited Problem

Solving or Routinized Response Behavior depending on the strength of Predisposition toward the brands. In the early phases of buying the buyer has not yet developed decision mediators well enough; specifically his product class concept is not well formed and predisposition is low. As he acquires information and gains experience in buying and consuming the brand, Decision Mediators become firm and Predisposition toward a brand is generally high.

In Extensive Problem Solving, Predisposition toward the brands is low. None of the brands is discriminated enough based on their criterial attributes for the buyer to show greater brand preference toward any one brand. At this state of decision making, brand ambiguity is high with the result that the buyer actively seeks information from his environment. Due to greater search for information, there exists a greater *latency of response*—the time interval from the initiation of a decision to its completion. Similarly, deliberation or reasoning will be high since he lacks a well-defined product class concept which is the denotative aspect of mediator. He is also likely to consider many brands as part of Evoked Set, and stimuli coming from the commercial environment are less likely to trigger any immediate purchase reaction.

When Predisposition toward the brands is moderate, the buyer's decision process can be called Limited Problem Solving. There still exists brand ambiguity since the buyer is not able to discriminate and compare brands so that he may prefer one brand over others. He is likely to see information but not to the extent that he seeks it in Extensive Problem Solving. More importantly, he seeks information more on a relative basis to compare and discriminate various brands rather than to compare them absolutely on each of the brands. His deliberation or thinking is much less since Decision Mediators are tentatively well defined. Evoked Set will consist of a small number of brands, each having about the same degree of preference.

In Routinized Response Behavior, the buyer will have a high level of Predisposition toward brands in his evoked set. Furthermore, he has now accumulated sufficient experience and information to have little brand ambiguity. He will in fact discriminate among brands enough to show a strong preference toward one or two brands in the evoked set. He is unlikely to actively seek any information from his environment since such information is not needed. Also, whatever information he passively or accidentally receives, he will subject it to selective perceptual processes so that only congruent information is allowed. Very often, the congruent information will act as "triggering cues" to motivate him to manifest purchase behavior. Much of impulse purchase, we believe, is really the outcome of a strong predisposition and such a facilitating commercial stimulus as store display. The buyer's evoked set will consist of a few brands toward which he is highly predisposed. However, he will have greater preference toward one or two brands in his evoked set and less toward others.

As mentioned earlier, Predisposition is an aggregate index of decision components. Thus, any changes in the components due to learning from experience or information imply some change in Predisposition. The greater the learning, the more the predisposition toward the brands in the evoked set. The exact nature of learning will be described later when we discuss the dynamics of buying behavior.

Perceptual Constructs. Another set of constructs serves the function of information procurement and processing relevant to a purchase decision. As mentioned earlier, information can come from any one of the three stimulus inputs—significative commercial stimuli, symbolic commercial stimuli, and social stimuli. Once again we will here only describe the constructs; their utilization by the buyer will be explained when we discuss the dynamics of buying behavior. The perceptual constructs in Figure 1 are: (a) Sensitivity to Information, (b) Perceptual Bias, and (c) Search for Information.

A perceptual phenomenon implies either ignoring a physical event which could be a stimulus, seeing it attentively or sometimes imagining what is not present in reality. All perceptual phenomena essentially create some change in quantity or quality of objective information.

Sensitivity to Information refers to the opening and closing of sensory receptors which control the intake of information. The manifestation of this phenomenon is generally called perceptual vigilance (paying attention) or perceptual defense (ignoring the information). Sensitivity to Information, therefore, primarily serves as a gatekeeper to information entering into the buyer's mental state. It thus controls the quantity of information input.

Sensitivity to Information, according to Berlyne,[12] is a function of the degree of ambiguity of the stimuli to which the buyer is exposed. If the stimulus is very familiar or too simple, the ambiguity is low and the buyer will not pay attention unless he is predisposed to such information from past learning. Furthermore, if ambiguity of the stimulus continues to be low, the buyer feels a sense of monotony and actually seeks other information, and this act can be said to *complicate* his environment. If the stimulus is very complex and ambiguous, the buyer finds it hard to comprehend and, therefore, he ignores it by resorting to perceptual defense. Only if the stimulus is in the moderate range of ambiguity is the buyer motivated to pay attention and to freely absorb the objective information.

In a single communication, the buyer may at first find the communication complex and ambiguous and so he will resort to perceptual defense and tend to ignore it. As some information enters, however, he finds that it is really at the medium level of ambiguity and so pays attention. On the other hand, it might be that the more he pays attention to it, the more he finds the communication too simple and, therefore, ignores it as the process of communication progresses.

A second variable which governs Sensitivity to Information is the buyer's predisposition toward the brand about which the information is concerned. The more interesting the information, the more likely the buyer is to open up his receptors and therefore to pay attention to the information. Hess has recently measured this by obtaining the strength of pupil dilation.

Perceptual Bias is the second perceptual construct. The buyer not only selectively attends to information, but he may actually distort it once it enters his mental state. In other words, quality of information can be altered by the buyer. This aspect of the perceptual process is summarized in Perceptual Bias. The buyer may distort the cognitive elements contained in information to make them congruent with his own frame of reference as determined by the amount of information he already has stored. A series of cognitive consistency theories have been recently developed to explain how this congruency is established and what the consequences are in terms of the distortion of information that we might expect.[13] Most of the qualitative change in information arises because of feedback from various decision components such as Motives, Evoked Set and Decision Mediators. These relations are too complex, however, to describe in the summary.

The perceptual phenomena described above are likely to be less operative if the information is received from the buyer's social environment. This is because: (i) the source of social information, such as a friend, is likely to be favorably regarded by the buyer and therefore proper, undistorted reception of information will occur, and (ii) the information itself is modified by the social environment (the friend) so that it conforms to the needs of the buyer and, therefore, further modification is less essential.

Search for Information is the third perceptual construct. During the total buying phase which extends over time and involves several repeat purchases of a product class, there are stages when the buyer *actively* seeks information. It is very important to distinguish the times when he passively receives information from the situations where he actively seeks it. We believe that perceptual distortion is less operative in the latter instances and that a commercial communication, therefore, at that stage has a high probability of influencing the buyer.

The active seeking of information occurs when the buyer senses ambiguity of the brands in his evoked set. As we saw earlier, this happens in the Extensive Problem Solving and Limited Problem Solving phases of the decision process. The ambiguity of brand exists because the buyer is not certain of the outcomes from each brand. In other words, he has not yet learned enough about the alternatives to establish an expectancy of potential of the brands to satisfy his motives. This type of brand ambiguity is essentially confined to initial buyer behavior which we have called Extensive Problem Solving. However, ambiguity may still exist despite knowledge of the potential of alternatives. The buyer may be unable to discriminate because his motives are not well structured: he does not know how to order them. He may then seek information which will resolve the conflict among goals, a resolution that is implied in his learning of the appropriate product class aspect of decision mediators that we discussed earlier.

There is yet another stage of total buying behavior in which the buyer is likely to seek information. It is when the buyer has not only routinized his decision process but he is so familiar and satiated with repeat buying that he feels bored. Then, all the existing alternatives in his evoked set including the most preferred brand become unacceptable to him. He seeks change or variety in that buying situation. In order to obtain this change, he actively searches for information on other alternatives (brands) that he never considered before. At this stage, he is particularly receptive to any information about new brands. Incidentally, here is an explanation for advertising in a highly stable industry. This phenomenon has long baffled both the critics and defenders of the institution of advertising. Newcomers to the market and forgetting do not provide a plausible explanation.

We have so far described the stimulus input variables and the hypothetical constructs. Now we proceed to describe the output of the system—the responses of the buyer.

Response Variables

The complexity of buyer behavior does not stop with the hypothetical constructs. Just as there is a variety of inputs, there exists a variety of buyer responses which becomes relevant for different areas of marketing strategy. This variety of consumer responses can be easily appreciated from the diversity of measures to evaluate advertising effectiveness. We have attempted to classify and order this diversity of buyer responses in the output variables. Most of the output variables are directly related to some and not other constructs. Each output variable serves different purposes both in marketing practice and fundamental research. Let us at first describe each variable and then provide a rationale for their interrelationships.

Attention. Attention is related to Sensitivity to Information. It is a response of the buyer which indicates the magnitude of his information intake. Attention is measured continuously during the time interval when the buyer receives information. There are several psychophysical methods of quantifying the degree of attention that the buyer pays to a message. The pupil dilation is one.

Comprehension. Comprehension refers to the store of knowledge about the brand that the buyer possesses at any point in time. This knowledge could vary from his simply being aware of a single brand's existence to a complete description of the attributes of the product class of which the brand is an element. It reflects the denotative meaning of the brand and in that sense it is strictly in the cognitive realm. It lacks the motivational aspects of behavior. Some of the standard measures of advertising effectiveness such as awareness, aided or unaided recall, and recognition may capture different aspects of the buyer's comprehension of the brand.

Attitude toward a Brand. Attitude toward a brand is the buyer's evaluation of the brand's potential to satisfy his motives. It, therefore, includes the connotative aspects of the brand concept: it contains those aspects of the brand which are relevant to the buyer's goals. Attitude is directly related to Predisposition and so it consists of both the evaluation of a brand in terms of the criteria of choice from Mediator and the confidence with which that evaluation is held.

Intention to Buy. Intention to buy is the buyer's forecast of his brand choice some time in the future. Like any forecast, it involves assumptions about future events including the likelihood of any perceived inhibitors creating barriers over the buyer's planning horizon. Intention to buy has been extensively used in the purchase of durable goods with some recent refinements in terms of the buyer's confidence in his own forecast; these studies are in terms of broadly defined product classes.[14] We may summarize this response of the buyer as something short of actual purchase behavior.

Purchase Behavior. Purchase Behavior refers to the overt act of purchasing a brand. What becomes a part of company's sales or what the consumer records in a diary as a panel member, however, is only the terminal act in the sequence of shopping and buying. Very often, it is useful to observe the complete movement of the buyer from his home to the store and his purchase in the store. Yoell, for example, shows several case histories where a time and motion study of consumer's purchase behavior have useful marketing implications.[15] We think that at times it may be helpful to go so far as to incorporate the act of consumption into the definition of Purchase Behavior. We have, for example, developed and used the technique of sequential decision making where the buyer verbally describes the sequential pattern of his purchase behavior in a given buying situation. Out of this description a "flow chart" of decision making is obtained which reveals the number and the structure of the decision rules that the buyer employs.

Purchase Behavior is the overt manifestation of the buyer's Predisposition in conjunction with any Inhibitors that may be present. It differs from Attitude to the extent that Inhibitors are taken into consideration. It differs from Intention to the extent that it is the actual manifestation of behavior which the buyer only forecasted in his intention.

Several characteristics of Purchase Behavior become useful if we observe the buyer in a repetitive buying situation. These include the incidence of buying a brand, the quantity bought, and the purchase cycle. Several stochastic models of brand loyalty, for example, have been developed in recent years.[16] Similarly, we could take the magnitude purchased and compare light buyers with heavy buyers to determine if heavy buyers are more loyal buyers.

Interrelationship of Response Variables. In Figure 1, it will be seen that we have ordered the five response variables to create a hierarchy. The hierarchy is similar to the variety of hierarchies used in practice such as AIDA (Attention, Interest, Desire and Action), to the Lavidge and Steiner hierarchy of advertising effectiveness,[17] as well as to the different mental states that a person is alleged by the anthropologists and sociologists to pass through when he adopts an innovation.[18] There are, however, some important differences which we believe will clarify certain conceptual and methodological issues raised by Palda and others[19]

First, we have added a response variable called Attention which is crucial since it reflects whether a communication is received by the buyer. Secondly, several different aspects of the cognitive realm of behavior such as awareness, recall, recognition, etc. are lumped into one category called Comprehension to suggest that they all are varying indicators of the buyer's storage of information about a brand which can be extended to *product class*, and in this way we obtain leverage toward understanding buyer innovation. Third, we have defined Attitude to include both affective and conative aspects since anyone who wants to establish casual relations between attitude and behavior must bring the motivational aspects into attitude. Furthermore, we separate the perceptual and the preference maps of the buyer into Comprehension and Attitude respectively. Fourth, we add another variable, Intention to Buy, because there are several product classes in both durable and semi-durable goods where properly defined and measured intentions have already proved useful. To the extent that Intention incoporates the buyer's forecast of his inhibitors, it might serve the useful functions of informing the firm how to remove the inhibitors before the actual purchase behavior is manifested.

Finally, and most importantly, we have incorporated several feedback effects which were described when we discussed the hypothetical constructs. We will now show the relations as direct connections among response variables but the reader should bear in mind that these "outside" relations are merely the reflection of relations among the hypothetical constructs. For example, Purchase Behavior via Satisfaction entails some consequences which affect Decision Mediators and brand potential in Evoked Set; any change in them can produce change in Predisposition. Attitude is related to Predisposition and, therefore, it can also be changed in the period from pre-purchase to post-purchase. In incorporating this feedback, we are opening the way to resolving the controversy whether Attitude causes Purchase Behavior or Purchase Behavior causes attitude. Over a period of time, the relation is interdependent, each affecting the other. Similarly, we have a feedback from Attitude to Comprehension and Attention, the rationale for which was given when we described the perceptual constructs.

Dynamics of Buying Behavior

Let us now explain the changes in the hypothetical constructs which occur due to learning.

The learning constructs are, of course, directly involved in the change that we label "learning." Since some of the learning constructs indirectly govern the perceptual constructs by way of feedbacks, there is also an indirect effect back upon the learning constructs themselves. As mentioned earlier, learning of Decision Mediators which structure Motives and Evoked Set of Brands which contain brand potentials can occur from two broad sources: (i) past experience and (ii) information. Experience can be further classified as having been derived from buying a specified product or buying some similar product. Similarly, information can come from the buyer's commercial environment or his social environment, and if commercial, it can be significative or symbolic.

We will look at the development and change in learning constructs as due to: (i) generalization from similar buying situations, (ii) repeat buying of the same product class, and (iii) information.

Generalization from Similar Purchase Situations

Some decision mediators are common across several product classes because many motives are common to a wide variety of purchasing activity. For example, a buyer may satisfy his health motive from many product classes by looking for nutrition. Similarly, many product classes are all bought at the same place which very often leads to spatial or contiguous generalization. The capacity to generalize provides the buyer with a truly enormous range of flexibility in adapting his purchase behavior to the myriad of varying market conditions he faces.

Generalization refers to the transfer of responses and of the relevance of stimuli from past situations to new situations which are similar. It saves the buyer time and effort in seeking information in the face of uncertainity that is inevitable in a new situation. Generalization can occur at any one of the several levels of purchase activity, but we are primarily interested in generalization of those decision mediators which only involve brand choice behavior in contrast to store choice or choice of shopping time and day. In other words, we are concerned with brand generalization.

Repeat Purchase Experiences

Another source of change in the learning constructs is the repeated purchase of the same product class over a period of time.

In Figure 1 the purchase of a brand entails two types of feedbacks, one affecting the decision mediators and the other affecting the brand potential of the evoked set. First, the experience of buying with all its cognitive aspects of memory, reasoning, etc. has a learning effect on the decision mediators. This occurs irrespective of which specific brand the buyer chooses in any one purchase decision because the decision mediators like the motives are product-specific and not limited to any one brand. Hence every purchase has an incremental effect in firmly establishing the decision mediators. This is easy to visualize if we remember that buying behavior is a series of mental and motor steps while the actual choice is only its terminal act.

Purchase of a brand creates certain satisfactions for the buyer which the consumer compares with his expectations of the brand's potential and this expectation is the basis on which he made his decision in the first place. This comparison of expected and actual consequences causes him to be satisfied or dissatisfied with his purchase of the brand. Hence, the second feedback from Purchase Behavior to Satisfaction changes the attractiveness of the brand purchased. If the buyer is satisfied with his consumption, he enhances the potential of the brand and this is likely to result in greater probability of its repeat purchase. If he is dissatisfied, the potential of the brand is diminished, and its probability of repeat purchase is also similarly reduced.

If there are no inhibitory forces which influence him, the buyer will continue to buy a brand which proves satisfactory. In the initial stages of decision making he may show some tendency to oscillate between brands in order to formulate his decision mediators. In other words, he may learn by trial-and-error at first and then settle on a brand and thereafter he may buy the brand with such regularity to suggest that he is brand loyal. Unless a product is of very high risk, however, there is a limit as to how long this brand loyalty will continue: he may become bored with his preferred brand and look for something new.

Information as a Source of Learning

The third major source by which the learning constructs are changed is information from the buyer's (i) commercial environment consisting of advertising, promotion, salesmanship and retail shelf display of the competing companies, and (ii) his social environment consisting of his family, friends, reference group and social class.

We will describe the influence of information at first as if the perceptual constructs were absent. In other words, we assume that the buyer receives information with perfect fidelity as it exists in the environment. Also, we will discuss separately the information from the commercial and social environments.

Commercial Environment. The company communicates about its offerings to the buyers either by the physical brand (significates) or by symbols (pictorial or linguistic) which represent the brand. In other words, significative and symbolic communication are the two major ways of interaction between the sellers and the buyers.

In Figure 1, the influence of information is shown on Motives, Decision Mediators, Evoked Set, and Inhibitors. We believe that the influence of commercial information on motives (specific and nonspecific) is limited. The main effect is primarily to *intensify* whatever motives the buyer has rather than to create new ones. For example, physical display of the brand may intensify his motives above the threshold level which combined with strong predisposition can result in impulse (unplanned) purchase. A similar reaction is possible when an ad creates sufficient intensity of motives to provide an impetus for the buyer to go to the store. A second way to influence motives is to show the *perceived instrumentality* of the brand and thereby make it a part of the buyer's defined set of alternatives. Finally, to a very limited extent, marketing stimuli may change the *content of the motives*. The general conception both among marketing men and laymen is that marketing stimuli change the buyer's motives. However, on a closer examination it would appear that what is changed is the *intensity* of buyer's motives already provided by the social environment. Many dormant or latent motives may become stimulated. The secret of success very often lies in identifying the change in motives created by social change and intensifying them as seems to be the case in the recent projection of youthfulness in many buying situations.

Marketing stimuli are also important in determining and changing the buyer's evoked set. Commercial information tells him of the existence of the brands (awareness), their identifying characteristics (Comprehension plus brand name) and their relevance to the satisfaction of the buyer's needs (Attitude).

Marketing stimuli are also important in creating and changing the buyer's decision mediators. They become important sources for learning decision mediators when the buyer has no prior experience to reply upon. In other words, when he is in the extensive problem-solving (ESP) stage, it is marketing and social stimuli which are the important sources of learning. Similarly, when the buyer actively seeks information because all the existing alternatives are unacceptable to him, marketing stimuli become important in *changing* his decision mediators.

Finally, marketing stimuli can unwittingly create inhibitors. For example, a company feels the need to emphasize price-quality association, but it may result in high-price inhibition in the mind of the buyer. Similarly, in emphasizing the details of usage and consumption of a product, the communication may create the inhibition related to time pressure.

Social Environment. The social environment of the buyer—family, friends, reference groups—is another major source of information in his buying behavior. Most of the inputs are likely to be symbolic (linguistic) although at times the physical product may be shown to the buyer.

Information from his social environment also affects the four learning constructs: Motives, Decision Mediators, Evoked Set and Inhibitors. However, the effect on these constructs is different from that of the commercial environment. First, the information about the brands will be considerably modified by the social environment before it reaches the buyer. Most of the modifications are likely to be in the nature of adding connotative meanings to brand descriptions, and of the biasing effects of the communication's perceptual variables like Sensitivity to Information and Perceptual Bias. Second, the buyer's social environment will probably have a very strong influence on the content of his motives and their ordering to establish a goal structure. Several research studies have concentrated on such influences.[20] Third, the social environment may also affect his evoked set. This will be particularly true when the buyer lacks experience. Furthermore, if the product class is important to the buyer and he is technically incompetent or uncertain in evaluating the consequences of the brand for his needs, he may rely more on the social than on the marketing environment for information. This is well documented by several studies using the perceived risk hypothesis.[21]

Exogenous Variables

Earlier we mentioned that there are several influences operating on the buyer's decisions which we treat as exogenous, that is, we do not explain their formation and change. Many of these influences come from the buyer's social environment and we wish to separate the effects of his environment which have occurred in the past and are not related to a specific decision from those which are current and directly affect the decisions that occur during the period the buyer is being observed. The inputs during the observation period provide information to the buyer to help his current decision making. The past influences are already imbedded in the values of the perceptual and learning constructs. Strictly speaking, therefore, there is no need for some of the exogenous variables which have influenced the buyer in the past. We bring them out explicitly, however, for the sake of research design where the research may control or take into account individual differences among buyers due to such past influences. Incorporating the effects of these exogenous variables will reduce the size of the unexplained variance or error in estimation which it is particularly essential to control under field conditions. Figure 1 presents a set of exogenous variables which we believe provide the control essential to obtaining satisfactory predictive relations between the inputs and the outputs of the system. Let us briefly discuss each of the exogenous variables.

Importance of Purchase refers to differential degrees of ego-involvement or commitment in different product classes. It, therefore, provides a mechanism which must be carefully examined in inter-product studies. Importance of Purchase will influence the size of the Evoked Set and the magnitude of Search for Information. The more important the product class, the larger the Evoked Set.

Time Pressure is a current exogenous variable and, therefore, specific to a decision situation. It refers to the situation when a buyer feels pressed for time due to any of several environmental influences and so must allocate his time among alternative uses. In this process a re-allocation unfavorable to the purchasing activity can occur. Time pressure will create Inhibition as mentioned earlier. It will also unfavorably affect Search for Information.

Financial Status refers to the constraint the buyer may feel because of lack of financial resources. This affects his purchase behavior to the extent that it creates a barrier to purchasing the most preferred brand. For example, a buyer may want to purchase a Mercedes-Benz but lacks sufficient financial resources and, therefore, he will settle for some low-priced American automobile such as a Ford or Chevrolet. Its effect is via Inhibitor.

Personality Traits take into consideration many of the variables such as self-confidence, self-esteem, authoritarianism and anxiety which have been researched to identify individual differences. It will be noted that these individual differences are "topic free" and, therefore, are supposed to exert their effect across product classes. We believe their effect is felt on: (i) nonspecific Motives and (ii) Evoked Set. For example, the more anxious a person, the greater the motivational arousal; dominant personalities are more likely by a small margin to buy a Ford instead of a Chevrolet; the more authoritarian a person, the narrower the category width of his evoked set.

Social and Organizational Setting (Organization) takes us to the group, to a higher level of social organization than the individual. It includes both the informal social organization such as family and reference groups which are relevant for *consumer behavior* and the formal organization which constitutes much of the environment for *industrial purchasing*. Organizational variables are those of small group interaction such as power, status and authority. We believe that the underlying process of intergroup conflicts in both industrial and consumer buying behavior are in principle very similar and that the differences are largely due to the formalization of industrial activity. Organization, both formal and social, is a crucial variable because it influences all the learning constructs.

Social Class refers to a still higher level of social organization, the social aggregate. Several indices are available to classify people into various classes. The most common perhaps is the Warner classification of people into upper-upper, lower-upper, upper-middle, lower-middle, upper-lower, and lower-lower classes. Social class mediates the relation between the input and the output by influencing: (i) specific Motives, (ii) Decision Mediators, (iii) Evoked Set, and (iv) Inhibitors. The latter influence is important particularly in the adoption of innovations.

Culture provides an even more comprehensive social framework than social class. Culture consists of patterns of behavior, symbols, ideas and their attached values. Culture will influence Motives, Decision Mediators, and Inhibitors.

Conclusions

In the preceding pages we have summarized a theory of buyer brand choice. It is complex. We strongly believe that complexity is essential to adequately describe buying behavior, from the point of view of both marketing practice and public policy.

We hope that the theory can provide new insights into past empirical data and to guide future research so as to instill with coherence and unity current research which now tends to be atomistic and unrelated. We are vigorously pursuing a large research program aimed at testing the validity of the theory. The research was designed in terms of the variables specified by the theory, and our most preliminary results cause us to believe that it was fruitful to use the theory in this way. Because it specifies a number of relationships, it has clearly been useful in interpreting the preliminary findings. Above all, it is an aid in communication among the researchers and with the companies involved.

Finally, a number of new ideas are set forth in the theory, but we would like to call attention to three in particular. The concept of evoked set provides a means of reducing the noise in many analyses of buying behavior. The product class concept offers a new dimension for incorporating many of the complexities of innovations and especially for integrating systematically the idea of innovation into a framework of psychological constructs. Anthropologists and sociologists have been pretty much content to deal with peripheral variables in their investigations of innovation. The habit-perception cycle in which perception and habit respond inversely offers hope for explaining a large proportion of the phenomenon that has long baffled both the critics and defenders of advertising: large advertising expenditures in a stable market where, on the surface, it would seem that people are already sated with information.

NOTES

1. Theodore Levitt, *Innovation in Marketing: New Perspectives for Growth* (New York: McGraw-Hill Book Company, 1962).
2. Jack B. McKitterick, "What Is the Marketing Management Concept?" in Frank M. Bass (ed.). *The Frontiers of Marketing Thought and Science* (Chicago: American Marketing Association, 1957), pp. 71–82.
3. George Katona, *The Powerful Consumer* (New York: McGraw-Hill Book Company, 1960).
4. John A. Howard, *Marketing Theory* (Boston: Allyn and Bacon, 1965), Chapter 1.
5. Lester Guest, "Consumer Analysis," *Annual Review of Psychology*, Vol. 13 (1962), pp. 315–344; Frederick May, "Buying Behavior: Some Research Findings," *Journal of Business* (October 1965), pp. 379–396; Dik Warren Twedt, "Consumer Psychology," *Annual Review of Psychology*, Vol. 16 (1965), pp. 265–294; Jagdish N. Sheth, "A Review of Buyer Behavior," *Management Science*, Vol. 13 (August 1967), pp. B718–B756.
6. Jagdish N. Sheth, *op. cit.*, p. B742.
7. Musafer Sherif and Carolyn Sherif, "Interdisciplinary Coordination as a Validity Check: Retrospect and Prospects" in M. Sherif (ed.) *Problems of Interdisciplinary Relationships in the Social Sciences* (Aldine Publishing Company, 1968).

8. William J. McGuire, "Some Impending Reorientations in Social Psychology," *Journal of Experimental Social Psychology*, Vol. 3 (1967), pp. 124–139.

9. Patrick Suppes, *Information Processing and Choice Behavior* (Technical Paper No. 9: Institute for Mathematical Studies in the Social Sciences, Stanford University, January 31, 1966), p. 27.

10. John A. Howard, *Marketing Management* (Revised edition; R. D. Irwin, Inc., 1963); J. A. Howard, *Marketing: Executive and Buyer Behavior* (Columbia University Press, 1963).

11. James G. March and Herbert A. Simon, *Organizations* (New York: John Wiley & Sons, 1958).

12. Terminology in a problem area that cuts across both economics and psychology is different because each discipline has often defined its terms differently from the other. We find the economist's definitions of exogenous versus endogenous and theory versus model more useful than those of the psychologist. The psychologist's distinction of hypothetical constructs and intervening variables, however, provides a helpful breakdown of endogenous variables. Finally, for the sake of exposition we have often here not clearly distinguished between the theory and its empirical counterparts. Although this practice encourages certain ambiguities and we lay ourselves open to the charge of reifying our theory, we believe that for most readers it will simplify the task of comprehending the material.

13. Clark C. Hull, *Principles of Behavior* (New York: Appleton-Century-Crofts, Inc., 1943); Clark C. Hull, *A Behavior System* (New Haven: Yale University Press, 1952).

14. Charles E. Osgood, "A Behavioristic Analysis of Perception and Meaning as Cognitive Phenomena" in *Symposium on Cognition, University of Colorado, 1955* (Cambridge, Harvard University Press, 1957), pp. 75–119; Charles E. Osgood, "Motivational Dynamics of Language Behavior" in J. R. Jones (ed.) *Nebraska Symposium on Motivation*, 1957 (Lincoln: University of Nebraska Press, 1957), pp. 348–423.

15. D. E. Berlyne, "Motivational Problems Raised by Exploratory and Epistemic Behavior" in Sigmund Koch (ed.) *Psychology: A Study of a Science*, Vol. 5 (New York: McGraw-Hill Book Company, 1963).

16. Rosser Reeves, *Reality in Advertising* (New York: Alfred A. Knopf, Inc., 1961).

17. J. S. Brown, *The Motivation of Behavior* (New York: McGraw-Hill Book Company, 1961).

18. George S. Day, "Buyer Attitudes and Brand Choice Behavior" (unpublished Ph.D. Dissertation, Graduate School of Business, Columbia University, 1967).

19. Berlyne, *op. cit.*

20. S. Feldman (ed.) *Cognitive Consistency: Motivational Antecedents and Behavioral Consequents* (Academic Press, 1966); Martin Fishbein (ed.) *Readings in Attitude Theory and Measurement* (New York: John Wiley & Sons, 1967).

21. Thomas F. Juster, *Anticipations and Purchases: An Analysis of Consumer Behavior* (Princeton University Press, 1964).

LEARNING REVIEW

Questions:

1. Stimulus variables come from a ____________ or a ____________ environment.

2. Development and change in learning constructs may be due to ____________ ____________, ____________________________, or____________.

3. The psychology of simplification is the phase of decision making in which the

buyer reduces the complexity of a buying situation with the help of ____________ and ____________.

Answers:

1. commercial, social 2. a) generalization from similar buying situations, b) repeat buying of the same product class, c) information 3. information, experience.

Retrospective Comment

Since this article was written, there have been, on the surface, profound changes. Yet, most of these could be said to be implied in this article. First, the structure of some of the individual constructs have been more fully explored. The most striking has been the case of attitude, where Professor Sheth in particular has continued pioneering work. Second, the system has become more sharply articulated and fully specified. Later research has shown, for example, that the system is more complex the constructs are more interrelated—than shown here. Third, the system, in general, has moved more from a traditional learning point of view to information processing and concept formation. Fourth, it has become almost fully mathematized. The earliest attempt is described in Farley, Howard and Ring (eds), *Consumer Behavior: Theory and Application*, Allyn and Bacon, 1974, with an introduction by the eminent sociologist Paul F. Lazarsfeld, who places this work in the mainstream of developments in social science. The earlier mathematization was linear in nature, but recently non-linear relations have been introduced. Still more recently, a non-linear dynamics system with feedbacks has been developed.

Finally, the work has moved much more in the direction of application. To ascertain the generality of the system, e.g. across cultures and products, it has been applied to the introduction of an instant breakfast (1966), to a perfumed soap in another culture (1969), and to a large consumer durable (1970). It has been articulated in the context of public policy, and criteria for socially evaluating marketing activity have been derived from it in Howard and Hulbert, *Advertising and the Public Interest: A Federal Trade Commission Report* (Crain Communications, Inc., 1973). In the area of social marketing, Professor Farley has applied it to population control problems in Kenya.

John A. Howard

Since publishing our theory of buyer behavior as a book in 1969 (J. A. Howard and J. N. Sheth, *The Theory of Buyer Behavior*, John Wiley and Sons), the theory has been widely accepted as a major scientific contribution to the development of marketing thought and practice. It provided impetus for a very large scale empirical research at Columbia University primarily to test the theory in its totality. Surprising to both of the authors, the theory has been utilized by marketing practitioners as a market research tool and perspective and some companies have even attempted to build their market research information systems based on the Howard-Sheth theory.

I have continued to extend the theory to more complicated areas of consumer behavior including family buying decisions and industrial buying decisions. The other author has extended it to provide a public policy viewpoint of advertising and its regulation. We are both continuing to empirically validate the theory by replicating studies.

Jagdish N. Sheth

PART 4

The Product Decision in the Marketing Mix

How do you define "sizzle?"

Brand extension, product life cycle, product management, product deletion, use-facilitating attributes. . . . a whole new vocabulary exists for the marketer to learn concerning just the product decision in the marketing mix. The thousands of salesmen who have been advised to *sell the sizzle* were pointed in the right direction. Fortunately the marketing literature did not stop there but went ahead to define the sizzle, to research the many dimensions of the *total product*.

Don't get locked in with the past

The product decision area of marketing is not independent, of course, from other decision variables in pricing, logistics, and advertising. The critical point is that the decision maker must not get locked into the traditional patterns of combining these variables. He must, as Lee Adler suggests in the first selection in this section, look for "A New Orientation for Plotting Marketing Strategy."

Crystal balls, interfaces, audits, and reconciliations

Chester Wasson's "How Predictable Are Fashion and Other Product Life Cycles," suggests that marketers are not wholly at the mercy of capricious consumers, but that an early warning system for selecting saleable inventory is possible. David Luck gives direction to the product manager role—an organizational arrangement which continues to be debated and often revised. Professor Alexander's "The Death and Burial of 'Sick' Products," adds a further dimension to the product life cycle concept. He emphasizes that the need for frequent auditing and phasing out of *sick* products is just as important as planning product introductions. In the last selection, William Mason reminds marketers that packaging is not the exclusive decision domain of production, shipping, sales, advertising, consumer protection, or any other single functional area. Rather, the product's package must represent a reconciliation of a variety of functions, all of which contribute toward satisfying the market target.

16

A New Orientation for Plotting Marketing Strategy

Lee Adler

PREVIEW

I. Companies need to return to fundamentals in setting their goals and objectives, and they need a clear definition of their purposes that is broad enough to allow growth.

II. There are twelve "weapons" that may be used successfully in marketing in conjunction with a successful underlying philosophy.

   A. The *end run* is to avoid unnecessary and undesirable battles with entrenched competitiors.
   B. *Domination* calls for enough concentration of funds, effort, manpower, or creativity in one area to dominate it.
   C. *Market segmentation* identifies and concentrates on fractions of total market.
   D. *Market stretching* may involve a redefinition of purpose in order for a company to create new markets.
   E. *Multibrand entries* into the market enable a company to capture more of available sales.
   F. *Brand extension* occurs when the same brand name covers a variety of products.
   G. *Product change* is at the heart of many strategies.
   H. *Overseas expansion* may offer tremendous potential.
   I. *Investment philosophy* should be such that a product is given proper support.
   J. *Distribution breakthroughs* offer a chance for growth.
   K. *Merger and acquisition* may work to the benefit of the companies involved.

Lee Adler, "A New Orientation for Plotting Marketing Strategy," is reprinted by permission from *Business Horizons* (Winter 1964), pp. 37–50.

L. *Iconoclasm*, or the willingness to depart from customary ways of doing things, is essential to a creative vision.

Since World War II ever intensifying competition and the need for profits have prompted alert companies to forge a number of new and productive marketing strategies, concepts, and tools. Unfortunately, however, there are signs that a grave illness affects many managements, preventing their effective use of these modern marketing instruments. Among the symptoms are:

1. A tendency to engage in bloody, knock-down-drag-out fights with entrenched competitors. Examples abound, especially in the packaged goods industries.

2. Haphazard or sophomoric application of theoretically sound marketing strategies—market segmentation, selection of companies for merger or acquisition and, above all, product differentiation. Products without truly demonstrable points of difference meaningful to the consumer are legion. Ask any advertising agency copywriter.

3. Devoted marriage to an existing business pattern despite evidence that it is in a declining phase. In the beauty aids business, for example, a famous company jealously guarded its department and drug store trade while sales volume in their product categories relentlessly shifted to supermarkets. To make matters worse, this company persisted in holding onto its older customers, despite ample evidence that women under thirty-five are the heavy users and are also becoming a larger proportion of the entire female population.

4. Emotional attachment to products that have outlived their viability. Take the case of the packaged breakfast food. It had been the foundation item in the original line, and, though tastes in breakfast foods had shifted and new products had been successful competitors for years, its manufacturer, like an indulgent parent, could find no fault with it. Or, when pressed to justify its continued existence, the company rationalized that the brand was a symbol for the company and that its old-time trade was still loyal to it.

5. A passion for the cachet conferred by volume without reckoning the cost of attaining that volume. This bit of irationality leads to a drive for volume for the sake of volume, rather than volume at a profit.

6. Failure to consider alternate routes to profitable volume. Thus, some companies continue to regard the United States as their sole territory while their peers are also vigorously expanding abroad where product potentials are easier to tap. Similarly, some marketers maintain safe advertising-to-sales ratios in fields where advertising makes a powerful contribution to total sales effect. In the meantime, their rivals have learned not to regard advertising as a cost, an inhibiting, negative viewpoint, but rather as an investment that can produce fabulous returns.

Marketing Vision

What is the nature of this illness that so inhibits creative marketing effort? Levitt called it "marketing myopia."[1] He argued that failure to define a business broadly enough leads to premature senescence. Levitt noted four conditions which tend to foster decay in the midst of apparent bounty: reliance on population growth, confidence in the infallibility of one's current product, reliance on the cost efficiences of mass production, and "preoccupation with products that lend themselves to carefully controlled scientific experimentation, improvement, and manufacturing cost reduction."[2]

Several other considerations that seem also to interfere with the achievement of marketing breakthroughs can be added to Levitt's discussion. The concern here is not so much with a whole industry as with the growth of individual companies, divisions, and brands.

Trapped in the Square

The problem is basically lack of vision and self-imposed limitations. There is no better analogy than to the nine-dot square, the familiar puzzle requiring the player to connect all nine dots arranged in the form of a square with no more than four lines, without lifting his pencil from the paper.

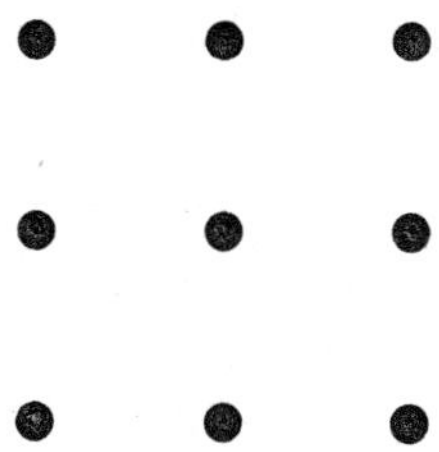

Most players don't succeed at first because, even without being told, they think that they have to remain within the square. It's only the bolder and more deeply reasoning who immediately realize that they must go outside the square in order to succeed.

Another factor responsible for this nearsightedness is the overdetailing of objectives. It used to be that if a man was asked what his business goal was he would say, "to make money." More likely, he wouldn't even have been asked the question in the first place. A corporate manager today will give some fancy responses, such as:

To implement the marketing concept
To build my share of market by five percentage points by January, 1966
To assure maximum use of our manpower, financial, and productive resources

To widen our distribution to 90 per cent of all supermarkets

To achieve an advertising penetration of 62 per cent by the end of the campaign, and so on.

It is vital to have goals. A steady parade of marketing experts are calling for businesses to lay down both broad corporate and divisional goals, and specific marketing objectives. But we should be aware of a danger inherent in setting objectives. To be workable a given objective must be concretized and aimed at a single target. While doing so, however, one tends to block his broader thinking. Thus, the objective of building Brand X's share of market from 18 per cent to 23 per cent within two years leaves out such other considerations as, "Maybe we should launch another brand in this market," or, "Would franchising help broaden our market, lessen our competitive burden?" or, "Our technical people say they can obsolete our brand and those of our competitors with a radically new idea. Should we market the idea, or suppress it for the time being?"

Although the process of detailing objectives is necessary, it tends at the same time to scatter objectives. The setting of numerous, detailed targets for an existing business bearing on advertising, sales management, sales channels, expense control, and so on, may not add up to an integrated system of goals leading to market breakthroughs. On the contrary, this process may perpetuate the status quo because it obscures the need for fresh approaches, because its benchmarks and building blocks all emerge from the existing situation, and because it administratively entangles marketers in today to the neglect of tomorrow.

Two other factors abet this tendency to blind business vision. The first is decentralization. Not decentralization itself, to be sure, for when unit managers are given the freedom and responsibility to operate, the spirit of innovation often flourishes. The trouble is with those managements who cannot keep their hands off the divisional steering wheels and insist that profit responsibility belongs to headquarters. When only lip service is paid to decentralization, both practical and psychological obstacles are raised to the free-thinking of divisional personnel.

The brand manager system, with all its merits, is an even worse offender in this respect. While acceptable in concept, in practice brand managers are often turned into production schedulers, inventory controllers, budget preparers, sales analysts, and expense control clerks. They are so busy with the mechanical details of their jobs that they have no time for its vital aspects—market planning, improving the creativity of their advertising, expanding their brands' domains. The growing roles of marketing consultants, package designers, sales promotion creators, and other outside business services testify to the sterility inside.

This problem is a serious one. It leads to such ill-advised actions as discordant mergers, copy-cat brands, and futile attacks on well-fortified positions. Or it leads to no action at all. The results are failure to grow and to manage change, and increased vulnerability to competition. This is a useless waste when powerful and proven marketing weapons are waiting to be deployed.

Breaking Out of the Square

To take advantage of opportunites, management needs a vision of the business.[3] This vision, McKay observes, should be spelled out in terms of (a) customers and markets, (b) products and services, (c) technology and production capability, and (d) corporate personality and character—all geared to the satisfaction of customer wants and needs.

Development of this vision enables a company or a division to apply marketing strategies in an orderly, consistent manner. It helps to plan and program marketing innovation. In a more detailed fashion, it guides the selection and use of each marketing weapon geared to the desired direction, pace, and timing of growth.

Put another way, this vision helps marketers break out of their nine-dot squares. It arises from a wholistic view of a business' *raison d'etre*, a return to fundamentals. And of all the fundamentals, the most basic is: a company is in business to make money by providing consumer gratifications. Within reason, it does not matter how the company makes money. No law says it must make money with Brand A if Brand A simply no longer has the capacity to make money. Brand B might do a much better job. Or, similarly, if Market C is exhausted, Market D may be wide open.

The vision necessary to grasp this fundamental reality has two dimensions. For breadth, according to Levitt,[4] industries should define their spheres broadly enough to assure continuing growth and to head off competition or, at least, to be fully prepared to deal with it. Thus, it is not sufficient for an oil company to conceive of itself as being in the oil business; it is far healthier if it regards itself as being in the fuel or energy business, or in the even broader petro-chemicals business.

The second dimension is depth. Every company has an essential being, a core, the commercial equivalent of a soul. Deepthinking managers learn to look for, identify, and capitalize on the essence of a company—that which gives it vitality and makes the crucial difference in dealing with rivals and making money.

Consider the Coca-Cola Company. It can be described as a manufacturer of a popular soft drink, or, more correctly, as the manufacturer of syrup used as the base of the soft drink. Or, more recently, as the parent of a whole line of soft drinks—Coca-Cola, Tab, Sprite, Fanta. But a definition of the Coca-Cola Company as a remarkable distribution network may be much closer to the truth. The company's great leader, Robert Woodruff, laid down the policy in the 1930s of putting Coca-Cola "within an arm's length of desire." Today, Coca-Cola is distributed in 1,600,000 outlets, more than any other product in the world. Every kind of retail outlet carries the brand. It is put into these outlets by over 1,000 local franchised bottlers in the United States. Because these bottlers, guided by the parent company, have created this extraordinary distribution, it is easier for the company to market new brands. So, with increasing competition on all sides, the heart of this success is the means of achieving widespread availability.

Procter & Gamble Company furnishes another good example. P&G manufactures soaps and detergents. To define their business in broader terms, as they keep adding products by internal development and by acquisition, P&G is in the household cleaner business, the food business, the health and beauty aids business, or in short, in the personal and household products business—a broad enough definition to keep even P&G going for years.

But P&G can also be viewed as a marketing management philosophy embodying such vital elements as careful market testing, the assurance of genuinely good products, a high order of merchandising skill, and well-supported brand managers. The application of these elements in a determined and unified manner brings marketing success whether the product is a detergent, a dentifrice, or a decaffeinated coffee.

Still another example is the Alberto-Culver Company, a manufacturer of hair preparations that has lately been broadening its line to include a headache remedy, a first-aid item, a dentifrice, and so on. Its president, Leonard Lavin has said: "If you judge us to be successful (the company went from sales of $400,000 in 1956 to over $80,000,000 in 1963), chalk it up to innovator products, excellent packaging, premium pricing, hard-driving promotions, and heavy TV backing of effective creative commercials."[5] Many marketers have innovator products and excellent packaging, and the rest, but not many have the kind of heavy TV backing Lavin refers to. For in my opinion the essence of Alberto-Culver is really a courageous media investment policy that results in their profit rate outdistancing their sales rate. The company has said as much: "We have found an astounding fact: the more we invest in advertising, the less our advertising-to-sales ratio becomes. The sales for our established brands are growing at a greater rate than their substantial advertising budgets. Where a million dollars in advertising used to buy for us $1 to $2 million in gross sales, for our leading brands it now buys added millions of dollars worth of sales, and the ceiling hasn't been reached. Our aggressiveness continues with the added incentive that once we get a brand off the ground, its ability to grow and return profits to the company accelerates at a much greater rate than the increased advertising expenditure."[6]

A company's definition of itself is at the root of marketing success. Only the company with unobstructed vision can use the marketing weapons with maximum effect.

Marketing Weapons System

There are an even dozen marketing weapons and together they make up a weapons system. They have been isolated by a qualitative analysis of the operations of many firms, mainly in the consumer nondurable packaged goods industries. Utilization of one or more of these marketing weapons was found to run as a common thread through the marketing practices of the successful companies in these fields. But these weapons were not used in a vacuum. Rather, an underlying philosophy gave them power and impact. By contrast, haphazard utilization of these weapons consistently characterized the less able marketers.

The End Run

The purpose of the end run is to avoid unnecessary, costly, time-consuming, or otherwise undesirable battles with entrenched competitors or other nearly insuperable obstacles. The objective is to create the arena rather than uncritically accept one made by the competitor. The following examples show how to do battle in one's own arena.

Those tobacco companies that are outflanking the serious problems of government regulation, public outcries and negative publicity revolving around the health issue are practicing the end run. A number of possible end runs are available to the industry. Defining oneself as being in the tobacco business, not just the cigarette business, leads to more vigorous activity in cigars and pipe tobaccos, which do not have the serious problem of cigarettes. The self-definition can refer to a technology-based firm using the tobacco plant as raw material. R. J. Reynolds' development of a fertilizer from tobacco stems is a step in this direction. The next step is to become a chemical processor of other vegetable matter.

Increased overseas marketing to escape or soften the strictures of the U.S. scene is another illustration. So, too, is a tobacco company's viewing itself as an expert in mass distribution rather than as a cigarette manufacturer. Philip Morris exemplifies this approach, as shown in their acquistion of Burma-Vita Company, American Safety Razor Company, and Clark Chewing Gum Company, all different products that rely on the same channels of distribution.

During the late 1940s and early 1950s, Lever Brothers Company made a number of unsuccessful assaults on P&G's solid position in the heavy-duty detergent field.[7] Finally, in 1957, Lever acquired "all" from Monsanto for the automatic washing machine market. In this way, Lever succeeded in outflanking P&G in a high-volume segment of the laundry market.

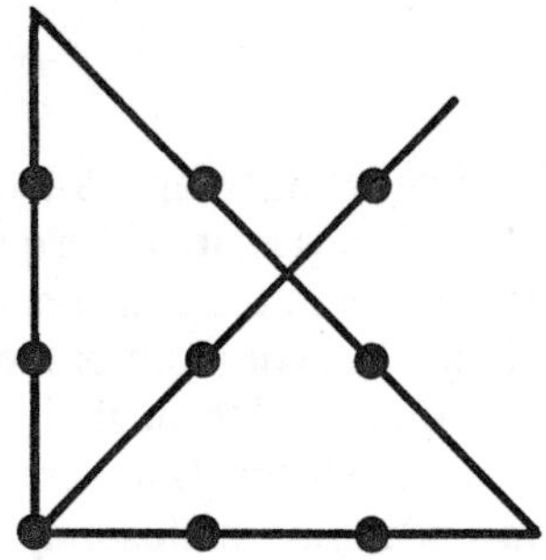

Solution to 9-dot puzzle

Not to be outdone, P&G counter-attacked "all" frontally with Dash. This tactic worked for a time, but by 1961 "all" had gained its lost ground. Then P&G launched its own end run—Salvo low-sudsing tablets. What P&G could not accomplish directly, it accomplished indirectly. Between Dash and Salvo P&G won half the low-sudsing business in several years. By 1963, P&G was well ahead of Lever with a 16.1 per cent share of the heavy-duty soap and detergent market with two brands as against only 12.7 per cent for Lever's "all" and Vim low-sudser combined.[8]

Thus, acceptance of the boundaries of a marketing battlefront, or of the weapons to be used, does not nurture the development of competitive advantage. But a penetrating vision of one's business strips away these restrictive definitions and leads to refreshing new horizons.

Domination

The principle of domination calls for sufficient concentration of effort, funds, manpower, or creativity (within the limits of one's resources) in one area to "own" that area rather than to spread oneself thin over a wider sector. Application of this principle calls for realistic self-perception. For example, one manufacturer of deodorants recognized that in his field, crowded with multimillion dollar advertisers relying heavily on television, his own modest resources would be insufficient. He therefore elected to use a medium then largely ignored by his competitors—radio. Put into radio, his budget was large enough to make him the dominant deodorant brand for radio listeners. This advertiser understood that it was not absolute dollars only that mattered but *share* of dollars too. Moreover, he saw that domination brought not only extra dollar volume but important psychological advantages in leadership and in the surety of a solid position, as well as a good jumping-off point to seize another segment of the business.

Market Segmentation

The concept of market segmentation is well known, and need not be discussed here. Its purpose is to identify and concentrate on fractions of a total market capable of yielding a disproportionate volume and profit. The key point of focus is on the skill with which factors that truly divide markets are identified, vital target groups are defined, marketing programs are tailored according to their motivations and needs, and segments harmonizing with a company's own talents are selected.

Some companies in the cosmetic industry, for instance, have developed an almost uncanny skill at grasping the psychology of beauty-conscious American women. The essence of their business is selling beauty rather than certain chemicals made up into cosmetics. "In the factory, we make cosmetics," says Charles Revson, president of Revlon, "in the drugstore, we sell hope." The subtle sale of hope has led to a profitable segmentation of the total cosmetics market.

Other companies have developed a flair for segmenting markets on a price basis. The heart of their business is efficient, low-cost production combined with low-margin marketing effort. Price segmentation also works at the other end of the scale—some firms have the taste for opulence that leads to success in "class" selling.

In this manner, insight into the heart of a business leads to use of the principle of market segmentation in ways that are uniquely right for the individual marketer. Market segmentation is no longer necessarily an unenlightening slicing of populations in terms of demographic and socioeconomic characteristics. It becomes a creative approach to markets that leads to real benefits.[9]

Consider what manufacturers of makeup and skin care preparations have achieved. Once upon a time there was a simple product called cold cream. Segmenting in terms of specialized consumer needs and desires, manner and occasion of use, age, motivation, and attitude, cold cream manufacturers now market foundation, cleansing, vanishing, nourishing, conditioning, hormone, astringent, lanolin, marrow, and wrinkle creams.

The vision of a business as a moneymaking operation also helps to secure concentration on key target groups, rather than dissipation of effort over a broad front. And so beauty aids companies zero in on young women, beer marketers direct their attention to young men, laxative and tonic producers to older, lower-income people, soft drink bottlers to teen-agers, floor wax makers to suburban housewives, cigarette manufacturers to men, and so on through all the heavy users in each field.

At the same time, this vision of a business reduces the dangers of the misuse of market segmentation. Three misapplications frequently observed are described below.

Pursuing the Wrong Segment One Western brewer, having won a good hold on the heart of the beer market—younger, lower-income male drinkers—aspired to win the favor of a more elegant, upper-income audience. Not only did his effort fail, but he also managed to alienate his original market. Contrast this with the case of other brewers who appeal to different social class and price segments with different brands. Thus, Anheuser Busch now offers two premium beers, Michelob and Budweiser, and one popular-priced brand, Busch Bavarian. Schlitz has two regional popular-priced brands, Burgemeister and Old Milwaukee, along with its premium-priced Schlitz.

Oversegmentation This phenomenon manifests itself in more specialization than the market requires. The deodorant industry is a case in point. Until the mid-1950s, women were the heart of the market and all products were named and promoted with feminine appeal uppermost. Men used women's products. By the early 1960s the female market was saturated and much had been done to evolve brands with masculine appeal. Gillette's Right Guard was a prominent example. The Gillette discovered that other family members were using Right Guard, too. Now the brand is being promoted for the whole family. Since men are willing to use "women's" deodorants and women are willing to use "men's" deodorants, one wonders whether segmentation by sex may not be overdone.

Overconcentration Sometimes companies, indeed whole industries, learn to concentrate too well. The brewery industry, for instance, has concentrated for many years on young men and justifiably so, in light of their heavy usage. But this has led to a sameness in advertising themes and subjects, media, and sports associations, and to near maximum penetration of the young male market at the expense of other segments worthy of further development. This may help to explain a static per capita level; annual gallons consumed per person were 18.0 in 1946, 16.8 in 1952, and 15.1 in 1962.

In the malt beverage field additional cultivation could include many other segments. The segments suggested in Figure 1 are necessarily an incomplete catalog and do not purport to be a set of recommendations to brewers. Rather, they are cited to demonstrate the potential in building new segments where competition is low-key or non-existent, while not neglecting established segments.

Soundly used, with guidance provided by a vision of the business, market segmentation is a creator of new markets markets rather than a constructor of established markets.

FIGURE 1. Possible Malt Beverage Market Segments for Additional Cultivation

Upper social class, "snob" appeal	via	Ale, imported beers
"With-meals" market	via	Advertising and store promotions depicting with-meals usc
With snack foods	via	Promotion such as Coca-Cola's "Nothing beatsa Coke 'n' Pizza," or "Coke 'n' Burger" promotions
Women	via	Feminine appeal brand name, small package sizes, recipes using beer, as the wine industry does*
Those who prefer strong beers	via	Malt liquor, some imports
Draught beer lovers	via	Bottled draught beer (for example, Michelob)

* These measures would be introduced to foster greater consumption of beer by women, in addition to the fact that they buy most of the beer sold in grocery stores (now over 40 per cent of total beer volume—and growing steadily) as their families' purchasing agents.

Market Stretching

New markets are created in many different fashions; the one a business uses depends on how it identifies itself. For example, it is becoming more common for industrial chemical producers to "go consumer." This can only come about from a redefinition of a business. Dow Chemical Company, for example, has broadened its horizon with plastic food wraps, oven cleaners, even Christmas tree decorative materials, among a long list of consumer products. A number of makers of hair care products have gone consumer another way; specialists serving the beauty salon trade, Helene Curtis, Rayette, Ozon, Breck, Clairol, and VO-5, have all made their mark by selling direct to the consumer.

Paradoxically, market segmentation can lead to the broadening of markets. Zealous specialization evokes a countervailing force: a strong desire is born for all-purpose products sold to and used by practically everyone. The detergent industry is ripe for one; now there are specialized products for heavy-duty laundering, fine laundering, manual dishwashing, automatic dishwashing, cleaning floors, kitchens, bathrooms, and so on. As a result, uses for even the most general cleansers are narrowing. The floor wax business is also setting the stage for an all-purpose product with its profusion of pastes, waxes, polishes—including a product that removes the other products. In this context, the recent burgeoning of one-step cleaning and waxing in floor waxes and one-step dusting, waxing, and polishing in furniture waxes may be the industry's way of broadening user segments. Thus, the sharp strategist recognizes when the time has come to throw the gears into reverse and use the tool of product or line simplification.

Multibrand Entries

Underlying this marketing strategy is a basic premise: two brands tend to capture more of the available sales than one. Marketers with a broad conception of their business have learned to overcome their passionate devotion to one brand. Their vision grants them detachment; they can see that their role in life is not to nurture their brand regardless of cost, but rather to maximize profitable volume. They can then also see that there will always be a few contrary consumers who will persist in buying a rival brand. So they reason that the other brand might just as well be theirs too. They know there may be some inroads into sales of the original brand, but that there will be in a *net* gain in volume with two brands instead of one.

Many packaged goods industries provide examples of the application of this strategy. In deodorants, Bristol-Myers has four brands and seven product variants: Ban (roll-on and cream), Mum (including Mum Mist and Mum Mist for Men), Trig, and Discreet. In soaps and detergents and tobacco products, examples of this strategy abound. Alberto-Culver has enunciated multibrand competition as a policy, and has begun to send second brands into markets in which they already compete.

Perhaps the shrewdest extension of this strategy, particularly applicable when a company is first with a truly new product and can realistically anticipate competition, is to lock out rivals by bringing out multiple offerings at the time of product introduction. One food manufacturer used this approach recently in a product category segmented by flavor. Similarly, a housewares producer applied this strategy to preempt the key position with different-featured models in a market that segments by price. The cigarette field also furnishes current examples: Philip Morris brought out no less than four new charcoal filter brands virtually at the same time—Philip Morris Multifilter, Galaxy, and Saratoga; and Liggett & Myers introduced two—Lark and Keith.

Brand Extension

Marketers' emotional attachment to products often includes the brand name. With brand extension strategy, too, a wholesome and realistic view of the business precludes the imposition of artificial and unnecessary limitations on the use of brand names. There is nothing holy about a brand name and if extension of it can bring about marketing good, while not discrediting or cheapening the original product or confusing the consumer, then extension can serve as a potent instrument. Thus, Dristan, first a decongestant tablet, is now a nasal spray, cough formula, and medicated room vaporizer. Lustre Creme, in addition to ignoring the literal meaning of its name and coming out as a liquid and a lotion shampoo, is now also a rinse and conditioner and a spray set. Ivory, as homey and hoary a brand name as any, is as vital as ever in Ivory Flakes, Ivory Snow, Ivory Soap, and Ivory Liquid.

Product Change

As in the case of market segmentation, the crucial importance of product innovation is so clear and so well understood that it requires no description here. Product change lies at the heart of many market strategies and is capable of application in a marvelous variety of ways. The essential prerequisite is a conception of a business that permits free scope to product change and, indeed, urgently demands ceaseless product change. The exact form and pattern of change will be conditioned by the nature and goals of the individual business.

End run candidates—and the concomitant avoidance of me-tooism—are evident in the development of essentially new products such as cold water detergents, hair sprays, electric toothbrushes, low-calorie foods and beverages, sustained-release cold tablets.

Flank attacks are also possible by what might be called extra benefit innovation, as contrasted with straight innovation. The typical example is in the use of an additive, for instance, lanolin, hexachlorophene, fluoride. The less typical example is the double-duty product; shampoos may also provide a color rinse, such as Helena Rubinstein's Wash 'n' Tint.

Product differentiation is the usual means of seeking a demonstrable point of difference. Taste, packaging size, and ways of using established products are the customary variations, as in orange-flavored analgesics for children, spray antiseptics, aerosol oven cleaners, liquid aspirin, mint-flavored laxatives, roll-on lipsticks, powdered deodorants, and travel-size packages of dentifrice.

To outflank competition or to carve out new segments, the ultimate in products must come from a policy of deliberate obsolescence. But this policy is applied reluctantly, and as a result, change is forced on companies by bold innovators, or by new competitors who have no vested interest to preserve. P&G changed the detergent industry with the introduction of Tide synthetic detergent in 1946, and thus widened the future of its own soap brands. Armstrong Cork Company entered the consumer field with a one-step floor cleaner and wax and had no compunctions about upsetting the established order. Gillette joined the stainless steel razor blade fray to protect its enormous franchise; because it was less than enthusiastic about it, the firm also demonstrated the high cost of being late.[10]

Overseas Expansion

Not only can the definition of a business be product-based, saying, "We are in the railroad industry, not the transportation industry," or conceptual in foundation, believing, "The strength of our company lies in the skillful use of media of communication rather than in our experience in this or that segment of the food trade," but the definition may also be geographic. Therefore, the vision of a business can also be liberating in this respect. Most American companies have, until recently, regarded themselves as serving the American market. The foreign market was truly foreign to their thoughts.

In contrast, companies that have the vision to see both the vast potential of the foreign market for basic goods, and their own role in supplying it, have profited enormously. In the case of Colgate-Palmolive, for instance, while its headquarters happens to be in New York, its spirit is global. This self-image is reflected in its sales and profit story. Faced with savage competition in most of its markets in the United States, Colgate has pushed its business abroad. Thus, its 1952 foreign sales were 36 per cent of its worldwide total; by 1962 this ratio had risen to 51 per cent. But the profit contribution from abroad soared from 45 per cent of total earnings in 1952 to a whopping 89 per cent in 1962. True, Colgate's overseas divisions do not have to absorb any of the costs of product development and testing, all of which are borne by the U.S. division. Nonetheless, the disproportionate overseas profit role is eloquent testimony to the benefit of this liberating vision. Another kind of corporate vision is working here in providing the extra margin necessary to overcome cost differentials, tariff barriers, and so forth, permitting overseas business to become feasible.

Investment Philosophy

The packaged goods world provides a sad, almost daily spectacle of products being sent into ferociously competitive markets by their loving or niggardly, but niggardly parents. To prevent nearly certain slaughter, products, especially new ones, require continued substantial support.

But again it takes a certain vision to see beyond the tendency to hold down on spending and seek as rapid as possible a return on investment. The vision includes a financial aspect in seeing the company as investor, not spender, and a temporal aspect in realizing that the company is going to be around for a long time and, if necessary, can wait for its money. It is surely going to have to wait longer as marketing rivalries intensify and greater resources are brought to bear. In the packaged goods field, a realistic vision is frequently identified by three policies:

Heavy weight in advertising, sales promotion, merchandising, and distribution-building, particularly in the introductory phase

Substantial share of weight in whatevever media and segment(s) one competes in

Prolongation of payout periods from a "traditional" three years to four or five years, where necessary, while maintaining a firm hold on future profit by sharp sales forecasting and margin control. (Obviously, this can't be done in fields where product life cycles are growing shorter.)

To challenge so well-established a brand as Listerine is a formidable undertaking. When Johnson & Johnson entered the market with Micrin, their investment in traceable advertising expenditures alone gave evidence of their awareness of these realities of the marketplace. Similarly, a deodorant brand of fairly recent vintage bought position by both heavy weight and deferment of profit taking to four and one-half years after launching. As the president of Alberto-Culver has observed, very heavy advertising appropriations build volume and market share to the point where, in that rarefied atmosphere where few marketers venture, the return becomes disproportionately higher than dollars invested, and the advertising-to-sales ratio actually drops.[11]

Distribution Breakthroughs

Almost as limiting in its effect on the vision of a business is being wedded to a given distribution system. It is also almost as frequent a manifestation of marketing backwardness because the forces of inertia, tradition, and myopia all exert their pull in the same direction. Helene Curtis' acquiring Studio Girl and Bristol-Myers' acquiring Luzier to tap the rich house-to-house sales channel are positive examples. So, too, is Chock Full o' Nuts' signing up local licensees for door-to-door selling. Cosmetics lines nationally sold to main-line department stores, and Class A drug stores that have now extended distribution to grocery stores are also cases in point. (Indeed, one must credit supermarkets more than manufacturers for breaking out of the traditional mold of being only food outlets and creating a vast enterprise in health and beauty aids and in packaged household necessities. Moreover, one must credit retailers in general for the postive effects of scrambled distribution in all manner of goods.) If a national beer brand were to franchise local brewers, taking a leaf from the book of the parent, soft drink companies, they would be acting on this principle.

Merger and Acquisition

The growing tide of mergers and acquisitions testifies to industry's awareness of the potential benefits of corporate marriages. Yet many curious matings raise questions about the vision of the corporations initiating them. This is not to argue against a most unlikely merger of a business whose vision is management talent for buying depressed situations and upgrading them or a business whose core is financial wizardry. But these are special circumstances. For most companies, mergers are a serious drain on manpower, time, and resources. Blind worship at the shrine of the Great God Diversification may hinder or arrest opportunities to blend the benefits of diversification with logical extensions of a business. Sound mergers take sound vision.

Chiclets are quite different from Bromo-Seltzer, Richard Hudnut Shampoo, Anahist, and DuBarry cosmetics, yet the purchase of American Chicle by Warner-Lambert marries dissimilar products with similar characteristics of packaging, rapid purchase-repurchase cycles, channels of merchandising, and advertising response. By the same principles, the subsequent merger of American Chicle with Smith Brothers cough drops is a further logical development of the Warner-Lambert vision.

The merger of Coca-Cola with Minute Maid and Duncan Coffee simultaneously with soft drink line extensions in different flavor categories with Spite and Fanta and the low calorie category with Tab represents the application of a two-fold vision of the business. One aspect of the vision has already been noted—an extraordinary distribution skill that Coca-Cola management can contribute to the acquired companies, though outside the bottler network, of course. The second is the definition of the firm as being not in the carbonated cola beverage field, not even in the soft drink field, but rather in the refreshment business, or indeed, in the beverage business. To these instances of horizontal mergers can be added vertical ones, such as cosmetics companies acquiring chemical interests or, more frequently, chemical and ethical drug producers centering cosmetic and proprietary drug fields. Philip Morris has effected mergers in both directions—horizontally with shaving cream and razor blades and vertically with Milprint.

Moreover, creativity and imagination in realizing a business' vision can lead to interesting symbiotic relationships. (Here I borrow the concept of symbiosis from biology where it refers to the living together of two dissimilar organisms in a mutually beneficial relationship.) International Breweries, for example, has undertaken to manufacture the product requirements of a small Cleveland brewer at one of International's own plants. The added volume will help amortize a goodly share of plant overhead and, at the same time, the Cleveland firm will become the distributor in the market for International's brands. The two companies remain independent while enjoying the benefits of a merger.

Iconoclasm

One of the hallmarks of practical application of a creative vision of a business is a willingness to depart from customary ways, to seek unorthodox solutions to orthodox problems. This iconoclasm runs as a common thread through the success stories of the period after World War II. Icon-breaking is necessary even in applying the most sophisticated marketing strategies. For example, it is by now axiomatic to concentrate on heavy users; yet this is not always the wisest strategy. In the wine industry, for example, a careful analysis of the characteristics of heavy users reveals a diverse assemblage of consumer segments. Marketing to each segment requires different tools and can be quite costly. Moreover, many confirmed users require only reminder advertising, but it is well worth promoting to the occasional user who can be cultivated to a greater frequency of usage.

To illustrate further, it is customary for national marketers to have advertising agencies serving them nationally. But Carling Breweries chose a quite different method to help bring the company from forty-ninth place to fourth place between 1950 and 1960. Reasoning that much of the beer business is local in character and competition, and that local advertising agencies are best suited to understand local circumstances, Carling worked up a network of eight local agencies, each of which serves the brewer in one of its marketing divisions, and is coordinated by the agency in the home city.

The advantages of marketing vision should be apparent. It is a mind-opening, horizon-stretching way of business life, keeping industries in the growth camp or converting them into growth situations. It fosters industry leadership, enabling companies to bypass competition and to manage change rather than to be managed by it. It helps decentralization to live up to its promise. Moreover, in providing a systematic framework for exploring new profit avenues, marketing vision is especially valuable in fields with built-in limitations. Some industries have trouble in new product development. Dentifrice manufacturers, for example, despite many efforts to give toothpaste companions in powder, liquid, and tablet forms, still find the paste in the collapsible tube owning the business. In their case, marketing vision found its practical expression in additives, including chlorophyll, antienzymes, hexachlorophene, and, most recently, the brilliantly successful fluoride development.

For another field, marketing vision might call for overseas expansion, diversification, or new distribution channels. But for each industry, for each company, for each division, and for each brand or line there is often one success factor that is more appropriate than other. The utilization of these marketing weapons cannot be generalized. What works well for one business will not work for another; what works well for one set of competitive circumstances will not work for another. Also, what works well at one point in time will not work at another. On the other hand, in some situations, two or more strategies may be applicable concurrently. Thus, a chart depicting various strategies at work in a multidivision, multibrand company might present a most haphazard appearance and yet make sense for each unit and harmonize with over-all corporate goals. To exemplify this point, Figure 2 shows the strategies at work over a recent five-year period for some of the components of one company. Some of these strategies can be developed within a brand management group; others, for example the acquisitions, have been worked out by top management.

It should be evident that these marketing strategies *interlock*. Segmenting a market helps one to dominate it. Product change is often an essential for segmentation. Brand extensions can lead to new distribution channels. And, in the final analysis, all other strategies are end runs, and all break with the rhythm and style of the past. It is this systematic yet bold imposition of a fresh image of a business that provides insurance against decay and a foundation for growth.

NOTES

1. Theodore Levitt, "Marketing Myopia," *Harvard Business Review,* XXXVIII (July-August, 1960), pp. 47–48.
2. "Marketing Myopia," pp. 47–48.
3. Edward S. McKay, "The Marketing and Advertising Role in Managing Change," in an address before the 54th meeting of the Association of National Advertisers, November 10–13, 1963.
4. "Marketing Myopia," pp. 52–53.
5. Address before the New York Marketing Executives Association, April, 1962.
6. John S. Lynch, "Turmoil in Toiletries—the Rise of Alberto-Culver," *Food Business* (November, 1962), p. 19.
7. Spencer Klaw, "The Soap Wars: A Strategic Analysis," *Fortune*, LXVII (June, 1963), p. 123 ff.
8. *The Gallagher Report*, XII (May 13, 1964).
9. Daniel Yankelovich, "New Criteria for Market Segmentation," *Harvard Business Review*, XLII (March-April, 1964), pp. 83–90.
10. Walter Guzzardi, Jr., "Gillette Faces the Stainless Steel Dragon," *Fortune*, LXVIII (July, 1963), p. 159 ff.

FIGURE 2. Multibrand Deployment of Marketing Strategies

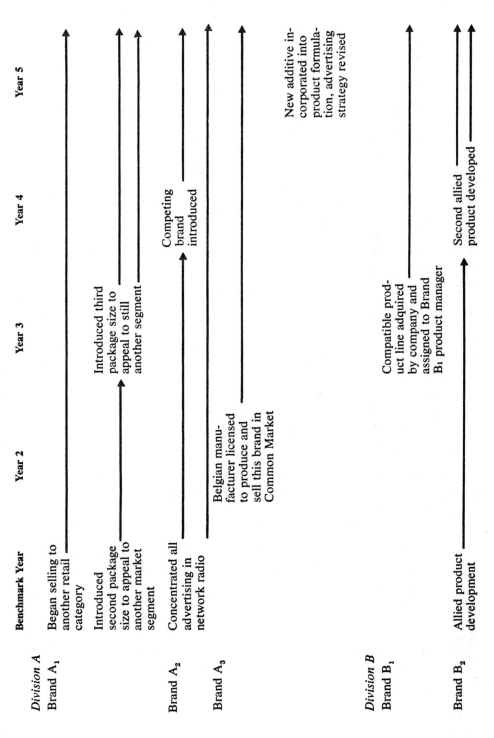

	Benchmark Year	Year 2	Year 3	Year 4	Year 5
Division A					
Brand A_1	Began selling to another retail category				
	Introduced second package size to appeal to another market segment		Introduced third package size to appeal to still another segment		
Brand A_2	Concentrated all advertising in network radio			Competing brand introduced	
Brand A_3		Belgian manufacturer licensed to produce and sell this brand in Common Market			
					New additive incorporated into product formulation, advertising strategy revised
Division B					
Brand B_1			Compatible product line adquired by company and assigned to Brand B_1 product manager		
Brand B_2	Allied product development			Second allied product developed	

11. Leonard Lavin, in an address before the New York Marketing Executives Association, April, 1962; and Alberto-Culver's 1963 annual report, p. 4.

LEARNING REVIEW

Questions:

1. ______________________ is at the root of marketing success.

2. Reynolds Tobacco Company's venture into fertilizer production is an example of the strategy called ______________________.

3. The three potential problems of segmentation are: ______________________, ______________________, and ______________________.

Answers:

1. A company's definition of itself 2. the end run 3. pursuing the wrong segment, oversegmentation, overconcentration.

Retrospective Comment

Re-examining this article some nine or ten years after I first wrote it, I would shift the emphasis from product to non-product means of achieving marketing success. More specifically, as I re-read the list of basic marketing strategies, many of them rely on product for competitive advantage. While by no means de-emphasizing those strategies, one can generalize that the quest for added volume and profit via product innovation or re-positioning, and multi-brand entries, has become more difficult for several reasons including higher development costs, shorter product life cycles, and intensified competition. I would therefore be inclined to recommend seeking distinctive strategies through innovations in distribution policies, practices, and channels; finding other markets for established products; linking a product offering to a set of services to create a system; pricing; and through departures from the conventional in advertising and sales promotion.

17

How Predictable Are Fashion and Other Product Life Cycles?

Chester R. Wasson

PREVIEW

I. It is possible to build a theory of product acceptance.

II. A theory must explain current behavior.
   A. There are three principles of product acceptance which explain the swings of fashion:
      1. *Inherent purchase compromise* refers to the compromise the buyer normally accepts between the ideal set of satisfactions sought and the reality the product offers.
      2. The *changing hierarchy of motivation* refers to the idea that the priority of motives shift when one is satisfied.
      3. The *tendency toward over-adoption* refers to the human drive for social approval which leads people to buy fashionable items that do not satisfy them.
   B. Changeless, always fashion acceptable, classics are explainable as midpoint compromises whose buyers seek only a few of the core attributes in the bundle for sale.
   C. Differences in the early acceptance pattern of a product may be partially explained by whether they call for new learning of three kinds:
      1. learning a new sequence of motor habits.
      2. learning to perceive new benefits as valuable and thus worth paying for.
      3. learning to perceive one's role in the use of the product as of less importance.

Chester R. Wasson, "How Predictable Are Fashion and Other Product Life Cycles?" is reprinted by permission from the *Journal of Marketing* published by the American Marketing Association (July 1968), pp. 36–43.

III. The validity of the model is supported by evidence of three kinds:
   A. Research shows that taste and fashion are predictable ahead of promotion and sales on the basis of analysis of consumer reaction.
   B. There are examples of situations in which a learning content analysis would have improved other research on product acceptance.
   C. Some limited observation and research has proved successful in prediction of a fashion cycle.

No aspect of marketing is so uncertain as the acceptance of new products, particularly those with a fashion element. Yet product introduction and fashion itself are such basic necessities for continued success that the gamble must be taken repeatedly. Clearly, a sound means of forecasting the onset of any popularity wave is needed, of predicting its course, and of recognizing the earliest symptoms of a forthcoming decline. Market planning needs a fundamental explanatory theory of the fashion cycle which would explain the clearly observable, ceaseless fluctuations and their subsequent course. The explanation can be sound only if based on known tendencies of human behavior and on the way human motives, both innate and socially conditioned, cause people to react to the kind of stimulus called a new product. To be useful the theory also must indicate at the minimum the general direction of the next fluctuation and detect the timing of at least the first signs of a new swing.

The thesis of this paper is that already a suitable framework exists for such a theory. It can be drawn from the documented results of product acceptance research when interpreted in the light of human reaction to product offerings and the social psychology of perception and motivation. Furthermore, the theory is at least testable for some kinds of products and corresponds with the results of some proprietary research, unfortunately not published. If valid, this theory is the direct antithesis of the popular myth of "created" fashion.

The Myth of Created Fashion

That fashion is a synthetic creation of the seller is an idea so entrenched that even marketing professionals are often blind to the observably low batting average of those who attempt such "creation." Even within the area of women's apparel, the fact most obvious to those who follow the news of new offerings is the diversity of their direction and the large numbers of "dictated" designs which fall by the wayside after every Paris showing. However, fashion is not limited to women's apparel, nor confined to matters of commercial exploitation.

There are fashions in politics and in business decision methods as marked as the documented cycles in styles of clothing and architecture.[1] A colleague once demonstrated similar cycles in religious interest in a study of church publications, and followers of the stock market are aware of the constantly changing identity of the "glamor" stocks. Whether on the dance floor, in the dress shop, or in the business conference room, the "in" thing changes with the calendar.

No seller can afford to ignore the state of the fashion cycle. Chrysler's misreading of the trend in taste caused real trouble for the firm on at least three occasions: with the 1934 Airflow Chrysler and De Soto, with the unpopular early 1950s designs, and with the "lean look" models of 1962. Ford's later correct reading of the trend gave the firm the well-publicized triumph of the Mustang introduction. In fact, even a superficial knowledge of the successes and failures of design introduction which dot the history of every major auto maker should long ago have convinced everyone that human behavior is not subject to the easy manipulation assumed by the created-fashions myth. The acceptance of a fashion is but one aspect of the process of new acceptance and rests on the same principles of individual and social behavior.

Fashion, Product Acceptance, and Human Behavior

Both fashions and fads are, of course, successful new product introductions. The distinction between the two is generally defined on an *ex post facto* basis—on the nature of their acceptance cycle. Fashions are generally thought to have an initially slower rise to popularity, a plateau of continuing popularity lacking in most fads, and a slow, rather than abrupt decline typical of the fad. (See Figures 1A and 1B) The acceptance cycle of a fashion is thus considered the same as the accepted theoretical course of the normal product life cycle (Figure 1A). Such an empirical after-the-fact basis for distinction, however, deprives any theory of most of its potential utility. It cannot be used for rational market planning. To be useful the theory must distinguish fads from other new products *in advance* on the basis of measurable product attributes, which explain why a market development period might be unnecessary and why acceptance disappears at the very peak of the market. If such an explanation is possible, it should be possible to identify and predict in advance another class of products: a class which requires little or nothing in the way of early market development, but rises in an active growth market from the moment of introduction and then remains popular for long periods. (See Figure 1C) Those who have observed any fashion-oriented market will also recognize the need to explain another related phenomenon with the

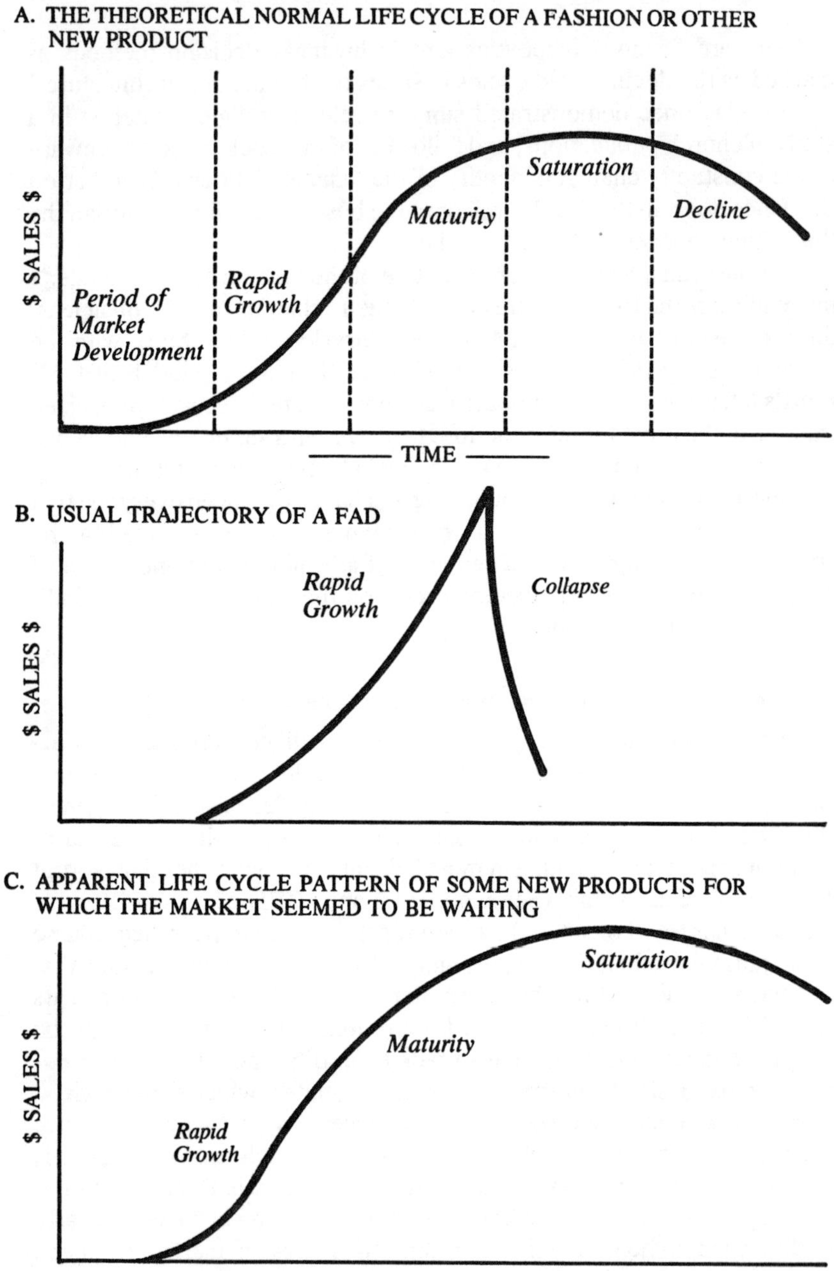

FIGURE 1. Three types of product life cycles.

same theory—the *classic*—the style which is never out of style for its market segment and is rarely the "rage."

To be really useful for product planning, a product acceptance theory should be based on known tendencies of individual and social behavior and encompass in a single model an explanation of:

1. Why and how any new product gains acceptance, and why about half of the seemingly well-screened and well-researched products fail.[2]
2. Why some products must pass through a slowly accelerating period of market development of some length before sales catch fire whereas others zoom to early popularity from the start.
3. Why some products succeed in attainment of a relatively solid niche in the culture, why the popularity of others tends to fluctuate, and why the popularity of fads collapses at their very sales peak.
4. How and why classics exist in a fashion environment.

The behavioral basis for such an explanation starts with the managerial economics view of a product as a compromise bundle of attributes perceived by buyers as an inseparable set of sources of satisfaction and also of some offsetting dissatisfactions for times for a set of desires.[3] To gain the satisfactions, the buyer must pay some price—he must sacrifice some measure of time, money, and/or effort. Whether he moves toward possession of this offering depends on his personal evaluation of the net gain in satisfaction its possession will bring.

Expressed in these forms, an operant psychologist would recognize the purchase as an *approach-avoidance* reaction. Satisfactions sought cause the buyer to approach the offering and seek its possession. The offering, however, includes a repelling force—the avoidance factors of the various prices exacted to obtain those satisfactions. Part of the price is monetary, part is search effort, and an important part can be the compromise enforced by the nature of product design—the denial of satisfaction for some of the elements in the desire-set whose appeasement is sought.

Product Compromise and the Hierarchy of Motives

The buyer usually seeks the simultaneous satisfaction of a set of several motivating desires in making a purchase. In practice, the product offering can seldom satisfy all at the same time and must strike some compromise in the kind and degree of satisfactions offered. Any offering will thus satisfy some buyers well, others partially; and some, perhaps not all, may even yield negative satisfaction for still others. The dress may be bought for physical warmth, figure enhancement, and freedom from restriction at the same time—attributes which cannot be equally well satisfied in the same design. The successful physician may long for the qualities of a prestige car but desire something sufficiently inconspicuous to avoid offending patients at billing time. Thus, the buyer must normally compromise between the ideal set of satisfactions sought and the reality of product design potentials. Nearly every purchase involves some compromise. This is evidenced by the fact that few, if any, products are immune to the inroads of differentiated offerings. Motivational compromise holds the key to an understanding of fashion oscillation when viewed as an extension of the knowledge of the hierarchical nature of motives and their dynamic character.

The intensity of any one desire varies over time within an individual, and, at any given moment, some motives gain priority over others. Even such basic motives as hunger and appetite dominate only until satisfied. As the meal is consumed, the drive to eat is extinguished and some other drive assumes top priority. This second drive was already inherently present before the meal but was not evoked until the hunger was appeased. The hierarchical nature of the motivating drives has long been recognized.[4] Individuals respond most actively to those stimuli that promise satisfaction of those most highly valued drives which are at the moment least well satisfied and at the same time felt to be important. Every satisfactory purchase thus becomes in time the initiator of a search for a somewhat different offering to satisfy newly felt drives. Thus, this continual restructuring of the motivational hierarchy gives the basis for a model explaining fashion oscillation and furnishes a framework for prediction of its new direction:

> The popularity of design attributes in a given utility-bundle will oscillate because no one design can encompass in full measure all of the attributes in the desire-set. The oscillation will tend to be polar, swinging from one extreme to the opposite, because the satisfaction-yield span of any one design will extinguish the very drives which led to its adoption and bring to the fore those drives least well fulfilled by the design.

Consider the example of the automobile design problem (Figure 2) and the oscillations of popular approval between the large and massive and the compact, relatively economical. The 1955 designs fulfilled all of the drives associated with massive appearance and power. In developing these designs, the automobile industry had to leave some other drives less well satisfied—for example, low cost of ownership and maintenance and such ease-of-use aspects as parking and roadability. Once most drivers had acquired the highly ornamented mammoths they desired, attention began to focus on the drives whose satisfaction had been neglected, and size became an avoidance factor for many. Buyers became attracted by mod-

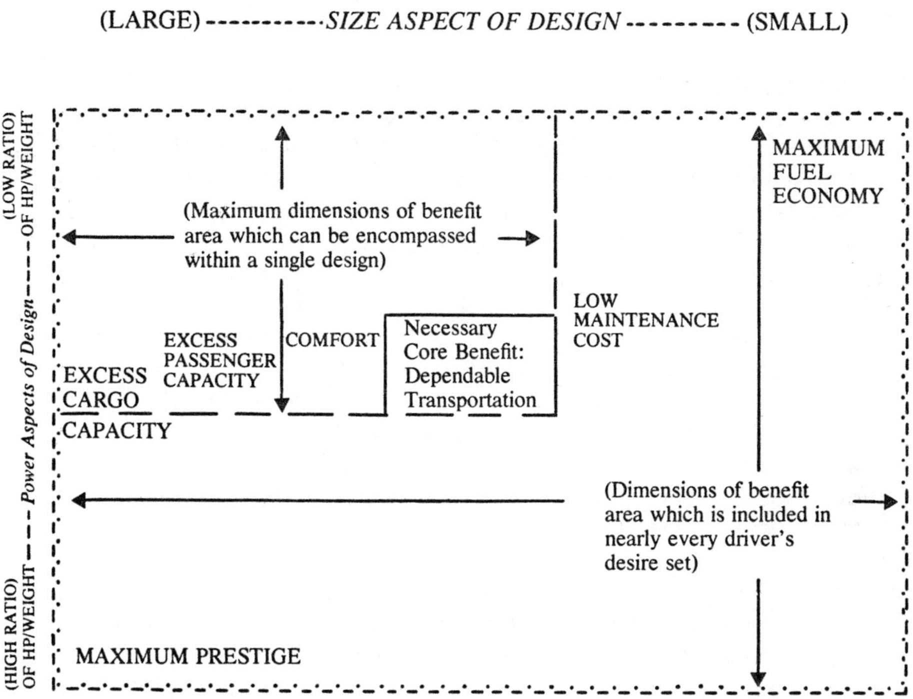

FIGURE 2. The automobile design puzzle: How to get as much of what the driver wants in a single design?

els offering high gasoline mileage, low physical and temporal depreciation, and ease of parking and handling. The sales of foreign makes which offered such attributes in abundance began a climb, and slowed down only when Detroit developed its own compacts in 1960. But the fickle customer, having a free choice of offerings giving most of what he desired, began to yearn again for the attributes associated with size, and the cycle restarted. By 1965, he was buying "compact" models almost as large as the 1955 "big" cars.

However, the composition of the desire-set varies so much from one person to another that the explanation needs one further element to account for the completeness of most new-fashion adoption and the rapidity of its spread. That element is furnished by the human drive for social approval—the desire to be "in the swim." The result is an almost universal tendency toward overadoption. Overadoption is painfully apparent with every extreme swing in the feminine fashion silhouette—the bandy-legged adopted mini-skirts which could only reveal physical deficiencies of the wearer. Overadoption became quite obvious in business management when organizations replaced an effective $300-a-month clerk with a $3,000-per-month computer which often did the clerk's job less efficiently. Overadoption has been documented in the studies of rural sociologists who found farmers adopting machinery which was uneconomic for their scale of operation.[5] The desire for social approval thus speeds adoption, but at the price of leading many to overadoption—to adoption of offerings which do not satisfy their desires well. The result is a considerable market segment which quickly develops an avoidance reaction to the fashion and triggers a decline from the peak.

The three principles of product acceptance—inherent purchase compromise, the changing hierarchy of motivation, and the tendency toward overadoption—furnish a necessary and sufficient explanation of the swings of fashion. However, they leave unexplained the existence of the classic—the style whose changes are minimal, but which remains always in the range of the acceptable. No theory of fashion can be adequate which omits an explanation of the classic and its appeal to a minority market which does not conform to major swings of fashion.

The Classic

The changeless, always acceptable classic is found in every recognized area of fashion. A woman can always feel comfortable in a tailored suit with a skirt line close to the knees. In automobiles, designs similar to the postwar Loewy-designed Studebaker still find a ready market around the world. The values placed by buyers on some security issues respond little to the gyrations of the bulk of those listed on the Big Board. Beige and off-white colors always sell well in automobiles and house paints. Such classics occasionally become the reigning fashion, but seldom are they "the rage."

What makes a classic? Observation seems to indicate that all classics are midpoint compromises and their buyers either have a special kind of personality or are prospects seeking only a few of the core attributes in the bundle for sale. The classic automobile design is neither starkly spartan nor highly ornamented; it is roomy but not gargantuan. The classic color is not found in the "hot" red end of the spectrum nor at the icy blue extreme; it is moderately pleasing but not conspicuous. The classic gives some measure of satisfaction to nearly all of the desire-set of drives, and probably does so at the expense of complete satisfaction of any drives except those at the core of product's physical functions. The classic buyer, then, has to be a person seeking only the core function attributes (such as convenient transportation in a Volkswagen) or one who recognizes that compromise is necessary in any case and who has chosen a compromise least likely to develop over time. He most certainly must be an individual who does not value highly the satisfaction of the drive for new experience. Such a consumer is a poor prospect for any fad, but may well be an excellent early-market customer for innovations of major functional import which others would be slow to accept, since he feels little need for complete conformity. If so, he is important in the early adoption of those products which are slow to catch on at first. Certainly, the differences in the speed of acceptance of various kinds of offerings is one of the most obvious puzzles of new product introduction which must be explained.

Differences in the Early Acceptance Pattern and Their Explanation

As already indicated, some products follow the standard conceptual curve of the product life cycle, but others, particularly fads, leap-frog the early market development phase of this curve with a rocket-like ascent to popularity. Clearly, the marketing mix must differ with the kind of sales acceleration likely to be experienced. Also, different levels of resource commitment are needed for the product which undergoes an extended period of slowly developing sales and those which attain their market potential early. When black-and-white television became a commercial reality, even fly-by-night electronic firms could get a profitable market share, and those who knew how to build on their early success could and did carve out a permanent market niche. Waiting out the ten long years until color television sales hit the growth phase, however, required the resources of an RCA.

A great many pairs of seeming anomalies can be cited from every kind of marketing operation. Soluble coffee existed for over a generation before World War II; and even when wartime developments brought its price down, six years were needed to develop the market potential. Frozen orange juice, another wartime beneficiary, rose from scratch to peak market in three years, as fast as facilities could be developed. The astonishing benefits of hybrid corn yields were not sufficient to get more than 6% of the farmers interested during the first six years on the market, although little else is planted today. However, another farm improvement—2-4-D and related insecticides were so avidly sought by farmers upon their release after the war that they became a real threat to health. Some textbooks take years to gain acceptance of the approach championed, yet Samuelson's *Economics* rose to quick dominance of the elementary course in colleges.

The anomaly disappears when we examine the value an adopter perceives in any product new or otherwise. To the purchaser, a product is only one element in the use-system which is the real source of the satisfaction of the desire-set. Products deliver their potential satisfactions only in the context of some established set of procedural habits organized around their use. Seed corn yields the sought-after crop only when procured, planted, cultivated, harvested and stored in a carefully planned and well-learned system of habitual practices. Television yields entertainment only when manipulated and viewed in another set of habit patterns.

The development of most habit patterns is a painful—or at least annoying—process for most of us. The extinction of one habit system leading to a satisfactory result and its replacement of another is even more so, as anyone who has gone from a three-speed manual automobile shift to a four-speed can testify. The degree to which a product offering involves habit pattern relearning will thus slow down its adoption. Conversely, innovative products which can simply replace old ones using the same set of procedures, or the same set simplified, should gain ready acceptance.

Good examples of products fitting neatly into existing procedures are the new insecticides, black-and-white television, and frozen orange juice. The new insecticides were applied by the same spray methods, with a similar timing, as the ones they displaced. They simply delivered a noticeably higher level of satisfaction—greater kill over a broader spectrum of pests. Black-and-white television entertained in the same way the movies did, by sitting and viewing a picture, but it avoided many nuisance steps—additional cost for every show, problems of travel, parking and getting tickets, and finding a desired seat position. Black-and-white television, too, simply delivered more value in the same system. (Eventually, of course, adoption of TV changed family living patterns. But such pattern changes were not a pre-condition for adoption.) Frozen orange juice fitted into kitchens long used to canned goods; the fact that it was frozen fitted into established perceptions of frozen foods being the equivalents of fresh ones. These products required no substantial learning of new habits or relearning of old. By contrast, hybrid seed corn, color television, and instant coffee all involved learning of some sort.

Any new offering can pose the problem of one or more of three kinds of learning:

1. Learning of a new sequence of motor habits (as in changing over from a three-speed shift to a four-speed, or from a wringer to an automatic washer);
2. Learning to perceive new benefits as valuable and thus worth paying for (as in learning to appreciate the cornering qualities offered by the small sports car);
3. Learning to perceive one's role in the use of the product as of less importance (as in the acceptance of an automatic transmission).

The acceptance of the use of hybrid seed required the learning of both a new sequential element and of the perception of relative value. Before its adoption, the farmer usually saved some of the better quality of the previous year's crop and replanted it. The use of hybrid seed meant the complete disposal of the crop and the repurchase of seed each year. (The farm journals of the period ran many an article warning farmers not to replant seed from hybrid crops.) Moreover, the seed he bought cost several times as much per bushel as the farmer received for the crop he sold. This resulted in a real value-perception problem.

The acceptance of color television in 1955 required no change in motor or other use-habits, but did involve a substantial change in value perception. It required seeing that the mere addition of color to the picture was worth hundreds of dollars—at a time when Technicolor movies had never achieved use in more than a minority of films. Color also deprived the viewer of the satisfaction of closure—the supplying of missing details himself. Psychologically, successful closure heightened the satisfaction gained, and has probably always been an element of successful entertainment. The double-meaning joke gets its whole point from the use of closure.

Soluble coffee certainly simplified the brewing process and required little in the way of motor learning. Once wartime experience had reduced its cost, any problem disappeared. But soluble coffee downgraded the homemaker's role; it required her to see her role in relation to mealmaking as less important. Coffee brewing is susceptible to individual skill, and many housewives pride themselves on their coffee. Acceptance of soluble coffee required admission that the housewife's kitchen role was less vital to family happiness than it had been. Is it any coincidence that the use of soluble increased with the growing acceptance of the housewife as a major contributor to the family's *outside* income?

The overnight success of radically new products like Samuelson's *Economics* are explainable as examples of product filling a missing link in an already developed system. They are products for which the market has been waiting. Economists began to pay increasing attention to the macro aspect of economic theory in the early 1930s. By 1946, when Samuelson's first edition was published, many economists were orienting their courses entirely in this direction. Since no satisfactory texts were available, a well-done text, as Samuelson's was, could hardly help but succeed. Rubber tractor tires provide a similar example. Mechanized farming became well established on the better-managed farms, but the steel-tired tractors compacted the soil, could not be run over paved roads, and did not always furnish the desired traction. Once a satisfactory tire was developed, the steel-wheeled tractor disappeared overnight. The supermarket was also a missing link in a developing food shopping and storing system. The automobile had widened the shopping range of the family; the need to park it called for a single stop. In addition, ownership of mechanical refrigerators was wide enough to eliminate the daily shopping trip. All that was needed was the foresight of a few independent entrepreneurs. Even though such missing link products do require learning of elements not required by the products they displace, the learning process is complete by the time of their introduction.

The rate of early-adoption acceleration is thus seen as contingent on the degree of learning required to accept and properly use any new offering. Both learning-content and attribute-compromise analyses are feasible, rendering the proposed model of product adoption speed and of fashion fluctuation subject to test and confirmation.

The Evidence of Testability

A model is valid if it has utility for prediction. The main recommendation for the proposed model is its testability—parts of it rather easily—and the fact that it is in harmony with some known successful proprietary unpublished private research predictions. Three kinds of evidence as to its validity can be cited:

1. Such known proprietary research clearly demonstrates that taste and fashion are predictable ahead of promotion and sales, and even in advance of design, on the basis of analysis of consumer reaction.
2. It is possible to cite at least a few examples of situations in which a simple learning-content analysis would have greatly improved otherwise extensive research on product acceptance.
3. Some limited observation and research has proved successful in prediction of a fashion cycle.

Sensing the Trend in Taste Ahead of Introduction

A sizable body of proprietary research has established the fact that rather simple, carefully administered checks of consumer reaction can reveal in advance which of an equally-promoted group of designs will succeed and which will fail. Dilman M. K. Smith[6] has sketched some of the results of successful Opinion Research studies in this area, some going back over three decades. The author of this article himself was able to develop a very simple ahead-of-the-season measure of relative demand in a line of dresses over 20 years ago—a test still in routine use by the employer for whom he developed it. A research director for a maker of permanent waves was able to alert his firm to a change in hair style tastes months before the change began to show up in beauty parlors and thus permitted a successful effort to buttress the firm's market position. Even more relevant was an unpublished Opinion Research triumph; the development of a new, instantly successful rug weave based on a revelation of an unsatisfactory consumer compromise. When research showed that housewives liked the texture of velvet rugs but were repelled by such a weave's tendency to show tracks, the firm advised a client to find a velvet weave which was trackless. After considerable prodding, designers came up with the sculptured wilton, which took off on a typical fast growth curve when introduced.

Unfortunately, understanding of consumer product acceptance has not gained much from this private research, since only fragments of a minor part could land in footnotable publications. The rest remains hidden in the files of those who pay for it and confined to conversations among a few research analysts. Confirmation of the learning content aspect of the proposed model, fortunately, does not always require access to any confidential data.

Learning Content and Prediction

The author has shown at length[7] elsewhere that use-systems learning requirements can be determined easily by means of simple comparison of flow diagrams—one diagram for the current means of obtaining the satisfaction desired and one for the system which would be the setting for use of the new product. Such a comparison quickly reveals both the advantages and the avoidance factors involved in adoption of the new. One need read only the preparation instructions on a pouch of dehydrated soup to discover why this thoroughly-researched product was a market failure which cost Campbell's alone some $10,000,000 in unsuccessful promotion,[8] according to news stories. The flow diagrams reveal a tremendous time-and-effort price disadvantage for the dehydrated product relative to the canned concentrate. It should have been clear that the housewife would not pay such a price for the kinds of satisfactions expected from soup in the American diet pattern. It may well be much of the failure of carefully investigated new products traces to the failure to investigate the learning-content requirements and the preparation-time price.

Perceptual-learning and value-learning requirements do not yield to as simple an analytical device as the flow chart, of course, but they are certainly possible to discover with currently available research techniques. And this singular aspect of the proposed model is manifestly testable against past history. Prediction of fashion oscillations is not so clearly testable against the past.

Checking Fashion Oscillation Predictability

Almost any hypothetical model must start with some classification and observation of past experience. But any model involving as many complex factors as the one proposed for fashion oscillation cannot be safely checked against history alone. This is true particularly when few observations from that past contain any substantial evidence of the psychological motives that buyers hope to appease with their adoptions. Most such observations have to be limited to studies in the fluctuations among physically measurable attributes which may or may not be the relevant items involved. The result can be a number of plausible but different explanations, each of which can be rationalized as fitting if the classifications and other data are carefully chosen. An acceptable theory must give more than a plausible explanation of past events: it must have pragmatic validity, be capable of predicting the future in some meaningful manner.

In this respect, the author can cite only a single documented successful prediction although he has attempted several others, unpublished, which have borne or are bearing fruit. As noted earlier, the author, writing in 1961 (for publication in 1964), traced the history of the swings in research fashion and noted that the current wave was at the peak of the recurrent mathematical emphasis. A swing to behavioral models and techniques was predicted. At the time of the analysis, the *Business Periodicals Index*[9] listed only two articles under "Innovation," neither of them in marketing journals and neither of them on research into the process. Concurrently, one of the marketing publications turned down Lionberger's *Adoption of New Ideas and Practices* as "not germane to the interests of" its readers. By 1965, both the Detroit and New York chapters of the AMA were holding New Products conferences, and "diffusion theory" is now the current shibboleth.

One such prediction success, or any number of them, does not constitute the final test of validity, however. A sound theory in any field must dig beneath any coincidence between its predictions and subsequent events to explain why the events can be expected to occur in the manner observed. A sound theory must have construct validity, be based on behavioral constructs which themselves are capable of test and confirmation or modification. The theory offered above is just such a theory. It is possible to test it pragmatically—to make predictions as to the next direction of a fashion swing or as to the speed of adoption of a projected new product and then to observe the objective events. But this theory also postulates a specific behavioral mechanism as responsible for the observed patterns, a mechanism fairly well established in behavioral knowledge and subject to test itself. What is being proposed is thus no mere attempt to invent plausible behavioral labels to explain known observations. Rather it starts from a series of established behavioral constructs derived independently of the kind of data to which they are being applied, and attempts to see if their implications fit the phenomena of fashion and product acceptance. This theory thus offers a framework for research into product acceptance in general as well as formulating an improvement for the practical problem of new product screening and testing.

Conclusion

Not only fashion, but product acceptance in general is far more predictable than is generally thought, providing we make full use of the basic concepts of a product as a compromise bundle of desire attributes, demand as a desire set based on social conditioning, and motives as existing in a dynamic hierarchy and constantly restructured in the very process of their appeasement. These concepts alone are adequate to explain both the existence of a constant oscillation in fashions and the directions these oscillations take. Fads are explainable within the framework of this model as products which satisfy solely a single utility-drive for new experience; thus they pose neither a learning requirement nor have much value once their newness has gone. The speed of adoption of products of any kind depends on the amount of required learning of three types: use-systems learning, value perception learning, and role-perception learning. All are researchable and describable in objective terms in advance.

NOTES

1. Chester R. Wasson, *The Strategy of Marketing Research* (New York: Appleton-Century-Crofts, 1964), pp. 67–77.

2. *Management of New Products* (Chicago: Booz, Allen & Hamilton, 1960).

3. Edward H. Chamberlin, *Theory of Monopolistic Competition*, 8th edition (Cambridge, Mass.: Harvard University Press, 1962), Appendix F, pp. 276–281; Chester R. Wasson, *The Economics of Managerial Decision* (New York: Appleton-Century-Crofts, 1965), pp. 55–87; and Chester R. Wasson, Frederick D. Sturdivant, and David McConaughy, *Competition and Human Behavior* (New York: Appleton-Century-Crofts, 1968), pp. 4–25.

4. A. H. Maslow, "A Dynamic Theory of Human Motivation," *Psychological Review*, Vol. 50 (March, 1963), pp. 370–396.

5. Everett Rogers, *The Diffusion of Innovations* (New York: The Free Press, 1962), pp. 142–145.

6. Dilman M. K. Smith, *How to Avoid Mistakes When Introducing New Products* (New York: Vantage Press, 1964).

7. Chester R. Wasson, Frederick D. Sturdivant, and David McConaughy, *Competition and Human Behavior* (New York: Appleton-Century-Crofts, 1968), pp. 83–91.

8. "Campbell's Drops Red Kettle Line," *Advertising Age* (August 29, 1966), p. 3.

9. *Business Periodicals Index* (New York: The H. W. Wilson Co., July 1961-June, 1962), p. 378.

LEARNING REVIEW

Questions:

1. The decline in fashion of a product may be explained by ____________.

2. According to the author, Campbell's Soup could have saved much money on unsuccessful promotion of dehydrated soup if they had conducted a simple ______________________________.

3. Nearly every purchase involves some ____________ in the kind and degree of satisfactions offered.

4. The main point of this article is that fashion may be ____________.

Answers:

1. over-adoption 2. learning content analysis 3. compromise 4. predicted

Retrospective Comment

At the time the article was written, the miniskirt, and its ultimate, the micro-mini, were nearing the height of their popularity. They were of a style best suited to the highly immature figure, and not all of these. It required a girl with minimum bust development, quite slender otherwise, with long, straight, slender legs (which only a minority of women of any age group possess).

In 1970–71, the fashion industry, with a wholly unaccustomed unanimity, tried promoting the *midi*—a dress dropping to mid-calf, but possessing little waist or bust emphasis. It was a major sales disaster, since it did nothing much to emphasize the feminine attributes the mini had neglected—the curves of the mature woman. Instead, a style which women themselves had been adopting over the combined opposition of designers, the trade, and even better restaurants and hotels—the dressy pants suit and the party dress—burst out of a slowly ascending trend into overnight popularity. This style hid the legs and was adopted in a version which accented the waist and bust to some degree. It was extremely functional, as well as attractive when well chosen. By 1974, it was well-entrenched in most women's wardrobes, with every indication it would become a perennial classic. Like all classics, however, the pants suit does not lend itself to the flash and glamor of the extremes, and so was only an interim solution for the woman who desired "something very special."

To get this something special, women themselves pushed another style the designers were neglecting. This style was exactly what the theory would predict, that is, the exact opposite of the mini—the *maxi*.

The attenuated skirt of the mini gave way to a flowing long skirt, belted or otherwise highly accented at the waist (against the virtually straight lines of the mini) and with a full bosom accent. The earlier models of this style were either made up by the women themselves or at their orders, many in a version known as the "prairie style" (pinafore bosom). By 1976 this had become the popular evening dress, with bare shoulders and back in some cases.

Thus, the trend of events followed guidelines which accorded with the theory in my article. And they came about in the face of industry and designer hostility and even institutionalized social opposition, indicating the very fundamental psychological foundations of fashion.

18

Interfaces of a Product Manager

David J. Luck

PREVIEW

I. The role of product manager is one involving several objectives and a number of important interfaces.

   A. The main purposes of product managers are seemingly being accomplished:

      1. Creation and conceptualization of strategies for improving and marketing the assigned product line or brands.
      2. Projection and determination of financial and operating plans for such projects.
      3. Monitoring execution and results of plans, with possible adaptations of tactics to evolving conditions.

   B. The interfaces of the product manager fall into six categories.

      1. The *buyers and users* compose the most important interface.
      2. *Wholesalers and retailers* play major roles in the market success of products.
      3. The *salesman* is a necessary ally. . . .
      4. The degree of involvement with *advertising agencies* varies.
      5. Involvement with *product development* depends on the firm's organizational structure.
      6. *Marketing research* supplies substantial amounts of data.

II. Product managers' interfaces are of high importance from each of three viewpoints.

   A. The *product manager* must serve as an information center, which requires much coordination of resources.
   B. The *firm* finds its main intelligence center in the properly functioning product manager.

David J. Luck, "Interfaces of a Product Manager," is reprinted by permission from the *Journal of Marketing*, published by the American Marketing Association (October 1969), pp. 32–36.

C. The *marketing institution* must interface fully with the buying public.

III. There are a number of obstacles to successful interfacing by the product manager.
  A. He may be preoccupied with trivial and distracting tasks.
  B. He may have a lack of assistance.
  C. He may find a lack of cooperation with functional departments.
  D. There may be a lack of well-conceived formal position descriptions.
  E. The product manager may be restricted to a single brand.
  F. Available time may be inadequately scheduled.
  G. The product manager may be inadequately trained.
  H. Job tenure may be short.
  I. There may be an excessive number of interfaces.

IV. There are four dimensions of development which may promote effective interfacing by product managers.
  A. The product manager's assignments may be re-aligned toward a market orientation.
  B. An improved atmosphere should be provided for the serious study by product managers of markets and alternative strategies in product, pricing, promotion, and distribution.
  C. Interfaces should be restricted to those that are most productive.
  D. Complete and realistic job descriptions should be developed, to be accompanied by more specific performance evaluation criteria.

The position of product manager was established over 40 years ago in a prominent marketing organization, that of Procter and Gamble. Despite this long history, scholarly research and writing have seemingly ignored the product management organization. Literature specifically treating product management organization is confined to perhaps three or four monographs or thin volumes which are largely descriptive.[1]

Does this obscurity imply that the product manager is a rare or unimportant functionary in modern business? Evidence points to the contrary. This writer's experience and that of other observers indicates that most large multiproduct companies have initiated the product management plan of organization.

Product managers operate on a horizontal plane, in contrast to the primarily vertical orientation of most marketing personnel. Their specialization is cross functional with primary focus on a specific product line or brand. They have numerous titles such as brand manager, product planning manager, or product marketing manager. These titles frequently denote varying emphases, but do not alter their basic responsibilities. The position of "product manager" is a radical departure in management that is not easily slotted into and absorbed by the existing organization. Consequently, it is not readily defined, staffed, and implemented.

Objectives of the Product Manager

Enthusiasts for product management have envisioned this position to the answer to the needs of large enterprises to create true profit centers within the organization. This vision has proved generally impracticable.[2] Product managers are seriously hampered by ambiguity of authority in the execution of their plans and decisions, in addition to the problems of a new type of position asserting its intended role. Undefined authority precludes clear-cut, enforceable responsibility. Despite such problems, the main purposes of product managers are seemingly being accomplished. They are:

1. Creation and conceptualization of strategies for improving and marketing the assigned product line or brands.
2. Projection and determination of financial and operating plans for such products.
3. Monitoring execution and results of plans, with possible adaptation of tactics to evolving conditions.

An underlying role of the product manager is that of becoming the information center on the assigned products.

Product management provides integrated planning which is intimately related to the market needs and opportunities of specific products. This contrasts with decisions that formerly were diffused among functional specialists who could not bring to bear comprehensive knowledge and analysis of factors peculiar to a product. The establishment of interfaces between product manager and these functional specialists is necessary in order to insure acquisition of the variety of information which these specialists can contribute. Simultaneously, the product manager needs to maintain interfaces with the functional personnel who execute the strategies and plans that he originates.

This leads us to the product managers as vital organizational loci for the focus of marketing interfaces. The subject of these interfaces and the means whereby they may be efficiently realized thus merits our serious concern.

Interfaces Vital to Product Managers

Research information obtained during studies of 17 product managers in the course of an advertising decision study[3] and during a current study of eight product managers for pharmaceutical manufacturers indicates that the interfaces which are important to a product manager's work are perhaps the most numerous and varied of any in middle management. They may be placed in the following six categories.

The Buying Public

In ultimate significance to marketing strategy and planning, the buyers and users of the particular product line overshadow all other interfaces. The man who is to conceive product and promotion strategies and prepare competitively viable plans can hardly be too well apprised of how, when, and for what purposes the product is bought and used. Market segments with unique needs may be identified and are often the clue to very effective strategies. Brand images, brand loyalties, consumer profiles, and the reception of advertising and sales promotion campaigns are further examples of the vast information the experienced product manager acquires and studies as he appraises the past and explores future possibilities.

Distributors

Wholesalers and retailers play major roles in the market success of products which they distribute. Relatively small shifts in shelf facings, out-of-stocks, displays, and other dealer support may produce favorable or dangerous trends. A significant portion of the product distribution strategy may be aimed at the distributors themselves to stimulate and maintain their interests through special programs, sales aids, and other trade promotion. Often the product manager's concern includes monitoring the inventories in the pipelines in order to control production rates.

Sales Force

The salesman is a necessary ally of the product manager, although often a very independent one. For most industrial products and for some consumer products, personal selling is the principal force in promoting the product. Since the salesman is frequently selling many products of the firm, product managers often compete with one another in seeking the salesman's support. Product managers are most concerned with the development of selling methods, sales aids, and applications literature. For industrial products, the product manager often makes sales calls with the salesman, particularly where technical expertise is needed.

Advertising Agencies

The degree of involvement with advertising agenices varies widely among product managers. For most industrial products it is of less concern than the sales force. In some consumer goods organizations, product managers are limited by policy to working with the agencies only to the extent of developing advertising strategies, with all other liaison conducted through advertising departments. At the other extreme, there are companies which place virtually all collaborations with the agencies in the hands of product managers. Typically a consumer goods product manager works intimately and continuously with his counterparts in the agency—a relationship that has received some criticism where inexperienced product managers have been troublesome to agencies.[4] Regardless of such views, agency account men tend to work as a team with product managers of major advertisers in developing advertising campaigns and in providing market information and merchandising ideas to the client.

Product Development

The product manager's involvement with new product development is dependent on the firm's organizational structure, the nature of the product itself, and the background of the manager. Where there is a separately designated manager for new products, the managers of current products are usually confined to planning modifications in existing products and packaging. With new products that can be designed relatively quickly, the product manager may maintain a close relationship with all stages of their development; in cases requiring prolonged research and development, product managers tend to have little contact with the emerging products until a market testing stage approaches. Another factor is that, typically, industrial products managers are technically trained and oriented, while the contrary is true in consumer goods. The former naturally have more frequent interface with research and development.

Marketing Research

In their roles of originating and formulating marketing plans and of monitoring the progress and obstacles of products, product managers require substantial marketing research information. Typically, they depend heavily on marketing research personnel to obtain and process this information. Within the enterprise, a marketing researcher may be the closest collaborator with a product manager.

Other Marketing and Corporate Personnel

The product manager's superior within the organization represents the interface most critical to the manager's personal career. Regardless of the superior's title, which will vary from firm to firm, this superior will usually bear the responsibility for marketing planning of a division or corporation. Very commonly these men are themselves former product managers and a high level of empathy tends to exist between these men, as the superior strives to develop the analytical and decision powers of his product managers.

When a product manager interprets his position broadly, he may have many intra-firm interfaces. For example, Scott Paper Company's diagram of its product manager relationships depicts up to 17 interfaces with other departments in the company and its advertising agency, not including the higher management line of responsibility.

Significance of Product Management Interfaces

One may assert that product managers' interfaces are exceedingly important to effective marketing, at the same time acknowledging the value of involving other corporate personnel. The much more numerous confrontations of salesmen with buyers might be considered of primary importance; yet these are relatively routine and remote from marketing strategy and policy. High echelon marketing executives' interfaces, both internal and external, are quite important since the more comprehensive and far-reaching decisions on goals, allocations, and programs are reached at that level. Regardless, product managers' interfaces are of high importance from each of three viewpoints.

Product Manager Viewpoint

Position descriptions for product managers are aptly counched in terms of "formulating" or "originating" product plans and strategies, or "centralizing" information about assigned products. A man placed in a conceptual and informational hub of the organization must personally be an intelligence headquarters. To maintain competitive position and profit of his products, with his performance starkly exposed to higher management, he must strive to be the best informed man about any aspect substantially affecting their future. He must arrange and nurture a number of information interfaces to achieve his functions.

The verb "coordinate" is often and aptly used to describe how a product manager should execute his "responsibilities." His interfaces are used to enthuse others about his plans and to obtain their concurrence and action. To a substantial degree, his success depends upon his effectiveness in motivating others to implement his plans without direct organizational authority.

The Firm's Viewpoint

The properly functioning product manager is the firm's main intelligence center for its product lines. Much more than a repository, he is an action center at which all strategy and plans for his product lines converge. A large company cannot rely on higher executives, functional middle managers, or committees to become sufficiently informed about the situation and opportunities facing an individual product line. Higher executives and committees should be well briefed in order to integrate various product managers' recommendations and make allocations fairly to each program; however, they cannot possess the depth of understanding and analysis of each product manager.

A General Marketing Viewpoint

The marketing institution viewpoint and the consumer or user viewpoint, taken broadly, should coincide in seeking what Paul Mazur considered marketing's goal to deliver a standard of living. This can be accomplished only when marketing interfaces with its buying publics as fully and intelligently as possible. The potential for effectively realizing this goal is enhanced when the information focus and the marketing strategy focus are centered within one position in the firm. This position ideally is that of a product manager who can devote all his powers and attention to his assigned product area. The man who serves as a gatekeeper in the firm at the spot where market needs and opportunities meet the firm's capabilities, objectives, and strategies, is most critical from a socially-aware marketing viewpoint.

Obstacles

While the number of interfaces realized by product managers may be adequate, the quality of these relationships tends to fall seriously short of the ideal. Product managers should be of gregarious nature, ready and anxious to meet others, and typically they are. Establishing a wide network of contacts is thus not overly difficult. The deficiency tends to arise from the failure of the product manager to develop the most productive associations in depth. Causes underlying this failure might include the following:

1. Preoccupation with trivial and distracting tasks. Many product managers find their time burdened with correspondence with salesmen and customers about minor problems and adjustments. Many allow themselves to become expediters of deliveries, and of the production and distribution of promotional literature.
2. Lack of assistance. This tends to prevent a product manager from allocating time to the interfaces which are most important. Most product managers have no help beyond a secretary (and some share secretaries). Some have trainees who are only temporary help before being elevated into full production managerships. More com-

panies are providing assistant product managers, but there has not been general recognition of the need.

3. Lack of cooperation with functional departments. This may result in the functional department either passing along to the product manager tasks that the functional department should assume, or conversely, encroaching on the decision sphere of a product manager by making decisions that are rightly his. At the extreme, a functional department may actually balk at cooperating in carrying out product plans.
4. Lack of well-conceived formal position descriptions. Where they exist, such descriptions either tend to assign the product manager too broad a responsibility, or list his duties in unrealistic detail. The interfaces implied for the manager may be too many and too unsystematic to be efficient. Sometimes the number of products and brands assigned a manager are excessive. In one case, for example, the author found a product manager responsible for 17 distinct nationally advertised products.
5. Restriction of the product manager to a single brand or type of a product with no supplemental participation regarding new products serving the same needs. While specific brand managers are needed where a single brand sells in enormous volume, product managers should not be excluded from the dynamics of product improvement and innovation.
6. Inadequate scheduling of available time. A specific set of priorities should be established and periodically reviewed, particularly for the novice product manager.
7. Inadequate training of product managers. Because the demands of the position are more varied than those of most other middle management jobs, training of product managers is relatively more important. Unfortunately many product managers learn under loose supervision or by trial and error. If each product manager kept explicit records of his planning and decision analyses and of the ensuing results, others could profit from this store of experience. This training technique, however, is often overlooked.
8. Short job tenure. The median in consumer products is about two years. The period is usually somewhat longer for industrial products managers. One product line, aggregating over $20,000,000 annual sales, was observed to have had three product managers in four years. In addition, new product managers appear to have little communication with their predecessors, although they are still working in the company.

9. Last, but very important, is the excessive number of interfaces that most product managers attempt, particularly intra-company. The product manager should be selective in the interfaces he establishes. This positions him to concentrate on decoding and analyzing the inputs he receives from these especially strategic linkages, and where necessary, to direct his communications skills toward them.

Some Recommendations

There appears to be a gradual shift in the positioning, functioning, and training of product managers as firms which utilize this approach gain experience. The writer has identified four dimensions of development which may promote effective interfacing by product managers.

1. Realignment of product managers' assignments toward a market orientation. The typical assignment is in terms of a particular product or products, and the concentration is on promoting their sales. The result can be a myopic vision of the market in terms of the given product. A more balanced and progressive view is likely when this manager is assigned a specific market or product-use area, in which he works to improve market penetration through innovation while simultaneously formulating the optimal strategy and marketing mix to increase the profitability of his existing products. This should result in a systematic market/product development while also accentuating the entirety of the market interface. Further, involvement with a homogeneous market may be less confusing for the product manager than a strict product alignment which often involves dealing with the heterogeneous uses and markets that a single product may serve.
2. Provision of an improved atmosphere for the serious study by product managers of markets and alternative strategies in product, pricing, promotion, and distribution. Some companies do provide sufficient privacy and, on a smaller scale, some seek to limit the many tasks and other distractions in order to provide product management with adequate time for marketing planning.
3. Restrictions of the interfaces attempted by product managers to the few that are most productive. This avoids the superficial contacts and fragmentary communications that are much too common. It is suggested that a consumer goods product manager restrict himself within the interfaces shown in Figure 1 and concentrate on those itemized below.

   Marketing research
   Advertising agency
   The market (dealers and buyers)

Sales management
Advertising management
Product development

His relationships should be conducted primarily through one liaison in the four named departments and the advertising agency. This is increasingly common with the market research interface, the chief and constant aid of many product managers. It is further suggested that the time saved by reducing intra-company communication be devoted to more personal interface with markets.

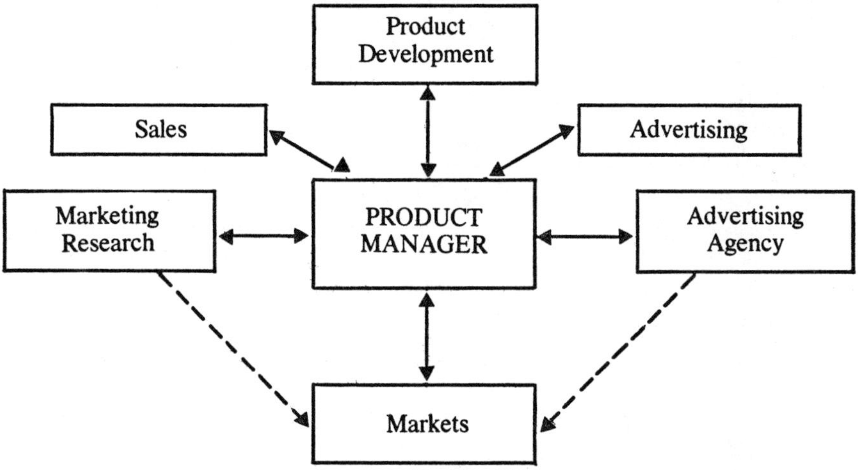

FIGURE 1. Interfaces of a product manager.

4. Development of complete and realistic job descriptions accompanied by more specific performance evaluation criteria. In addition to removing much of the vagueness that contributes to inefficient product manager work, this would relieve personal frustration and direct the manager's efforts, including those related to interfacing within and outside the firm. In providing a solid basis for extensive job training and manpower development, this procedure can make a long-range contribution to the product manager concept.

Conclusion

Product managers are surely here to stay, for it appears that no other organizational arrangement so well promotes efficient marketing planning in the spirit of the marketing concept. Clear recognition of the fundamental role that effective interfaces play, both within the firm and with the external publics who shape the firm's destiny, will be a long first step to realization of the profit potential of the product manager system.

NOTES

1. The more thorough analyses of product manager's work are in: Gordon H. Evans, *The Product Manager's Job* (New York: American Management Association, 1964) and Gordon Medcalf, *Marketing and the Brand Manager* (London, England: Pergamon Press, Ltd., 1967).
2. David J. Luck and Theodore Nowak, "Product Management: Vision Unfilled," *Harvard Business Review*, Vol. 43 (May, 1965), pp. 143–150.
3. This study under sponsorship of the Marketing Science Institute contributed to the volume: P. J. Robinson and D. J. Luck, *Promotional Decision Making* (New York: McGraw-Hill Book Company, 1964)
4. In *Management and Advertising Problems* (New York: Association of National Advertisers, 1965) this problem is discussed on page 53. The study reported in this volume, however, later affirmed the continuous growth of product management, but in more effective relationships with advertising agencies. (p. 92.)

LEARNING REVIEW

Questions:

1. The product manager may have too many ____________________.

2. A deficiency with product managers is not a shortage of contacts but the failure to____.

3. The six interfaces most important to the product manager are
   a) ____________, b) ____________, c) ____________,
   d) ____________, e) ____________, f) ____________.

Answers:

1. interfaces 2. develop them in depth 3. a) marketing research, b) advertising agency, c) the market, d) sales management, e) advertising management, f) product development.

Retrospective Comment

The *Interfaces* article stated some fundamentals of a product manager's situation that were too universal to produce any controversial sequel, although a few product managers did protest that their involvements with manufacturing departments were understated. My fascination with product management has continued with additional study of their organization, the publication of a short book on their strategic functions, and writing a longer book on the same subject. The research has confirmed the pervasiveness of the indicated interfaces, as well as the widening use of the product manager system. In the petroleum crisis of 1973–76, another interface has arisen urgently for many managers of products using petroleum byproducts: directly working with *materials sources* to meet critical manufacturing schedules. The implication: an economy of scarcity may find product managers interfacing *suppliers* as importantly as markets.

19

The Death and Burial of "Sick" Products

R. S. Alexander

PREVIEW

I. Several factors should be considered in selection of products for possible elimination:
   A. A sales decline over a period of time merits attention
   B. A downward trend in the price of an established product should be examined
   C. Declining profit should raise questions
   D. When a substitute product appears on the market and is an improvement, elimination of the old product should be considered
   E. If the product loses some of its effectiveness, deletion should be considered
   F. If a product requires excessive executive time, it should be examined carefully.

II. In analyzing a product, the decision maker needs information on several factors:
   A. Profit should be important, but should not be the sole factor
      1. An attempt should be made to assign costs to individual products in the line
      2. Management should set a target profit for products and evaluate them in terms of this profit goal
   B. Decision makers must weigh the effect of the deletion on the capital structure of the firm
   C. If deletion means discharging or transferring union employees, the company must consider the effect on union-company relations

---

R. S. Alexander, "The Death and Burial of 'Sick' Products," is reprinted by permission from the *Journal of Marketing*, published by the American Marketing Association (April 1964), pp. 1–7.

   D. Marketing factors, such as the effect of deletion on the sale of other products in the line, should be researched carefully.

III. Decision makers should consider alternatives other than deletion:
   A. Methods of cost reductions might be sought
   B. Changes in the marketing mix (such as varying advertising and sales efforts) should be examined
   C. Price adjustments should be considered as an alternative.

IV. Once the deletion decision has been made, a number of factors must be considered:
   A. Timing of the deletion is critical to financial, human resources, and production facility needs; and the deletion should cause minimum disturbance to customers
   B. If the deleted product is a durable one, the company should consider the necessity of parts and replacements for customers
   C. The deletion plan should clear out accumulated inventory
   D. Holdover demand might be dealt with by having another firm assume manufacture of the product.

Euthanasia applied to human beings is criminal; but aging products enjoy or suffer no such legal protection. This is a sad fact of business life.

The word "product" is used here not in its broad economic sense of anything produced—such as wheat, coal, a car, or a chair—but in its narrower meaning of an article made to distinct specifications and intended for sale under a separate brand or catalogue number. In the broader sense of the word, certain products may last as long as industrial civilization endures; in the narrow sense, most of them are playthings of change.

Much has been written about managing the development and marketing of new products, but business literature is largely devoid of material on product deletion.

This is not surprising. New products have glamor. Their management is fraught with great risks. Their successful introduction promises growth in sales and profits that may be fantastic.

But putting products to death—or letting them die—is a drab business, and often engenders much of the sadness of a final parting with old and tried friends. "The portable 6-sided, pretzel polisher was the first product The Company ever made. Our line will no longer be our line without it."

But while deletion is an uninspiring and depressing process, in a changing market it is almost as vital as the addition of new products. The old product that is a "football" of competition or has lost much of its market appeal is likely to generate more than its share of small unprofitable orders; to make necessary short, costly production runs; to demand an exorbitant amount of executive attention; and to tie up capital that could be used more profitably in other ventures.

Just as a crust of barnacles on the hold of a ship retards the vessel's movement, so do a number of worn-out items in a company's product mix affect the company's progress.

Most of the costs that result from the lack of an effective deletion system are hidden and become apparent only after careful analysis. As a result, management often overlooks them. The need for examining the product line to discover outworn members, and for analysis to arrive at intelligent decisions to discard or to keep them, very rarely assumes the urgency of a crisis. Too often, management thinks of this as something that should be done but that can wait until tomorrow.

This is why a definite procedure for deletion of products should be set up, and why the authority and responsibility for the various activities involved should be clearly and definitely assigned. This is especially important because this work usually requires the cooperation of several functional groups within the business firm, including at least marketing, production, finance, and sometimes personnel.

Definite responsibility should be assigned for at least the following activities involved in the process:(1) selecting products which are candidates for elimination; (2) gathering information about them and analyzing the information; (3) making decisions about elimination; and (4) if necessary, removing the doomed products from the line.

Selection of Products for Possible Elimination

As a first step, we are not seeking the factors on which the final decision to delete or to retain turns, but merely those which indicate that the product's continuation in the product mix should be considered carefully with elimination as a possibility. Although removal from the product line may seem to be the prime aim, the result is not inevitably deletion from the line; instead, careful analysis may lead to changes in the product itself or in the methods of making or marketing it.

Sales Trend. If the trend of a product's sales is downward over a time period that is significant in relation to the normal life of others like it, its continuation in the mix deserves careful examination. There may be many reasons for such a decline that in no way point toward deletion; but when decline continues over a period of time the situation needs to be studied.

Price Trend. A downward trend in the price of a new product may be expected if the firm introducing it pursues a skimming-price policy, or if all firms making it realize substantial cost savings as a result of volume production and increased processing know-how. But when the price of an established product whose competitive pattern has been relatively stabilized shows a downward trend over a significant period of time, the future of that product should receive attention.

Profit Trend. A declining profit either in dollars or as a per cent of sales or investment should raise questions about a product's continued place in the product line. Such a trend usually is the result of a price-factory cost squeeze, although it may be the outcome of a loss in market appeal or a change in the method of customer purchase which forces higher marketing expenditures.

Substitute Products. When a substitute article appears on the market, especially if it represents an improvement over an old product, management must face the question of whether to retain or discard the old product. This is true regardless of who introduces the substitute. The problem is especially difficult when the new product serves the same general purpose as the old one but is not an exact substitute for it.

Product Effectiveness. Certain products may lose some of their effectiveness for the purposes they serve. For example, disease germs may develop strains that are resistant to a certain antibiotic. When this happens, the question of whether to keep or delete the drug involve issues not only of the interests of the firm but of the public welfare.

Executive Time. A possible tipoff as to the location of "illness" in a product mix lies in a study of the amount of executive time and attention devoted to each of the items in the product line. Sick products, like sick people, demand a lot of care; but one must be careful to distinguish the "growing pains" of a new product from the more serious disorders of one that has matured and is now declining.

The six indicators mentioned do not of themselves provide evidence justifying deletion. But they can help management to single out from a line of products those upon which it can profitably spend time and money in analyzing them, with elimination from the line as a *possibility*.

Analysis and Decision Making About "Sick" Products

Although the work of analyzing a sick or decrepit product is usually done by people other than the management executives who decide what to do about it, the two processes are interdependent. Unless the right factors are chosen for analysis and unless the work is properly done, the decision is not likely to be an intelligent one. Accordingly, these two factors will be discussed together.

What information does a decision-maker need about a product, and what sort of analysis of it should he have in order to render a sound verdict as to its future? The deletion decision should not turn on the sole issue of profitability. Profit is the most important objective of a business; but individual firms often seek to achieve both long-run and short-run objectives other than profit.

So, in any individual case the critical factors and the weights assigned them in making a decision must be chosen in the light of the situation of the firm and the management objectives.

Profits

Profit management in a firm with a multi-product line (the usual situation in our economy) is not the simple operation generally contemplated in economic theory. Such a firm usually has in its product mix (1) items in various stages of introduction and development, some of which may be fantastically profitable and others deep "in the red"; (2) items which are mature but not "superannuated," whose profit rate is likely to be satisfactory; and (3) declining items which may yield a net profit somewhat less than adequate or may show heavy losses.

The task is to manage the whole line or mix so that it will show a satisfactory profit for the company. In the process, two questions are vital; What is a profit? How much profit is satisfactory?

Operating-statement accounting makes it possible to determine with reasonable accuracy the total amount of net profit a company earns on an overall basis. But when the management of a multi-product firm seeks to determine how much of this total is generated by its activities in making and marketing each product in its mix, the process is almost incredibly complex; and the results are almost certain to be conditioned on a tissue of assumptions which are so debatable that no management can feel entirely comfortable in basing decisions on them.

This is because such a large portion of the costs of the average multi-product firm are or behave like overhead or joint expense. Almost inevitably several of the items in the product mix are made of common materials, with the same equipment, and by manpower which is interchangeable. Most of the company's marketing efforts and expenses are devoted to selling and distributing the mix or a line within the mix, rather than individual items.

In general, the more varied the product mix of a firm, the greater is the portion of its total expense that must be classified as joint or overhead. In such a company, many types of cost which ordinarily can be considered direct tend to behave like overhead or joint expenses. This is particularly true of marketing costs such as advertising that does not feature specific items; personal selling; order handling; and delivery.

This means that a large part of a company's costs must be assigned to products on some arbitrary basis and that however logical this basis may be, it is subject to considerable reasonable doubt in specific cases. It also means that if one product is removed from the mix, many of these costs remain to be reassigned to the items that stay in the line. As a result, any attempt to "prune" the product mix entirely on the basis of the profit contribution, or lack of it, of specific items is almost certain to be disappointing and in some cases disastrous.

But if a multi-product firm could allocate costs to individual items in the mix on some basis recognized as sound and thus compute product-profit accurately, what standard of profit should be set up, the failure to meet which would justify deletion?

Probably most managements either formally or unconsciously set overall company profit targets. Such targets may be expressed in terms of dollars, although to be most useful in product management they usually must be translated into percentages on investment, or money used. As an example, a company may have as its profit target 15% on investment before taxes.

Certainly *every* product in the mix should not be required to achieve the target, which really amounts to an average. To do so would be to deny the inevitable variations in profit potential among products.

Probably a practical minimum standard can be worked out, below which a product should be eliminated unless other considerations demand its retention. Such a standard can be derived from a balancing out of the profit rates among products in the mix, so as to arrive at the overall company target as an average. The minimum standard then represents a figure that would tip the balance enough to endanger the overall target.

What role, then, should considerations of product profit play in managerial decisions as to deletion or retention?

1. Management probably will be wise to recognize an overall company target profit in dollars or rate on investment, and to set in relation to it a minimum below which the profit on an individual product should not fall without marking that item for deletion (unless other special considerations demand its retention).

2. Management should cast a "bilious eye" on all arguments that a questionable product be kept in the mix because it helps to defray overhead and joint costs. Down that road, at the end of a series of decisions to retain such products, lies a mix entirely or largely composed of items each busily "sopping up" overhead, but few or none contributing anything to net profit.

3. This does not mean that management should ignore the effect of a

product deletion on overhead or joint costs. Decision-makers must be keenly aware of the fact that the total of such costs borne by a sick product must, after it is deleted, be reallocated to other products, and with the result that they may become of doubtful profitability. A detailed examination of the joint or overhead costs charged against an ailing product may indicate that some of them can be eliminated in whole or in part if it is eliminated. Such costs are notoriously "sticky" and difficult to get rid of; but every pretext should be used to try to find ways to reduce them.

4. If a deletion decision involves a product or a group of products responsible for a significant portion of a firm's total sales volume, decision-makers can assess the effects of overhead and joint costs on the problem, by compiling an estimated company operating statement after the deletion and comparing it with the current one. Such a forecasted statement should include expected net income from the use of the capital and facilities released by deletion if an opportunity for their use is ready to hand. Surviving joint and overhead expenses can even be reallocated to the remaining products, in order to arrive at an estimate of the effect that deletion might have, not only on the total company net income but on the profitability of each of the remaining products as well. Obviously such a cost analysis is likely to be expensive, and so is not justified unless the sales volume stakes are high.

Financial Considerations

Deletion is likely not only to affect the profit performance of a firm but to modify its financial structure as well.

To make and sell a product, a company must invest some of its capital. In considering its deletion, the decision-makers must estimate what will happen to the capital funds presently used in making and marketing it.

When a product is dropped from the mix, most or all of the circulating capital invested in it—such as inventories of materials, goods in process, and finished goods and accounts receivable—should drain back into the cash account; and if carried out in an orderly fashion, deletion will not disturb this part of the capital structure except to increase the ratio of cash to other assets.

This will be true, unless the deletion decison is deferred until product deterioration has gone so far that the decision assumes the aspect of a crisis and its execution that of a catastrophe.

The funds invested in the equipment and other facilities needed to make and market the "sick" product are a different matter. If the equipment is versatile and standard, it may be diverted to other uses. If the firm has no need of it and if the equipment has been properly depreciated, management may find a market for it at a price approaching or even exceeding its book value.

In either case, the capital structure of the company is not disturbed except by a shift from equipment to cash in the case of sale. In such a case management would be wise, before making a deletion decision, to determine how much cash this action promises to release as well as the chances for its reinvestment.

If the equipment is suited for only one purpose, it is highly unlikely that management can either find another use for it or sell it on favorable terms. If it is old and almost completely depreciated, it can probably be scrapped and its remaining value "written off" without serious impairment of the firm's capital structure.

But if it is only partly depreciated, the decision-makers must weigh the relative desirability of two possible courses of action: (1) to delete immediately, hoping that the ensuing improvement in the firm's operating results will more than offset the impairment in capital structure that deletion will cause; or (2) to seek to recapture as much as possible of its value, by continuing to make and market the product as long as its price is enough to cover out-of-pocket costs and leaving something over to apply to depreciation.

This choice depends largely on two things: the relation between the amount of fixed and circulating capital that is involved; and the opportunities available to use the funds, executive abilities, manpower, and transferable facilities released by deletion for making profits in other ventures.

This matter of opportunity costs is a factor in every deletion decision. The dropping of a product is almost certain to release some capital, facilities, manpower skills, and executive abilities. If opportunities can be found in which these assets can be invested without undue risk and with promise of attractive profits, it may be good management to absorb considerable immediate loss in deleting a sick product.

If no such opportunities can be found, it is probably wise to retain the product so long as the cash inflow from its sales covers out-of-pocket costs and contributes something to depreciation and other overhead expenses. In such a case, however, it is the part of good management to seek actively for new ventures which promise satisfactory profits, and to be ready to delete promptly when such an opportunity is found.

Employee Relations

The effect which product elimination may have on the employees of a firm is often an important factor in decisions either to drop or to retain products.

This is not likely to be a deciding factor if new product projects are under development to which the people employed in making and marketing the doubtful product can be transferred, unless such transfer would deprive them of the earning power of special skills. But when deletion of a product means discharging or transferring unionized employees, the decision-makers must give careful thought to the effect their action is likely to have on company-union relations.

Even in the absence of union pressure, management usually feels a strong sense of responsibility for the people in its employ. Just how far management can go in conserving specific jobs at the expense of deferring or foregoing necessary deletions before it endangers the livelihood of all the employees of the firm is a nice question of balance.

Marketing Factors

Many multi-product firms retain in their marketing mixes one or more items which, on the basis of profits and the company financial structure, should be deleted. To continue to make and market a losing product is no managerial crime. It is reprehensible only when management does not know the product is a losing one or, knowing the facts, does not have sound reasons for retaining it. Such reasons are very likely to lie in the marketing area.

Deletions of products are often deferred or neglected because of management's desire to carry a "full line," whatever that means. This desire may be grounded on sound reasons of consumer patronage or on a dubious yearning for the "prestige" that a full line is supposed to engender. But there is no magic about a full line or the prestige that is supposed to flow from it. Both should be evaluated on the basis of their effects on the firm's sales volume, profits, and capacity to survive and grow.

Products are often associated in the marketing process. The sale of one is helped by the presence of another in the product mix.

When elimination of a product forces a customer who buys all or a large part of his requirements of a group of profitable items from the firm to turn to another supplier for his needs of the dropped product, he might shift some or all of his other patronage as well. Accordingly, it is sometimes wise for management to retain in its mix a no-profit item, in order to hold sales volume of highly profitable products. But this should not be done blindly without analysis.

Rarely can management tell ahead of time exactly how much other business will be lost by deleting a product, or in what proportions the losses will fall among the remaining items. But in many cases the amount of sales volume can be computed that will be *hazarded* by such action; what other products will be subject to that hazard; and what portion of their volume will be involved. When this marketing interdependence exists in a deletion problem, the decision-makers should seek to discover the customers who buy the sick product; what other items in the mix they buy; in what quantities; and how much profit they contribute.

The firm using direct marketing channels can do this with precision and at relatively little cost. The firm marketing through indirect channels will find it more difficult, and the information will be less exact; but it still may be worth-while. If the stakes are high enough, marketing research may be conducted to discover the extent to which the customer purchases of profitable items actually are associated with that of the sick product. Although the results may not be precise, they may supply an order-of-magnitude idea of the interlocking patronage situation.

Product interrelationships in marketing constitute a significant factor in making deletion decisions, but should never be accepted as the deciding factor without careful study to disclose at least the extent of the hazards they involve.

Other Possibilities

The fact that a product's market is declining or that its profit performance is substandard does not mean that deletion is the *only* remedy.

Profits can be made in a shrinking market. There are things other than elimination of a product that can be done about deteriorating profit performance. They tend to fall into four categories.

(1) *Costs*. A careful study may uncover ways of reducing factory costs. This may result from improved processes that either eliminate manpower or equipment time or else increase yield; or from the elimination of forms or features that once were necessary or worth-while but are no longer needed. The natural first recourse of allocating joint and overhead costs on a basis that is "kinder" to the doubtful product is not to be viewed with enthusiasm. After reallocation, these costs still remain in the business; and the general profit picture has not been improved in the least.

(2) *Marketing*. Before deleting a product, management will be wise to examine the methods of marketing it, to see if they can be changed to improve its profit picture.

Can advertising and sales effort be reduced without serious loss of volume? A holding operation requires much less effort and money than a promotional one.

Are services being given that the product no longer needs?

Can savings be made in order handling and delivery, even at some loss of customer satisfaction? For example, customers may be buying the product in small orders that are expensive to handle.

On the other hand, by spending more marketing effort, can volume be increased so as to bring about a reduction in factory cost greater than the added marketing expense? In this attempt, an unexpected "assist" may come from competitors who delete the product and leave more of the field to the firm.

By remodeling the product, "dressing it up," and using a new marketing approach, can it be brought back to a state of health and profit? Here the decision-makers must be careful not to use funds and facilities that could be more profitably invested in developing and marketing new products.

(3) *Price*. It is natural to assume that the price of a failing product cannot be raised. At least in part, its plight is probably due to the fact that it is "kicked around" by competition, and thus that competition will not allow any increases.

But competitors may be tired of the game, too. One company that tried increasing prices found that wholesalers and retailers did not resent a larger cost-of-goods-sold base on which to apply their customary gross profit rates, and that consumers continued to buy and competitors soon followed suit.

Although a price rise will not usually add to the sum total of user happiness, it may not subtract materially from total purchases. The decision-makers should not ignore the possibility of using a price reduction to gain enough physical volume to bring about a more-than-offseting decline in unit costs, although at this stage the success of such a gambit is not likely.

(4) *Cross Production*. In the materials field, when small production runs make costs prohibitive, arrangements may sometimes be made for Firm A to make the *entire* supply of Product X for itself and Competitor B. Then B reciprocates with another similar product. Such "trades," for instance, are to be found in the chemical business.

Summation for Decision

In solving deletion problems, the decision-makers must draw together into a single pattern the results of the analysis of all the factors bearing on the matter. Although this is probably most often done on an intangible, subjective basis, some firms have experimented with the formula method.

For example, a manufacturer of electric motors included in its formula the following factors:

Profitability
Position on growth curve
Product leadership
Market position
Marketing dependence of other products

Each factor was assigned a weight in terms of possible "counts" against the product. For instance, if the doubtful item promised no profits for the next three years, it had a count of 50 points against it, while more promising prospects were assigned lesser counts. A critical total for all factors was set in advance which would automatically doom a product. Such a system can include other factors—such as recapturability of invested capital, alternate available uses of facilities, effects on labor force, or other variables peculiar to the individual case.

The use of a formula lends an aura of precision to the act of decision-making and assures a degree of uniformity in it. But obviously the weights assigned to different factors cannot be the same in all cases. For example, if the deletion of a doubtful product endangers a large volume of sales of other highly profitable items, that alone should probably decide the matter.

The same thing is true if deletion will force so heavy a writeoff of invested funds as to impair the firm's capital structure. Certainly this will be true if all or most of the investment can be recaptured by the depreciation route if the product stays in the mix.

This kind of decision requires that the factors be weighted differently in each case. But when managers are given a formula, they may tend to quit thinking and do too much "weighing."

The Deletion of a Product

Once the decision to eliminate a product is made, plans must be drawn for its death and burial with the least disturbance of customer relations and of the other operations of the firm.

Such plans must deal with a variety of detailed problems. Probably the most important fall into four categories: timing; parts and replacements; stocks; and holdover demand.

Timing. It is desirable that deletion be timed so as to dovetail with the financial, manpower, and facilities needs for new products. As manpower and facilities are released from the dying product and as the capital devoted to it flows back into the cash account, it is ideal if these can be immediately used in a new venture. Although this can never be completely achieved, it may be approximated.

The death of a product should be timed so as to cause the least disturbance to customers. They should be informed about the elimination of the product far enough in advance so they can make arrangements for replacement, if any are available, but not so far in advance that they will switch to new suppliers before the deleting firm's inventories of the product are sold. Deletion at the beginning of a selling season or in the middle of it probably will create maximum customer inconvenience, whereas at the end of the season it will be the least disturbing.

Parts and Replacements. If the product to be killed off is a durable one, probably the deleting firm will find it necessary to maintain stocks of repair parts for about the expected life of the units most recently sold. The firm that leaves a trail of uncared-for "orphan" products cannot expect to engender much good will from dealers or users. Provision for the care and maintenance of the orphan is a necessary cost of deletion.

This problem is much more widespread than is commonly understood. The woman who buys a set of china or silverware and finds that she cannot replace broken or lost pieces does not entertain an affectionate regard for the maker. The same sort of thing is true if she installs draperies and later, when one of them is damaged, finds that the pattern is no longer available.

Stocks. The deletion plan should provide for clearing out of the stocks of the dying product and materials used in its production, so as to recover the maximum amount of the working capital invested in it. This is very largely a matter of timing—the tapering off of purchase, production, and selling activities. However, this objective may conflict with those of minimizing inconvenience to customers and servicing the orphan units in use after deletion.

Holdover Demand. However much the demand for a product may decline, it probably will retain some following of devoted users. They are bound to be disturbed by its deletion and are likely to be vocal about it; and usually there is little that management can do to mitigate this situation.

Sometimes a firm can avoid all these difficulties by finding another firm to purchase the product. This should usually be tried before any other deletion steps are taken. A product with a volume too small for a big firm to handle profitably may be a money-maker for a smaller one with less overhead and more flexibility.

Neglect or Action?

The process of product deletion is important. The more dynamic the business, the more important it is.

But it is something that most company executives prefer not to do; and therefore it will not get done unless management establishes definite, clearcut policies to guide it, sets up carefully articulated procedures for doing it, and makes a positive and unmistakable assignment of authority and responsibility for it.

Exactly what these policies should be, what form these procedures should take, and to whom the job should be assigned are matters that must vary with the structure and operating methods of the firm and with its position in the industry and the market.

In any case, though, the need for managerial attention, planning, and supervision of the deletion function cannot be overemphasized. Many business firms are paying dearly for their neglect of this problem, but unfortunately do not realize how much this is costing them.

LEARNING REVIEW

Questions:

1. In a changing market ____________ is almost as vital as the addition of new products.

2. A clue to the location of *illness* in a product mix lies in a study of the amount of ____________________ devoted to each of the items in the product line.

3. The four factors to consider in analyzing a product for deletion are:
   a) ____________, b) ________________________,
   c) ________________________________,
   and d) ______________.

4. Two possible effects of retaining a sick product are:
   a) ________________________________
   b) ________________________________

5. The three stages in analyzing a sick product are:
   a) ________________________________
   b) ________________________________
   c) ________________________________

6. Other possibilities less drastic than deletion of an unprofitable product include:
   a) ____________, b) ________________,
   c) ____________, and d) ________________
   ________________________________.

Answers:

1. deletion; 2. executive time and attention; 3. a) profit, b) financial considerations, c) employee relations (due to displacement or discharge), d) marketing factors; 4. a) slow growth potential, b) economic inefficiencies; 5. a) selection of products for elimination, b) analyze and decide product's fate, c) actual deletion; 6. a) reducing costs, b) improving marketing strategy, c) raising the price, d) subcontracting or cross production with another firm

Retrospective Comment

If I were writing the article for current publication, I would have to include at least two, possibly three, mathematical formulas. Otherwise, I doubt if I would get it published. But if I was merely revising the article for republication, I think I would make at least two significant changes.

I would urge that any firm with a multiple product mix conduct what might be called a *product audit* every five years, perhaps every two or three years depending on the volatility of the industry, to select products to consider for deletion. Such an audit should be a matter of company policy. A product audit should cover the factors mentioned in the article—sales trend, substitute products, product effectiveness, executive time devoted to the product—and such other factors as might be applicable in specific cases.

Second, in discussing attempts to revive a failing product, I would point out that such attempts, especially of the promotional variety, would be much less likely to succeed in the case of an industrial product than when applied to a consumer good. An industrial product is likely to go into a decline because it no longer suits the purpose. When this happens, no amount of cost reduction, dressing up, or promotion is likely to do any good. Of course, this sometimes happens with a consumer product, but much less often.

Without the field research which is well beyond the financial resources of a retired professor, I can have no idea of what the current practice or procedure for deleting products may be. So I can say nothing on that point. Conpanies do not usually announce in the trade press the demise of their products. Most product funerals are private and the more private the better.

20

A Theory of Packaging in the Marketing Mix

William R. Mason

PREVIEW

I. There are six functions of a product's package:
   A. Protecting the product
   B. Adapting to production line speeds
   C. Promoting the product
   D. Increasing product density
   E. Facilitating the use of the product
   F. Having re-use value for the consumer

II. Each of the six functions interrelates with the others in such a way that all functions must be considered, but each function remains to some extent mutually exclusive of the others.

III. The most successful package changes are those which help to maximize product inventory as close to a point of use as possible.
   A. Changes involving package size or count either cause the consumer to store larger quantities or to store in more than one place.
   B. Changes of package shape allow easier storage at all points along the marketing line.
   C. Changes involving addition of *ease of opening* or *ease of use* attributes aid movement at the retail level.

It is axiomatic that the job of packaging is to sell. But after that banality has been voiced, what guides to management judgement—what theories, if you will—influence the choice of a package?

William R. Mason, "A Theory of Packaging in the Marketing Mix," is reprinted by permission from *Business Horizons* (Summer 1958), pp. 91–95.

This article is not a check list of features that should be built into a package, but a rough guide to basic judgments management must bring to bear in its choice of packaging before the particulars of type face, combination of colors, package count, or printing method are up for decision.

The critical judgments that must be made on the packaging choice concern the "mix" of packaging attributes best able to perform, in different degrees, the particular functions of the package that are believed to be important to sales. The basic judgment in choice of packaging is "What jobs should the package do, and how completely should it do each?" The answers to the lesser decisions can fall into place once the "mix" of desirable packaging attributes has been determined, once the assignment of basic functions desired of the package has been made. Frequently, too much effort and time are devoted to making lesser decisions, usually on questions of graphic art, rather than this basic judgment.

The packager may accept as a guide, when making basic decisions on product "mix," that:

> *The major purpose of any package is to influence or control the location of product storage within the marketing channel.*

"Storage," as I am using the term, means the holding of goods for future use at any level along the marketing channel, *including the level of the ultimate consumer*. Even at the ultimate consumer level, the product may be stored in several places—sugar, for example, may be stored on a shelf or on the table. The packager is interested in getting the bulk of his product's storage as near as possible to the point of ultimate use.

The functions of the product's package are:

Protecting the product
Adapting to production line speeds
Promoting the product
Increasing product density[1]
Facilitating the use of the product
Having re-use value for the consumer.

The performance of a package in the first two of these basic functions is relatively easy to measure through physical testing procedures. And, because it is comparatively easy to evaluate the degrees to which these functions are fulfilled by any package under consideration, such measurement is very common. Today, it must be a rare package that reaches its market without being rated objectively on its degrees of protection and production line adaptability. However, these ratings seem to be applied too often without consideration of the package's ability to fulfill its other possible functions.

There are four other major jobs that the package can do at least partially; these should be assigned priority by company management, but often they seem to be neglected.

All packages have the opportunity to perform, at least partially, each of these functions. But it is an unusual package that performs each to the same degree. That the package gives a superior performance of one function does not necessarily mean that it will give a superior performance of another. Because he needs to choose a package, the packager, whether he recognizes it or not, must assign priorities to the value of each of these functions to further his product's sale and use.

To illustrate, it is usually easy to create a package that has uniquely promotable features quite aside from graphic arts; that is, a package that could eminently perform the promotional function. But something else has to give. Using such a package may require sacrificing a good job in one of the other areas, for example in adaptability to production line speeds or in failure to increase package density. In like fashion, it is frequently possible to build a feature facilitating product use into a package—but not always without sacrificing some measure of product protection.

After all, when a package is criticized as a poor sales- or use-builder, it can be criticized fairly only when its performance of *each* of the basic functions is evaluated. A product may seem "overpackaged" simply because the packager's assignment of priorities differs from the critic's.

Interrelationships

Let's examine in a little more detail the way each function impinges on the others:

Protecting the Product

Beyond the requirements imposed by various governmental, carrier, and trade practice rulings, there usually are a substantial number of alternatives open to management with regard to product protection—even during the period when the product is in its distribution channel. To illustrate, even though a carrier ruling may require the product's 24-count carton to have a minimum corrugated fiberboard strength of, say, a 100-pound test, a company's management may choose board that meets more severe tests in order to permit higher stacking or use of mechanized materials-handling equipment by certain important handlers at various levels in the product's distribution channel. Accordingly, in such a situation, an opportunity to tailor the product's package to its product-protection job alone is relinquished because of a desire to better the package's performance of its density-increasing and promotional jobs.

But perhaps a more important range of product-protection considerations occurs at the time of product use—especially when the product is partially used. How much protection should the bread wrapper give a partially used loaf of bread? Will incorporating the use-facilitating features of a pouring spout or a tear tape opening require yielding too much product protection?

Adapting to Production Line Speeds

Sometimes the operating speeds of packaging equipment do not match the speeds of other equipment in the production line. Until recently, for instance, the normal operating speeds of wrapping machinery that would handle polyethylene film did not match the normal production line speeds for many products. Two or more wrapping machines were often required in a production line, and the results were poor space utilization, greater capital investment, and sometimes greater labor costs. As an alternative to these wastes, the packager "made do" with other types of film that could be handled by high-speed wrapping equipment but lacked some of polyethylene's protective attributes. New types of wrapping machines have largely corrected this situation. But the point is that the freedom of the packagers to better their packages' protective attributes was limited.

The question of a package's adaptability to production line speeds, however, usually crops up before the package is actually used. The packager's advertising agency or his sales department suggests a new package with striking promise of being able to fulfill the promotional or use-facilitating function better than current packaging; but, upon analysis, the suggested new package is found to require either slowdowns in production line speeds or investment in new packaging equipment. The company's management is then obliged to judge whether or not the suggested package's better performance of the promotional or use-facilitating functions justifies the slower line speed or the different packaging equipment.

Promoting the Product

Features may be built into a package which are promotable to consumers, to customers, and to intermediaries in its product's distribution channel. But sometimes a feature desirable for promotion to one of the three is not desirable for one of the others. Features that minimize a retailer's loss or pilferage are, presumably, important to him; but they are not necessarily of any interest to consumers. Features that minimize a consumer's embarrassment at purchase can increase a retailer's stacking or display difficulties and make inventory control more trying.

Even granting a package feature that is promotable regardless of level in its product's distribution or use, incorporation of the feature into the package frequently requires sacrificing some good package performance of one of the other basic package functions. For example, a gift-wrapped set-up box complete with nosegay of artificial flowers is a highly promotable candy package, as is a rigid plastic, reusable package for razors that is large enough to hold a fishing lure. But both packages sacrifice density for better promotion.

Increasing Product Density

This seems to be the area where the packager's sales department on the one hand, and his purchasing and production departments on the other, are most often in disagreement about the choice of packaging. Except on those occasions when the sales department recommends yielding a package's higher density in order to improve its promotional value, the sales department is usually advocating increased package density. It improves relations with carriers; it permits better utilization of space throughout the distribution channel, thus encouraging fuller inventory stocks in the pipeline; and it permits more units to be displayed per assigned running foot of self-service display space. But it frequently slows production line speeds and increases per-unit packaging cost.

Usually this issue turns on package shape. The cylinder, for instance, is an efficient package shape for liquids; a given measure of liquid can be packaged cylindrically with less material than is necessary for any rectangular container holding the same amount of liquid. But the normal 12-count (3×4 put-up) layer of a 24-count carton will occupy significantly less shelf space if it holds rectangular packages rather than the same number of cylindrical packages with the same amount of liquid.

But bettering a package's performance of its density-increasing functions can inhibit good performance in other areas too. The density of many candy packages, for instance, could be improved significantly, but not without loss of their value as items specifically tailored for re-use as sewing baskets or cookie tins. Increasing density could also lessen the package's value as a promotional vehicle or as a promotable item in itself. Package designers seem better able to build points of brand differentiation into a 12-ounce beer bottle than into the higher-density 12-ounce beer can.

Facilitating the Use of the Product

Excluding changes in the graphic art of packages, most package changes in recent years have been in facilitating the product's use. All the changes to tear tapes, pouring spouts, squeeze bottles, aerosol cans, and so forth would have to be included here. And, as is obvious to anyone exposed to the mass advertising media, bettering the package's fulfillment of this function has proved to be a means of bettering the package's performance in promotion.

In many cases, however, where the use-facilitating function of a package has been improved, a case can be built that some degree of product protection has been sacrificed. And, bettering the package's use-facilitating job sometimes means relinquishing some package value as a re-use container for the consumer. The flow of a viscous liquid perhaps can be directed a little more accurately or easily from the mouth of a narrow-necked glass jar than from a tin can, but packaging the liquid in the glass jar means sacrificing the protection against impact provided by the tin can. The tear tape makes a corrugated carton easier to open but, for many purposes, lessens its value as a re-usable container. Some shaker openings make cleanser or spice packages easy to use but, once used, leave the product exposed.

Having Re-Use Value for the Consumer

Perhaps the competition of the various functions of the package for recognition by company managements is most apparent in this area. In recent years, according much recognition to this function of the package seems not to have been in vogue. Typically, designing a package to do its other jobs well has meant slighting its re-use value—the previous illustrations of candy and razors notwithstanding. A package's re-use value generally has suffered with successive changes unless its reusability has been very promotable.

The Principle, The Corollary, and Recent Trends

How does management know whether it is better to sacrifice a measure of product protection for a more promotable package or to build a use-facilitating attribute into the package instead of a density-increasing attribute?

Assuming that two "mixes" are in conflict or partial conflict, management may find the answer by deciding which will be more likely to push product storage as far from the packager as possible. This is, of course, another way of saying that the basic purpose of a product's package should be as much as possible to maximize product inventory near the point of use or possible use. If neither "mix" holds promise of increasing product inventory at the point of use, does either hold promise of increasing product storage at the next level back from the point of use? If neither "mix" aids in getting the product stored on the dining-room table, does either help in getting more of the product inventoried on the kitchen shelves? If neither helps there, which encourages the greater amount of well-placed open display at retail? If it is a tie between the two package "mixes" at this level, which of the two has promise of encouraging the greater retailer inventory—regardless whether in open display or not?

It follows, then, that the most successful package changes are those whose impact is greatest at a level in the product's marketing one step forward from the level currently storing the channel's largest share of the product.

Most recent packaging changes can be understood a little better if viewed against the backdrop of these generalizations. Interestingly, they explain current trends in package design that, on the surface, seem to be running in opposite directions. For instance, recently some company managements have been increasing package size or package count. Other managements have unit-packaged, lessened package size, or reduced package count. But both apparently contradictory approaches have the same purpose—*to maximize product inventory as close to a point of use as possible*. Let's examine a few recent packages changes in light of these generalizations (I am referring to those changes that typically affect more than just the package's graphic art):

Changes Involving Package Size or Count

Proprietary medicine, soap powder or detergent, beverages, and toilet tissue are among those widely distributed consumer products whose recent package changes have included addition of "king" or "giant economy" size packages to their lines. Table salt, facial tissue, crackers, and cereal on the other hand are among the items, distributed in large part through the same marketing channel, which have added smaller-size packages or "unitized" packages to their lines. In each case, promotion turning on "convenience" to the user frequently has accompanied the introduction of the new package size. Where the move has been to increase the package size, packagers are trying to encourage the consumer to maintain inventories of their particular brands far in excess of the consumer's normal needs for the product during any reasonable time span between shopping trips. In effect, the packagers are trying to move a greater share of their channel's total storage function closer to the point of use—from retailer to consumer in this particular illustration. Where the move has been to lessen package size, it is apparent that the packagers are trying to move storage location further forward: to get facial tissues into purses as well as on the vanity; to get brand-identified salt on the dining-room, breakfast, TV, or barbecue table as well as on the pantry shelf; to get half a dozen varieties of cereal in the home rather than in the store in anticipation of a family's vacillating demands. Again, the packagers are trying to move a greater share of the channel's total storage closer to the point of use.

Changes Involving Package Shape

Ice cream and milk, in both powdered and liquid forms, are examples of items that have been undergoing changes from cylindrical to space-saving rectangular packages. In part, at least, the change has been precipitated by increased recognition of the marketing channel's limited capacity to store items under refrigeration and of its eagerness to husband its shelf space. In effect, the change permits a greater share of the inventory to be moved forward.

Changes Involving Packaging Materials

This is the area where packagers' desires to push storage forward probably have been most apparent. And, incidentally, it is in this area that the lie is put to the belief that a package's prime job is protection of the product. If product protection were the prevailing consideration, few if any of certain kinds of change in packaging materials would ever have taken place. For example:

Changes from opaque to transparent materials usually have been represented as irrefutable evidence of the packager's good faith in allowing his customers to see his product. Understandably, the suppliers of transparent packaging materials have done what they could to further this impression. But conversion from opaque to transparent packaging typically has meant something else as well; *It has been a means of obtaining favorable open display shelf space at retail*, where the product could be seen by the consumers. In effect, it has meant moving part of the storage function forward in the channel from concealed storage or low-traffic locations to prominent, high-traffic locations. Small wonder that such a premium has come to be placed on transparency—even for products not especially attractive to the eye.

Changes from rigid to flexible materials have almost always meant relinquishing some measure of product protection—and the recent changes from rigid to semirigid or flexible packaging are legion. The changes, while requiring some loss of product-protection value, typically have given the product an especially promotable package, one with conspicuous promise of moving product storage closer to a point of use.

Changes Involving Addition of "Ease-of-opening" or "Ease-of-use" Attributes

I believe that, where they have been successful, package changes incorporating this kind of feature have tended to move product storage increasingly closer—however slightly—to the point of use. Typically, the movement of storage effected by such "ease-of-opening" package changes has not been at the consumer level in the product's marketing channel; it has been at the retail level. Perhaps it could be argued that the extremely successful rigid flip-top cigarette package has helped move the smoker's storage of his cigarettes a little closer to the point of their use, but the main value of the package with regard to its movement of product storage has been at the retail level. The package, again, was a means of obtaining a good, high-traffic position in open display for the particular brands of cigarette that pioneered this packaging change. It was something distinctively new that could be promoted to the marketing channel itself—quite aside from its being amenable to use in effective promotion to smokers—for brands not having so extensive or complete retail inventories as those enjoyed by more popular brands.

In summary, the choice of a product's package, no less than the choice of the total selling effort brought to bear on the product, has to represent a reconciliation of a variety of functions, each of which has potential merit in furthering the sale of the product, but all of which are, in part at least, mutually exclusive.

The most successful reconciliation will be the one that, to return to our original axiom, produces the most sales. It will emphasize that function which pushes the bulk of product storage one step farther along the marketing channel and one step closer to the ultimate consumer.

NOTES

1. That is, increasing the ratio of product volume to package volume.

LEARNING REVIEW

Questions:

1. Because of ease of measurement of these functions, it is a rare package that reaches its market without being rated objectively on its degrees of ____________ and ____________________________.

2. The major purpose of any package is to ________________________
____
____.

3. A package function which has been accorded very little recognition in recent years is ____.

Answers:

1. protection, production line adaptability; 2. influence or control the location of product storage within the marketing channel; 3. having re-use value for the customer

Retrospective Comment

This theory was developed initially about two decades ago and first appeared in print in the Summer 1958 issue of *Business Horizons*, published by Indiana University. Since then, it has been reproduced several times in the marketing literature without change. In subsequent use of the theory, I have found little reason to alter its basics. I have felt an increased assurance that intelligent choice of a package should entail: (1) determining the importance, within a product's marketing channel, of each location at which the product is stored or inventoried, (2) addressing, with new package choice, that specific location at which the greatest amount of in-channel product storage occurs, (3) doing so in ways that attempt to encourage product storage one step forward in the channel, and (4) doing so in ways that reconcile well a number of package features perceived as useful in furthering sale of the product.

I have, on the other hand, found ample reason to feel that—as developed in 1958—*the theory today does not treat adequately the difficulty of reconciling well the variety of package-features that realistically can be perceived as potentially useful*. In particular, I feel that the theory today is flawed by its failure to recognize the contribution that can be made by the package itself to the packager's efforts to focus his product and its marketing toward a market segment perceived as the most worthy candidate for his resource commitments. And, in this context, the theory ought to be able to accommodate those segments of many markets that today ascribe importance to the re-use value of packaging materials.

PART 5

The Channels Decision in the Marketing Mix

"She ain't what she used to be."

Oldtimers are often quoted as noting that "things ain't what they used to be." That comment is certainly appropriate when discussing marketing channels. Marketers who insist upon retaining the distribution patterns of twenty years ago are in danger of being bypassed by their competitors if, indeed, this has not already occurred.

The basic concepts are still insightful

Concepts discussed in the selections which follow, however, have not been outdated. That marketing channel strategy is not always dictated by the manufacturer as *channel commander* but may be determined by middlemen and must ultimately be reflective of consumer *commands* is as true today as when William Davidson's article first appeared in 1961. The idea of channel leadership and direction is further developed by Bruce Mallen in "Conflict and Cooperation in Marketing Channels." Recognizing the areas of probable channel conflict will permit the marketer to turn problems into opportunities rather than blithely assuming that the channel is necessarily an extension of his own organization.

"This is where I came in!"

Stanley Hollander's "The Wheel of Retailing" continues with minor adjustments to be observable today. It is axiomatic that no retailer can be all things to all customers. As one retailer reaches out to appeal to another, possibly more profitable segment, an opening is created for a more tailored appeal by another retailer to the customers on which the business was built; the wheel turns a notch. Louis Bucklin's classification of consumer goods and retail stores also remains a useful framework today. Marketing strategy and the selection of a successful marketing mix will be facilitated through first perceiving the product or store in terms of the effort the consumer is willing to extend to gain advantages which may or may not have acceptable substitutes.

It's a fast pace

"The Logistics of Distribution," the article by John Magee, represents a marketing frontier that continues to be expanded. The changes in this area have been accelerated by technological growth in transportation, materials handling, inventory control, and related areas.

21

Channels of Distribution—One Aspect of Marketing Strategy

William R. Davidson

PREVIEW

I. Channels of distribution are one aspect of the total marketing mix and decisions concerning them should be made in light of their relationship to an overall strategy of marketing.
   A. While there are many definitions of *channel of distribution,* the most realistic definition is *the course taken in the transfer of title to a commodity.*
   B. There is an increasing tendency in a number of fields for the physical flow of merchandise NOT to accompany the route of exchange, which may lead eventually to considering methods for effecting changes in ownership as an element in the marketing mix distinct from arrangements for physical supply.

II. There is some difference in the *commander* of the channel situation.
   A. The manufacturer, as commander, makes two types of decisions in choosing a channel:
      1. Vertical considerations relating to the number of different levels or stages in the route used to effect transfers of title.
      2. Horizontal considerations pertaining to the density or selectivity of distribution and the classes and number of outlets on a given plane.
   B. The middleman, in his role as buyer and selector of sources of supply, often really determines the nature of the channel of distribution.
   C. In the long run, it is the buying decisions of consumers that determine the adjustments that occur in the relative importance of different kinds of channels of distribution.

William R. Davidson, "Channels of Distribution—One Aspect of Marketing Strategy," is reprinted by permission from *Business Horizons* (Special Issue—First International Seminar on Marketing Management, February 1961), pp. 84–90.

III. Manufacturers must look beyond their own circumstances and beyond the situation of intermediaries in the channel, so that they are attuned to the wants and interests of the consumers in the market segment they are trying to reach.

In recent years, increasing emphasis has been placed upon modern concepts of "customer-oriented marketing management"; it has become more and more common to administer marketing activities with reference to some defined marketing strategy.

The formulation of a marketing strategy[1] consists of two steps:

1. Identification of a market target: the selection of an objective stated in terms of the segment of the market (group of consumers or industrial users) to which the company wishes to appeal.
2. Development of a marketing mix: the choice of the relative emphasis to be accorded to different aspects of the total marketing effort, in order to best attain the objective of reaching the identified market.

While the number of separate, identifiable aspects of the total marketing effort will vary from one company to another, it may be helpful to enumerate some rather common ingredients. These are: marketing research, product planning, channels of distribution, physical availability of product, advertising and sales promotion, personal selling, and pricing.

Decisions concerning the relative emphasis to be placed upon each aspect involve alternative uses of marketing man power and capital resources. Within a particular company at a given time, it is not possible to increase greatly the relative emphasis upon one aspect without decreasing the relative importance of other ingredients of the marketing mix. Hence, decisions that enlarge or reduce the importance of one item in the mix can be made intelligently only by considering the potential effects of changing the relative importance of others, and by evaluating the total impact of such changes upon the firm's ability to reach the market identified in the first step of formulating a marketing strategy.

These introductory remarks set the stage for viewing channels of distribution as one aspect of marketing strategy. While such channels can be singled out for special attention and discussion, managerial decisions concerning the selection of trade channels and maintenance of relationships with agencies in these channels should be made in the light of their relationship to an overall strategy of marketing.

This discussion will deal primarily with the marketing of consumer goods within the domestic market. This restriction offers some advantages. First, channels are usually lengthier and more complex in consumer goods marketing than in the industrial goods field, even though important generalizations apply equally under similar conditions. Furthermore, discussion of channel problems in industrial marketing tends to be more difficult, because of different vocabulary and operating conditions among industries; in consumer goods marketing, on the other hand, all of us have the perspective and experience of consumers, and hence can more readily grasp the implications of examples and generalizations.

Channels Defined

The term "channel of distribution" is part of the working vocabulary of every business executive, yet many would be hard pressed to define its meaning precisely. This is not surprising because a wide variety of interpretations are available in the literature on the subject.

For example, the channel has been defined by one author as "the pipline through which a product flows on its way to the consumer. The manufacturer puts his product into the pipeline, or marketing channel, and various marketing people move it along to the consumer at the other end of the channel."[2]

Another authority states, "Marketing channels are the combination of agencies through which the seller, who is often, though not necessarily, the manufacturer, markets his product to the ultimate user."[3]

A third scholar views marketing channels as consisting of "intermediary sellers who intervene between the original source of supply and the ultimate consumer." In his view, the number and character of such intermediaries "are determined primarily by the requirements of sorting and by the opportunity to effect economies by suitable sorting arrangements."[4] On another occasion, the same writer described a marketing channel as a group of firms that "constitute a loose coalition engaged in exploiting a joint opportunity in the market."[5]

Another well-known source states that "the trade channel is made up of the middlemen who move goods from producers to consumers" and that "we usually think of the channel as being made up of those merchants who own the goods and of those agent middlemen who effect sales."[6]

This variety of viewpoint leads to lack of clarity on several points. Does the channel have to do primarily with the change of ownership of goods or with the physical movement of product? Is the nature of a given channel determined by the manufacturer, acting as a seller, or by middlemen and consumers, carrying out their role as buyers? Is the channel made up only of middlemen or intervening intermediaries, or does it include the manufacturer at one end and the consumer at the other?

Given some product to be marketed, several jobs must be done. First, there is the question of arrangements for bringing about changes in ownership by performance of the functions of exchange, buying, and selling. Second, there is the matter of availability of physical supply, which involves the functions of transportation and storage, and related activities such as physical handling and control of inventories. Third, there is the necessity of various facilitating or auxiliary functions, such as the collection and dissemination of marketing information, management of market risks, financing of marketing activities, and standardization and grading.

Generally speaking, the functions of exchange may be considered as paramount because planning for physical supply and performance of facilitating functions do not become relevant in the typical marketing organization unless there is profitable opportunity for transfers of ownership.

It appears, therefore, most realistic to define the channel of distribution as consisting of "the course taken in the transfer of title to a commodity."[7] It is the route taken in transferring the title of a product from its first owner (usually a manufacturer) to its last owner, the business user or ultimate consumer. Such a route necessarily includes both the origin and the destination; hence, it should be viewed as including the manufacturer and the ultimate consumer, as well as any intervening middlemen, inasmuch as all three are originators and performers of much marketing activity. Middlemen in the channel include both merchants, who assume title and resell on their own account, and various kinds of agents or brokers, who do not take title but are nonetheless instrumental along the route taken to effect transfers of ownership. Broadly speaking, the channel also includes marketing establishments owned by vertically integrated companies, that is, those performing marketing functions on more than one plane or level of distribution. Examples are chain-store distribution warehouses and manufacturers' branch sales offices. There is no legal transfer of title between a factory and a sales branch operated by the same company nor between a chain-store warehouse and the retail units it serves; however, there are intracompany transactions that have the nature of sales or shipments, and which are comparable in nature to the transactions made by alternative suppliers or distributors performing similar functions on the same plane of distribution.

Physical Distribution

The general tendency is for the physical flow of merchandise to accompany the route of exchange. This is not, however, universally the case, and there are indications that separate structural arrangements for physical distribution are increasingly important. A few examples will illustrate a variety of arrangements for providing physical supply apart from the channel of distribution.

In the field of *industrial marketing* and in many lines of consumer goods, manufacturers' agents are used in lieu of manufacturers' sales branches. In combining the product lines of several manufacturers, the manufacturers' agent provides economical sales coverage of a given area, and often reaches certain customers who would be difficult to contact by other means. While such agents are links in the channel used to effect transfers of title, they do not ordinarily carry stocks. The physical flow of goods is another arrangement, one that is usually direct from the factory to the customer of the agent.

In the *wholesale paper trade* (as in many other lines of wholesaling), most transactions are handled from warehouse stocks owned and stored by the merchant. A large proportion of the total dollar and physical volume of sales consists, however, of so-called "direct" sales. On individual orders of large size, the wholesale merchant buys from the manufacturer and takes title at the point where merchandise is loaded on cars, but the merchandise itself flows directly from factory to customer as a drop shipment, never coming near the establishment where the sale was negotiated.

Several retail *mail-order companies* have worked out arrangements to establish catalogue order departments in retail establishments operated by supermarket chains. While the facilities of another retailing organization are used as part of the route through which sales contact is made with the consuming public, the merchandise is shipped directly from the mail-order establishment.

In the field of *food-product manufacturing*, several companies with factories located in various parts of the country and wide product lines have recently established gigantic regional food distribution warehouses. Such warehouses consolidate in each region, a reservoir of all products in the line, permitting fast delivery of mixed cars at low freight rates to wholesalers and chain warehouses. This form of physical distribution tends to be separate from organizational responsibility for sales handled through branch offices or through food brokers, and the geographic flow of merchandise does not correspond to the location of establishments responsible for making sales contacts with customers.

In the *appliance industry*, some wide-line manufacturers have concentrated a physical supply of various items in the line, either by centralizing all manufacturing facilities or by providing for distribution warehouses. The wholesale distributor remains as the institution making sales contact with the retailer and assumes responsibility for developing the desired share of available market potential in the area of his operation. Many types of dealers at the retail level are able to purchase full cars containing a mixture of various items in the manufacturers' assortment, with the flow of goods direct from factory or manufacturers' warehouse. The retailer still has contact with the wholesaler as the next link in the distribution channel but, in many instances, this is related to transfer of title, financing arrangements, and sales promotion assistance, and has little to do with the physical flow of merchandise.

The last two examples, in particular, reflect a growing tendency to streamline physical distribution by setting it apart from the complex of channel links used for obtaining sales. In some companies, a new department of physical distribution combines a number of previously scattered activities, including finished goods inventory control, transportation and traffic warehousing, order processing, container design, and sometimes even manufacturing scheduling.[8]

As this practice becomes more widespread, there will be an increasing tendency to consider institutional arrangements in the channel used for effecting changes in ownership to be an element in the marketing mix, distinct from the arrangements for the availability of physical supply. In the majority of instances, however, both ownership changes and physical flow may continue along all or a major part of the same route.

Channel "Commanders"

In many discussions of the subject, the manufacturer is cast in the role of "commander"of the channel situation. When introducing a new product or when making a major change in distribution policies, he examines a wide range of possible alternatives with respect to kinds and numbers of wholesale and retail outlets, weighs a number of factors that have a bearing upon sales volume, costs, and profitability, and selects the arrangements that best serve his purpose.

The types of decisions to be made by a manufacturer in choosing a channel may be divided into two classes: vertical considerations, which relate to the number of different levels or stages in the route used to effect transfers of title; and horizontal considerations, which pertain to the density or selectivity of distribution and the classes and number of outlets on a given plane (for example, wholesale or retail level).[9]

Vertical choices may be illustrated by alternatives of the following kind that might be available to a manufacturer of home furnishings. He could choose (1) to sell direct to the consumer without use of any middlemen, perhaps by means of catalogues; (2) to sell retail furniture stores by means of a manufacturer-employed sales organization; (3) to sell to furniture stores through wholesale merchants; (4) to sell to wholesale merchants by means of manufacturers' agents who also sell other related lines; (5) to use manufacturers' agents who call directly upon retailers; or (6) to use some combination of the above channels in order to reach different geographic markets or various classes of stores, perhaps differentiated on the basis of sales volume.

Horizontal choices may be illustrated by listing the channels open to a manufacturer of home furnishings who has his own sales organization calling directly upon the retail furniture trade. He must decide whether to (1) continue confining his distribution to retail furniture stores; (2) sell also to furniture departments in regular department stores; (3) offer his merchandise also to variety-department stores operated by certain variety chains who are expanding their merchandise offerings of this general type of merchandise; or (4) sell to various forms of discount houses.

Conventional discussions of channel problems have tended to devote more emphasis to questions of the vertical kind by stressing the factors that determine whether or when it is feasible for the manufacturer to move forward in the channel, assuming within his own organization the functions normally performed by various types of middlemen. He thereby carries his own marketing effort as close as possible to the final user. Among the various factors generally believed to contribute to the feasibility of short channels are a high unit value of product, a wide line of items marketed together, geographically concentrated markets, and financial strength and marketing know-how in the manufacturing company's organization.

In recent years, several factors have tended to make decisions of the horizontal type appear as matters of greater decision-making significance. For one thing, various types of retail outlets have greatly diversified their merchandise offerings, thereby invading what was once considered the private province of establishments in other categories. As a consequence, there is a wider range of alternatives at the retail level, and each class has unique operating problems, buying procedures, and operating philosophies. Second, choices at the horizontal level are more likely to cause frictions and tensions in channel relationship. For example, antagonism among regular household appliance stores and a possible withdrawal of sales support by them may occur when a manufacturer decides to aggressively solicit business from various types of discount houses. Similar frictions exist at the wholesale level when distributors in one line of trade find that new outlets in another trade classification are selling identical products formerly distributed in a more confined way. Third, decisions to use particular types of outlets at the retail level—a horizontal choice—may often dictate the kind of channel to be used in a vertical sense, since the retailer customarily uses certain sources of supply and a traditional outlook on buying arrangements.

The Middleman

In numerous situations, the manufacturer can realistically be regarded as the channel commander, at least in the short run. It is rather common for the manufacturer to call the plays when he is large and powerful, when he has developed high public status by his demand creation activities, when he finds it feasible to use a limited number of distribution outlets, and when distribution outlets operate under the terms of a franchise and would be seriously handicapped by the withdrawal of it. This tends to be the case with automobiles, major household appliances, and automotive petroleum products sold through gasoline service stations.

In many other instances, the manufacturer is channel commander not in any basic way but only in a derivative sense, owing to the strong position of middlemen in the channel. This circumstance stems from the twofold role of middlemen as distributors of manufacturers' goods and as suppliers of the purchasing requirements of their customers. When the middleman carries a variety of items drawn from many original sources, he tends to be more strongly oriented to the latter role than to the former.

Briefly, it may be noted that the manufacturers' freedom to select among conceptually available alternatives is practically limited by conditions and attitudes prevailing among middlemen. Many circumstances limit the potentialities for distribution in certain types of channel situations, whether the choice be of a vertical or horizontal nature. Examples of these circumstances follow:

> The manufacturer finds that the most desirable types of outlets have already been pre-empted by strongly entrenched competitive organizations.
>
> The middleman, already using his space and capital resources to the maximum, is reluctant to add additional items to his line, since such proliferation poses serious logistics problems, particularly in terms of available display space, warehousing space, catalogue or stock control listings, capital required for inventory investment, and so forth.
>
> The pricing or discount structure on the item is not sufficiently attractive to induce middlemen to devote promotional effort adequate to ensure movement to the consumer.
>
> The manufacturer mishandles consumer packaging or shipping containers so that neither is acceptable under the conditions of selling or merchandise handling typical in a particular line of trade.
>
> The manufacturer has created tensions or frictions in trade channels, either

by using distribution techniques that place him in direct competition with some possible outlets or by distributing through various outlets in different lines of trade with varying margin and sales supporting requirements. He thereby generates antagonism, which makes his products unacceptable or, at best, only marginally acceptable to certain types of potential outlets.

When the manufacturer encounters conditions of such a nature, he often learns that the middleman, in his role as a buyer and selector of sources of supply, really determines the nature of the channel of distribution.

The Consumer

Even when middlemen, whether they be wholesale distributors or retailers, are more strongly entrenched than manufacturers as channel commanders, their role too is more derivative than basic, owing to their need to adjust to constant changes. In a private enterprise economy characterized by high levels of buying income per family, the consumer has a wide range of choices when it comes to satisfying those wants that can be met in the market place. The consumer can, for example, decide whether to use more of his purchasing power to eat better, to travel more, to buy more clothes, or to purchase new appliances for his home. If the choice is for appliances, he can satisfy his needs at a department store, an appliance store, a mail-order company, a furniture store, a discount house, an automobile accessories store or, in some areas, a supermarket or consumers' cooperative organization. His choice will ordinarily be the outlet that has best harmonized its marketing mix with the buying interests of the group of consumers of which the individual purchaser is a member.

In the long run, therefore, the buying decisions of consumers determine the adjustments that occur in the relative importance of different kinds of channels of distribution. As adjustments occur at the retail level, they naturally have their impact in a vertical sense, by modifying the relative positions of various kinds of channel links between the manufacturer and the retailer.

Channel Choice

The discussion thus far indicates why certain manufacturers have found it necessary to modify their concept of factors that determine the choice of channels. In the company that follows a program of modern, consumer-oriented marketing management, considerations relating to consumer requirements are elevated to paramount status, and factors relating to company situation are subordinated, at least in the sense that the latter must be adjusted to the former. This means that the manufacturer must look beyond his own circumstances and beyond the situation of intermediaries in the channel, so that he is attuned to the wants and interests of the consumers in the market segment he is trying to reach.

Evaluating Channel Relationships

Too often, channel relationships do not receive due attention since they involve matters that are "outside" the company and, hence, are more easily taken for granted than other activities such as marketing research, advertising, or personal selling. These "internal" functions come up for more frequent review or appraisal since responsibility for them tends to be fixed on the organizational chart or in job descriptions, and the cost of them is conspicuously identified on accounting statements.

In manufacturing companies, opportunities for more frequent and more realistic appraisal of channel problems and relationships might be provided by new approaches to charting the organization of marketing activities. A new version of an organization chart might well show not only the various departments within the marketing division of the company, but also all of the vertical links in the channel used to effect transfers of title to eventual users, and, moreover, the different types of outlets on each horizontal plane or stage of distribution.

A related possibility is to prepare operating statements that reveal sales performance and cost situations through the channels used. At the top of such a statement would be sales, stated in terms of prices paid by the ultimate user, and showing as expenses the costs of marketing through the various channels in use.

In any event, manufacturers will have made progress in solving channel of distribution problems when they recognize two considerations. *First*, channel activities must be thought of as only one aspect of the total marketing mix and one that must be coordinated with other ingredients, as these contribute to the objective of reaching a defined market; *second*, in the long-run, the nature of channels is determined from "the bottom up" rather than from "the top down."

NOTES

1. For further discussion, see Alfred R. Oxenfeldt, "The Formulation of a Market Strategy," in Eugene J. Kelley and William Lazer, *Managerial Marketing: Perspectives and Viewpoints* (Homewood, Ill.: Richard D. Irwin, Inc., 1958), pp. 264 ff.

2. Richard M. Clewett, *Checking Your Marketing Channels* (No. 120; Washington: U.S. Small Business Administration, Management Aids for Small Manufacturers, January, 1961).

3. John A. Howard, *Marketing Management: Analysis and Decision* (Homewood, Ill.: Richard D. Irwin, Inc., 1957), p. 179.

4. Wroe Alderson, *Marketing Behavior and Executive Action* (Homewood, Ill.: Richard D. Irwin, Inc., 1957), p. 211.

5. Wroe Alderson, "The Development of Marketing Channels," in Richard M. Clewett, ed., *Marketing Channels for Manufactured Goods* (Homewood, Ill.: Richard D. Irwin, Inc., 1954), p. 30.

6. Paul D. Converse, Harvey W. Huegy, and Robert V. Mitchell, *Elements of Marketing* (Englewood Cliffs: Prentice-Hall, Inc., 1958), p. 119.

7. Theodore N. Beckman, Harold H. Maynard, and William R. Davidson, *Principles of Marketing* (New York: The Ronald Press Company, 1957), p. 39.

8. "New-Fangled Routes Deliver the Goods—Faster and Cheaper," *Business Week* (Nov. 14, 1959), pp. 108 ff; John F. Magee, "The Logistics of Distribution," *Harvard Business Review*, XXXVIII (July-Aug., 1960), 89 ff; Edward W. Smykay, Donald J. Bowersox, and Frank H. Mossman, *Physical Distribution Management* (New York: The Macmillan Company, 1961).

9. For more comprehensive treatment, see *Principles of Marketing*, pp. 39 ff. (Fn. 7 above).

LEARNING REVIEW

Questions:

1. The route taken in transferring the title of a product from first to last owner may be thought of as ____________.

2. What three groups represent *potential* channel commanders?
   a. ________________________
   b. ________________________
   c. ________________________

3. Channel activities must be thought of as only one aspect of the ____________.

4. In the long run, it is the ________________ that determine the channels of distribution.

5. In the majority of instances, both ownership changes and ____________ may continue along all or a major part of the distribution channel.

Answers:

1. The channel of distribution; 2. a) Manufacturer, b) Middleman, c) Consumer; 3. total marketing mix; 4. buying decisions of consumers; 5. physical flow

Retrospective Comment

During the first half of the 1970s, all of the trends discussed in my article have proceeded at an accelerated pace, as important components of the Retailing Revolution. Through the Retail Intelligence System, a subscription service of *Management Horizons*, many leading retailers and their wholesaler and manufacturer suppliers, are monitoring the impact of these changes on a regular basis.

For a variety of reasons, the pace of retail store expansion is expected to be more moderate in the latter part of the 1970s than was the case in recent years. Some such reasons are:

1. Selective scarcities related to the energy crisis.
2. Increases in the *cost of living* which have tended to reduce consumer expenditures (in real terms) for some lines of trade.
3. High interest rates and high rates of inflation in commercial construction, which have curtailed some expansion plans.
4. A slower pace of construction of new regional mall shopping centers, which are approaching a mature phase of their institutional life cycle.
5. More government control over locations for large facilities owing to the growth of agencies and regulations dealing with environmental impact.

However, the qualitative characteristics of changes in distributive institutions are expected to persist as originally outlined in my 1970 article.

22

Conflict and Cooperation in Marketing Channels

Bruce Mallen

PREVIEW

I. Conflict in marketing channels may be of three types:
   A. *Horizontal competition* is between middlemen of the same type.
   B. *Intertype competition* is between middlemen of different types in the same channel sector.
   C. *Vertical conflict* is between channel members of different levels.
      1. While there are many sources of conflict between channel members, the basic source is the exchange act in which one member is buyer and the other is seller.
      2. The exchange act brings out the element of price conflict.
      3. Non-price sources of conflict include differences of opinion on promotion, distribution, and philosophy.

II. A channel can adjust to its conflicting-cooperating environment in three ways:
   A. It can have a leader who forces members to cooperate.
   B. It can have a leader who helps members to cooperate, creating a democratic relationship.
   C. It can do nothing and have an anarchistic relationship.

III. In a situation of controlled cooperation, there is generally a channel leader, but historically the leadership has varied and even now there is disagreement about who the leader should be.
   A. In the 19th century the wholesaler was the channel leader, but in the 20th century the manufacturer became the leader.

Bruce Mallen, "Conflict and Cooperation in Marketing Channels," is reprinted by permission from L. George Smith (editor) *Progress in Marketing* (Chicago: American Marketing Association, 1964), pp. 65–85.

B. There is disagreement among scholars as to who the channel leader should be.
   1. The pro-manufacturer argument is that the manufacturer must lead in order to assure himself of increasing volume.
   2. The pro-retailer argument is that the retailer stands closest to the consumer and knows what he wants.
   3. The pro-wholesaler argument is that the wholesaler is the most significant part of the entire marketing organization.

IV. Each channel leader dominates the other members by using a number of weapons.
   A. Manufacturers maintain domination with promotional, legal, negative, suggestive, and voluntary cooperative compartments.
   B. Retailer dominance weapons include promotion, concentration of purchasing power, legal contracts, semiproduction, and others.

V. An emphasis on the cooperating, rather than the conflicting objectives of channel members has led to the oversimplified concept of the channel as an extension of one's own internal organization. The goal is to minimize conflict and maximize cooperation.

The purpose of this article is to advance the hypotheses that between member firms of a marketing channel there exists a dynamic field of conflicting and cooperating objectives; that if the conflicting objectives outweigh the cooperating ones, the effectiveness of the channel will be reduced and efficient distribution impeded; and that implementation of certain methods of cooperation will lead to increased channel efficiency.

Definition of Channel

The concept of a marketing channel is slightly more involved than expected on initial study. One author in a recent paper[1] has identified "trading" channels, "non-trading" channels, "type" channels, "enterprise" channels, and "business-unit" channels. Another source[2] refers to channels as all the flows extending from the producer to the user. These include the flows of physical possession, ownership, promotion, negotiation, financing, risking, ordering, and payment.

The concept of channels to be used here involves only two of the above-mentioned flows: ownership and negotiation. The first draws merchants, both wholesalers and retailers, into the channel definition, and the second draws in agent middlemen. Both, of course, include producers and consumers. This definition roughly corresponds to Professor Breyer's "trading channel," though the latter does not restrict (nor will this paper) the definition to actual flows, but to "flow-capacity." "A trading channel is formed when trading relations, making possible the passage of title and/or possession (usually both) of goods from the producer to the ultimate consumer, is consummated by the component trading concerns of the system."[3] In addition, this paper will deal with trading channels in the broadest manner and so will be concentrating on "type-trading" channels rather than "enterprise" or "business-unit" channels. This means that there will be little discussion of problems peculiar to integrated or semi-integrated channels, or peculiar to specific channels and firms.

Conflict

Palamountain isolated three forms of distributive conflict.[4]

1. Horizontal competition—this is competition between middlemen of the same type; for example, discount store *versus* discount store.
2. Intertype competition—this is competition between middlemen of different types in the same channel sector; for example, discount store *versus* department store.
3. Vertical conflict—this is conflict between channel members of different levels; for example, discount store *versus* manufacturer.

The first form, horizontal competition, is well covered in traditional economic analysis and is usually referred to simply as "competition." However, both intertype competition and vertical conflict, particularly the latter, are neglected in the usual micro-economic discussion.

The concepts of "intertype competition" and "distributive innovation" are closely related and require some discussion. Intertype competition will be divided into two categories; (a) "traditional intertype competition" and (b) "innovative intertype competition." The first category includes the usual price and promotional competition between two or more different types of channel members at the same channel level. The second category involves the action on the part of traditional channel members to prevent channel innovators from establishing themselves. For example, in Canada there is a strong campaign, on the part of traditional department stores, to prevent the discount operation from taking a firm hold on the Canadian market.[5]

Distributive innovation will also be divided into two categories; a) "intrafirm innovative conflict" and b) "innovative intertype competition." The first category involves the action of channel member firms to prevent sweeping changes within their own companies. The second category "innovative intertype competition" is identical to the second category of intertype competition.

Thus the concepts of intertype competition and distributive innovation give rise to three forms of conflict, the second of which is a combination of both: (1) traditional intertype competition, (2) innovative intertype competition, and (3) intrafirm innovative conflict.

It is to this second form that this paper now turns before going on to vertical conflict.

Innovative Intertype Competition

Professor McCammon has identified several sources, both intrafirm and intertype, of innovative conflict in distribution, i.e., where there are barriers to change within the marketing structure.[6]

Traditional members of a channel have several motives for maintaining the channel status quo against outside innovators. The traditional members are particularly strong in this conflict where they can band together in some formal or informal manner—when there is strong reseller solidarity.

Both entrepreneurs and professional managers may resist outside innovators, not only for economic reasons, but because change "violates group norms, creates uncertainty, and results in a loss of status." The traditional channel members (the insiders) and their affiliated members (the strivers and complementors) are emotionally and financially committed to the dominant channel and are interested in perpetuating it against the minor irritations of the "transient" channel members and the major attacks of the "outside innovators."

Thus, against a background of horizontal and intertype channel conflict, this paper now moves to its area of major concern; vertical conflict and cooperation.

Vertical Conflict–Price

The Exchange Act. The act of exchange is composed of two elements: a sale and a purchase. It is to the advantage of the seller to obtain the highest return possible from such an exchange and the exact opposite is the desire of the buyer. The exchange act takes place between any kind of buyer and seller. If the consumer is the buyer, then that side of the act is termed shopping; if the manufacturer, purchasing; if the government, procurement; and if a retailer, buying. Thus, between each level in the channel an exchange will take place (except if a channel member is an agent rather than a merchant).

One must look to the process of the exchange act for the basic source of conflict between channel members. This is not to say the exchange act itself is a conflict. Indeed, the act or transaction is a sign that the element of price conflict has been resolved to the mutual satisfaction of both principals. Only along the road to this mutual satisfaction point or exchange price do the principals have opposing interests. This is no less true even if they work out the exchange price together, as in mass retailers' specification-buying programs.

It is quite natural for the selling member in an exchange to want a higher price than the buying member. The conflict is subdued through persuasion or force by one member over the other, or it is subdued by the fact that the exchange act or transaction does not take place, or finally, as mentioned above, it is eliminated if the act does take place.

Suppliers may emphasize the customer aspect of a reseller rather than the channel member aspect. As a customer the reseller is somebody to persuade, manipulate, or even fool. Conversely, under the marketing concept, the view of the reseller as a customer or channel member is identical. Under this philosophy he is somebody to aid, help, and serve. However, it is by no means certain that even a large minority of suppliers have accepted the marketing concept.

To view the reseller as simply the opposing principal in the act of exchange may be channel myopia, but this view exists. On the other hand, failure to recognize his basic opposing interest is also a conceptual fault.

When the opposite principals in an exchange act are of unequal strength, the stronger is very likely to force or persuade the weaker to adhere to the former's desires. However, when they are of equal strength, the basic conflict cannot so easily be resolved. Hence, the growth of big retailers who can match the power of big producers has possibly led to greater open conflict between channel members, not only with regard to exchange, but also to other conflict sources.

There are other sources of conflict within the pricing area outside of the basic one discussed above.

A supplier may force a product onto its resellers, who dare not oppose, but who retaliate in other ways, such as using it as a loss leader. Large manufacturers may try to dictate the resale price of their merchandise; this may be less or more than the price at which resellers wish to sell it. Occasionally, a local market may be more competitive for a reseller than is true nationally. The manufacturer may not recognize the difference in competition and refuse to help this channel member.

Resellers complain of manufacturers' special price concessions to competitors and rebel at the attempt of manufacturers to control resale prices. Manufacturers complain of resellers' deceptive and misleading price advertising, nonadherence to resale price suggestions, bootlegging to unauthorized outlets, seeking special price concessions by unfair methods, and misrepresenting offers by competitive suppliers.

Other points of price conflict are the paper-work aspects of pricing. Resellers complain of delays in price change notices and complicated price sheets.

Price Theory. If one looks upon a channel as a series of markets or as the vertical exchange mechanism between buyers and sellers, one can adapt several theories and concepts to the channel situation which can aid marketing theory in this important area of channel conflict.[7] For example, the exchange mechanism between a manufacturer as a seller and a wholesaler as a buyer is one market. A second market is the exchange mechanism between the wholesaler as a seller and the retailer as a buyer. Finally, the exchange mechanism between the retailer as a seller and the consumer as a buyer is a third market. Thus, a manufacturer-wholesaler-retailer-consumer channel can be looked upon as a series of three markets.

The type of market can be defined according to its degree of competitiveness, which depends to a great extent on the number of buyers and sellers in a market. Some possible combinations are shown in Table 1.

Suppliers (sellers)	*Middlemen (buyers)*	*Market situation*
Pure competitor	Pure competitor	Pure competition
Olgopolist	Pure competitor	Oligopoly
Monopolist	Pure competitor	Monopoly
Pure competitor	Oligopsonist	Oligoposony
Pure competitor	Monopsonist	Monopsony
Oligopoly	Oligoposonist	Bilateral oligopoly
Monopolist	Monopsonist	Bilateral monopoly
Monopolist	Monopolist	Successive monopoly

TABLE 1. Classification of Economic Markets

A discussion of monopoly in a channel context may show the value of integrating economic theory with channel concepts.

If one channel member is a monopolist and the others pure competitors, the consumer pays a price equivalent to that of an integrated monpolist; and the monopolist member reaps all the channel's pure profits; that is, the sum of the pure profits of all channel members. Pure profits are, of course, the economist's concept of those profits over and above the minimum return on investment required to keep a firm in business.

Assume that the retailer is the monopolist and the others (wholesalers and manufacturers) are pure competitors, as for example, a single department store in an isolated town. Total costs to the retailer are composed of the total cost of the other levels plus his own costs. No pure profits of the other levels are included in his costs, as they make none by definition (they are pure competitors).

The retailer would be in the same buying price position, so far as the lack of suppliers' profits are concerned, as would the vertically integrated firm. Thus, he charges the same price as the integrated monopolist and makes the same profits.

If the manufacturer were the monopolist and the other channel members pure competitors, he would calculate the maximizing profits for the channel and then charge the wholesaler his cost plus the total channel's pure profits—all of which would go to him since the others are pure competitors. The wholesaler would take this price, add it on to his own costs, and the result would be the price to retailers. Then the retailers would do likewise for the consumer price.

Thus, the prices to the wholesaler and to the retailer are higher than in the first case (retailer monopoly), since the channel's pure profits are added on before the retail level. The price to the consumer is the same as in the first case. It is of no concern to the consumer if the pure profit elements in his price are added on by the manufacturer, wholesaler, or retailer.

Thus, under integrated monopoly, manufacturer monopoly, wholesaler monopoly, or retailer monopoly, the consumer price is the same; but the prices within the channel are the lowest with the retailer monopoly and the highest with the manufacturer monopoly. Of course, the non-monopolistic channel members' pure profits are not affected by this intrachannel price variation, as they have no such profits in any case.

Vertical Conflict–Non Price

Channel conflict not only finds its source in the exchange act and pricing, but it permeates all areas of marketing. Thus, a manufacturer may wish to promote a product in one manner or to a certain degree while his resellers oppose this. Another manufacturer may wish to get information from his resellers on a certain aspect relating to his product, but his resellers may refuse to provide this information. A producer may want to distribute his product extensively, but his resellers may demand exclusives.

There is also conflict because of the tendency for both manufacturers and retailers to want the elimination of the wholesaler.

One very basic source of channel conflict is the possible difference in the primary business philosophy of channel members. Writing in the Harvard Business Review, Wittreich says:

> In essence, then, the key to understanding management's problem of crossed purpose is the recognition that the fundamental (philosophy) in life of the high-level corporate manager and the typical (small) retail dealer in the distribution system are quite different. The former's (philosophy) can be characterized as being essentially dynamic in nature, continuously evolving and emerging; the latter, which are in sharp contrast, can be characterized as being essentially static in nature, reaching a point and leveling off into a continuously satisfying plateau.[8]

While the big members of the channel may want growth, the small retail members may be satisfied with stability and a "good living."

Anarchy[9]

The channel can adjust to its conflicting-cooperating environment in three distinct ways. *First*, it can have a leader (one of the channel members) who "forces" members to cooperate; this is an autocratic relationship. *Second*, it can have a leader who "helps" members to cooperate, creating a democratic relationship. *Finally*, it can do nothing, and so have an anarchistic relationship. Lewis B. Sappington and C. G. Browne, writing on the problem of internal company organizations, state:

> The first classification may be called "autocracy." In this approach to the group the leader determines the policy and dictates or assigns the work tasks. There are no group deliberations, no group decisions . . .
>
> The second classification may be called "democracy." In this approach the leader allows all policies to be decided by the group with his participation. The group members work with each other as they wish. The group determines the division and assignment of tasks . . .
>
> The third classification may be called "anarchy." In anarchy there is complete freedom of the group or the individual regarding policies or task assignments, without leader participation.[10]

Advanced in this paper is the hypothesis that if anarchy exists, there is a great chance of the conflicting dynamics destroying the channel. If autocracy exists, there is less chance of this happening. However, the latter method creates a state of cooperation based on power and control. This controlled cooperation is really subdued conflict and makes for a more unstable equilibrium than does voluntary democratic cooperation.

Controlled Cooperation

The usual pattern in the establishment of channel relationships is that there is a leader, an initiator who puts structure into this relationship and who holds it together. This leader controls, whether through command or cooperation, i.e., through an autocratic or a democratic system.

Too often it is automatically assumed that the manufacturer or producer will be the channel leader and that the middlemen will be the channel followers. This has not always been so, nor will it necessarily be so in the future. The growth of mass retailers is increasingly challenging the manufacturer for channel leadership, as the manufacturer challenged the wholesaler in the early part of this century.

The following historical discussion will concentrate on the three-ring struggle between manufacturer, wholesaler, and retailer rather than on the changing patterns of distribution within a channel sector, i.e., between service wholesaler and agent middleman or discount and department store. This will lay the necessary background for a discussion of the present-day manufacturer-dominated *versus* retailer-dominated struggle.

Early History

The simple distribution system of Colonial days gave way to a more complex one. Among the forces of change were the growth of population, the long distances involved, the increasing complexity of new products, the increase of wealth, and the increase of consumption.

The United States was ready for specialists to provide a growing and widely dispersed populace with the many new goods and services required. The more primitive methods of public markets and barter could not efficiently handle the situation. This type of system required short distances, few products, and a small population, to operate properly.

19th Century History

In the same period that this older system was dissolving the retailer was still a very small merchant who, especially in the West, lived in relative isolation from his supply sources. Aside from being small, he further diminished his power position by spreading himself thin over many merchandise lines. The retailer certainly was no specialist but was as general as a general store can be. His opposite channel member, the manufacturer, was also a small businessman, too concerned with production and financial problems to fuss with marketing.

Obviously, both these channel members were in no position to assume leadership. However, somebody had to perform all the various marketing functions between production and retailing if the economy was to function. The wholesaler filled this vacuum and became the channel leader of the 19th century.

The wholesaler became the selling force of the manufacturer and the latter's link to the widely scattered retailers over the nation. He became the retailer's life line to these distant domestic and even more important foreign sources of supply.

These wholesalers carried any type of product from any manufacturer and sold any type of product to the general retailers. They can be described as general merchandise wholesalers. They were concentrated at those transportation points in the country which gave them access to both the interior and its retailers, and the exterior and its foreign suppliers.

Early 20th Century

The end of the century saw the wholesaler's power on the decline. The manufacturer had grown larger and more financially secure with the shift from a foreign-oriented economy to a domestic-oriented one. He could now finance his marketing in a manner impossible to him in early times. His thoughts shifted to some extent from production problems to marketing problems.

Prodding the manufacturer on was the increased rivalry of his other domestic competitors. The increased investment in capital and inventory made it necessary that he maintain volume. He tended to locate himself in the larger market areas, and thus, did not have great distances to travel to see his retail customers. In addition, he started to produce various products; and because of his new multi-product production, he could reach—even more efficiently—these already more accessible markets.

The advent of the automobile and highways almost clinched the manufacturer's bid for power. For now he could reach a much vaster market (and they could reach him) and reap the benefits of economies of scale.

The branding of his products projected him to the channel leadership. No longer did he have as great a need for a specialist in reaching widely dispersed customers, nor did he need them to the same extent for their contacts. The market knew where the product came from. The age of wholesaler dominance declined. That of manufacturer dominance emerged.

Is it still here? What is its future? How strong is the challenge by retailers? Is one "better" than the other? These are the questions of the next section.

Disagreement Among Scholars

No topic seems to generate so much heat and bias in marketing as the question of who should be the channel leader, and more strangely, who is the channel leader. Depending on where the author sits, he can give numerous reasons why his particular choice should take the channel initiative.

Authors of sales management and general marketing books say the manufacturer is and should be the chief institution in the channel. Retailing authors feel the same way about retailers, and wholesaling authors (as few as there are), though not blinded to the fact that wholesaling is not "captain," still imply that they should be, and talk about the coming resurrection of wholesalers. Yet a final and compromising view is put forth by those who believe that a balance of power, rather than a general and prolonged dominance of any channel member, is best.

> The truth is that an immediate reaction would set in against any temporary dominance by a channel member. In that sense, there is a constant tendency toward the equilibrium of market forces. The present view is that public interest is served by a balance of power rather than by a general and prolonged predominance of any one level in marketing channels.[11]

John Kenneth Galbraith's concept of countervailing power also holds to this last view.

For the retailer:

> In the opinion of the writer, "retailer-dominated marketing" has yielded, and will continue to yield in the future greater net benefits to consumers than "manufacturer-dominated marketing," as the central-buying mass distributor continues to play a role of ever-increasing importance in the marketing of goods in our economy. . . .
>
> . . . In the years to come, as more and more large-scale multiple-unit retailers follow the central buying patterns set by Sears and Penneys, as leaders in their respective fields (hard lines and soft goods), ever-greater benefits should flow to consumers in the way of more goods better adjusted to their demands, at lower prices.[12]
>
> . . . In a long run buyer's market, such as we probably face in this country, the retailers have the inherent advantage of economy in distribution and will, therefore, become increasingly important.[13]
>
> The retailer cannot be the selling agent of the manufacturer because he holds a higher commission; he is the purchasing agent for the public.[14]

For the wholesaler:

> The wholesaling sector is, first of all, the most significant part of the entire marketing organization.[15]
>
> . . . The orthodox wholesaler and affiliated types have had a resurgence to previous 1929 levels of sales importance.[16]
>
> . . . Wholesalers have since made a comeback.[17] This revival of wholesaling has resulted from infusion of new management blood and the adoption of new techniques.[18]

For the manufacturer:

> . . . The final decision in channel selection rests with the seller, manufacturer and will continue to rest with him as long as he has the legal right to choose to sell to some potential customers and refuse to sell to others.[19]

> These channel decisions are primarily problems for the manufacturer. They rarely arise for general wholesalers. . . .[20]
>
> Of all the historical tendencies in the field of marketing, no other is so distinctly apparent as the tendency for the manufacturer to assume greater control over the distribution of his product. . . .[21]
>
> . . . Marketing policies at other levels can be viewed as extensions of policies established by marketing managers in manufacturing firms; and, furthermore, . . . the nature and function can adequately be surveyed by looking at the relationship to manufacturers.[22]

Pro Manufacture

The argument for manufacturer leadership is production oriented. It claims that they must assure themselves of increasing volume. This is needed to derive the benefits of production scale economies, to spread their overhead over many units, to meet increasingly stiff competition, and to justify the investment risk they, not the retailers, are taking. Since retailers will not do this job for them properly, the manufacturer must control the channel.

Another major argumentative point for manufacturer dominance is that neither the public nor retailers can create new products even under a market-oriented system. The most the public can do is to select and choose among those the manufacturers have developed. They cannot select products that they cannot conceive. This argument would say that it is of no use to ask consumers and retailers what they want because they cannot articulate abstract needs into tangible goods; indeed, the need can be created by the goods rather than vice-versa.

This argument may hold well when applied to consumers, but a study of the specification-buying programs of the mass retailers will show that the latter can indeed create new products and need not be relegated to simply selecting among alternatives.

Pro-Retailer

This writer sees the mass retailer as the natural leader of the channel for consumer goods under the marketing concept. The retailer stands closest to the consumer; he feels the pulse of consumer wants and needs day in and day out. The retailer can easily undertake consumer research right on his own premises and can best interpret what is wanted, how much is wanted, and when it is wanted.

An equilibrium in the channel conflict may come about when small retailers join forces with big manufacturers in a manufacturer leadership channel to compete with a small manufacturer-big retailer leadership channel.

Pro-Wholesaler

It would seem that the wholesaler has a choice in this domination problem as well. Unlike the manufacturer and retailer though, his method is not mainly through a power struggle. This problem is almost settled for him once he chooses the type of wholesaling business he wishes to enter. A manufacturers' agent and purchasing agent are manufacturer-dominated, a sales agent dominates the manufacturer. A resident buyer and voluntary group wholesaler are retail-dominated.

Methods of Manufacturer Domination

How does a channel leader dominate his fellow members? What are his tools in this channel power struggle? A manufacturer has many domination weapons at his disposal. His arsenal can be divided into promotional, legal, negative, suggestive, and ironically, voluntary cooperative compartments.

Promotional. Probably the major method that the manufacturer has used is the building of a consumer franchise through advertising, sales promotion, and packaging of his branded products. When he has developed some degree of consumer loyalty, the other channel members must bow to his leadership. The more successful this identification through the promotion process, the more assured is the manufacturer of his leadership.

Legal. The legal weapon has also been a poignant force for the manufacturer. It can take many forms, such as, where permissible, resale price maintenance. Other contractual methods are franchises, where the channel members may become mere shells of legal entities. Through this weapon the automobile manufacturers have achieved an almost absolute dominance over their dealers.

Even more absolute is resort to legal ownership of channel members, called forward vertical integration. Vertical integration is the ultimate in manufacturer dominance of the channel. Another legal weapon is the use of consignment sales. Under this method the channel members must by law sell the goods as designated by the owner (manufacturer). Consignment selling is in a sense vertical integration; it is keeping legal ownership of the goods until they reach the consumer, rather than keeping legal ownership of the institutions which are involved in the process.

Negative Methods. Among the "negative" methods of dominance are refusal to sell to possibly uncooperative retailers or refusal to concentrate a large percentage of one's volume with any one customer.

A spreading of sales makes for a concentrating of manufacturer power, while a concentrating of sales may make for a thinning of manufacturer power. Of course, if a manufacturer is one of the few resources available and if there are many available retailers, then a concentrating of sales will also make for a concentrating of power.

The avoidance and refusal tactics, of course, eliminate the possibility of opposing dominating institutions.

Suggestives. A rather weak group of dominating weapons are the "suggestives." Thus, a manufacturer can issue price sheets and discounts, preticket and premark resale prices on goods, recommend, suggest, and advertise resale prices.

These methods are not powerful unless supplemented by promotional, legal, and/or negative weapons. It is common for these methods to boomerang. Thus a manufacturer pretickets or advertises resale prices, and a retailer cuts this price, pointing with pride to the manufacturer's suggested retail price.

Voluntary Cooperative Devices. There is one more group of dominating weapons, and these are really all the voluntary cooperating weapons to be mentioned later. The promise to provide these, or to withdraw them, can have a "whip and carrot" effect on the channel members.

Retailers' Dominating Weapons

Retailers also have numerous domination weapons at their disposal. As with manufacturers, their strongest weapon is the building of a consumer franchise through advertising, sales promotion, and branding. The growth of private brands is the growth of retail dominance.

Attempts at concentrating a retailer's purchasing power are a further group of weapons and are analogous to a manufacturer's attempts to disperse his volume. The more a retailer can concentrate his purchasing, the more dominating he can become; the more he spreads his purchasing, the more dominated he becomes. Again, if the resource is one of only a few, this generalization reverses itself.

Such legal contracts as specification buying, vertical integration (or the threat of it), and entry into manufacturing can also be effective. Even semiproduction, such as the packaging of goods received in bulk by the supermarket can be a weapon of dominance.

Retailers can dilute the dominance of manufacturers by patronizing those with excess capacity and those who are "hungry" for the extra volume. There is also the subtlety, which retailers may recognize, that a strong manufacturer may concede to their wishes just to avoid an open conflict with a customer.

Voluntary Cooperation

But despite some of the conflict dynamics and forced cooperation, channel members usually have more harmonious and common interests than conflicting ones. A team effort to market a producer's product will probably help all involved. All members have a common interest in selling the product; only in the division of total channel profits are they in conflict. They have a singular goal to reach, and here they are allies. If any one of them fails in the team effort, this weak link in the chain can destroy them all. As such, all members are concerned with one another's welfare (unless a member can be easily replaced).

Organizational Extension Concept

This emphasis on the cooperating, rather than the conflicting objectives of channel members, has led to the concept of the channel as simply an extension of one's own internal organization. Conflict in such a system is to be expected even as it is to be expected within an organization. However, it is the common or "macro-objective" that is the center of concentration. Members are to sacrifice their selfish "micro-objectives" to this cause. By increasing the profit pie they will all be better off than squabbling over pieces of a smaller one. The goal is to minimize conflict and maximize cooperation. This view has been expounded in various articles by Peter Drucker, Ralph Alexander, and Valentine Ridgeway.

> Together, the manufacturer with his suppliers and/or dealers comprise a system in which the manufacturer may be designated the primary organization and the dealers and suppliers designated as secondary organizations. This system is in competition with similar systems in the economy; and in order for the system to operate effectively as an integrated whole, there must be some administration of the system as a whole, not merely administration of the separate organizations within that system.[23]

Peter Drucker[24] has pleaded against the conceptual blindness that the idea of the legal entity generates. A legal entity is not a marketing entity. Since often half of the cost to the consumer is added on after the product leaves the producer, the latter should think of his channel members as part of his firm. General Motors is an example of an organization which does this.

> Both businessmen and students of marketing often define too narrowly the problem of marketing channels. Many of them tend to define the term channels of distribution as a complex of relationships between the firm on the one hand, and marketing establishments exterior to the firm by which the products of the firm are moved to market, on the other. . . . A much broader

more constructive concept embraces the relationships with external agents or units as part of the marketing organization of the company. From this viewpoint, the complex of external relationships may be regarded as merely an extension of the marketing organization of the firm. When we look at the problem in this way, we are much less likely to lose sight of the interdependence of the two structures and more likely to be constantly aware that they are closely related parts of the marketing machine. The fact that the internal organization structure is linked together by a system of employment contracts, while the external one is set up and maintained by a series of transactions, contracts of purchase and sale, tends to obscure their common purpose and close relationship.[25]

Cooperation Methods

But how does a supplier project its organization into the channel? How does it make organization and channel into one? It accomplishes this by doing many things for its resellers that it does for its own organization. It sells, advertises, trains, plans, and promotes for these firms. A brief elaboration of these methods follows.

Missionary salesmen aid the sales of channel members, as well as bolster the whole system's level of activity and selling effort. Training of resellers' salesmen and executives is an effective weapon of cooperation. The channels operate more efficiently when all are educated in the promotional techniques and uses of the products involved.

Involvement in the planning functions of its channel members could be another poignant weapon of the supplier. Helping resellers to set quotas for their customers, studying the market potential for them, forecasting a member's sales volume, inventory planning and protection, etc., are all aspects of this latter method.

Aid in promotion through the provision of advertising materials (mats, displays, commercials, literature, direct-mail pieces), ideas, funds (cooperative advertising), sales contests, store layout designs, push money (PM's or spiffs), is another form of cooperation.

The big supplier can act as management consultant to the members, dispensing advice in all areas of their business, including accounting, personnel, planning, control, finance, buying, paper systems or office procedure, and site selection. Aid in financing may include extended credit terms, consignment selling, and loans.

By no means do these methods of coordination take a one-way route. All members of the channel, including supplier and reseller, see their own organizations meshing with the others, and so provide coordinating weapons in accordance with their ability. Thus, the manufacturer would undertake a marketing research project for his channel, and also expect his resellers to keep records and vital information for the manufacturer's

1. Cooperative advertising allowances
2. Payments for interior displays including shelf-extenders, dump displays, "A" locations, aisle displays, etc.
3. P.M.'s for salespeople
4. Contests for buyers, salespeople, etc.
5. Allowances for a variety of warehousing functions
6. Payments for window display space, plus installation costs
7. Detail men who check inventory, put up stock, set up complete promotions, etc.
8. Demonstrators
9. On certain canned food, a "swell" allowance
10. Label allowance
11. Coupon handling allowance
12. Free goods
13. Guaranteed sales
14. In-store and window display material
15. Local research work
16. Mail-in premium offers to consumer
17. Preticketing
18. Automatic reorder systems
19. Delivery costs to individual stores of large retailers
20. Studies of innumerable types, such as studies of merchandise management accounting
21. Payments for mailings to store lists
22. Liberal return privileges
23. Contributions to favorite charities of store personnel
24. Contributions to special store anniversaries
25. Prizes, etc., to store buyers when visiting showrooms—plus entertainment, of course
26. Training retail salespeople
27. Payments for store fixtures
28. Payments for new store costs, for more improvements, including painting
29. An infinite variety of promotion allowances
30. Special payments for exclusive franchises
31. Payments of part of salary of retail salespeople
32. Deals of innumerable types
33. Time spent on actual selling floor by manufacturer, salesmen
34. Inventory price adjustments
35. Store name mention in manufacutrer's advertising

TABLE 2. Methods of Cooperation as Listed[27]

use. A supplier may also expect his channel members to service the product after the sale.

A useful device for fostering cooperation is a channel advisory council composed of the supplier and his resellers.

Finally, a manufacturer or reseller can avoid associations with potentially uncooperative channel members. Thus, a price-conservative manufacturer may avoid linking to a price-cutting retailer.

E. B. Weiss has developed an impressive, though admittedly incomplete list of cooperation methods (Table 2). Paradoxically, many of these instruments of cooperation are also weapons of control (forced cooperation) to be used by both middlemen and manufacturers. However, this is not so strange if one keeps in mind that control is subdued conflict and a form of cooperation even though perhaps involuntary cooperation.

Extension Concept is the Marketing Concept

The philosophy of cooperation is described in the following quote:

> The essence of the marketing concept is of course customer orientation at all levels of distribution. It is particularly important that customer orientation motivate all relations between a manufacturer and his customer—both immediate and ultimate. It must permeate his entire channels-of-distribution policy.[26]

This quote synthesizes the extension-of-the-organization system concept of channels with the marketing concept. Indeed, it shows that the former is, in essence, "the" marketing concept applied to the channel area in marketing. To continue:

> The characteristics of the highly competitive markets of today naturally put a distinct premium on harmonious manufacturer-distributor relationships. Their very mutuality of interest demands that the manufacturer base his distribution program not only on what he would like from distributors, but perhaps more importantly, on what they would like from him. In order to get the cooperation of the best distributors, and thus maximum exposure for his line among the various market segments, he must adjust his policies to serve their best interest and, thereby, his own. In other words, he must put the principles of the marketing concept to work for him. By so doing, he will inspire in his customers a feeling of mutual interest and trust and will help convince them that they are essential members of his marketing team.[28]

Summary

Figure 1 summarizes this whole paper. Each person within each department will cooperate, control, and conflict with each other (notice arrows). Together they form a department (notice department box contains person boxes) which will be best off when cooperating (or cooperation through control) forces weigh heavier than conflicting forces. Now each department cooperates, controls, and conflicts with each other. Departments together also form a higher level organization—the firm (manufacturer, wholesaler, and retailer). Again, the firm will be better off if department cooperation is maximized and conflict minimized. Finally, firms standing vertically to each other cooperate, control, and conflict. Together they form a distribution channel that will be best off under conditions of optimum cooperation leading to consumer and profit satisfaction.

Conclusions and Hypotheses

1. Channel relationships are set against a background of cooperation and conflict; horizontal, intertype, and vertical.

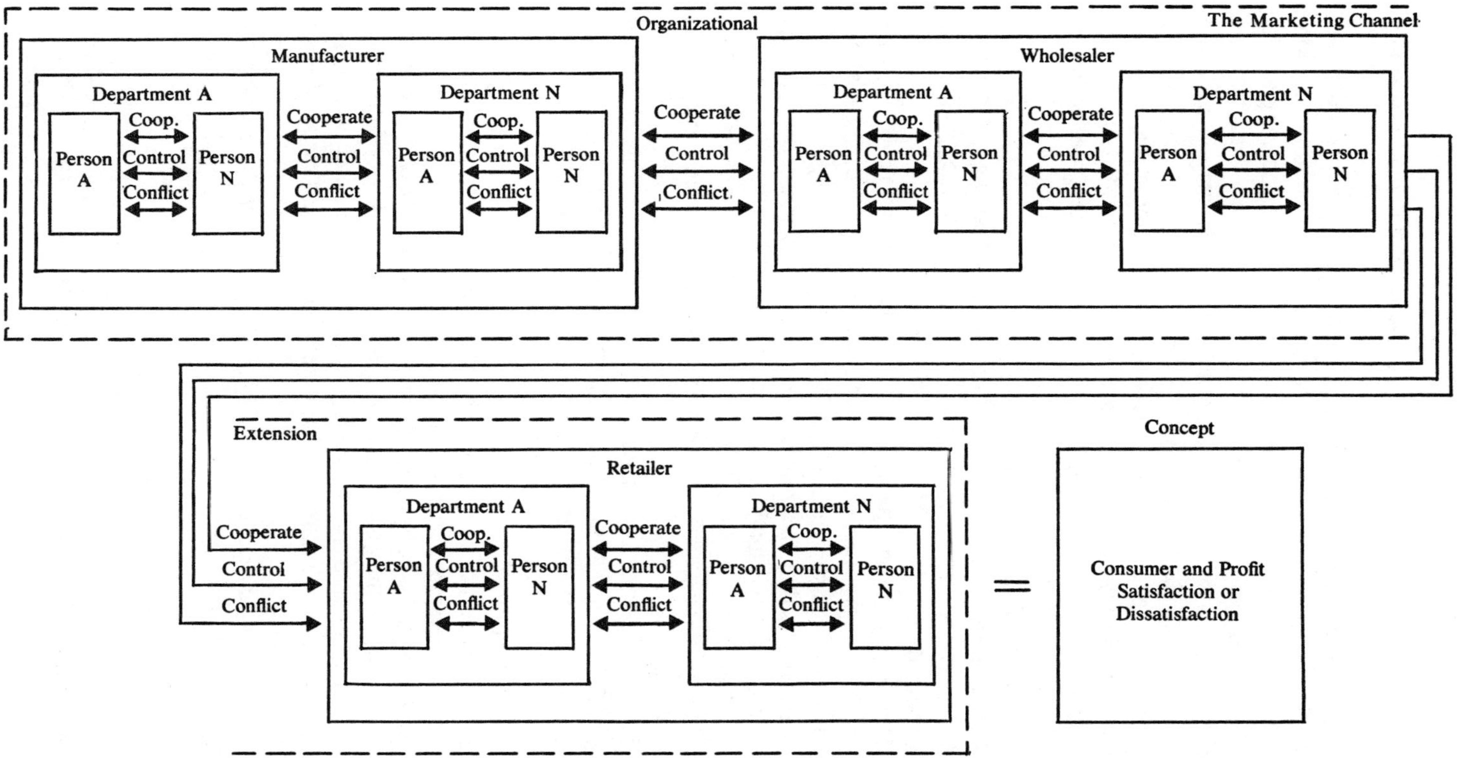
Organizational
The Marketing Channel
Manufacturer
Department A
Person A
Coop.
Control
Conflict
Person N
Cooperate
Control
Conflict
Department N
Person A
Coop.
Control
Conflict
Person N
Cooperate
Control
Conflict
Wholesaler
Department A
Person A
Coop.
Control
Conflict
Person N
Cooperate
Control
Conflict
Department N
Person A
Coop.
Control
Conflict
Person N
Extension
Cooperate
Control
Conflict
Retailer
Department A
Person A
Coop.
Control
Conflict
Person N
Cooperate
Control
Conflict
Department N
Person A
Coop.
Control
Conflict
Person N
=
Concept
Consumer and Profit
Satisfaction or
Dissatisfaction

FIGURE 1.

2. An autocratic relationship exists when one channel member controls conflict and forces the others to cooperate. A democratic relationship exists when all members agree to cooperate without a power play. An anarchistic relationship exists when there is open conflict, with no member able to impose his will on the others. This last form could destroy or seriously reduce the effectiveness of the channel.

3. The process of the exchange act where one member is a seller and the other is a buyer is the basic source of channel conflict. Economic theory can aid in comprehending this phenomenon. There are, however, many other areas of conflict, such as differences in business philosophy or primary objectives.

4. Reasons for cooperation, however, usually outweigh reasons for conflict. This had led to the concept of the channel as an extension of a firm's organization.

5. This concept drops the facade of "legal entity" and treats channel members as one great organization with the leader providing each with various forms of assistance. These are called cooperating weapons.

6. It is argued that this concept is actually the marketing concept adapted to a channel situation.

7. In an autocratic or democratic channel relationship, there must be a leader. This leadership has shifted and is shifting between the various channel levels.

8. The wholesaler was the leader in the last century, the manufacturer now, and it appears that the mass retailer is next in line.

9. There is much disagreement on the above point, however, especially on who should be the leader. Various authors have differing arguments to advance for their choice.

10. In the opinion of this writer, the mass retailer appears to be best adapted for leadership under the marketing concept.

11. As there are weapons of cooperation, so are there weapons of domination. Indeed the former paradoxically are one group of the latter. The other groups are promotional, legal, negative, and suggestive methods. Both manufacturers and retailers have at their disposal these dominating weapons.

12. *For maximization of channel profits and consumer satisfaction, the channel must act as a unit.*

NOTES

1. Ralph F. Breyer, "Some Observations on Structural Formation And The Growth of Marketing Channels," in *Theory In Marketing*, Reavis Cox, Wroe Alderson, Stanley J. Shapiro, Editors. (Homewood, Illinois: Richard D. Irwin, Inc., 1964), pp. 163–175.

2. Ronald S. Vaile, E. T. Grether, and Reavis Cox, *Marketing In the American Economy* (New York: Ronald Press, 1952), pp. 121 and 124.
3. Breyer, *op. cit.*, p. 165.
4. Joseph C. Palamountain, *The Politics of Distribution* (Cambridge: Harvard University Press, 1955).
5. Isaiah A. Litvak and Bruce E. Mallen, *Marketing: Canada* (Toronto: McGraw-Hill of Canada, Limited, 1964), pp. 196–197.
6. This section is based on Bert C. McCammon, Jr., "Alternative Explanations of Institutional Change And Channel Evolution," in *Toward Scientific Marketing*, Stephen A. Greyser, ed. (Chicago: American Marketing Association, 1963), pp. 477–490.
7. Bruce Mallen, "Introducing The Marketing Channel To Price Theory," *Journal of Marketing*, July, 1964, pp. 29–33.
8. Warren J. Wittreich, "Misunderstanding The Retailer," *Harvard Business Review*, May-June, 1962, p. 149.
9. The term "anarchy" as used in this paper connotes "no leadership" and nothing more.
10. Lewis B. Sappington and C. G. Browne, "The Skills of Creative Leadership," in *Managerial Marketing*, rev. ed., William Lazer and Eugene J. Kelley, ed. (Homewood, Ill.: Richard D. Irwin, Inc., 1962), p. 350.
11. Wroe Alderson "Factors Governing The Development of Marketing Channels," in *Marketing Channels For Manufactured Products*, Richard M. Clewett, Editor. (Homewood, Richard D. Irwin, Inc., 1954), p. 30.
12. Arnold Corbin, *Central Buying in Relation To The Merchandising of Multiple Retail Units* (New York, Unpublished Doctoral Dissertation at New York University, 1954), pp. 708–709.
13. David Craig and Werner Gabler, "The Competitive Struggle for Market Control," in *Readings in Marketing*, Howard J. Westing, ed. (New York, Prentice-Hall, 1953), p. 46.
14. Lew Hahn, *Stores, Merchants and Customers* (New York, Fairchild Publications, 1952), p. 12.
15. David A. Revzan, *Wholesaling in Marketing Organization* (New York: John Wiley & Sons, Inc., 1961), p. 606.
16. *Ibid.*, p. 202.
17. E. Jerome McCarthy, *Basic Marketing* (Homewood, Illinois: Richard D. Irwin, Inc., 1960), p. 419.
18. *Ibid.*, p. 420.
19. Eli P. Cox, *Federal Quantity Discount Limitations and Its Possible Effects on Distribution Channel Dynamics* (Unpublished Doctoral Dissertation, University of Texas, 1956), p. 12.
20. Milton Brown, Wilbur B. England, John B. Matthews, Jr., *Problems in Marketing*, 3rd ed. (New York: McGraw-Hill Book Co., Inc., 1961), p. 239.
21. Maynard D. Phelps and Howard J. Westing, *Marketing Management*, Revised Edition. (Homewood, Ill.: Richard D. Irwin, Inc., 1960), p. 11.
22. Kenneth Davis, *Marketing Management* (New York: The Ronald Press Co., 1961), p. 131.
23. Valentine F. Ridgeway, "Administration of Manufacturer-Dealer Systems," in *Managerial Marketing*, rev. ed. William Lazer and Eugene J. Kelley, eds. (Homewood, Ill.: Richard D. Irwin, Inc., 1962), p. 480.
24. Peter Drucker, "The Economy's Dark Continent," *Fortune*, April 1962, pp. 103 ff.
25. Ralph S. Alexander, James S. Cross, Ross M. Cunningham, *Industrial Marketing*, rev. ed. (Homewood, Ill.: Richard D. Irwin, Inc., 1961), p. 266.
26. Hector Lazo and Arnold Corbin, *Management in Marketing* (New York: McGraw Hill Book Company, Inc., 1961), p. 379.
27. Edward B. Weiss, "How Much of a Retailer Is the Manufacturer," in *Advertising Age*, July 21, 1958, p. 68.
28. Lazo and Corbin, *loc. cit.*

LEARNING REVIEW

Questions:

1. Mallen's hypothesis of channel conflict and cooperation is concerned with optimizing ____________________________.

2. The three forms of distributive conflict that Mallen suggests are:
   a) ____________________________
   b) ____________________________
   c) ____________________________

3. Mallen suggests several *weapons* a manufacturer may use to become dominant as a leader in a controlled cooperation situation. Name three of these *weapons* suggested.
   a) ____________________________
   b) ____________________________
   c) ____________________________

4. Although there is considerable disagreement on this point, Mallen sees the ______________ as the natural leader of the channel for consumer goods.

5. The emphasis on the cooperating, rather than the conflicting objectives of channel members, has led to oversimplifying the concept of the channel as ____________________.

Answers:

1. channel efficiency; 2. a) horizontal competition b) intertype competition c) vertical conflict; 3. a) successful promotion which builds channel member "franchises", b) careful contractual agreements, c) refusal to sell; 4. mass retailer; 5. an extension of a firm's own organization

Retrospective Comment

Since writing this article (which actually first appeared in a shorter version a year earlier in the Summer, 1963 issue of the *Journal of Retailing*) there have been a number of significant developments in the application of behavioral science concepts and theory to the study of marketing channel systems. Some of these concepts would today lead me to modify some conclusions of my article as follows:

1. Most channels, *but not all*, are probably social systems, i.e. they interact because of their mutual dependence.
2. In some cases, the free market mechanism or lack of centralized channel control may lead to the most efficient form of distribution.
3. There is a conflict threshold level up to which conflict need not be dysfunctional and may very well be functional. There, in fact, may be multi-threshold levels, e.g. where conflict is first neutral, then functional, then dysfunctional. (The first two levels may be reversed.)
4. The fundamental causes of channel conflict are differences over goals and roles and communication distortion.
5. A channel leader's leadership may be based on sociological reference position as well as, or instead of, economic power.
6. Two sub-classes of channel social systems can be identified—contractual marketing systems (e.g. franchising) and corporate vertical integration—to distinguish them from the non-contractual, non-ownership form of controlled channel systems, i.e. autocratic administered systems.
7. For maximization of channel profits and consumer satisfaction, the channel must usually, *but need not always*, act as a unit.

23

The Wheel of Retailing

Stanley C. Hollander

PREVIEW

I. There are several explanations for the wheel of retailing:
   A. The personality of the entrepreneur is such that he is thrifty at first but becomes less so with age and wealth, or else someone else assumes management and is less competent.
   B. Trade journals may coax merchants into modernization.
   C. Imperfect competition may cause merchants to provide increasingly elaborate services at higher prices.
   D. Excess capacity in imperfect competition may occur as more dealers enter a branch of retail trade.
   E. There may be a general long-run increase in the standard of living which may allow steps up as well as opportunities for new operations.
   F. Present tendencies toward scrambled merchandising may create the illusion of the wheel phenomenon.

II. An examination of the actual development of retail institutions helps shed light on the wheel hypothesis and its explanations:
   A. Problems with data concerning margin cause some difficulty in analysis.
   B. There are a number of examples of conformity to the wheel pattern both in Britain and America.
      1. British grocery trade and department stores have conformed to the wheel pattern.
      2. Trends toward increasing margins were apparent in many branches of American business following the Civil War.
   C. There are a number of examples of businesses which do not conform to the wheel pattern.
      1. In foreign countries, supermarkets and other stores have been introduced at the top of the social and price scales.

Stanley C. Hollander, "The Wheel of Retailing," is reprinted by permission from the *Journal of Marketing*, published by the American Marketing Association (July 1960), pp. 37–42.

2. In America, automatic merchandising started as a high-cost, high-margin, high-convenience type of retailing.
3. American department-store branch movement and shopping centers have also progressed contrary to the wheel.

III. The wheel hypothesis is not valid for all retailing but describes a fairly common pattern best accounted for by the general, long-term rise in the standard of living.

"The wheel of retailing" is the name Professor Malcolm P. McNair has suggested for a major hypothesis concerning patterns of retail development. This hypothesis holds that new types of retailers usually enter the market as low-status, low-margin, low-price operators. Gradually they acquire more elaborate establishments and facilities, with both increased investments and higher operating costs. Finally they mature as high-cost, high-price merchants, vulnerable to newer types who, in turn, go through the same pattern. Department-store merchants, who originally appeared as vigorous competitors to the smaller retailers and who have now become vulnerable to discount house and supermarket competition, are often cited as prime examples of the wheel pattern.[1]

Many examples of conformity to this pattern can be found. Nevertheless, we may ask: (1) Is the hypothesis valid for all retailing under all conditions? (2) How accurately does it describe total American retail development? (3) What factors cause wheel-pattern changes in retail institutions?

The following discussion assembles some of the slender empirical evidence available that might shed some light on these three questions. In attempting to answer the third question, a number of hypotheses should be considered that marketing students have advanced concerning the forces that have shaped retail development.

Tentative Explanations of the Wheel

(A) *Retail Personalities*. New types of retail institutions are often established by highly aggressive, cost-conscious entrepreneurs who make every penny count and who have no interest in unprofitable frills. But, as P. D. Converse has suggested, these men may relax their vigilance and control over costs as they acquire age and wealth. Their successors may be less competent. Either the innovators or their successors may be unwilling, or unable, to adjust to changing conditions. Consequently, according to this view, deterioration in management causes movement along the wheel.[2]

(B) *Misguidance*. Hermann Levy has advanced the ingenious, if implausible, explanation that retail trade journals, seduced by profitable advertising from the store equipment and supply industry, coax merchants into superfluous "modernization" and into the installation of overly elaborate facilities.[3]

(C) *Imperfect Competition*. Although retail trade is often cited as the one type of business that approaches the Adam Smith concept of perfect competition, some economists have argued that retailing actually is a good example of imperfect competition. These economists believe that most retailers avoid direct price competition because of several forces, including resale price maintenance, trade association rules in some countries, and, most important, the fear of immediate retaliation. Contrariwise, the same retailers feel that service improvements, including improvements in location, are not susceptible to direct retaliation by competitors. Hence, through a ratchet process, merchants in any established branch of trade tend to provide increasingly elaborate services at increasingly higher margins.[4]

(D) *Excess Capacity*. McNair attributes much of the wheel effect to the development of excess capacity, as more and more dealers enter any branch of retail trade.[5] This hypothesis rests upon an imperfect competition assumption, since, under perfect competition excess capacity would simply reduce margins until the excess vendors were eliminated.

(E) *Secular Trend*. J. B. Jefferys has pointed out that a general, but uneven, long-run increase in the British standard of living provided established merchants with profitable opportunities for trading up. Jefferys thus credits adjustments to changing and wealthier market segments as causing some movement along the wheel. At the same time, pockets of opportunity have remained for new, low-margin operations because of the uneven distribution of living-standard increases.[6]

(F) *Illusion*. Professor B. Holdren has suggested in a recent letter that present tendencies toward scrambled merchandising may create totally illusory impressions of the wheel phenomenon. Store-wide average margins may increase as new, high-markup lines are added to the product mix, even though the margins charged on the original components of that mix remain unchanged.

Difficulties of Analysis

An examination of the actual development of retail institutions here and abroad does shed some light on both the wheel hypothesis and its various explanations. However, a number of significant difficulties hinder the process.

(1) Statements concerning changes in retail margins and expenses are the central core of the wheel hypothesis. Yet valid information on historical retail expense rates is very scarce. Long-run changes in percentage margins probably do furnish fairly reliable clues to expense changes, but this is not true over short or intermediate periods. For example, 1957 furniture-store expense rates were about 5 percentage points higher than their 1949–1951 average, yet gross margins actually declined slightly over the same period.[7]

(2) Historical margin data are somewhat more plentiful, but these also have to be dredged up from fragmentary sources.[8]

(3) Available series on both expenses and margins merely note changes in retailers' outlays and receipts. They do not indicate what caused those changes and they do not report changes in the costs borne by suppliers, consumers, or the community at large.

(4) Margin data are usually published as averages that may, and frequently do, mask highly divergent tendencies.

(5) A conceptual difficulty presents an even more serious problem than the paucity of statistics. When we talk about "types" of retailers, we think of classifications based upon ways of doing business and upon differences in price policy. Yet census categories and other systems for reporting retail statistics are usually based upon major differences in commodity lines. For example, the "pineboard" druggists who appeared in the 1930s are a "type" of retailing for our purposes. Those dealers had cruder fixtures, charged lower prices, carried smaller assortments, gave more attention to turnover, and had less interest in prescriptions than did conventional druggists. Yet census reports for drugstores necessarily included all of the pineboards that maintained any sort of prescription department.

Discount houses provide another example of an important, but amorphous, category not reflected in census classifications. The label "discount house" covers a variety of retailers. Some carry stocks, others do not. Some have conventional store facilities, whereas others operate in office buildings, lofts, and warehouses. Some feature electrical appliances and hard goods, while others emphasize soft goods. Some pose as wholesalers, and others are practically indistinguishable from all other popular priced retailers in their fields. Consequently discount dealers' operating figures are likely to be merged into the statistics reported for other appliance, hardware, or apparel merchants.

Examples of Conformity

British

British retailing provides several examples of conformity to the wheel pattern. The grocery trade has gone through several wheel-like evolutions, according to a detailed analysis made by F. G. Pennance and B. S. Yamey.[9] Established firms did initiate some changes and some margin reductions, so that the pattern is obscured by many cross currents. But the major changes seem to have been due to the appearance and then the maturation, first, of department-store food counters; then, of chain stores; and finally, of cut-price cash-and-carry stores. Now supermarkets seem to be carrying the pattern through another evolution.[10]

Jefferys also has noted a general long-run upgrading in both British department stores and chains.[11] Vague complaints in the co-operative press and a decline in consumer dividend rates suggest that wheel-like changes may have occurred in the British co-operative movement.[12]

American

Very little is known about retail margins in this country before the Civil War. Our early retail history seems to have involved the appearance, first, of hawkers, walkers, and peddlers; then, of general stores; next, of specialty stores; and finally, of department stores. Each of these types apparently came in as a lower-margin, lower-price competitor to the established outlets, and thus was consistent with the wheel pattern. We do not know, however, whether there was simply a long-run decline in retail margins through successive improvements in retail efficiency from one type to another (contrary to the wheel pattern), or whether each of the early types was started on a low-margin basis, gradually "up-graded," and so provided room for the next entrant (in accordance with the pattern).

The trends toward increasing margins can be more easily discerned in many branches of retailing after the Civil War. Barger has described increases over the years 1869—1947 among important retail segments, including department stores, mail-order firms, variety stores, and jewelry dealers. He attributes much of the pre-World War I rise in department-store margins to the absorption of wholesaling functions. Changes in merchandise mix, such as the addition of soda fountains and cafeterias to variety stores and the upgrading of mail-order merchandise, seem to have caused some of the other increases. Finally, he believes changes in customer services have been a major force in raising margins.[13] Fabian Linden has extended Barger's observations to note similar 1949–1957 margin increases for department stores, variety chains, and appliance dealers.[14]

Some other examples of at least partial conformity to the wheel pattern may be cited. Many observers feel that both discount-house services and margins have increased substantially in recent years.[15] One major discount-house operator has stated that he has been able to keep his average markup below 12%, in spite of considerable expansion in his facilities and commodity mix.[16] However, the concensus seems to be that this probably is an exception to the general rule.

A study of gasoline pricing has pointed out how many of the so-called "off-brand" outlets have changed from the "trackside" stations of pre-war days. The trackside dealers typically maintained unattractive and poorly equipped installations, at out-of-the-way locations where un-branded gasoline was sold on a price basis. Today many of them sell well-promoted regional and local brands, maintain attractive, efficient stations, and provide prompt and courteous service. Some still offer cut prices, but may have raised their prices and margins up to or above national brand levels.[17] Over time, many of the pineboard druggists also seem to have become converted to fairly conventional operations.[18]

Non-Conforming Examples

Foreign

In underdeveloped countries, the relatively small middle- and upper-income groups have formed the major markets for "modern" types of retailing. Supermarkets and other modern stores have been introduced in those countries largely at the top of the social and price scales, contrary to the wheel pattern.[19] Some non-conforming examples may also be found in somewhat more industrialized environments. The vigorous price competition that developed among Japanese department stores during the first three decades of this century seems directly contrary to the wheel hypothesis.[20] B. S. Yamey's history of resale price maintenance also reports some price-cutting by traditional, well-established British merchants who departed from the wheel pattern in the 1880s and 1890s.[21] Unfortunately, our ignorance of foreign retail history hinders any judgment of the representativeness of these examples.

American

Automatic merchandising, perhaps the most "modern" of all American retail institutions, departed from the wheel pattern by starting as a high-cost, high-margin, high-convenience type of retailing.[22] The department-store branch movement and the concomitant rise of planned shopping centers also has progressed directly contrary to the wheel pattern. The early department-store branches consisted of a few stores in exclusive suburbs and some equally high-fashion college and resort shops.

Only in relatively recent years have the branches been adjusted to the changing and more democratic characteristics of the contemporary dormitory suburbs. Suburban shopping centers, too, seem to have appeared first as "Manhasset Miracle Miles" and "Ardmores" before reaching out to the popular price customers. In fact, complaints are still heard that the regional shopping centers have displayed excessive resistance to the entry of really aggressive, low-margin outlets.[23] E. R. A. Seligman and R. A. Love's study of retail pricing in the 1930s suggests that pressures on prices and margins were generated by all types of retailers. The mass retailing institutions, such as the department and chain stores, that had existed as types for many decades were responsible for a goodly portion of the price cutting.[24] As McNair has pointed out, the wheel operated very slowly in the case of department stores.

Finally, Harold Barger has described the remarkable stability of overall distributive margins during the years 1919–1947.[25] Some shifting of distributive work from wholesalers to retailers apparently affected their relative shares of the total margins during this period, but this is not the type of change contemplated by the wheel pattern. Of course, the stability Barger notes conceivably could have been the result of a perfectly smooth functioning of the pattern, with the entrance of low-margin innovators providing exactly the right balance for the upcreep of margins in the longer established types. But economic changes do not come in smooth and synchronized fashion, and Barger's data probably should indicate considerably wider oscillations if the wheel really set the mold for all retailing in the post-war period.

Conclusions

The number of non-conforming examples suggests that the wheel hypothesis is not valid for all retailing. The hypothesis, however, does seem to describe a fairly common pattern in industrialized, expanding economies. Moreover, the wheel is not simply an illusion created by scrambled merchandising, as Holdren suggests. Undoubtedly some of the recent "upcreep" in supermarket average margins is due to the addition of nonfood and other high margin lines. But in recent years the wheel pattern has also been characteristic of department-store retailing, a field that has been relatively unreceptive to new commodity groups.[26]

In some ways, Jefferys' secular trend explanation appears most reasonable. The tendency of many established retailers to reduce prices and margins during depressions suggests also that increase may be a result of generally prospering environments. This explanation helps to resolve an apparent paradox inherent in the wheel concept. Why should reasonably skilled businessmen make decisions that consistently lead their firms along seemingly profitable routes to positions of vulnerability? Jefferys sees movement along the wheel as the result of sensible, businesslike decisions to change with prospering market segments and to leave the poorer customers to low-margin innovators. His explanation is supported by the fact that the vulnerability contemplated by the wheel hypothesis usually means only a loss of market share, not a loss of absolute volume. At least in the United States, though, this explanation is partially contradicted by studies showing that prosperous consumers are especially prone to patronize discount houses. Also they are equally as likely to shop in supermarkets as are poorer consumers.[27]

The imperfect competition and excess capacity hypotheses also appear highly plausible. Considerably more investigation is needed before their validity can be appraised properly. The wheel pattern developed very slowly, and very recently in the department-store field. Yet market imperfections in that field probably were greater before the automobile gave the consumer shopping mobility. Major portions of the supermarket growth in food retailing and discount-house growth in appliance distribution occurred during periods of vastly expanding consumption, when excess capacity probably was at relatively low levels. At the moment there is little evidence to suggest any clear-cut correlation between the degree of market imperfection and the appearance of the wheel pattern. However, this lack may well be the result of the scarcity of empirical studies of retail competition.

Managerial deterioration certainly must explain some manifestations of the wheel, but not all. Empires rise and fall with changes in the quality of their leadership, and the same thing seems true in business. But the wheel hypothesis is a hypothesis concerning types of retailing and not merely individual firms. Consequently, the managerial-deterioration explanation holds true only if it is assumed that new people entering any established type of retailing as the heads of both old and new companies are consistently less competent than the first generation. Again, the fact that the wheel has operated very slowly in some fields suggests that several successive managerial generations can avoid wheel-like maturation and decay.

NOTES

1. M. P. McNair, "Significant Trends and Developments in the Postwar Period," in A. B. Smith (editor), *Competitive Distribution in a Free, High-Level Economy and Its Implications for the University* (Pittsburgh: University of Pittsburgh Press, 1958), pp. 1–25 at pp. 17–18.

2. P. D. Converse, "Mediocrity in Retailing," *Journal of Marketing*, Vol. 23 (April, 1959), pp. 419–420.

3. Hermann Levy, *The Shops of Britain* (London: Kegan Paul, Trench, Trubner & Co., 1947), pp. 210–211.

4. D. L. Shawver, *The Development of Theories of Retail Price Determination*, (Urbana; University of Illinois Press, 1956), p. 92.

5. Same reference as footnote 1.

6. J. B. Jefferys, *Retail Trading in Great Britain*, 1859–1950 (Cambridge: Cambridge University Press, 1954), various pages, especially p. 96.

7. Cited in Fabian Linden, "Department Store Operations," *Conference Board Business Record*, Vol. 14 (October, 1958), pp. 410–414, at p. 411.

8. See Harold Barger, *Distribution's Place in the American Economy Since 1869* (Princeton: Princeton University Press, 1955).

9. F. G. Pennance and B. S. Yamey, "Competition in the Retail Grocery Trade, 1850–1939," *Economica*, Vol. 22 (March, 1955), pp. 303–317.

10. "La Methode Americaine," *Time*, Vol. 74, (November 16, 1959), pp. 105–106.

11. Same reference as footnote 6.

12. "Battle of the Dividend," *Co-operative Review*, Vol. 36 (August, 1956), p. 183; "Independent Commission's Report," *Co-operative Review*, Vol. 38 (April, 1958), pp. 84–89; "£52 Million Dividend in 1957," *Co-operative Review* (August, 1958), pp. 171–182.

13. Same reference as footnote 8, p. 82.

14. See footnote 7.

15. D. A. Loehwing, "Resourceful Merchants," *Barron's*, Vol. 38 (November 17, 1958), p. 3.

16. S. Masters, quoted in "Three Concepts of Retail Service," *Stores*, Vol. 41 (July-August, 1959), pp. 18–21.

17. S. M. Livingston and T. Levitt, "Competition and Retail Gasoline Prices," *The Review of Economics and Statistics*, Vol. 41 (May, 1959, pp. 119–132 at p. 132.

18. Paul C. Olsen, *The Marketing of Drug Products* (New Brunswick: Rutgers University Press, 1948, pp. 130–132.

19. H. S. Hettinger, "Marketing in Persia," *Journal of Marketing*, Vol. 15 (January 1951), pp. 289–297; H. W. Boyd, Jr., R. M. Clewett, R. L. Westfall, "The Marketing Structure of Venezuela," *Journal of Marketing*, Vol. 22 (April, 1958), pp. 391–397; D. A. Taylor, "Retailing in Brazil," *Journal of Marketing*, Vol. 24 (July, 1959), pp. 54–58; J. K. Galbraith and R. Holton, *Marketing Efficiency in Puerto Rico* (Cambridge: Harvard University Press, 1955), p. 35.

20. G. Fukami, "Japanese Department Stores," *Journal of Marketing*, Vol. 18 (July, 1953), pp. 41–49 at p. 42.

21. "The Origins of Resale Price Maintenance," *The Economic Journal*, Vol. 62 (September, 1952), pp. 522–545.

22. W. S. Fishman, "Sense Makes Dollars," *1959 Directory of Automatic Merchandising* (Chicago: National Automatic Merchandising Association, 1959), p. 52; M. V. Marshall, *Automatic Merchandising* (Boston: Graduate School of Business Administration, Harvard University, 1954), pp. 108–109, 122.

23. P. E. Smith, *Shopping Centers* (New York: National Retail Merchants' Association, 1956), pp. 11–12; M. L. Sweet, "Tenant-Selection Policies of Regional Shopping Centers," *Journal of Marketing*, Vol. 23 (April, 1959), pp. 399–404.

24. E. R. A. Seligman and R. A. Love, *Price Cutting and Price Maintenance* (New York: Harper & Brothers, 1932).

25. Same reference as footnote 8, pp. ix, x.

26. R. D. Entenberg, *The Changing Competitive Position of Department Stores in the United States by Merchandise Lines* (Pittsburgh: University of Pittsburgh Press, 1957), p. 52.

27. R. Holton, *The Supply and Demand Structure of Food Retailing Services, A Case Study* (Cambridge: Harvard University Press, 1954).

LEARNING REVIEW

Questions:

1. The Wheel of Retailing describes the situation where a new type of retailing starts small, grows, and gradually imposes higher ____________.

2. Jefferys' secular trend explanation of the wheel refers to a general, long-run increase in ______________________________.

3. Studies in the United States show that prosperous customers are especially prone to patronize ______________________________.

Answers:

1. margins; 2. standard of living; 3. discount houses

Retrospective Comment

The Wheel of Retailing concept describes many, but not all, of the institutional developments in American and Western European retail trade during the last ten to fifteen years.[1] Wadinambiaratchi, drawing upon Cundiff[2] and upon his own research in Ceylon, agrees that the Wheel does not seem applicable in underdeveloped economies. He claims, in fact, that it is specifically related to the *early industrial* phase of economic development, i.e. the fifth stage in a six stage progression.[3]

But in North America and Western Europe many of the newer store types, such as discount department stores, furniture warehouse showrooms and catalog discount appliance showrooms started off with price and margin advantages that gradually weakened as competition increased and as new services and amenities were added to attract customers. Hypermarkets seem to be going through similar Wheel phases in Europe and appear likely to encounter the same stages if introduced into the U. S. In contrast, however, convenience food stores, which might or might not be considered to be a new type of outlet, entered the market with relatively high prices and margins. Moreover, many old-line retailers, such as the traditional variety store chain companies that converted to discount department store operation or the supermarket chains that adopted *economy* or *discount pricing* tactics, demonstrated that the Wheel need not describe the behavior of individual firms regardless of what it might say about store types.

In this connection, it is worthwhile to remember that M. P. McNair used the Wheel of Retailing as warning of what could happen, rather than as a prediction of what must happen. He used it as a sermon, based upon free choice rather than predestination. He felt that merchants could avert the Wheel through vigorous and forthright competitive action. That view of the Wheel involves no fundamental conflict with writers such as Ronald Gist[4] and Dov Izraeli[5] who describe even broader patterns of, to use Gist's Hegelian terms, thesis (the older established type of retail institution), antithesis (the newer rival), and synthesis (the joint process of moving toward greater similarity).

The greatest limitation to such more general and comprehensive pictures of retail evolution is that they fail to deal with the most interesting and puzzling aspect of the whole process: the fact that in the so-called developed or industrialized countries, new types of outlets have generally entered the market at the low end of the cost, margin, price and status spectrum. Why have there been so few new luxury types of retailing? Why has so little retailing development resembled the familiar *skimming* the *cream* pattern of new product introduction, in which the innovation is first offered at high prices and then gradually reaches a wider market? One possible answer is that most new types of retailing (with the exception of the unWheel-like convenience stores) have not offered really new services or benefits. Instead they have attracted patronage through the promise of traditional services, or even some reduced package of services, at reduced prices. For example, television sets offered satisfactions not available from radio, and color television offered satisfactions not available from black and white sets. Thus, both were suitable candidates for a *skimming* policy. In contrast, the proprietors of new types of retail establishments have apparently had to claim benefits on the input (cost) rather than output (satisfaction) side. Conceivably, closed circuit TV shopping systems and other forecasted revolutionary methods of distribution may deviate substantially from the Wheel of Retailing and enter at the top of the market if they ever become viable marketing techniques.

With regard to causation, Thomas considers the Wheel to be "a reasonable framework for interpreting institutional change in retailing," at least in the industrialized countries. However, he feels that it can only be properly understood through appreciation of changes in consumer expectations of retailing.[6] Unlike Thomas, who emphasizes a pattern of first increased consumer demand for vicarious status through intensive retail service and then a shift away from ostentatious shopping, L. P. Bucklin concentrates on consumer desire for enlarged services. He argues that the cost and margin increases that are part of the Wheel pattern are not entirely or even mainly the unfortunate effects of a ratchetlike oligopolistic competitive process, but are primarily sound response to that demand for increased services.[7] Clearly, as already noted, such increases are not irreversible if management is willing to take drastic action and reconvert to a simpler and more spartan form of operation. But the fact that simpler, low-cost, low-service, low-price outlets (whether new entrants or converted older firms) have generally been able to divert trade from the higher-priced firms indicates the weaknesses of the supposed current demand for increased services.

The problem, of course, is that very high volume and productivity are required to support a truly drastic low-price policy. Such productivity becomes difficult to maintain as intratype competition increases and the business is shared among more firms. (This would be an argument for limitation of entry if such a policy did not involve other dangers of detriment to the consumer). Consumers may more readily perceive small increases in service and amenities than they do similar increases in price. This can continue until creeping costs and margins result in vulnerability to dramatic new competition. The Wheel of Retailing is a vague concept, and it is a reversible one, but it has continued to roll somewhat erratically during the past ten or fifteen years.

NOTES TO RETROSPECTIVE COMMENT

1. For an extensive discussion of the Wheel of Retailing from a European point of view, see A. C. R. Dreesmann, "Patterns of Evolution in Retailing," *Journal of Retailing* 44 (Spring 1968) 64–81.
2. Edward Cundiff, "Concepts in Comparative Retailing," *Journal of Marketing* 29 (January 1965) 59–63.
3. G. Wadinambiaratchi, "Theories of Retail Development," *Social and Economic Studies* (University of the West Indies) 4 (December 1972) 391–200.
4. *Retailing: Concepts and Decisions*. New York: John Wiley & Sons, Inc., 1968, Chap. 4, espec. pp. 106–12.
5. "The Three Wheels of Retailing: A Theoretical Note," *European Journal of Marketing* 7 (No. 1, 1973) 70–74.
6. R. E. Thomas, "Change in the Distribution Systems of Western Industrialized Nations," *British* (now European) *Journal of Marketing* 4 (Summer 1970) 62–69.
7. *Competition and Evolution in the Distributive Trades*. Englewood Cliffs, N. J.: Prentice-Hall, Inc., 1972, p. 166.

24

Retail Strategy and the Classification of Consumer Goods

Louis P. Bucklin

PREVIEW

I. Consumer buying efforts may be divided into two categories called shopping and nonshopping goods.
   A. Shopping goods are those whose suitability is determined by search before the consumer buys.
   B. Nonshopping goods are those for which the consumer is both willing and able to use past experience or stored information for buying.
      1. A convenience good is a nonshopping item for which the consumer will readily accept any number of substitutes and buy the most accessible.
      2. A specialty good is a nonshopping item for which the consumer will accept only one brand as satisfactory for her needs.

II. In addition to buyers' attitudes toward the product for retailing purposes the buyer's attitude toward the store must be considered.
   A. Consumers' attitudes toward stores may be divided into three categories:
      1. For convenience stores the key factor is accessibility.
      2. Shopping stores are those for which the buyer has developed no preference, so she searches.
      3. Specialty stores are those for which the buyer has a divided preference.
   B. It is possible to construct a three-by-three matrix of product motives by patronage motives in order to classify consumer buying behavior.

Louis P. Bucklin, "Retail Strategy and the Classification of Consumer Goods," is reprinted by permission from the *Journal of Marketing*, published by the American Marketing Association (January 1963), pp. 50–55.

III. The retailer may use the extended classification system to plan his marketing strategy through three basic steps.
   A. First, the retailer's potential customers for some product are classified by market segment, using the matrix.
   B. Next the retailer determines the marketing strategy necessary to appeal to each market segment.
   C. Finally the retailer selects the market segment, and the strategy associated with it, to which he will sell.

When Melvin T. Copeland published his famous discussion of the classification of consumer goods, shopping, convenience, and specialty goods, his intent was clearly to create a guide for the development of marketing strategies by manufacturers.[1] Although his discussion involved retailers and retailing, his purpose was to show how consumer buying habits affected the type of channel of distribution and promotional strategy that a manufacturer should adopt. Despite the controversy which still surrounds his classification, his success in creating such a guide may be judged by the fact that through the years few marketing texts have failed to make use of his ideas.

The purpose of this article is to attempt to clarify some of the issues that exist with respect to the classification, and to extend the concept to include the retailer and the study of retail strategy.

Controversy Over the Classification System

The starting point for the discussion lies with the definitions adopted by the American Marketing Association's Committee on Definitions for the classification system in 1948.[2] These are:

> *Convenience Goods*: Those consumers' goods which the customer purchases frequently, immediately, and with the minimum of effort.
>
> *Shopping Goods*: Those consumers' goods which the customer in the process of selection and purchase characteristically compares on such bases as suitability, quality, price and style.
>
> *Specialty Goods*: Those consumers' goods on which a significant group of buyers are habitually willing to make a special purchasing effort.

This set of definitions was retained in virtually the same form by the Committee on Definitions in its latest publication.[3]

Opposing these accepted definitions stands a critique by Richard H. Holton.[4] Finding the Committee's definitions too imprecise to be able to measure consumer buying behavior, he suggested that the following definitions not only would represent the essence of Copeland's original idea, but be operationally more useful as well.

> *Convenience Goods*: Those goods for which the consumer regards the probable gain from making price and quality comparisons as small compared to the cost of making such comparisons.
>
> *Shopping Goods*: Those goods for which the consumer regards the probable gain from making price and quality comparisons as large relative to the cost of making such comparisons.
>
> *Specialty Goods*: Those convenience or shopping goods which have such a limited market as to require the consumer to make a special effort to purchase them.

Holton's definitions have particular merit because they make explicit the underlying conditions that control the extent of a consumer's shopping activities. They show that a consumer's buying behavior will be determined not only by the strength of his desire to secure some good, but by his perception of the cost of shopping to obtain it. In other words, the consumer continues to shop *for all goods* so long as he feels that the additional satisfactions from further comparisons are at least equal to the cost of making the additional effort. The distinction between shopping and convenience goods lies principally in the degree of satisfaction to be secured from further comparisons.

The Specialty Good Issue

While Holton's conceptualization makes an important contribution, he has sacrificed some of the richness of Copeland's original ideas. This is essentially David J. Luck's complaint in a criticism of Holton's proposal.[5] Luck objected to the abandonment of the *willingness* of consumers to make a special effort to buy as the rationale for the concept of specialty goods. He regarded this type of consumer behavior as based upon unique consumer attitudes toward certain goods and not the density of distribution of those goods. Holton, in a reply, rejected Luck's point; he remained convinced that the real meaning of specialty goods could be derived from his convenience goods, shopping goods continuum, and market conditions.[6]

The root of the matter appears to be that insufficient attention has been paid to the fact that the consumer, once embarked upon some buying expedition, may have only one of two possible objectives in mind. A discussion of this aspect of consumer behavior will make possible a closer synthesis of Holton's contribution with the more traditional point of view.

A Forgotten Idea

The basis for this discussion is afforded by certain statements, which the marketing profession has largely ignored over the years, in Copeland's original presentation of his ideas. These have regard to the extend of the consumer's awareness of the precise nature of the item he wishes to buy, *before* he starts his shopping trip. Copeland stated that the consumer, in both the case of convenience goods and specialty goods, has full knowledge of the particular good, or its acceptable substitutes, that he will buy before he commences his buying trip. The consumer, however, lacks this knowledge in the case of a shopping good.[7] This means that the buying trip must not only serve the objective of purchasing the good, but must enable the consumer to discover which item he wants to buy.

The behavior of the consumer during any shopping expedition may, as a result, be regarded as heavily dependent upon the state of his decision as to what he wants to buy. If the consumer knows precisely what he wants, he needs only to undertake communication activities sufficient to take title to the desired product. He may also undertake ancillary physical activities involving the handling of the product and delivery. If the consumer is uncertain as to what he wants to buy, then an additional activity will have to be performed. This involves the work of making comparisons between possible alternative purchases, or simply search.

There would be little point, with respect to the problem of classifying consumer goods, in distinguishing between the activity of search and that of making a commitment to buy, if a consumer always performed both before purchasing a good. The crucial point is that he does not. While most of the items that a consumer buys have probably been subjected to comparison at some point in his life, he does not make a search before each purchase. Instead, a past solution to the need is frequently remembered and, if satisfactory, is implemented.[8] Use of these past decisions for many products quickly moves the consumer past any perceived necessity of undertaking new comparisons and leaves only the task of exchange to be discharged.

Redefinition of the System

Use of this concept of problem solving permits one to classify consumer buying efforts into two broad categories which may be called shopping and nonshopping goods.

Shopping Goods

Shopping goods are those for which the consumer *regularly* formulates a new solution to his need each time it is aroused. They are goods whose suitability is determined through search before the consumer commits himself to each purchase.

The motivation behind this behavior stems from circumstances which tend to perpetuate a lack of complete consumer knowledge about the nature of the product that he would like to buy.[9] Frequent changes in price, style, or product technology cause consumer information to become obsolete. The greater the time lapse between purchases, the more obsolete will his information be. The consumer's needs are also subject to change, or he may seek variety in his purchases as an actual goal. These forces will tend to make past information inappropriate. New search, due to forces internal and external to the consumer, is continuously required for products with purchase determinants which the consumer regards as both important and subject to change.[10]

The number of comparisons that the consumer will make in purchasing a shopping good may be determined by use of Holton's hypothesis on effort. The consumer, in other words, will undertake search for a product until the perceived value to be secured through additional comparisons is less than the estimated cost of making those comparisons. Thus, shopping effort will vary according to the intensity of the desire of the consumer to find the right product, the type of product and the availability of retail facilities. Whether the consumer searches diligently, superficially, or even buys at the first opportunity, however, does not alter the shopping nature of the product.

Nonshopping Goods

Turning now to nonshopping goods, one may define these as products for which the consumer is both willing and able to use stored solutions to the problem of finding a product to answer a need. From the remarks on shopping goods it may be generalized that nonshopping goods have purchase determinants which do not change, or which are perceived as changing inconsequentially, between purchases.[11] The consumer, for example, may assume that price for some product never changes or that price is unimportant. It may be unimportant because either the price is low, or the consumer is very wealthy.

Nonshopping goods may be divided into convenience and specialty goods by means of the concept of a preference map. Bayton introduces this concept as the means to show how the consumer stores information about products.[12] It is a rough ranking of the relative desirability of the different kinds of products that the consumer sees as possible satisfiers for his needs. For present purposes, two basic types of preference maps may be envisaged. One type ranks all known product alternatives equally in terms of desirability. The other ranks one particular product as so superior to all others that the consumer, in effect, believes this product is the only answer to his need.

Distinguishing the Specialty Good

This distinction in preference maps creates the basis for discriminating between a convenience good and a specialty good. Clearly, where the consumer is indifferent to the precise item among a number of substitutes which he could buy, he will purchase the most accessible one and look no further. This is a convenience good. On the other hand, where the consumer recognizes only one brand of a product as capable of satisfying his needs, he will be willing to bypass more readily accessible substitutes in order to secure the wanted item. This is a specialty good.

However, most nonshopping goods will probably fall in between these two polar extremes. Preference maps will exist where the difference between the relative desirability of substitutes may range from the slim to the well marked. In order to distinguish between convenience goods and specialty goods in these cases, Holton's hypothesis regarding consumer effort may be employed again. A convenience good, in these terms, becomes one for which the consumer has such little preference among his perceived choices that he buys the item which is most readily available. A specialty good is one for which consumer preference is so strong that he bypasses, or would be willing to bypass, the purchase of more accessible substitutes in order to secure his most wanted item.

It should be noted that this decision on the part of the consumer as to how much effort he should expend takes place under somewhat different conditions than the one for shopping goods. In the nonshopping good instance the consumer has a reasonably good estimate of the additional value to be achieved by purchasing his preferred item. The estimate of the additional cost required to make this purchase may also be made fairly accurately. Consequently, the consumer will be in a much better position to justify the expenditure of additional effort here than in the case of shopping goods where much uncertainty must exist with regard to both of these factors.

The New Classification

The classification of consumer goods that results from the analysis is as follows:

> *Convenience Goods*: Those goods for which the consumer, before his need arises, possesses a preference map that indicates a willingness to purchase any of a number of known substitutes rather than to make the additional effort required to buy a particular item.

Shopping Goods: Those goods for which the consumer has not developed a complete preference map before the need arises, requiring him to undertake search to construct such a map before purchase.

Specialty Goods: Those goods for which the consumer, before his need arises, possesses a preference map that indicates a willingness to expend the additional effort required to purchase the most preferred item rather than to buy a more readily accessible substitute.

Extension to Retailing

The classification of the goods concept developed above may now be extended to retailing. As the concept now stands, it is derived from consumer attitudes or motives toward a *product*. These attitudes, or product motives, are based upon the consumer's interpretation of a product's styling, special features, quality, and social status of its brand name, if any. Occasionally the price may also be closely associated with the product by the consumer.

Classification of Patronage Motives

The extension of the concept to retailing may be made through the notion of patronage motives, a term long used in marketing. Patronage motives are derived from consumer attitudes concerning the retail establishment. They are related to factors which the consumer is likely to regard as controlled by the retailer. These will include assortment, credit service, guarantee, shopping ease and enjoyment, and usually price. Patronage motives, however, have never been systematically categorized. It is proposed that the procedure developed above to discriminate among product motives be used to classify consumer buying motives with respect to retail stores as well.

This will provide the basis for the consideration of retail marketing strategy and will aid in clearing up certain ambiguities that would otherwise exist if consumer buying motives were solely classified by product factors. These ambiguities appear, for example, when the consumer has a strong affinity for some particular brand of a product, but little interest in where he buys it. The manufacturer of the product, as a result, would be correct in defining the product as a specialty item if the consumer's preferences were so strong as to cause him to eschew more readily available substitutes. The retailer may regard it as a convenience good, however, since the consumer will make no special effort to purchase the good from any particular store. This problem is clearly avoided by separately classifying product and patronage motives.

The categorization of patronage motives by the above procedure results in the following three definitions. These are:

Convenience Stores: Those stores for which the consumer, before his need for some product arises, possesses a preference map that indicates a willingness to buy from the most accessible store.

Shopping Stores: Those stores for which the consumer has not developed a complete preference map relative to the product he wishes to buy, requiring him to undertake a search to construct such a map before purchase.

Specialty Stores: Those stores for which the consumer, before his need for some product arises, possesses a preference map that indicates a willingness to buy the item from a particular establishment even though it may not be the most accessible.

The Product-Patronage Matrix

Although this basis will now afford the retailer a means to consider alternative strategies, a finer classification system may be obtained by relating consumer product motives to consumer patronage motives. By cross-classifying each product motive with each patronage motive, one creates a three by three matrix, representing nine possible types of consumer buying behavior. Each of the nine cells in the matrix may be described as follows:

1. *Convenience Store—Convenience Good*: The consumer, represented by this category, prefers to buy the most readily available brand of product at the most accessible store.
2. *Convenience Store—Shopping Good*: The consumer selects his purchase from among the assortment carried by the most accessible store.
3. *Convenience Store—Specialty Good*: The consumer purchases his favored brand from the most accessible store which has the item in stock.
4. *Shopping Store—Convenience Good*: The consumer is indifferent to the brand of product he buys, but shops among different stores in order to secure better retail service and/or lower retail price.
5. *Shopping Store—Shopping Good*: The consumer makes comparisons among both retail controlled factors and factors associated with the product (brand).
6. *Shopping Store—Specialty Good*: The consumer has a strong preference with respect to the brand of the product, but shops among a number of stores in order to secure the best retail service and/or price for this brand.
7. *Specialty Store—Convenience Good*: The consumer prefers to trade at a specific store, but is indifferent to the brand of product purchased.
8. *Specialty Store—Shopping Good*: The consumer prefers to trade at a certain store, but is uncertain as to which product he wishes to buy and examines the store's assortment for the best purchase.
9. *Specialty Store—Specialty Good*: The consumer has both a preference for a particular store and a specific brand.

Conceivably, each of these nine types of behavior might characterize the buying patterns of some consumers for a given product. It seems more likely, however, that the behavior of consumers toward a product could be represented by only three or four of the categories. The remaining cells would be empty, indicating that no consumers bought the product by these methods. Different cells, of course, would be empty for different products.

The Formation of Retail Strategy

The extended classification system developed above clearly provides additional information important to the manufacturer in planning of his marketing strategy. Of principal interest here, however, is the means by which the retailer might use the classification system in planning his marketing strategy.

Three Basic Steps

The procedure involves three steps. The first is the classification of the retailer's potential customers for some product by market segment, using the nine categories in the consumer buying habit matrix to define the principal segments. The second requires the retailer to determine the nature of the marketing strategies necessary to appeal to each market segment. The final step is the retailer's selection of the market segment, and the strategy associated with it, to which he will sell. A simplified, hypothetical example may help to clarify this process.

A former buyer of dresses for a department store decided to open her own dress shop. She rented a small store in the downtown area of a city of 50,000, ten miles distant from a metropolitan center of several hundred thousand population. In contemplating her marketing strategy, she was certain that the different incomes, educational backgrounds, and tastes of the potential customers in her city meant that various groups of these women were using sharply different buying methods for dresses. Her initial problem was to determine, by use of the consumer buying habit matrix, what proportion of her potential market bought dresses in what manner.

By drawing on her own experience, discussions with other retailers in the area, census and other market data, the former buyer estimated that her potential market was divided, according to the matrix, in the following porportions.

This analysis revealed four market segments that she believed were worth further consideration. (In an actual situation, each of these four should be further divided into submarket segments according to other possible factors such as age, incomes, dress size required, location of residence, etc.) Her next task was to determine the type of marketing mix which would most effectively appeal to each of these segments. The information for these decisions was derived from the characteristics of consumer behavior associated with each of the defined segments. The following is a brief description of her assessment of how elements of the marketing mix ought to be weighted in order to formulate a strategy for each segment.

A Strategy for Each Segment

To appeal to the convenience store-specialty good segment she felt that the two most important elements in the mix should be a highly accessible location and a selection of widely-accepted brand merchandise. Of somewhat lesser importance, she found, were depth of assortment, personal selling, and price. Minimal emphasis should be given to store promotion and facilities.

She reasoned that the shopping store-shopping good requires a good central location, emphasis on price, and a broad assortment. She ranked store promotion, accepted brand names and personal selling as secondary. Store facilities would, once again, receive minor emphasis.

The specialty store-shopping good market would, she believed, have to be catered to with an exceptionally strong assortment, a high level of personal selling and more elaborate store facilities. Less emphasis would be needed upon prominent brand names, store promotions, and price. Location was of minor importance.

The specialty store-specialty good category, she thought, would require a marketing mix heavily emphasizing personal selling and highly elaborate store facilities and services. She also felt that prominent brand names would be required, but that these would probably have to include the top names in fashion, including labels from Paris. Depth of assortment would

Buying Habit	*% of Market*
Convenience store—Convenience good	0
Convenience store—Shopping good	3
Convenience store—Specialty good	20
Shopping store—Convenience good	0
Shopping store—Shopping good	35
Shopping store—Specialty good	2
Specialty store—Convenience good	0
Specialty store—Shopping good	25
Specialty store—Specialty good	15
	100

TABLE 1. Proportion of Potential Dress Market in Each Matrix Cell

be secondary, while least emphasis would be placed upon store promotion, price, and location.

Evaluation of Alternatives

The final step in the analysis required the former dress buyer to assess her abilities to implement any one of these strategies, given the degree of competition existing in each segment. Her considerations were as follows. With regard to the specialty store-specialty good market, she was unprepared to make the investment in store facilities and services that she felt would be necessary. She also thought, since a considerable period of time would probably be required for her to build up the necessary reputation, that this strategy involved substantial risk. Lastly, she believed that her experience in buying high fashion was somewhat limited and that trips to European fashion centers would prove burdensome.

She also doubted her ability to cater to the specialty store-shopping good market, principally because she knew that her store would not be large enough to carry the necessary assortment depth. She felt that this same factor would limit her in attempting to sell to the shopping store-shopping good market as well. Despite the presence of the large market in this segment, she believed that she would not be able to create sufficient volume in her proposed quarters to enable her to compete effectively with the local department store and several large department stores in the neighboring city.

The former buyer believed her best opportunity was in selling to the convenience store-specialty good segment. While there were already two other stores in her city which were serving this segment, she believed that a number of important brands were still not represented. Her past contacts with resources led her to believe that she would stand an excellent chance of securing a number of these lines. By stocking these brands, she thought that she could capture a considerable number of local customers who currently were purchasing them in the large city. In this way, she believed, she would avoid the full force of local competition.

Decision

The conclusion of the former buyer to use her store to appeal to the convenience store-specialty good segment represents the culmination to the process of analysis suggested here. It shows how the use of the three-by-three matrix of consumer buying habits may aid the retailer in developing his marketing strategy. It is a device which can isolate the important market segments. It provides further help in enabling the retailer to associate the various types of consumer behavior with those elements of the marketing mix to which they are sensitive. Finally, the analysis forces the retailer to assess the probability of his success in attempting to use the necessary strategy in order to sell each possible market.

NOTES

1. Melvin T. Copeland, "Relation of Consumers' Buying Habits of Marketing Methods," *Harvard Business Review*, Vol. 1 (April, 1923), pp. 282–289.

2. Definitions Committee, American Marketing Association, "Report of the Definitions Committee," *Journal of Marketing*, Vol. 13 (October, 1948), pp. 202–217, at p. 206, p. 215.

3. Definitions Committee, American Marketing Association, *Marketing Definitions*, (Chicago: American Marketing Association, 1960), p. 11, 21, 22.

4. Richard H. Holton, "The Distinction Between Convenience Goods, Shopping Goods, and Specialty Goods," *Journal of Marketing*, Vol. 23 (July, 1958), pp. 53–56.

5. David J. Luck, "On the Nature of Specialty Goods," *Journal of Marketing*, Vol. 24 (July, 1959), pp. 61–64.

6. Richard H. Holton, "What is Really Meant by 'Specialty' Goods?" *Journal of Marketing*, Vol. 24 (July, 1959), pp. 64–67.

7. Melvin T. Copeland, same reference as footnote 1, pp. 283–284.

8. George Katona, *Psychological Analysis of Economic Behavior* (New York: McGraw-Hill Book Co., Inc., 1951), p. 47.

9. Same reference, pp. 67–68.

10. George Katona and Eva Mueller, "A Study of Purchase Decisions in Consumer Behavior," Lincoln Clark, editor, *Consumer Behavior* (New York: University Press, 1954), pp. 30–87.

11. Katona, same reference as footnote 8, p. 68.

12. James A. Bayton, "Motivation, Cognition, Learning—Basic Factors in Consumer Behavior," *Journal of Marketing*, Vol. 22 (January, 1958), pp. 282–289, at p. 287.

LEARNING REVIEW

Questions:

1. For a convenience store-specialty goods approach, the two most important elements might be ____________ and ____________.

2. ____________ goods are those for which the buyer is willing to make comparisons.

3. A major point of this article is that a classification system for marketing strategy must consider both the ____________ motives and the ____________ motives of the consumer.

Answers:

1. good location, brand-name merchandise; 2. Shopping; 3. product, patronage

---

Retrospective Comment

Since its inception, Copeland's imaginative and original theory of marketing strategy (3) based upon a classification of goods has both captured the fancy of marketing educators and their interest in attempting to improve upon its design. The article *Retail Strategy and the Classification of Consumer Goods* is but one of many efforts (1, 5, 7, 10, 13, 14) to make the theory more precise and useful in the solution of marketing problems. In reflecting upon the article for purposes of writing this commentary, what strikes one most is how much more must be done in order to achieve that end. While marketing technology has progressed significantly since its publication, and offers some possible fresh solutions, our new knowledge has heightened awareness of the formidable difficulties that remain. The intent of this commentary is to deal with the nature of these problems, hopefully both for the purpose of clarification and of suggesting possible approaches.

To appreciate the nature of the difficulties, it is important to remember that the purpose behind the theory *is* to provide a guide for developing marketing strategy. Most discussions of the theory, including the retail strategy article, deal predominantly with the conceptual framework for classifying consumer buying behavior. Yet, this is just one part of the theory. There are two others.

One of these is another classification scheme. This is for marketing strategies. Such a scheme is necessary if the implications of the theory are to be respected. It must be possible to discriminate clearly between one type of strategy and another so that empirical referents of these may be identified for testing purposes.

The third part of the theory is a mapping process. This is some functional relationship which indicates the specific strategy most appropriate for each product category. The degree of success to be obtained through use of the theory is obviously dependent upon the accuracy of this process in identifying the optimal strategy. The extent of this success becomes the empirical criterion upon which the theory must be validated.

Each of these components of the theory will now be discussed in some greater detail.

The Strategy Classification

Perhaps the most painful questions of all with respect to the theory emerge with respect to the quality of the classification scheme developed to categorize marketing strategies. In the earliest developments of the theory, strategies were organized in accord with distribution patterns, intensive, selective, and exclusive. Advertising and price were sometimes considered, but not always in a very coherent pattern. In some instances it was presumed that certain modes of advertising would be associated with the method of distribution, *broadcast* promotion with intensive distribution and "rifle shots" with selective. While this is but a rudimentary basis, little has been done to significantly improve it and there is no evidence of any active research in the area.

While in a loose sense this original orientation is appealing, it is obviously inadequate. There are, no doubt, more than three types of marketing strategies; heavy broadcast advertising does not necessarily accompany efforts to obtain intensive distribution; and the role of price is most obscure.

In a more fundamental sense, it may be appropriate to ask whether it is possible to conceive of marketing strategies in terms of categories. The concept of the marketing mix in vogue over the last several decades views the development of strategy as a process of adjusting the proportions of a firm's resources devoted to promotion, product quality, product line, price, and distribution intensity. In this posture there are an infinite number of possible resource allocation patterns. Whether some small number of these would represent the great proportion of viable strategies to be utilized, is a conjecture both little considered and open to some doubt. To the extent that patterns do not exist, it may be necessary to abandon the concept of a classification of strategies. In its place it may be possible to substitute the size of the response coefficients (for elasticities) for each of the elements of the marketing mix.

The Mapping Procedure

The mapping procedure, whereby specific goods categories and strategies are joined, also has not been well developed. For the most part, the relationships have been set forth in terms of what might be regarded as *self-evident rationalizations*. For example, if in the purchase of convenience goods consumers buy the item which is maximally accessible, then it follows that manufacturers marketing products in that category must have their wares widely distributed if they hope to tap their full market potential.

Several difficulties emerge with this approach. Perhaps the most obvious is that it is never verified through empirical research. If we are to follow the scientific method, then we should have tests of the extent to which goods classified in the convenience category are actually successfully distributed under intensive distribution and mass advertising. However, there have been no tests of distribution patterns let alone advertising policies.

Were tests to be made, one might have suspicions that the results in the form of simple correlations might not be as clear cut as desired. One reason is that while consumer buying habits are likely to be a major determinant of strategy, other facets of the market may play a role as well. For example, the structure of the market, as reflected in the number of manufacturers, the degree of concentration, barriers to entry, the significance of private brands and the bargaining power of distributors are conditions which will affect the viability of alternative marketing strategies. Testing procedures may well be required to hold these and other factors constant if the real impact of consumer buying patterns on strategy is to be ascertained. While this is not necessarily an impossible task, it obviously adds to the burden.

Another concern with the types of results that might emerge from tests, emanates from the absence of full control over marketing strategies by manufacturers. While, for example, some might seek intensive distribution, the limited capacities of the available system to accommodate all who might desire this may thwart the intentions of many. Such a barrier is apt to be sufficient cause for many firms to adopt strategies quite dissimilar to those that otherwise might be optimal.

Most vexing of all, however, is issue of the direction of causation in the process. Implicitly we assume that product category determines strategy. But, might not marketing strategies influence the buying patterns which are the basis for the product categories? Firms are wont to develop means to move their products toward the insulated speciality category. To the extent that R&D and advertising can accomplish this, the meaning of any observed relationship between strategy and product category may well be obscure.

The Goods Classification

With regard to the goods classification element of the theory several questions on fundamental level must be raised. These involve the specific choice of the criteria to form the categories and the number of categories to be formed. On the empirical level there is the question of how these criteria are to be defined and measured so that validation of the theory may proceed.

With respect to the first issue, some authors (1, 14) have attempted to formulate the classification of goods theory from a number of explicit measures, e.g. frequency of purchase, customer need for service. While these encompass some of Copeland's framework, they go substantially beyond it.

The test of which set of criteria are the best can be made by logic and intuition, but this may not offer satisfactory resolution of the problem. When confronted with alternative approaches, we should use the one which provides the best parsimonious set of indicators. Yet, unfortunately, as indicated, we are not close to being ready to make such a test.

One possible solution would be to employ some empirical techniques which would allow the basic descriptors of a wide range of consumer buying practices to identify the criteria. For example, for a given set of buying practices, one could obtain from consumers, and/or other market data, measures for a large number of varied product classes. These criteria could be reduced, through factor analysis, to that set which are most independent of each other. (Clearly it serves no purpose to have several criteria closely correlated with each other. This offers no improvement in predictive value and serves but to clutter up the analysis.)

A variety of techniques could then be employed to develop natural clusters of product classes. Procedures that could be employed include numerical taxonomy, cluster analysis, Q-type factor analysis, and some multi-dimensional scaling routines. Application of any of these would derive from the data a set of product clusters which could be named and used directly in the process of determining whether they are predictive of successful marketing strategies.

One possible drawback to this approach is that there is no guarantee that the clusters so formed will have any clear intuitive meaning. Marketing managers may regard these with some skepticism and be unwilling to invest time and funds necessary to develop the analysis and apply it. The approach could fail because of its own complexity.

Were further work to be undertaken with the framework of Copeland's thesis, major opportunities exist in terms of developing more operational measures of the classification criteria (8, pp. 216–220). From my article, two criteria were identified. These were the degree of closeness of consumer preference for products and the extent to which such preference maps were clearly formulated. Both criteria are related to the type of search activity the consumer is likely to employ in buying a product.

The first of these measures may be recast in terms of the substantial research work that has taken place in regard to the concept and measure of product similarities, developments that paralleled the growth of multidimensional scaling techniques for identifying product space and spatial relationships among the brands in a product class. Our first criterion, then, would be defined as the degree of perceived brand similarity within a product class.

The second criterion on the degree of completeness of the preference map may be recast in terms of the degree of uncertainty that the consumers feel about making choices among the brands of a given product class. Here, too, a relatively extensive development in research has occurred (4), making possible empirical measures of this dimension of consumer behavior.

Using these two variables as the axes in a two dimensional space, as shown in Figure 1, we find that specialty goods appear in quadrant III (perceived differences are high and little uncertainty is involved in the judgments). Convenience goods appear in quadrant II (perceived differences are low and, again little uncertainty is involved in the judgment). Shopping goods appear in quadrants I and IV. Those in the first quadrant are labeled as low intensity and those in IV as high intensity.

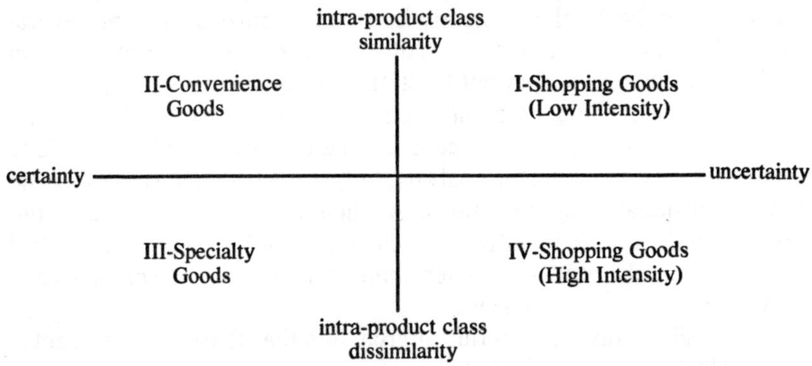

FIGURE 1. The classification of goods via the criteria of degree of intra-product class similarity and degree of uncertainty held by consumers in ranking intra-product class similarities.

Identification of the degree of perceived product dissimilarity for various product classes, e.g. automobiles, television sets, canned soup, would proceed through the development of product space maps for each. An example of how such maps are derived through the use of consumer perceptions of the product attributes held by each brand is developed by Johnson (9). Once the maps for each are developed, Euclidian distance measures of each pair of brands could be summed and the mean or median distance regarded as the degree of product similarity.

A possible difficulty with this approach is the probable lack of perceptual comparability of the differences in distance in the various product space maps. Some method of normalization will be necessary if the similarity measures for each product class are to be comprarable.

A less complex approach would be to obtain paired comparison judgments for all brands in a class. In this consumers would not only be requested to make known the preferred brand of each pair, but to estimate the price differential required to equate the values inherent in both. These price differentials may be summed to find the mean differential in value among all the brands. This mean value would represent the level of product class similarity. The continuum of such values would then form the basis for the horizontal axis in Figure I.

In the literature of consumer risk taking and uncertainty, two measures have been implemented. The first (12) and simplest was developed in a study of cognitive dissonance on race track betting. Betters were requested to estimate on a seven point scale their confidence of winning. Such a procedure could be readily applied to evaluate the level of consumer confidence in their estimates of the price differentials involved in the paired comparison technique explained above.

A more detailed technique to probe uncertainty involves consumer elaboration of their entire prior distribution of probabilities that specific product brands possess given attributes (16). Whether the richness, as well as the complexity, of this approach is warranted for the present purposes, however, seems somewhat doubtful.

Through implementation of data gathering procedures such as these, it would appear possible to place on Figure 1 the locus of most, if not all, consumer product classes. Such an arrangement would provide the basis for tests to determine whether there were similarities among the marketing strategies for the classes in each of the four quadrants. Barring this full-fledged test, it would be simple to evaluate the extent to which these categories did reflect major differences in consumer search patterns. Procedures for making these types of tests have long been identified (2, 5, 11, 15).

Conclusions

In reflecting upon the manifold barriers that lie in the way of attempting to validate any classification of goods theory, it is perhaps understandable why specific reference to the theory appears so infrequently in the literature of marketing research. Outside of some of the publications cited here, very little has been done with the theory as a whole and the vast preponderance of existing work has been qualitative in nature.

It might, therefore, appear somewhat surprising to find the frequent reference to and use of the theory in basic marketing texts and edited readings books intended to instruct practitioners in the profession. The reason is that, qualitative as it is, the classification theory provides a broad and essential integration of much material in marketing. It provides a framework for the analysis of marketing problems, at least at rudimentary level, and suggests where students might look to devise answers to marketing strategy problems. It provides a logic which can be readily understood and appreciated.

It is this very integrative character of the theory that makes it so difficult, perhaps intractable, to evaluate in its fullest. Being human, marketing researchers are more prone to study smaller issues where hopes of making some progress within their limits of time and funds seem possible.

While each of the bits of knowledge provided by this narrower base builds a necessary base for future work, the bits are not always meaningful to the student or intelligible to the practitioner. It may be a sign that marketing research has truly come of age when it develops the capability of testing large scale theories encompassing elements of strategy as well as consumer behavior. At that time, the classification of goods theories, or their lineal descendants, may become sophisticated tools of value to expanding the insights of student, practitioner, and marketing researcher.

REFERENCES

1. Leo Aspinwall, "The Characteristics of Goods and Parallel System Theories." In *Managerial Marketing: Perspectives and Viewpoints*, E. J. Kelley and W. Lazer, eds. (Homewood, Illinois: Richard D. Irwin, Inc., 1958).
2. Louis P. Bucklin, "Testing Propensities to Shop." *Journal of Marketing*, 30 (January 1966), pp. 22–27.
3. Melvin T. Copeland, "Relation of Consumer's Buying Habits to Marketing Methods." *Harvard Business Review*, I (April 1923), pp. 282–289.
4. Donald F. Cox, ed., *Risk Taking and Information Handling in Consumer Behavior* (Boston: Graduate School of Business Administration, Harvard University, 1967).
5. William P. Dommermuth, "The Shopping Matrix and Marketing Strategy." *Journal of Marketing Research*, II (May 1965), pp. 128–132.
6. William P. Dommermuth and Edward W. Cundiff, "Shopping Goods, Shopping Centers, and Selling Strategies." *Journal of Marketing*, 31 (October 1967), pp. 32–36.
7. Richard H. Holton, "The Distinction Between Convenience Goods, Shopping Goods, and Specialty Goods." *Journal of Marketing*, 23 (July 1958).
8. John A. Howard and Jagdish N. Sheth, *The Theory of Buyer Behavior*, (New York: John Wiley and Sons, 1969), pp. 216–220.
9. Richard M. Johnson, "Marketing Segmentation: A Strategic Management Tool." *Journal of Marketing Research*, VIII (February 1971), pp. 13–18.
10. Stanley Kaish, "Cognitive Dissonance and the Classifications of Consumer Goods." *Journal of Marketing*, 31 (October 1967), pp. 28–31.
11. Arno K. Kleimenhagen, "Shopping, Specialty or Convenience Goods." *Journal of Retailing*, 42 (Winter, 1966–1967), pp. 32–39.
12. Robert T. Knox and James A. Inkster, "Post Decision Dissonance at Post Time." *Journal of Personality and Social Psychology*, 8, No. 4 (1968), pp. 319–323.
13. David J. Luck, "On the Nature of Specialty Goods." *Journal of Marketing*, 24 (July 1959).
14. Gordon E. Miracle, "Product Characteristics and Marketing Strategy." *Journal of Marketing*, 29 (January 1965).
15. Joseph W. Newman and Richard Staelin, "Prepurchase Information Seeking for New Cars and Major Household Appliances." *Journal of Marketing Research*, IX (August 1972), pp. 249–257.
16. Robert B. Woodruff, "Measu. ment of Consumers' Prior Brand Information." *Journal of Marketing Research*. IX (August 1972), pp. 258–263.

25

The Logistics of Distribution

John F. Magee

PREVIEW

I. Many pressures have strained current distribution systems:
   A. Competition has taken the form of availability of goods and reliability of delivery.
   B. Product changes, especially through use of style as a merchandising practice, have increased demand for service.
   C. The need to stabilize production and insulate production levels from short-term fluctuations in sales are internal pressures.

II. Many changes have occurred in distribution to meet increasing demands:
   A. Trucks, railroads, and airlines have all improved their freight-handling methods.
   B. Data-processing methods, especially through use of computers, have improved greatly.
   C. New materials-handling methods have gained acceptance.
   D. Progress has been made in ways of looking at the logistics problem and at methods for analyzing distribution systems.

III. Long-term planning of distribution methods may affect product design and other aspects of business by providing at least two methods of making a wide variety of products available in local markets:
   A. Manufacturers may move toward centralized production in large volume and moved quickly to local markets as needed.
   B. Diversity may be through superficial differences, with the basic product manufactured centrally and moved to widespread local assembly or modification plants.

John F. Magee, "The Logistics of Distribution," is reprinted by permission from *Harvard Business Review* (July-August 1960), pp. 89–101.

American business is awakening to a new, exciting opportunity to improve service and reduce costs—better management of the flow of goods from plant to user. Capitalizing on this opportunity means:

1. Thinking of the physical distribution process as a *system* in which, just as in a good hi-fi system, all the components and functions must be properly balanced.
2. Taking a fresh look at the responsibilities, capabilities, and organizational positions of executives in traffic, warehouse management, inventory control, and other functions which make up the over-all system.
3. Re-examining the company's physical plant and distribution procedures in the light of technical advances in such areas as transportation, data processing, and materials handling.

Stubborn Pressures

The need for progress in distribution is a product of not one but several trends—trends in costs, in product-line policy, and in the market place. More often than not, the challenge posed is to the system as a whole, not just to the particular part or function where trouble is most obvious.

Rising Costs

For years, businessmen and economists have looked with mixed feelings on the increase in distribution costs in our economy. Over the past half century, tremendous strides have been made in reducing the costs of production, but these feats have not been duplicated in other areas. If the over-all efficiency of companies is to continue to improve, management must turn its attention increasingly to holding distribution costs in line. Physical distribution costs in particular, estimated by some to represent the third largest component in the total cost of business operation, are a logical center for management attention.

The problems of cutting these costs pose certain new and interesting questions for business. Whereas in many production operations it has been possible in the past to substitute a machine for human labor and to cut the cost of one operation without seriously disturbing the rest of the production system, this is hardly the case in efforts to cut physical distribution costs. Indiscriminate cost reduction in any one of the individual cost elements, such as inventory maintenance, warehousing, transportation, or clerical activities, can have a disastrous effect on the efficiency of the system as a whole. To illustrate this point:

1. Suppose we cut inventories. Certainly a reduction in inventories will save capital investment and the costs of supplying capital, and it may save some expenses in storage, taxes, and insurance. On the other hand, an

indiscriminate reduction in inventory levels may seriously impair the reliability of delivery service to customers and the availability of products in the field. An inventory reduction which saves money but destroys competitive position is hardly a contribution to a more effective distribution system.

2. We can cut transportation costs, perhaps, by changing to methods showing lower cost per ton-mile, or by shipping in larger quantities and taking advantage of volume carload or truckload rates. But if lower transportation costs are achieved at the expense of slower or less frequent movement of goods, we face the risk of: (a) cutting the flexibility and responsiveness of the distribution system to changes in customer requirements; (b) requiring greater field inventories to maintain service; (c) creating greater investment requirements and obsolescence risks.

Similarly, blanket refusal to allow cost increases in any one part can wipe out opportunities to make the system as a whole more efficient. For instance: New methods of high-speed data communications and processing may in fact increase the clerical costs of operating the distribution system. On the other hand, they may cut down delays in feeding information back to govern production operations and to control lags in getting material moving into the distribution system in response to customer demand. Thus, they may actually cut *total* distribution system costs because of their impact on improved production and inventory control.

It takes a careful analysis of the total physical distribution system to know whether net costs will be increased or decreased by efforts to cut the cost of any one component.

Proliferating Product Lines

Physical distribution systems in recent years have been put under tremendous pressure induced by changes in product-line characteristics. Until recently, for example, products like typewriters, light bulbs, appliances, and plumbing fixtures were largely utilitarian, with differences in product characteristics rather closely related to function. A typewriter manufacturer did not have to worry about matching typewriter color to office decor or type style to company "image." Light bulbs used to be white and sometimes clear, and they varied by wattage. Now, however, typewriters come in pastels and two-tones. Light bulbs are sold not only to provide light but atmosphere, with a corresponding increase in the number of products that have to be shipped, stocked, and controlled. Appliances and plumbing fixtures are available to customers not only in the classical antiseptic white, but in a wide range of color and style combinations. In short, style and individuality have become strong competitive weapons.

In an almost unending list of products in the consumer field, variations in color, packaging, and other features have imposed heavy burdens on the distribution system. In the marketing of industrial goods, variations in grade, color, and size have had a similar impact. In paper manufacture, for example, the wide variety of package sizes required for consumer products has led carton manufacturers to demand correspondingly wide ranges of kraft board roll widths from paper manufacturers, and these demands have created difficult problems of scheduling, inventory control, and distribution.

The growth and change in product-line characteristics in both consumer and industrial products have meant that manufacturing plants have had more items to make, and the distribution system has had more items to handle and stock. More items mean lower volume per item and correspondingly higher unit handling inventory and storage costs.

Alternative Courses

Increased cost, selling, and product-line pressures suggest that management should take a hard look at alternative distribution patterns, as a means of cutting logistics costs without a major sacrifice in service. Here are a few of the possibilities:

1. The company can carry central stocks of low-selling items only. To get the right balance of transportation costs, handling costs, and service, it may be necessary to stock these items at one central point and ship them against individual customer orders as the latter arise, perhaps by expedited service or air freight.
2. For many items in the line, a good compromise may be to carry some low- or middle-volume items in only a few large regional warehouses, as a compromise between the excessive storage costs incurred from broad-scale stocking and the transportation and service penalties incurred by attempting to meet demand from manufacturing points alone.
3. Warehouse points can be consolidated. With improvements in transportation and in mechanical material- and data-handling methods, large opportunities exist in many businesses for cutting down on the number of field warehouse points. With increased volume through the individual warehouses, carrying a broader product line at the local points begins to make greater economic sense.

Sales-Generating Capacity

The first and most basic job of the distribution system is to get customers, to turn interest and orders into sales. As business has grown more competitive and the public has become harder to please, management has focused increasing attention on the *quality* of its logistical operations. What can be done to make products more readily available for purchase in local markets? What improvements can be made in backing up product merchandising and advertising programs with adequate deliveries and service? Obviously, questions like these are affected by cost considerations, but as marketing objectives they deserve individual attention.

In analyzing the capacity of a distribution system to produce sales, executives will do well to examine three key characteristics:

1. *Location*. It has been estimated, for example, that from 5 distribution points a company can reach 33% of the United States consumer market within a day; while from 25 warehouse locations, 80% can be reached in one day.

2. *Inventories*. Judging from my own and associates' experience, approximately 80% more inventory is needed in a typical business to fill 95% of the customers' orders out of stock than to fill only 80%.

3. *Responsiveness*. The ability of a system to transmit needs back to the supplying plant and get material needed into the field determines how quickly the business can shift with changes in customer preferences to meet demand with minimum investment and cost.

Revolution in Technology

The pressures on distribution methods have led to exciting new technological advances for getting goods to the user at lower cost to the company—with less labor and materials expended and less capital tied up in inventories and facilities. When these advances are introduced in proper balance, the distribution process can better meet the needs of the consumer. Major technological changes are now taking place in transportation, information handling, and material handling. Let us examine each of them in turn.

Costs vs. Transport Time

Transportation thinking has been dominated too long by preoccupation with the direct traffic bill. Too much attention has been paid to transport cost per ton-mile and not enough to the contribution transportation makes to the effectiveness of the distribution system as a whole.

Railroad rate structures are to an outsider an eye-opening illustration of what can happen when a transportation system is put under the cost-per-ton-mile pressure for too long. Rail rate structures, despite frequent attempts to introduce some rationale, have degenerated into an unbelievable hodgepodge of unrealistic and uneconomic rate compromises as the roads have succumbed to the pressure of giving each shipper the lowest cost per ton-mile, often at the expense of service. While improvements in equipment, such as the introduction of the diesel locomotive, have led to greater efficiency on the track, in some cases at least the longer trains and increased classification problems that have resulted have meant little or no net increase in over-all distribution efficiency. The gap between traffic and marketing thinking is painfully evident in many companies' distribution methods; little has been done to relate transportation methods and service to the objectives of the distribution system in support of marketing efforts.

Transportation costs are important indeed, but they are only part of the story. For example, think of the value of materials in transit:

1. Data collected on sample shipments in various parts of the country indicate that material may spend one to two weeks in transit and that the capital value of assets tied up in the transportation system may, depending on the pressure for capital, add as much as to the economic costs of the goods.
2. Service, or reliability of the transport system, is also important. Goods must get to the user promptly and reliably, to permit him to operate systematically with low inventories.
3. The direct and indirect costs of damage in transport are another large item in the traffic bill that at times gets overlooked in the pressure for low cost per ton-mile.

Clearly, transport time is one of the key determinants of the efficiency of the distribution system. Its impact is not vivid or dramatic, and executives do not always appreciate what a difference it makes, but in a great many companies it is a significant factor in financing. To take a simple illustration: Suppose that in a company doing an annual business of $100 million, time in transit is reduced from 14 days to 2. Time between reorders is 14 days, communication and processing time is 4 days, and field stocks average $12.5 million. In such a situation the reduction in transit time might well lead to a reduction in distribution inventory investment of $6 million, made up of: (1) a reduction of $3.3 million in transit, i.e., 12 days' sales; (2) a reduction of $2.7 million in inventories required to protect customer service resulting from a faster, more flexible distribution system response.

Speeding Up Service

Changes in transportation leading to improved opportunities in distribution have been truly revolutionary since World War II. Major superhighway systems have been built, truck speeds have increased substantially and so have trailer capacities. The growth in the use of trucking for industrial distribution is now well known. The stimulus from subsidies is only part of the story; trucks have been able to compete at characteristically higher ton-mile costs because they have offered speed, reliability, and flexibility to shippers.

Without doubt, railroads are responding to this challenge. A recent survey showed that almost all Class I railroads are offering some form of piggyback or expedited motor-carrier service. At least some railroads are showing new merchandising awareness in concentrating on customer service. Whether the industry will be able, in the face of inherent limitations, to reverse the decline in its share of manufacturers' freight business is still an open question.

Air freight represents a challenge to both rail and over-the-road haulers. Today most industry executives still tend to view air freight as a luxury, as a service available for "orchids and emergencies." However, the trend in air freight rates has been sharply downward in recent years. With new planes coming into service, even further reductions can be projected—down to 8 cents to 12 cents a ton-mile from present-day rates of approximately 22 cents. Much depends on the success of efforts to develop aircraft equipped for freight handling and for flexible operation under a wide range of conditions (for example, modest runway lengths), and to build up the ground service needed to match air-handling speeds so as to avoid the danger faced by the railroads—the collapse of service as a result of concentration on mass, low-cost, terminal-to-terminal movement.

Impact of New Methods

What is the significance of the ferment in transportation methods? For one thing, improvement in local truck service opens up opportunities to serve wide-flung markets through fewer and larger distribution points. With larger distribution centers, the chance that mechanized material handling and storage systems will pay off is enhanced, and inventory requirements are reduced through consolidation.

To suggest the size of the opportunity, one analysis with which I am familiar showed that cutting the number of field distribution points for a national product line from 50 to 25 would increase total transport costs 7% but cut inventories 20% and cut *total* physical distribution costs 8% (the latter representing roughly a 1% cut in the total cost of delivered product). This was accomplished at the cost of serving a few small markets—about 5% of the total—with second-day instead of first-day delivery.

Rapid truck or air service increases the feasibility of relying on shipments from a few central points to back up service. Here are two ways in which this can be employed:

1. The many low-volume items in the typical product line, the items on which local storage and handling costs outweigh the penalty costs of expedited shipment, can be held centrally and moved to the market where they are needed as needed. For example, the bottom 50% of the product line, which often accounts for only 4% of sales, may require 25% or more

of the warehousing costs and inventory capital charges. Turnover of the stocks of these items is often only one eighth that of the high-volume half of the line. In a *relatively* high number of cases, special shipments could be made at a cost well below that of storing the items at local distribution centers.

2. If there are substantial reserve stocks designed to protect customer service located in the field, it is possible to pare them down in the knowledge that additional supplies can be moved in promptly to meet sudden customer demands.

In a typical distribution system a large share of the inventory—as much as 90%—is carried to protect delivery service to customers in the face of fluctuating demand and system delays. This safety stock is most likely to be used at the end of the reorder cycle, when stocks hit their low point before new receipts. Fig. 1 illustrates a common situation, with safety stocks being partly depleted at intervals just before a new shipment arrives. During the period of the first reorder, demand has been heavy. In many reorder cycles, however, stocks will not be touched at all; this is the case before the second reorder in the illustration (middle of the chart) comes in. Note that inventory in transit represents a fairly significant proportion of the whole.

How much of safety stocks is actually used depends on the reorder system and level of service maintained. Typically, the last 10% may be needed only once or twice a year—a turnover rate roughly one sixth the average; and the last 30% may be needed only two to four times a year. Warehouses and inventory carrying charges on this portion of inventory, then, may easily run to 10%–20% of the sales they make possible.

There is an opportunity in many companies for management to cut material held in the field and back up customer service through regularized high-speed delivery service. This possibility will deserve increasing attention from management as the costs of high-speed transport, communication, and data processing drop.

Information Processing

Revolutionary data-processing methods were noisily battering at established business methods some six or seven years ago, but the impact was more in noise generated than in accomplishment. Now that a lot of the superficial excitement has died away, however, a broad and solid structure of accomplishment in modern data-processing techniques is quietly being built.

For one thing, computers seem to have become much more broadly accepted than anticipated. When the earliest internally programed machines were announced, computer manufacturers' optimistic estimates

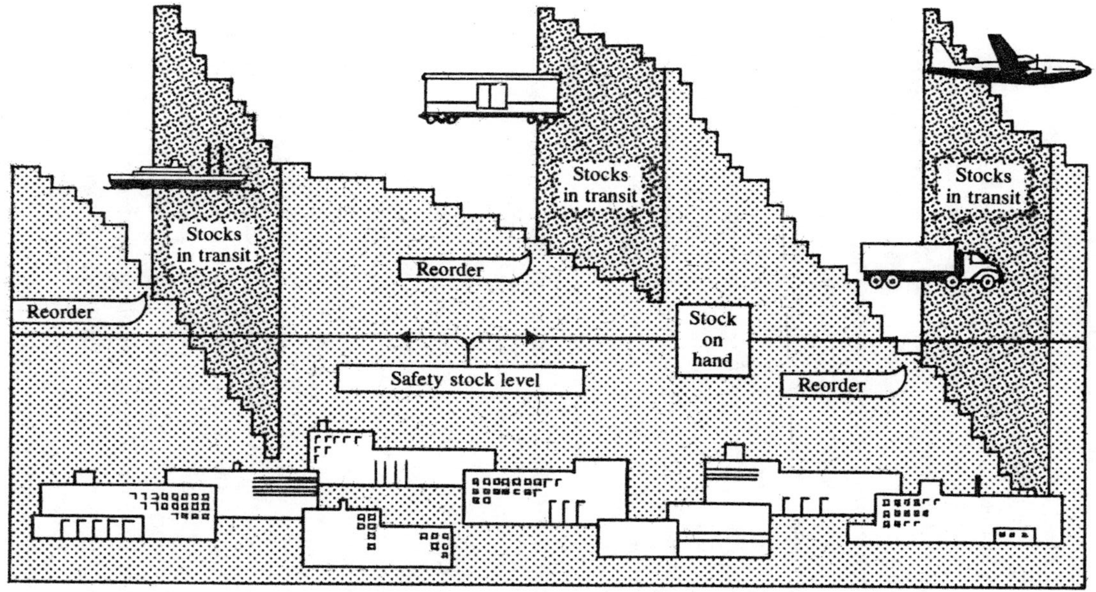

FIGURE 1. What is the characteristic inventory pattern of stocks on hand in the typical company?

were in the dozens. Today the number of machines installed or in the process of installation is in the thousands. In support of computing or processing facilities, great improvements are taking place in communications systems, especially systems designed to feed into or out of computers. In distribution management, fast, reliable communication is equally as important as fast, reliable processing.

The *use* being made of modern information-processing equipment in distribution is just as significant as its broad market acceptance. For instance, machines are being used to maintain local inventory balances, forecast near-term demand, employ forecasts and inventory balances as inputs in calculating item orders, prepare tentative purchase orders, allocate item balances among stock points, and draw up production schedules and work force requirements. These are not mere compiling and accounting functions, nor is it fair to call them "decision making." In these functions, the machine systems are interpreting rules or procedures to work out the decisions implicit in them in light of the facts of the situation. In other words, the equipment is doing what we would like intelligent clerks to do: diligently following policy and weighing costs to arrive at day-to-day actions.

The forecasting function in particular deserves special attention. I refer not to the longer term economic forecasts, annual business forecasts, or even shorter term (e.g., quarterly) business predictions, but to short-term forecasts of sales, item by item, over the replenishment lead time. These forecasts are made implicitly or explicitly in every inventory control system. In most companies they are left up to the individual stock clerk or inventory controller to make as best he can, usually with little or no training or guides. Management will spend hundreds of hours of industrial engineering time simplifying or improving a job method here and there to take a few pennies out of labor cost. Yet the stock clerk making inventory control forecasts may, through his control over product distribution and assets tied up in inventories, be costing his company many pennies indeed.

Many people still argue that one cannot forecast routinely because intuition and background knowledge count too heavily. They fail to recognize that objective procedures for short-term prediction of item sales have the same merits as say, routing and tooling lists in a shop. Experience leaves little doubt that great gains can be made by substituting powerful systematic methods for casual or unrecognized ones.[1]

Changes in Material Handling

Mechanization is slowly spreading from the making of things to their handling in distribution. For instance: One company in the clothing industry has installed a new data-processing system first to handle sales orders and then inventory control and production-scheduling systems. At the same time, it has been developing a bin-and-conveyer system which will permit economical mechanization of order-filling activities. The goal toward which both of these efforts are directed is a unified system in which the customer order not only serves as an input in automatic order handling but will also, after suitable internal mechanical processing, activate the warehouse system to select and consolidate the customer's order. This customer order data will also be processed internally for inventory management and production planning purposes.

How will such changes in warehousing and materials handling influence the planning of distribution systems? The effects will take at least three forms:

1. *Integration of systems for (a) material storage and transport and (b) information handling.* This development should create opportunities for significant "automation" of the distribution function and for reduction of manual drudgery. Ultimate full-scale mechanization of materials handling will not only require redesign of warehouse and transport facilities, but will have an impact on design of products and packages as well.

2. *Pressure to reduce the number of distribution points or warehouses.* Mechanized warehouses cost money. One way to improve the efficiency of capital utilization is of course to increase throughput.

3. *Pressure to concentrate ownership of warehousing facilities.* Mechanization takes capital: This factor will be another force behind the tendency for manufacture, distribution, and maintenance service to become integrated under one ownership roof.

Getting Started

Some managers view the opportunities presented by changes in distribution technology with about the same air with which a bear views a porcupine: the possibilities look interesting, but where can you start to get your teeth in?

Improvements in distribution efficiency cost money. Higher speed, more flexible transport generally costs more per ton-mile. Mechanized warehousing systems or material-handling systems are not cheap. The cost of working out, installing, and testing new information-processing systems may make direct clerical cost savings look like a rather thin return on investment. In fact, direct payoffs from distribution changes (e.g., modified transport methods leading to a direct cut in transport costs) may often be small or nonexistent. The payoffs, often handsome ones, are likely to be indirect, coming about from "tradeoffs" such as paying a higher transport bill to save material investment, putting in warehouse investment to cut over-all shipping costs, and so on.

Because tradeoffs so often are involved, it is not always easy for management to get an aggressive, functionally operated group of people to think *through* the problems. It is not easy for men in production, sales, warehousing, traffic, merchandising, and accounting to grasp other functions' needs or express their own needs in terms which make the advantages of tradeoff and balance clear. Many times the distribution *system* has been run too long as a collection of more or less independent *functions*. Any changes, any tradeoffs to get the system into better, more economical balance, any modifications to take advantage in the whole system of new technical developments—these are bound to be disruptive and to some extent resisted.

The difficulties in facing up to a searching look at the distribution system are not confined to the individual functions concerned. Some of the toughest questions arise at the general management level. For example:

1. What degree of sales service is the system to provide? How far will the firm go to meet customers' service desires?

2. What standards are to be used to judge investment in facilities and inventory so that it can be weighed against any cost savings that are made possible?

3. What policy will the company take toward ownership and operation of the distribution, transport, warehousing, and information-processing facilities? Will the company operate its own facilities, lease them, contract for services, or rely on independent businesses to perform some or all of the necessary distribution system functions?

4. What is the company's policy toward employment stabilization? To what extent is the company prepared to pay higher distribution costs to absorb demand variations and to level employment?

Approach to the Issues

Grappling with all of these problems is like untangling a tangled skein of yarn. Each decision has an impact on other choices and for this reason is hard to pin down. The distribution problem is a system problem, and it must be looked at as such. If it is examined in total and if the experience and methods available for studying it are used, the issues just mentioned can be resolved in an orderly, mutually compatible way.

In my experience, three key conditions have, when present, made for a sound distribution system study and an effective implementation program:

1. Recognition by company management that improving distribution means examining the full physical distribution system.

2. Use of quantitative systems analysis or operations research methods to show clearly the nature of tradeoffs and the relation between system operation and company policies.

3. Cooperative work by men knowledgeable in sales and marketing, transportation, materials handling, materials control, and information handling.

Conclusion

To sum up, a number of pressures have piled up on today's distribution systems. As manufacturing efficiency has increased and product cost has come down, costs have grown. Physical distribution costs are a significant share of these.

Business in many fields is becoming increasingly competitive, with competition taking new forms, including availability of goods and reliability of delivery. Product changes are forcing new pressures on the distribution system—more items to carry, faster obsolescence, lower unit sales and inventory turnover. In particular, changes in merchandising practices, such as the introduction of style as a merchandising weapon, have significantly complicated this distribution problem. Pressures for improvement in logistics also include internal forces—for example, the need to stabilize production and insulate production levels from short-term fluctuations in sales.

In the face of these trends, a number of revolutionary changes have taken place. Substantial improvements have come about in essentially all forms of transportation methods. Tremendous strides forward have been made in information-handling methods, including schemes for assimilating and processing data dealing with product demand and with the need for replenishment. Materials-handling methods, ranging from mechanized stock keeping to extensions of the pallet concept to eliminate item-by-item handling, have been gaining acceptance. Finally, and perhaps as important as improvement in physical facilities and concepts, there has been progress in ways of looking at the logistics problem and at methods for analyzing distribution systems.

Long-Run Implications

So far, we have seen farsighted companies taking advantage of the changes I have described by redesigning their distribution systems to cut costs and increase the support given to sales programs. The next step is now beginning to be felt—the insinuation of distribution concepts into certain aspects of long-term planning and capital budgeting, especially the analysis of facility requirements, the location of distribution points, and the determination of financial requirements to support distribution.

Of course, we must avoid the trap of thinking that all management problems will be resolved in terms of efficient distribution. Nevertheless, the long-range impact of distribution-system thinking on production, on product design, and on manufacturing location may be substantial. Perhaps one of the most significant changes will be in concepts of organization, in the assisgnment of functions and responsibilities. Efficient physical distribution poses a challenge to business in integrating what is essentially a system approach with the functional approaches that hitherto have tended to govern business organization planning.

In the long run, at least two possible directions are open for making a wide variety of products available in local markets. On the one hand, manufacturers can move toward centralized manufacture, with the specialty or small-volume items being made in enough volume to permit reasonable manufacturing economy and then being moved rapidly, perhaps by air freight, to the local markets as needed. On the other hand, management can try to achieve diversity through superficial differences built into a few basic product lines. Low-cost mass transport methods, perhaps rail freight, can be used to move parts and components from centralized manufacturing points with heavy equipment into widespread local assembly or modification plants. At the local points, the final touches can be put on the product to meet customer demand.

One thing seems sure: the choice of distribution system each company makes will have a significant impact on product design, plant investment, and organization. Industrial logistics and trends in logistics technology will receive increasing attention from business, along with markets, capital resources, and product development, in the formulation of corporate plans for the decade ahead.

NOTES

1. See Robert G. Brown, "Less Risk in Inventory Estimates," *Harvard Business Review*, July-August 1959, p. 104.

LEARNING REVIEW

Questions:

1. A major point in this article is that direct payoffs from distribution changes may be small or nonexistent and that payoffs may be in the form of ____________.

2. The author says changes in material handling will create pressure to ____________ the number of distribution plants.

3. In analyzing the capacity of a distribution system to produce sales, executives should examine these three characteristics:
   a) ____________________
   b) ____________________
   c) ____________________

Answers:

1. trade offs; 2. reduce; 3. a) location, b) inventories, c) responsiveness

---

Retrospective Comment by James C. Johnson*

Every breakthrough in management thought is typically precipitated by a classic article or book which discusses the basic concepts and parameters of the innovative idea. Thus Alfred Marshall's *Principles of Economics* (1890) greatly clarified the theory of value and introduced the idea of elasticity of demand. Frederick W. Taylor's *Principles of Scientific Management* (1911) introduced the concept of systematic and precise measurement of business activities. In business logistics, the undisputed classic writing is John F. Magee's "The Logistics of Distribution" (1960). This article was very influential in achieving the explosive growth and acceptance of logistics by the business community.

It should be noted that the study of *business logistics* (which is also commonly referred to as physical distribution) is still a relative neophyte compared to the traditional functional areas of business, such as accounting, production, finance, management and marketing. As recently as 1962, Peter F. Drucker observed, "We know little more about distribution today than Napoleon's contemporaries knew about the interior of Africa. We know it is there, and we know it is big; and that's about all."[1]

The reader should be especially careful in his perusal of Magee's article, because it masterfully discusses the key concepts of business logistics. He guides the reader quickly but thoroughly through (1) the reasons for physical distribution's growth, (2) the information needed to perform a logistics study, and (3) the long-run benefits that accrue to a firm that makes a strong commitment to implementing the physical distribution concept.

Today, while business logistics still stresses the twin objectives of decreasing operational costs and improving customer service standards, it appears that the latter goal is assuming somewhat greater emphasis than the former. Harvey N. Shycon has recently noted, "We in distribution have recognized that providing a proper level of service to the customer is one of the major objectives of the physical distribution operation. Getting the product to the customer *when* he wants it and *where* he wants it is the most important thing that we do. And performing this operation at a reasonable cost is the primary objective of every good distribution operation. I believe that is going to be the major objective of every successful manufacturer during the balance of the 1970s."[2]

Business logistics is a dynamic and challenging aspect of business. Upon completion of Magee's article, the reader will appreciate Drucker's oft quoted statement in which he referred to physical distribution as the *most exciting area of business today.*[3]

* Dr. Johnson is currently Associate Professor of Marketing and Transportation at The University of Tulsa and the author of numerous articles and several books in his field.

1. Peter F. Drucker, "The Economy's Dark Continent," *Fortune* (April, 1962), p. 265.
2. Harvey N. Shycon, "Customer Service—Measuring Its Value," *Annual Proceedings of the National Council of Physical Distribution Management* (1973), p. 420.
3. Peter F. Drucker, "Physical Distribution: The Frontier of Modern Management," in Donald J. Bowersox, *et. al.*, (eds.), *Readings in Physical Distribution Management* (New York: The Macmillan Company, 1969), p. 5.

PART 6

The Promotion Decision in the Marketing Mix

Start here: a primer on promotion

Many volumes have been and will be written about the promotion decision. Still it remains an imprecise art, not a science, even while it represents billions of dollars in annual expenses. In order to develop a broad understanding of this area, the reader needs a foundation of basic information. The foundation provided by the next four articles should sharpen the reader's interest in the literature of promotion and furnish some insight into the complex nature of the topic.

Some ABC's rather than "buzz words"

No attempt is made here to provide a complete vocabulary of promotion; that will come from the classroom, from the textbook on advertising or promotional strategy, from the current literature, and from the job. But Wilbur Schramm describes "How Communication Works" and Irving White explains " . . . that the function of advertising is to help to organize and modify the basic perceptual processes of the consumer, so that he is guided toward seeing and feeling a product in a given predictable way."

Return on investment . . . . and prestige

Next Joel Deal provides a rationale for treating advertising as an investment having futurity rather than considering it as entirely a current expense. Finally, Carl Rieser puts to rest the Willy Loman, *Death of a Salesman*, image which has turned away many who might otherwise have chosen a promotional career in this well-paid direct sales field.

26

How Communication Works

Wilbur Schramm

PREVIEW

I. Communication is the process of establishing *commonness* with someone.
   A. The process of communication has three essential elements:
      1. The source may be an individual or an organization who tries to encode in such a way as to make it easy for the destination to tune in the message.
      2. The message is a signal that stands for something in experience.
      3. The destination may be an individual or a group which decodes the message to produce the desired response.
   B. The operation of the process depends on a number of factors.
      1. All parts of the system must function properly.
      2. The system will have a maximum capacity for handling information.
      3. The nature of language affects the degree of relative freedom.
   C. Feedback tells us how our messages are being interpreted.
   D. Almost any kind of communication is sent out in more than one channel.

II. There are four conditions necessary for success in communication:
   A. The message must gain the attention of the intended destination.
   B. The message must employ signs which refer to experience common to source and destination.
   C. The message must arouse personality needs in the destination and suggest some ways to meet those needs.
   D. The message must suggest a way to meet these personality needs which is appropriate to the group in which the destination finds himself at the time a response is desired.

III. Mass communication has the same process as communication in general but there are differences.

Wilbur Schramm, "How Communication Works," is reprinted by permission from Wilbur Schramm (editor) *The Process and Effects of Mass Communication* (Urbana: University of Illinois Press, 1955), pp. 3–26.

A. Mass Communication differs in several ways from individual communication.
   1. The chief source is a communication organization or an institutionalized person.
   2. The organization has a very high ratio of output to input.
   3. There is very little direct feedback from the receivers to the sender.
   4. Mass communication audiences have very little contact with each other.

B. The effects of mass communication are strong.
   1. It has taken over the function of society communicating.
   2. The effect on the mass audience cannot be predicted; only the effect on the individual can be predicted.

The Process

It will be easier to see how mass communication works if we first look at the communication process in general.

Communication comes from the Latin *communis*, common. When we communicate we are trying to establish a "commonness" with someone. That is, we are trying to share information, an idea, or an attitude. At this moment I am trying to communicate to you the idea that the essence of communication is getting the receiver and the sender "tuned" together for a particular message. At this same moment, someone somewhere is excitedly phoning the fire department that the house is on fire. Somewhere else a young man in a parked automobile is trying to convey the understanding that he is moon-eyed because he loves the young lady. Somewhere else a newspaper is trying to persuade its readers to believe as it does about the Republican Party. All these are forms of communciation, and the process in each case is essentially the same.

Communication always requires at least three elements—the source, the message, and the destination. A *source* may be an individual (speaking, writing, drawing, gesturing) or a communication organization (like a newspaper, publishing house, television station or motion picture studio). The *message* may be in the form of ink on paper, sound waves in the air, impulses in an electric current, a wave of the hand, a flag in the air, or any other signal capable of being interpreted meaningfully. The *destination* may be an *individual* listening, watching, or reading; or a member of a *group*, such as a discussion group, a lecture audience, a football crowd, or a mob; or an individual member of the particular group we call the *mass audience*, such as the reader of a newspaper or a viewer of television.

Now what happens when the source tries to build up this "commonness" with his intended receiver? First, the source encodes his message. That is, he takes the information or feeling he wants to share and puts it into a form that can be transmitted. The "pictures in our heads" can't be transmitted until they are coded. When they are coded into spoken words, they can be transmitted easily and effectively, but they can't travel very far unless radio carries them. If they are coded into written words, they go more slowly than spoken words, but they go farther and last longer. Indeed, some messages long outlive their senders—the *Iliad*, for instance; the Gettysburg address; Chartres cathedral. Once coded and sent, a message is quite free of its sender, and what it does is beyond the power of the sender to change. Every writer feels a sense of helplessness when he finally commits his story or his poem to print; you doubtless feel the same way when you mail an important letter. Will it reach the right person? Will he understand it as you intend him to? Will he respond as you want him to? For in order to complete the act of communication the message must be decoded. And there is good reason, as we shall see, for the sender to wonder whether his receiver will really be in tune with him, whether the message will be interpreted without distortion, whether the "picture in the head" of the receiver will bear any resemblance to that in the sender.

We are talking about something very like a radio or telephone circuit. In fact, it is perfectly possible to draw a picture of the human communication system that way:

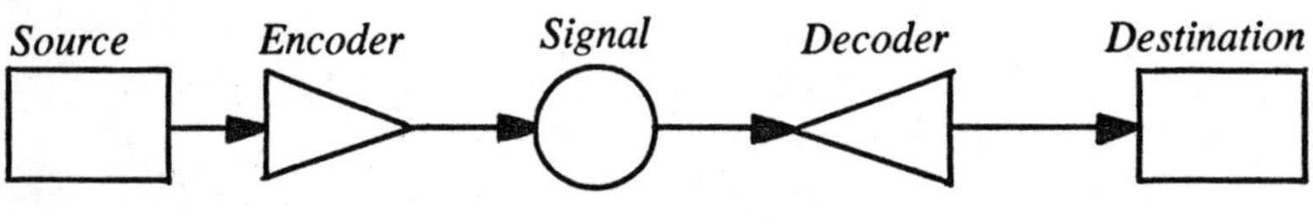

Substitute "microphone" for encoder, and "earphone" for decoder and you are talking about electronic communication. Consider that the "source" and "encoder" are one person, "decoder" and "destination" are another, and the signal is language, and you are talking about human communication.

Now it is perfectly possible by looking at these diagrams to predict how such a system will work. For one thing, such a system can be no stronger than its weakest link. In engineering terms, there may be filtering or distortion at any stage. In human terms, if the source does not have adequate or clear information; if the message is not encoded fully, accurately, effectively in transmittible signs; if these are not transmitted fast enough and accurately enough, despite interference and competition, to the desired receiver; if the message is not decoded in a pattern that corresponds to the encoding; and finally, if the destination is unable to handle the decoded mesage so as to produce the desired response—then, obviously, the system is working at less than top efficiency. When we realize that *all* these steps must be accomplished with relatively high efficiency if any communication is to be successful, the everyday act of explaining something to a stranger, or writing a letter, seems a minor miracle.

A system like this will have a maximum capacity for handling information and this will depend on the separate capacities of each unit on the chain—for example, the capacity of the channel (how fast can one talk?) or the capacity of the encoder (can your student understand something explained quickly?). If the coding is good (for example, no unnecessary words) the capacity of the channel can be approached, but it can never be exceeded. You can readily see that one of the great skills of communication will lie in knowing how near capacity to operate a channel.

This is partly determined for us by the nature of the language. English, like every other lanaguage, has its sequences of words and sounds governed by certain probabilities. If it were organized so that no set of probabilities governed the likelihood that certain words would follow certain other words (for example, that a noun would follow an adjective, or that "States" or "Nations" would follow "United") then we would have nonsense. As a matter of fact, we can calculate the relative amount of freedom open to us in writing any language. For English, the freedom is about 50 per cent. (Incidentally, this is about the required amount of freedom to enable us to construct interesting crossword puzzles. Shannon has estimated that if we had about 70 per cent freedom, we could construct three-dimensional crossword puzzles. If we had only 20 per cent, crossword puzzle making would not be worthwhile.)

So much for language *redundancy*, as communication theorists call it, meaning the percentage of the message which is not open to free choice. But there is also the communicator's redundancy, and this is an important aspect of constructing a message. For if we think our audience may have a hard time understanding the message, we can deliberately introduce more redundancy; we can repeat (just as the radio operator on a ship may send "SOS" over and over again to make sure it is heard and decoded), or we can give examples and analogies. In other words, we always have to choose between transmitting more information in a given time, or transmitting less and repeating more in the hope of being better understood. And as you know, it is often a delicate choice, because too slow a rate will bore an audience, whereas too fast a rate may confuse it.

Perhaps the most important thing about such a system is one we have been talking about all too glibly—the fact that receiver and sender must be in tune. This is clear enough in the case of a radio transmitter and receiver, but somewhat more complicated when it means that a human receiver must be able to understand a human sender.

Let us redraw our diagram in very simple form, like this:

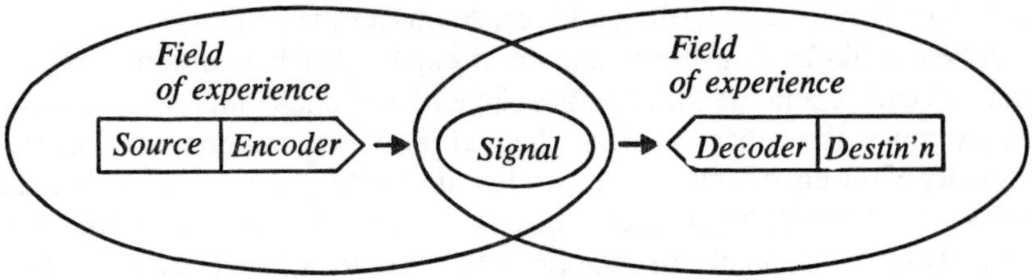

Think of those circles as the accumulated experience of the two individuals trying to communicate. The source can encode, and the destination can decode, only in terms of the experience each has had. If we have never learned any Russian, we can neither code nor decode in that language. If an African tribesman has never seen or heard of an airplane, he can only decode the sight of a plane in terms of whatever experience he has had. The plane may seem to him to be a bird, and the aviator a god borne on wings. If the circles have a large area in common, then communication is easy. If the circles do not meet—if there has been no common experience—then communication is impossible. If the circles have only a small area in common—that is, if the experiences of source and destination have been strikingly unlike–then it is going to be very difficult to get an intended meaning across from one to the other. This is the difficulty we face when a non-science-trained person tries to read Einstein, or when we try to communicate with another culture much different from ours.

The source, then, tries to encode in such a way as to make it easy for the destination to tune in the message—to relate it to parts of his experience which are much like those of the source. What does he have to work with?

Messages are made up of signs. A sign is a signal that stands for something in experience. The word "dog" is a sign that stands for our generalized experience with dogs. The word would be meaningless to a person who came from a dog-less island and had never read of a heard of a dog. But most of us have learned that word by association, just as we learn most signs. Someone called our attention to an animal, and said "dog." When we learned the word, it produced in us much the same response as the object it stood for. That is, when we heard "dog" we could recall the appearance of dogs, their sound, their feel, perhaps their smell. But there is an important difference between the sign and the object: the sign always represents the object at a reduced level of cues. By this we mean simply that the sign will not call forth all the responses that the object itself will call forth. The sign "dog," for example, will probably not call forth in us the same wariness or attention a strange dog might attract if it wandered into our presence. This is the price we pay for portability in language. We have a sign system that we can use in place of the less portable originals (for example, Margaret Mitchell could re-create the burning of Atlanta in a novel, and a photograph could transport world-wide the appearance of a bursting atomic bomb), but our sign system is merely a kind of shorthand. The coder has to be able to write the shorthand, the decoder to read it. And no two persons have learned exactly the same system. For example, a person who had known only Arctic huskies will not have learned exactly the same meaning for the shorthand sign "dog" as will a person who comes from a city where he has known only pekes and poms.

We have come now to a point where we need to tinker a little more with our diagram of the communication process. It is obvious that each person in the communication process is both an encoder and a decoder. He receives and transmits. He must be able to write readable shorthand, and to read other people's shorthand. Therefore, it is possible to describe either sender or receiver in a human communication system thus:

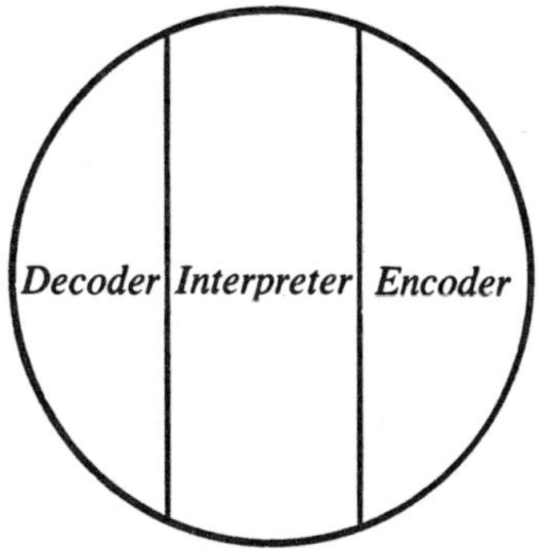

What happens when a signal comes to you? Remember that it comes in the form of a sign. If you have learned the sign, you have learned certain responses with it. We can call these mediatory responses, because they mediate what happens to the message in your nervous system. These responses are the *meaning* the sign has for you. They are learned from experience, as we said, but they are affected by the state of your organism at the moment. For example, if you are hungry, a picture of a steak may not arouse exactly the same response in you as when you are overfed.

But subject to these effects, the mediatory responses will then determine what you do about the sign. For you have learned other sets of reactions connected to the mediatory responses. A sign that means a certain thing to you will start certain other processes in your nerves and muscles. A sign that means "fire," for example, will certainly trigger off some activity in you. A sign that means you are in danger may start the process in your nerves and muscles that makes you say "help!" In other words, the meaning that results from your decoding of a sign will start you *en*coding. Exactly *what* you encode will depend on your choice of the responses available in the situation and connected with the meaning.

Whether this encoding actually results in some overt communication or action depends partly on the barriers in the way. You may think it better to keep silent. And if an action does occur, the nature of the action will also depend on the avenues for action available to you and the barriers in your way. The code of your group may not sanction the action you want to take. The meaning of a sign may make you want to hit the person who has said it, but he may be too big, or you may be in the wrong social situation. You may merely ignore him, or "look murder at him," or say something nasty about him to someone else.

But whatever the exact result, this is the process in which you are constantly engaged. You are constantly decoding signs from your environment, interpreting these signs, and encoding something as a result. In fact, it is misleading to think of the communication process as starting somewhere and ending somewhere. It is really endless. We are little switchboard centers handling and rerouting the great endless current of communication. We can accurately think of communication as passing through us—changed, to be sure, by our interpretations, our habits, our abilities and capabilities, but the input still being reflected in the output.

We need now to add another element to our description of the communication process. Consider what happens in a conversation between two people. One is constantly communicating back to the other, thus:

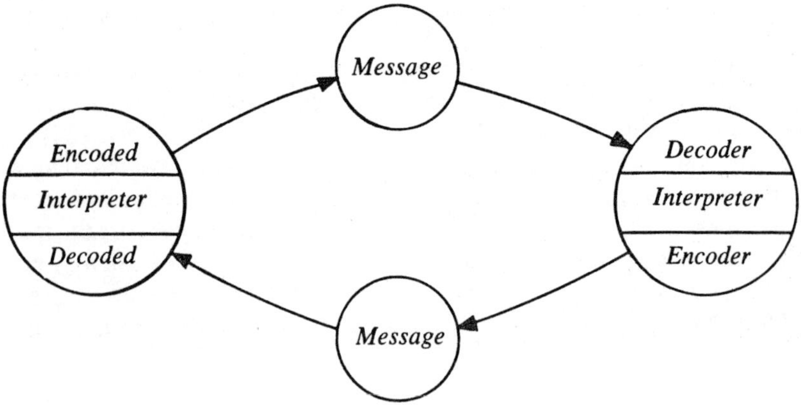

The return process is called *feedback*, and plays a very important part in communication because it tells us how our messages are being interpreted. Does the hearer say, "Yes, yes, that's right," as we try to persuade him? Does he nod his head in agreement? Does a puzzled frown appear on his forehead? Does he look away as though he were losing interest? All these are feedback. So is a letter to the editor of a newspaper, protesting an editorial. So is an answer to a letter. So is the applause of a lecture audience. An experienced communicator is attentive to feedback, and constantly modifies his messages in light of what he observes in or hears from his audience.

At least one other example of feedback, also, is familiar to all of us. We get feedback from our own messages. That is, we hear our own voices and can correct mispronunciations. We see the words we have written on paper, and can correct misspellings or change the style. When we do that, here is what is happening:

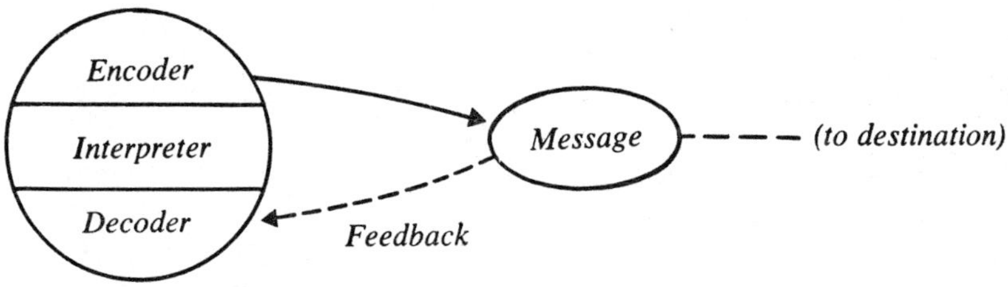

It is clear that in any kind of communication we rarely send out messages in a single channel, and this is the final element we must add to our account of the communication process. When you speak to me, the sound waves from your voice are the primary message. But there are others: the expression on your face, your gestures, the relation of a given message to past messages. Even the primary message conveys information on several levels. It gives me words to decode. It emphasizes certain words above others. It presents the words in a pattern of intonation and timing which contribute to the total meaning. The quality of your voice (deep, high, shrill, rasping, rich, thin, loud, soft), itself, carries information about you and what you are saying.

This multiple channel situation exists even in printed mass communication, where the channels are perhaps most restricted. Meaning is conveyed, not only by the words in a news item, but also by the size of the headline, the position on the page and the page in the paper, the association with pictures, the use of boldface and other typographical devices. All these tell us something about the item. Thus we can visualize the typical channel of communication, not as a simple telegraph circuit, in which current does or does not flow, but rather as a sort of coaxial cable in which many signals flow in parallel from source toward the destination.

These parallel relationships are complex, but you can see their general pattern. A communicator can emphasize a point by adding as many parallel messages as he feels are deserved. If he is communicating by speaking, he can stress a word, pause just before it, say it with a rising inflection, gesture while he says it, look earnestly at his audience. Or he can keep all the signals parallel—except *one*. He can speak solemnly, but wink, as Lowell Thomas sometimes does. He can stress a word in a way that makes it mean something else—for example: "That's a *fine* job you did!" And by so doing he conveys secondary meanings of sarcasm or humor or doubt.

The same thing can be done with printed prose, with broadcast, with television or films. The secondary channels of the sight-sound media are especially rich. I am reminded of a skillful but deadly job done entirely with secondary channels on a certain politicial candidate. A sidewalk interview program was filmed to run in local theaters. Ostensibly it was a completely impartial program. An equal number of followers of each candidate were interviewed—first, one who favored Candidate A, then one who favored Candidate B, and so on. They were asked exactly the same questions, and said about the same things, although on opposite sides of the political fence, of course. But there was one interesting difference. Whereas the supporters of Candidate A were ordinary folks, not outstandingly attractive or impressive, the followers of Candidate B who were chosen to be interviewed invariably had something slightly wrong with them.

They looked wildeyed, or they stuttered, or they wore unpressed suits. The extra meaning was communicated. Need I say which candidate won?

But this is the process by which communication works, whether it is mass communication, or communication in a group, or communication between individuals.

Communication in Terms of Learning Theory

So far we have avoided talking about this complicated process in what may seem to you to be the obvious way to talk about it—in the terminology and symbols of learning theory.[1] We have done so for the sake of simplicity. Now in order to fill in the picture it seems desirable to sketch the diagram of how communication looks to a psychologist of learning. If psychological diagrams bother you, you can skip to section 3.

Let's start with the diagram, then explain it.

The diagram isn't as complicated as it looks. Remember that time in the diagram moves from left to right, and then follow the numbers and you won't get far off the road.

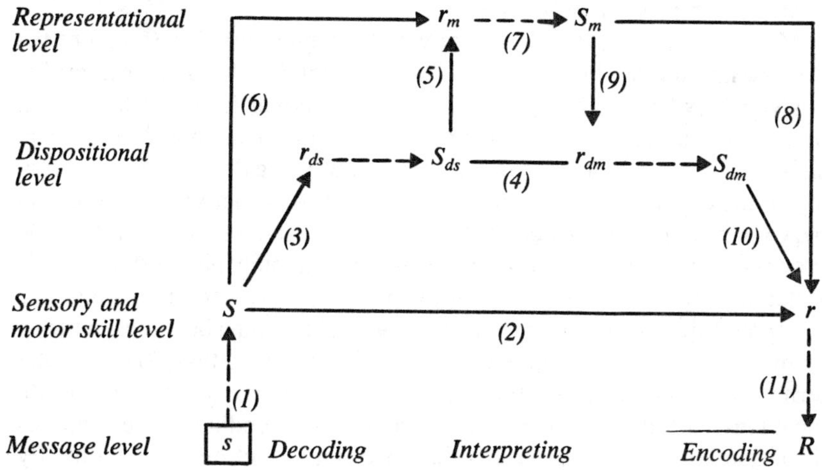

Begin with (1). This is input. At the message level we have a collection of objectively measurable signs [s]. These come to your sense organs, where they constitute a stimulus for action. This stimulus we call S. When the process gets as far as S, you are paying attention. The message has been accepted. It may not have been accepted as intended; S may not equal [s]; the sensory mechanism may have seen or heard it incompletely. But everying else that happens as a result of the message in that particular destination will now necessarily be the result of the stimulus accepted by your sense organs.

Now look at number (2). The message may not have to go to any other level in order to bring about a response. If a man waves his fist near your nose, you may dodge. If he squeezes your hand, you may say "ouch!" These are learned, almost automatic, responses on the sensory and motor skill level.

But the stimulus may also bring about other kinds of activity within your nervous system. Look at number (3). The stimulus S may be translated into a grammatical response on your dispositional level—by which we mean the level of learned integrations (attitudes, values, sets, etc.) which make it so easy for you to dispose of the variety of stimuli that come to you in the course of a day. These are what we call the intervening variables. Suppose the stimulus stirs up activity in this area of intervening variables. Two things may happen. Look at number (4). The response may be so well learned that it doesn't even have to go to the level of thinking. You hear a line of a poem, and almost automatically say the second line. In that case the activity is through numbers (4) and (10).

More often, however, the activity goes through number (5). Here the original stimulus has been decoded into grammar, fed through the intervening variables, and sent up to the representational level of the central nervous system, where meanings are assigned and ideas considered. Occasionally a stimulus comes to that level without going through the intervening variables—as in number (6). These stimuli create activity in the central nervous system (rm) which is the terminus of the decoding part of the process. This is equivalent to the meaning or significance of the signs $\boxed{S}$. What happens in number (7), then, is what we have been referring to as interpretation. The response rm which we call meaning becomes in turn a stimulus which sets the encoding process in action, so that (7) is both the terminus of decoding and the start of encoding. We learn to associate meanings with desired responses. And so the encoding process moves through (8) or (9). That is, we give certain orders which either pass directly to the neuromuscular system (through 8) or are passed through the intervening variables (through 9 and 10). In any case, all this activity of the nervous system finally results in a response on the motor skill level (r), which results in output (number 11). If the output is an overt response (R), then we have another message, which may offer itself as a collection of signs $\boxed{S}$ and be accepted by still another person as a stimulus (S).

This is what we believe happens when someone says to you, "cigarette?" and you answer "yes, please," or "no, thanks." If you are interested in doing so, you can translate all that is said about the communication process in this paper into the psychological symbols we have just been using. But to make the account simpler, we are going to shift gears at this point and talk about communication effects and mass communication in the terms we used in the first section of this article.

How Communication Has an Effect

The chief reason we study this process is to learn something about how it achieves effects. We want to know what a given kind of communication does to people. Given a certain message content, we should like to be able to predict what effect that content will have on its receivers.

Every time we insert an advertisment in a newspaper, put up a sign, explain something to a class, scold a child, write a letter, or put our political candidate on radio or television, we are making a prediction about the effect communication will have. I am predicting now that what I am writing will help you understand the common everyday miracle of communication. Perhaps I am wrong. Certainly many political parties have been proved wrong in their predictions about the effects of their candidates' radio speeches. Some ads sell goods; others don't. Some class teaching "goes over"; some does not. For it is apparent to you, from what you have read so far, that there is no such thing as a simple and easily predictable relationship between message content and effect.

Nevertheless, it is possible to describe simply what might be called the conditions of success in communication—by which we mean the conditions that must be fulfilled if the message is to arouse its intended response. Let us set them down here briefly, and then talk about them:

1. The message must be so designed and delivered as to gain the attention of the intended destination.

2. The message must employ signs which refer to experience common to source and destination, so as to "get the meaning across."

3. The message must arouse personality needs in the destination and suggest some ways to meet those needs.

4. The message must suggest a way to meet those needs which is appropriate to the group situation in which the destination finds himself at the time when he is moved to make the desired response.

You can see, by looking at these requirements, why the expert communicator usually begins by finding out as much as he can about his intended destination, and why "know your audience" is the first rule of practical mass communication. For it is important to know the right timing for a message, the kind of language one must use to be understood, the attitudes and values one must appeal to in order to be effective, and the group standards in which the desired action will have to take place. This is relatively easy in face-to-face communication, more difficult in mass communication. In either case, it is necessary.

Let us talk about these four requirements.

1. *The message must be so designed and delivered as to gain the attention of the intended destination*. This is not so easy as it sounds. For one thing, the message must be made available. There will be no communication if we don't talk loudly enough to be heard, or if our letter is not delivered, or if we smile at the right person when she isn't looking. And even if the message is available, it may not be selected. Each of us has available far more communication than we can possibly accept or decode. We therefore scan our environment in much the same way as we scan newspaper headlines or read a table of contents. We choose messages according to our impression of their general characteristics—whether they fit our needs and interests. We choose usually on the basis of an impression we get

from one cue in the message, which may be a headline, a name in a radio news story, a picture, a patch of color, or a sound. If that cue does not appeal to us, we may never open our senses to the message. In different situations, of course, we choose differently among these cues. For example, if you are speaking to me at a time when I am relaxed and unbusy, or when I am waiting for the kind of message you have (for instance, that my friends have come to take me fishing), then you are more likely to get good attention than if you address me when noise blots out what you say, or when all my attention is given to some competing message, or when I am too sleepy to pay attention, or when I am thinking about something else and have simply "tuned out." (How many times have you finished speaking and realized that your intended receiver had simply not heard a word you said?) The designing of a message for attention, then, involves timing, and placing, and equipping it with cues which will appeal to the receiver's interests.

2. *The message must employ signs which refer to experience common to both source and destination, in order to "get the meaning across."* We have already talked about this problem of getting the receiver in tune with the sender. Let us add now that as our experience with environment grows, we tend to classify and catalog experience in terms of how it relates to other experience and to our needs and interests. As we grow older that catalog system grows harder and firmer. It tends to reject messages that do not fit its structure, or distort them so that they do fit. It will reject Einstein, perhaps, because it feels it can't understand him. If an airplane is a completely new experience, but a bird is not, it may, as we have said, interpret the plane as a large, noisy bird. If it is Republican it will tend to reject Democratic radio speeches or to recall only the parts that can be made into pro-Republican arguments; this is one of the things we have found out about voting behavior. Therefore, in designing a message we have to be sure not only that we speak the "same language" as the receiver, and that we don't "write over his head," but also that we don't conflict too directly with the way he sees and catalogs the world. There are some circumstances, true, in which it works well to conflict directly, but for the most part these are the circumstances in which our understandings and attitudes are not yet firm or fixed, and they are relatively few and far between. In communicating, as in flying an airplane, the rule is that when a stiff wind is blowing, one doesn't land cross-wind unless he has to.

3. *The message must arouse personality needs in the destination and suggest some way to meet those needs*. We take action because of need and toward goals. In certain simple situations, the action response is quite automatic. When our nerves signal "pain-heat-finger" we jerk our fingers back from the hot pan. When our optic nerve signals "red traffic light" we stop the car. In more complicated situations we usually have more free-

dom of choice, and we choose the action which, in the given situation, will come closest to meeting our needs or goals. The first requisite of an effective message, therefore (as every advertising man knows), is that it relate itself to one of our personality needs—the needs for security, status, belongingness, understanding, freedom from constraint, love, freedom from anxiety, and so forth. It must arouse a drive. It must make the individual feel a need or a tension which he can satisfy by action. Then the message can try to control the resulting action by suggesting what action to take. Thus an advertisement usually tells you to buy, what, and where. Propaganda to enemy troops usually suggests a specific action, such as surrender, subversion, or malingering. The suggested action, of course, is not always the one taken. If an easier, cheaper, or otherwise more acceptable action leading to the same goal is seen, that will probably be selected instead. For instance, it may be that the receiver is not the kind of person to take vigorous action, even though that seems called for. The person's values may inhibit him from doing what is suggested. Or his group role and membership may control what action he takes, and it is this control we must talk about now.

4. *The message must suggest a way to meet those needs which is appropriate to the group situation in which the destination finds himself at the time when he is moved to make the desired response*. We live in groups. We get our first education in the primary group of our family. We learn most of our standards and values from groups. We learn roles in groups, because those roles give us the most orderly and satisfying routine of life. We make most of our communication responses in groups. And if communication is going to bring about change in our behavior, the first place we look for approval of this new behavior is to the group. We are scarcely aware of the great importance our group involvements have for us, or of the loyalties we develop toward our several groups and institutions, until our place in the group or the group itself is threatened. But yet if our groups do not sanction the response we are inclined to make to communication, then we are very unlikely to make it. On the other hand, if our group strongly approves of a certain kind of action, that is the one we are likely to select out of several otherwise even choices.

You can see how this works in practical situations. The Jewish culture does not approve the eating of pork; the Indian culture does not approve the slaughter of cows, and the eating of beef. Therefore, it is highly unlikely that even the most eloquent advertisement will persuade an orthodox Jewish family to go contrary to its group sanctions, and buy pork; or an orthodox Hindu family, to buy beef. Or take the very simple communication situation of a young man and a young woman in a parked automobile. The young man communicates the idea that he wants a kiss. There isn't much likelihood of his not gaining attention for that communication or of its not being understood. But how the young woman responds will depend on a number of factors, partly individual, partly group. Does she want to be kissed at that moment? Does she want to be kissed by that young man? Is the situation at the moment—a moon, soft music from the radio, a convertible—conducive to the response the young man wants? But then, how about the group customs under which the girl lives? If this is a first date, is it "done" to kiss a boy on a first date? Is petting condoned in the case of a girl her age? What has she learned from her parents and her friends about these things? Of course, she won't knowingly have a little debate with herself such as we have suggested here, but all these elements and more will enter into the decision as to whether she tilts up her chin or says, "No, Jerry. Let's go home."

There are two things we can say with confidence about predicting communication effects. One is that a message is much more likely to succeed if it fits the patterns of understandings, attitudes, values and goals that a receiver has; or at least if it starts with this pattern and tries to reshape it slightly. Communication research men call this latter process "canalizing," meaning that the sender provides a channel to direct the already existing motives in the receiver. Advertising men and propagandists say it more bluntly; they say that a communicator must "start where the audience is." You can see why this is. Our personalities—our patterns of habits, attitudes, drives, values, and so forth—grow very slowly but firmly. I have elsewhere compared the process to the slow, sure, ponderous growth of a stalagmite on a cave floor. The stalagmite builds up from the calcareous residue of the water dripping on it from the cave roof. Each drop leaves only a tiny residue, and it is very seldom that we can detect the residue of any single drop, or that any single drop will make a fundamental change in the shape or appearance of the stalagmite. Yet together all these drops do build the stalagmite, and over the years it changes considerably in size and somewhat in shape. This is the way our environment drips into us, drop by drop, each drop leaving a little residue, each tending to follow the existing pattern. This personality pattern we are talking about is, of course, an active thing—not passive, like the stalagmite—but still the similarity is there. When we introduce one drop of communication into a person where millions of drops have already fallen and left their residue, we can hardly expect to reshape the personality fundamentally by that one drop. If we are communicating to a child, it is easier, because the situation is not so firmly fixed. If we are communicating in an area where ideas and values are not yet determined—if our drop of communication falls where not many have fallen before—then we may be able to see a change as a result of our communication.

But in general we must admit that the best thing we can do is to build on what already exists. If we take advantage of the existing pattern of understanding, drives, and attitudes, to gain acceptance for our message, then we may hope to divert the pattern slightly in the direction we want to move it. Let's go back to elections again for an example. It is very hard to change the minds of convinced Republicans or Democrats through communication, or even to get them to listen to the arguments of the opposing party. On the other hand, it is possible to start with a Republican or Democratic viewpoint and slightly modify the existing party viewpoints in one way or other. If this process goes on for long enough, it may even be possible to get confirmed partymen to reverse their voting pattern. This is what the Republicans were trying to do in the 1952 election by stressing "the mess in Washington," "time for a change," "the mistakes in Korea," and "the threat of Communism," and apparently they were successful in getting some ordinarily Democratic votes. But in 1952, as in every campaign, the real objectives of the campaigning were the new voters and the undecided voters.

The second thing we can say with confidence about communication effects is that they are resultants of a number of forces, of which the communicator can really control only one. The sender, that is, can shape his message and can decide when and where to introduce it. But the message is only one of at least four important elements that determine what response occurs. The other three are the situation in which the communication is received and in which the response, if any, must occur; the personality state of the receiver; and his group relationships and standards. This is why it is so dangerous to try to predict exactly what will be the effect of any message except the simplest one in the simplest situation.

Let us take an example. In Korea, in the first year of the war there, I was interviewing a North Korean prisoner of war who had recently surrendered with one of our surrender leaflets on his person. It looked like an open and shut case: the man had picked up the leaflet, thought it over, and decided to surrender. But I was interviewing him anyway, trying to see just how the leaflet had its effect. This is what he told me.

He said that when he picked up the leaflet, it actually made him fight harder. It rather irritated him, and he didn't like the idea of having to surrender. He wasn't exactly a warlike man; he had been a clerk, and was quiet and rather slow; but the message actually aroused a lot of aggression in him. Then the situation deteriorated. His division was hit hard and thrown back, and he lost contact with the command post. He had no food, except what he could find in the fields, and little ammunition. What was left of his company was isolated by itself in a rocky valley. Even then, he said, the morale was good, and there was no talk of surrendering. As a matter of fact, he said, the others would have shot him if he had tried to surrender. But then a couple of our planes spotted them, shot up their hideout, and dropped some napalm. When it was over, he found himself alone, a half mile from where he had been, with half his jacket burned off, and no sign of any of his company. A couple of hours later some of our tanks came along. And only then did the leaflet have an effect. He remembered it had told him to surrender with his hands up, and he did so.

In other words, the communication had no effect (even had an opposite effect from the one intended) so long as the situation, the personality, and the group norms were not favorable. When the situation deteriorated, the group influence was removed, and the personality aggression was burned up, then finally the message had an effect. I tell you this story hoping it will teach you what it taught me: that it is dangerous to assume any simple and direct relationship between a message and its effect without knowing all the other elements in the process.

The Nature of Mass Communication

Now let us look at mass communication in the light of what we have already said about communication in general.

The process is exactly what we have described, but the elements in the process are not the same.

The chief source, in mass communication, is a communication organization or an institutionalized person. By a communication organization we mean a newspaper, a broadcasting network or station, a film studio, a book or magazine publishing house. By an institutionalized person we mean such a person as the editor of a newspaper, who speaks in his editorial columns through the facilities of the institution and with more voice and prestige than he would have if he were speaking without the institution.

The organization works exactly as the individual communicator does. It operates as decoder, interpreter, and encoder. On a newspaper, for example, the input to be decoded flows in through the news wires and the reporters. It is evaluated, checked, amplified where necessary, written into a story, assigned headline and position, printed, distributed. This is the same process as goes on within an individual communicator, but it is carried out by a group of persons rather than by one individual. The quality of organization required to get a group of reporters, editors, and printers working together as a smooth communication unit, decoding, interpreting, and encoding so that the whole operation and product has an individual quality, is a quite remarkable thing. We have become so used to this performance that we have forgotten how remarkable it is.

Another difference between the communication organization and the individual communicator is that the organization has a very high ratio of output to input. Individuals vary, of course, in their out-input ratios. Persons who are in the business of communicating (preachers or teachers, for example) ordinarily have higher ratios than others, and so do naturally talkative persons who are not professional communicators. Very quiet persons have relatively higher input. But the communication institution is so designed as to be able to encode thousands—sometimes millions—of identical messages at the same time. To carry these, intricate and efficient channels must be provided. There have to be provisions for printing and delivering thousands of newspapers, magazines, or books, for making prints of a film and showing them in hundreds or thousands of theaters, for translating sound waves into electricity and distributing it through wires and through the air to millions of receiving sets.

The *destinations* of mass communication are individuals at the ends of these channels—individuals reading the evening paper, looking through the new magazine, reading the new book, sitting in the motion picture theater, turning the dial on the radio set. This receiving situation is much different from that which pertains in face-to-face communication, for one thing, because there is very little direct *feedback* from the receivers to the sender. The destination who, in a face-to-face situation, will nod his head and smile or frown while the sender is speaking, and then encode a reply himself, will very seldom talk back to the radio network or write a letter to the editor. Indeed, the kind of feedback that comes to a mass communication organization is a kind of inferential expression—receivers stop buying the publication, or no longer listen to the program, or cease to buy the product advertised. Only in rare instances do these organizations have an opportunity to see, more directly than that, how their messages are going over. That is one reason why mass communication conducts so much audience research, to find out what programs are being listened to, what stories are being read, what ads attended to. It is one of their few substitutes for the feedback which makes interpersonal communication so relatively easy to plan and control.

There are other discussions about the audiences of the different media, and we need not discuss them in any detail here. These audiences cluster, not only around a newspaper, magazine, or television station, but also around certain stories in the paper, certain parts of the magazine, certain television or radio programs. For example, Station A will not have the same audience at 8:00 as it had at 7:00, because some of these listeners will have moved to Stations B or C, and some of the listeners from B and C will have moved to A. Newspaper D will not have the same audience on its sports pages as on its society pages, although there will be some overlap. What determines which offering of mass communication will be selected by any given individual? Perhaps the easiest way to put it is to say that choice is determined by the Fraction of Selection—

$$\frac{\text{Expectation of reward}}{\text{Effort required}}$$

You can increase the value of that fraction either by increasing the numerator or decreasing the denominator, which is to say that an individual is more likely to select a certain communication if it promises him more reward or requires less effort than comparable communications. You can see how this works in your own experience. You are much more likely to read the newspaper or magazine at hand than to walk six blocks to the newsstand to buy a bigger newspaper or magazine. You are more likely to listen to a station which had a loud clear signal than to one which is faint and fading and requires constant effort from you to hear at all. But if the big game of the week is on that faint station, or if your favorite author is in the magazine at the newsstand, then there is more likelihood that you will make the additional effort. If you were a member of the underground in occupied France during World War II, you probably risked your life to hear news from the forbidden Allied radio. You aren't likely to stay up until 2 A.M. simply to hear a radio program, but if by staying up that long you can find out how the Normandy invasion is coming or who has won the Presidential election—then you will probably make the extra effort just as most of the rest of us did. It is hardly necessary to point out that no two receivers may have exactly the same fraction of selection. One of them may expect more reward from Milton Berle than will the other. One of them may consider it less effort to walk six blocks to the newsstand than does the other. But according to how this fraction looks to individuals in any given situation, the audience of mass communication is determined.

Unlike lecture audiences and small groups, mass communication audiences (with the exception of the people in a motion picture theater at the same time) have very little contact with each other. People in one house listening to Jack Benny don't know whether anybody in the next house is listening to him or not. A person reading an editorial in the New York *Times* has little group feeling for the other people in this country who read editorials in the New York *Times*. These audiences are individuals, rather than groups. But each individual is connected with a group or groups—his family, his close friends, his occupational or school group—and this is a very important thing to remember about mass communication. The more we study it, the more we are coming to think that the great effects of mass communication are gained by feeding ideas and information into small groups through individual receivers. In some groups, as you well know, it is a sign of status to be familiar with some part of mass communication (for example, in the teen-age group to hear the currently screamable crooner, or in some business groups to read the *Wall Street Journal*). In many a group, it is a news story from the radio, or an editorial from the *Tribune*, or an article from the *Times*, or an article from one of the big magazines, that furnishes the subject of conversation on a given day. The story, or article, or editorial, is then re-interpreted by the group, and the result is encoded in group opinion and perhaps in group action. Thus it may well be that the chief influence of mass communication on individuals is really a kind of secondary influence, reflected to the group and back again.

We are ready now to draw a diagram of mass communication, and to talk about the kinds of messages this sort of system requires and what we know about predicting their effects. This is the way mass communication seems to work:

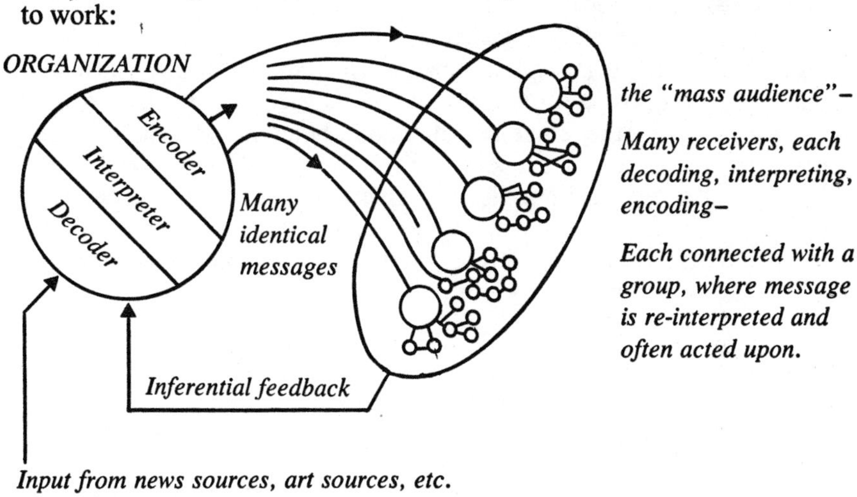

Now it is easy to see that there will be certain restrictions on the kinds of program which can be carried over these identical circuits to these little-known and changing audiences. The communication organization knows it is dealing with individuals, yet does not know them as individuals. Its audience research classifies, rather than individualizes, the audience. Audience research, that is, says that so many people are listening at a given time, or that so many men and so many women are likely to read a given kind of article, or that the readers of a given magazine are in the upper economic bracket and have had on the average twelve years of schooling. Whereas the individual communicator is dealing with individuals and able to watch the way his message is received and modify it if necessary, the organization is dealing only with averages and classes. It must pitch its reading level somewhere below the estimated average of its audience, in order not to cut off too many of the lower half of the audience. It must choose its content according to the best estimate it can make of what the broadest classes of receivers want and need. Whereas the individual communicator is free to experiment because he can instantly correct any mistake, the organization is loath to experiment. When it finds an apparently successful formula, it keeps on that way. Or it changes the details but not the essentials. If one organization makes a great success with a given kind of message, others tend to copy it—not because of any lack of originality, but because this is one of the few kinds of feedback available from the mass audience. That is why we have so much sameness on the radio, why one successful comic strip tends to be followed by others of the same kind, one successful news or digest magazine by others, one kind of comedy program by others of the same kind, and so forth.

What can we say about the effects of these mass communication messages? For one thing, mass communication has pervasive effect because in many respects it has taken over the function of *society communicating*. Our society, like any other communication unit, functions as decoder, interpreter, and encoder. It decodes our environment for us, watches the horizon for danger and promise and entertainment. It then operates to interpret what it has decoded, arrives at a consensus so that it can put policy into effect, keeps the ordinary interactions of communal life going, and helps its members enjoy life.

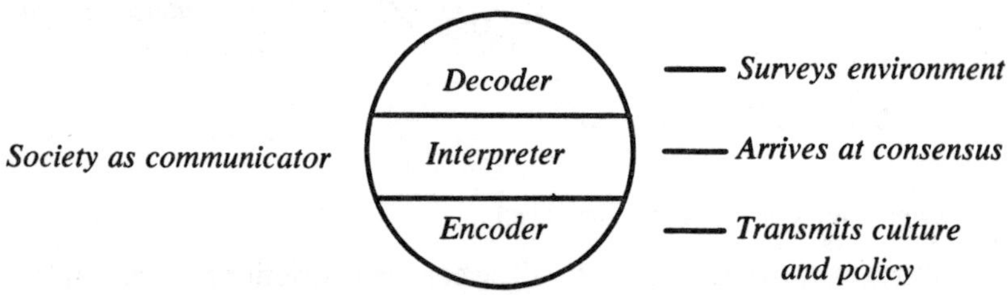

It also encodes messages to maintain our relations with other societies in the world, and messages to transmit our culture to its new members. Mass communication, which has the power to extend our eyes and ears almost indefinite distances, and to multiply our voices and written words as far as we can find listeners or readers, has taken over a large share of the responsibility for this social communication. Newspapers, radio, television watch the horizon for us. By telling us what our leaders and experts think, by conducting a discussion of public issues, these media, and magazines and films as well, help us to interpret what is seen on the horizon and decide what to do about it. The textbook and educational films have led all the other media in encoding our culture so that the young persons coming into our society may learn as quickly and easily as possible the history, standards, roles, and skills they must know in order to be good members of society. This is not to say that all the media do not contribute in some degree to all these functions. For example, a book like *1984* may be as much a report of the horizon as the most current news story. And on the other hand, it is certainly true that a great deal of our culture is transmitted currently through television, radio, newspapers, and magazines. But the faster media are better equipped to be watchmen, and are more often so used. The slower, longer lasting media are better equipped to be teaching aids and are so used. The important thing is that *all* the mass media have important uses in providing the network of understandings without which the modern large community could not exist.

So much for the basic effect, which we see every day in the kind of customs around us, the people and problems talked about, and the language we speak. This is the slow, imperceptible effect. This is like building the stalagmite. But how about the specific effect of a given message transmitted by mass communication? How can we predict what the effect will be on the mass audience?

We can't predict the effect on the mass audience. We can only predict the effect on individuals. Communication organizations have developed group encoding, but there is only individual decoding. Therefore, we can predict the effect of mass communication only in the way we try to predict the effect of other communication—that is, in terms of the interaction of message, situation, personality, and group.

The first thing which becomes obvious, therefore, is that inasmuch as there are many different combinations of personality, situation, and group in any mass audience, there are likely to be many different kinds of effects. It is equally obvious that since mass communication doesn't know much about the individuals in its audience, predicting effects is going to be extremely difficult.

Nevertheless, there are certain things to be said. The problem of attention constantly faces mass communication. The average American (whoever he is) probably gives four or five hours a day to mass communication. If he lives in a big city, he gets a paper that would itself take half that time to read. (He doesn't read all of it.) He is offered the equivalent of two weeks of radio and television every day from which he can choose. He is offered a bewildering array of magazines and books and films. From these also he must choose. Other attractive ways to spend leisure compete with communication. He sometimes combines them—listening to music while he reads, playing cards or eating while he hears a newscast, playing with the baby while he watches television. Therefore, we can predict at least that any individual will have a fairly small chance of selecting any given item in mass communication, and that if he does select it, his level of attention may be rather low. This is responsible for many cases of "mis-hearing" radio. We know also that readership of the average newspaper story falls off sharply after the first few paragraphs, so that a member of the mass audience is likely not to see at all the latter part of a long newspaper story.

There are of course many cases in which markedly high attention is aroused by mass communication, and plentiful instances of listeners identifying closely with radio characters and adopting the mannerisms and language of movie heroes. It has been said that the mass media have brought Hollywood, Broadway, and Washington nearer than the next town, and there is a great deal of truth in this. There are also some cases in which very spectacular overt results have been accomplished by mass communication.

Let us recall one of them. Can you remember when CBS broadcast Orson Welles' performance of H. G. Wells' "War of the Worlds"? The script featured the invasion of the United States by armies from outer space. Perhaps you were one of the people who ran screaming for the hills, or armed yourself to wait for the invaders, or tried to call your loved ones long distance for a farewell talk. Or perhaps you were not. Perhaps you were one of those who heard the CBS announcers explain carefully that it was a play made from a book of fiction. Those who didn't hear those announcements were engaged in proving what we have just said about the low level of attention to some parts of mass communication.

But that doesn't entirely explain why people became hysterical and did things they were rather ashamed of the next day. And in truth, this is one of the really spectacular examples of mass communication effect. This happened without any specific reference to groups; it happened spontaneously in thousands of homes near the supposed scene of invasion. Why did it happen? Research men have studied the incident, and think they have put together the puzzle. For one thing, it was a tense time. People were full of anxiety, which could have been triggered off in many ways. In the second place, people trusted—still trust—radio news; the play was in the form of newscasts and commentaries. Therefore, the communication as it was interpreted really represented a spectacular change in the situation: the Martians were invading! Apparently the group element played no large part in this event, but the other three did. The message was accepted (minus the important identification as fiction). The listeners had a good deal of anxiety ready to be used. The message convinced them that the situation had indeed changed for the worse. Each according to his own personality and situation then took action.

As we have said, that was, fortunately, one of the few really spectacular examples of mass behavior. Another one was the Gold Rush that resulted in the 1890s when the newspapers brought word of gold in Alaska. Some people might say that what the Communists have been able to accomplish is a spectacular advertisement for the power of mass communication, and that subject is worth looking at because it shows us not only some of the differences between the ways we use the mass media and the way dictators use them, but also some of the principles of communication effect.

It is true that one of the first acts of the Communists, when they take over a country, is to seize the mass communication system. (That was also one of Hitler's first acts.) They also seize the police power and the control of productive resources, and they organize an intricate system of Party groups and meetings. I don't know of any case in which the Communists have put the whole burden of convincing people and gaining members on mass communications alone. They always provide a group structure where a convert can get reinforcement, and meetings to which a potential convert can be drawn. They use mass communication almost as an adjunct to these groups. In Korea and China, the mass media actually become texts for the groups. And the Communists do one thing more. If at all possible, they secure a monopoly on the communication reaching the people whom they are taking over. When they took Seoul, Korea, in 1950, they confiscated radio receivers wherever they found receivers despite the fact that they had captured Radio Seoul, intact, the most powerful transmitter in that part of Asia. They were willing to give up the use of Radio Seoul, if by so doing they could keep their subjects from foreign radio.

Now obviously, a state monopoly on communication, as well as control of resources and organization of a police state, is a long way from our system. And as long as our mass media are permitted free criticism and reporting, and as long as they represent more than one political point of view, we have little to worry about in a political way from them. But even though we may look with revulsion at the Communist way of using mass communication, still we can study it. And let us refer back to the four elements which we said were instrumental in bringing about communication effects—message, situation, personality, and group. The Communists control the messages. By their police power, control of resources (and hence of food and pay), they can structure the situation as they see fit.

Their group organization is most careful, and offers a place—in fact compels a place—for every person. Thus they control three of the four elements, and can use those three to work on the fourth—the personalities of their receivers.

The Communists, who have now had thirty-five years' practice in the intensive use of mass communication for accomplishing specified effects, are apparently unwilling to predict the results of their communication unless they can control three of the four chief elements which enter into the effect.

Let us take one final example. There is a great deal of violence in mass communication content today. Violence is interesting to children. Yet only a few children actually engage in acts of criminal violence. Most children do no such things. They sample the violent material, and decide they would rather play football. Or they attend faithfully to the violent material, use it to clear out vicariously some of the aggressions they have been building up, and emerge none the worse for the experience. Or they adopt some of the patterns in a mild and inoffensive way when they play cops and robbers. Only a few children learn, from the mass media, techniques of crime and violence which they and their pals actually try out. Now what is it that determines which of those children will be affected harmfully by those messages of violence, and which will not?

We can attempt to answer this question from cases we have studied. And the answer is simply that the other three elements—personality, situation, and group influence—will probably determine the use made of the message. If the child is busy with athletics, Scouts, church, or other wholesome activities, he is not likely to feel the need of violent and antisocial actions. On the other hand, if he is bored and frustrated, he may experiment with dangerous excitement. If he has a healthy personality, if he has learned a desirable set of values from his family group, he is less likely to give in to motivation toward violence. On the other hand, if his value standards are less certain, if he has lost some of his sense of belonging and being loved (possibly because of a broken home), he may entertain more hospitably the invitation to violence. If the group he admires has a wholesome set of standards, he is not likely to try an undesirable response, because the group will not reinforce it. On the other hand, if he belongs to a "gang" there is every reason to expect that he will try some of the violence, because in so doing he will win admiration and status in the group. Therefore, what he does will depend on the delicate balancing of these influences at a given time. Certainly no one could predict—except possibly on an actuarial basis—from merely seeing such a message exactly what the response to it would be. And it is entirely probable in the case we have mentioned that the community, the home, and the school—because they influence so greatly the other three elements—would have much more to do with the young person's response than would the message itself.

The all-pervasive effect of mass communication, the ground swell of learning that derives from mass communication acting as *society communicating*—this we can be sure of, and over a long period we can identify its results in our lives and beliefs. The more specific effects, however, we must predict only with caution, and never from the message alone without knowing a great deal about the situation, the personality, and the group relationship where the message is to be acted upon.

NOTES

1. For the model in the following pages the author is indebted to his colleague, Dr. Charles E. Osgood. Dr. Osgood has since published the model in a more advanced form.

LEARNING REVIEW

Questions:

1. With mass communications, an individual will more likely choose a certain communication if it promises more ____________ or requires less ____________ than other comparable communications.

2. The essential elements in the general process of communication are ____________, ____________, and ____________.

3. The four elements affecting success of the communication are the message, situation, ____________, and ____________.

Answers:

1. reward, effort; 2. source, message, destination; 3. personalities, group influence

---

Retrospective Comment

Readers who wish to "update" my thinking on the topics dealt with in this paper may wish to read the introductory essays in the 1970 edition of

Process and Effects of Mass Communication (Schramm and Roberts, University of Illinois Press) or pages 37–57 and 300–301 of *Men, Messages and Media* (Wilbur Schramm, published by Harper and Row, 1973). These newer books do not change essentially what is said in this paper, but develop more fully the nature of the communication process.

For one thing, they emphasize that communication is *relationship* and they de-emphasize its linearity. Nothing passes directly from sender to receiver, of course; there is no *bullet* or *hypodermic* effect. Rather, one party to the relationship puts out a set of information signs, and the other party does something with them. Thus, both parties to communication have to process the information separately, actually making the *act* of communication two acts in two people.

When one thinks of communication as a relationship, then one can ask some interesting questions about it. What do the parties to the relationship bring to it? What kind of experience, what kind of life space, what kinds of ability to process information, and consequently, what kind of relationship is likely to build up over the shared signs? Again, what are they seeking in the relationship? What roles are they playing? For example, a teacher and a student will play quite different roles in a communication relationship than will a salesman and prospective purchaser, or a lover and his lass. They expect different things of each other. The student comes, supposedly, with respect and a wish to learn; the teacher's role requires him, if possible, to be interesting and accurate and informed. The prospective purchaser comes with his fists up to protect himself against a sales pitch; the young lover comes with a quite different approach. There is, in fact, a kind of unwritten contract between the parties to a communication relationship, depending on the goal of the relationship, the roles they are playing, and how society has taught them to behave in such roles.

Furthermore, it is apparent that the relationship will be considerably different in one-way and in two-way communication, for the one-way relationship is efficient for certain goals and certain roles, but not for others. These are some of the newer lines of approach that readers will find when they go about "updating" what they read here.

27

The Functions of Advertising in Our Culture

Irving S. White

PREVIEW

I. The function of advertising is to assist in organizing and modifying the basic perceptual processes of the consumer so that he is guided toward seeing and feeling a product in a given predictable way.

II. There are three sources of meanings in the interaction between the consumer and the product that may be affected by advertising:
   A. *Culture* places the product in a social context and gives it meaning.
      1. Advertising must understand and reflect the value-structure of society before it can win approval for a product.
      2. Advertising may reformulate societal definitions of a product by pointing out more pleasant aspects of the product.
   B. The *brand image* is a relatively stable organization of percepts about a product.
      1. The function of advertising is to create strong sub-categories of values and needs within the social structure, and to associate these with the product.
      2. Advertising causes the brand to be associated with a certain type of personality, causing a segmentation of the market.
   C. *Direct experience* gives consumers "feedback" in terms of social gratifications and primary sensory experiences that the brand image and cultural definition have set up for them.
      1. The function of advertising is to supply the terms in which the product is valued.

Irving S. White, "The Functions of Advertising in our Culture," is reprinted by permission from the *Journal of Marketing*, published by the American Marketing Association (July 1959), pp. 8–14.

2. Direct experience is patterned by what the consumer has heard and seen through advertising.

The function of advertising in our culture may be characterized in two theoretical ways.

First, there are those who state the theory within the framework of economic laws, asserting that advertising affects knowledge about and demand for a product.

This article attempts to develop a second orientation. It is that the function of advertising is to help to organize and modify the *basic perceptual processes* of the consumer, so that he is guided toward *seeing* and *feeling* a product in a given predictable way.

Advertising as a Perceptual Process

With the recently formed partnership between the social scientist and the marketing professional, some foundation has been laid for a general reorientation toward understanding this influence as a dynamic process between communicators and perceivers. David Ogilvy and other advertising practitioners have formally incorporated terms such as "brand image" as applied to various advertised products. Journalists such as Martin Mayer have come to see advertising as affecting the "values" of a product.[1]

Yet "images" and "values" have no meaning outside of the experience and outlook of the consumer as a personality and the consumer-market as a social group. Gardner and Levy, influenced by the social psychology of George Herbert Mead, have shown how consumers are swayed toward or against a product because of the way a brand image is perceived.[2] And Martineau's *Motivation in Advertising* is a practical and lucid application of that proposition.[3]

It is a truism that the function of advertising is to inform and sell. But the more basic theoretical question is, how does advertising perform this function?

The Variables of Consumer Experience

Most advertisers would agree that advertising should orient the consumer toward a consistent, and usually pleasurable, relationship with their products. Consistency implies a rather stable organization of meanings and values centering around a product as an "object" in one's life. It is this consistency which gives what is often called "character" to a product or service. Cadillacs, for example, have traditionally meant specific mechanical, aesthetic, and social experiences to their adherents. Buying a Cadillac has often meant success and power to the purchaser, and the conviction that in several years from the time of purchase his car would still connote the same qualities. Pleasure merely means that the consumer derives gratifications out of this object-relationship that motivate him toward repeating and reinforcing the experience.

To structure the experience of the potential consumer along lines of consistent and predictable satisfactions requires an understanding of the total source of meanings, the *whole* interaction between the consumer and the product. For any advertiser, there is a certain amount of realistic humility inherent in the knowledge that advertising is only one of the several sources of stimulation that a product contains for the individual in society. The influences of culture and of private sensations modify and intermingle with the stimuli of advertising to achieve the final pattern of relationship between the seller's product (or ideas and services) and the consumer. What perceptions can advertising influence, and what can it not?

Even to begin to answer this question means an investigation of the structure of the product as an "object" in relationship with the individual. After interviewing hundreds of consumers, utilizing techniques of different levels of penetration, getting at "unconscious" and "conscious" attitudes and needs, three sources of meaning about a product have been isolated.

The first source is the set of meanings stemming from the *cultural definition* of the product. The second source of meaning comes from the consumer's organized set of notions about the brand, that is, the *brand image*. The third source of meaning is from direct *experience with the product*.

Cultural Definition of the Product

Social psychology and anthropology have dealt with the problem of objects in culture. That is, how do people come to understand and relate in a socially consistent manner to artifacts that are with them from time of birth?

The concept of "object" implies more than just a unidirectional flow of activity from the manipulator to the manipulated. It also implies a set of stimulations and communications in the reverse direction that guide the actions of the user. This means a dynamic relationship between the artifact and the user, wherein the latter perceives and acts upon the former according to the organized meanings that the culture and its subcultures have formulated for it.

The fact that few objects are naturally and intrinsically what they seem to be has been clearly indicated by such thinkers as George Herbert Mead, Jean Piaget, and Heinz Werner. A child growing up within a society begins by viewing an object in an idiosyncratic, self-centered way, and gradually redefines his relationship to it in terms of the broader, adult society. The acculturated individual internalizes the way the general society view the artifact, and sees the product in a setting of needs and values that control his action and attitudes about it. For example, there is nothing intrinsic in a baseball bat to account for its relationship to its user; a member of a primitive society could easily mistake it for a weapon.

It is perhaps more accurate to think of culture as involving a "climate of valuations" rather than being a thing apart from people. "Climate" implies the possibility for shift, and "valuations" suggests that the climate is made up of ideas, beliefs, feelings, and actions expressed by people. Yet the word "culture" as an abstraction also implies that the whole is greater than the sum of its parts, and that people learn from and conform to the patterns of people as a whole.

Elvis Presley in his early exposure on television and in popular music was responded to by a host of individual teen-agers who reacted to him with their own private senses. As Presley grew as an ideal, teen-agers were no longer free to accept him or reject him simply as individuals. They had to cope with a new level of values—that of the teen-age *society*.

Sometimes the important patterns of behavior and perception are learned from smaller reference groups, as adolescents, for example, respond to popular records. Sometimes learning is funneled through the larger, common culture, as in the singing of "The Star Spangled Banner." Although adults live in the same culture, they do not see a popular hit in the same light as teen-agers. Nor do non-Americans respond to the national anthem in the same way as Americans. An object or an idea differentiates itself along lines of the implied *membership* behind it.

Culture places the product in a social context and imbues it with meanings that set the broadest limitations on how it is experienced. A commercial product becomes culturally defined by the broad history of interaction with its market. In particular, the definition is determined by the social, biological, and psychic needs the product fulfills for its user. Thus, when a product achieves a niche in its cultural context, it is an object which denotes *consistent* (*not* unalterable) and *predictable* behavior within the social structure.

The ballpoint pen, for example, is intrinsically nothing but a complex set of tactile and visual sensations. These sensations are selected and modified by its user, according to the cultural definition of a ballpoint pen, and purposively placed in a social setting. That is, the object becomes perceived by the consumer. The result is that the user experiences a handy, easy-to-use, and relatively inexpensive tool for communicating his thoughts.

Advertising and Culture

Cultural influence is obvious when one thinks of how a cigarette in the mouth of a woman may be perceived today as compared to how it was perceived thirty or forty years ago. The above-the-ankle skirt might have indicated many qualities about its wearer during the last century that would be fallacious today.

Advertising must take account of the current values and product-definitions of the society (or subsociety) in which it intends to operate. In other words, advertisers must be aware of the role of the object in the life of the consumer. Likewise, advertisers must understand the limits of these broader cultural definitions before trying to amplify the product into a brand image.

For example, the social values implied by the concept "perfume" are such that its users are necessarily considered feminine. Any attempt by advertising to contradict the strong mores inherent in such a cultural definition might backfire as a commercial enterprise. Advertisers of male cosmetics and other self-indulgent items have discovered that they must carefully conceal the femininity and narcissism involved in colognes.

Culturally, then, the function of advertising is to understand, to reflect, and in most instances to accept the value-structure of society before it can go about its creative task of helping to organize in a consistent, gratifying manner the numerous stimulations a product contains for the potential consumer. Advertising can help to select and reinforce certain values and needs inherent in the role of the product. It can operate within the limits of culture to create new expectations for the consumer.

Occasionally an entire society may entertain negative or distorted notions about a product that may be a result of an unfortunate long-standing history between object and consumer. The potential for a limited, positive redefinition on a societal or subsocietal scale may exist in the case of such products.

The reader may think of numerous examples of products and services, the mere mention of which sends a wave of disdain, fear, digust, discomfort, and other negative reactions through him. Spinach, dentists, hypodermic needles, and long underwear are examples of "objects" with a positive function subordinated to the unfavorable experiences behind them.

In these cases, advertising can embark on the Herculean task of pointing up new avenues of more pleasurable interaction between the product and the consumer, and reformulate aspects of the cultural definitions of a product class. Of course, true reformulation lies in the response by the consumer society to the communicator's message. If the message is consistent with the society's experiences, an advertising-success story may indeed occur in a social movement toward a product. In such instances, reformulation is based on a pleasure-pain principle that promises to take the consumer from an unsatisfying relationship to a gratifying one.

For example, dental care in the mind of the average American is fraught with annoyance and discomfort, on the one hand, or with special precaution, compulsiveness, and concern on the other. Dental care and dentists are too often associated with a conception of teeth as a set of nuisances which nature ordained shall be in one's mouth. The American Dental Association is trying to reorient the client toward conceiving of his teeth and their care in the positive light of self-grooming and social reward in much the manner of the cosmetic industries.[4]

And when the Tea Bureau suggested that tea is the "hefty, hale, and hearty" drink for the average man, it was attempting to counter the stereotyped notions of effeteness, femininity, and snobbishness culturally attributed to the drink.

If the program of redefinition dramatically and effectively brings a product closer to the experience of the consumer, a new cognitive orientation toward the product will take place. Success in changing a popular concept depends upon how intense and stable, how true to experience, is the cultural tradition concerning products, ideas, or services.

Although advertising can help to reorganize some of the social interaction between a consumer and a product, it must be sensitive enough to these patterns to recognize their intensity and stability. An extremely exotic product, perhaps suitable for a small elite group, cannot be converted into a mundane, mass product *merely* by advertising.

The Brand Image as a Source of Meaning

The cultural definition of a product is too broad and generalized to allow a consumer to select a brand. It helps to create the initial set of expectations about the product which is then qualified by the second variable in product-consumer interaction, the brand image.

The brand image, as a source of meaning, helps the consumer further to select and organize the stimulations of the product, display, and other communications directed to him. Mead's social psychology suggests that an "image" guides one's actions and attitudes toward the object.[5]

It has been further suggested that the *meaning* of any message is the "change which it produces in the (already existing) image" that an individual harbors about the object in question.[6] This means that the message value of a television commercial, for example, lies in the degree and direction of change in a brand image previously held by the viewer. (Reinforcement of an already existing image implies a change in degree.)

Differences among brand images represent much more than literal product differences. A whole different set of notions and actions are inherent in the name "Lincoln" as compared with the name "Jaguar," despite the fact that each make has at least one or two models that are functionally comparable. It is somewhat difficult to imagine the typical Lincoln owner sitting behind the wheel of the typical Jaguar. The difference in the two images is, therefore, more intricate than the simple differences between the two lines of cars.

Tests of consumer reactions to various products and their advertisements indicate that the brand image may undergo change more quickly then the basic cultural definition of the product. Perception of the brand image is more capable of being influenced than is the perception of the general class of the product. This is logical, as the image is formulated within the limits of a culture.

The changes which took place in the brand images of certain filter cigarettes, for example, were fairly swift once the underlying cultural attitudes about filter cigarettes were modified by broader social influences affecting their definition, such as science, medicine, group hysteria. Marlboro could become a *manly* cigarette rather quickly once society relaxed its notions about who might smoke such a cigarette.

The image of the brand appears to be a relatively stable organization of percepts about a product. Once established, a brand image lends the consistency and predictability in the consumer's relationship with the product which allow him to select and experience those aspects of the product he values. Schweppes quinine water must indeed be a different experience to those who have responded to its image than is that of several other brands. The senses become attuned differently, and the social values inherent in the product-consumer interaction are different from brand to brand.

Advertising and the Brand Image

The major influence of advertising appears to be felt in the area of consumer perception of the brand. The brand image is the major organizing concept through which the consumer is guided toward perceiving unified patterns of stimulation. This imagery provides the emotional and sensual qualities which distinguish a brand from the general product-class and help the consumer discriminate from brand to brand.

Jello is not just a gelatin dessert, nor are Jello and Royal simply two products united by their common class. For the purchaser of a brand, there is usually a feeling that one has purchased a product distinctly different from another brand. This is probably most obvious in the case of beer and cigarettes.

This is the clue to what is often termed the "irrational" motive of the consumer in purchasing products. Skeptics, classic economists, and behaviorists in market research might demonstrate by blindfold tests how suggestible the average consumer is. They point out that the average consumer cannot distinguish between a Camel or a Philip Morris, or between Schlitz and Miller.

What such a literal understanding of the product-consumer relationship fails to consider is that *the value of a brand and its over-all symbolic effects on the consumer cannot be teased apart by tests oriented toward seeing the product in its barest, utilitarian terms.*

Another way of saying this is that the consumer purchases the brand and its cluster of meanings as much as he purchases the literal product. What Vance Packard calls "hidden persuasion" is probably the reference-group and other symbolic values implied in most social communications.[7]

The function of advertising is to create strong sub-categories of values and needs within the social structure, and to associate these with the product. Consumers may then select those brands whose sets of implied experiences fit into the sub-group with which he identifies.

The *Chicago Tribune* study on cigarettes and smokers clearly indicated that it is as reasonable to talk about the man who smokes Camels, for example, as having a "Camel personality" as it is to say that the brand itself has a personality.[8] It is reasonable because the two are correlates of each other. To the extent that the consumer perceives the brand image in this stable, predictable (and pleasurable) manner, the brand becomes a need-satisfying monopoly rather than a competitor with other brands. The power of the monopoly is dependent on the degree to which the brand is differentiated from other brands and is pleasurable at the same time.

If this aspect of the function of advertising is recognized, much of the arrogant and sanctimonious tone in some advertising can be relieved and a positive program of distinctive image development put in its place.

This relationship between the consumer and the brand must be understood by the advertiser in the earliest stages of planning if some measure of control and predictability in one's message is to be realized. If it is believed that facial tissue "A" can appeal to an important part of the market not adequately tapped by facial tissue "B," its advertisers must understand both the expectancies of the market and how advertising might serve to fit in with, reinforce, and organize these sets into a satisfying perceptual whole.

Direct Experience with the Product as a Source of Meaning

The third perceptual area is that of direct experience, the *use* which classical theory states determines the *utility* of the product and ultimately its demand. By direct experience with a product, a consumer finally gets his "feedback" in terms of social gratifications and primary sensory experiences that the brand image and cultural definitions have set up for him.

In a sense, the consumer is not fully open to his experiences and is not likely to perceive all the stimuli of a product. His own needs, in conjunction with the social conceptions reinforced by the imagery surrounding the product, emphasize certain aspects of direct experience and weed out others.

In some research on the ballpoint pen, for example, consumers were asked to describe their *writing* experiences with three brands of pens. One of these pens is a brand which stresses efficiency and predictability. The second brand emphasizes a general quality of competence, including prestige and status. The third brand focuses on inexpensiveness and dispensability.

Consumers described their experiences with the pens in terms of the generalized brand image, giving evidence of an awareness of how they were oriented toward the product. It is fairly evident that technical product improvements alone, unless they are highly dramatic or extreme, do not radically alter the consumer's previous ideas about the product. Some outside agent must serve to create a new expectation about the product that will allow the consumer to perceive the difference.

Advertising and Direct Experience with the Product

The function of advertising in this third area of consumer perception is to supply the *terms* in which the product is valued. In some ways advertising sets up a "self-fulfilling prophecy."[9] Most researchers are aware that a consumer's reaction to use is channeled in an important way by what he expects to experience. The terms in which the consumer responds to use are, in good part, supplied by advertising. The facets of experience beyond the scope of advertising are the concrete physiological sensations of the consumer.

Nor can broad organizing concepts, such as a cultural definition or a brand image, account for the unpredicted idiosyncrasies of either the consumer or the product. However, by the time the consumer has selected and organized all the communications of the product, he will evaluate the use experience in a fairly patterned manner.

Too often, the advertiser is so close to competitive aspects of his product that he has personally defined it in a manner that is not of optimum value to the consumer. Competition often causes advertisers to "hop on the current bandwagon" of advertising claims and to shout loudly about values that have little positive meaning to the consumer. In the automobile industry, a complex language of power dynamics has been foisted upon the consumer. Is this the optimum language of use available for him? In filter cigarettes, the language of use among certain competitive brands has been the number of filter-traps contained in the cigarette. Is the filter-cigarette smoker aided in getting gratification out of a cigarette by a terminology that concentrates upon the negatives of smoking?

The advertiser might improve his relationship with the consumer if he realized that his characterization of the consumer's use-experience helps the latter selectively perceive out of the product's numerous stimulations. Direct experience with a product is patterned by the communicable language of the product which has been created or reinforced by advertising.

NOTES

1. Martin Mayer, *Madison Avenue, U.S.A.* (New York: Harper and Brother, 1958).

2. Burleigh B. Gardner and Sidney J. Levy, "The Product and the Brand," *Harvard Business Review*, Vol. 33-No. 2 (March-April, 1955), pp. 33–39.

3. Pierre Martineau, *Motivation in Advertising* (New York: McGraw-Hill Book Company, Inc., 1957).

4. "A Motivational Study of Dental Care: A Pilot Investigation," prepared for the American Dental Association by Social Research, Inc., in the *Journal of the American Dental Association*, serialized in Vol. 56 (March, April, May, and June, 1958).

5. George Herbert Mead, *Mind, Self, and Society*, edited by Charles W. Morris (Chicago, University of Chicago Press, 1934).

6. Kenneth E. Boulding, *The Image* (Ann Arbor: University of Michigan Press, 1956), p. 7.

7. Vance Packard, *The Hidden Persuaders* (New York, David McKay Company, Inc., 1957).

8. *Cigarettes: Their Role and Function, A Study for the Chicago Tribune*, prepared by Social Research, Inc., Chicago, 1953.

9. Robert K. Merton, "The Self-Fulfilling Prophecy," in Robert K. Merton, *Social Theory and Social Structure* (Glencoe, The Free Press, 1949).

LEARNING REVIEW

Questions:

1. The three sources of meanings in the interaction of the consumer and product are ___________, ___________, and ___________.

2. The source of meaning most affected by advertising is ___________.

3. The author's thesis is that the function of advertising is to help to organize and modify the ______________________ of the consumer.

Answers:

1. cultural definition, brand image, direct experience; 2. brand image; 3. basic perceptual processes

Retrospective Comment

Since the writing of this article, which was the first formal theoretical statement of the relationship between cultural meanings, psychological values, and the physical product in advertising, the role of perceptual processes in evaluating advertising has been elevated to the forefront of advertising research. Yet, surprisingly, the clash between social scientifically-oriented marketers and *intuitivists*, those creative personnel who prefer to initiate advertising out of their instinctive sense of the product, still rages unabated. Shall the creative process be disciplined to function within an established cultural and psychological framework, or shall the opportunity for unbridled innovation be kept intact? From the advertiser's point of view, the controversy is not merely academic, for upon its resolution may depend many dollars, as well as the effectiveness of an advertising campaign.

To this day, there is reasonable agreement that a brand must ideally become *unique* through advertising. Yet the dictum of many in the advertising world that it is better to have a distinct *attention-getter* (apparently even if all falls outside of the consumer culture) than an appropriate, but commonplace brand is still powerful.

The underlying issue *still remains* as to whether advertising as a medium can create new cultural definitions of products or whether it must function within the evolving framework or meanings selected by the culture. As a social scientist, I have become more convinced that advertising is only one instrument of communication, still quite subordinate to the larger *epiphenomenological* instruments of value-formation such as political events, the economy, scientific breakthroughs, and value-revolution exemplified by the women's liberation movement, civil rights, racial and ethnic identity affirmation, and others.

It is still amazing to me, as a consultant to America's largest companies and to their advertising agencies, that the role of advertising has not been encompassed by an appreciation of the limited framework of the social and psychological values of the consumer world.*

* Dr. White is currently President of CRA, Inc., Los Angeles.

28

Does Advertising Belong in the Capital Budget?

Joel Dean

PREVIEW

I. There are several important concepts to understand in determining whether promotion is an investment.
   A. An investment is an outlay made today to achieve benefits in the future.
   B. Promotional costs are outlays to augment the demand for the product, while production costs are all outlays required to meet this demand.
   C. Promotional investments differ from traditional corporate investments in a number of ways, but these differences should not disqualify promotion for investment treatment.

II. Considering advertising as an investment, there are a number of questions and concerns important to the question of how much a corporation should invest in promotion.
   A. The problem of how much to spend on advertising has not been solved.
   B. There are three reasons why the problem is unsolved:
      1. There is a failure to acknowledge the importance of futurity.
      2. There is a lack of a conceptual apparatus whose orientation is economic.
      3. There is the difficulty of measuring the effectiveness of promotional outlays.
   C. The solution for the problem of how much to invest should be geared to the goal of profitability.
   D. Promotion relates in a complex way to two other ways of increasing sales: by cutting price and by improving the product.
   E. The productivity of an investment in promotion is the relation of its earnings to the amount of invested capital.

Joel Dean, "Does Advertising Belong in the Capital Budget?" is reprinted by permission from the *Journal of Marketing*, published by the American Marketing Association (October 1966), pp. 15–21.

F. There are four concepts of measurement useful for calibrating return on investment: *alternatives*, *futurity*, *increments*, and *cash flows*.
G. The best yardstick for investments in promotion is true profitability as measured by discounted-cash-flow analysis.
H. The standard of minimum acceptable profitability should be the same for all capital proposals: the company's market cost-of-capital or its opportunity cost-of-capital, whichever is higher.

III. Putting advertising in the capital budget does not guarantee success, but it does provide a reasonable means for having promotion compete for funds on the basis of merit.

Should advertising be budgeted as an expense or as an investment?

Advertising is now book-kept and budgeted as though its benefits were used up immediately, like purchased electricity. Management thinks about advertising as it is book-kept, as a current expense. The decision as to how much a corporation should spend on persuasion is made by the same criteria as for materials used up in the factory—impact upon the current P&L. The advertising budget is part of the *operating* budget.

So far as is known, no corporation puts advertising in its capital budget. But maybe it belongs there. Several disinterested parties say so:

The stock market says it belongs there. It says the benefits derived from promotional outlays are just as capitalizable as the tangible assets that the bookkeeper does capitalize. It says this when Bristol Myers sells at ten times its book value.

Corporation presidents occasionally say it belongs there, especially when they evoke *investment* in advertising to justify poor current profits.

New entrants into an industry say advertising belongs in the capital budget. They say it by including the promotional outlays required to build brand-acceptance as an integral part of the total investment required to break into the business.

Antitrust economists say advertising belongs in the capital budget. They say it by viewing brand-acceptance, which is built up by promotion, as just as substantial a barrier to entry as the investment required in buildings and machinery.

It is just possible that the bookkeeper's guide to top-management thinking about advertising is wrong.

The Approach

The plan of this article is, first, to find whether promotion is an investment; second, to consider how to optimize it if it is an investment; and third, to speculate on the probabilities that this novel approach, even if theoretically valid, will do any good.

The approach here to the problem of how much to invest in advertising is formal and objective, rather than intuitive. The premise is that the overriding goal of the corporation is to maximize profits. The viewpoint is that of an economist concerned with managerial finance.

This article is confined to the conceptual framework for deciding how much to invest in promotion. Measurement problems are not examined, nor the mechanics of application. The analysis is presented in terms of advertising, but is equally applicable to all forms of persuasion. Advertising is used as an example simply because it is the purest and most indisputable form of selling cost, and for many firms also the largest.

My thesis is as follows. Most advertising is, in economic essence, an investment. How much to spend on advertising is, therefore, a problem of investment economics. A new approach is required—economic and financial analysis of futurities. This approach focuses on future after-tax cash flows and centers on the profit-productivity of capital.

Is Promotion an Investment?

To determine whether, as a matter of economics, outlays for advertising and other forms of promotion constitute an investment, rather than a current expense, is our first task.

So we must bravely face three basic questions concerning the economics of investment in corporate persuasion:

A. Precisely what is a business investment; how is it distinguished from a current expense?

B. Just what are promotional costs; how should they be distinguished from production costs?

C. What are the distinctive characteristics of promotional outlays; do they disqualify promotion for investment treatment?

A. Concept of Investment

What distinguishes a business investment from a current expense?

An investment is an outlay made today to achieve benefits in the future. A current expense is an outlay whose benefits are immediate. The question is not how the outlay is treated in conventional accounting, how it is taxed, or whether the asset is tangible or intangible. The hallmark of an investment is futurity.

B. Concept of Promotional Costs

Precisely what are promotional costs? How do they differ from production costs?

Promotional costs are outlays to augment the demand for the product—that is, to shift its price-quantity demand schedule upward, so that more will be sold at a given price. In contrast, production costs are all outlays required to meet this demand.

This different dividing line means that some costs which are conventionally classified as marketing costs, for example, physical distribution, are here viewed as part of production costs. It means also that some costs usually viewed as production costs, for example, inspection, are here viewed as promotional costs, even though they are incurred in the factory.

This is the cost-dichotomy needed for clear thinking about promotional investments. A clear idea of the purpose of an outlay is indispensable for a useful estimate of its effectiveness. Moreover, the criterion for optimization is quite different for production costs than for promotional costs. For production, it is sheer cost-minimization; for promotion, it is not cost-minimization but something much more intricate, as we shall see.

C. Distinctive Traits of Promotional Outlays

Do promotional investments differ from unimpeachable corporate investments in ways that make it impractical to manage them like true investments?

Promotional investments *are* different from traditional corporate investments—for example, capital tied up in machinery. The question is whether these differences call for a different intellectual apparatus for measuring productivity and rationing the firm's capital.

Promotional investments *are book-kept differently*. They are not capitalized and not depreciated. But this does not keep them from being investments. They tie up capital with equal inflexibility and do so with similar expectation of future benefits.

Promotional investments *are taxed differently*. Unlike acknowledged investments, they are deductible against income fully at the time of outlay, regardless of the delay of benefits. The fact that the tax collector is oblivious to promotional investments increases their productivity. Immediate tax writeoff of the entire outlay halves the investment after tax and steps up its true rate of return.

Promotional investments *are generally spread out over time* and usually can be adjusted in amount in relatively small steps. However, this is irrelevant in determining whether or not they are true investments.

Most promotional investments *have an indeterminate economic life*. Brand-acceptance "planted in the head" of a teenager by television may influence his purchases for 50 minutes or 50 years. But uncertainty of duration of the benefits does not make the promotional outlay any less an investment. The obsolescence-life of a computer is also quite uncertain.

Promotional investments *have multiple benefits* which can be reaped in optional ways. The profitability of augmented demand may be taken out either in higher prices or in larger volume. But this is not unique to promotional investments. Usually factory modernization not only saves labor, but also increases capacity and improves product-quality and employee morale.

Promotional investments *usually have irregular and diverse time-shapes in their benefits streams*. But this is a common characteristic of many tangible investments. Some oil wells, for example, come in as gushers, have an unexpected midlife rejuvenation from repressuring, and live out a tranquil old age as pumpers.

Promotional investments *have a benefit-stream which is difficult to measure and to predict*. But they share this characteristic with many forms of outlay conventionally classified as capital expenditures. Obsolescence of chemical-processing equipment, for example, is hard to predict, yet vitally affects its rate of return.

Promotional investments *are provocative*; they may induce rivals to retaliate. This adds to the difficulty of measuring and predicting benefits. Tangible investments, however, can also provoke competitors' reactions in ways that erode their profitability (for example, retail store modernization).

All this adds up to the fact that the promotional investments *do* have unusual characteristics, different from many other investments that now fight for funds in the capital budget. However, these traits either are not distinctive, or if they are, do not destroy the essential investment-character of the promotional outlays.

All promotional outlays are now conventionally viewed exclusively as current expenses. Some are, if the time lag of benefits is sufficiently short; but others are instead true investments, because the delay in their benefits is substantial. Most promotion is a *mixture*, and the richness of the investment-mix varies over a wide range.

How to Optimize Investment in Promotion

Granted that much advertising is largely an investment in economic reality, how should a corporation determine how much it should invest in promotion? To solve this problem, we need answers to the following questions:

a. Does a satisfactory solution for the problem already exist?
b. Why has such an important problem remained unsolved?
c. To what corporate goal should the solution be geared?
d. How does promotion tie into other ways of getting business?
e. What are the determinants of the productivity of capital?

f. What concepts of measurement are needed to calibrate productivity of capital?
g. What is the most appropriate yardstick of capital productivity for promotional investments?
h. How would rate-of-return rationing work for investments in corporate persuasion?

A. Problem Unsolved

Has the problem of how much a corporation should spend on advertising and other forms of persuasion been already satisfactorily solved?

The problem is important. The answer is crucial to the competitive success of many firms, and may involve vast expenditures.

In the future, it is likely to be even more vital. Depersonalized distribution, increased urbanization, rising consumer affluence, revolutionary advances in technology, and bigger economies of scale in some promotional media are dynamic forces which will make the decision as to how much to invest in promotion a jugular issue for many corporations in the next decade.

Surprisingly, this crucial problem is not yet solved. Despite yards of computer print-outs and millions of dollars spent on advertising research, most corporations do not really know whether their promotional outlays should be half or twice as large as they now are.

B. Reasons for Failure

Why has such an important problem remained unsolved? There are three main causes.

The first cause is *failure to acknowledge the importance of futurity*. The full impact of most promotional outlays upon demand is delayed with associated uncertainty. Hence, the conceptual framework of analysis that management needs for solving this problem is the kind that is used in modern, sophisticated management of conventional corporate capital appropriations.

A second cause is *lack of a conceptual apparatus whose orientation is economic*. The problem of optimizing promotional investment is basically a matter of managerial economics, that is, balancing incremental promotional investment against predicted benefits, so as to augment sales most profitably.

The third cause of failure is *the difficulty of measuring the effectiveness of promotional outlays*. Their impacts on demand are diffused, delayed, and intricately interwoven with other forces. To make the kind of investment approach needed to produce practical benefits will require an open mind, fresh concepts, substantial research spending, and great patience.

C. Overriding Corporate Goal

What is the corporate goal to which the solution of optimum investment in promotion should be geared?

Promotional outlays, like other expenditures, should be judged in terms of their contribution to attainment of the corporation's objectives. Most companies have several goals, some of which conflict; but the solution for the problem of how much to invest in promotion should be geared primarily to the goal of profitability.

The master goal of the modern corporation should be maximum profits in the long run. More explicitly, it should be to maximize the present worth at the corporation's cost of capital of the future stream of benefits to the stockholder.

All other objectives—such as growth or market-share or eternal life—should be either intermediate or subsidiary to this overriding corporate objective.

D. Business-Getters

How does promotion relate to other ways of getting business?

A company has three ways to augment its sales: by cutting price, by spending more on promotion, and by bettering its product. The three members of the business-getting threesome pull together. But being alternatives, they are at the margin rivalrous substitutes.

The three reinforce each other in a complex symbiotic relationship. For a product that is superior to rivals in wanted ways, promotional outlays will be more effective than for an inferior product. A given amount and quality of promotion will produce more sales of a product priced in correct economic relationship to buyers' alternatives than for an overpriced product.

Each of the three business-getters can have delayed impacts and hence be a business investment. Their delayed and intertwining effects on sales, now and in the future, increase the problem of measuring the effects of promotional investment.

E. Determinants of Capital Productivity

What are the determinants of the productivity of capital invested in promotion?

These need to be identified to find out whether capital tied up in advertising will yield enough profits to earn its keep. Its yield must pay for the cost of this capital in the marketplace, or its opportunity costs in benefits passed up by not investing the money somewhere else.

The productivity of an investment in promotion is the relation of its earnings to the amount of capital tied up. This relationship requires explicit recognition of four economic determinants to be measured: (1) the amount and timing of *added investment*; (2) the amount and timing of *added earnings*; (3) the *duration of the earnings*; and (4) the *risks and imponderable benefits* associated with the project.

1. *Added Investment*. The appropriate investment base for calculating rate of return is the added outlay which will be occasioned by the adoption of a promotion project as opposed to its rejection.

The investment should include the entire amount of the original added outlay, regardless of how it is classified on the accounts. Any additional oulay for point-of-purchase displays or for distribution of samples to consumers should be included in the investment amount, as should future research expenses caused by the proposal.

The timing of these added investments has an important effect upon true profitability and should, therefore, be reflected in the rate-of-return computation.

2. *Added Earnings*. Concern with capital productivity implies, of course, that the company's goal is profits.

The productivity of the capital tied up is determined by the increase in earnings or savings, that is, net cash receipts, caused by making the investment as opposed to not making it. These earnings should be measured in terms of their after-tax cash or cash equivalents.

Only costs and revenues that will be different as a result of the adoption of the proposal should be included. The concept of earnings should be broad enough to encompass intangible and often unquantifiable benefits. When these have to be omitted from the formal earnings-estimates, they should be noted for subsequent appraisal of the project.

3. *Durability of Earnings*. The duration of the benefits from a promotional investment has a vital effect on its rate of return.

Economic life of promotion depends (a) on frequency of purchase; (b) on loyalty-life-expectancy, that is, longevity of customers; (c) on gestation period of the purchase decision; and (d) on erosion by the promotional efforts of rivals.

For advertising investments, durability is often the most difficult dimension of project value to quantify. But the problem cannot be avoided. Some estimate is better than none; and estimates can be improved by well-directed research.

4. *Risks and Imponderable Benefits*. Appraising the risks and uncertainties associated with a project requires a high order of judgment. It is only disparities in risk among projects which need to be allowed for, since the company's cost of capital reflects the overall risks. Although

measurement of this sort of dispersion is difficult, some headway can sometimes be made by a necessarily arbitrary risk-ranking of candidate projects or categories of projects.

Most projects have some added benefits over and above the measurable ones. If excessive weight is given to these imponderables, then there is danger that rate-of-return rationing will occur. When a low rate-of-return project is preferred to a high one on the grounds of imponderable benefits, the burden of proof clearly should rest on the imponderables.

F. Concepts of Measurement

For calibrating these four determinants of return on investment, what concepts of measurement are needed? Four are particularly useful:

1. *Alternatives*. The proper benchmark for measuring added investment and the corresponding added earnings is the best alternative way to do it.
2. *Futurity*. Future earnings and future outlays of the project are all that matter.
3. *Increments*. Added earnings and added investment of the project alone are material.
4. *Cash flows*. After-tax cash flows (or their equivalents) alone are significant for measuring capital productivity.

1. *Alternatives*. There is always an alternative to the proposed capital expenditure.

The alternative may be so catastrophic that refined measurement is unnecessary to reject it; but in any case, the proper benchmark for the proposal is the next profitable alternative way of doing it.

2. *Futurity*. The value of a proposed capital project depends on its future earnings.

The past is irrelevant, except as a benchmark for forecasting the future. Consequently, earnings estimates need to be based on the best available projections. The outlays and earnings need to be estimated year by year over the economic life of the proposed promotion, and their time shape needs to be taken into account explicitly.

3. *Increments*. A correct estimate of both earnings and investment must be based on the simple principle that the earnings from the promotional proposal are measured by the total *added* earnings by making the investment, as opposed to *not* making it . . . and that the same is true for the investment amount.

Project costs should be unaffected by allocation of existing overheads, but should reflect the changes in total overhead and other costs likely to result from the project. No costs of revenues which will be the same, regardless of whether the proposal is accepted or rejected, should be included and the same goes for investment.

4. *Cash flows.* To be economically realistic, attention should be directed exclusively at the after-tax flows of cash or cash equivalents which will result from making the promotional investment.

Book costs are confusing and immaterial. But taxes do matter, because advertising investments are favored over depreciable investments in after-tax rate of return.

G. Yardstick of Financial Worth

The productivity of capital in a business investment is the relationship between its earnings and the amount of capital tied up. To measure this productivity for promotional investments, we not only must have a correct conceptual framework of measurements, but also must choose the most appropriate yardstick of investment worth.

The concept of advertising as an investment already has some limited acceptance in new-product introduction. The measure of productivity of capital often used is the payout period—a crude yardstick. The cutoff criterion is also set rather arbitrarily to get the original outlay back in two years or three years. Such standards have no objective justification as compared with corporate cost of capital.

What is the best yardstick of economic worth for investments in persuasion? Clearly, the yardstick that is economically appropriate for investments in promotion is true profitability as measured by discounted-cash-flow analysis.

1. *Discounted-Cash-Flow Analysis.* The discounted-cash-flow (DCF) method is a new approach to measuring the productivity of capital and measuring the cost of capital.

The application is new, not the principle. Discounting has long been used in the financial community, where precision and realism are indispensable. The essential contributions of discounted-cash-flow analysis to management thinking about investment in promotion are three:

a. An explicit recognition that time has economic value—and hence, that near money is more valuable than distant money.

b. A recognition that cash flows are what matter—and hence, that book costs are irrelevant for capital-decisions except as they affect taxes.

c. A recognition that income taxes have such an important effect upon cash flows that they must be explicitly figured into project worth.

The discounted-cash-flow method has two computational variants.

The first is a rate-of-return computation, which consists essentially of finding the interest rate that discounts gross future after-tax cash earnings of a project down to a present value equal to the project cost. This interest rate is the rate of return on that particular investment.

The second variant is a present-value computation which discounts gross future after-tax cash earnings of all projects at the same rate of interest. This rate of interest is the company's minimum acceptable rate of return. This should be based on the company's cost of capital. Special risk should be reflected either by deflating project earnings or by adjusting the cutoff rate for projects of different categories of risk. The resulting present-value is then compared with the project cost investment. If the present value exceeds it, the project is acceptable. If it falls below, it is rejected.

In addition, projects can by this variant be ranked by various kinds of profitability indexes which reflect the amount or ratios of excess of present value over project cost.

Both variants of the discounted-cash-flow approach require a timetable of after-tax cash flows of investment and of gross earnings which cover the entire economic life of the project.

In practice, the timetable can be simplified by grouping years in blocks. For projects for which investment is substantially instantaneous and gross earnings are level, simple computational charts and tables can be used to estimate the discounted-cash-flow rate of return directly from estimated economic life and after-tax payback. For projects with rising or declining earnings streams, this conversion is more complex.

2. *Superiorities of DCF.* The discounted-cash-flow method of analysis is particularly needed for measuring the profitability of promotional investments, for two reasons.

First, the outlays are usually spread out. Second, benefits, mainly incremental profits from added sales in the future, are always spread out and usually have a non-level time-shape.

The superiorities of discounted-cash-flow analysis over rival yardsticks for measuring the productivity of capital in promotional investments are imposing:

a. It is economically realistic in confining the analysis to cash-flows and forgetting about book-allocations.
b. It forces guided thinking about the whole life of the project, and concentration on the lifetime earnings.
c. It weights the time-pattern of the investment outlay and the cash earnings, so as to reflect real and important differences in the value of near and distant cash-flows.
d. It reflects accurately and without ambiguity the timing of tax-savings.

e. It permits simple allowances for risks and uncertainties, and can be adapted readily to increasing the risk allowance over time.
f. It is strictly comparable to cost-of-capital, correctly measured, so that decisions can be made quickly and safely by comparing rate of return and the value of money to the firm.

H. Rate-of-return Rationing

How should rationing of capital work for persuasion-investments?

Rate-of-return "battling" among capital proposals is the essence of capital rationing. The standard of minimum acceptable profitability should (after proper allowance for special risks and for imponderables) be the same for all, namely, the company's market cost-of-capital or its opportunity cost-of-capital, whichever is higher.

Market cost-of-capital is what the company probably will pay for equity and debt funds, on the average, over the future. For a large publicly-held company, this cost can be measured with adequate precision for rationing purposes. There is no better cutoff criterion.

Opportunity cost-of-capital is the sacrificed profit-yield from alternative investments. Only when a company refuses to go to market for funds can its opportunity costs stay long above market cost-of-capital.

Practical Values

Will putting advertising in the capital budget do any good?

Granted that as a matter of economic principle much advertising and other forms of promotional spending are investments . . . and granted also that conceptually correct and pragmatically proved techniques for optimizing investment outlays are available for promotional investment . . . the question is whether this sophisticated and powerful mechanism, applied to promotional investments, will have any practical value.

Most business investments are not made in ignorance of their probable impacts, whereas, many of the outlays for persuasion now are. Characteristically, the amount and timing of the effects of advertising are unknown. The duration of their impact on economic life is unknown, and the probabilities of effectiveness are also unknown. Quite possibly, attempting to estimate these unknowns cannot improve overall results.

The problem of how much to invest in promotion can be solved either by intuitive and perhaps artistic processes, or through a more formal and more systematic study of objective evidence. Quite possibly men of experience and good judgment can determine how much the corporation should invest in promotion by subjective judgment, regardless of whether advertising is formally put in the capital budget. This article is nevertheless confined to a consideration of ways in which sophisticated economic models and systematic quantitative study can help to find the appropriate size of the appropriation for corporate persuasion.

In Summary

1. Much advertising (and other corporate persuasion) is in economic reality partly an investment. The investment-mix varies over a wide spectrum.

2. Investments in promotion are different from conventional capital expenditures; but these distinctive characteristics do not disqualify promotion for investment treatment.

3. Profitability must be the basic measurement of the productivity of capital invested in promotion. Despite the multiplicity of conflicting corporate goals, the overriding objective for decisions or investment of corporate capital should be to make money.

4. The main determinants of profitability of an advertising investment that need to be estimated are the amount and timing of added investment and of added earnings, the duration of advertising effects and risks.

5. The measurement concepts of capital productivity that must be estimated are future, time-spotted, incremental, after-tax cash flows of investment outlays and of added profits from added sales.

6. Discounted-Cash-Flow (DCF) analysis supplies the financial yardstick most appropriate for promotional investments. By comparison, payback period, although widely used, has no merit.

7. Advertising belongs in the capital budget. Promotional investments should be made to compete for funds on the basis of profitability, that is, DCF rate of return.

8. The criterion for rationing scarce capital among competing investment proposals should be DCF rate of return. The criterion of the minimum acceptable return should be the corporation's cost of capital—outside market-cost or internal opportunity-cost, whichever is higher.

9. Putting advertising into the capital budget will not perform a miracle. Judgment cannot be displaced by DCF analysis and computers. But judgment can be economized and improved. The most that it can do is to open the way for a research approach which is oriented to the kind of estimates that are relevant and that will permit advertising investment in promotion to fight for funds on the basis of financial merit rather than on the basis of personal persuasiveness of their sponsor.

10. An investment approach to produce practical benefits will require fresh concepts, substantial research-spending, and great patience.

LEARNING REVIEW

Questions:

1. The best yardstick for investments in promotion is true profitability as measured by ______________________________.

2. A company has three ways to augment its sales: a) ____________, b) ____________, c) ____________.

3. The author's central idea is that most advertising is ____________.

Answers:

1. discounted-cash-flow analysis; 2. a) by cutting price; b) by spending more on promotion; c) by improving its product; 3. an investment

Retrospective Comment

Not all advertising (or other promotion) is an investment, but much of it is. Each nationwide new-product launch demonstrates again that a large part of advertising belongs in the capital budget. The $15 million that Procter & Gamble reportedly spent to launch *Sure* aerosol deodorant (*Advertising Age*, September 3, 1972, p. 1) was surely viewed by management as an investment.

The measure of the goodness of promotional investments is prospective profitability. Promotional outlays should be made to compete on this basis with other investments in the capital budget. The objection that promotion is defensive should not dissuade top management from perceiving launch outlays as investments. Most promotional investments are defensive. But so are most investments in plant modernization and in product quality. Their profitability must be measured against what would have happened in the absence of investment: promotional outlays to prevent loss of patronage can be just as profitable as investments to conquer new markets. Similarly, the argument that it is difficult to measure returns on persuasion investments should not deter investment thinking or contaminate capital rationing. A guess at the right concept is better than a precise measure of an irrelevant one. Other objections—that returns on promotional outlays are uncertain, that mortality rates are high and product lives short—also do not hold.

Uncertainty is characteristic of most important investment projects, and all capital projects have a limited and hard-to-estimate life expectancy.

Recognition of economic reality rather than reform of accounting or of budgetary procedures is what I plead for.

In reports to stockholders and to tax collectors, promotional investments will continue to be expensed rather than capitalized. Management cannot change stockholder accounting over the opposition of a conservative and tradition-conscious accounting profession, nor should it want to change tax accounting. Accounting theology should not, however, deter top management from recognizing that all forms of persuasion are, in economic reality, mainly investments.

29

The Salesman Isn't Dead—He's Different

Carl Rieser

PREVIEW

I. The marketing concept has had very decided and significant structural effects on sales forces.
   A. Salesmen may sell a whole group of products to a particular market; therefore, they must be generalists.
   B. Salesmen must have more executive ability, for they are being given more authority to make important decisions in the field.
   C. There remains a need for aggressive salesmen who open new accounts, but this is becoming the specialty of a few rather than the primary function of all salesmen.

II. Other changes that have taken place in business have greatly affected the role and function of the salesman.
   A. Salesmen today have access to much more information about their customers and are backed by technical and other kinds of assistance.
   B. Development of sophisticated electronic data-processing systems have relieved salesmen of a great deal of detail that formerly occupied their time.
   C. In business, fewer and bigger customers are responsible for a large part of any company's sales, making the role of the salesman shift more toward a service orientation.
   D. Because decisions to buy are often made among the customer's top management, more top executives have been drawn more directly into the selling act.
   E. Personal selling is now a company-wide endeavor, and contact with the customer takes place at many levels in an organized, formal way.

Carl Rieser, "The Salesman Isn't Dead—He's Different," is reprinted by permission from *Fortune* Magazine (November 1962), pp. 124ff. © 1962 Time Inc.

III. There is a lag in public recognition of the changes that have taken place in the nature of selling that needs to be eliminated in order to make the position of the salesman more prestigious.

There is no more abused figure in American life than the salesman. One group of critics scorns him for certain qualities that another group sneers at him for losing. To many novelists, playwrights, sociologists, college students, and many others, he is aggressively forcing on people goods that they don't want. He is the drummer, with a dubious set of social values—Willy Loman in the Arthur Miller play. The second group of critics, which includes the Secretary of Commerce and many business executives all over the U.S., charges the salesman with lacking good, old-fashioned, hard-hitting salesmanship. He was spoiled by the postwar days when competition was easy. If only he would get up off his duff, and get out and *sell*, the goods would move and business would be in fine shape.

Both sets of critics are swatting at a target that doesn't matter much any more. The plain fact is that, as one Boston sales executive recently said, "The old drummer type of salesman has gone by the board." Nor are his talents especially needed in today's economy. To be sure, there are plenty of aggressive, hard-hitting salesmen still and there will always be a place for their brand of selling. But this kind of man is no longer the archetype.

From bits and pieces of evidence in all sectors of U.S. business, it is now possible to discern the emergence of a new dominant type, a man with a softer touch and greater breadth, a new kind of man to do a new—much more significant—kind of job. Whereas the old-time salesman devoted himself primarily to pushing a product, or a line of products, the new-era salesman is involved with the whole distribution pipeline, beginning with the tailoring of products to the customer's desire and extending through their promotion and advertising to final delivery to the ultimate consumer.

The salesman has been cast in his new role by "the marketing concept," a term that originated at General Electric around 1950 and has gained wide currency recently. It means essentially that companies are orienting their organization and effort toward the market, toward the ever changing needs of the customer, and the ever shifting calculations of their own production costs and opportunities. The emphasis is less concentrated on the isolated point-of-sale; it is spread forward, into the buyer's operations, and backward into the seller's operations. The profound consequences of this trend have been suggested by Orm Henning, marketing manager of industrial products at Texas Instruments:

"One should remind oneself that selling is only part of marketing—particularly in the scientific-industrial world. Marketing is communicating back to your factory your individual customer's needs and particular problems. When you realize and practice this, you open an entirely new vista in the area of sales. You cannot afford to sell a product, a static product—not in our business."

And what's true today in the electronics business—and many others—is going to be true of more and more businesses tomorrow.

The great change in selling affects practically all industries and all kinds of goods, whether they are what the marketing profession calls "pull-through" or "push-through" products. Pull-through refers generally to mass-produced consumer items, where a sort of siphon is already working. Pull-through products and services are presold by the manufacturer to the final consumer by mass advertising and promotion, which in effect creates a demand that almost literally pulls the goods through the distribution pipeline. Push-through products are wholly new consumer goods for which the siphon has not yet begun to work or, more commonly, they are industrial materials and equipment. Since the latter are usually highly technical in nature, they must be explained to the buyer and they require more personal selling so as to generate in the buyer the idea that he needs the product.

The distinction between pull-through and push-through is becoming less important. The retailer now stocks Kleenex tissues, for example, because he is persuaded that Kimberly-Clark Corp. will maintain public recognition of the brand and will see to it that thousands of boxes are siphoned rapidly and profitably right through his warehouse and off his store shelves. The job of the Kimberly-Clark salesman is to service the account so that the buyer will keep buying. He expedites and consolidates the shipments, keeps track of the retailer's inventory, sees that the goods get the greatest display and promotion possible, keeps himself available in case of any trouble or emergency. The job of the man who sells computers is much the same. The computer is one element in a whole system of mechanical devices and programming techniques, which is sold on the basis of what the customer is persuaded it can do for him.

The salesman's responsibility becomes greater as technology advances and producers offer products of ever mounting complexity. "We are tending toward the marketing of systems and services," says James Jewell, marketing vice president of Westinghouse. "The customers want to buy greater production—not equipment. We take the full responsibility for engineering and installing, and we are moving further into servicing."

This orientation toward the customer's needs is pointed up in a recent book that has received wide attention in the trade—*Innovation in Marketing*, by Theodore Levitt, a management consultant and a member of the faculty of Harvard Business School. Levitt, who speaks for a new generation of believers in "the marketing concept," states flatly that "a strictly sales-oriented approach to doing business can be suicidal. The difference between selling and marketing is more than semantic. Selling focuses on the needs of the seller, marketing on the needs of the buyer. Selling is preoccupied with the seller's need to convert his product or service into cash; marketing with the idea of satisfying the needs of the customer by means of the product or service and by the whole cluster of customer-getting value satisfactions associated with creating, delivering, and finally consuming it."

In this quotation Levitt seems to be oversimplifying the contrast between selling and marketing. Any implication that "the marketing concept" isn't motivated by the seller's desire for profits is, of course, mistaken. While his motives remain the same, the seller now sees marketing as a more elaborate link between production and consumption, a link that has to be carefully constructed and maintained.

Two situations may illustrate the change. In the past, a factory would overproduce the market and unload on the sales force the responsibility for unloading the goods on the customers. In the other situation, the salesmen kept their volume up by selling those products in their line that were easiest to sell—even those that were the least profitable. The incidence of both these cases tends to be diminished by the new trend with its more delicate alignment of markets and production, and its careful analysis of product profitability. The salesman is less often stuck with the necessity of a fast, hard sell. But he is steadily pressed to make the sales where the profit lies. Altogether, the marketing concept has played a vital role in developing the enormous velocity in the flow of goods, a phenomenon that has been described earlier in this series as the "short-order economy" (*Fortune*, August, 1962).

The Mirror of the Markets

There is little doubt that the impact of "the marketing concept" has reduced the stature of the sales manager in scores of companies. He has lost his former autonomy and now reports to the marketing vice president rather than directly to the president. He has less say over such vital matters as pricing and credit policies. The sales force must fit its work into an over-all corporation marketing policy. Furthermore, over the decade, the autonomy of the sales manager has been further trimmed in many companies by the creation of the job of product manager, who has both line and staff authority for a given product or group of products and coordinates production with advertising, research, and field selling.

The marketing concept has had very decided and significant structural effects on sales forces. This can be seen very clearly at General Electric, father of the marketing concept. G.E.'s salesmen used to be essentially product specialists, each selling only the line of a specific manufacturing department, even though it went into a variety of markets. It took time for G.E. to orient its sales forces toward markets rather than products, but this process finally began seven years ago in the company's electrical-apparatus business. Instead of specializing in one product, e.g., cord sets, fan motors, push buttons, the salesman began selling a whole group of products to a particular market—for example, the air-conditioning industry. Early this year more than a dozen separate departments selling G.E.'s biggest single customer, the government, were reorganized into one defense sales force. In other words, instead of being product-oriented, the sales organizations have become "mirrors" of the markets G.E. serves.

Recently, Westinghouse reorganized its entire 13,600-man field sales organization along somewhat similar lines, in accord with what the company calls the "province concept." The company wants to be represented wherever possible by a "Mr. Westinghouse" rather than by a confusing bevy of different salesmen from various production divisions. (Significantly, in reorganizing, Westinghouse also seized the opportunity to put more salesmen in jobs where they actually meet customers and eliminated virtually an entire "staff" layer of some 104 sales managers who never called on customers).

The same kind of reorganization has gone on in scores of companies in such diverse fields as motor trucks and optical equipment. At American Optical Co., for example, salesmen who used to be product specialists now sell a line that includes every piece of furniture and equipment for the doctor's office, from lenses to tables.

Thus the kind of man needed for this new kind of sales job has to be a generalist. The trend is away from the "sales engineer," the technically trained salesman, of a few years ago. His successor is a man capable of absorbing stacks of information churned out by the marketing department, and of applying it to his customers' problems. He goes forth armed with a tremendous amount of data on his customers' needs, their products, their corporate organizations, and their supply and delivery schedules.

He is also a man with more executive ability than the salesman of yesterday. A Boston sales manager describes the new salesmen as simply "businessmen who travel." One Milwaukee executive notes that increasingly the new salesman is being given the authority and stature to make important decisions in the field without having to go back to corporate headquarters for an O.K. General Foods has adopted a new title of prestige for its senior salesmen, each of whom lives with one food-chain customer and attends to its needs. They are called "account executives" and they command the services of junior salesmen, who do the routine housekeeping chores of servicing the customers' stores.

In the new order of things there is obviously still a need for hard-selling, aggressive salesmen to open up new accounts, to introduce new and untried products, to sell the wares of new companies that have no national reputation. Since the service-oriented sales staff has turned away from this kind of pioneering effort, the door has been opened to a new kind of specialist, typified by a New York firm called the George N. Kahn Co. This company provides a crew of highly aggressive young salesmen who open up new territories for companies that don't want to retrain their own sales forces for such sporadically necessary missions. (Kahn is not a manufacturer's representative; it works on a flat-fee basis rather than a commission and, after pioneering the sale of a product, expects that the manufacturer will take it back for handling by his own sales staff.) There is now some thought in the top management of a number of companies that the way to deal with this basic problem is to set up special sections of sales staffs with the specific function of going after new business. Thus what has been commonly thought of as the primary function of all salesmen is now becoming the specialty of a few.

The Service Troops

The new salesman has a tremendous advantage over his predecessors. Not only does he have access to much more information about his customers, but he is also backed up by formidable technical and other kinds of assistance. For example, in reshaping its inorganic-chemical sales recently, FMC Corp. (formerly Food Machinery & Chemical Corp.) has beefed up the number of its technical people directly behind the salesmen by some 20 per cent. The present ratio: one technical man to every four salesmen. The great pioneer in this development was du Pont, which years ago saw the close connection between selling and customer service. Today, at Chestnut Run, outside Wilmington, du Pont has an impressive $20-million, campus-like complex of laboratories and workshops, employing 1,700 scientists, technicians, and others devoted to providing sales literature, solving technical problems, providing all kinds of services for customers or potential buyers of du Pont products, and otherwise aiding the sales effort. Companies selling all kinds of goods have developed similar assistance, though, naturally, the more complex the technology, the more elaborate the technical backup.

The development of sophisticated electronic data-processing systems, which was described earlier in this series, is revolutionizing inventory handling, ordering, warehousing, and other physical aspects of marketing. This, in turn, relieves the salesman of a great deal of detail that used to absorb valuable hours of his time—writing up orders and reports, checking whether goods are available and how soon they can be delivered, and performing other niggling drudgery.

At the same time, the computer also introduces an element of impersonality in the relations between a seller and a buyer. Much of today's ordering of goods and materials, from packaged foods to industrial chemicals, is done, as it were, by a computer, which tells the buyer when to reorder; the transaction is handled routinely and a salesman never enters into it. This disencumbering of the salesman releases him to function on a new level of performance, to use his time more creatively. At Allis-Chalmers, which has just set up a department of marketing, an executive says, "Now our salespeople won't get bogged down in a lot of detail that goes hand in hand with selling, like the preparation of presentations, charts, convention exhibits, and whatnot. We'll do all the work, including the training of salesmen, in cooperation with company divisions."

"You Lose One of the Big Babies . . . "

The rise of the new salesman is the result of changes in the marketplace that have drastically altered the relationship of buyer to seller. One of the most significant developments has been the growing importance of the big customer. In almost every line of business, fewer and bigger customers are responsible for an increasingly large part of any given company's sales. Twenty-five years ago, when independent grocers were an important factor in food retailing, food processors did the bulk of their business with thousands upon thousands of chains and stores. Today, with the concentration of business in the hands of a relatively few big chains, some 300 buying offices throughout the U.S. account for 80 per cent of all food bought at wholesale. Preoccupation with the "key customer" affects every industry, from steel to office supplies. Sighs an officer of the Acme Chemical Co. in Milwaukee, "You lose one of the big babies and you're in trouble."

This whole trend is building up momentum as smaller buyers band together to increase their purchasing power and efficiency by buying cooperatively. It affects suppliers of school equipment, for example, because schools are consolidating on a county basis. Independent hardware stores and even hospitals are doing it.

How this has affected the food business has been fully explored in a new book with a provocative title, *The Vanishing Salesman*, by E. B. Weiss, a New York marketing specialist in the consumer-goods field. Actually, Weiss does not believe that the salesman is vanishing; his point is that the shift to the service-oriented sales function has so greatly altered the nature of personal selling that companies are faced with entirely new conditions in the hiring, training, and organization of salesmen. Weiss also notes that as retail food chains have become bigger and bigger, and their purchases have reached stupendous volume, the position of the individual buyer, once regarded as the salesman's opposite number, has greatly diminished. The buyer in a food chain used to be an important figure; he made the decisions on what the chain was going to buy. Now his power has been usurped by buying committees. The buyer has become merely a technician who interviews the salesmen from the food processor and passes on his findings to his superiors. Says Weiss: "Members of the buying committee tend not to be buying specialists. Moreover, they made decisions covering the entire range of merchandise inventoried by the organization. Since they tend to be at executive levels considerably higher than that of the buyer who appears before them, they are more apt to depend on their own judgment than that of the buyer. And, by the same token, the buyer is not apt to put up much of a battle . . . In buying committee sessions, it is presumably the majority that rules. But since it is traditional in large organizations for so many committee members to vote with the head of the table, the majority rule prevails more in theory than in fact."

So the man that the seller must get to is the man at the head of the table. And this is true not only in the food field. Throughout U.S. industry, key buying power has steadily risen up through the corporate structure to higher echelons of authority. In industrial selling, an increasing number of purchasing decisions tend to involve bigger and bigger outlays of capital. In large part this is the result of the rise of what is now commonly called *systems selling*. Instead of buying components from many suppliers, a company often buys a whole integrated system, be it a system for heating and air conditioning, protecting a plant from theft and fire, automating a production line, or handling materials. As technology becomes more complex, users, intent on eliminating technical headaches, are ever more anxious to buy such systems, while suppliers, intent on greater profit, are ever more anxious to design and sell a whole package. Naturally, the final approval for such an expenditure or commitment moves up the line, from the plant superintendent or manager, to the corporate controller or treasurer, perhaps all the way to the president or board chairman.

"The President's Project"

Not only has this created the need for salesmen with sufficient stature to talk to the customer's top management, but it has also drawn top executives more directly into the selling act. In company after company, higher officials now make a very determined effort to get out in the field and call on the big customers, and even to do considerable pioneer work with potential customers. This kind of thing, of course, is not new. Many companies were built by star salesmen at the top, a very good example being the late Thomas J. Watson Sr. at I.B.M. ("What my father used to do when people began to talk about the great complexity of the products," says Tom Watson Jr., the present head of the company, "would be to sweep his hand and say, 'It's all so simple. All it does is add, subtract, and multiply!' ") And in industries where enormous capital investment is required, such as the utility business, intimate and continued contact between seller and buyer at a high level has always been important. But now personal selling by top executives is becoming much more common. Raytheon, for example, has divided up its list of big customers among managers and officers of the company, and assigned each the responsibility of keeping in touch with a few accounts, with a view to bolstering the salesman's efforts.

General Foods was one of the pioneers in this. When Charles Mortimer was president of the company, he started "The President's Project," a series of meetings with customers all over the country. "In the beginning the meetings started out 100 per cent social," explains Wayne Marks, now president of the company. "They were strictly for pleasure—and we invited more than one customer to a meeting. But we found that nothing *happened*. Except that we got acquainted. We didn't find out what to improve in our business operation. So the format was quickly changed."

Now Marks's office sets up his customer-visiting schedule at least a month in advance. The customer is requested to have all his key people at the meeting, and several weeks before the encounter, G.F. sends along a "questionnaire" to elicit comments on G.F.'s performance and suggestions for items to dicuss. In the past eighteen months Marks, accompanied by a team of executives and salesmen, has visited fifty-four customers throughout the U.S.

Marks has found the customer "avid" for this kind of contact. Not only does G.F. come out of these encounters (some of them lasting for five or six hours over dinner and drinks) with a fuller idea of what it should be doing—but the customers learn a great deal about their own organizations that they weren't aware of. Says Marks: "Many a meeting, at the end the boss man will say, 'Why don't *we* go out and find out what's happening in our own stores' At the end of a recent meeting the top man told me, 'I've been frank with you and told you what I don't like about your operations. Would you be willing to report back to us on what you think of us?'"

The "Sellingest" Firm

Personal selling is now a company-wide endeavor, and the contact with the customer takes place at many levels in an organized, formal way. The best illustration of how this has changed fundamentally the relations between buyer and seller is offered by National Cash Register, long known as perhaps the "sellingest" firm in the country. N.C.R.'s founder, the late John H. Patterson, has been called the father of many of the standard techniques of modern selling. He established the first formal training courses for salesmen, the first yearly sales quotas, the first guaranteed sales territories for salesmen, the first annual sales convention. Patterson's earlier sales methods were comparatively crude; cash registers were sold to storekeepers by appealing to their fear that dishonest clerks were pocketing money out of the till. But over the years the company refined its appeals, and forty years ago, when it began selling accounting machines, it even evolved a primitive kind of systems selling. But its big leap came about five years ago when the company introduced, somewhat belatedly as compared with the competition, its first electronic computer.

N.C.R. had to set up a whole new sales force for the computer, and in doing so it made a profound discovery: it was not easy to make a salesman of accounting machinery into a computer salesman. Says one N.C.R. senior salesman: "It was the death of salesmen like Willy Loman. At N.C.R. a few were left behind. They couldn't make the switch. It wasn't that they were too old—some were in their forties. But men's intellectual capabilities get set at various ages, and some *were* too old at that age." The company also found that it had to alter its time-honored compensation system. Normally, the N.C.R. salesman collects an advance that is charged against the commission he makes on his sales. Says marketing director Harry Keesecker, "Computer selling is still incentive selling, but due to the kind of product—sometimes the long time between sales—we have to compensate the salesmen by salary plus commission."

At the same time N.C.R. set up an elaborate organization to give the salesmen technical support. This now includes 325 mathematicians and technical people; the number has doubled in size in the past twelve months. They develop manuals and presentations, help the customer define his problems, train his computer operators for him, set up his E.D.P. system, and produce the programming for it. The support organization also trains the computer salesman, a departure for N.C.R., which years ago built its whole sales-training program around the use of experienced salesmen, borrowed from the field, as instructors. (The total computer sales and support staff numbers about 500 people, as against 2,100 in accounting machines, but the company is supplementing the small computer force by training as many of the accounting-machine men as possible to sell both kinds of equipment.)

The Willy Lomans Are No Longer Feasible

The difference between the old and new eras at N.C.R.—and in salesmanship in general—is dramatically illustrated by the story of how the company landed a rather sensational contract for the sale of a computer to the Dime Savings Bank of Brooklyn, New York, the country's second-largest mutual savings bank. The bank and the company had longstanding ties dating back to 1929, when the Dime bought its first N.C.R. posting machines for the tellers' windows. In subsequent decades the bank bought other N.C.R. equipment. In those years the chief link between the two was an N.C.R. salesman, Anthony de Florio, now district manager of sales for accounting and computer systems, and Karl Stad, who is now vice president of methods and systems at the Dime. The relationship was a cordial one, and N.C.R., which is mainly known for its experience in retailing and banking, was solidly in with the Dime.

In the late 1950s, however, there was a sudden change in the old easygoing ways. The bank decided, in 1957, that it was time to think about tying its entire bookkeeping operations into a computer to keep up with its bounding growth, and Stad was told to set up a task force to study the entire field and to recommend the "ideal" system. De Florio observes, "This was the beginning of group selling. The salesman had to understand the problems and systems of the customer. The staff at the bank had to define what was required. And we at N.C.R. had to be sure that the bank wasn't running away from us in know-how." (To N.C.R., as to many another company, the growing sophistication of the buyer has become an important factor to reckon with.) N.C.R. also had to reckon with competition; every other computer manufacturer came in for the kill at Dime. For the next two years Stad and his team studied the field and enlarged their expertise. By 1959 they had winnowed the choice down to four systems, including N.C.R.'s, and asked the competitors for feasibility studies. (Says de Florio: "By the time you get to feasibility studies, the Willy Lomans are no longer feasible.")

Now the contacts between the company and the bank multiplied. N.C.R. sent teams of technical people from Dayton headquarters to confer with Stad—they submitted a technical proposal two inches thick—and Stad went out to Dayton to talk to N.C.R.'s research people. He was put up at N.C.R.'s plush Moraine Farm, the estate of a former board chairman, which the company now uses to entertain groups of customers and potential customers. (Like du Pont and other companies, N.C.R. uses its factories and laboratories as a sales showcase.) By the end of 1959, Stad decided that computer, N.C.R.'s 304 then just being delivered to the first purchasers, was the one for the Dime.

Thereupon the Dime's board of trustees decided that Stad's decision ought to be second-guessed by an independent consultant in the electronic data-processing field. This, of course, opened up the whole matter again, and brought the competitors back in. Fortunately for N.C.R., the consultant confirmed the decision, and the affair between the bank and the company again resumed, in a deliberate and measured way. The Dime's board selected a committee of three trustees to study the proposal. They went out to Dayton—staying at an even more posh N.C.R. guest house, the old home of Orville Wright—and they talked with everyone from technicians to N.C.R.'s president, R. S. Oelman, and its then board chairman, S. C. Allyn. On the way back in the plane, the trustees decided to sign with N.C.R. It was an $800,000 decision, and it was a key one not only to the bank but to N.C.R., which closed some other bank contracts on the strength of the Dime's decision.

N.C.R. was in the middle of a training program for the Dime's employees when, early in 1960, a crisis arose. N.C.R.'s technicians reached the chilling conclusion that the 304 computer would not have the capacity to do what the Dime eventually would require—i.e., a direct linkage from the posting machines at the tellers' windows to the computer without the intermediate use of tabulating equipment. The next model in the design stage, the 315 random-access computer, would do the job—but not the 304. De Florio had to come clean with the bank. "I called up Karl and said, 'Let's have lunch at the Brooklyn Club,' " recalls de Florio, still wincing at the ensuing conversation. De Florio offered to tear up the contract for the 304. The Dime's board accepted the proposal, and the whole computer question was back in the soup again.

Rival manufacturers had another chance to make presentations, and N.C.R. had to start all over again selling its 315 model, then two years from delivery. De Florio kept pounding on one main point: the bank already was using N.C.R. machines at its windows, and any company that finally got the computer contract would have to tie in to N.C.R.'s equipment. In the end the argument prevailed; Stad recommended the 315 computer on the grounds that it would be "just as good" as other computers—though no better—and that N.C.R. had "window experience." Along with the computer, the bank also agreed to use other N.C.R. equipment in its integrated system, so the total package came to $2 million. Says de Florio, looking back on the whole transaction, "In this kind of selling you can't see everything you buy. A lot has to be bought on faith. Therefore a company likes to work with big companies. Come hell or high water, they have to deliver."

One of N.C.R.'s brightest and most successful young computer salesmen recently expanded this doctrine. "A salesman is important," he remarked, "because the policy makers today come from a previous generation of doing business. They don't have the technical equipment necessary to make a decision about a computer that requires technical sophistication. So the salesman has to take the language of the computer man and turn it into language his customer understands. I used to think that those decisions would be made on a scientific basis—but it's a gross act of faith." The salesman's job, he said, is "to create an environment in which an act of faith can take place."

The "Foot Soldiers" Need Upgrading

There is doubtless still plenty of faith in sales transactions. But as the Dime Savings Bank affair shows, there is a great deal more. And this is the fact that salesmen do not seem to realize when they talk about their jobs. They are still trained to have a kind of emotionalism about their craft, and they carry with them a heavy load of outworn notions about their role. They view selling as both warfare and love, hostility and benevolence. They see themselves as "the men on the firing line," and "the foot soldiers of democracy." The combative nature of selling is stressed in almost every book on the subject, as in one of the most famous and widely sold of all books on selling, *Open the Mind and Close the Sale*, by John M. Wilson, who recently retired as N.C.R.'s sales manager. Wilson speaks of the "tension in every buyer-seller relationship," of the "challenge" in each encounter, of the need for "handling" the customer—though, of course, "in the way he wants to be handled."

This lag in the recognition of what has happened to selling is harmful, because the sales profession is still held in low esteem by the public. Just how low was indicated recently in a survey by *Sales Management* magazine of college students and their attitude toward selling. Selling ranked a very poor fourth, after teaching, law, and medicine, as a choice for a career. Only 6 per cent of the students favored it. (Of seventy-one students whose fathers are in sales, only *five* wanted to go into selling.)

The students did not particularly object to the working conditions in selling; relatively few said they were put off by too much traveling, for example. Nor did many feel that the financial reward was inadequate. The chief objections to a selling career (some even denied that selling *is* a career) were these: "I don't want to force people to buy things they don't need." "Job security is poor." "I'm not extrovert enough." "Selling has no prestige."

One student unwittingly put his finger on the ironic predicament business faces. He remarked that selling simply does not require "a college education or intelligence." The main feature of the new kind of personal selling, of course, is that it does require men who are able and intelligent; the new salesmen, quite obviously, must be recruited from among the better college graduates. But how are they going to be recruited if the better college graduates think selling is beneath them? The experience of Scott Paper illustrates the difficulties business has in luring these men into selling. The company prides itself on the fact that 95 per cent of its sales staff are college graduates. Each year, to keep the staff replenished, it interviews some 2,000 students, invites about 100 of these men to visit its Philadelphia headquarters, makes offers to about seventy-five—and lands thirty-five or forty of them.

The trouble is that business has signally failed to get across the idea that there has been a tremendous change in selling. (The *Sales Management* poll shows that this generation of students has not grasped one of the simplest and most fundamental changes—i.e., that by and large salesmen are no longer paid on commission but are salaried.) Business has a massive educational job to do. Perhaps as a start it might throw away a lot of the old inspirational literature on selling and let the facts of the new situation do the inspiring.

LEARNING REVIEW

Questions:

1. The ____________ concept has a strong effect on the structure of sales forces.

2. Buyers today are likely to be ____________ who interview salesmen and pass their findings on to their ____________.

3. The lag in recognition of what has happened to salesmen is dangerous, because

the sales profession still has ____________ in the eyes of the public and a serious shortage of sales professionals may continue if new persons are not attracted to these careers.

Answers:

1. marketing; 2. technicians, superiors; 3. low esteem

Retrospective Comment by Harry A. Lipson*

Carl Rieser in this classic article identified the trend of the times. He managed to give greater clarity and depth to his presentation concerning the growing importance of the marketing and sales function than many of his contemporaries.

Other writers were, however, addressing themselves to the same subject. In "Gearing Up for the Hard Sell,"[1] the author identified the increased emphasis on marketing research, increased status by top salespersons, a shift from general to specialized sales, the increased use of staff specialists, and the shift from geographic territories to a type of industry coverage. At about the same time the article "What's Happened to Salesmanship" reported on the changing economic and business conditions requiring a new breed of salesman.[2]

More recent articles have described the changing emphasis in sales management in the decade of the 1970s. Leslie Dawson in "Towards a New Concept of Sales Management" sees three changes from the previous to the present decade: (1) business response to perceived dominant environmental conditions shifting from a marketing orientation to a human orientation; (2) emphasis in management's conception of the sales job shifting from professionalism to personal fulfillment; and (3) emphasis in sales management from strategies and profits to total human resource development.[3]

Benson Shapiro, in a more recent *Harvard Business Review* article, has added a new dimension to the discussion. He takes the view that the real focus of management should be upon customers rather than the salesman. He argues that management should be trying to generate greater profits and return on investment through determining the role of personal selling in the company's marketing strategy. Changes suggested include a more careful assigning of customers and prospects, products, territories, and selling tasks; giving more attention to developing and maintaining account relationships; and continuous auditing of the fixed and variable costs and benefits received from different kinds of selling efforts.[4]

It remains to be seen whether this approach will significantly change the status of the salesperson in the eves of the public. Perhaps this will not occur until the public recognizes that the type of salesman described in Rieser's article is an important if not senior corporate executive—and until the esteem of corporate executives also rises.

* Dr. Lipson is currently Board of Visitors Research Professor and Professor of Marketing at The University of Alabama.

1. *Conference Board Business Record* (June 1961), pp. 34–44.
2. *Sales Management* (April 7, 1961), pp. 37–39.
3. *Journal of Marketing* (April 1970), pp. 33–38.
4. "Manage the Customer, Not Just the Sales Force," *Harvard Business Review* (September-October 1974), pp. 127–137.

PART 7
The Pricing Variable of the Marketing Mix

This is pricing strategy?

Examples of successful pricing strategy may be drawn from various sources. A favorite illustration of the editor's was told by Harry Lipson, one of the surrogate authors in the previous section. The story goes like this. . . .

"Lost money on every sale. . . . had good volume, however!"

Two discount drug stores faced one another on opposite sides of the street. Both had the price policy that *we have the lowest prices in town*, and both had lunch counters. One morning one of the managers placed a sign outside announcing breakfast for only 79¢. The competitor retaliated by posting a sign announcing breakfast for 69¢. The prices continued to be marked down that morning to 59¢, 49¢, 39¢, and the only reason they did not go lower was that it was well past the time of day for offering breakfast at all. But that afternoon the price competition resumed as the manager across the street brought out his sign advertising ice cream sundaes at 35¢. The price was quickly bested by his competition with sundaes at 30¢. Again the prices dropped rather quickly to 25¢, 20¢, 15¢, 10¢, and 5¢. At this point price strategy across the street underwent a drastic change. It was a warm bright spring day and the sidewalks were beginning to fill with children on their way home from school. Now armed with nickels rather than sign paint, the momentarily undersold manager placed himself beside his competitor's *5¢* sign and offered every child who passed a free nickel, at the same time directing them into the competitor's store!

There's a better way

John Udell's article puts the above mania for price-leadership-into-oblivion in its proper perspective as he points out how pricing freedom and customer demand are generated through product/customer research. Joel Dean discusses "Techniques for Pricing New Products and Services;" the emphasis here is on the manner in which pricing strategy might change as a newly introduced product progresses through its life cycle. Alfred Oxenfeldt shows a way to arrive at the approximate price by dividing the decision into six successive stages, each one narrowing the alternatives available from the previous stage.

30

How Important Is Pricing in Competitive Strategy?

Jon G. Udell

PREVIEW

I. A study of twelve general policy areas of marketing management showed that product research and development is more important than pricing.
   A. The competitive activities relating to the product and to sales effort were selected as most important to success.
   B. The lack of emphasis on pricing may be accounted for by three factors:
      1. Supply generally exceeds demand.
      2. Customers today are interested in more than price.
      3. A manufacturer obtains pricing freedom through product differentiation.

II. A breakdown of respondents by type of industry revealed some differences.
   A. Producers of industrial goods stressed the product facet of competitive strategy.
   B. Manufacturers of consumer goods placed a much greater emphasis on the sales effort facet of competitive strategy.

In an effort to ascertain the key elements of business success in the market place, the author conducted a study among 200 producers of industrial and consumer goods. A sample of fairly well-known and successful manufacturing companies was selected from *Martindell's Manual of Excellent Management*. Listed are companies which are supposedly well managed, evaluated according to the criteria developed by the American Institute of

---

Jon G. Udell, "How Important Is Pricing in Competitive Strategy?" is reprinted by permission from the *Journal of Marketing*, published by the American Marketing Association (January 1964), pp. 44–48.

Management. The use of the manual seemed appropriate in that the two most heavily weighted criteria are sales vigor and management efficiency.

The present study attempted to answer the question: "What are the key policies and procedures common to successful marketing managements in various manufacturing industries?"

Management's interest in the study was reflected by a 75% response to a 4-page mail questionnaire. The first section of the questionnaire listed 12 general policy areas of marketing management—among them, sales research and sales planning, pricing, management of sales personnel, and product service. The respondent, usually the vice president in charge of marketing, was asked to select the five areas which he regarded as most vital in his company's marketing success.

Importance of Product Development

The results indicate that product research and development, selected by almost 80% of the respondents, is most important in modern-day competitive strategy. Four other policy areas, relating to either product or sales effort, were selected by more than half of the respondents. Table 1 presents a percentage analysis of the responses.

TABLE 1. How Management Ranks the Factors of Marketing Success

Rank	*Policy areas*	*% of firms selecting the policy area**
1	Product research and development	79
2	Sales research and sales planning	73
3	Management of sales personnel	59
4	Advertising and sales promotion	56
5	Product service	52
6	Pricing	50
7	Organizational structure	44
8	Distribution channels and their control	41
9	Marketing cost budgeting and control	17
10	Financing and credit	14
11	Transportation and storage	7
12	Public relations	7

*Based on a tabulation of 135 usable questionnaires. Percentages here are rounded.

It appears that business management did not agree with the economic views of the importance of pricing—one-half of the respondents did *not* select pricing as *one of the five* most important policy areas in their firm's marketing success.

Also, the two major facets of nonprice competition (product and sales effort) were subdivided into a number of policy areas; for example, sales effort was subdivided into sales research and sales planning, management of sales personnel, and advertising and sales promotion. In short, *the competitive activities relating to the product and to sales effort were selected as most important in the success of these firms*.

Pricing

The emphasis on product and sales effort does not imply that price is unimportant. Three factors probably account for the relatively low ranking of pricing:

1. In today's competitive economy, *supply*—or production capacity—*generally exceeds demand*; and, therefore, nearly all sellers are forced to be either completely competitive or almost collusive in their pricing. Because there may be little or no freedom for a company to deviate from the market price, heavy reliance must be placed on product differentiation and sales effort.

2. *The relatively well-to-do consumers of today are interested in more than just price*. They are interested in product quality, distinctiveness, style, and many other factors which lead to both physical and psychological satisfaction. Consumers not only can afford but want product differentiation and sales promotion. From them the consumer receives a great deal of psychological satisfaction and utility. It is only logical that consumer-oriented managements would choose to emphasize products and sales efforts in an attempt to satisfy consumer desires.

3. *It is through successful product differentiation that a manufacturer may obtain some pricing freedom*. Products known to be identical must be priced identically in the market place. A departure from identical prices would result in all patronage going to the seller or sellers with the lowest price.

Marketing Strategies According to Products and Customers

Economists have proposed several theories that give recognition to the nonprice factors of competitive strategy.[1] However, they have not credited the nature of the product and the characteristics of the buyers as the dominant factors in explaining how companies organize to market their products. Instead, the dominant factor is usually assumed to be the market structure of the industry (competitive, oligopolistic, or monopolistic).

A producer of machine tools would not be expected to compete in the same manner as a producer of perfume; and a comparison of the structures of the machine-tool and perfume industries would not explain the differences in their marketing strategies. *Common business sense would lead one to believe that a company's use of nonprice competitive strategy should vary according to the nature of a firm's product and the characteristics of the buyers for that product.*

Accordingly, the data were classified according to the respondents' type of industry: industrial goods, consumer durable goods, and consumer non-durable goods.

TABLE 2. Policy Areas Selected by Industrial Goods Producers

Policy areas	*% of firms selecting the policy area**
Product:	
Product research and development	79
Product service	79
Average product selection ratio	79
Sales efforts:	
Sales research and sales planning	63
Management of sales personnel	49
Advertising and sales promotion	37
Average sales efforts selection ratio	50
Pricing	47
Other areas:	
Organizational structure	50
Distribution channels and their control	34
Financing and credit	18
Marketing cost budgeting and control	12
Transportation and storage	9
Public relations	7

*Based on the questionnaires of 68 industrial goods producers. Percentages here are rounded.

Producers of Industrial Goods

The producers of industrial goods stressed the product facet of competitive strategy.

Two of the policy areas listed in the marketing management study pertain directly to the product—product research and development, and product service. (Product service refers to those activities performed by a manufacturer in the attempt to guarantee that a product gives satisfactory performance to its users.)

As shown in Table 2, both of these policy areas were selected by about 80% of the industrial users.

The policy areas relating to sales effort were relegated to a lesser role by the successful manufacturers of industrial goods. The average selection for the policy areas pertaining to sales effort was 50%, as compared with the average product selection of 80%.

The industrial-goods producers' primary emphasis on the product facet of marketing strategy was also emphasized in letters received from various respondents. A Pratt & Whitney Aircraft executive said: "Our two most valuable assets sales-wise are the technical excellence of our products, and our policy of rendering the best possible product service to our customers both before and after the sale."

Producers of Consumer Goods

The manufacturers of consumer goods placed a much greater emphasis on the sales effort facet of competitive strategy. This emphasis was especially great in the case of the firms producing nondurable goods.

TABLE 3. Policy Areas Selected by Consumer Goods Manufacturers

Policy areas	*Manufacturers of nondurable goods*	*Manufacturers of durable goods**
Sales efforts:		
Advertising and sales promotion	89	73
Management of sales personnel	64	91
Sales research and sales planning	82	73
Average sales efforts selection ratio	85	79
Product:		
Product research and development	83	75
Product service	14	36
Average product selection ratio	45	60
Pricing	50	46
Other areas:		
Distribution channels and their control	54	46
Organizational structure	39	27
Marketing cost budgeting and control	29	9
Financing and credit	11	9
Transportation and storage	4	9
Public relations	7	—

* Based on the questionnaires of 28 nondurable goods producers and 11 durable goods producers. Figures here are rounded.

As shown in Table 3, the nondurable goods producers had an average sales effort selection of 85%, as compared with an average product selection of 45%. Durable goods producers had an average sales efforts selection of 79%, as compared with the product selection of 60%.

The differences were accounted for by the low selection ratios for product service, in that most consumer goods manufacturers selected product research and development.

It is understandable that consumer-goods producers selected product research and development with such a high degree of frequency in light of their emphasis on sales efforts. It is less difficult to promote a differentiated product than it is to promote an undifferentiated product.

Product research and development are important, but sales efforts are *most* important to manufacturers of consumer goods.

Product research and development was not broken down into research related to physical (real) product improvement and research related to psychological (fancied) product improvement. It would be immaterial to the consumer-goods manufacturer if a product change were *real* or *fancied*, so long as the change was regarded as an improvement by his customers.

The second section of the questionnaire subdivided the general areas of policies and procedures into more specific categories of business activities. When product research and development was subdivided into three categories of activities, the following selections were obtained:

	Manufacturers of		
	Industrial goods	*Consumer nondurables*	*Consumer durables*
Technical research and development	75	54	56
Marketing research related to new products	30	62	56
Product evaluation	16	19	22

As might be expected, the technical development of products was most emphasized by the industrial-goods producers, whereas marketing research related to new products was most emphasized by the consumer-goods producers.

This analysis indicated that all three groups of manufacturers—industrial, consumer durable, and consumer nondurable—stressed the nonprice facets of competitive strategy, and that *the relative emphasis on product and sales efforts varied according to the nature of the products and the characteristics of the buyers.*

To further test this proposition, the questionnaires were grouped according to specific industries. If the proposition were valid, there should have been a high degree of similarity in the marketing strategies of respondents of a specific industry. That is, the respondents of a given industry, producing similar products for like customers, should select similar policy areas as most important in their marketing success.

Here are three examples that demonstrate the validity of this proposition.

TABLE 4. Selection of Major Policy Areas Twelve Producers of Major Installations

Rank	*Policy areas*	*Selection ratio %*
1	Product research and development	100
2	Product service	100
3	Distribution channels and their control	67
4	Organizational structure	42
5	Management of sales personnel	42
6	Sales research and sales planning	42
7	Advertising and sales promotion	33
8	Pricing	25
9	Financing and credit	17
10	Public relations	17
11	Marketing cost budgeting and control	8
12	Transportation and storage	8

Case No. 1—Capital Goods Industry

The most homogeneous grouping of companies with similar products and similar customers consisted of 12 producers of major installations—capital goods. As Table 4 illustrates, *all 12 producers selected product research and development and product service*.

Distribution channels and their control was selected by 8 of the 12 producers. This may be because sales servicing before and after is often performed by the distributors of capital goods.

The 100% selection for product research and development and for product service were high. Statistically one would expect such an occurrence only twice in 100,000 trials due to random sampling error.

Assuming that each policy area is actually of equal importance, there is a .00002 probability of getting a policy area with a 100% selection ratio due to random sampling error (binomial theorum used). The fact that *both* of the policy areas pertaining to product were selected by all 12 respondents provides further statistical proof that the selection ratios are *not* due to chance.

TABLE 5. Selection of Major Policy Areas by Eight Producers of Metals

Rank	*Policy areas*	*Selection ratio %*
1	Product service	100
2	Product research and development	75
3	Sales research and sales planning	63
4	Pricing	63
5	Distribution channels and their control	50
6	Management of sales personnel	38
7	Organizational structure	25
8	Transportation and storage	25
9	Financing and credit	25
10	Public relations	13
11	Advertising and sales promotion	13
12	Marketing cost budgeting and control	—

Case No. 2—Metals Industry

Another grouping of companies was comprised of producers of steel, zinc, aluminum, and other processed metals. The companies have similar markets and similar products, in that their products are the raw materials for the manufacture of other goods.

It would be anticipated that the product facet of competition would have prevailed in the competitive strategies of these companies; and Table 5 shows that this was true.

TABLE 6. Selection of Major Policy Areas by Chemical and Drug Producers

Policy areas	*Selection ratio of industrial chemical producers (3)*		*Selection ratio of consumer chemical producers (3)*	
Product research and development	100		100	
Product service	67		—	
Average product selection ratio		83		50
Advertising and sales promotions	—		100	
Sales research and sales planning	100		67	
Management of sales personnel	33		67	
Average sales efforts selection ratio		44		78

Case No. 3—Chemical Industry

A third grouping of companies highlights the importance of customers in determining marketing strategy. Of the six chemical manufacturers participating in the study, three produced for the consumer market and three for the industrial market.

All six firms responded by selecting product research and development, but at this point the similarities ceased.

As shown in Table 6, the average product selection ratio of the industrial chemical manufacturers was much higher than that of the consumer chemical manufacturers. The average sales effort selection ratio of the consumer products manufacturers was higher than that of the industrial producers.

How Important Is Size?

To ascertain the influence of company size on management's selection of the facets of marketing strategy, the responses were classified according to the sales volume of each company: less than $50 million, $50 to $100 million, $100 to $500 million, and over $500 million.

The differences among the selection ratios of the various size classifications were so small that none was found to be statistically significant. Apparently size had little influence on the relative importance that a company attached to the various facets of its marketing mix.

In Conclusion

The ranking method provided only a rough measure of the importance of price, product, and sales efforts; *but it was a measurement.*

As for another possible limitation—lack of differentiation between responses related to "what is" and what the respondents felt "should be"—one might ask, "Who is better qualified to select the most important areas of a successful firm's marketing program than the firm's marketing management?"

The study reported illustrates two major points:

1. In today's market, the nonprice facets of competition occupy a prominent role.
2. The explanation of the roles of nonprice competitive facets does *not* lie solely in the structure of the industry (or the size of the firm), but instead primarily in the nature of the product and its market.

The importance of the nonprice aspects of the marketing mix and the variations among industries can be explained by the nature of today's economy. To compete successfully in a setting characterized by oligopolistic firms offering rival products to a customer-dominated market, the firm must be customer-oriented. In appealing to the customer, management finds success in utilizing the nonprice facets of competitive activity, adjusting its strategy to the needs and desires of the buyer.

NOTES

1. Lawrence Abbott, *Quality and Competition* (New York: Columbia University Press, 1951); Hans Brems, "The Interdependence of Quality Variations, Selling Effort and Price," *Quarterly Journal of Economics*, Vol. 62 (May 1948), pp. 418–440; C. A. Stocking, "Advertising and Economic Theory," *American Economic Review*, Vol. 21 (March, 1931), pp. 43–55.

LEARNING REVIEW

Questions:

1. The study revealed that the relative emphasis on product and sales effort varied according to the nature of the ____________ and the characteristics of the ____________.

2. Product research and development are important, but ____________ are recognized as most important by manufacturers of consumer goods.

3. Three factors that might account for the low ranking of pricing among the 200 producers Udell studied were: a) ____________
b) ____________
and c) ____________
____________.

Answers:

1. products, buyers; 2. sales efforts; 3. a) supply generally exceeds demand; b) consumers are interested in more than price; c) product differentiation may give the manufacturer pricing freedom

---

Retrospective Comment

The findings concerning the relative importance of pricing and the other elements of competitive strategy were substantiated and advanced by a more recent study of 485 highly successful products. The latter study used a scaling device with 100 points representing the total importance of all elements of marketing and competitive strategy. Pricing received an average of only 18.4 points. Sales efforts and marketing communications were most important in the sales and profitability of successful products, being followed by product development and service, pricing, and distribution, in that order.

By a wide margin, the most important of 20 specific marketing activities were sales management and personal selling. These selling activities were especially important among industrial goods producers. Product service and technical research and development were second and third in importance among the industrial goods.

Within the pricing arena, pricing according to the competitive level was the most important pricing policy for all types of producers other than aerospace and defense contractors. Cost-plus-pricing was second in importance.

In the recent study, the importance of each marketing activity was analyzed by industry classification. More importantly, the study related marketing strategies to the behavioral characteristics of the market and the product and, in so doing, provided a conceptual foundation for the design of effective marketing strategies. The findings, plus discussions of such topics as the role of science and theory in business, the impact of a dynamic environment on marketing, a decision model for non-price strategy, and successful marketing strategies in all major industries are presented in my book, *Successful Marketing Strategies in American Industry*. In the book I also examine the relationship between marketing strategy and share of market, corporate size, and marketing costs.

31

Techniques for Pricing New Products and Services

Joel Dean

PREVIEW

I. A new product goes through different stages in its life cycle, and appropriate pricing reflects the development of three different aspects of maturity:
   A. *Technical maturity* is indicated by declining rate of product development, uniformity of competing brands, and increasing stability of manufacturing processes.
   B. *Market maturity* is indicated by consumer acceptance of the basic service idea and by enough consumer familiarity with the product to compare brands competently.
   C. *Competitive maturity* is indicated by increasing stability of market shares and price factors.

II. Pricing is influenced by several factors:
   A. The competition a product faces, or the lack of it, has a strong effect on pricing.
   B. In pricing, the buyer's viewpoint is controlling.
      1. The buyers' alternatives to a new product must be carefully weighed.
      2. The value to the customer of the innovational superiority of the new product is the most challenging problem.
      3. Rate-of-return pricing looks at a price through the investment eyes of the customer.
   C. Three kinds of cost must be considered:
      1. The cost to the buyer should be such as to make the product attractive from an economic standpoint.

Joel Dean, "Techniques for Pricing New Products and Services," is reprinted by permission from Victor Buell (editor) *Handbook of Modern Marketing* (New York: McGraw-Hill Book Co., Inc., 1970), pp. 5-51–5-61.

2. Competitors' costs may determine their staying power and ability to defend retaliation pricing.
3. Producer's costs determine whether a product should ever be produced, and also set a price floor.

III. A business should choose a marketing strategy consistent with the corporate goals of maximizing profit in the long-run.
   A. There are different strategies for pricing so as to maximize long-run profit.
      1. *Skimming pricing* calls for high prices and large promotional expenditure early in market development, with lower prices later.
      2. *Penetration pricing* uses low prices as an entering wedge to get into mass markets early.
   B. Promotion and distribution are closely related to pricing in determining the best way to maximize profits.

Pricing a new product or service is one of the most important and puzzling of marketing problems. The high proportion of new products which fail in the marketplace is partly due to the difficulty of pricing them correctly.

A *new* product (or service)[1] is here defined as one which incorporates a major innovation. It is new to the world, not just new to the company. This means that its market is, at the outset, ill defined. Potential applications cannot be foreseen with precision. Pricing decisions usually have to be made with little knowledge and with wide margins of error in the forecasts of demand, cost, and competitors' capabilities.

This section deals with the price level, not the price structure; e.g., the average price per ton-mile of air freight, not the structure of price differentials by size of shipment, density, distance, etc.

The difficulty of pricing new products is enhanced by the dynamic deterioration of the competitive status of most new products, which is speeded by today's high rate of innovation. This makes the evolution of a new product's economic status a strategic consideration in practical pricing.

Dynamic Competitive Setting

A product which is new to the world, as opposed to being merely new to the company, passes through distinctive competitive stages in its life cycle. The appropriate pricing policy is likely to be different for each stage.

New products have a protected distinctiveness which is doomed to progressive degeneration from competitive inroads. As new competitors enter the field and innovations narrow the gap of distinctiveness between the product and its substitutes, the seller's zone of pricing discretion narrows. His distinctive "specialty" fades into a pedestrian "commodity" which is so little differentiated from other products that the seller has limited independence in pricing, even if rivals are few.

Throughout the cycle, continual changes occur in promotional and price elasticity and in costs of production and distribution. These changes call for adjustments in price policy.

Appropriate pricing over the cycle depends on the development of three different aspects of maturity which usually move in approximately parallel time paths: (1) *technical maturity*, indicated by declining rate of product development, increasing uniformity of competing brands, and increasing stability of manufacturing processes and knowledge about them; (2) *market maturity*, indicated by consumer acceptance of the basic service idea, by widespread belief that the products of most manufacturers will perform satisfactorily, and by enough familiarity and sophistication to permit consumers to compare brands competently; and (3) *competitive maturity*, indicated by increasing stability of market shares and price structures.

The rate at which the cycle of degeneration progresses varies widely among products. What are the factors that set its pace? An overriding determinant is technical—the extent to which the economic environment must be reorganized to use the innovation effectively. The scale of plant investment and technical reaction called forth by telephone, electric power, the automobile, or the jet airplane makes for a long gestation period as compared with even such major innovations as cellophane or frozen foods. Development comes fastest when the new gadget fills a new vacuum.

Monopoly Pricing

New product pricing, if the product is truly novel, is in essence monopoly pricing. Stark monopoly pricing, which is the core of new product pricing, considers only what the traffic will bear—the price which will maximize profits, taking into account the price sensitivity of demand and the incremental promotional and production cost of the seller. What the product is worth to the buyer, not what it costs the seller, is the controlling consideration.

The competitive setting of the new product has, however, peculiar features that modify monopoly pricing. The monopoly power of the new product is (1) restricted (i.e., buyers have alternatives in the form of products that compete indirectly), (2) ephemeral (i.e., subject to inevitable erosion by imitation and obsolescence), and (3) controllable (i.e., capable of some degree of expansion and prolongation by actions of the seller).

For example, Quanta Welding's new diffusion bonding system, based on a millisecond-shaped power pulse, is a patented monopoly. But its pricing power is restricted by alternatives. For supersonic aircraft, these are resistance-welding or riveting, which are candidate pricing benchmarks. The market power of Quanta's superior metals-joining process will be eventually eroded. Solid-state devices may make obsolete the mercury vapor tube that supplies the controllable massive pulses of electrical energy on which the process depends. Penetration pricing might discourage this competitive entry.

These peculiarities of the new-product monopoly introduce dynamism and uncertainty which call for dynamic modifications of monopoly pricing. Exampies include:

1. Substitute ways to get the service. These set limits on the market power of a new product and hence serve as benchmarks for pricing it.

2. The perishability of the new product's wanted distinctiveness. This makes the timing of price, promotion, and capacity competition crucial (e.g., choice between skimming and penetration pricing).

3. The ability to influence the amount and the durability of the new product's market power some degree by specially planned pricing and promotion actions. This gives added weight to the effect of today's pricing upon tomorrow's demand.

Demand: Sensitivity of Volume to Price

Profitable monopoly pricing of a new product, even with these dynamic competitive modifications, requires an estimate of how price will affect sales. This relationship can be explored in two steps, by (1) finding what range of price will make the product economically attractive to buyers, and (2) estimating what sales volumes can be expected at various points in this price range.

Price Range

The price range is determined by the indirect competition of substitutes, which sets limits to the monopoly power of the new product. In this sense, no product is really new; the most novel product merely plugs an abnormally large gap in the chain of substitutes. This gap marks out the potential range of its price.

For industrial products, a relatively quick and cheap way to find this range is to "pick the brains" of professionals experienced in looking at comparative product performance in terms of buyers' cost and requirements—for example, distributors, prime contractors, and consulting engineers, as well as purchasing analysts and engineers of prospect companies.

For consumers' goods, different methods are needed. In guessing the price range of a radically novel product of small unit value, the concept of barter equivalent can be useful. For example, a manufacturer of paper specialties tests a dramatic new product this way: A wide variety of consumer products totally unlike the new product were purchased and spread out on a big table. Consumers selected the products they would swap for the new product.

Price-Volume Relationship

The effect of the price of the new product upon its volume of sales is the most important and most difficult estimate in pricing. We know in general that the lower the price, the greater the volume of sales and the faster its rate of growth. The air-freight growth rate is about 18 per cent; priced higher, it will grow more slowly. But to know the precise position and shape of the price-quantity demand schedule or how much faster sales will grow if the price is 20 percent lower is not possible. But we must estimate.

The best way to predict the effect of price on sales volume for a new product is by controlled experiments: offering it at several different prices in comparable test markets under realistic sales conditions. For example, frozen orange juice was thus tested at three prices. When test marketing is not feasible, another method is to broaden the study of the cost of buyers' alternatives and include forecasts of the sales volume of substitutes (and other indications of the volume to customers of different categories). This approach is most promising for industrial customers, because performance comparisons are more explicit and measurable and economics more completely controls purchases. When buyers' alternatives differ widely in service value, the difficulty of translating this disparity into superiority premiums adds to the imprecision of this method of estimating price-volume relationships.

Pricing Benchmarks

The buyers' viewpoint should be controlling in pricing. For every new product there are alternatives. Buyers' best alternatives are usually products already tested in the marketplace. The new product will, presumably, supply a superior solution to the problem of some categories of buyers. The superiority differential over existing products differs widely among new products. The degree of superiority of any one new product over its substitutes usually also differs widely as viewed by different buyers.

Buyers' Alternatives

The prospective buyer of any new product does have alternatives. These indirectly competitive products are the benchmark for his appraisal of the price-performance package of a new product. This comparison with existing products determines its relative attractiveness to potential buyers. Such an analysis of demand can be made in the following steps:

1. Determine the major uses for the new product. For each application, determine the product's performance characteristics.
2. For each important usage area, specify the products that are the buyer's best alternative to the new product. Determine the performance characteristics and requirements which buyers view as crucial in determining their product selection.
3. For each major use, determine how well the product's performance characteristics meet the requirements of customers compared with the performance of these buyers' alternative products.
4. Forecast the prices of alternative products in terms of transaction prices, adjusted for the impact of thc new product and translated into units of use. Estimate from the prices of these benchmark substitutes the alternative costs to the buyer per unit of the new product. Real transactions prices (after all discounts), rather than list prices, should be the benchmark in order to reflect marketplace realities. Prices should bc predicted, after the introduction of the new product, so as to reflect probable competitive adaptation to the new product. Where eventual displacement of existing substitutes appears likely, short-run incremental cost supplies a Jeremiah forecast of defender's pricing retaliation.
5. Estimate the superiority premium; i.e., price the performance differential in terms of what the superior solution supplied by the new product is worth to buyers of various categories.
6. Figure a "parity price" for the product relative to the buyer's best alternative product in each use, and do this for major categories of customers. Parity is a price which encompasses the premium a customer would be willing to pay for comparative superiority in performance characteristics.

Pricing the Superiority Differential

Determining this price premium over benchmark products which the new product's superiority will most profitably warrant is the most intricate and challenging problem of new-product pricing.

The value to the customer of the innovational superiority of the new product is surrounded by uncertainties: whether the product will work, whether it will attain its designed superiorities, what its reliability and durability performance will be, and how soon it in turn will become obsolete. These uncertainties influence the price a customer would pay and the promotional outlay that would be required to persuade him to buy. Thus, customers' uncertainties will cost the seller something, either in price or promotion.

In essence, the superiority premium requires translation of differential performance characteristics into dollars, based on value analysis from the buyer's viewpoint. The premium will differ among uses, among alternative products, and among categories of customers. For some, it will be negative. Unless it proves practical to segment the market by application and to have widely discriminatory prices, the new product is likely to be priced out of some markets.

A simplistic, single-point premium reflecting "what the product can command in the marketplace" will not do. The customer-response pattern that is needed is the relationship between (1) a series of prospective superiority premiums and (2) the corresponding potential volumes.

What matters is superiority as *buyers* value it, not superiority as calibrated by technicians' measurements or by the sellers' costs. This means that more and better promotion can raise the premium-volume schedule and make a higher superiority premium achieve the same sales volume or rate of sales growth as would a lower premium without the promotion. This premium-volume schedule will be kicked about by retaliatory pricing of displaceable substitutes as well as by the imitative and innovative new-product competition of rivals.

The optimizing premium—i.e., the price that would maximize profits in any specified time period—will depend upon future costs as well as upon the hazy and dynamic demand schedule. It will be hard to find. Uncertainty about the future thus makes the appropriate pricing strategy for the long run a matter of sophisticated judgment.

Rate-of-Return Pricing

Application of the principles of economic pricing is illustrated by rate-of-return pricing of new capital equipment. Industrial goods are sold to businessmen in their capacity as profit-makers. The technique is different for a producer's good (e.g., a truck) than for a customer's good (e.g., a sports car).

The difference is caused by the fact that the essential service purchased if a product is a producer's good is added profits. A product represents an investment by the customer. The test of whether or not this investment is a desirable one should be its profitability to the customer. The pricing guide that this suggests is rate of return on the capital a customer ties up by his investment in a product.

Rate of Return on Customer's Investment

Rate-of-return pricing looks at a price through the investment eyes of the customer. It recognizes that the upper limit is the price which will produce the minimum acceptable rate of return on the customer's investment. The added profits obtainable from the use of equipment differ among customers and among applications for the same customer.

Cutoff criteria of required return also differ, so prospective customers differ in the rate of return which will induce them to invest in a given product. Thus, the rate-of-return approach opens up a new kind of demand analysis for industrial goods. This analysis consists of inqury into (a) the costs to buyers from displaceable alternative ways to do the job; (b) the cost-saving and profit-producing capability of equipment in different applications and for different prospects; and (c) the capital budgeting policies of customers, with particular emphasis on their cost-of-capital and their minimum rate-of-return requirements.

The rate-of-return analysis just outlined is particularly useful in the pioneering stages of new products when the competition consists of only obsolescent ways of doing the job. At more mature stages in the life cycle of a new product, competitive imitation improves prospective customers' alternatives. These rival investment alternatives must then be taken explicitly into the analysis.

One way is to use a competitor's product as the benchmark in measuring the rate of return which a given product will produce for specified categories of prospects. The profitability from the product is measured in terms of its superiority over the best alternative new equipment offered by rivals rather than by its superiority over the customer's old equipment. Rate-of-return pricing translates this competitive superiority into dollars of added profit for the customer and relates this added profit to the added investment. In effect, one would say: "To be sure, buying my competitor's product will give you a 25 per cent rate of return, and that is better than keeping your old equipment; but buying *my* product will give you a 30 per cent rate of return." For each customer category, rate-of-return analysis reveals a price for a given product that makes it an irresistibly good investment to the customer in view of his alternatives and at the same time extracts from the customer all that can safely be demanded.

Investigation of (1) the productivity of the buyers' capital invested in your new product and (2) the required rate of return of prospective customers has proven a practical way to predict the demand for industrial goods. It must be coupled with forecasts of costs to find the immediately most profitable price, and with considerations of competitive strategy for the longer run.

The Role of Cost

To get maximum practical use from costs in new product pricing, three questions of theory must be answered: (1) Whose cost? (2) Which cost? and (3) What role? As to whose cost, three classes of costs are important: (1) those of prospective buyers, (2) those of existent and potential competitors, and (3) those of the producer of the new product. Cost should play a different role for each of the three, and the pertinent concept of cost will differ accordingly.

Buyers' Cost

How should costs of prospective customers be used in setting the price of a new product? By applying value analysis to prices and performance of alternative products to find the superiority premium that will make the new product attractive from an economic standpoint to buyers of specified categories. Rate-of-return pricing of capital goods illustrates this buyer's-cost approach, which is applicable in principle to all new products.

Competitors' Costs

Competitors' costs are usually the crucial estimate in appraisal of competitors' capabilities.

Costs of two kinds of competitive products can be helpful. The first kind are products already in the marketplace. The objectives are to estimate (1) their staying power and (2) the floor of retaliation pricing. For the first objective, the pertinent cost concept is the competitor's long-run incremental cost. For the second, his short-run incremental cost.

The second kind is the unborn competing product that could blight a new product's future or eventually displace it. Forecasts of competitors' costs for such products can help assess this crucial dimension of capability of prospective competitors and estimate the effectiveness of a strategy of pricing the new product so as to discourage entry. For this purpose, the cost behavior to forecast is the relationship between unit production cost and plant size as the new producer and his rivals move from pilot plant to small-scale test production plant to large-scale mass production. The cost forecasts should take into account technological progress and should be spotted on a time scale that reflects the potential head-start cost advantages that could be attained under a policy of penetration pricing and under skimming pricing.

Estimates of cost of unborn competitive products are necessarily rough, but evaluation of major differences between competitors' costs and the new producer's costs can nevertheless be useful. Thus cost estimates can help forecast a defending product's retaliation pricing and an invading product's conquest pricing.

Producer's Costs

The cost of the producer plays several roles in pricing a new product. The first is birth control. A new product must be prepriced provisionally early in the R&D stage and then again periodically as it progresses toward market. Forecasts of production and promotional costs at matching stages should play the role of forecasting its economic feasibility in determining whether to continue product development and ultimately to commercialize. The concept of cost relevant for this birth-control role is a prediction of full cost at a series of prospective volumes and corresponding technologies, and encompassing imputed cost of capital on intangible as well as tangible investment.

A second role is to establish a price floor which is also the threshold for selecting from candidate prices that which will maximize return on a new product investment over the long run.

For both jobs, the relevant concept is future costs, forecast over a range of volume, production technologies and promotional outlays in the marketing plan.

Two categories of cost require separate forecasts and have quite different impacts on new-product pricing: (1) Production costs (including physical distribution), and (2) Persuasion costs, which are discretionary and rivalrous with price.

The production costs that matter are the future costs over the long run that will be added by making this product on the predicted scale (or scales) versus not making it. The added investment necessary to manufacture and distribute the new product should be estimated. Investment should include intangibles such as R&D, promotion, and launching outlays as well as increased working capital. Then the added costs of manufacturing and selling the product at various possible sales volumes should be estimated. It is important to calculate total costs (rather than unit costs) with and without the new product. The difference can then be assigned to the new product. Present overhead that will be the same whether or not the addition to the product line is adopted should be ignored. Future additions to overhead caused by the new product are alone relevant in pricing it. Two sets of cost and investment figures must be built up—one showing the situation *without* the new product and the other showing the situation *with* the new product added to the line, and at several possible volumes. High costs of pilot-plant production and of early small-scale production plants should be viewed as intangible capital investment rather than as the current operating costs. The losses of a break-in period are part of the investment on which a satisfactory return should be made.

Long-run future incremental costs, including costs of equity capital (i.e., satisfactory return on the added investment), supply the base line above which contribution profits of a new product should be maximized—not an impenetrable floor, but a calculation benchmark for optimization.

Strategy Choices

A major strategy decision in pricing a new product is the choice between (1) skimming pricing and (2) penetration pricing. There are intermediate positions, but the issues are made clearer by comparing the two extremes.

Skimming Pricing

Some products represent drastic improvements upon accepted ways of performing a service or filling a demand. For these products a strategy of high prices with large promotional expenditure in the early stages of market development (and lower prices at later stages) has frequently proved successful. This can be termed a "skimming-price" policy. There are four main reasons for its success:

1. Sales of the product are likely to be less sensitive to price in the early stages than when the product is "full-grown" and competitive imitations have appeared. In the early stages, the product usually has so few close rivals that cross elasticity of demand is low. Promotional sensitivity is, on the other hand, quite high, particularly for products with high unit prices, since it is difficult for the customer to value the service of the product.

2. Launching a new product with a high price is an efficient device for breaking the market up into segments that differ in price elasticity of demand. The initial high price serves to skim the cream of the market that is relatively insensitive to price. Subsequent price reductions tap successively more elastic sectors of the market. This pricing strategy is exemplified by the systematic succession of editions of a book, sometimes starting with a $50 limited personal edition and ending up with a 75-cent paperback book.

3. A skimming policy is safer, or at least it appears so. Facing an unknown elasticity of demand, a high initial price serves as a "refusal" price during the stage of exploration. How much costs can be reduced as the market expands and as the design of the product is improved by increasing production efficiency with new techniques is difficult to predict.

4. High prices frequently produce a greater dollar volume of sales in the early stages of market development than are produced by low initial prices. When this is the case, skimming pricing will provide funds to finance expansion into the larger volume sectors of a given market.

Penetration Pricing

Despite its many advantages, a skimming-price policy is not appropriate for all new product problems. Although high initial prices may maximize profits during the early stages of product introduction, they may also prevent sales to many of the buyers upon whom you must rely for a mass market. The alternative is to use low prices as an entering wedge to get into mass markets early. This may be termed penetration pricing. Such an approach is likely to be desirable under any of these conditions:

First, when sales volume of the product is very sensitive to price, even in the early stages of introduction.

Second, when it is possible to achieve substantial economies in unit cost of manufacturing and distributing the product by operating at large volume.

Third, when a product faces threats of strong potential competition very soon after introduction.

Fourth, when there is no "elite" market—that is, no class of buyers willing to pay a higher price to obtain the newest and the best.

While a penetration pricing policy can be adopted at any stage in the product's life cycle, this pricing strategy should always be examined before a new product is marketed at all. Its possibility should be explored again as soon as the product has established an elite market. Sometimes a product can be rescued from premature death by adoption of a penetration price after the cream of the market has been skimmed.

One important consideration in the choice between skimming and penetration pricing at the time a new product is introduced is the ease and speed with which competitors can bring out substitute products. If you decide to set your initial price low enough, your large competitor may not feel it worthwhile to make a big investment for slim profit margins. The speed with which your product loses its uniqueness and sinks from its sheltered status to the level of just another competitive product depends on several factors:

1. Its total sales potential. A big potential market entices competitive imitation.

2. The investment required for rivals to manufacture and distribute the product. A big investment barrier deters invasion.

3. The strength of patent and know-how protection.

4. The alertness and power of competitors.

Although competitive imitation is almost inevitable, the company that introduces a new product can use price to discourage or delay the introduction of competitive products. Keep-out prices can be achieved quickly by penetration pricing.

Pricing in Maturity

To price appropriately for later stages in the cycle of competitive maturity, it is important to be able to tell when a product is approaching maturity. When the new product is about to slip into the commodity category, it is sometimes desirable to reduce real prices promptly as soon as symptoms of deterioration appear. Some of the symptoms of degeneration of competitive status toward the commodity level are:

1. Weakening in brand preference. This may be evidenced by a higher cross elasticity of demand among leading products, the leading brand not being able to continue demanding as much price premium as initially without losing position.
2. Narrowing physical variation among products as the best designs are developed and standardized. This has been dramatically demonstrated in automobiles and is still in process in television receivers.
3. The entry in force of private-label competitors. This is exemplified by the mail-order houses' sale of own-label refrigerators and paint sprayers.
4. Market saturation. The ratio of replacement sales to new-equipment sales serves as an indicator of the competitive degeneration of durable goods, but in general it must be kept in mind that both market size and degree of saturation are hard to define (e.g., saturation of the radio market, which was initially thought to be one radio per home and later had to be expanded to one radio per room).
5. The stabilization of production methods, indicated by slow rate of technological advance, high average age of equipment, and great uniformity among competitors' introduction technology.

Promotion and Distribution

Promotion

Closely related to pricing is promotional strategy. An innovator must not only sell his product, but frequently he must also make people recognize their need for a new *kind* of product. The problem is one of "creating a market."

Initial promotion outlays are an investment in the product that cannot be recovered until some kind of market has been established. The innovator shoulders the burden of educating consumers to the existence and uses of the product. Later imitators will never have to do this job; so if the innovator does not want to be simply a benefactor to his future competitors, he must make pricing plans to earn a return on all his initial outlays before his pricing discretion evaporates.

The basic strategic problem is to find the right mixture of price and promotion to maximize long-run profits. A relatively high price may be chosen in pioneering stages, together with large advertising and dealer discounts, and the plan may be to get the promotion investment back early; or low prices and lean margins may be used from the very outset in order to discourage potential competition when the barriers of patents and investment in production capacity, distribution channels, or production techniques become inadequate.

Channels of Distribution

Choice of channels of distribution should be consistent with strategy for initial pricing and for promotional outlays. Penetration pricing and explosive promotion call for distribution channels that promptly make the product broadly available. Otherwise advertising is wasted or mass-market pricing stymied. Distribution policy also concerns the role the dealer is to play in pushing a given product, the margins he must be paid to induce this action, and the amount of protection of territory and of inventory required to do so.

Estimation of the costs of moving the new product through the channels of distribution to the final consumer must enter into the pricing procedure, since these costs govern the factory price that will result in a specified final price. Distributive margins are partly pure promotional costs and partly physical distribution costs. Margins must at least cover the distributors' costs of warehousing, handling, and order taking. These costs are similar to factory production costs in being related to physical capacity and its utilization; i.e., fluctuations in production or sales volume. Hence these set a floor to trade-channel discounts. But distributors usually also contribute promotional effort—in point-of-sale pushing, local advertising, and display—when it is made worth their while. These pure promotional costs are more optional.

Distributors' margins are best determined by study of distributors' alternatives. This does not mean that the distributor gross margin on a given product must be the same as that of rival products. It should instead produce a competitive rate of return on the distributors' investment (in inventory, shelf space and sales capacity).

Summary

Pricing new products is an art. The important determinants in economic pricing of pioneering innovations are complex, interrelated, and hard to forecast. Experienced judgment is required in pricing and repricing the product to fit its changing competitive environment. This judgment may possibly be improved by some pricing precepts suggested by the preceding analysis:

1. Corporate goals must be clearly defined. Pricing a new product is an occasion for rethinking them. This chapter has assumed that the overriding corporate goal is long-run profit maximization; e.g., making the stock worth the most by maximizing the present worth, at the corporation's cost of capital, of its per-share earnings.

2. Pricing a new product should begin long before its birth. Prospective prices, coupled with forecast costs, should play the decisive role in product birth control.

3. Pricing a new product should be a continuing process of bracketing the truth by successive approximations. Rough estimates of the relevant concepts are preferable to precise knowledge of historical irrelevancies.

4. Costs can supply useful guidance in new-product pricing, but not by the conventional wisdom; i.e., cost-plus pricing. Three categories of costs are pertinent: those of the buyer, those of the seller, and those of the seller's rivals. The role of cost differs among the three, as does the concept of cost that is pertinent to that role: different costs for different purposes.

5. The role of cost is to set a reference base for picking the most profitable price. For this job the only costs that are pertinent to pricing a new product on the verge of commercialization (i.e., already developed and tested) are incremental costs; the added costs of going ahead at different plant scales. Costs of R&D and of market testing are now sunk and hence irrelevant.

6. The pricing implications of the changing economic status and competitive environment of a product must be recognized as it passes through its life cycle from birth to obsolescence. This cycle, and the plans that are made to influence it, are of paramount importance for pricing policy.

7. The product should be seen through the eyes of the customer and priced just low enough to make it an irresistible investment in view of his alternatives as he sees them. To estimate successfully how much a given product is worth to the prospect is never easy, but it is usually rewarding.

8. Customers' rate of return should be the main consideration in pricing novel capital goods. Buyers' cost savings (and other earnings) expressed as a return on his investment in the new product are the key to predicting the price sensitivity of demand and to pricing profitably.

9. The strategic choice between skimming and penetration pricing should be based on economics. The skimming policy—i.e., relatively high prices in the pioneering stage, cascading downward thereafter—is particularly appropriate for products whose sales initially are comparatively unresponsive to price but quite responsive to education. A policy of penetration pricing—i.e., relatively low prices in the pioneering stage in anticipation of the cost savings resulting from an expanding market—is best when scale economies are big, demand is price sensitive, and invasion is threatened. Low starting prices sacrifice short-run profits for long-run profits and discourage potential competitors.

NOTES

1. Hereafter, the term "new product" will encompass new services as well.

SELECTIVE BIBLIOGRAPHY

Dean, Joel, *Managerial Economics*, Prentice-Hall, Englewood Cliffs, N.J., 1951 (especially pp. 419–424).

Harper, Donald, *Price Policy and Procedure*, Harcourt, Brace & World, New York, 1966.

Mulvihill, D. F., and S. Paranka, *Price Policies and Practices: A Source Book in Readings*, Wiley, New York, 1967.

Thompson, G. Clark, and M. M. MacDonald, "Pricing New Products," *Conference Board Record*, National Industrial Conference Board, New York, 1964.

LEARNING REVIEW

Questions:

1. The optimizing premium of a new product will depend on ____________ and ____________.

2. Appropriate pricing over the life cycle of a product depends on three dif- aspects of maturity: a) ____________, b) ____________, and c) ____________.

3. Using high prices and large promotional expenditures in the early stages of market development is called ____________, while using low prices as an entering wedge to get into mass markets early is called ____________.

Answers:

1. future costs, demand schedule; 2. a) technical maturity; b) market maturity; c) competitive maturity; 3. skimming pricing, penetration pricing

Retrospective Comment

Two major developments in recent years that affect new-product pricing are super-inflation and speedier technological progress.

How does double-digit inflation affect new-product pricing?

(1) It forces forecasting of costs and raises the predicted costs of making and selling the new product. (2) It raises the parity benchmark of the product's competitive alternatives (*everything costs more*). (3) It lifts the buyer-benefits obtained from the new product's protected distinctiveness (e.g., saves more wage dollars). (4) It increases goal profits of the seller and raises the customer's cutoff point of minimum acceptable rate of return, because the cost of equity capital and of debt capital must compensate suppliers for anticipated inflation. (5) It heightens the importance of prebirth pricing, which (to reduce uncertainty) increases stillbirths of marginal new products and lowers infant mortality.

Generally speaking, super-inflation makes numerical benchmarks and projections quickly obsolete. It does not, however, change the essential economics of new-product pricing. Inflation's principal consequence is to make an economic attack on the pricing problem more compelling.

How will speedier technical progress, such as the quantum leap in microprocessor technology, affect new product pricing? The microprocessor, which is a functional computer on a single chip, offers high performance at such low cost that almost any operation now performed electromechanically will be done by microprocessors much more reliably and cheaply. Today, the same computation that cost about $100, twenty-five years ago, can be performed by semiconductors for a penny. The sophisticated large-scale integrated circuit, coupled with the new plasma-panel technology of flat-tube displays and hardcopy printouts will create awesome obsolescence. New products will be launched in profusion, and many of them will embody giant advances (in contrast with the mincing progress of technology which normally occurs in tiny steps).

Every new product has in early life a protected distinctiveness which is doomed to progressive deterioration as competitors imitate and innovate. With the new microprocessor technology, a profusion of new products will make existing products of even recent vintage obsolete. Products will move through the life cycle more quickly and pricing strategy will have to change faster to keep pace as the products mature competitively. Promotional and price responsiveness will also change faster, as will the prospective costs of competitor buyers and of producers of the new microcomputer-geared products. Hence the pricing of new products will have to be even more vigilant and dynamic.

Penetration pricing strategy will become especially important in this new era. By using price to sharpen the effectiveness of promotion, penetration pricing speeds demand expansion and attains competitor-frustrating economies of size more quickly.

Learning-curve pricing has great importance for products on the technological edge of tomorrow. It epitomizes penetration pricing by condensing the process of cutting prices ahead of forecasted cost-savings to beat competitors to the bigger market that is opened by creative pricing. This pricing strategy, which took a decade for the Model T, is condensed into a few months for the integrated circuit. In the case of the Model T, the sources of forecasted cost reductions were economies of scale and increased mechanization. In the case of the integrated circuit, the sources of cost reductions are savings from learning, routinization, and managerial innovation and, above all, savings from the dramatic reduction in subquality rejects. But though the sources of savings are different, the principle is the same: learning-curves call for penetration pricing which is most powerful when costs will come down as a consequence of the greater volume created by pricing ahead of cost reductions, and by gearing price to buyer benefits in price-responsive sectors of the market.

32

Multi-Stage Approach to Pricing

Alfred R. Oxenfeldt

PREVIEW

I. A helpful tool in pricing may be a multi-stage approach which sorts the major elements in a pricing decision into six successive stages, each of which narrows the alternatives from the previous stage.
   A. The first stage is to select market targets which a firm can reasonably hope to capture with its specified resources.
   B. The second stage, the selection of a company and brand image, should be dictated by the types of customers the firm is trying to attract.
   C. The third stage calls for the selection of a combination of sales promotional devices that will create and reinforce the desired company and product brand image and achieve maximum sales for the planned level of dollar outlays.
   D. The fourth stage calls for the selection of a pricing policy.
   E. The fifth stage is to determine pricing strategy to guide management in setting price during special situations.
   F. The final step is setting specific price.

II. There are a number of advantages to a multi-stage approach to pricing.
   A. It breaks up the pricing decision into six relatively manageable pieces.
   B. It reduces risk that the price setter will destroy the firm's valuable investments in corporate and brand images.
   C. It should be valuable to executives who are compelled to delegate pricing responsibilities.
   D. It puts considerable emphasis on the intangibles that are involved in pricing.

Alfred Oxenfeldt, "Multistage Approach to Pricing," is reprinted by permission from *Harvard Business Review* (July–August 1960), pp. 125–133.

III. There are limitations to a multi-stage approach to pricing.
   A. This approach does not indicate all the considerations that should be taken into account at each stage in the pricing decision.
   B. This approach does not indicate what price to charge in any specific situation.
   C. This method does not guide price setters in recognizing the factors that dominate the market at any time and in knowing when to switch basic strategies.

Of all the areas of executive decision, pricing is perhaps the most fuzzy. Whenever a price problem is discussed by a committee, divergent figures are likely to be recommended without a semblance of consensus. Although unanimity in marketing decisions is a custom more remarkable in its occurrence than in its absence, agreement in pricing decisions is even more rare.

This article accordingly presents a long-run, policy-oriented approach to pricing which should reduce the range of prices considered in specific situations and consequently improve the decisions which result. This approach, which to the best of my knowledge is new, calls for the price decision to be made in six successive steps, each one narrowing the alternatives to be considered at the next step.

Is this method just another mechanical pricing formula? Hardly, for it is my conviction that the quest for mechanical pricing methods is unduly optimistic, if not downright naive. Nevertheless, many businessmen consistently employ almost mechanical formulas for pricing. They do this even though they scoff at the claim that there are reliable fixed formulas for handling personnel problems or making advertising or capital outlay decisions. Certainly, experience has not produced recipes that guarantee correct decisions in any sphere of business. The best of them only apply under normal conditions, and it is most rare indeed that conditions resembling normalcy prevail.

On the other hand, many discussions of pricing present a long list of factors to be "taken into account," carefully weighed and balanced, and then subjected to a process called "judgment." While a specific price is thus arrived at, this does not alter the fact that intelligent and experienced business executives using the method will arrive at widely different price decisions—all based on the same information.

Yet, even if mechanical pricing formulas are the hope of the optimistic, it would be excessively pessimistic to resign ourselves to a *formless* consideration of all the relevant factors and to a random exercise of judgment. Many things are known about the subject that would be extremely helpful to those responsible for making such decisions.

Sequential Stages

In order to organize the various pieces of information and considerations that bear on price decisions, a multi-stage approach to pricing can be a very helpful tool. This method sorts the major elements in a pricing decision into six successive stages:

1. Selecting market targets.
2. Choosing a brand "image."
3. Composing a marketing mix.
4. Selecting a pricing policy.
5. Determining a pricing strategy.
6. Arriving at a specific price.

The sequence of the stages is an essential part of the method, for each step is calculated to simplify the succeeding stage and to reduce the likelihood of error. One might say that this method divides the price decision into manageable parts, each one logically antecedent to the next. In this way, the decision at each stage facilitates all subsequent decisions. This approach might also be regarded as a process of selective search, where the number of alternatives deserving close consideration is reduced drastically by making the decision in successive stages. Of course, one could arrive at the same result by simultaneously considering all the factors mentioned—but it might require a computer to do so.

While it appears that this approach is applicable over a broad range of industry and trade, the great diversity of business situations precludes the possibility of its being a universally applicable method. No rigid approach, and certainly not the one presented here, offers a guarantee of reaching the best—or even a satisfactory—price decision. It must be adapted to prevailing circumstances; consequently, information, experience, and the application of rigorous logic are required for its optimum utilization.

I. Market Targets

A going concern is "committed," confined, and tied down by several important circumstances which can be altered only over a considerable period of time. It must live with many conditions, even while it may attempt to alter them. Also, an operating business possesses specified resources on which it will strive to capitalize in achieving its objectives. For example, a firm will have:

A fixed production location, given physical facilities, and a particular production and sales labor force.

A set of distribution arrangements through which the firm generally sells, including particular distributors with whom it has established relationships.

Contracts with suppliers, customers, laborers, and lenders of funds.

A portfolio of customers who have a definite opinion of the firm's reliability, and the quality of its offerings and service.

These commitments and resources of a firm contain pricing implications. Mainly, they determine the type of product that it can make, the type of service it can render, and its probable costs of operation. What is more, these circumstances form the basis for the most fundamental pricing decision that management should make—namely, the types of customers, or market segments, it will attempt to cultivate.

By virtue of its fixed commitments, then, a firm is limited to the several market segments it can reasonably hope to capture. It has customer connections on which it can capitalize, and it has a variety of strengths and weaknesses that limit its choice among potential submarkets for intensive cultivation.

Two examples drawn from the TV set industry will help to clarify this crucial first stage. Certainly, no two firms could possibly exemplify all situations, nor is it possible for an outsider to explain satisfactorily why specific decisions were made in specific cases. However, these illustrations are intended to indicate what factors management must consider if it is to apply the multi-stage approach. They do *not* describe how management reasoned or what would have been the best decision under the circumstances.

Zenith Radio

First, consider the pricing problem of the Zenith Radio Corporation at the time it started to produce TV sets in 1948:

This company, which is one of the two largest TV set producers now, dropped out of the automobile radio business in order to manufacture television sets. (At that time, it was the largest single producer of automobile radios, but this business was not very profitable). Zenith possessed these resources and was subject to these commitments and limitations that could have influenced its selection of market targets in the business—

It had production facilities in Chicago that had been designed for and used in radio production for many years; its labor force and supervisory personnel were familiar with the electronics business. The firm had substantial manufacturing skills in electronics because of its work for the military during and after World War II. Zenith could assess its manufacturing capabilities as very substantial, but not outstanding.

> Financially, Zenith was also in a very strong and liquid position and could readily have undertaken heavy expenditures at this time.
>
> But Zenith's outstanding resource was a distributor and dealer organization that was as good as that possessed by any other firm in the nation. Its dealers commanded strong loyalty among their clientele not only in small communities but also in large cities—a most vital fact in view of the technical character of TV and the great power that retailers wield over consumer choices of such products. Here Zenith was helped by the fact that it had acquired an excellent reputation for quality products in radios; for many years, it was the Cadillac of the radio industry. Zenith management, like all other radio manufacturers who entered the television business, decided to sell its sets through the distributor organization it had already created; its distributors, in turn, would sell them mainly to dealers already buying Zenith radios.
>
> There were also several other peripheral advantages. Zenith was closely identified, in the minds of many consumers, with hearing aids which were widely advertised as much on grounds of moderate price as in terms of high quality. Further, Zenith started to telecast, experimentally, in the Chicago market even before World War II and had some local identification as a telecaster, as well as a manufacturer. Its products were strongly favored in the Chicago market.
>
> In summary, Zenith Radio could count on its strong distributor and retail organizations as its outstanding resource, while recognizing that it did not possess any particular advantage in costs of manufacture or quality of product and, in fact, that its behavior in the television business was necessarily circumscribed by its radio and hearing aid business. Zenith's management would have required very strong reasons to choose as its market targets customers who were very different from those who bought its radios and hearing aids.

Under these circumstances, Zenith management might have decided to attempt to reach customers at almost all levels of income. Partly, it could do this by including "low-end" and promotional models in its line; partly because television sets were sold on installment credit involving modest monthly charges; and partly because, at least in the early years, television purchases were spread rather evenly over all income groups.

On the other hand, Zenith management, as its first step, might well expect to cultivate particularly those consumers who were conservative and quality-conscious, who felt a strong loyalty to particular appliance retailers, and who were located mainly in small cities and towns. On this basis, the Zenith customer targets would not include "snobs" who, at that time, favored the Dumont brand and, to a lesser degree, the RCA set. Also they would not include bargain hunters. Rather Zenith's customers would be the the kind of people who feel that "you get what you pay for." (Zenith would presumably capitalize on its strong position in the Chicago area by special measures aimed at that market.)

Columbia Broadcasting

Now contrast Zenith's position with that of Columbia Broadcasting System, Inc. when it started to produce and sell TV sets under its own brand name in 1953:

> CBS resources and commitments were altogether different from those possessed by Zenith, with the result that the two companies could have been expected to cultivate different market targets. Specifically, in the case of Columbia Broadcasting—
>
> CBS executives were primarily familiar with the management of entertainment talent and the creation and servicing of a network of stations. Although its phonograph record and Hi-Fi phonograph business did involve a type of production and distribution experience, CBS was completely new to major appliance manufacturing and possessed no suitable distribution facilities whatsoever for appliances.
>
> In addition, CBS acquired production facilities when it entered the TV business that were of relatively poor quality. The size, location, equipment, plant layout, and employee facilities of the Air King firm, which CBS acquired, were widely recognized as mediocre or below. Many people familiar with that company and with the TV industry strongly doubted that Air King's management was capable of establishing a prestige national brand and producing the high quality product needed to support a quality reputation.
>
> On the other hand, CBS had some genuine pluses in its favor. Its radio and television networks were the largest, and enjoyed great prestige at the time CBS entered the TV set business. Also, by virtue of its telecasting facilities, it could, moreover, get the advertising support—mainly through testimonials from outstanding personalities like Arthur Godfrey, Edward R. Murrow, Jack Benny, and others—for little or no cost.

To what kinds of customers could a firm with these resources and limitations appeal?

One way that CBS might have adjusted to its particular combination of resources and weaknesses would have been to select as its chief consumer market target the metropolitan customer who is anxious to be associated with prestigeful figures, vulnerable to advertising over radio and TV, prepared to pay a premium price, and relatively unfamiliar with or insensitive to technical performance features. But this market target would hardly have been very large in the first instance; moreover, CBS management must have recognized that many other firms were cultivating this type of customer.

It would appear, then, that CBS was compelled to select its market targets mainly in terms of distributors and retailers, rather than ultimate consumers. Whereas Zenith already possessed a strong distributor and dealer organization, CBS had to construct one. Only after it secured representation on the market could it hope to sell to consumers.

CBS management must have realized that whatever it did in an effort to win distributors and dealers would also influence the kind of customers it could hope to attract. For example, if it had to extend big markups to distributors and retailers to get them to handle its sets (combined with the fact that its production facilities were mediocre), CBS would be compelled to charge a relatively high retail price for its sets. In turn, it would have to rely on intensive advertising to persuade consumers to pay these higher prices and find methods of making its sets appear luxurious and worth the high price.

In addition to having to accept the fact of a relatively high-price product, CBS would feel pressure to concentrate on customers in the large metropolitan centers, because of the need to build large sales volume rapidly in order to get its production costs in line with those of its competitors. Even as early as 1953, the large metropolitan markets were pervaded by severe price competition among set manufacturers and relatively little emphasis on quality and brand loyalty on the part of retailers. Independent distributors were leaving the business because of great manufacturer pressure to gain heavy sales volume. Hence CBS could not have much hope of obtaining strong independent distributors for its line in most metropolitan markets, but would have to look ahead to a considerable period during which it "supported" both distributors and key retailers to obtain an organization that would distribute its sets.

Other Cases

Zenith and CBS have been cited as companies that would have been justified in placing relatively little weight on price in their selection of target submarkets. These companies mainly had to avoid alienating customers by charging prices that were far out of line with other companies' prices. Not all TV set manufacturers could have taken this approach, however. Thus:

> Companies like Admiral, Emerson, and producers of private brands were under pressure to cultivate customers who place heavy emphasis on price. Why? Because in some cases they lacked the personnel and financial resources to sustain a claim of quality and style superiority; or, because their experience in the major appliance business before adding a line of TV receivers could have indicated that they had won acceptance mainly among

customers who want moderate quality at prices below the average; or, finally, because their chief asset was a very efficient manufacturing organization that could imitate the products of their more progressive rivals at low cost.

Other industries offer clear examples of firms that selected as market targets persons who were not particularly interested in high intrinsic quality or style. Specifically:

> A fairly obvious example is the Scripto pencil, which offers satisfactory performance at minimum cost. Apparently the customers Scripto selected for intensive cultivation were those who would want a pencil to write with and not for display, a pencil they could afford to lose or misplace.
>
> Some producers of private brands of aspirin likewise have selected as market targets those persons who know of the fundamental similarity of aspirin quality and who actively desire to minimize their outlays for this product.

These examples illustrate a point that may not have been particularly clear in the discussion of the Zenith and CBS examples: *one important criterion in the selection of market targets is customer awareness of and sensitivity to price.*

II. Brand "Image"

Once management has defined the submarkets it wishes to cultivate most actively, it must select the methods it will use to achieve its goal.

Success in the market place for more and more products seems to depend on creating a favorable general image (often vague and formless) of the product or company among prospective customers. The selection and development of this image become of prime importance and have a direct bearing on price, as will be explained subsequently. A favorable image is especially important when one sells consumers' goods, but only rarely is it completey unimportant even in the sales of producers' goods. Buyers' very perceptions are affected by their prior attitudes, the actions and opinions of others, first impressions and early associations. It is a rare firm that can ignore the total impression its potential customers have of it and of what it is selling.

The firm's selection of its company and brand image should be dictated by the types of customers it is trying to attract. Submarkets may be likened to targets at which the seller is firing, and "images" are powerful weapons that can be used to hit the targets.

Almost every going concern has invested—often very heavily—in the creation of a favorable image. Most businesses know what image they wish to achieve and are concerned lest they or their products fail to have a favorable "meaning" to potential customers. At the very minimum, almost every management knows there are certain images that customers might have of it and its product that would prove disastrous.

The type of image a firm can create of itself and its wares depends to a considerable degree, again, on its fixed commitments and resources. With its physical and personnel resources, there is a limit to what it can do to alter the prevailing opinions—for they reflect all that the company was and did in the past. In that sense, the basic commitments limit the type of image a firm can establish, how much time it will require to establish it, and the cost. Even as brand image is frequently an effective weapon in cultivating particular submarkets, price helps to create the brand image. It is for this reason that the selection of a brand image which is consistent with the firm's market targets implies particular forms of price behavior.

Let us carry our original examples a little further. Given the market targets that they might have selected, as explained earlier, what brand image could Zenith and CBS try to create?

Alternative Qualities

As in the selecting of market targets, every firm has only a few *reasonable* alternatives from which to choose its desired image. For example:

> Zenith already possessed a brand image that contributed strongly to its success in the radio and hearing aid business. Even if another image might have been advantageous for its television business, Zenith's management could hardly afford to injure the bird already in hand. Consequently, Zenith would be obliged to perpetuate for its TV line the brand image it had already established in its other activities. As it happened, that image was altogether suitable for its TV set business.
>
> To implement this line of thinking, Zenith would be obliged to establish the image of a "premium" product and of a company that was old-time, conservative, and mainly concerned with quality and craftsmanship. Above all, it would seek to avoid high-pressure selling, emphasis on price, and shoddiness of product. In styling, it could pursue a safe policy of including a wide variety of styles, while being especially careful not to alienate its conservative small-town customers with models too far in the vanguard of modern design.
>
> CBS faced a very different choice with regard to brand image. It, too, could not afford to jeopardize its eminent position in the radio and network field, for those activites were very profitable and would always remain its major sources of income. Except for this limitation, CBS had a relatively free choice of brand images.
>
> CBS could well undertake to be the style leader in the industry. This image would be consistent with relatively inefficient manufacturing facilities, concentration on selling in the metropolitan market, and the necessity of charging a high retail price. It would appear that few brand images other than for

advanced styling and for gimmicks would have been consistent with the resources and limitations on CBS at this time.

In contrast to Zenith and CBS, other TV set producers sought a brand image that did have an important price ingredient. Again, most producers of private brands, Admiral, Emerson, and others, often featured price in their advertising and apparently sought to sensitize prospective customers to price. They could purposely become identified as firms that were not afraid to discuss price and that seemed confident they offered better values than their competitors.

Many firms outside the TV set industry attempt to establish a brand image that has a heavy price ingredient. Among producers, one finds Caron boasting that its Joy perfume is the most expensive, and Chock-Full-of-Nuts implying much the same thing about its coffee. Without being explicit, some retailers seem to claim that no stores charge more than they—and, strangely, this image is a source of strength. The retail world is full of stores that claim that they are never knowingly undersold; on the other hand, it is difficult to name manufacturers who claim that their product is the cheapest on the market—probably because of the implication that theirs is also the brand of lowest quality. (Automobile manufacturers occasionally claim to be the "cheapest of the low-price three," but none has occupied that position long.)

III. Marketing Mix

The third stage in multi-stage pricing calls for the selection of a combination of sales promotion devices that will create and re-enforce the desired company and product brand image and achieve maximum sales for the planned level of dollar outlays. In this stage, a role must be assigned to price. The role in which price is cast should be selected only after assessment is made as to the relative effectiveness and appropriateness of each sales promotion device that might be employed. The short-term gains of certain sales promotion devices may entail injury to the image objectives of the firm. Conflicts of such a nature must be resolved at this stage.

Then, too, a firm might achieve precisely the *desired* image and still find customers very hard to get. It is not enough to establish the desired image; it must be an *effective* image. Furthermore, even though a firm may establish highly favorable impressions of itself and its wares, the company and its products must live up to the image they foster. Not only must its product be "within reach" in price, but it must be accessible by being offered through convenient channels of distribution, and must be sold in outlets where customers like to buy.

The third stage builds directly upon the second. The need to conform to the prior decision about company and brand image greatly limits the number of price alternatives that a price setter can reasonably consider.

The marketing mix decision at this stage need not be translated into specific dollars and cents amounts to be devoted to each sales promotion device; however, it does at least call for crude answers to the following questions:

How heavily to advertise?
How much for salesmen?
How much for product improvement?
How much of an assortment to carry?
How large an inventory to hold?
How best to provide speedy delivery?
How much emphasis on price appeal?

The composition of a marketing mix (arrived at by answering the type of questions just listed) is admittedly very difficult and highly subjective. But the job is facilitated greatly when answers are subjected to the test of conforming to the desired company and brand image and to the firm's fixed commitments.

Few firms can afford to switch "images," usually because they have invested heavily in them in prior years and should, therefore, not abandon them lightly. Moreover, past images persist and blur any future attempts at image building. Although it cannot easily scrap its brand image, a firm can vary its marketing mix within moderate limits and remain consistent with the image it seeks to create. Thus, the selection of an image sets limits and gives direction to the decision about the elements to be included in the marketing mix. In that way, it facilitates the decision and also increases the likelihood that it will be correct. However, it does not isolate a single marketing mix as the only correct one.

Marketing the Image

How might have Zenith, CBS, and other TV set manufacturers composed a marketing mix, if they had reasoned about market targets and brand image along the lines of the foregoing discussion? Let us see:

> In Zenith's case, price clearly would have had to be subordinated as a sales appeal. The company could have placed major emphasis on quality of product, subdued advertising, and reliable service, while placing its product with retailers who would enhance the reputation of the brand. By these measures, Zenith could have re-enforced the image of a high quality and reliable producer.
>
> In the case of CBS, the role of price in the marketing mix would not have been subject to much control. As explained, it might have been forced to charge a high price; if so, most of its other actions would have been dictated by that fact. It could have relied very heavily on radio and TV advertising to generate consumer preference, and justified its high price by adding externals

to the set—particularly attractive styling, an expensive furniture appearance, or special features of some sort. It could not have reasonably hoped to get very much support from retailers who commanded strong loyalty among their patrons.

Other TV set producers adopted quite different market mixes from those that Zenith and CBS would have selected if they had reasoned along these lines. Some, however, apparently had no conscious marketing mix philosophy and, therefore, seemed to improvise and stumble from one crisis to another. Nevertheless, in their bids for patronage, some set producers apparently placed relatively heavy reliance on advertising (including mainly RCA, General Electric, Westinghouse, and Sylvania). Others made strong quality claims (like Dumont and Andrea). Still others placed chief emphasis on styling (Magnavox.)

IV. Determining Policy

The fourth stage in multi-stage pricing calls for the selection of a pricing policy. But before a pricing policy can be determined, answers to the following questions must be obtained:

How should our price compare with "average" prices in the industry? Specifically, should we be 2% above or 4% below the average? And, when we speak of the average, which firms' prices are we going to include in the computation?

How fast will we meet price reductions or increases by rivals?

How frequently will it be advisable to vary price? To what extent is stability of price advantageous?

Should the firm make use of "fair trade" price maintenance?

How frequently should the firm run price promotions?

These are simply illustrative of the aspects of a pricing policy which management can and should spell out—in proper sequence. By virtue of having made the evaluations and decisions called for in the first three stages, management will find itself limited in the number of choices on these points.

In addition, each company must take account of the valuations placed on its product-service "package" as well as the valuations of rival products by the market segments it is most anxious to cultivate. On the basis of such considerations, plus its target market segments and marketing mix, it will decide whether it can afford to charge much more or less than its rivals.

"Bracketing" the Price

Before proceeding further, let us summarize. Surely, a price setter would be some distance from a specific price decision even after completing the fourth step. We must ask ourselves whether he would not also have covered considerable distance toward a price decision. By taking account of the firm's basic commitments and resources, the images it desires to establish, its decision about marketing mix, and the selection of a detailed pricing policy, has not the price setter reached the point where he is very strongly circumscribed in the price decision he will ultimately make? To illustrate Step Four, let us carry our two main examples—Zenith and CBS—about as far as they can be taken and see what pricing policy these companies might have adopted:

> If the Zenith management had selected the market targets set forth here and made the same decisions regarding brand image and marketing mix, it would have had little trouble in selecting a pricing policy. It would have felt obliged to charge a price somewhat above the average in the market and to minimize emphasis on price in its advertising. Moreover, it could have varied price relatively infrequently to the consumer—except possibly in some of the large metropolitan markets where neither consumers nor retailers are loyal to anything or anyone, except their own pecuniary interests.
>
> In Zenith's pricing policy, the preservation of distributor and retailer loyalty would have figured very prominently in its thinking. It would be compelled to sacrifice long-term price advantages in order to protect its distributors and retailers from financial loss due to price change.
>
> CBS, on the other hand, need not have concerned itself much with dealer and retailer loyalty. It had none and must have realized that it would not have been able to create a loyal distribution structure unless it were willing to make very large financial outlays. If it had reconciled itself to a not-too-loyal distributor and dealer organization, CBS could have conducted sales promotions and varied price frequently and by large amounts. It could have emphasized price in these promotions, but presumably only when combined with strong emphasis on alleged high quality and superior styling. CBS need not have felt obliged to match the prices charged by its competitors, but it could not have afforded to have its retailers' margins be out of line on the low side.
>
> Since it commanded no loyalty from its retailers, CBS was, in fact, compelled to buy their sales support. This it could do, primarily by offering a higher than average margin. (CBS could also have attempted to solve its distribution problem by granting exclusive privileges to a small number of retail outlets. In the case of the TV industry, such a policy has been used successfully by Magnavox. However, this company had already sewed up the strong quality retailers who were capable of producing large volume. As a result, CBS was shut out of this pattern of distribution.)

Although Zenith and CBS apparently would have been obliged to charge more than the average by the foregoing line of thinking, other TV producers were wise to take a very different tack, mainly because of their different resources and commitments. For example, Admiral and Emerson have tended to charge somewhat less than average, while General Electric has not adopted a very consistent price position.

V. Pricing Strategy

It is difficult to draw a sharp line between policy and strategy, but it is possible and useful to make some sort of distinction between them. Policy is formulated to deal with anticipated and foreseeable situations of a recurrent type. However, markets frequently are beset and dominated by *special* situations that basic policy was not designed to meet. For example:

> A Congressional committee might threaten to investigate the company's or the industry's pricing arrangements.
>
> A sizable firm may have fallen into a desperate financial situation so that it was forced to raise cash through a liquidation of its inventories.
>
> A large new firm may have entered the market.
>
> Business may have fallen off precipitately for the entire industry or economy.
>
> The company may have introduced a model that is either a "dud" or a "sure winner."

Special situations like these ordinarily require an adjustment in price—and the formulation of a strategy to guide management in setting price *during the time that the special* situation endures.

There generally are several strategies which would be compatible with the firm's basic commitments and resources, its market targets, its image objectives, its convictions about the relative emphasis to attach to various elements in the marketing mix, and its specific pricing policies. Others would be incompatible with earlier decisions and therefore might endanger precious values. A threat to one's very survival might justify a scrapping of these, but impetuousness, shortsightedness, or avarice would not. Explicit recognition of these earlier stages of the pricing decision should prevent hasty short-run actions that are painful, but quite common.

No effort will be made to discuss the Zenith and CBS examples in connection with the formulation of a pricing strategy. They have already been stretched far enough to illustrate the application of the multi-stage approach to pricing—especially in the most difficult stages. The reader might, however, speculate about how, within the framework of the approach outlined here, both Zenith and CBS management could have responded to a great pricing crisis in the TV set industry. This occurred in the fall of 1953 when Westinghouse suddenly reduced its TV sets by approximately 20% during the very heart of the selling season. We may speculate that adherence to decisions regarding market targets, brand image, marketing mix, and price policy would have prevented both Zenith and CBS from reducing their prices to the levels set by Westinghouse Electric Corporation.

VI. Specific Price

Here is the final step—the selection of a specific price. At this point, the price setter will usually find himself sharply circumscribed in the specific sums he can charge. Nevertheless, he usually will have some range of price possibilities that are consistent with the decisions made in the preceding five stages of the price decision. How may he best select among the alternatives?

To the extent that he is able, he should be guided by the arithmetic of pricing—that is, by a comparison of the costs and revenues of the alternative prices within the zone delimited by the prior stages of his pricing decision. Once he has taken into account his market targets, brand image, marketing mix, pricing policy, and strategy, he can afford to ignore everything but the calculations of costs and revenues. *The first five stages of decision are designed to take account of the business considerations which may be ignored if one selects price solely on the basis of prevailing cost and revenue conditions.*

It often is impossible to obtain reliable information about sales at different prices; this difficulty is present whatever method of pricing one employs. But the multi-stage policy approach facilitates research and experimentation into demand conditions by limiting the number of alternatives to be considered.

The price that would be established under this multi-stage policy approach would rarely be the same as that set by balancing marginal cost and marginal revenue. The former probably would exclude, as incompatible with the firm's basic commitments and resources, desired brand image, and so on, the prices that would be most profitable in the very short term.

The Advantages

First, this approach breaks up the pricing decision into six relatively manageable pieces. In that way, it introduces order into the weighing of the many considerations bearing on price. This approach, therefore, should increase the likelihood that all major factors will be taken into account and that their large number will not overwhelm the price setter.

Second, this method of pricing reduces the risk that the price setter will destroy the firm's valuable investments in corporate and brand images.

Also, it requires the price setter to determine and take into account the limitation on the firm's freedom of decision. In that way, it would discourage the pricing executive from undertaking what he is powerless to accomplish. Similarly, the multi-stage policy approach should militate against a short-run policy of opportunism that would sacrifice long-term values.

Third, the multi-stage policy approach to pricing should be valuable to those executives who are compelled to delegate pricing responsibilities. In the first place, high-level executives are virtually required by the method to make the decisions for several stages, which thus limits their dependence on their subordinates. In the second place, as explained, it simplifies the making of a price decision so that greater success can be expected. Then, too, its use should make it easier for subordinates to raise questions and obtain advice from their superiors, should they be unable to reach a decision.

Fourth, this approach to pricing puts considerable emphasis on the intangibles that are involved in pricing—particularly on the total impression that customers have of the vendor and of the things he sells. Price is far more than a rationing device that determines which potential customers will be able to afford to make a purchase. Generally it is one of the most important actions in creating an impression of the firm among potential customers. Especially as tangible differences among rival products shrink, these intangibles will grow in significance for marketing success.

The Limitations

This approach does not indicate all the considerations that should be taken into account at each stage in the pricing decision. In other words, the price setter is compelled to isolate the significant factors operating at each stage and weigh them for himself.

Second, this approach does not indicate what price to charge in any specific situation. The most that can be claimed for it is that it narrows down the zone of possible prices to the point where it may not matter a great deal which particular price is selected. As stated at the outset, one must beware of any pricing method that does lead to a single price, for such a method could not possibly take into account all of the special circumstances which are relevant to a price decision and which vary so greatly from market to market and from time to time.

Third, this method does not guide price setters in recognizing the factors that dominate the market at any time and in knowing when to switch basic strategies. Also, there may well be more than one dominant condition which must be considered in selecting a basic strategy.

On balance, then, the multi-stage approach to pricing at best only takes an executive fairly close to his ultimate destination. Although the multi-stage policy approach does not do the whole job of pricing, the part of the job that is left is relatively easy to finish in many cases. Where this is not so, one can only assume that the task would be almost hopeless without the assistance of a method that reduces the pricing decision to a series of relatively manageable steps in a prescribed sequence.

Conclusion

The multi-stage policy approach outlined here differs from usual approaches to pricing in two major respects. First, it demands a long-range view of price by emphasizing the enduring effects of most price actions on company and brand image. One might say this approach constructs a policy framework for the price decision. And, second, it allows the price decision to be made in stages, rather than requiring a simultaneous solution of the entire price problem.

LEARNING REVIEW

Questions:

1. ______________ helps to create the brand image.

2. The most fundamental pricing decision that management should make is ______________________________.

3. Not only must a product be *"within reach"* in price, it must also be accesible through______________________________ ______________________________.

Answers:

1. price; 2. the types of customers it will try to cultivate; 3. convenient channels of distribution

---

Retrospective Comment

My article offers a general approach for all marketing-mix decisions, not for price decisions alone. Possibly for that reason, it does not lead the price-setter to a specific price. The article also says very little about how resellers, rivals, colleagues, and suppliers should figure in price decisions.

This article, like the rest of the literature dealing with pricing, concentrates on ultimate customers or rivals, neglects other parties, and fails to indicate the behavioral impact of price changes or price differentials on all parties. We still know very little about the functional relationship between price and customer desire, reseller sales support, colleagues' cooperation, and salesmen's calling patterns.

Only if one explicitly deals with the several central parties to the pricing process and discusses the varied behavioral effects of price changes can one help executives to set price. Of course, this could not be done in the confines of a single article.

PART 8
International Marketing

The conversation went something like this . . .

A: "People are pretty much the same the world over. Right?"
B: "Wrong."

A: "Well, what sells well in St. Louis would sell well in Sao Paulo, would't it?"
B: "Not likely without considerable modifications."

A: "But once you've got it sold somewhere in Brazil, that's sort of like additional money in the bank."
B: "Sort of, but whose bank in whose country also makes a difference."

A: "Anyway, once you learn the rules, national policies, and traditions in a country; once you've established some good contacts over there; well, then international marketing is not much different from domestic marketing, is it?"
B: "Maybe, but those rules and policies can change fast. Let me give you a few examples . . ."

The only constant is . . . change

The section which follows was assembled to assist readers who may have conceptual problems similar to those suggested by the above conversation. The reader wanting a review or an introduction to the areas questioned above will find excellent illustrations in the order mentioned in Ernest Dichter's "The World Customer," Warren Keegan's "Multinational Product Planning: Strategic Alternatives," and David Leighton's "The Internationalization of American Business—The Third Industrial Revolution."

33

The World Customer

Ernest Dichter

PREVIEW

I. In the future an understanding of cultural anthropology will be an important tool of competitive marketing as business appeals to a world customer.

II. There are a number of characteristics of European markets of which the American businessman needs to be aware.
   A. Anti-Americanism is often coupled with a desire for American products.
   B. There are a number of ingrained stereotypes of which the businessman must beware.
   C. There are a number of hidden competitors in European markets that are unfamiliar in America.

III. Nationalism plays a major role in determining whether foreign markets accept American goods.
   A. National pride can be a motivating sales factor usable by the overseas marketer as an asset.
   B. Cultural traditions in a nation may dictate changes in advertising approaches that have been successful elsewhere.
   C. Stereotyped national self-illusions can alter the direction of marketing strategy.

IV. There are essentially six stages of development of various world customers.
   A. The almost classless society of contented countries view reliability and economy as important with a conservative attitude toward style.
   B. Affluent countries with room still at the top of the class structure, pay attention to functional values in products like automobiles.

Ernest Dichter, "The World Customer," is reprinted by permission from *Harvard Business Review* (July–August 1962), pp. 113–122.

C. Countries in transition still have a working class and wealthy upper classes, and prestige plays an important role.
D. Revolutionary countries with more extremely rich people and a very large group of extremely poor view products like automobiles as luxury items.
E. Primitive countries have very few literate people and they exist in a preconsumer stage.
F. The new class society with an aristocracy of bureaucrats and a large low middle class has much interest in prestige products.

V. The world market presents a great opportunity for American businessmen willing to understand and cater to it.

Only one Frenchman out of three brushes his teeth.

Automobiles have become a must for the self-esteem of even the lowliest postal clerk in Naples or the Bantu street cleaner in Durban.

There is a supermarket in Apia, the capital of Western Samoa (which received its independence in January of this year). I found can openers and the cans to go with them in a remote village on the island of Upolu.

Four out of five Germans change their shirts but once a week.

Amazon Indians use outboard motors in deep green water alleyways.

What do these facts, and many others like them, portend for the future marketing manager? For top management in companies with foresight to capitalize on international opportunities? They mean that an understanding of cultural anthropology will be an important tool of competitive marketing. They mean that knowledge of the basic differences, as well as basic similarities, among consumers in different parts of the world will be essential. They mean that the successful marketer of the future will have to think not of a United States customer, nor even of a Western European or Atlantic community customer, but of a *world customer*.

For Western European countries, it is specific marketing facts and consumer purchasing behavior patterns which are of moment to today's businessman seeking new customers. At present, these countries comprise the biggest potential overseas market for most products. They are also the countries about whose consumers the most research information has been gathered. However, as some of the above examples illustrate, other parts of the world too are becoming potential markets, as human desires break the barricades of centuries in South America, Africa, and Asia.

Emergence of the European Common Market has forced businessmen and philosophers alike to take a look at the European as a distinct species.

We now see the European as more than a Frenchman or an Austrian. The Atlantic community market and the world market may make us yet take a fresh look at what is alike and what is really different in humans, their desires, hopes, fears—in short, their motivations. Close observation of customers, and potential customers, all over the world reveals that there *are* some striking similarities, yet at the same time a considerable degree of permanent difference. From objective examination of these basic cultural similarities and differences, one may discern clues for serving the World Customer today.

In this article, I shall first point to a number of consumer behavior patterns relevant to international marketing, particularly within the Western European market but also in some of the less developed areas. Then I shall examine the differential role of national pride, which obviously affects and will affect the success of American-made products in Western European and other countries in the Atlantic market. Finally, in an effort to define and interpret the economic and psychological differences among world customers, I shall postulate six world market groups of nations, measured by the yardstick of middle class development.

The Distinctive European

The United States company going into Europe has to study the culture and the psychology of the people of the country, not just its manufacturing facilities and markets in the technological sense. The advertising and sales managers have to learn that reaching customers in a given country involves a real understanding of the basic motivations which operate within that country.

In dealing with various European markets, the American businessman must open his eyes to certain paradoxes, stereotypes, and hidden competitors.

Apparent Paradoxes

There are paradoxes between the way in which American products are perceived and the way they are used. Thus, anti-Americanism is strongly coupled with a desire for many United States products, often out of pure snobbery, often because they are symbols of an affluent society. The Italian housewife considers her American sister a poor cook and a lady of leisure, but dreams day and night of owning a Hollywood kitchen.

A similar paradox is that of the West German businessman who scoffs at American know-how, pointing out the technical superiority of many of his natural products, but proudly puts his elegantly uniformed chauffeur in a Ford, polished up to the last fold of its lacquered steel hull tuxedo.

Ingrained Stereotypes

The American businessman must cast off deeply ingrained stereotypes in analyzing the purchasing behavior of European consumers, in reference to product meaning, "purchasing morality," and quality consciousness.

We all "know" that French women are very fashion conscious. Yet a study recently showed that this was exactly one of those glib stereotypes that have little if any basis in reality. The purchase of a dress or coat is much more of an investment for the Frenchwoman than for the American woman. This results from differences both in income and in prices of fashion products. It is not enough, therefore, to tell a French shopper that a garment is fashionable. She also wants to know, in a way, the "trade-in value" of the dress or blouse. How long will the fabric last? How many years will she be able to wear it? These are promises and appeals which have to a very large extent lost their attraction to the American woman.

The European is very conscious of preservation. He collects and retains things. The only parallel that we have had in this country was during the period of World War II, when we developed a new kind of pride, a pride in doing without, a pride in not having bought a new car for several years, for example. This pride did not last very long. Just as soon as cars became available again, we reverted to our somewhat affluent American habit of replacing models quite rapidly. Yet this concept of "purchasing morality" still exerts influence in the United States for some products. For example, the average male still hesitates to buy two or three suits at one time because he feels that suits, together with many other articles of clothing, are highly overvalued, and therefore it is extravagant to buy more than one at the same time. On the other hand, most of us have learned that it no longer pays to resole shoes more than twice.

As for quality consciousness, as well as confidence in the trustworthiness of the manufacturer, this is quite different in different countries. In Australia or South Africa—and for that matter in England—you find on most toilet tissues the reassuring message that the manufacturer guarantees that the paper was not made out of secondhand rags, but only new rags and new raw materials.

Such a promise has become completely unnecessary in North America. Whatever advertising may be accused of, in many areas it provides the consumer, particularly in branded merchandise, with an assurance that he will not be cheated as long as he buys a well-known brand. It is true today that whether we buy a Westinghouse, a General Electric, or a Kelvinator refrigerator, we get more or less equal values as long as we pay about the same amount of money. What we have learned to buy is the freedom of individual choice. We buy images; we buy the sizzle because we have been reassured that the steak itself is of generally good quality. *In many European countries this confidence*, this almost blind reliance on the promise of the manufacturer, *has not yet been established.* Therefore, advertising approaches have to be based much more on definite proofs of quality.

Hidden Competitors

Another problem facing Atlantic marketers is that in many areas they are still dealing with hidden competitors, lurking in places unfamiliar in domestic marketing. Taking toilet tissue again, in some recent motivational research done in West Germany I found it was much too premature to promise the German consumer luxury softness or colors compatible with the bathroom fixtures. Instead, the hidden but real competitor with which the toilet tissue manufacturer has to contend is the newspaper and the old standby of the German equivalent of the Sears, Roebuck catalog. The West German family feels that toilet tissue, particularly the American luxury type, is wasteful and unnecessary. The advertising approach, then, has to deal much more with providing absolution and selling the concept that good quality toilet tissue is a part of modern life.

Ethos of Nationalism

Nationalism obviously plays a major role in determining consumer acceptance of nondomestically made products. Understanding its manifold aspects is a *sine qua non* for United States businessmen operating overseas.

National feeling manifests itself in many ways. Some of these have already been touched on briefly before. In this section, I shall show in greater detail how: (1) national pride can be a motivating sales factor employable by the astute overseas marketer as an asset; (2) longstanding cultural traditions in one nation can dictate the *discard* of advertising approaches proven successful in another nation; (3) stereotyped national *self*-illusions can alter the direction of marketing strategy.

National Pride

Admiration of foreign products often goes together with *hidden inferiority feelings* which are overcompensated by tearing the foreigner down. These products are the tangible symbols of foreign superiority. For example:

> In Venezuela, despite various forms of anti-Yankee sentiment, it is considered chic to smoke United States cigarettes. Even when the American brand

name is used and the Venezuelan smoker can discover the little phrase "Hecho en Venezuela" on his package, the almost completely identical cigarette suffers at least a 50% prestige loss. A successful approach used in overcoming this problem was to convince Venezuelans that the people they secretly admired in a form of love-hatred—the Americans—indeed liked Venezuelan tobacco, used it for their own cigarettes, and had no negative feeling toward Venezuelan cigarettes.

A similar solution was found in connection with Venezuelan rum by serving this rum in hotels in Caracas frequented by United States businessmen and tourists. The Venezuelan could be convinced that if it was good enough for the supposed foreign connoisseur, then it certainly ought to be good enough for him.

The French gasoline, *Total*, had a domestic marketing problem arising from a national inferiority complex. Gasoline, to the Frenchman, was for a long time represented by American and British companies. Gasoline and oil (to a lesser extent) are symbols of power. The Frenchman was not convinced that his own gasoline would have the same power as the foreign brands. The approach calculated to overcome this sentiment was to present *Total* as an international brand that happened to originate in France and the Sahara, but was accepted and well-liked in many other countries.

In Morocco, sales of French pasteurized milk had dropped considerably with the advent of Morocco's independence. This stemmed partly from the exodus of the French army with its families, and also from Moroccan unfamiliarity with drinking pasteurized milk.

But the drop in milk sales was also due to other factors, psychological in nature. One was the lack of confidence in the quality of pasteurized milk—Moroccan women were accustomed to buying from street vendors who milked the cows in front of their own eyes and then ladled the milk out of the pail. The soulless, odorless, clean pasteurized milk in bottles was simply too far removed from the original natural source of milk for the women to realize that they were still receiving the same quality of product.

But even more interesting was a factor dealing again with the phenomenon of national pride. The company had changed the lettering on its milk bottles and milk cartons from French to Arabic. The purpose was to please the newly independent consumers. Research showed, however, that instead of being pleased, consumers reacted negatively to this attempt at flattery. They stated it in the following way: "What is good enough for the French people is good enough for us. We don't want Arab milk. We want good French milk that the Frenchmen drink themselves."

For *marketing purposes* it thus was necessary to re-establish confidence in the naturalness of pasteurized bottled milk by showing cows and having street vendors also peddle pasteurized milk. A second measure was to change the lettering on the milk bottles back to French. Both steps resulted in increased sales.

The little phrase "Made in . . . " can have a tremendous influence on the acceptance and success of products over and above the specific advertising techniques used by themselves.

In a recent study in West Germany, this query was posed as part of a projective test: "An important discovery has been made in the technical field which has a great influence on our daily life. Which country has made this discovery?" As many as 78% answered: "Germany." (The study is being repeated in other countries. It will be interesting to examine the answers.) We also asked the Germans to think of a new product which through an error in production caused the death of several hundred people. The task of the respondents was to indicate which country would be most likely to manufacture such a product. We found that Germans considered this most likely to happen in the East zone, Russia, or the satellite countries, and then up to 30% in Italy or France.

The strong positive attitude evidenced by Germans toward their own technical product influenced an advertising approach developed for Ford in Germany. Research showed that the name Ford had a strong American association. The reaction of Germans was: "Americans drive our cars, Volkswagen and Mercedes; therefore they must be convinced that German cars are better than their own; so why should we buy their cars?" When the German Ford was presented as an example of cooperation between American ingenuity and know-how and German thoroughness and efficiency, considerable sales success was achieved.

Inverted Morality

The influence of cultural traditions permeates a host of consumer behavior patterns.

The fact that 64% of Frenchmen don't brush their teeth is in part caused by the lack of running water in many communities. But a far more interesting aspect of the behavior could be explained on the basis of what I call "inverted morality." Here is an illustration of what can happen: In Puritanical cultures it is customary to think of cleanliness as being next to godliness. The body and its functions are covered up as much as possible.

But, in Catholic and Latin countries, to fool too much with one's body, to overindulge in bathing or toiletries, has the opposite meaning. It is *that* type of behavior which is considered immoral and improper. Accordingly, an advertising approach based on Puritanical principles, threatening Frenchmen that if they didn't brush their teeth regularly, they would develop cavities or would not find a lover, failed to impress.

To fit the accepted concept of morality, the French advertising agency changed this approach to a permissive one. The new approach presented the brushing of teeth as modern and chic but not as an absolute necessity which when neglected would result in dire consequences.

In line with the "inverted morality" notion is the fact that deodorant sales in France are lower than in most other countries. The majority, up to 80% of French housewives, use laundry soap instead of toilet soap. Only 20% of them have discovered perfumed, feminine soap which in the United States is frequently referred to as a "French type" of soap.

Self-Illusions

Often nationals of a particular country are completely mistaken themselves about their own main characteristics. Successful marketers must be as cognizant of these national self-illusions as they must be aware of the mistaken stereotypes noted earlier. For example:

> Germans still refer to themselves as a nation of poets and thinkers; yet the largest selling newspaper, *The Bildzeitung*, has a circulation of 2½ million based largely on sensationalism and tabloid treatment of news. Even German *advertisers* had to be shown that this circulation, although proven by audits, was indeed psychologically possible. The only way this could be done was to force the German advertiser to look at his own people, including himself, without hypocrisy and in the harsh light of reality.

> All references to economy, comfort, and warmth had only a minimal effect in getting Englishmen to install central heating. They all ran up against a barrier of traditional self-illusion that Englishmen are of a hardy race that does not need the softening and effeminate effect of central heating. Inroads could be made only when the health of babies was used as a rationalization and after reassurance was given to the English "he-man" that to feel comfortably warm would not be detrimental to his self-image of virility.

> Most Europeans are convinced that they are individualists and nonconformists. Studies have shown that this is to a very large extent an illusion. There is a widely expressed fear of losing individuality, but right now it is the European who is becoming the representative of the mass market while it is the American market which in turn relies more and more on psychological segmentations. United States manufacturers may produce individuality on a mass scale, but individuality has become the decisive appeal in many products and services.

National self-illusions are hardly restricted to other nations. In the United States, as in quite a few other countries, many of our ethical principles are still based on the concept that we have to work by the sweat of our brow. In Germany, this is even more so. *The more you work, the more moral you feel*. Yet at the same time our modern psychological development and automation have resulted in a situation where fewer and fewer people work with their hands. Service fields are increasing, and we have more and more leisure time. The recent victory of the electricians' union in New York introducing a five-hour day aroused the nation for many reasons. Particularly pertinent here is that it clashed with most of our cherished beliefs of the importance of achieving happiness through work.

We are now confronted with increasing leisure time. Our discomfort results to a large extent from a lack of hedonistic morality such as prevailed among the Greeks for whom life was here to be enjoyed by a few people who did not have to work and did not have to feel guilty about it.

Leisure pursuits are spreading rapidly. Labor-saving devices are multiplying, and they are being adopted all over the world. The major difference lies in the degree of manifest or latent guilt feelings which are aroused:

> Instant coffee is used by the Dutch housewife accompanied by the verbal protest that she only uses it in an emergency. What happens, however, is that the number of emergencies has increased amazingly.
>
> French farmwives are inclined to say that they need large kitchen stoves in order to do the cooking for their large farm families. Young farmwives, however, have begun to admire and gradually buy the smaller units used by their city sisters. They have discovered that they do not have to stay as long behind the stove, and so are finding interests in other roles than that of a kitchen slave.

Breaking Boundaries

Politically, in recent years we have watched a host of new nations emerge from erstwhile colonial status. It may be argued that many colonies would have been better off staying under the protection of enlightened colonial powers. Yet their desire for independence, no matter how premature we consider it to be, is so impulsive, explosive, and uncontrollable that no other solution remains than to satisfy this emotionally, humanly understandable hunger.

More important to the marketer is the fact that the same desire which spurred these political events has another dimension—viz., *in terms of consumption, whole centuries are being skipped in a world revolution of human expectations.*

Thus, from the viewpoint of the international psychologist's concern with the people still living in national units, we see the gradual development of the World Customer who breaks all boundaries:

> When a South African clothing manufacturer asks how to sell more long pants to previously half-naked Bantus, he is the first one to smash the barrier

of apartheid, no matter how segregationistic his views may be. The moment one starts thinking of 10 million natives as consumers, one has to concern himself with their emotions and motivations.

Research revealed a great psychological parallel between the emancipated Zulu and the emancipated white worker than between the nonemancipated Zulu and his emancipated tribal brother. The latter is ashamed when visited by his former ethnic peers. He has learned to speak English Afrikaans, has started to wear long pants, and often owns a car—a secondhand, dilapidated car, but nevertheless a car. He represents in many ways the same emotional conflict as that which existed between the first- and second-generation immigrants during the period of heavy immigration in the United States.

In Australia until a few years ago 10% of the population was represented each year by newcomers, migrants, or—more euphemistically—"new Australians." These new Australians will change the basic Australian character in unrecognizable fashion within another ten years or so. As consumers, on the one hand, they want to eat, drink, and use the same products as the established Australians; on the other hand, they bring in their own customs and often superimpose Italian, German, or Spanish culture on the Australians.

Six Market Groups

How can we locate the World Customer at various stages of development? How can we measure nations?

The "consumer revolution" which we are witnessing is basically not a proletarian one, but is *a revolution of the middle class*. It is the degree of development of a large middle class which makes the difference between a backward and a modern country both economically and psychologically. That is the clue for appraising and interpreting different cultures, for measuring their achievement.

The most important symbol of middle class development in the world today is the automobile. It is the automobile which represents achievement and personal freedom for the middle class. And this restless middle class is the most important factor in the constructive discontent which motivates people's desires and truly moves them forward. In some countries, like the United States, West Germany, Switzerland, Sweden, and Norway, most people have enough to eat and are reasonably well housed. Having achieved this thousand-year-old dream of humanity, they now reach out for further satisfactions. They want to travel, discover, be at least physically independent. The automobile is the symbol of mobility; the automobile has become the self-mobile!

Using middle class development as a measure of achievement, if we were to visualize the social composition of each country in terms of a scale showing the size of its middle class, upper class, and lower class, we could probably define some six groups.

Group One: The Almost Classless Society, Contented Countries. In this group we would include primarily the Scandinavian countries. The middle class takes up almost all of the scale, with very few people left who could be considered really poor and few who are really rich. We are dealing with a socialistic security and equalization which sounds like paradise, but often leads to loss of incentives.

In these countries, products are viewed in a rather sober fashion. The car, for instance, is strictly utilitarian, and showing off with one's auto is not considered correct.

Studies have shown that reliability and economy are very important. Attitudes toward products are rational: they do not represent a special status value. There is generally a conservative attitude toward new gadgets and styles. Second cars are practically nonexistent.

Group Two: The Affluent Countries. This group includes the United States, West Germany, Switzerland, Holland, and Canada. Few people starve, and there is still some room at the top. The top of the middle class itself, however, often is high and desirable enough so that there is no need to break through and trespass into the unpopular and threatened class of financial aristocracy.

Among these cou tries the most advanced is the United States. What happens in many areas in the United States represents the latest and leading trends and permits us to predict what will happen in the next few years in the other affluent countries. People in affluent countries want great individuality in their products. They dream of high-quality, repair-proof, almost custom-tailored articles.

While the German still uses his car for prestige purposes, in the United States the status value of cars has substantially diminished and has been shifted to other products and services such as swimming pools, travel, and education. The average American considers his car more like an appliance than a status symbol. Conspicuous cars like the Cadillac or the Lincoln try to emphasize their quiet elegance to avoid being considered cars for show-offs. There is increased attention to functional values and integration in car designs. Cars are not pampered; they are expected to do their job.

Group Three: Countries in Transition. In this group we may place England, France, Italy, Australia, South Africa, and Japan. These countries still have a working class in the nineteenth century sense. But this class is trying to break out of its bondage and join the comfortable middle class. The upper classes still have privileges and can afford maids, Rolls-Royces, and castles; but their privileges are being rapidly whittled away. These countries have not had complete social revolutions. (The Labor government in England represented such an attempt but failed). Servants are still cheap but rapidly getting more expensive and less easily available. Many wage-earning groups suffer from low wages. Living standards are behind those of the United States and West Germany. The white-collar worker often makes less money than the factory worker, but he has not integrated yet with the developing labor-based middle class. Prestige still plays an important role.

Cars are pampered in these countries. They are an extension of one's personality. They are given pet names. They represent major investments. Cars are outward symbols of success. There are still many first-car people, who have only now bought their first proof of "having arrived." Price plays an important role as an invitation to enter the automobile world—upgrading the buyer from bicycles and motorcycles. For top classes, some very expensive cars are available. Style plays a role with certain groups; there is much experimentation, curiosity, and desire for product adventure. Markets are still fluid, have not stabilized yet. There is resistance in all these countries against planned obsolescence. A lot of people hold onto their cars for six to ten years or more. American cars are considered to be too flashy and also too expensive.

Group Four: Revolutionary Countries. Venezuela, Mexico, Argentina, Brazil, Spain, India, China, and the Philippines are in this group. In these areas large groups of people are just emerging from near-starvation and are discovering industrialization. Relatively speaking, there are more extremely rich people, a small but expanding middle class, and a very large body of depressed economic groups that are beginning to discover the possibilities of enjoying life through the revolution in industry.

In these countries large sections of the population have not even reached the level of being consumers. These are the Indians living in many South American countries, the people living in villages in India and Indonesia, and so on.

Automobiles are available only to a relatively small group. They are expensive and considered a luxury. They are taxed so highly that they are beyond the reach of most people. American cars are considered the ideal. People want to show off. Small cars are bought as a way to get started. As the middle class develops, there should be an even further increase in the sale of small and compact cars, with the really rich people preferring big American cars.

Group Five: Primitive Countries. The newly liberated countries of

Africa and the remaining colonies comprise the fifth group. In these countries there exists only a very small group of wealthy indigenous and foreign businessmen, new political leaders, and foreign advisers. The rest of the population is most often illiterate and ignorant and exists in a preconsumer stage, characterized either by barter or by almost complete primitive "self-sufficiency." The few cars that are sold are primarily for the government bureaucracy. There is no real car market as yet.

Group Six: The New Class Society. In Russia and its satellite countries, there is emerging a class of bureaucrats who represent a new form of aristocracy, while everybody else represents a slowly improving, low middle class. True, in these countries the extremely low income and the starving proletarians have disappeared.

The automobile, the modern home with its mechanized kitchen and mass-produced food items, and supermarket distribution represent the symbols of a new industrial society. By understanding the basic position of a country on this scale of development one can understand the role of products at present and one can also predict their future possibilities.

There is an interest in prestige cars. All the bourgeois symbols of capitalist countries are being copied—particularly those of the United States.

Our Greatest Opportunity

Many recent stories in the press—most of them picked up in foreign countries—make it appear that we ought to be ashamed of the good life we are leading. This recanting has its origin in a deep-seated guilt feeling which is unhealthy and dangerous. Some of the recanting is directed against a number of specific products, such as electrical gadgets, big cars, luxury and leisure time, and merchandise.

The real measuring rod of the success of one system over another should be based on the happiness of the citizens, their creativeness, and their constructive discontent. The desire to grow, to improve oneself, and to enjoy life to the fullest is at least equal, if not decidedly superior, to the goal of being ahead in a missile or a satellite program.

Our present life, therefore, should be presented as a challenge to the outside world—not in a boastful way, but as a life attainable by everyone through democratic and peaceful pursuits.

Conclusion

In most countries I have visited, I find that human desires are pretty much alike. The big difference lies in the level of achievement, in its many different forms.

In Iquitos, on the Amazon River, I recently visited an Indian tribe. They live in blissful fashion, hunting and planting bananas and yuccas. Who is smarter—we, the hard-working "civilized people"—or the contented Indians? Part of the answer was provided by the fact that our guide complained that there were fewer and fewer Indians for tourists to see. They were becoming "too civilized." In other words, these primitive people who were supposed to be happy are caught in the inevitable maelstrom of development. They smoke cigarettes and are beginning to wear jeans and shirts.

Growth and progress are the only possible goals of life. I believe that the clue to man's destiny lies in his relentless training toward independence, not only politically, but also in the psychological sense. We are beset by fears, by inhibitions, by narrow-minded routine thinking. Step by step, year by year, we free ourselves more and more. Jets reduce physical distances; international trade and mass communications break down barriers. The world is opening up. The Common Market will broaden into an Atlantic Market and finally into a World Market. In order to participate effectively in this progressive development of mankind, it is essential to have a creative awareness of human desire and its strategy throughout the world—to understand and prepare to serve the new World Customer.

LEARNING REVIEW

Questions:

1. Advertising approaches in Europe have to be based much more on definite proofs of ______________.

2. The successful marketer of the future will have to think not of an American customer, but of ______________.

3. Long-standing cultural traditions in one nation can dictate the ______________ of advertising approaches proven successful in another nation.

Answers:

1. quality; 2. a world customer; 3. discarding

Retrospective Comment

In my article I stressed the significant role of the car, its prestige value, and the possibility of using it as a measuring tool for the position of a country. The car in the United States, Europe, and many Scandinavian countries has lost its prestige value to a large extent. However, some of the statements made about developing countries still hold true.

The recent energy crisis has raised a much broader question: whether or not energy benefits the citizens of a particular country. Do they become more advanced by having better highways and cars? Such movements as *The Limits of Growth, The Club of Rome, The Protection of the Environment,* and *the Consumer's Movement*, all have had their impact on our value systems.

While some philosophers and writers demand that progress be halted and stress the dangers of a post-industrial society, directing their criticism to the very advanced countries such as the United States, it still holds true that most of the newer and less fully developed countries are more interested in first acquiring all the so-called, *devilish,* dangerous, immoral parts of the consumer society. In other words, world customers will resemble each other whether we like it or not.

In my own work, I am very frequently called upon by a country like Portugal or Spain, or countries of Latin America. They want to know what can be done to make women use deodorants or to shave their legs and under their arms.

In a recent visit to such fairly undiscovered islands as the Azores, I found a considerable degree of migration taking place. They claim they don't want any tourists; yet on the other hand, a labor shortage is taking place because of the migration. Many new hotels are being built to attract more tourists and with this development come all the evils of civilization.

Therefore, bringing my original article up to date, I must conclude that, despite the more sober attitude towards progress in highly developed countries, we are still moving at the same rapid pace. We are striving more and more towards a world market and a world customer.

Possibly the only major change is that we are paying a little bit more attention to multinational concepts, rather than trying to Americanize the world. Equally, another new trend has been started by a number of European countries as they have begun to introduce aspects of the connoisseur, the gourmet, as well as to rediscover individualism, through the influence of the United States.

34

Multinational Product Planning: Strategic Alternatives

Warren J. Keegan

PREVIEW

I. There are five strategic alternatives available to international marketers.
   A. Strategy one is to extend the same product world-wide and use the same advertising and promotional appeals.
      1. This is the most economical strategy.
      2. It does not work in all markets because there are differences in consumer preferences.
   B. Strategy two involves extending the same product with advertising adapted to have the product serve a different function.
   C. Strategy three is to adapt the product to meet different environmental conditions and to extend the same advertising appeals.
   D. Strategy four involves adaptation of both the product and the advertising to meet differences in environmental conditions and in the function the product serves.
   E. Strategy five is the invention or development of an entirely new product to satisfy the identified need or function at a price the potential customer can afford.

II. The best market strategy is the one which creates the most profit over the long term.

III. There are several steps in formulating international product policy.
   A. The first step is to apply the systems analysis technique to each product in question to determine whether adaptation, if feasible, is necessary or desirable.

Warren J. Keegan, "Multinational Product Planning: Strategic Alternatives," is reprinted by permission from the *Journal of Marketing*, published by the American Marketing Association (January 1969), pp. 58–62.

B. Company analysis dictates that any product or communication adaptation strategy must survive the test of profit effectiveness.

Inadequate product planning is a major factor inhibiting growth and profitability in international business operations today. The purpose of this article is to identify five strategic alternatives available to international marketers, and to identify the factors which determine the strategy which a company should use. Table 1 summarizes the proposed strategic alternatives.

Strategy One: One Product, One Message, Worldwide

When PepsiCo extends its operations internationally, it employs the easiest and in many cases the most profitable marketing strategy—that of product extension. In every country in which it operates, PepsiCo sells exactly the same product, and does it with the same advertising and promotional themes and appeals that it uses in the United States. PepsiCo's outstanding international performance is perhaps the most eloquent and persuasive justification of this practice.

Unfortunately, PepsiCo's approach does not work for all products. When Campbell soup tried to sell its U.S. tomato soup formulations to the British, it discovered, after considerable losses, that the English prefer a more bitter taste. Another U.S. company spent several million dollars in an unsuccessful effort to capture the British cake mix market with U.S.-style fancy frosting and cake mixes only to discover that Britons consume their cake at tea time, and that the cake they prefer is dry, spongy, and suitable to being picked up with the left hand while the right manages a cup of tea. Another U.S. company that asked a panel of British housewives to bake their favorite cakes discovered this important fact and has since acquired a major share of the British cake mix market with a dry, spongy cake mix.

Closer to home, Philip Morris attempted to take advantage of U.S. television advertising campaigns which have a sizable Canadian audience in border areas. The Canadian cigarette market is a Virginia or straight tobacco market in contrast to the U.S. market which is a blended tobacco market. Philip Morris officials decided to ignore market research evidence which indicated that Canadians would not accept a blended cigarette, and went ahead with programs which achieved retail distribution of U.S.-blended brands in the Canadian border areas served by U.S. television. Unfortunately, the Canadian preference for the straight cigarette remained unchanged. American-style cigarettes sold right up to the border but no further. Philip Morris had to withdraw its U.S. brands.

The unfortunate experience of discovering consumer preferences that do not favor a product is not confined to U.S. products in foreign markets. Corn Products Company discovered this in an abortive attempt to popularize Knorr dry soups in the United States. Dry soups dominate the soup market in Europe, and Corn Products tried to transfer some of this success to the United States. Corn Products based its decision to push ahead with Knorr on reports of taste panel comparisons of Knorr dry soups with popular liquid soups. The results of these panel tests strongly favored the Knorr product. Unfortunately these taste panel tests did not simulate the actual market environment for soup which includes not only eating but also preparation. Dry soups require 15 to 20 minutes cooking,

TABLE 1. Multinational Product-Communications Mix: Strategic Alternatives

Strategy	*Product Function or Need Satisfied*	*Conditions of Product Use*	*Ability to Buy Product*	*Recommended Product Strategy*	*Recommended Communications Strategy*	*Relative Cost of Adjustments*	*Product Examples*
1	Same	Same	Yes	Extension	Extension	1	Soft drinks
2	Different	Same	Yes	Extension	Adaptation	2	Bicycles, Motor-scooters
3	Same	Different	Yes	Adaptation	Extension	3	Gasoline, Detergents
4	Different	Different	Yes	Adaptation	Adaptation	4	Clothing, Greeting Cards
5	Same	——	No	Invention	Develop New Communications	5	Hand-powered Washing Machine

whereas liquid soups are ready to serve as soon as heated. This difference is apparently a critical factor in the soup buyer's choice, and it was the reason for another failure of the extension strategy.

The product-communications extension strategy has an enormous appeal to most multinational companies because of the cost savings associated with this approach. Two sources of savings, manufacturing economies of scale and elimination of product R and D costs, are well known and understood. Less well known, but still important, are the substantial economies associated with the standardization of marketing communications. For a company with worldwide operations, the cost of preparing separate print and TV-cinema films for each market would be enormous. PepsiCo international marketers have estimated, for example, that production costs for specially prepared advertising for foreign markets would cost them $8 million per annum, which is considerably more than the amounts now spent by PepsiCo International for advertising production in these markets. Although these cost savings are important, they should not distract executives from the more important objective of maximum profit performance, which may require the use of an adjustment or invention strategy. As shown above, product extension in spite of its immediate cost savings may in fact prove to be a financially disastrous undertaking.

Strategy Two: Product Extension—Communications Adaptation

When a product fills a different need or serves a different function under use conditions identical or similar to those in the domestic market, the only adjustment required is in marketing communications. Bicycles and motorscooters are illustrations of products in this category. They satisfy needs mainly for recreation in the United States but provide basic transportation in many foreign countries. Outboard motors are sold primarily to a recreation market in the United States, while the same motors in many foreign countries are sold mainly to fishing and transportation fleets.

In effect, when this approach is pursued (or, as is often the case, when it is stumbled upon quite by accident), a product transformation occurs. The same physical product ends up serving a different function or use than that for which it was originally designed. An actual example of a very successful transformation is provided by a U.S. farm machinery company which decided to market its U.S. line of suburban lawn and garden power equipment as agricultural implements in less-developed countries. The company's line of garden equipment was ideally suited to the farming task in many less-developed countries, and, most importantly, it was priced at almost a third less than competing equipment especially designed for small acreage farming offered by various foreign manufacturers.

There are many examples of food product transformation. Many dry soup powders, for example, are sold mainly as soups in Europe but as sauces or cocktail dips in the United States. The products are identical; the only change is in marketing communications. In this case, the main communications adjustment is in the labeling of the powder. In Europe, the label illustrates and describes how to make soup out of the powder. In the United States, the label illustrates and describes how to make sauce and dip as well as soup.

The appeal of the product extension communications adaptation strategy is its relatively low cost of implementation. Since the product in this strategy is unchanged, R and D, tooling, manufacturing setup, and inventory costs associated with additions to the product line are avoided.

The only costs of this approach are in identifying different product functions and reformulating marketing communications (advertising, sales promotion, point-of-sale material, and so on) around the newly identified function.

Strategy Three: Product Adaptation—Communications Extension

A third approach to international product planning is to extend without change the basic communications strategy developed for the U.S. or home market, but to adapt the U.S. or home product to local use conditions. The product adaptation-communications extension strategy assumes that the product will serve the same function in foreign markets under different use conditions.

Esso followed this approach when it adapted its gasoline formulations to meet the weather conditions prevailing in foreign market areas, but employed without change its basic communications appeal, "Put a Tiger in Your Tank." There are many other examples of products that have been adjusted to perform the same function internationally under different environmental conditions. International soap and detergent manufacturers have adjusted their product formulations to meet local water conditions and the characteristics of washing equipment with no change in their basic communications approach. Agricultural chemicals have been adjusted to meet different soil conditions as well as different types and levels of insect resistance. Household appliances have been scaled to sizes appropriate to different use environments, and clothing has been adapted to meet fashion criteria.

Strategy Four: Dual Adaptation

Market conditions indicate a strategy of adaptation of both the product and communications when differences exist in environmental conditions of use and in the function which a product serves. In essence, this is a combination of the market conditions of strategies two and three. U.S. greeting card manufacturers have faced these circumstances in Europe where the conditions under which greeting cards are purchased are different than in the United States. In Europe, the function of a greeting card is to provide a space for the sender to write his own message in contrast to the U.S. card which contains a prepared message or what is known in the greeting card industry as "sentiment." European greeting cards are cellophane wrapped, necessitating a product alteration by American greeting card manufacturers selling in the European market. American manufacturers pursuing an adjustment strategy have changed both their product and their marketing communications in response to this set of environmental differences.

Strategy Five: Product Invention

The adaptation and adjustment strategies are effective approaches to international marketing when potential customers have the ability, or purchasing power, to buy the product. When potential customers cannot afford a product, the strategy indicated is invention or the development of an entirely new product designed to satisfy the identified need or function at a price within reach of the potential customer. This is a demanding but, if product development costs are not excessive, a potentially rewarding product strategy for the mass markets in the middle and less-developed countries of the world.

Although potential opportunities for the utilization of the invention strategy in international marketing are legion, the number of instances where companies have responded is disappointingly small. For example, there are an estimated 600 million women in the world who still scrub their clothes by hand. These women have been served by multinational soap and detergent companies for decades, yet until this year not one of these companies had attempted to develop an inexpensive manual washing device.

Robert Young, Vice President of Marketing-Worldwide of Colgate-Palmolive, has shown what can be done when product development efforts are focused upon market needs. He asked the leading inventor of modern mechanical washing processes to consider "inventing backwards"—to apply his knowledge not to a better mechanical washing device, but to a much better manual device. The device developed by the inventor is an inexpensive (under $10), all-plastic, hand-powered washer that has the tumbling action of a modern automatic machine. The response to this washer in a Mexican test market is reported to be enthusiastic.

How to Choose a Strategy

The best product strategy is one which optimizes company profits over the long term, or, stated more precisely, it is one which maximizes the present value of cash flows associated with business operations. Which strategy for international markets best achieves this goal? There is, unfortunately, no general answer to this question. Rather, the answer depends upon the specific product-market-company mix.

Some products demand adaptation, others lend themselves to adaptation, and others are best left unchanged. The same is true of markets. Some are so similar to the U.S. markets as to require little adaptation. No country's markets, however, are exactly like the U.S., Canada's included. Indeed, even within the United States, for some products regional and ethnic differences are sufficiently important to require product adaptation.

Other markets are moderately different and lead themselves to adaptation, and still others are so different as to require adaptation of the majority of products. Finally, companies differ not only in their manufacturing costs, but also in their capability to identify and produce profitable product adaptations.

Product-Market Analysis

The first step in formulating international product policy is to apply the systems analysis technique to each product in question. How is the product used? Does it require power sources, linkage to other systems, maintenance, preparation, style matching, and so on? Examples of almost mandatory adaptation situations are products designed for 60-cycle power going into 50-cycle markets, products calibrated in inches going to metric markets, products which require maintenance going into markets where maintenance standards and practices differ from the original design market, and products which might be used under different conditions than those for which they were originally designed. Renault discovered this latter factor too late with the ill-fated Dauphine which acquired a notorious reputation for breakdown frequency in the United States. Renault executives attribute the frequent mechanical failure of the Dauphine in the United States to the high-speed turnpike driving and relatively infrequent U.S. maintenance. These turned out to be critical differences for the product, which was designed for the roads of France and the almost daily maintenance which a Frenchman lavishes upon his car.

Even more difficult are the product adaptations which are clearly not mandatory, but which are of critical importance in determining whether the product will appeal to a narrow market segment rather than a broad mass market. The most frequent offender in this category is price. Too often, U.S. companies believe they have adequately adapted their international product offering by making adaptations to the physical features of products (for example, converting 120 volts to 220 volts) but they extend U.S. prices. The effect of such practice in most markets of the world where average incomes are lower than those in the United States is to put the U.S. product in a specialty market for the relatively wealthy consumers rather than in the mass market. An extreme case of this occurs when the product for the foreign market is exported from the United States and undergoes the often substantial price escalation that occurs when products are sold via multi-layer export channels and exposed to import duties. When price constraints are considered in international marketing, the result can range from margin reduction and feature elimination to the "inventing backwards" approach used by Colgate.

Company Analysis

Even if product-market analysis indicates an adaptation opportunity, each company must examine its own product/communication development and manufacturing costs. Clearly, any product or communication adaptation strategy must survive the test of profit effectiveness. The often-repeated exhortation that in international marketing a company should always adapt its products' advertising and promotion is clearly superficial, for it does not take into account the cost of adjusting or adapting products and communications programs.

What Are Adaptation Costs?

They fall under two broad categories—development and production. Development costs will vary depending on the cost effectiveness of product/communications development groups within the company. The range in costs from company to company and product to product is great. Often, the company with international product development facilities has a strategic cost advantage. The vice-president of a leading U.S. machinery company told recently of an example of this kind of advantage:

> We have a machinery development group both here in the States and also in Europe. I tried to get our U.S. group to develop a machine for making the elliptical cigars that dominate the European market. At first they said "who would want an elliptical cigar machine?" Then they gradually admitted that they could produce such a machine for $500,000. I went to our Italian product development group with the same proposal, and they developed the machine I wanted for $50,000. The differences were partly relative wage costs but very importantly they were psychological. The Europeans see elliptical cigars every day, and they do not find the elliptical cigar unusual. Our American engineers were negative on elliptical cigars at the outset and I think this affected their overall response.

Analysis of a company's manufacturing costs is essentially a matter of identifying potential opportunity losses. If a company is reaping economies of scale from large-scale production of a single product, then any shift to variations of the single product will raise manufacturing costs. In general, the more decentralized a company's manufacturing setup, the smaller the manufacturing cost of producing different versions of the basic product. Indeed, in the company with local manufacturing facilities for each international market, the additional *manufacturing* cost of producing an adapted product for each market is zero.

A more fundamental form of company analysis occurs when a firm is considering in general whether or not to pursue explicitly a strategy of product adaptation. At this level, analysis must focus not only on the manufacturing cost structure of the firm, but also on the basic capability of the firm to identify product adaptation opportunities and to convert these perceptions into profitable products. The ability to identify preferences will depend to an important degree on the creativity of people in the organization and the effectiveness of information systems in this organization. The latter capability is as important as the former. For example, the existence of salesmen who are creative in identifying profitable product adaptation opportunities is no assurance that their ideas will be translated into reality by the organization. Information, in the form of their ideas and perceptions, must move through the organization to those who are involved in the product development decision-making process; and this movement, as any student of information systems in organizations will attest, is not automatic. Companies which lack perceptual and information system capabilities are not well equipped to pursue a product adaptation strategy, and should either concentrate on products which can be extended or should develop these capabilities before turning to a product adaptation strategy.

Summary

The choice of product and communications strategy in international marketing is a function of three key factors: (1) the product itself defined in terms of the function or need it serves; (2) the market defined in terms of the conditions under which the product is used, including the preferences of potential customers and the ability to buy the products in question; and (3) the costs of adaptation and manufacture to the company considering these product-communications approaches. Only after analysis of the product-market fit and of company capabilities and costs can executives choose the most profitable international strategy.

LEARNING REVIEW

Questions:

1. The choice of product and communications strategy in international marketing is a function of three key factors: a) ____________, b) ____________, and c) ____________.

2. Adaptation costs fall under two broad categories: ____________ and ____________.

3. The ______________________________
   strategy assumes that the product will serve the same function in foreign markets under different use conditions.

Answers:

1. product, market, company; 2. development, production; 3. product adaptation-communications extension

---

Retrospective Comment

The basic models for multinational product and communications planning as outlined in my article have proved to be remarkably durable. Many teachers and practitioners have extended the model to pricing and distribution decisions, thus applying it to the entire multinational marketing plan.

At the time the article was written, the strategy of *invention* was a theoretical output of my model rather than a description of actual marketing practice. Since the article was written, several companies have pursued invention strategies. Perhaps the most interesting examples are the vehicles especially developed and designed for less-developed countries by Ford and General Motors. The General Motors vehicle, called a basic transportation vehicle (*BTV*) can be made in a less-developed country in a plant that costs about $50,000. GM provides the difficult-to-manufacture parts which are assembled by a labor, rather than capital, intensive process. This results in training and employment opportunities in the developing country as well as a vehicle which is suited to the country's environments both in design performance and cost characteristics.

It is, in short, a perfect expression of the idea that I suggested in my article. While I do not, of course, take credit for the BTV or Ford's *Fiera*, I think that my model does provide a framework for arriving at this kind of output and that it is a robust and durable contribution to the ever-challenging and exciting world of multinational marketing.

35

The Internationalization of American Business—The Third Industrial Revolution

David S. R. Leighton

PREVIEW

I. Changes in business management in the last fifteen years, marked by substantial growth of overseas investment, have been so vast as to be called a third industrial revolution.

II. The economics of managing a modern industrial enterprise have changed dramatically.
   A. Improved communications and travel permit continuous monitoring of subsidiaries.
   B. Electronic equipment and management specialists permit the management and control of large-scale operations.
   C. Management has become the key resource for large multinational firms.

III. The implications of the huge changes in business mangement are many and complex.
   A. The traditional approach to international business is entirely inadequate for the 1970s.
   B. Business needs to adopt a micro orientation, focusing on the decision processes of individual firms, both buyers and sellers.
   C. Business should look more to the study of direct investment and less to the study of international flows of goods.

David S. R. Leighton, "The Internationalization of American Business—The Third Industrial Revolution," is reprinted by permission from the *Journal of Marketing*, published by the American Marketing Association (July 1970), pp. 3–6.

D. The skills of the international marketing man are crucial in direct investment.

Changes in business management have been so vast in the last 15 years that this period might be described as "The Third Industrial Revolution." The principal characteristic of this revolution has been the emergence of corporations of unprecedented size, complexity, breadth and international scope. For example:

> In 1969, International Business Machines Corporation had total sales of $7.2 *billion* with $2.5 *billion* coming from outside the U.S. This company operated in 108 countries with 99,000 foreign employees, one-third of the company's total payroll.
>
> The International Telephone and Telegraph Corporation had worldwide sales of over $5.4 *billion from 200 companies and divisions in 67 countries employing a total of 300,000 persons*. It derived 40% of its sales and a substantial share of its $300,000,000 before-tax income from assets outside the U.S

Manufacturing or service companies of this scale of international operations were virtually unknown 15 years ago, at least in the U.S. Today, these are merely two of several hundred U.S.-based corporations that meet the test of multinationality, owning and operating a significant proportion of their assets abroad. The really substantial movement of U.S. firms abroad that began in the late 1950s marked the true beginning of The Third Industrial Revolution.

This movement continues unabated; growth of U.S. direct investments abroad has maintained a consistent 10% per-annum rate over the last 10 years. A development of this magnitude will inevitably shape the international environment for business in the 70s and beyond. Its implications for academicians, businessmen, and government policy makers have not yet been fully appreciated.

The Three Industrial Revolutions

The First Industrial Revolution occurred in England in the last third of the eighteenth century. It was triggered by the invention of the steam engine, the replacement of hand labor, and the shift to more capital-intensive methods of production.[1] This spelled the end of the craft and "putting-out" systems, brought workers together under one roof, led to specialization and the division of labor, and put us on the road toward the industrial world of today.

The Second Industrial Revolution came in the 1880's and 1890's in the United States with the evolution of the national corporation. This was made possible in part by developments in communication, and in part by facilitating legal instruments. These developments enabled multiplant operation, opened markets, provided a vehicle for large-scale financing, and led to the growth of centralized staff and geographically decentralized line operations. They eventually pushed the corporation into large, vertically-integrated structures embracing research and development, marketing and distribution, and manufacturing.[2]

The Third Industrial Revolution began in the last half of the 1950s, with the sudden explosion of U.S. corporations beyond national and continental limits. From a modest level of direct investment of $20 billion in 1955, most of it in Canada, U.S. private direct investment abroad increased to $65.7 billion by 1968, with Europe the main recipient.[3] This development has helped transform U.S. business' inward-looking, parochial point of view to one of considerable international sophistication. At the same time it has wrought an even greater upheaval in the ways of foreign-based firms.

The Changing Economics of Management

The point that has been largely missed in writings on the subject is that this recent revolution in business has been primarily a revolution in management. The economics of managing a modern industrial enterprise have changed dramatically in little over a decade, making possible for the first time in history the successful operation of concerns of the size and scope of an IBM or ITT. These companies manufacture many diverse products, operate in a large number of different countries, and employ hundreds of thousands of people.

Less than half a century ago, it was very difficult to operate a company with foreign-based manufacturing facilities. Alfred Sloan and his associates travelled by boat to Germany to consummate their first real overseas venture, the General Motors purchase of Adam Opel A.G. in March, 1929.[4] The round-trip crossing took approximately two weeks. In addition, they spent several weeks on the Continent. During this time communication was difficult, and limited largely to telegraphic cable. Absence of top management for such an extended period would have been unthinkable for most companies. Sloan, however, had successfully delegated most operating decisions to relatively autonomous divisions. Once management had returned to Detroit, control over Opel's operating decisions rested largely with the man in Germany, I. J. Reuter. It was significant that he was a "company man," known and trusted by Detroit management. Reports were long in transit, and it was difficult for head office staff to check and interpret data once received. Reaction time at the center was slow; however, with the state of the art of management of the time, this was also true for other firms. It was not surprising that the few U.S. firms looking for other worlds to conquer turned their attention first to Canada. This neighboring country had the advances of proximity, a common language, and similar cultural heritage.

Today's jet travel enables businessmen to cross the Atlantic and back simply to attend a single meeting. With improved telecommunications, large amounts of data can be quickly and inexpensively transmitted from overseas plant to head office. There they may be digested by digital computer and critical operating data channeled to the executives concerned.

The health of hundreds of operating subsidiaries may thus be continuously monitored, fed back to corporate management, and corrective steps taken quickly before events get out of control. This is simply the application of the feedback and control principles of cybernetics to management of the overall corporation.

Organizations such as the modern-day ITT would have been impossible to administer economically prior to these developments. The thousands of clerks, bushels of records, and untold quantities of management time that would have been necessary to manage such an enterprise were out of the question only 15 years ago. Today, the job is being performed largely by electronic equipment and related planning and information systems coupled with a cadre of highly paid management specialists. This system of hardware, software and people, unlike a primarily clerical operation, represents a large capital investment and high fixed costs of operation. Such systems not only make possible the management and control of large-scale operations, but they also constitute a powerful force *compelling* businesses to extend their scope to make efficient use of the system itself.

At ITT, for example, each subsidiary works on the basis of annual, two- and five-year plans designed in detail and reviewed at least annually with the top officers of the corporation. Reports flow daily in to ITT's European headquarters in Brussels from subsidiaries in vastly differing lines of business. Even a small operating unit must submit as many as 13 reports per month, plus a number of others on quarterly, semi-annual or annual bases. The reports are processed by computer and analyzed by a highly skilled staff of financial and general business analysts. Where operations diverge from the plan, inquiries follow by Telex. Where trouble persists, teams of specialists converge upon the subsidiary and work with it until it is back on plan. Meanwhile, staff product line managers oversee various groupings of products seeking opportunities for intra-company sales, product improvements, or other business opportunities.

The core of ITT's business is this highly sophisticated planning and control system and, even more important, the talented team of about 2,000 managers who make it work. One criterion constantly in the forefront in the analysis of potential acquisitions is the opportunity to improve management under ITT control; i.e., by applying the ITT system. The central nature of the system to ITT's operation is underlined by the fact that several years ago the company stopped considering the acquisition of companies with less than $10 million in sales. This was due in part to the fact that small companies could not support the costs and effort required by the ITT control system.

This indicated that top managers in such situations, instead of facing eventually increasing marginal costs of management, as in classical theory, are actually facing a management cost curve which for all practical purposes is constantly declining. *The economics of management have undergone a complete transformation,* and it is this which has really been both the cause and effect of the growth of large multinational firms. It is significant that the growth of conglomerates also began to take off at about the same time as the growth of multinational companies, and for many of the same reasons. A principal task of top management in such firms has become to manage managers.

These developments imply that for the large multinational firm, management is not only a key resource, it is *the* key resource both in terms of people and systems. Having developed a large, sophisticated, and well-organized group of managers skilled in acquisitions and in operating complex systems, this team must be operated at a high level of its capacity. Continuous attention must be focused on acquiring new businesses, and more operating units must be integrated into the elaborate and expensive system for monitoring operations. Growth begets growth; expansion begets expansion. As yet the end is not in sight.

Some Implications

The implications are many and complex, and some are still obscure. These implications pose serious questions to business leaders, to national policy makers, and to teachers and researchers in economics and business administration.

Because of the growth of multinational corporations, world business is no longer primarily concerned with trade, but with direct investment. In 1967, world output from foreign-owned subsidiaries of international corporations was about $240 billion, while exports from the major nations totalled $130 billion. Sidney Rolfe, who developed these figures, has pointed out the following:

> It is therefore clear that for the whole developed world, international investment has bypassed exports as the major channel of international economic relations, and there has been a massive shift from the original extractive industry investments to manufacturing and trade, banking, services and a further shift from developing to developed countries.[5]

Unfortunately, neither national policies nor conventional wisdom at the universities have yet caught up with these changes. Much of the theory by which we attempt to understand and predict events in the world of international business is derived from international trade theory. This has largely been considered from the point of view of the nation as a whole; i.e., it has been macro in nature, a tradition that dates back to the mercantilists and Adam Smith. Its principal cornerstone has been the theory of comparative advantage, which attributes trade patterns to a country's relative advantages in the factors of production—land, labor, capital and, more recently, management. The theory's main concern has been with flows of goods and capital across national boundaries.

It is becoming increasingly evident that this traditional approach is entirely inadequate for the 1970s. The theory does not explain real-world trade flows very well, and in concentrating on nation-to-nation flows the theory deals with phenomena that are becoming less significant. In looking at trade from the country's point of view, we have lost sight of the fact that, except in certain special cases, countries do not trade with each other, companies do. The statistics we gather are aggregates, representing the sum of many thousands of transactions made by business firms with other business firms. Many of these business firms' critical decisions involve decisions on reinvestment of earnings or raising funds in foreign countries, neither of which results in any flow across borders. The decision to export, usually seen as something quite separate from capital flows, is coming to be looked upon as inextricably interlinked with the decision to invest; to decide to export is a decision *not* to invest in plant, and vice-versa. Contrary to classical theory, such decisions are based more often on demand and competitive considerations than on seeking lowest cost production sites. Most of these points become clear only when trade and investment are perceived as part of the decision-making process of business managers.

If we wish to explain phenomena in the world of international economics, we must adopt a micro orientation, focusing on the decision processes of individual firms, both buyers and sellers. We should look more to the study of direct investment and less to the study of international flows of goods. Kindleberger and Vernon, for example, have carried us part of the way; however, much is yet to be covered.[6]

The skills of the international marketing man are crucial in direct investment. Traditional international trade theory has ignored marketing; it has assumed perfect knowledge and has overlooked the key importance of demand functions. What we are seeing in an early stage of its development is the creation of a new body of theory in international economic relations, in which demand analysis and imperfections in knowledge will play a central role. There is hope that such a body of theory will bridge the gap that has for too long existed between the fields of international economics and international marketing. One example, already being explored, lies in the tremendous potential contribution of diffusion theory to understanding and improving the processes of economic development.

Conclusion

The revolution that has taken place in the economics of business management in the last 15 years has been profound. It has resulted in an international environment in which the old rules, policies, and theories are no longer adequate. New theories are desperately needed to help explain past events and to help us predict future developments.

The author has suggested that more useful theory can only come if a completely new orientation is adopted. A start could be made by looking at the decision processes in individual business firms operating under conditions of imperfect information. In the development of new theory, demand considerations must play a much more important part than they have in the past, and here the potential contribution of marketing is great. Above all, it must be recognized that the old world of trade has been largely superseded by the multinational corporation and direct investment. This will be the central fact of international business in the decade that lies ahead.

NOTES

1. This development has been documented in many books and articles. See, for example, Paul Mantoux, *The Industrial Revolution in the Eighteenth Century*, Revised Edition (New York: Harper & Row, 1961).

2. For an excellent summary of these events, see Alfred D. Chandler, Jr., *Strategy and Structure* (New York: Doubleday Anchor, 1966), Chapter 1.

3. These and other statistics on foreign investment are given in N. William Hazen, "Overseas High Stakes of Multinational Firms," in *Marketing in a Changing World*, Bernard A. Morin, ed. (Chicago, Ill.: American Marketing Association, June, 1969), pp. 47–52.

4. The events surrounding the Opel purchase are detailed in Alfred P. Sloan, Jr., *My Years with General Motors* (New York: Macfadden-Bartell, 1963), Chapter 18.
5. Dr. Rolfe is so quoted in the Toronto *Globe and Mail* Report on Business, Friday, May 2, 1969, in a report on an international conference on trade held in Washington, D.C.
6. Charles Kindleberger, *American Business Abroad, Six Lectures on Direct Foreign Investment* (New Haven and London: Yale University Press, 1969); and Raymond Vernon, "International Investment and International Trade in the Product Cycle," *Quarterly Journal of Economics*, Vol. LXXX (May, 1966), pp. 190–207.

LEARNING REVIEW

Questions:

1. The recent revolution in business has been primarily a revolution in ____________.

2. For the large multinational firm, the key resource is ____________.

3. World business is no longer primarily concerned with trade, but with ____________.

Answers:

1. management; 2. management; 3. direct investment

Retrospective Comment

Since this article appeared in July, 1970, the environment of international business has suffered a succession of violent paroxysms—radically new economic policy; the petroleum crisis and its effects on payments balances, commodity shortages and rising world prices; the decision to float currencies; and the rising price of gold. The old stability of trade and investment has been replaced by a situation in which nothing is certain. In such an environment, international trade and investment has entered a new era. One can only speculate as to its future direction, but a few features appear to be taking shape.

1. Growing nationalist sentiment, and a drive towards greater economic self-sufficiency.
2. A move towards diversification of supply sources by the industrialized nations, especially for strategic raw materials.

3. A drastic shift in the balance of power in world economics, away from industry-intensive nations and toward those with control over raw materials.
4. Serious limitations on the flow of capital across borders, caused as much by uncertainty as by overt governmental intervention in both sending and receiving nations.

As for the established multinational companies, there can be no turning the clock back. The basic forces that led to their establishment in the first place are still there. The challenge is to governments to harness this potent economic force.

The multinational corporation is potentially an extremely powerful device. But by itself it is neither good nor bad, only neutral. If properly harnessed, it holds the promise of being a major force for the solution of some of the world's most perplexing problems. If badly handled, it can serve to inflame nationalistic passions and trigger hostilities among the United States' trading partners.

As Professor Charles Kindleberger has said:

> " . . . the international corporation can develop as a monopolist or as an instrument of national goals which conflict with world efficiency, or it can operate in the cosmopolitan interest to spread technology, reallocate capital, and enlarge competition. The choice is not solely up to the corporation. It depends largely on national policies towards the corporation. Policy may be laissez-faire . . . or it may be interventionist in one or more directions: to maximize national income, regardless of the effect on the rest of the world, or to join with other countries in harmonized policies in the general interest.
>
> "Dependent then on the nature of their behaviour and the character of the environment within which they operate, as determined by governmental policies of an independent, contradictory, or harmonized type, international corporations can represent a boon, a bane, or a nullity."[1]

What Kindleberger is saying is that as businessmen, as academics, or simply as private citizens in a democratic society, we have three options:

One, we can bury our heads in the sand and ignore the problem in the hope that it will go away. But it won't go away, and to take this approach means abandoning control over national policies with regard to key economic and political goals, such as employment levels and inflation, the balance of payments, and regional development. No politician can do this and survive.

Two, we can attempt to exert greater control over the economy and hence over the multinational corporations themselves. This is what is being called for by Professor Galbraith, among others. Essentially the argument runs that what we need is a planned economy, based on a grand strategy as to what industries should be supported and which abandoned, and involving close control over the levers that affect economic levels in the interest of preserving the high domestic standard of living, employment, and minimal inflation. In this view, the U.S.-based multinational corporation should serve the goals of the domestic economy, and policies should be adopted which force these corporations to act in ways that suit the interest of the U.S. government. When the balance of payments is in trouble, force U.S. multinationals to repatriate funds. When it is against U.S. interest to trade with China, force the U.S. multinational to prohibit its subsidiaries from dealing with China. When employment levels are low, force the U.S. multinational to base its new plants in the U.S. rather than abroad so that American jobs may be created.

Carried to an extreme, the concern over jobs can and is being used by politicians in all countries to fan the flames of nationalism in order to win votes. At the same time, this approach propels the government into an even greater measure of control over the individual than it has today. This is in fact what is happening in Canada today, and is in danger of happening to the U.S. To have the cancer of nationalism used as a rationale for even greater centralism and state control seems to me to be a gross felony, compounded.

The third option, and in my view our only real hope, is for a serious attempt to harmonize the approaches of individual nations towards the regulation and taxation of multinational corporations. This would inevitably mean giving up, voluntarily, some measure of individual national sovereignty in the interests of the whole. But make no mistake—it is the concept of national sovereignty and the independent nation-state that is challenged most by the multinational corporation. And what we need, above all, are new institutional arrangements and mechanisms to cope with the challenge. The initiative in this *must* come from the United States, as the home base of the majority of multinational corporations. Yet, to be realistic, there appear to be few if any signs that this initiative is likely to be taken. In fact, many of the pronouncements that come from Washington seem to be carrying us in precisely the opposite direction: towards hostility and competition in our policies.

1. Charles Kindleberger, *American Business Abroad, Six Lectures on Direct Foreign Investment* (New Haven and London: Yale University Press, 1969).

PART 9

Ethics, Consumerism, and Social Responsibility—The Challenges of Marketing

Again, and again, and again, and . . .

How many times has it been said, and in how many ways from how many sources?

> "You must really *believe* in what you are selling."
> "Don't worry about how much money you're going to make—if people know you can provide a product or service that they need and want, you will be well paid."
> "You can fool all of the people some of the time, and some of the people all of the time, but never all of the people all of the time."
> "Do unto others as you would have them do unto you."

Another form of myopia

It is axiomatic that shortsightedness brings difficulties in the long run. Shortsighted marketing practices in the past have led to corrections to which present-day marketers are having to adjust, sometimes with great discomfort. Marketing is a powerful force in our society and with this power must be accepted the responsibility for its use. If marketers do not accept this responsibility with farsightedness, the countervailing forces of consumerism will make the adjustment for them. Exercising responsibility does not require the neglect of one's self-interest, however, To ignore this would be to remove the capitalistic spark which has rewarded through the provision of the largest gross national product the world has known.

There is a way . . .

In these last three selections, William Lazer examines marketing's growing recognition of social responsibility; George Day and David Aaker explain why consumerism has become and will remain the concern of the public, the news media, and legislative bodies; and Louis Stern offers a plan for reducing the incidence and enormity of future abuses.

36

Marketing's Changing Social Relationships

William Lazer

PREVIEW

I. Marketing has an important impact on our lifestyles today.
   A. The American lifestyle is a materialistic one which is optimistic of continued growth and expansion.
   B. One of marketing's roles is to encourage increasing expenditures by consumers of dollars and time in order to develop themselves socially, intellectually, and morally.
   C. Another role of marketing is to help solve some of the fundamental problems that nations face today.

II. Americans may feel guilty about the abundance in which they live and hence view marketing in a negative way.
   A. Abundant lifestyle must be accepted as moral and ethical.
   B. Marketing is a necessary condition of our high standard of living.

III. The boundaries of marketing have changed in modern society.
   A. Marketing can be viewed as a social instrument in a highly industrialized society.
   B. Marketing's responsibility is only partially fulfilled through economic processes.

Marketing is not an end in itself. It is not the exclusive province of business management. Marketing must serve not only business but also the goals of society. It must act in concert with broad public interest. For

---

William Lazer, "Marketing's Changing Social Relationships," is reprinted by permission from the *Journal of Marketing*, published by the American Marketing Association (January 1969), pp. 3–9.

marketing does not end with the buy-sell transaction—its responsibilities extend well beyond making profits. Marketing shares in the problems and goals of society and its contributions extend well beyond the formal boundaries of the firm.

The purpose of this article is to present some viewpoints and ideas on topics concerning marketing's changing social relationships. The author hopes to stimulate discussion and encourage work by others concerned with the marketing discipline, rather than to present a definitive set of statements. He first presents a brief discussion of marketing and our life style, and marketing's role beyond the realm of profit. This is followed by the development of some ideas and viewpoints on marketing and consumption under conditions of abundance, with a particular focus on changing consumption norms. The last section is concerned with changing marketing boundaries and emerging social perspectives.

Marketing and Life Style

Recent developments in such areas as consumer safety and protection, product warranties, government investigations, and a host of urban issues, including air and water pollution, and poverty, are stimulating thoughtful executives and academicians to pay increasing attention to marketing's fundamental interfaces with society. They highlight the fact that marketers are inevitably concerned with societal segments. Since the American economy is a materialistic, acquisitive, thing-minded, abundant market economy, marketing becomes one of the cores for understanding and influencing life styles; and marketers assume the role of taste counselors. Since American tastes are being emulated in other parts of the world such as Europe, Japan, and Latin America, the impact of our values and norms reverberate throughout a broad international community.

Yet a basic difference exists between the orientation of the American life style, which is interwoven with marketing, and the life style of many other countries, particularly of the emerging and lesser-developed countries, although the differences are blurring. American norms include a general belief in equality of opportunity to strive for a better standard of living; the achievement of status and success through individual initiative, sacrifice, and personal skills; the provision and maintenance of a relatively open society with upward economic and social movement; the availability of education which is a route for social achievement, occupational advancement, and higher income. Yet, there are contradictory and conflicting concepts operating within this value system. One contradiction is seen in the conflict between concepts of equality for all on the one hand and the visible rank and status orderings in society. Another conflict much discussed today concerns the conflicts between the coexisting values of our affluent society and the pockets of poverty in the United States.

In their scheme of norms the majority of Americans, even younger Americans, exude optimism in the materialistic productivity of our society. They feel confident that the economic future will be much better than the present, that our standard of living and consumption will expand and increase, that pleasure will be multiplied, and that there is little need to curb desires. They are certain that increasing purchasing power will be made available to them.

This is not to deny the existence of discontent in our economy of plenty, or the challenging and questioning of values. There is evidence that some younger members are critical of our hedonistic culture, of our economic institutions and achievements. Questions have been raised about priorities of expenditures, and authority has been challenged. Various marketing processes and institutions have been attacked. But, by and large, there exists a general expectation of increasing growth, the availability of more and more, and a brighter and better future. As a result of this perspective, economic opportunities and growth are perceived not so much in terms of curbing consumer desires as is the case in many other societies, particularly in underdeveloped economies, but in increasing desires; in attempting to stimulate people to try to realize themselves to the fullest extent of their resources and capabilities by acquiring complementary goods and symbols. Whereas other societies have often hoped that tomorrow will be no worse than today, we would certainly be dismayed if present expectations did not indicate that tomorrow will be much better than today. Similarly, the emerging nations now have rising economic expectations and aspiration levels, and their life style perspectives are changing. They expect to share in the economic abundance achieved by highly industrialized economies.

The growth orientation which reverberates throughout the American society has its impact on our norms and on marketing practices. It is reflected in such marketing concepts and techniques as product planning, new product development, installment credit, pricing practices, advertising campaigns, sales promotion, personal selling campaigns, and a host of merchandising activities.

Beyond the Realm of Profit

One of the next marketing frontiers may well be related to markets that extend beyond mere profit considerations to intrinsic values—to markets based on social concern, markets of the mind, and markets concerned with the development of people to the fullest extent of their capabilities. This may be considered a macro frontier of marketing, one geared to interpersonal and social development, to social concern.

From this perspective one of marketing's roles may be to encourage increasing expenditures by consumers of dollars and time to develop themselves socially, intellectually, and morally. Another may be the direction of marketing to help solve some of the fundamental problems that nations face today. Included are such problems as the search for peace, since peace and economic progress are closely intertwined; the renewal of our urban areas which is closely related to marketing development and practices, particularly in the area of retailing; the reduction and elimination of poverty, for marketing should have a major role here; the preservation of our natural resources; the reshaping of governmental interfaces with business; and the stimulation of economic growth. To help solve such problems, in addition to its current sense of purpose in the firm, marketing must develop its sense of community, its societal commitments and obligations, and accept the challenges inherent in any institution of social control.

But one may ask whether social welfare is consonant with the bilateral transfer characteristics of an exchange or market economy, or can it be realized only through the unilateral transfer of a grants economy? This is a pregnant social question now confronting marketing.

Business executives operating in a market economy can achieve the degree of adaptation necessary to accept their social responsibilities and still meet the demands of both markets and the business enterprise. At the very least, the exchange economy will support the necessary supplementary grants economy. Currently we are witnessing several examples of this.[1] The National Alliance for Businessmen composed of 50 top business executives is seeking jobs in 50 of our largest cities for 500,000 hard-core unemployed; the Urban Coalition, composed of religious, labor, government, and business leaders, as well as several individual companies, is actively seeking ways of attacking the problem of unemployment among the disadvantaged; and the insurance companies are investing and spending millions for new housing developments in slum areas. It even seems likely that business executives, operating in a market environment, stimulated by the profit motive, may well succeed in meeting certain challenges of social responsibility where social planners and governmental agencies have not.

Governmental agencies alone cannot meet the social tasks. A spirit of mutual endeavor must be developed encompassing a marketing thrust.

For marketing cannot insulate itself from societal responsibilities and problems that do not bear immediately on profit. Marketing practice must be reconciled with the concept of community involvement, and marketing leaders must respond to pressures to accept a new social role.[2]

The development of the societal dimensions of marketing by industry and/or other institutions is necessary to mold a society in which every person has the opportunity to grow to the fullest extent of his capabilities, in which older people can play out their roles in a dignified manner, in which human potentials are recognized and nurtured, and in which the dignity of the individual is accepted. While prone to point out the undesirable impact of marketing in our life style (as they should), social critics have neglected to indicate the progress and the contributions that have been made.

In achieving its sense of broad community interest and participation, marketing performs its social role in two ways. First, marketing faces social challenges in the same sense as the government and other institutions. But unlike the government, marketing finds its major social justification through offering product-service mixes and commercially unified applications of the results of technology to the marketplace for a profit. Second, it participates in welfare and cultural efforts extending beyond mere profit considerations, and these include various community services and charitable and welfare activities. For example, marketing has had a hand in the renewed support for the arts in general, the increasing demand for good books, the attendance at operas and symphony concerts, the sale of classical records, the purchase of fine paintings through mail-order catalogues, and the attention being given to meeting educational needs. These worthy activities, while sometimes used as a social measure, do not determine the degree of social concern or the acceptance of social responsibility.

A fundamental value question to be answered is not one of the absolute morality or lack of problems in our economic system and marketing activities, as many critics suggest. Rather, it is one concerning the *relative* desirability of our life style with its norms, its emphasis on materialism, its hedonistic thrust, its imperfections, injustices, and poverty, as contrasted with other life styles that have different emphases. Great materialistic stress and accomplishment is not inherently sinful and bad. Moral values are not vitiated (as many critics might lead one to believe) by substantial material acquisitions. Increasing leisure time does not automatically lead to the decay and decline of a civilization. In reality, the improvement of material situations is a stimulus for recognition of intrinsic values, the general lifting of taste, the enhancement of a moral climate, the direction of more attention to the appreciation of arts and esthetics. History seems to confirm this; for great artistic and cultural advancements were at least accompanied by, if not directly stimulated by, periods of flourishing trade and commerce.

Marketing and Consumption under Abundance

American consumers are confronted wth a dilemma. On the one hand, they live in a very abundant, automated economy that provides a surplus of products, an increasing amount of leisure, and an opportunity for a relative life of ease. On the other hand, they have a rich tradition of hard physical work, sweat, perseverance in the face of adversity, earning a living through hard labor, being thrifty, and "saving for a rainy day." There is more than token acceptance of a philosophy that a life of ease is sinful, immoral, and wrong. Some consumers appear to fear the abundance we have and the potential life style that it can bring, and are basically uncomfortable with such a way of life.

Yet, for continued economic growth and expansion, this feeling of guilt must be overcome. American consumers still adhere to many puritanical concepts of consumption, which are relevant in an economy of scarcity but not in our economy of abundance. Our society faces a task of making consumers accept comfortably the fact that a life style of relative leisure and luxury that eliminates much hard physical labor and drudgery, and permits us to alter unpleasant environments, is actually one of the major accomplishments of our age, rather than the indication of a sick, failing, or decaying society. Those activities resulting in the acquisition of more material benefits and greater enjoyment of life are not to be feared or automatically belittled, nor is the reduction of drudgery and hard physical tasks to be regretted.

Some of the very fundamental precepts underlying consumption have changed. For example, consumption is no longer an exclusive home-centered activity as it once was; consumption of large quantities of many goods and services outside the home on a regular basis is very common. Similarly, the hard work and drudgery of the home is being replaced by machines and services. The inherent values of thrift and saving are now being challenged by the benefits of spending and the security of new financial and employment arrangements.[3] In fact, the intriguing problems of consumption must now receive the attention previously accorded to those of physical production.

In essence, our consumption philosophy must change. It must be brought into line with our age of plenty, with an age of automation and mass production, with a highly industrialized mass-consumption society.

To do so, the abundant life style must be accepted as a moral one, as an ethical one, as a life which can be inherently good. The criteria for judging our economic system and our marketing activities should include opportunity for consumers to develop themselves to the fullest extent, personally and professionally; to realize and express themselves in a creative manner; to accept their societal responsibilities; and to achieve large measures of happiness. Abundance should not lead to a sense of guilt stemming from the automatic declaration of the immorality of a comfortable way of life spurred on by marketing practices.

In our society, is it not desirable to urge consumers to acquire additional material objects? Cannot the extension of consumer wants and needs be a great force for improvement and for increasing societal awareness and social contributions? Is it not part of marketing's social responsibility to help stimulate the desire to improve the quality of life—particularly the economic quality—and so serve the public interest?

In assessing consumption norms, we should recognize that consumer expenditures and investments are not merely the functions of increased income. They stem from and reflect our life style. Thus, new consumption standards should be established, including the acceptance of self-indulgence, of luxurious surroundings, and of non-utilitarian products. Obviously, products that permit consumers to indulge themselves are not "strict necessities." Their purchase does not, and should not, appeal to a "utilitarian rationale." For if our economic system produced only "utilitarian products," products that were absolute necessities, it would incur severe economic and social problems, including unemployment.

Yet some very significant questions may be posed. Can or should American consumers feel comfortable, physically and psychologically, with a life of relative luxury while they are fully cognizant of the existence of poverty in the midst of plenty, of practice of discrimination in a democratic society, the feeling of hopelessness and despair among many in our expanding and increasingly productive economy, and the prevalence of ignorance in a relatively enlightened age? Or, on a broader base, can or should Americans feel comfortable with their luxuries, regular model and style changes, gadgetry, packaging variations, and waste while people in other nations of the world confront starvation? These are among the questions related to priorities in the allocation of our resources, particularly between the public and private sectors and between the national and international boundaries that have been discussed by social and economic commentators such as Galbraith[4] and Toynbee.

These are not easy questions to answer. The answers depend on the perspective adopted (whether macro or micro), on the personal philosophy adhered to (religious and otherwise), and on the social concern of individuals, groups, and nations. No perfect economic system has or will ever exist, and the market system is no exception. Economic and social problems and conflicts will remain, but we should strive to eliminate the undesirable features of our market system. And it is clear that when abundance prevails individuals and nations can afford to, and do, exercise increasing social concern.

Toynbee, in assessing our norms and value systems (particularly advertising), wrote that if it is true that personal consumption stimulated by advertising is essential for growth and full employment in our economy (which we in marketing believe), then it demonstrates automatically to his mind that an economy of abundance is a spiritually unhealthy way of life and that the sooner it is reformed, the better.[5] Thus, he concluded that our way of life, based on personal consumption stimulated by advertising, needs immediate reform. But let us ponder for a moment these rather strong indictments of our norms and the impact of marketing on our value systems and life style.

When economic abundance prevails, the limitations and constraints on both our economic system and various parts of our life style shift. The most critical point in the functioning of society shifts from physical production to consumption. Accordingly, the culture must be reoriented: a producers' culture must be converted into a consumers' culture. Society must adjust to a new set of drives and values in which consumption, and hence marketing activities, becomes paramount. Buckminster Fuller has referred to the necessity of creating regenerative consumers in our affluent society.[6] The need for consumers willing and able to expand their purchases both quantitatively and qualitatively is now apparent in the United States. It is becoming increasingly so in Russia, and it will be so in the future among the underdeveloped and emerging nations. Herein lies a challenge for marketing—the challenge of changing norms and values to bring them into line with the requirements of an abundant economy.

Although some social critics and observers might lead us to believe that we should be ashamed of our life style, and although our affluent society is widely criticized, it is circumspect to observe that other nations of the world are struggling to achieve the stage of affluence that has been delivered by our economic system. When they achieve it, they will be forced to wrestle with similar problems of abundance, materialism, consumption, and marketing that we now face.

Consumption Activities and Norms

The relative significance of consumers and consumption as economic determinants has been underemphasized in our system.[7] Consumption should not be considered an automatic or a happenstance activity. We must understand and establish the necessary conditions for consumption to proceed on a continuing and orderly basis. This has rich meaning for marketing. New marketing concepts and tools that encourage continuing production rather than disruptive production or the placement of consumer orders far in advance, or new contractual obligations, must be developed.[8] To achieve our stated economic goals of stability, growth, and full employment, marketing must be viewed as a force that will shape economic destiny by expanding and stabilizing consumption.

To date the major determinant of consumption has been income. But as economic abundance increases, the consumption constraints change. By the year 2000 it has been noted that the customer will experience as his first constraint not money, but time.[9] As time takes on greater utility, affluence will permit the purchase of more time-saving products and services. Interestingly enough, although time is an important by-product of our industrial productivity, many consumers are not presently prepared to consume time in any great quantities, which in turn presents another opportunity for marketing. The manner in which leisure time is consumed will affect the quality of our life style.

In other ages, the wealthy achieved more free time through the purchase of personal services and the use of servants. In our society, a multitude of products with built-in services extend free time to consumers on a broad base. Included are such products as automobiles, jet planes, mechanized products in the home, prepared foods, "throw-aways," and leased facilities. Related to this is the concept that many consumers now desire the use of products rather than mere ownership. The symbolism of ownership appears to take on lesser importance with increasing wealth.[10]

We live in a sensate culture, one which stresses materialism and sensory enjoyment. Consumers desire and can obtain the use of products and symbols associated with status, achievement, and accomplishments. Material values which are visible have become more important to a broader segment of society, and marketing responds to and reinforces such norms. But our basic underlying value system is not merely the result of the whims of marketers—it has its roots in human nature and our cultural and economic environments.

The concept of consumption usually conjures a false image. Consumption generally seems to be related to chronic scarcity. It is associated with hunger, with the bare necessities of life, and with the struggle to obtain adequate food, shelter, and clothing.[11] It is associated with the perception of economics as the "dismal science," with the study of the allocation of scarce resources.

But, it has been noted that in the future consumption and consuming activities will occur in a society suffering from obesity and not hunger; in a society emerged from a state of chronic scarcity, one confronting problems of satiation—full stomachs, garages, closets and houses.[12] Such an environment requires a contemporary perspective and concept of consumption and consumers. It requires a recognition and appreciation of the importance of stimulating the consumption of goods. For consumers will find that their financial capabilities for acquiring new products are outstripping their natural inclinations to do so.

But what happens to norms and values when people have suitably gratified their "needs"? What happens after the acquisition of the third automobile, the second color television set, and three or four larger and more luxurious houses? Maslow has noted that consumers then become motivated in a manner different from that explained by his hierarchy of motives. They become devoted to tasks outside themselves. The differences between work and play are transcended; one blends into the other, and work is defined in a different manner. Consumers become concerned with different norms and values reflected in metamotives or metaneeds, motives or needs beyond physical love, safety, esteem, and self-actualization.[13]

The tasks to which people become dedicated, given the gratification of their "needs," are those concerned with intrinsic values. The tasks are enjoyed because they embody these values. The self then becomes enlarged to include other aspects of the world. Under those conditions, Maslow maintains that the highest values, the spiritual life, and the highest aspirations of mankind become proper subjects for scientific study and research. The hierarchy of basic needs such as physical, safety, and social is prepotent to metaneeds. The latter, metaneeds, are equally potent among themselves.

Maslow also makes a distinction between the realm of being, the "B-realm," and the realm of deficiencies, the "D-realm,"—between the external and the practical. For example, in the practical realm of marketing with its daily pressures, executives tend to be responders. They react to stimuli, rewards, punishments, emergencies, and the demands of others. However, given an economy of abundance with a "saturation of materialism," they can turn attentions to the intrinsic values and implied norms—seeking to expose themselves to great cultural activities, to natural beauty, to the developments of those "B" values.

Our society has reached the stage of affluence without having developed an acceptable justification for our economic system, and for the eventual life of abundance and relative leisure that it will supply. Herein lies a challenge for marketing: to justify and stimulate our age of consumption. We must learn to realize ourselves in an affluent life and to enjoy it without pangs of guilt. What is required is a set of norms and a concept of morality and ethics that corresponds to our age. This means that basic concepts must be changed, which is difficult to achieve because people have been trained for centuries to expect little more than subsistence, and to gird for a fight with the elements. They have been governed by a puritanical philosophy, and often view luxurious, new, convenient products and services with suspicion.

When we think of abundance, we usually consider only the physical resources, capabilities, and potentialities of our society. But abundance depends on more than this. Abundance is also dependent on the society and culture itself. It requires psychological and sociological environments that encourage and stimulate achievement. *In large measure, our economic abundance results from certain institutions in our society which affect our pattern of living, and not the least of these institutions is marketing.*

Advertising is the institution uniquely identified with abundance, particularly in America. But the institution that is actually brought into being by abundance without previous emphasis or existence in the same form is marketing.[14] It is marketing expressed not only through advertising. It is also expressed in the emphasis on consumption in our society, new approaches to product development, the role of credit, the use of marketing research and marketing planning, the implementation of the marketing concept, the management of innovation, the utilization of effective merchandising techniques, and the cultivation of mass markets. Such institutions and techniques as self-service, supermarkets, discount houses, advertising, credit plans, and marketing research are spreading marketing and the American life style through other parts of the world.

Marketing is truly an institution of social control in a relatively abundant economy, in the same sense as the school and the home. It is one of the fundamental influences of our life style. It is a necessary condition of our high standard of living. It is a social process for satisfying the wants and needs of our society. It is a very formative force in our culture. In fact, it is impossible to understand fully the American culture without a comprehension of marketing. But, unlike some other social institutions, marketing is confronted with great conflicts that cloud its social role.

Changing Marketing Boundaries

We may well ask, what are the boundaries of marketing in modern society? This is an important question that cannot be answered simply. But surely these boundaries have changed and now extend beyond the profit motive. Marketing ethics, values, responsibilities, and marketing-government relationships are involved. These marketing dimensions will unquestionably receive increasing scrutiny by practitioners and academicians in a variety of areas, and the result will be some very challenging and basic questions that must be answered.

We might ask, for example, can or should marketing, as a function of business, possess a social role distinct from the personal social roles of individuals who are charged with marketing responsibilities?[15] Does the business as a legal entity possess a conscience and a personality whose sum is greater than the respective attributes of its individual managers and owners? Should each member of management be held personally accountable for social acts committed or omitted in the name of the business? Answers to such questions change with times and situations, but the trend is surely to a broadening recognition of greater social responsibilities—the development of marketing's social role.

Few marketing practitioners or academicians disagree totally with the concept that marketing has important social dimensions and can be viewed as a social instrument in a highly industrialized society. Disagreement exists, however, about the relative importance of marketing's social dimensions as compared to its managerial or technical dimensions.

The more traditional view has been that marketing management fulfills the greater part of its responsibility by providing products and services to satisfy consumer needs profitably and efficiently. Those adopting this view believe that as a natural consequence of its efficiency, customers are satisfied, firms prosper, and the well-being of society follows automatically. They fear that the acceptance of any other responsibilities by marketing managers, particularly social responsibilities, tends to threaten the very foundation of our economic system. Moot questions about who will establish the guidelines, who will determine what these social responsibilities should be, and who will enforce departures from any standards established, are raised.

However, an emerging view is one that does not take issue with the ends of customer satisfaction, the profit focus, the market economy, and economic growth. Rather, its premise seems to be that the tasks of marketing and its concomitant responsibilities are much wider than purely economic concerns. It views the market process as one of the controlling elements of the world's social and economic growth. Because marketing is a social instrument through which a standard of living is transmitted to society, as a discipline it is a social one with commensurate social responsibilities that cannot merely be the exclusive concern of companies and consumers.

Perhaps nowhere is the inner self of the populace more openly demonstrated than in the marketplace; for the marketplace is an arena where actions are the proof of words and transactions represent values, both physical and moral. One theologian has written, "the saintly cannot be separated from the marketplace, for it is in the marketplace that man's future is being decided and the saintly must be schooled in the arts of the marketplace as in the discipline of saintliness itself."[16]

In this context, marketing's responsibility is only partially fulfilled through economic processes. There is a greater responsibility to consumers and to the human dignity that is vital to the marketplace—the concern for marketing beyond the profit motive.

Academicians and executives will be forced to rethink and reevaluate such situations in the immediate future just by the sheer weight of government concern and decisions if by nothing else.[17] In the last year, there have been governmental decisions about safety standards, devices for controlling air pollution, implied product warranties, packaging rules and regulations, the relationship of national brands to private labels, pricing practices, credit practices, and mergers. There have been discussions about limiting the amount that can be spent on advertising for a product, about controlling trading stamps, about investigating various promotional devices and marketing activities. Such actions pose serious questions about marketing's social role. If we do not answer them, others will; and perhaps in a manner not too pleasing, or even realistic.

There need be no wide chasm between the profit motive and social responsibility, between corporate marketing objectives and social goals, between marketing actions and public welfare. What is required is a broader perception and definition of marketing than has hitherto been the case—one that recognizes marketing's societal dimensions and perceives of marketing as more than just a technology of the firm. For the multiple contributions of marketing that are so necessary to meet business challenges, here and abroad, are also necessary to meet the nation's social and cultural problems.

NOTES

1. For a discussion of this point see Robert J. Holloway, "Total Involvement in Our Society," in *Changing Marketing Systems*, Reed Moyer (ed.) (Washington, D.C.: American Marketing Association 1967 Winter Conference Proceedings, December, 1967), pp. 6–8; Robert Lekachman, "Business Must Lead the Way," *Dun's Review*, Vol. 91 (April, 1968), p. 11; and Charles B. McCoy, "Business and the Community," *Dun's Review*, Vol. 91 (May, 1968), pp. 110–11.

2. Among the recent articles discussing management's new social role are "Business Must Pursue Social Goals: Gardner," *Advertising Age*, Vol. 39 (February, 1968), p. 2; B. K.

Wickstrum, "Managers Must Master Social Problems," *Administrative Management*, Vol. 28 (August, 1967), p. 34; and G. H. Wyman, "Role of Industry in Social Change," *Advanced Management Journal*, Vol. 33 (April, 1968), pp. 70–4.

3. Some aspects of the economic ambivalence of economic values are discussed by David P. Eastburn, "Economic Discipline and the Middle Generation," *Business Review*, Federal Reserve Bank of Philadelphia (July, 1968), pp. 3–8.

4. John K. Galbraith, "The Theory of Social Balance," in *Social Issues in Marketing*, Lee E. Preston (ed.), (Glenview, Illinois: Scott, Foresman and Company 1968), pp. 247–252.

5. "Toynbee vs. Bernbach: Is Advertising Morally Defensible?" *Yale Daily News* (Special Issue, 1963), p. 2.

6. Buckminster Fuller, *Education Automation: Freeing the Scholar to Return to his Studies* (Carbondale, Ill.: Southern Illinois University Press, 1961).

7. George Katona, "Consumer Investment and Business Investment," *Michigan Business Review* (June, 1961), pp. 17–22.

8. Ferdinand F. Mauser, "A Universe-in-Motion Approach to Marketing," in *Managerial Marketing—Perspectives and Viewpoints*, Eugene J. Kelley and William Lazer (eds.) (Homewood, Illinois: Richard D. Irwin, Inc., 1967), pp. 46–56.

9. Nelson N. Foote, "The Image of the Consumer in the Year 2000," Proceedings, Thirty-Fifth Annual Boston Conference on Distribution, 1963, pp. 13–18.

10. Same reference as footnote 8.

11. Same reference as footnote 9.

12. Same reference as footnote 9.

13. Abraham Maslow, "Metamotivation," *The Humanist* (May-June, 1967), pp. 82–84.

14. David M. Potter, "People of Plenty" (Chicago, Ill.: The University of Chicago Press, 1954), p. 167.

15. For a discussion of the social responsibilities of executives see James M. Patterson, "What are the Social and Ethical Responsibilities of Marketing Executives?" *Journal of Marketing*, Vol. 30 (July, 1966), pp. 12–15, and K. Davis, "Understanding the Social Responsibility Puzzle," *Business Horizons*, Vol. 10 (Winter, 1967), pp. 45–50.

16. Louis Finkelstein in Conference On The American Character, Bulletin Center for the Study of Democratic Institutions (October, 1961), p. 6.

17. The reader can gain some insight into government concern from such articles as "Consumer Advisory Council: First Report," in *Social Issues in Marketing*, Lee E. Preston, editor (Glenview, Ill.: Scott, Foresman and Company, 1968), pp. 282–294; Betty Furness, "Responsibility in Marketing," in *Changing Marketing Systems . . . ,*" Reed Moyer, editor (Washington, D.C.: American Marketing Association 1967 Winter Conference Proceedings, December, 1967), pp. 25–27; Galbraith, same reference as footnote 4; Richard H. Holton, "The Consumer and the Business Community," in *Social Issues in Marketing*, Lee E. Preston, editor (Glenview, Ill.: Scott, Foresman and Company, 1968), pp. 295–303; George H. Koch, "Government-Consumer Interest: From the Business Point of View," in *Changing Marketing Systems . . . ,*" Reed Moyer, editor (Washington, D.C.: American Marketing Association 1967 Winter Conference Proceedings, December, 1967), pp. 156–60.

LEARNING REVIEW

Questions:

1. ____________ is one of the fundamental influences on our lifestyle.

2. Marketing is a ____________ through which a standard of living is transmitted to society.

3. The ______________ lifestyle must be accepted as a moral one.

4. A compromise between those who stress the importance of marketing's social dimensions and those who stress marketing's responsibility to satisfy consumer needs profitably and efficiently is the position that does not take issue with the ends of consumer satisfaction, profit, and growth but rather views the market process as ____.

Answers:

1. Marketing; 2. social instrument; 3. abundant; 4. one of the controlling elements of the world's social and economic growth

Retrospective Comment

The question was asked of me, "What else might be said if the article were being written today rather than back in 1968?" I would have to answer, "Very little!" The general thrust is the same and the trends which I indicated seem to be unfolding. There are additional examples and a wide variety of experiences that may be noted reinforcing these observations.

Just as the 1950s ushered in a managerial orientation, the latter part of the 1960s brought forth a leading edge of social responsibility. It was noted initially by a few businessmen and professors, but received relatively little emphasis. However, by 1970 it was well-entrenched in business and institutionalized by government and numerous articles and some books appeared. Perhaps history will show the next decade to be a period during which the social responsibility concept grew and matured.

It appears that the 1970s will be a decade during which marketers will look beyond merely satisfying consumer needs and wants in specific markets by products and services, and will become more concerned with social goals. The discipline of social marketing is being established. Marketing under conditions of scarcity and shortages is being considered. Greater recognition is being given to ecological and environmental goals and marketing's impact on them and on the quality of our life.

The social relationships of marketing have changed and, as a result, the marketing discipline is increasingly reflecting these developments. But this does not mean that economic goals and the profit orientation will be ignored. They must be a primary but not sole focus of a marketing-oriented business.

37

A Guide to Consumerism

George S. Day
and
David A. Aaker

PREVIEW

I. The most common understanding of consumerism is in reference to the activities designed to protect individuals from practices that infringe upon their rights as consumers.
   A. The oldest and least controversial aspect is protection against clear-cut abuses.
   B. Provision of adequate information involves the economic interests of the consumer.
   C. The protection of consumers against themselves and other consumers is a controversial facet.

II. The scope of consumerism will probably eventually subsume or be subsumed by two other areas of social concern:
   A. Distortions and inequities in the *economic environment* have been a concern since the end of the 19th century.
   B. The declining quality of the *physical environment* is a recent concern.

III. There are a number of underlying reasons for the upsurge in consumerism.
   A. A number of causes are associated with the discontented consumer.
      1. Problems of the marketplace, such as the proliferation of products, make it impossible for the consumer to have all the information he needs to make useful price and quality comparisons.
      2. Changes in the social fabric, such as the new visibility of the low income consumer and a dissatisfaction with the impersonalization of society, have been catalysts for consumerism.

George S. Day and David Aaker, "A Guide to Consumerism," is reprinted by permission from the *Journal of Marketing*, published by the American Marketing Association (July 1970), pp. 12–19.

B. The consumer has found more effective ways to express feelings and press for change than ever before.
C. The legal and political structure has been much more willing to take action than ever before.

IV. Consumerism activity is not likely to decline significantly in the future; therefore, effective programs to protect the rights of the consumer should be developed using information gained from planned research.

Consumerism has played an expanding role in the environment of business decision makers. Despite wishful thinking by some, the following analysis of consumerism is as relevant today as it was in 1964 when it was written:

1. As evidenced by consumer agitation at the local-state-federal levels, business has failed to meet the total needs and desires of today's consumers.
2. Into this business-created vacuum, government forces have quickly moved to answer this consumer need.
3. The areas of consumer interest are so diverse that they offer government agencies and legislators almost limitless reasons for additional regulation of business and commerce.
4. If business managers want to avoid such new government regulations (with the attendant possibilities of excessive and punitive legislation), they will have to take positive action to demonstrate that the business interest is in more general accord with consumer's needs and wants.[1]

The ensuing six years has seen the passage of considerable consumerism legislation and a substantial broadening of the concept's scope. During this period one constant factor has been a lack of agreement on the extent of the influence of consumerism or its long-range implications. Businessmen have suffered from a myopia that comes from perceiving consumerism primarily in terms of markets with which they are very familiar. Their emphasis on the peculiarities of these few markets often leads them to overlook similar problems in other contexts and, thus, to discount the seriousness of the overall problem they face. Legislators and members of the consumer movement are more responsive to the broad problems facing consumers, but their lack of understanding of specific market situations too often leads to inappropriate diagnoses and solutions. Fortunately the two basic perspectives are demonstrating a healthy convergence. The goal of this paper is to encourage this convergence by putting consumerism into a perspective that will facilitate understanding.

The Scope of Consumerism

The term *consumerism* appears to be uniquely associated with the past decade. Even in this short period it has undergone a number of changes in meaning. Vance Packard, one of the earliest adopters of the term, linked consumerism with strategies for persuading consumers to quickly expand their needs and wants by making them "voracious, compulsive (and wasteful)."[2] His usage clearly reflected the concerns of the fifties with planned obsolescence, declining quality, and poor service in saturated consumer goods markets. The term was not put to wider use until 1963 or 1964, when a variety of commentators identified it with the very visible concerns triggered indirectly by Rachel Carson, and directly by Ralph Nader's auto safety investigations and President Kennedy's efforts to establish the rights of consumers: to safety, to be informed, to choose, and to be heard.[3]

The most common understanding of consumerism is in reference to the *widening* range of activities of government, business, and independent organizations that are designed to protect individuals from practices (of both business and government) that infringe upon their rights as consumers. This view of consumerism emphasizes the direct relationship between the individual consumer and the business firm. Because it is an evolving concept, there is no accepted list of the various facets of this relationship. The following is representative:

1. *Protection against clear-cut abuses*. This encompasses outright fraud and deceit that are a part of the "dark side of the marketplace,"[4] as well as dangers to health and safety from *voluntary use of a product*. There is substantial agreement in principle between business and consumer spokesmen that such abuses must be prevented, but there is often a wide divergence of opinion on the extent of the problem. As a result the government has taken the initiative in this area, usually after the divulgence of a sensational abuse. This has been the case with much of the legislation dealing with drug, tire, auto, and pipeline safety, and meat and fish inspection. Even so, this is the least controversial and oldest aspect of consumerism.

2. *Provision of adequate information*. The concern here is with the economic interests of the consumer. The question is whether the right to information goes beyond the right not to be deceived, to include the provision of performance information that will ensure a wise purchase. Much of the controversy and confusion over consumerism revolves

around this basic issue.[5] The two polar positions identified by Bauer and Greyser are the business view that the buyer should be guided by his judgment of the manufacturer's reputation and the quality of the brand, versus the view of the consumer spokesmen that information should be provided by impartial sources and reveal performance characteristics.[6]

3. *The protection of consumers against themselves and other consumers*. Some of the thrust behind consumerism comes from the growing acceptance of the position that paternalism is a legitimate policy. Thus, the National Traffic and Motor Vehicle Safety Act of 1966 is not concerned with the possibility that the buyer has an expressed but unsatisfied need for safety, and emphasizes instead that carelessness may have undesirable consequences for innocent participants.[7] There is a sound basis in economic theory for such intervention whenever the action of a buyer serves only his own best interest and fails to take into account the effects on others. However, this principle is being extended to situations of "implied consumer interest" where the individual is deemed unable to even identify his own best interest (e.g., the mandatory installation of seat belts and the provision for a "cooling off" period after a door-to-door sale). This is a strong justification for the protection of inexperienced, poorly educated, and generally disadvantaged consumers. More controversial by far is the extension of this notion to all consumers on the grounds that manipulated preferences may be disregarded when the consumer is not acting in his best interest.[8]

The above three facets of consumerism suggest the current thrust of the movement. Yet, it would be naive to portray consumerism as a static entity. It has had a dynamic past and continues to evolve and change at an increasingly rapid rate. For example, the emphasis of the consumer movement of the thirties and later was on dangerous and unhealthy products and "dishonest or questionable practices which are believed to hamper the consumer in making wise decisions . . . and obtaining useful information."[9] The emphasis today is clearly much broader.

There is a high probability that the scope of consumerism will eventually subsume, or be subsumed by two other areas of social concern; distortions and inequities in the economic environment and the declining quality of the physical environment. The forecast of a greater identity between these social problems and consumerism rests on the fact that they are associated with many of the same basic causes, have common spokesmen, and seem to be moving in the same direction in many respects. Yohalem has indicated that the ultimate challenge of consumerism to industry is "toward ending hunger and malnutrition . . . toward alleviating pollution of the air, water and soil . . . toward educating and training the disadvantaged . . . toward solving these and other problems of a society rather than strictly of an industrial nature."[10]

Concern over the *economic environment* dates back to the end of the last century. The long-run manifestation of this concern has been antitrust law and enforcement, which has swung back and forth between protecting competition and protecting competitors. Despite various ambiguities in antitrust interpretation, this has been a major effort to ensure consumers' "right to choose" by increasing the number of competitors. Some regard it as "the fundamental consumer edifice on which all other measures are bottomed."[11] Judging from the recent intensification of concern over the economic role of advertising and promotion (insofar as they increase price and raise barriers to entry to new markets), reciprocity, restrictive distributive arrangements, conglomerate mergers, and related topics, it appears that antitrust issues will be a continuing impetus to consumerism. In a period of rapid inflation it is not surprising that advertising and promotion costs have come under additional scrutiny for their role in contributing to high prices, particularly food prices. This promises to be a durable issue, considering a task force of the White House conference on food, nutrition, and health has recommended lower food prices, by reducing promotion not related to nutritional or other food values, as a major item in a national nutrition policy.[12]

More recently, consumerism has become identified with the widespread concern with the quality of the *physical environment*. The problems of air, water, and noise pollution have become increasingly salient as the tolerance of the public for these abuses has decreased. In effect a "critical mass" of explosive concern has suddenly been created. The consumer movement has rapidly rearranged its priorities to become a part of this critical mass. This shift is not surprising in view of the desire to broaden consumerism to include problems arising from indirect influences on the consumer interest. It also follows naturally from the long standing concern with built-in obsolescence and poor quality and repairability, for these problems contribute to pollution in a "disposable" society.

As the consumer movement joins with conservationists and interested legislators there is a growing likelihood of government action. The argument for such intervention has been well stated by Andrew Shonfield:

> Increasingly the realization is forced upon us that the market, which purports to be the reflection of the way in which people spontaneously value their individual wants and efforts, is a poor guide to the best means of satisfying the real wishes of consumers. That is because market prices generally fail to measure either social costs or social benefits. In our civilization these grow constantly more important. Simply because some

> amenity—let it be a pleasant view or an uncongested road or a reasonably quiet environment—is not paid for directly by those who enjoy it, there is no measure of the cost of the disinvestment which occurs when a profitable economic activity destroys what already exists. Unless the State actively intervenes, and on an increasing scale, to compel private enterprise to adapt its investment decisions to considerations such as these, the process of economic growth may positively impede the attainment of things that people most deeply want.[13]

The result may well be increased controls on producer-controlled emittants and, perhaps, "quality standards . . . or other regulatory devices in the interest of upgrading product quality and repairability."[14]

The Underlying Causes of Consumerism

Additional insights come from a consideration of the factors underlying the recent upsurge of interest in consumerism. It appears that increasingly discontented and aroused consumers have combined with a growing number of formal and informal institutions capable of focusing discontent, to create enough pressure to overcome the advantage of the traditionally more effective lobbies representing the producer's interests. Since a particular government action means much more to the individual producer (who will be totally affected), than to the individual consumer (who divides his concern among many items), this clearly involved a significant effort.

The Discontented Consumer

The discontented consumer is not part of a homogeneous group with easily described complaints. The fact is great variation exists among consumers in the extent of their discontent and there is a wide variety of underlying causes. Nonetheless, it is possible to distinguish specific sources of discontent that are traceable to the marketing environment from other more pervasive concerns with the nature of society.

Problems in the marketplace. To some observers the leading problem is imperfections in the state of information in consumer markets.[15] They believe consumers would be adequately cared for by competition *if* they could learn quickly about available brands and their prices and characteristics. However, as products and ingredients proliferate, each consumer is less and less able to make useful price and quality comparisons. This inability leads to "increasing shopper confusion, consequent irritation and consequent resentment."[16] The problem is most severe for products which are purchased infrequently, exhibit a rapid rate of technological change, and whose performance characteristics are not readily apparent. Hence, increasing pressure is applied for tire standards, unit prices, truth-in-lending, truth-in-funds, information about the design-life of durable goods, and so on. The truth-in-packaging bill is another manifestation of this problem, for it aims to help the consumer cope with the volume of information available relative to grocery and drug products. Since advertising has not been notable as a source of adequate, or even accurate information that could alleviate the problem, it has been under continuing attack.[17] To the extent that retailing is becoming more and more impersonal, the whole situation may become worse. Thus,

> . . . as a result of the character of contemporary retail establishments, the vastly increased number of consumer products, and the misleading, deceptive and generally uninformative aspects of advertising and packaging, the consumer simply lacks the information necessary to enable him to buy wisely.[18]

This is not an unusually intemperate charge; nor is it denied by the finding that 53% of a sample of adults disagreed with the statement that, "In general, advertisements present a true picture of the product advertised." This response measures both a concern over genuine deception and differences in people's tolerance for fantasy.[19] Nonetheless the potential for dissatisfaction is large.

The proliferation and improvement of products, resulting from attempts to better satisfy specific needs and/or reduce direct competition, has also had other consequences. As one appliance executive noted, " . . . the public is staging a revolt of rising expectancy. Customers today expect products to perform satisfactorily, to provide dependable functional performance and to be safe. This threshold of acceptable performance is steadily rising . . . "[20] Unfortunately the complexity and malfunction potential of many products has also been rising.[21] The result is an uncomfortable level of dissatisfaction with quality, compounded by inadequate service facilities.[22] This situation is not confined to hard goods, for one result of rapidly rising sales is overburdened retail and manufacturing facilities, which leads to deteriorating quality and service for almost all mass-merchandised goods.[23]

These problems are occurring at a time when consumers are generally less willing to give industry the benefit of the doubt—an understandable reaction to the well-publicized shortcomings of the drug, auto, and appliance manufacturers. Even without these problems, more skepticism is to be expected from consumers who have found that their assumptions about the adequacy of laws covering reasonable aspects of health, safety, and truthfulness are wrong. Recent disclosures involving such vital issues as meat inspection and auto and drug safety have hurt both government and industry by contributing to an atmosphere of distrust. According to Stanley Cohen, the meat inspection battle was particularly important here, "because for the first time the public had a clear cut demonstration of the jurisdictional gap (between state and federal governments) that limits the effectiveness of virtually all consumer protection legislation."[24]

Problems in the social fabric. The present imperfections in the marketplace would probably not have generated nearly the same depth of concern in earlier periods. The difference is several changes deep in society that have served as catalysts to magnify the seriousness of these imperfections.

The first catalyst has been the new visibility of the low-income consumer. These consumers suffer the most from fraud, excessive prices, exorbitant credit charges, or poor quality merchandise and service. Unfortunately, solutions oriented toward improving the amount and quality of product information have little relevance to low-income buyers who lack most of the characteristics of the prototype middle-income consumer.[25]

> Low income consumers are often unaware of the benefits of comparative shopping.
>
> They lack the education and knowledge necessary to choose the best buy, even if it were available. Because of their low income they have fewer opportunities to learn through experience.
>
> They often lack the freedom to go outside their local community to engage in comparative shopping.
>
> They lack even a superficial appreciation of their rights and liabilities in post-sale legal conflicts.
>
> Nothing in their experience has reinforced the benefits of seeking better value for their money; consequently, the low-income buyer lacks the motivation to make improvements in his situation.

Thus, the low-income consumer environment is a perfect breeding ground for exploitation and fraud. The extent of the distortion in the ghetto marketplace has only recently been widely comprehended and related to the overall failure of society to help the disadvantaged.[26]

The second catalyst is best described as a basic dissatisfaction with the impersonalization of society in general, and the market system in particular. Evidence for this point of view is not difficult to find, particularly among young people. A survey of college student opinion found 65% of the sample in strong or partial agreement with the statement that "American society is characterized by injustice, insensitivity, lack of candor, and inhumanity."[27] Similar levels of disenchantment were reported among parents and nonstudents of the same age. The need seems to be felt for social organizations that are responsive—and perhaps the impression of responsiveness is as important as the specific responses that are made.

There is little doubt that large American corporations are not regarded as responsive by their customers. According to Weiss, both manufacturers and retailers are "turning a deaf ear," while increasingly sophisticated consumers are demanding more personal relationships and security in their purchases.[28] This situation stems from a series of changes in the marketing environment—the rise of self-service and discounting (in part because of the difficulty of obtaining good sales employees), the high cost of trained service personnel, and the intervention of the computer into the relationship with consequent rigidifying of customer policies and practices. The prospects for improvement are dim, because the benefits of good service and prompt personal attention to complaints are difficult to quantify and consequently are given low priority when investment decisions are made. As more consumers are seeing the government as being more sympathetic, if not more helpful, the prospect for arbitration procedures to settle complaints is increased.

The most disturbing feature of the catalyzing effects of the recently visible low-income consumer, the growing dissatisfaction with the impersonalization of society, and concern over the quality of the physical environment is their intractability. These problems are almost impervious to piecemeal attempts at correction. In view of the small likelihood of large-scale changes in social priorities or social structures, these problems will be a part of the environment for the foreseeable future.

The final and most enduring catalyst is the consequence of an increasingly better educated consumer. The Chamber of Commerce recently noted that the consumer of the present and future "expects more information about the products and services he buys. He places greater emphasis on product performance, quality and safety. He is more aware of his 'rights' as a consumer and is more responsive than ever before to political initiatives to protect these rights."[29]

The Activist Consumer

The discontented consumer found many more effective ways to express feelings and press for change during the 1960s than ever before. The development of means of translating discontent into effective pressure distinguishes recent consumer efforts from those of the 1910 and 1935 eras.

The consumer has been more ably represented by advocates such as Ralph Nader, Senator Warren Magnuson, and a number of journalists who pursue similar interests. These men are able to identify and publicize problems, and to follow up with workable programs for improvement. In a real sense, they are self-elected legal counsels to a typically unrepresented constituency. Many consumer problems would have remained smoldering but unfocused discontents without their attention. New product researchers have frequently found consumers do not seem to know what is bothering them or realize that others are similarly troubled until the extent of the problem is publicized or an alternative is provided.

The institutional framework has also been expanded and strengthened in recent years. Traditional bodies, such as Consumers Union and Consumers Research, Inc., have now received support from permanent bodies in the government such as the Consumer Advisory Council and the Office of the Special Assistant to the President for Consumer Affairs. These agencies have been specifically developed to avoid the problems of excessive identification with regulated industries which plague some of the older regulated bodies.

This decade has also seen greater willingness on the part of consumers to take direct action. Consider the protest of housewives in Denver over the costs of trading stamps and games. While this was probably due to general dissatisfaction over the effects of inflation on food prices, it did represent an important precedent. More sobering is the extreme form of protest documented by the National Commission on Civil Disorders. "Much of the violence in recent civil disorders has been directed at stores and other commerical establishments in disadvantaged Negro areas. In some cases, rioters focused on stores operated by white merchants who, they apparently believed, had been charging exorbitant prices or selling inferior goods. Not all the violence against these stores can be attributed to 'revenge' for such practices. Yet, it is clear that many residents of disadvantaged Negro neighborhoods believe they suffer constant abuses by local merchants."[30]

The Changing Legal and Political Scene

Pressures for change have been directed at a legal and political structure that is much more willing to take action than before:

1. Overall, there is more acceptance of government involvement in issues of consumer protection. Also, the federal government has been more prepared to take action because the state and local governments have generally defaulted their early legal responsibility in this area.[31]

2. A combination of factors has contributed to the expanded role of the federal government. Congress is no longer so dominated by the rural constituencies who appear less interested in these matters; consumer legislation is relatively cheap and appears to generate goodwill among

voters; and various tests of the influence of business lobbyists have shown that their power is not as great as originally feared.[32] In fact, many observers feel that industry may have been its own worst enemy by often opposing all consumer legislation without admitting any room for improvement or providing constructive alternatives.[33] Worse, they may have demonstrated that industry self-regulation is not workable.[34]

3. The consequence is a Congress that is responsive to the economic interests of consumers. A significant proportion of the enacted or pending legislation is a result of Congressional initiative and is directed toward ensuring that consumers have adequate and accurate shopping information. This is very different from earlier legislation which was enacted because a tragedy dramatized the need to protect health and safety.[35]

4. A large number of legal reforms have been slowly instituted which attempt to correct the imbalance of power held by the manufacturers; e.g., the expansion of the implied warranty, and the elimination of privity of contract.[36] Of special interest are current efforts to give the individual consumer more leverage by making the practice of consumer law profitable for attorneys. The mechanism being promoted is the consumer class action which permits suits by one or a few consumers on behalf of all consumers similarly abused.[37] This will make fraud cases, where individual claims are smaller than legal costs, more more attractive to investigate and litigate.

The Future of Consumerism

One of the main conclusions from past efforts to forecast social phenomena is that naive extrapolations are likely to be wrong. A better approach in this situation is to utilize the interpretation that consumerism is, at least partially, a reflection of many social problems that are certain to persist, and perhaps be magnified in the future. This diagnosis rules out the possibility that consumerism activity will decline significantly in the future; the unanswered questions concern the rate of increase in this activity and the areas of greatest sensitivity.

One index of activity, the amount of federal consumer legislation pending, should slow its rate of increase. Only a limited number of consumer bills can be considered at a time; over 400 such bills were pending in Congressional committees at the end of 1969.[38] Also more attention will have to be given to implementing and improving existing legislation, rather than writing new legislation. For example, there is evidence that the truth-in-lending bill will not achieve its original goals; partly because of lack of understanding of the problem and partly because of inadequacies and confusion in the enacted legislation.[39] Similarly, it is dismaying that after two years of experience with the truth-in-packaging bill it is being referred to as "one of the best non-laws in the book."[40] In this particular situation the problem seems to lie with the interest and ability of the various regulatory agencies to implement the law. This is not an isolated example of enforcement failures. The Food and Drug Administration (FDA) recently estimated that fewer than two-thirds of all food processors have complied with standards to prevent some forms of food contamination. One result has been an increased pressure for a powerful central consumer agency[41] to implement, modify and coordinate the 269 consumer programs that are presently administered by 33 different federal agencies.[42]

The very nature of the contemporary marketplace will probably continue to inhibit basic changes in business operations. Weiss points out some manufacturers and retailers will always equate responsible with legal behavior.[43] These tendencies are reinforced by the competitive structure of many markets where success depends on an ability to appeal directly to the "marginal float." One view of this group is that they constitute a minority who are "fickle . . . particularly susceptible to innovation that may not be relevant, and to attention getters such as sexy TV jokes or giveaway games."[44] While research support is lacking, this widely held view helps explain some of the behavior consumerists complain about.

There are signs that concerned parties are making efforts to rise above emotion to rationally identify and realistically attack the problems. Two major, if embryonic, research efforts are under way which aim at providing decision makers in business and government with empirically based knowledge to supplement the intuition on which they now too often solely rely. The first is the Consumer Research Institute sponsored by the Grocery Manufacturers Association, and the second is an effort by the Marketing Science Institute.[45] Although both research organizations have close ties with business, neither was established to justify or defend vested interests. Their objectives are to promote basic, academic research that will be respected by all parties. The MSI group specifically proposes to obtain participation at the research-design phase of each project of those who would potentially disagree about policy. Although the government now has no comparable effort, it is reasonable to expect movement in this direction. Cohen has suggested that the FTC should establish a Bureau of Behavioral Studies "whose function would be to gather and analyze data on consumer buying behavior relevant to the regulations of advertising in the consumer interest."[46]

An early study, which might be regarded as a prototype to the CRI and

MSI efforts, experimentally examined the relationship between deceptive packaging (with respect to content weight) and brand preference.[47] It demonstrated that experimentation can provide useful information to policy makers.

These research approaches and the forces behind them should not only generate influential information, but should also help stimulate some basic changes in orientation. We can expect to see, for example, the simplistic "economic man" model of consumer behavior enriched.[48] The last decade has seen great progress made in the study of consumer behavior. This progress should contribute directly to a deeper analysis of consumerism issues. Hopefully, the dissemination of relevant knowledge will help eliminate present semantic problems.[49] Such a development must accompany rational discourse.

Business managers, whether progressive or defensive, can be expected to develop new, flexible approaches toward insuring that the rights of the consumer will be protected. Even though the motives may be mixed, there is no reason why effective programs cannot be developed.

NOTES

1. Tom M. Hopkins, "New Battleground—Consumer Interest," *Harvard Business Review*, Vol. 42 (September-October, 1964), pp. 97–104.

2. Vance Packard, *The Waste Makers* (New York: David McKay, 1960), p. 23.

3. Rachel Carson, *Silent Spring* (Boston, Mass.: Houghton Mifflin Company, 1962); Ralph Nader, *Unsafe At Any Speed* (New York: Pocket Books, 1966); and "Consumer Advisory Council, First Report," Executive Office of the President (Washington, D.C.: U.S. Government Printing Office, October, 1963).

4. Senator Warren Magnuson and Jean Carper, *The Dark Side of the Marketplace* (Englewood Cliffs: Prentice-Hall, 1968).

5. *Freedom of Information in the Market Place* (Columbus, Mo.: F.O.I. Center, 1967).

6. Raymond A. Bauer and Stephen A. Greyser, "The Dialogue That Never Happens," *Harvard Business Review*, Vol. 45 (November-December, 1967), p. 2.

7. Robert L. Birmingham, "The Consumer As King: The Economics of Precarious Sovereignty." *Case Western Reserve Law Journal*, Vol. 20 (May, 1969).

8. Same reference as footnote 7, p. 374.

9. Fred E. Clark and Carrie P. Clark, *Principles of Marketing* (New York: The Macmillan Company 1942), p. 406.

10. Aaron S. Yohalem, "Consumerism's Ultimate Challenge: Is Business Equal to the Task?" address before the American Management Association, New York, November 10, 1969.

11. Statement of Leslie Dix (on behalf of the Special Committee on Consumer Interests), Federal Trade Commission, *National Consumer Protection Hearings* (Washington: U.S. Government Printing Office, November, 1968), p. 16.

12. "Food Ads to Get Wide Ranging Scrutiny at White House Session," *Advertising Age*, Vol. 41 (December 1, 1969), p. 1.

13. Andrew Shonfield, *Modern Capitalism: The Changing Balance of Public and Private Power* (New York: Oxford University Press, 1965), p. 227.

14. Stanley E. Cohen, "Pollution Threat May Do More for Consumers Than Laws, Regulations," *Advertising Age*, Vol. 41 (March 2, 1970), p. 72.

15. Richard H. Holton, "Government-Consumer Interest: The University Point of View," in *Changing Marketing Systems*, Reed Moyer, ed. (Chicago, Ill.: American Marketing Association, Winter, 1967), pp. 15–17.

16. E. B. Weiss, "Line Profusion in Consumerism," *Advertising Age*, Vol. 39 (April 1, 1968), p. 72.

17. Louis L. Stern, "Consumer Protection Via Increased Information," *Journal of Marketing*, Vol. 31 (April, 1967), pp. 48–52.

18. Richard J. Barber, "Government and the Consumer," *Michigan Law Review*, Vol. 64 (May, 1966), p. 1226.

19. Raymond A. Bauer and Stephen A. Greyser, *Advertising in America: The Consumer View* (Boston: Graduate School of Business Administration, Harvard, 1968), p. 345.

20. Robert C. Wells, quoted in James Bishop and Henry W. Hubbard, *Let the Seller Beware* (Washington: The National Press, 1969), p. 14.

21. "Rattles, Pings, Dents, Leaks, Creaks—and Costs," *Newsweek*, Vol. 45 (November 25, 1968), p. 93.

22. See, Federal Trade Commission, "Staff Report on Automobile Warranties" (Washington: no date), and "Report of the Task Force on Appliance Warranties and Service" (Washington: January, 1969).

23. "Consumers Upset Experts," *New York Times* (April 13, 1969), F. 17.

24. Stanley E. Cohen, "Business Should Prepare for Wider Probe of Consumer Protection Laws," *Advertising Age*, Vol. 39 (January 8, 1968), p. 59.

25. Lewis Schnapper, "Consumer Legislation and the Poor," *The Yale Law Journal*, Vol. 76 (1967).

26. David Caplovitz, *The Poor Pay More* (New York: The Free Press, 1963).

27. Jeremy Main, "A Special Report on Youth," *Fortune*, Vol. 79 (June, 1969), pp. 73–74.

28. E. B. Weiss, "The Corporate Deaf Ear," *Business Horizons*, Vol. XI (December, 1968), pp. 5–15.

29. Report of Council on Trends and Perspective on, "Business and the Consumer—A Program for the Seventies" (Washington, D.C.: Chamber of Commerce of the United States, 1969).

30. "Exploitation of Disadvantaged Consumers by Retail Merchants," *Report of the National Commission on Civil Disorders* (New York: Bantam Books, 1968), pp. 274–277.

31. Ralph Nader, "The Great American Gyp," *New York Review of Books*, Vol. 9 (November 21, 1968), p. 28.

32. Stanley E. Cohen, "'Giant Killers' Upset Notions That Business 'Clout' Runs Government," *Advertising Age*, Vol. 40 (July 14, 1969), p. 73.

33. Jeremy Main, "Industry Still has Something to Learn About Congress," *Fortune*, Vol. 77 (February, 1967), pp. 128–130.

34. Harper W. Boyd, Jr., and Henry J. Claycamp, "Industrial Self-Regulation and the Consumer Interest," *Michigan Law Review*, Vol. 64 (May, 1966), pp. 1239–1254.

35. Philip A. Hart, "Can Federal Legislation Affecting Consumers' Economic Interests Be Enacted?" *Michigan Law Review*, Vol. 64 (May, 1966), pp. 1255–1268.

36. David L. Rados, "Product Liability: Tougher Ground Rules," *Harvard Business Review*, Vol. 47 (July-August, 1969), pp. 144–152.

37. David Sanford, "Giving the Consumer Class," *The New Republic*, Vol. 40 (July 26, 1969), p. 15. Partial support for this concept was given by President Nixon in his "Buyer's Bill of Rights" proposal of October 30, 1969.

38. See, "Nixon shops for consumer protection," *Business Week* (November 1, 1969), p. 32.

39. "A Foggy First Week for the Lending Law," *Business Week* (July 5, 1969), p. 13. This result was accurately forecasted by Homer Kripke, "Gesture and Reality in Consumer Credit Reform," *New York University Law Review*, Vol. 44 (March, 1969), pp. 1–52.

40. Stanley E. Cohen, "Packaging Law Is on Books, But Ills It Aimed to Cure Are Still Troublesome," *Advertising Age*, Vol. 40 (September 1, 1969), p. 10.

41. Same reference as footnote 18, and Louis M. Kohlmeier, Jr., "The Regulatory Agencies: What Should Be Done?" *Washington Monthly*, Vol. 1 (August, 1969), pp. 42–59.

42. "Wide Gaps Exist in Consumer Food Safety," *Congressional Quarterly* (November, 1969).

43. E. B. Weiss, "Marketeers Fiddle While Consumers Burn," *Harvard Business Review*, Vol. 46 (July-August, 1968), pp. 45–53.

44. See Stanley E. Cohen, "Consumer Interests Drift in Vacuum as Business Pursues Marginal Float," *Advertising Age*, Vol. 40 (March 24, 1969), p. 112.

45. "Business Responds to Consumerism," *Business Week* (September 6, 1969), p. 98, and Robert Moran, "Consumerism and Marketing," *Marketing Science Institute Preliminary Statement* (May, 1969).

46. Dorothy Cohen, "The Federal Trade Commission and the Regulation of Advertising in the Consumer Interest," *Journal of Marketing*, Vol. 33 (January, 1969), pp. 40–44.

47. James C. Naylor, "Deceptive Packaging: Are Deceivers Being Deceived?" *Journal of Applied Psychology*, Vol. 6 (December, 1962), pp. 393–398.

48. David M. Gardner, "The Package, Legislation, and the Shopper," *Business Horizons*, Vol. 2 (October, 1968), pp. 53–58.

49. Same reference as footnote 6.

LEARNING REVIEW

Questions:

1. There is a forecast of a closer identity between consumerism and social problems involving the ____________ environment and the ____________ environment.

2. Changes in society that have served as catalysts to the development of consumerism are a) ______________________________ and b) ____________________.

Answers:

1. economic, physical; 2. a) new visibility of low income consumer; b) impersonalization of society, and the marketplace in particular.

Retrospective Comment

The term *consumerism* identifies the modern consumer movement launched in the mid-1960s by the concerns triggered indirectly by Rachel Carson[1] and directly by Ralph Nader's auto safety investigation,[2] and by

President Kennedy's efforts to establish the rights of consumers to safety, to be informed, to choose and to be heard.[3] It encompasses the evolving set of activities of government, business, independent organizations, and concerned consumers that are designed to protect the rights of consumers. It is an evolving dynamic movement with an enlarging scope and changing spokesmen and issues.

The core of consumerism remains the four rights set forth by President Kennedy. The meaning of each of these rights has been broadened considerably during the past decade to represent many new concerns. Perhaps most significantly, the past five years has seen a growing recognition that the scope of consumerism includes the right to an environment that will enhance the quality of life.

The *right to safety* implies protection against the marketing of goods which are hazardous to health or life. Such a right has motivated numerous laws which protect the consumer when he cannot be expected to have sufficient knowledge to protect himself.

The right to safety has been broadened to include the protection of people from themselves, a policy with which there is more disagreement. It is argued that people should not always be permitted to make decisions which are not in their best long-run interests, even when such decisions are deliberate and informed. This orientation reflects a growing acceptance of paternalism as a legitimate policy.[4]

The *right to be informed* is a fundamental economic interest of the consumer. There is wide acceptance that the consumer should not be deceived. Just what constitutes deception is more controversial and constantly changing.

The right to be informed also now goes beyond avoiding deception. It involves providing the consumer with sufficient information for him to make wise purchase decisions. To this end there has been a great deal of legislation designed to provide the consumer with useful, comparative information—such as the true rate of interest (*Truth-in-Lending*), the cost of food products on a per unit basis (*unit pricing*), product ingredients, and nutritional quality.

Concern over the *right to choose* dates back to the end of the last century when the Sherman Anti-Trust Act was passed as a means to counteract the monopoly power of the giant firms of the day. Initially, the focus was on protecting competitors from each other, particularly the small firm from the large one. However, anti-trust legislation and enforcement has gradually evolved toward an emphasis upon protecting and encouraging competition. Thus, the major effort is toward increasing the number of competitors and toward ensuring that the competitors that do exist actually compete and do not have understandings which would not be in the long-run best interest of the consumer.

President Kennedy indicated that the *right to be heard* involved an assurance that consumer interests would be considered in the formulation of government policy and during regulatory proceedings.

The right to be heard further implies the existence of mechanisms through which other rights can be asserted; in particular by ensuring redress for legitimate consumer grievances. A variety of innovations, including free legal service for the poor, consumer class action suits, and arbitration procedures have substantially enhanced this right.[5]

It is becoming clear, as well, that firms have difficulty "listening" to their customers. Thus, many firms have created *ombudsman* positions, people in the organization who act as a representative and advocate of the consumer interest during the policy-making process. Even assuming this formal apparatus is effective at representing the consumer to those making high level decisions, there is still the individual consumer and his or her problem. How can large organizations be adapted so that the consumer can truly be heard? The firm ombudsman and the government consumer affairs departments often receive complaints and attempt to resolve them, but the political realities of large, impersonal organizations tend to inhibit such efforts.[6]

To the above list of consumer rights has recently been added the *right to a physical environment that will enhance the quality of life*. Indeed, consumerism has been defined more broadly as an organized expression for an improved quality of life. A beer can or phosphates from detergents can substantially degrade the physical environment. Advertising clutter on the television screen or on the highway can similarly have a negative impact on the quality of life. These environmental problems differ from many of the other consumer problems in that the purchase and consumption decision of the individual consumer does not by itself directly create a problem for him. Because of this characteristic of environmental problems, government action is usually sought in any solution.

1. Rachel Carson, *Silent Spring* (Boston: Houghton, Mifflin, 1962).
2. Ralph Nader, *Unsafe At Any Speed* (New York: Pocket Books, 1966).
3. For discussion see "Consumer Advisory Council: First Report," Executive Office of the President (Washington, D.C.: United States Government Printing Office, October 1963).
4. See Robert L. Birmingham, "The Consumer as King: The Economics of Precarious Sovereignty," David A. Aaker and George S. Day, *Consumerism: Search for the Consumer Interest*, Second Edition (New York: The Free Press, 1975).
5. See Philip Schrag, "Consumer Rights," in our book *Consumerism: Search for the*

Consumer Interest; see also Thomas L. Eovalde and Joan E. Gestren, "Justice for Consumers: The Mechanisms of Redress," *Northwestern University Law Review*, *66* (July-August 1971).

6. See our article, "Corporate Responses to Consumerism Pressure," in *Consumerism: Search for the Consumer Interest*.

38

Consumer Protection Via Increased Information

Louis L. Stern

PREVIEW

I. There is more interest in consumer protection by government and others than ever before.

II. Consumers have a right to be informed as distinct from a right not to be deceived.
   A. The loss of personal relationships in the marketplace has reduced the availability and reliability of product information.
   B. The rising level of technology makes consumers less capable personally of evaluating products.
   C. The language of advertising has contributed to the problem of product evaluation.

III. The methods of providing product information may be both voluntary and compulsory.
   A. Private industry has done much to provide information to consumers and to forestall government activity.
   B. Government intervention may involve several areas:
      1. The greatest need for consumer protection is in regard to clarity of terms of sale.
      2. Standards of minimum quality or performance may be useful where health or safety is involved.
      3. Grade-labeling is not an effective way of indicating quality.

Louis L. Stern, "Consumer Protection via Increased Information," is reprinted by permission from the *Journal of Marketing*, published by the American Marketing Association (April 1967), pp. 48–52

4. Consumer advisory services might have serious disadvantages because of the power they would come to have over the fate of individual companies.

IV. *Full disclosure* has a variety of implications:
   A. It implies disclosure of the dangerous nature of a product.
   B. It might compel the disclosure of component ingredients, not contents, and other terms-of-sale information.
   C. It might mean revelation of a product's performance characteristics.
   D. At another level it pertains to disclosure of potentially derogatory information unrelated to health, safety, terms of sale, or performance.

V. The best compromise about disclosures would be to have certain information included with the product and more extensive information available upon request.

What about consumer protection?

The great concern of businessmen about recent demands for consumer protection is indicated by the establishment of: (1) a consumer-information service by the National Association of Manufacturers, known as Techniques in Product Selection (TIPS); and (2) a program of cooperation between the Association of Better Business Bureaus and federal departments and agencies that affect consumer-business relationships.

Although the NAM and ABBB programs may be public-relations efforts to mollify demands for consumer protection, nevertheless their creation reflects businessmen's concern that, "Unless business moves to organize some communication apparatus, it will soon be confronted with a benevolent, bureaucratic structure that will take over such functions."[1]

Nor is such concern unfounded. Consider recent proposals to establish an Office or Department of Consumers, and for the federal government to engage in "Consumers Union" types of product-evaluation and reporting. Is it madness to speculate that the precedents set by the Drug Amendments of 1962 (1962) and the "fair labeling and packaging" bill might lead to proposals for a "fair advertising" law?

Probably no other Congress ever faced as many consumer-protection proposals as the 89th. Even the U.S. Supreme Court showed an interest in consumer protection, as evidenced by its handling of the Rapid Shave case.[2]

Other signs of increasing government interest in consumer protection include:

1. Completion by Congress, the Food and Drug Administration, the

National Commission on Food Marketing, and the Consumer Advisory Council of voluminous reports relating to consumer protection

2. Establishment of a special division within the U.S. Department of Agriculture to handle the Department's labeling programs

3. Establishment by the Office of Economic Opportunity of an experimental program of consumer education

4. Within the Federal Trade Commisssion, setting up of a new office of federal-state cooperation; new studies of consumer-goods marketing practices; and new trade-regulation guides and rules pertaining to the marketing of consumer goods.

But perhaps the best indication of the great amount of government interest in consumer protection is the statement of Charles Sweeny, Chief of the FTC's Bureau of Deceptive Practices: "The present Commission is more deeply determined to combat consumer deception than any Commission I have known in my 30 years of service."[3]

Why is there so much interest in consumer protection?

One reason is that rising incomes and a cornucopia of new products has multiplied the number, value, and variety of consumers' market transactions. Therefore, there are far more opportunities for consumer deception than ever before. Furthermore, the mounting variety of consumer products is increasing the competitiveness of our economic system. In turn, this may be leading to a deterioration of business ethics, thus giving rise to added interest in consumer protection.

Yet it is not at all clear that deception in the marketplace has, in fact, increased. What is clear is that the history of the United States is a record of accumulated social and technological efforts to protect the individual from adversity of every sort. The drive for consumer protection may be viewed as simply a continuation of those efforts.

The Need for Product Information

Do consumers have a right to be informed, as distinct from a right not to be deceived?

Our economic system is based on the belief that free and intelligent decisions in the marketplace, rather than by government fiat, will produce the most efficient allocation of resources toward the achievement of private and social goals. To exercise free and intelligent choices in the marketplace, consumers must have access to terms of sale and product information.

However, it is likely that the loss of personal relationships in the marketplace has reduced both the availability and the reliability of product information.

A second factor contributing to the problem is the rising level of technology. New materials, new operating principles, new functions, new designs, and new packaging have increased the difficulty of choosing one product or brand over another. The growing number of synthetic textiles and textile mixtures with varying prices and performance characteristics amply illustrates this situation.

Because of their usually greater complexity, durable products may reflect more advances in technology than nondurable products. Hence, the problem of adequacy and comprehension of product-performance information may be compounded in the case of durable goods. Furthermore, consumers are less capable of personally evaluating durable products because the long life and varied conditions under which these products are used cloud post-purchase brand comparisons. To make matters even more difficult, the reports of such organizations as *Consumers Union* are quickly rendered obsolete by model changes or model number changes.

A third factor contributing to the problem of adequacy of product information is the language of advertising. From Martineau to Weir, many advertisers and copywriters have preached the sermon of *image*.

In the words of Pierre Martineau, "It is generally insufficient to convince a person on intellectual grounds. His feelings must be involved. And this we achieve by affective or esthetic suggestion and imagery, by the meanings behind the words and pictures."[4]

Consider also the "heretical" words of William D. Tyler, *Advertising Age* columnist: "Most advertising down the years has done little more than say sweet nothings about a product. . . . It has contained the least information, the fewest facts, of almost anything ever written. We have relied mainly on adjectives, on charm, on manner of presentation, coupled with unspecific, unsupported claims of superiority."[5]

The question is how greater disclosure of product and terms-of-sale information can be achieved. The difficulties of attempting to provide greater information to consumers are substantial. The problem of communicating technical information to a non-technical audience, the time and space limitations of the vehicle of communication, and the cost of the time and space used must all be taken into account.

On the other hand, there is the question of *methods*. Will the methods of information be voluntary or compulsory? Will they involve standards, labeling requirements, consumer-advisory services, consumer-education programs, or some combination of these?

Voluntary Disclosure

Private industry has made great strides in attempting to provide information to consumers and to forestall government activity. Consider the following:

1. Formation over the years of codes of ethics by various associations in the packaging field.

2. Adoption by the 50th National Conference on Weights and Measures (June, 1965) of a standard for conspicuous labeling, as an amendment to the Model State Regulation Pertaining to Packages. (The new standard defines officially and nationally for the first time what constitutes a "clear and conspicuous" statement of net contents on package labels.)

3. Adoption by the American Standards Association, the National Bureau of Standards, and many other groups of standards for the size, shape, or performance ratings (such as BTU output) of innumerable products and containers.

Government Intervention

Of course, government regulations are sometimes unduly rigid, and create legal hazards for even the conscientious corporate citizen. (For example, the present standard of identity for butter was formulated at the turn of the century and does not permit the addition of emulsifiers or preservatives to butter, an unconscionable shackle to the butter industry's competition with margarine. Neither does it provide for the addition of vitamins to butter or the continuous-process method of manufacturing butter, both of which are common today.) Nevertheless, even more regulations probably are in prospect.

Terms of Sale

Aside from regulations pertaining to safety or gross misrepresentation, the greatest need for consumer protection is in regard to clarity of terms of sale. The least restrictive measure would require merely a statement of net contents on the package. However, mere knowledge of the weight or quantity of a product is an inadequate basis for intelligent choice; and if the statement of net contents is inconspicuous or the shopper unobservant, not even that much information will be known.

A further level of protection would be to provide for standardization of weights and quantities in which a consumer product may be distributed for retail sale. State laws already provide for standard package sizes for a few staple food products such as bread, butter, margarine, milk, cream, and flour.

Standardization of weights and quantities would provide informational gains to consumers. It would enable many shoppers to compare the price of equivalent amounts of alternative brands. In contrast, indications of price per ounce carried out to several decimal places would be no real improvement, and actually might distract consumers from making price comparisons of total amounts.

Standardization of weights and quantities would also call attention to price increases, which are otherwise hidden from some consumers in the form of a reduction in quantity.

It would be desirable, therefore, to establish standard weights or quantities in which selected consumer goods might be distributed. Provision for variations from these standards in multiples of 25% of the standard amounts would probably satisfy most consumer preferences for size of unit of purchase.

Establishment of standard weights and quantities might reduce the number of opportunities for using one size and style of container for packaging a variety of products as soup, cracker, and cereal companies now do. Considerable expense would also be involved in adjusting packaging machinery to the new weight or quantity standards. Nevertheless, the long-run advantages to consumers probably would exceed these disadvantages.

A still higher level of restriction, to regulate container sizes and shapes, is not only unnecessary but contrary to consumers' interests. It would severely inhibit package innovation. However, the International Organization for Standardization, whose standards may acquire the effect of law in over 50 member nations, has launched a program to develop retail package size standards that would affect *all* consumer products. Its program could, within a few years, force U.S. manufacturers to adopt similar standards for export purposes.

Standards and Grade-labeling

Compulsory standards of minimum quality or performance can be a useful form of consumer protection where health or safety is involved. Minimum standards can also serve to prevent consumers from being sold grossly inferior products.

Product standards usually impose minimum product requirements. On the other hand, grade-labeling involves an attempt to communicate in one or more symbols the relative quality of a product as influenced by a variety of characteristics.

Because grade-labeling requires a high degree of agreement as to what constitutes the best combination of product characteristics, its utility is limited to simple products having few attributes. Yet these products tend to be those which consumers are most capable of evaluating themselves. And even for these products, the whirlwind pace of product and package innovation occurring today would present an enormous grade-labeling task.

Furthermore, the effects of grade-labeling upon product research and innovation must also be considered. Grade-labeling would reduce product differentiation and thereby tend to promote price competition. As a result, smaller marketing margins would yield less research-and-development revenues.

Consumer Advisory Services

As proposed by Donald Turner, Chief of the U.S. Justice Department's Antitrust Division, another means of communicating more information to consumers would be for the federal government to evaluate products and publish its evaluations, or to subsidize organizations such as *Consumers Union*.[6] Such publications as *Consumers Bulletin* or *Consumer Reports* provide a source of clear and continuing product information; and their evaluations can be both capsulized and detailed.

On the other hand, their value is limited by their remoteness from the point of purchase. A more serious disadvantage, were they to achieve widespread consumer influence, would be the power they would come to possess over the economic fate of individual companies. If the majority of consumers followed their brand recommendations, producers of lower-rated brands would be strongly induced to imitate the preferred brand as closely as possible.

Accordingly, product differentiation might be expected to decrease, and this would be to consumers' disadvantage. Simultaneously, a loss of product differentiation might lead to a reduction in the number of producers, another undesirable effect.

Full Disclosure

"Full disclosure" has a variety of implications. Most commonly, it is assumed to imply disclosure of the dangerous nature of a product. Such laws as the Flammable Fabrics Act (1953), the Hazardous Substances Labeling Act (1960) the Drug Amendments of 1962 (1962), and the Cigarette Labeling Act (1965) already impose this level of meaning.

A second level of meaning would compel disclosure of component ingredients, net contents, and other terms-of-sale information, such as interest and related charges. Laws such as the Food, Drug and Cosmetics Act (1938), the Wool Products Labeling Act (1939), the Fur Products Labeling Act (1951), the Textile Fiber Products Identification Act (1958), and the Automobile Information Disclosure Act (1958) are intended to provide legislative mandate for this type of disclosure. Disclosure of component ingredients is primarily useful in relation to determining the healthfulness, safety, value, or performance of a product. Over and above this, compulsion of such disclosure might be interpreted as protection for and responsiveness to the existence of individual preferences for certain products.

The next higher level of disclosure is the revelation of a product's performance characteristics. To some extent this level of disclosure is implemented voluntarily by manufacturers of above-average quality products who employ rational selling appeals. Horsepower ratings, BTU ratings, and lumber ratings are familiar voluntary disclosures by manufacturers and distributors of performance characteristics. But unfortunately, many voluntary performance descriptions are meaningless or unreliable and sometimes refer to inputs rather than outputs.

Most manufacturers prefer to avoid direct performance statements in favor of evocative expressions or episodes. This is especially likely to be the case where no substantial differences in performance exist among rival brands, because for these products disclosure of meaningful performance information would tend to reduce the apparent differentiation among brands.

The Drug Amendments of 1962 (1962), although passed in the wake of the thalidomide scare and applying to a narrow and emotionally-charged area of consumption, provide a legislative precedent for regulatory agency concern with a product performance *even where health or safety are not involved.* Witness the FDA's attempt to require vitamins to be labeled with the statement: " . . . Except for persons with special medical needs, there is no scientific basis for recommending routine use of dietary supplements." A likely outcome of regulations pertaining to *nonperformance* would be regulations pertaining to *degrees* of performance.

As to the question of consumers' abilities to understand performance information, this problem will diminish over time in response to rising levels of education, the enormous capacity of consumers to learn informally, the effectiveness of media in informing consumers, and, most importantly, the challenge to learn presented by the availability of such information.

A still higher level of disclosure pertains to potentially derogatory information unrelated to health, safety, terms of sale, or performance of a product—illustrated by the FTC requirement of disclosure, where applicable, of the foreign origin of a product or component part. Conceivably, the FTC requirement could be extended to include disclosure, where applicable, of ratings by such groups as *Consumers Union*, production by companies not subscribing to voluntary codes of advertising practice, or production by nonunionized labor, etc.

The U.S. Supreme Court decision pertaining to disclosure of use of television mockups falls within this category of compulsory disclosure.[7]

The Court took the extreme position that not only misrepresentations, but also deceptive presentations of valid claims, even if necessary to compensate for the technical deficiencies of communications media, are illegal.

Implementation

Note especially that the FTC may be capable of expanding its disclosure requirements without the aid of new legislation. FTC Commissioner Everette MacIntyre has been quite explicit on this matter.[8]

Furthermore, the position taken by the Commission is this: "The question . . . is not whether the Commission may declare substantive standards and principles, for it plainly may and must. The question is whether the Commission may . . . promulgate them only in the course of adjudication."[9]

In the Commission's opinion, it is also free to promulgate them in formal rule-making proceedings.

The issue is whether consumers have expectations of receiving some standard of product performance, say, average for that industry's product. If they do, then failure to disclose the fact that a particular brand is below that standard of expectation would appear to be deceptive. If, in addition, the performance factor in question is material to the consumer's purchase decision, its nondisclosure violates the FTC Act.

The principle that nondisclosure of material information constitutes a misrepresentation is well established in law.[10] Moreover, the U.S. Supreme Court made abundantly clear in the Rapid Shave case that reviewing courts should ordinarily accept the Commission's judgment as to what constitutes deception.[11] " . . . When the Commission finds deception it is also authorized, within the bounds of reason, to infer that the deception will constitute a material factor in a purchaser's decision to buy."[12] Accordingly, the opportunity for the FTC to widen its requirements for full disclosure is clear.

The selection of what additional disclosures should be required is admittedly a difficult administrative decision, particularly so the more complex the product involved.

Nevertheless, a reasonable compromise could be reached whereby certain information would have to be provided with the product, and whereby other, more extensive, information would have to be made readily available on request. Nothing in this proposal would prevent a manufacturer from extolling additional characteristics of his products. Nor does this proposal imply that compulsory disclosures should be included in advertising or in promotion.

In short, this proposal would improve the functioning of the marketplace by increasing the amount of information therein. It would enable consumers to choose products rationally *if* they wished to do so.

In Conclusion

The consumer-protection movement is definitely in the ascendancy. The issue is not whether consumers will be better protected, but what form the protection will take.

Better and more reliable product and terms-of-sale information on package labels is perhaps the most economical and least restrictive type of consumer protection. Moreover, *full disclosure* might help to dissuade current demands for additional restrictions on advertising.

NOTES

1. "GF's Cleaves Calls for Food Industry Consumer Information Unit," *Advertising Age*, Vol. 36 (April 19, 1965), p. 16.
2. Colgate Palmolive Co. v. FTC, 85 S. Ct. 1035.
3. "Druggist May Be Liable for Brand Copy in His Ads," *Advertising Age*, Vol. 36 (June 7, 1965), pp. 1 and 135, at p.1.
4. Pierre Martineau, *Motivation in Advertising* (New York: McGraw-Hill Book Co., 1957), 187.
5. William D. Tyler, "Is Competitive Comparison Really Bad in Advertising? Reform With Care," *Advertising Age*, Vol. 37 (March 14, 1966), pp. 61–62, at p. 61.
6. "Anti-Trust Chief Urges Alternative to Advertising," *Advertising Age*, Vol. 37 (June 6, 1966), pp. 1 and 147–158, at p. 147.
7. Same reference as footnote 2.
8. *The Packaging-Labeling Controls Bill* (Washington, D.C.: Chamber of Commerce of the United States, 1965), p. 14.
9. Same reference as footnote 8, at p. 18.
10. P. Lorilard Co. v. FTC, 186 F2d 52; Raladam Co. v. FTC, 283 U.S. 643. But see also Alberty v. FTC, 182 F2d 36, Certiorari denied, 340 U.S. 818.
11. Same reference as footnote 2 at p. 1043.
12. Same reference as footnote 2 at p. 1046.

LEARNING REVIEW

Questions:

1. The greatest need for consumer protection is in regard to clarity of ______ ______________.

2. Consumers have a need for increased product information due to the development of these three factors: a) ______________, b) ______________ and c) ______________.

Answers:

1. terms of sale; 2. a) loss of personal relationship in the market place; b) rising level of technology; c) advertising techniques

---

Retrospective Comment

The call for consumer protection via increased information is louder today and more widespread than in 1967 when my article was written. The continuing popularity of the idea results from the fact that it strikes at the most serious and most pervasive of all consumer problems.

Since 1967, laws or regulations have been established to require disclosure of credit terms and annual rates of finance charges on loans and installment credit; terms and conditions of the proposed disposal of land and of access to utilities on interstate land sales; credit dossiers; gasoline octane ratings; and performance characteristics of light bulbs. Prominent candidates for mandatory disclosure include automobile mileage per gallon of gasoline, appliance energy consumption, nutritional characteristics of food, food chain gross margins by department, and detergent performance.

Where or when will demands for still more consumer information stop? More precisely, will the demand subside? Not in the foreseeable future. On the contrary, the process of defining consumer information needs which are material to the purchase decision is gathering steam. "'The (FTC's) goal is to facilitate marketplace competition for the consumer dollar through better informed buyers. '"[1]

Buttressed by the octane rating decision[2] (which confirmed the FTC's rule-making power) and the drug price advertising decision[3] (which implies consumer rights to market information), the FTC may be expected to require an expanding list of affirmative disclosures. Looking ahead to the day of product information data banks accessible by home computer, the FTC may be expected to specify standard terminology in order to provide comparability of data.

In a larger sense, consumer protection via increased information includes avoidance of deceptive "information." Puffery, long acceptable under common law, is being called into question.[4] Advertisements which consumers interpret falsely because the ads are ambiguous or literally meaningless are drawing increasing attention. Thus, it has been proposed[5] that advertising agencies be held strictly accountable for the meanings which the public derives from advertising messages.

Inference substantiation is meritorious—particularly for researchers—but not without limitations. For example, suppose a buyer infers from advertising that a particular brand of product will increase his prestige or sex appeal. Proving or disproving the (inferred) claim should be interesting indeed. Alternatively, suppose the buyer infers from advertising that virile people use "x" brand cigarettes. How should a virile population be defined in order to test the proposition?

1. Stanley E. Cohen, "FTC's Budget Memos Show New Objectives; Old Targets Disappear," *Advertising Age* (March 11, 1974), p. 62.

2. National Petroleum Refiners Assn. v. FTC, CA DC, 482, F2d 672, Cert. Denied.

3. "Warning on Nader Victory," *Advertising Age* (April 18, 1974), p. 14; see also Virginia Citizens Consumer Council, Inc., *et al*. v. State Board of Pharmacy, *et al*., D.C.

4. Ivan L. Preston, "Challenges Stand That Puffery May Be A Low-Priority Problem," *Advertising Age* (November 27, 1972), p. 47. For a profound defense of puffery, see Theodore Levitt, "The Morality (?) of Advertising," *Harvard Business Review* (July-August 1970), p. 84.

5. Dorothy Cohen, "Surrogate Indicators and Deception in Advertising," *Journal of Marketing* (July 1972), pp. 10–15; Gary M. Armstrong and James P. McLennan, "The Federal Trade Commission and the Investigation and Regulation of Deception in Advertising," Thomas V. Greer (editor) *Combined Proceedings of the American Marketing Association* (Chicago: American Marketing Association, 1974), pp. 430–434; *FTC News* (Washington: Federal Trade Commission), February 26, 1974.

Name Index

General Index